The Victorian
Economy

The Victorian Economy

FRANÇOIS CROUZET

Translated by Anthony Forster

METHUEN & CO LTD LONDON

To Sir Michael Postan
In Memoriam

First published in 1982 by
Methuen & Co. Ltd.
11 New Fetter Lane, London EC4P 4EE
Published in the USA by
©1982 François Crouzet
Printed in Great Britain

British Library Cataloguing in Publication Data

Crouzet, François
The Victorian Economy
1. Great Britain – Economic conditions – 19th
century
I. Title II. L'economie de la Grande Bretagne
victorienne. English
330.9'41'081   HC255

ISBN 0-416-31110-5
ISBN 0-416-31120-2 Pbk

Contents

List of tables

Preface

This volume was intended as a textbook for French students reading history, who were in their third or fourth year at university. As they could not be expected to be familiar either with Britain's economic history or with economics, nothing could be taken for granted and a fair number of elementary definitions and summaries had to be given; everything had to be in simple terms and without using cliometrics. On the other hand, it was hoped that discussions at a moderate level of sophistication could be followed. This is basically straightforward economic history, though some problems of social history closely linked with economic affairs – for instance the pattern of landownership – had occasionally to be considered. Unlike some other works which deal with England only and leave out Scotland, this book is concerned with Great Britain, but it excludes Ireland, whose economic structures and economic history were radically different.

This book has no pretension to be an exhaustive or original study, except modestly in the timespan it covers. While many others have the mid-nineteenth century as *terminus ad quem* or *a quo,* it is centred on the Victorian period (1837–1901). But neither the beginning nor the end of Victoria's long reign were significant breaks in the economic and social history of Great Britain. It is even doubtful whether they have much value in regard to political history, for the role of the Queen should not be overrated. If a Victorian era did exist, it must be defined by cultural criteria based on mental attitudes; and even on this count this long period saw such important changes that it is difficult to find in it a true unity. In fact, British historians usually divide the era into early, mid- and late Victorian. For economic historians a *terminus a quo* other than 1837 might be attractive, for instance the beginning of the Railway Age, as in Sir John Clapham's classic work, marked by the inauguration of the Liverpool and Manchester Railway in 1830, or the abolition of the Corn Laws in 1846.

On the other hand, the sixty-odd years of Victoria's reign form an integral part of the century of peace, economic growth and reform which extends in a continuous and homogeneous sweep from the end of the interminable wars against revolutionary and Napoleonic France (a period, even from the economic point of view, with its own distinct character and special problems) up to the outbreak of the first world war. 1914 certainly saw a major break or even a split in Great Britain's economic history. By disrupting the world economy, the Great War upset the foundations on which England's wealth was based and led to England's crisis in the interwar period. So it has seemed necessary to insert the actual Victorian period in the long-term context of the nineteenth century and to look at the pre-1837 as well as the post-1901 years. However, the special characters of the Victorian age, when they do exist, have been emphasized.

As regards the quantitative data, which readers may find excessive, but without which there can be no genuine economic history, it must be stressed that, although statistical materials about nineteenth-century Britain are abundant and of good quality, there are serious gaps, especially at the beginning of the century when governments, which were addicted to *laissez-faire* and anyway did not possess the powers or the administrative means to do so, did not trouble to gather statistical data on many aspects of economic and social life. Thus civil registration only started in England in 1836, and in Scotland in 1855. There are no annual series for coal or pig-iron production before 1854. Furthermore, the aggregate series, e.g. industrial production, national product, capital formation, etc., recently worked out by economists and statisticians, despite the remarkable care and ingenuity which their creators have displayed, can only give rough orders of magnitude, especially for the first decades of the nineteenth century. It is unwise to take them at their face value or draw precise conclusions from them, let alone to build elaborate theories on these frail foundations. Readers should also pay attention to the different geographical areas covered by the statistical data quoted. Some of them apply only to England (which, in fact, is always England and Wales); others apply to Great Britain (England and Wales plus Scotland); finally others to the United Kingdom (Great Britain and Ireland). In some cases the conclusions to be drawn from these data have to be qualified with due attention paid to the exact territory they cover. On the other hand, in the text we have sometimes used the terms 'England', 'Great Britain' and 'Britain' synonymously, to avoid repetition.

The British school of economic history has a long and distinguished tradition. There are many scholars now active and their work is of high quality. Yet the Victorian era has been studied less thoroughly than the Industrial Revolution period that preceded it, so that there are hazy patches. Furthermore, such is the activity of British economic historians and such is their taste for criticism, not to say hypercriticism, that the research front is in constant flux; unlike in France, the conclusions of the most eminent writers do not become dogmas and are soon challenged; and the liveliest controversies rage around many important problems. This book endeavours to give a survey of the problems and the debates. Readers must not be surprised if they do not find verdicts on various questions, or if they come across opinions different from those stated in textbooks that are reputable but now out of date. Conversely it was not possible to include every hypothesis and every conclusion formulated in the countless works published by British historians and economists, not to mention important contributions hailing from across the Atlantic.

One last word of warning. In some respects the Victorian era is quite close to us. Our parents or our grandparents were generally born before 1901 or at least 1914 (an English newspaper recently reproduced a photograph of the present King of Norway as a child sitting on the knees of Edward VII). In spite of the second-world-war bombings and of recent development, the urban landscape of Britain remains largely Victorian, from the Houses of Parliament to whole streets or terraces of well-to-do or modest homes, not to mention the main railway stations – those cathedrals of the nineteenth century – and neo-Gothic town halls and churches. Victorian literature, especially the work of the great novelists, is easy to read and widely read – as well as regularly watched on television. But in other respects, in its outlook and in the assumptions that lie behind its *Weltanschauung,* Victorian society is lightyears away from our own. Thus, it believed in immutable economic laws, in face of which human action and above all state intervention were not only impotent but positively harmful. The Victorians considered inequality to be part of the universal order decreed by Providence, and poverty either an element in that order or the result of the failings of those who endured it. So one must make a strenuous effort of understanding in order to penetrate to the heart of this civilization – and an effort of sympathy too. For more than half a century a spate of books has excoriated or ridiculed the society, attitudes, mentality, morals, tastes and taboos of the Victorians. Certainly the Victorian age has many blemishes and absurdities to show us, but many of those Eminent Victorians, whom Lytton Strachey ridiculed in a famous book published in 1918, and many others who remain unsung, struggled tirelessly to promote reforms and improve 'the condition of England'. At her zenith as a superpower, Victorian Britain was lacking neither in greatness nor in human virtues.

Introduction

Opening symbolically with Wellington's victory at Waterloo, the nineteenth century of the historians – 1815-1914 – was the century of England and of English supremacy. The political system of the classic land of liberty was an inspiration and often a model for many countries then called civilized. Thanks to a fleet that was easily the first in the world, 'Britannia ruled the waves'. She also possessed the foremost colonial empire which was to extend over nearly a quarter of the earth's land-surface and in which nearly a quarter of the human race would live. The United Kingdom was the only truly global power, the only superpower, whose intervention or abstention was decisive for the balance of power, not only in Europe but in the world.

On the economic plane the preponderance of Great Britain and her lead over the other countries were no less marked – just the opposite in fact, hard though it is to imagine it today. For contemporaries, during a large part of the nineteenth century at least, England was (and deserved to be) what the United States has been in the eyes of the twentieth-century world – the country which excited fascination and repulsion at the same time by her riches, the massive scale of her achievements and her extreme contrasts. It was the country which was forging a new civilization that was destined to sweep through the world. It was the 'mirror for our future', according to Stendhal, in which could be discerned, with hope for some and with terror for others, the 'scenes of future life'.

Indeed, Britain was certainly the 'dominant' economy, not to say the 'super-dominant' economy, of the nineteenth century (P.Bairoch),[1] i.e. it was not only the most advanced and powerful economy but also the one which had the capacity to influence all the economies involved in

---

[1] P. Bairoch, *Commerce extérieur et développement économique de l'Europe au XIXe siècle* (Paris – The Hague, 1976), p. 168.

world trade, whereas the converse was only true in a limited way (though this preponderant position was weakened by the end of Victoria's reign). Britain was the 'First Industrial Nation'–the striking title of Peter Mathias's book[2]–and she merited that description in the double sense of priority in time and superiority in power. She was the first country to industrialize and to create not only an economy dominated by industry (and especially large-scale industry) but a new type of society and a new civilization, predominantly industrial and urban. She was thus confirmed for a long time as an economic power of crushing superiority, enjoying a commanding lead over other countries.

It was in fact in England that the Industrial Revolution started in the last third of the eighteenth century. It consisted of a complex series of technological innovations based mainly on the use of machinery in the textile industry and of coal in the iron industry, and on the exploitation of a new source of energy, steam; and this led to a radical transformation of the methods and structure of industry. Furthermore this revolution in industry was preceded, accompanied or followed by important changes in the other sectors of the economy–agriculture, transport and finance. It would be outside the scope of this book to analyse the reasons why this revolution occurred in England and at the end of the eighteenth century. What counts was the result–the creation of a new type of economy. While traditional economies were characterized by the predominance of agriculture, by low productivity (and a low average standard of living), and by slow, irregular growth, the Industrial Revolution was the onset in Great Britain of modern economic growth–that is growth which is sustained and relatively rapid, with industry as the leading sector, while productivity and the standard of living are constantly improved by technological progress.

Britain got away first in the race and was not to be overtaken for a long time, for her role of pioneer continued to assure her enormous advantages and had a determining effect on her relative economic strength vis-à-vis not only her traditional rival, France, but also her future competitors, the United States and Germany. In the eighteenth century and at the beginning of the nineteenth century the spread of new technology was slow, and moreover it was retarded by the wars and upheavals of the revolutionary and Napoleonic period, which also had negative effects for England's potential rivals. The delay in the general spread of the first great British innovations (as opposed to the sporadic adoption of new techniques) in the most advanced continental

---

[2]   P. Mathias, *The First Industrial Nation: An Economic History of Britain, 1700–1914* (London, 1969).

countries was between twenty and forty years, and even then these countries had serious difficulties in mastering and exploiting them effectively[3]. Furthermore, far from resting on her first laurels, England constantly improved her techniques and remained the dominating centre of technological innovation right up to the middle of the nineteenth century. It has been calculated that, out of seventy-eight important inventions made between 1800 and 1839, forty-two occurred in the United Kingdom and thirty-six on the continent and in the United States[4].

Certainly, after 1800 (and more obviously 1815) some continental countries – Belgium, Switzerland, France and Germany – and also the United States had successfully resisted the deindustrialization which had threatened them as the result of English competition. They had launched their own Industrial Revolution and made fair progress, acquiring modern industrial sectors, mechanizing their textile industries in part, renovating their iron industries and improving their transport systems. But their rates of growth and modernization had probably been inferior, or at best equal to British rates, and so they had not been able to catch up. Furthermore, they laboured under several serious handicaps, whereas England enjoyed comparative advantages that were considerable and indeed overwhelming. She had an abundant supply of cheap coal (an indispensable raw material for the new industry), plenty of capital, a competent labour-force used to the new work-conditions in factories, and an abundance of entrepreneurs who were dynamic and open to technical progress. She had also assured herself of a very strong position, in fact a near monopoly, in many overseas markets[5].

In these conditions, the *relative* gap between Britain and the most advanced countries diminished very little during the first half of the nineteenth century. In *absolute* terms it widened and in the modern sectors of the economy it became formidable indeed[6]. Over the other

[3] Bairoch, *Commerce extérieur*, p. 27, also pp. 142–3, M. Lévy-Leboyer, *Les Banques européennes et l'industrialisation internationale dans la première moitié du XIXe siècle* (Paris, 1964), pp. 15, 23, 32.

[4] Data from T.K. Derry and T.I. Williams, *A Short History of Technology* (London, 1960), pp. 738–43, printed by Bairoch, *Commerce extérieur*, p. 141 (table 45).

[5] F. Crouzet, 'Western Europe and Great Britain: catching up in the first half of the nineteenth century', in A.J. Youngson (ed.), *Economic Development in the Long Run* (London, 1972), pp. 98ff; Lévy-Leboyer, pp. 15, 23, 32, 170.

[6] According to J. Marczewski, the real value of France's total industrial production up to about 1820 remained superior to Great Britain's; but its per-capita value was much less. In 1850, the UK produced 2,249,000 tons of pig-iron against 763,000 tons made by Germany, Belgium and France combined. She possessed 21 million cotton-spindles against slightly over 6 million for western Europe; Crouzet, 'Western Europe', p. 107; D.S. Landes, *The Unbound Prometheus: Technological Change and Industrial Development in Western Europe, 1750 to the Present* (Cambridge, 1969), p. 194 (table 4).

countries of Europe (where changes were very limited, or non-existent), even Europe as a whole,and overseas countries too, apart from the United States, Britain's lead grew relatively as well. Paul Bairoch, despite the dearth of satisfactory statistical data, has made some ingenious estimates of the comparative levels of industrialization and economic development in the United Kingdom and on the continent (taken overall and by countries).

For instance, he presents (see table 1) two indicators of the level of industrialization[7].

Table 1   Indicators of the level of industrialization

	Production of pig-iron (in kg. per inhabitant)		Consumption of raw cotton (in kg. per inhabitant)	
	1830	1860	1830	1860
United Kingdom	29	132	4.7	15.1
Continental Europe	4	10	0.3	1.1
France	7	26	0.9	2.5
Germany	3	13	0.1	1.5

The gaps between Britain and other economies are enormous, even with the most advanced countries[8]. Certainly we are looking at the two branches of industry where British superiority was especially marked. It was much less the case for total industrial production *per head* of population, and Bairoch reckons that in Germany, Belgium and France, industrial production increased more rapidly than in England between 1830 and 1860, to such an extent that these three countries had caught up 12 per cent on the lead held by Britain in 1830[9].

With statistics becoming more abundant after 1850, Bairoch has been able to estimate (see table 2) with a certain degree of precision the weight of the United Kingdom in the European and in the world economy towards 1860[10].

With 2 per cent of the world's population and 10 per cent of Europe's, the United Kingdom would seem to have had a capacity in modern

[7]   Bairoch, *Commerce extérieur*, p. 138 (table 43).
[8]   It is true that Belgium and Sweden in 1830 had very high figures (24 and 37 kg) for iron production, but these were exceptional cases. For cotton consumption, Switzerland held second place with 1.9 kg in 1830 and 5.1 in 1860.
[9]   Bairoch, *Commerce extérieur*, p. 290. He admits that there is a wide margin of error in his calculations.
[10]   To be precise, the average of 1858/62, Cf. Bairoch, *Commerce extérieur*, (table 52), also pp. 171–2, 177, 182. Cotton consumption doubtless applies to the total earmarked for commercial production. The share of world production of coal was taken from another source and applies to 1870.

Table 2   UK share of total output (%)   ⟨$858-$⟩62⟩

	World	Europe
Iron production	53	58
Coal and lignite production	(50)	68
Raw cotton consumption	49	59
Energy consumption	27	45
Exports	25	30
Merchant navy	34	43

industries equal to 40–45 per cent of the world's potential and 55–60 per cent of that of Europe. According to an older estimate she still produced in 1870 nearly one-third of all the articles manufactured in the world[11]. This implies enormous advances over the rest of mankind in terms of production and consumption of industrial products per head. The dominating position of England in world industry was much more pronounced than that of the United States in the mid-twentieth century, and in western European industry than that of Germany today[12].

It is true that from the GNP standpoint, and notably as regards product per capita (which is a satisfactory measure of the level of economic development) the United Kingdom's superiority though very real, was much less marked, for the differences with the continent were much smaller in the agriculture and service sectors[13].

It is probable that at the end of the seventeenth century England had had an average per-capita income superior to that of all European countries, with the possible exception of the Netherlands. This margin of superiority had doubtless grown at the end of the eighteenth and beginning of the nineteenth century, thanks to the early start of England's economic revolution, and Bairoch reckons that the gap increased again between 1830 and 1860 (except with Belgium and Switzerland), for the increase in per-capita product was probably faster in the United Kingdom than on the continent (a conclusion that is, in our view, not beyond dispute). Towards 1860 the United Kingdom's

[11]   Estimate of a League of Nations publication (1945), quoted by Phyllis Deane, in H.J. Habakkuk and M.M. Postan(eds), *The Cambridge Economic History of Europe*, VI: *The Industrial Revolutions and After* (Cambridge, 1965), p. 25 (table 2).

[12]   Bairoch, *Commerce extérieur*, gives an index of 'modern industrial power' and also the 'level of development of modern industrial sectors' in European countries around 1860. On the base of 100 for the UK (but GB alone would be 125), these indices are respectively: France 22–27 and 17–22, Germany 13–16 and 10–15. Taking the second criterion, the continent is 10 (including Russia, or 25–30 without Russia), Switzerland 60 and Belgium 50.

[13]   Bairoch, *Commerce extérieur*, p. 175, estimates that British productivity in agriculture per active male worker was only double what it was on the continent.

total GNP was probably 20-22 per cent of that of the continent, or 18 per cent that of all Europe, and her per-capita product roughly double the continent's[14].

Be that as it may, there is no doubt that during the whole of the nineteenth century the United Kingdom (and so *a fortiori* Britain) was the richest country in Europe, i.e. the country which enjoyed the highest GNP per head. This first place, which she held in 1815, 1837, 1850 and 1860, would be hers up to 1914, even though from the 1880s and 1890s the lead over the continent's most advanced countries – Belgium, Germany, Switzerland, Denmark and France – was sharply reduced. From the same point of view the United Kingdom was the richest country in the world up to around 1880, when she had to concede first position to the United States (whose GNP per head was to be 40 per cent higher than the United Kingdom's in 1913), and at the end of the century Canada took over the second place. On the other hand, Britain's lead over the poor countries of Europe and even more over those of the Third World, which was already considerable at the beginning of the nineteenth century, never ceased to increase in the course of the nineteenth century[15]. Towards 1830, GNP per head of the United Kingdom was, at constant prices, more than double that of Africa and Asia in 1960.

So during the whole of the first half of the nineteenth century, and even beyond, the quantitative superiority of Britain over the other countries was crushing, and the difference really spectacular. None of them, even Switzerland or Belgium, came near to Britain's level of industrialization. The scale of her economy was unrivalled; it was 'unique in being the first'[16].

During this same period Britain was also first qualitatively, because

[14]   Bairoch, *Commerce extérieur*, pp. 16, 73 (table 15), 149 (table 47), 151 (table 48), 155 (table 50), 175, 289–93 (tables 76, 79, 80). Also Crouzet, 'Western Europe', p. 199. In 1830, GNP per head for the continent was probably 65 per cent of what it was in the UK.

[15]   Bairoch, *Commerce extérieur*, pp. 19, 154–6; P. Bairoch, 'Europe's gross national product: 1800–1975', *Journal of European Economic History*, v(2), Autumn 1976, 278, 281, 285–7. Of course things were different from the point of view of total GNP (which was much less important, even in terms of 'economic power'). For this Russia probably held first place in Europe up to about 1850, but the UK replaced her between 1850 and the beginning of the twentieth century, when Germany took the lead. The UK's share in the total GNP of Europe might have risen from 9 per cent around 1800 to 14 per cent in 1830, to reach a peak of 20 per cent in 1890 and fall back to 17 per cent in 1913.

[16]   P. Mathias, 'British industrialization: unique or not?', in P. Léon, F. Crouzet and R. Gascon (eds), *L'Industrialisation en Europe au XIXe siècle* (Paris, 1972), pp. 497–510; also Mathias, *The First Industrial Nation*, pp. 251–2. See Chapter 9, p. 287, for British superiority in railways, which was to be expected since they were an English invention.

of the technological superiority which she had secured by her early Industrial Revolution. She also succeeded in maintaining this superiority and even increasing it despite other countries' efforts to imitate her. Very few of Europe's most progressive enterprises came up to the level of the 'best British practice'. In England machines were more sophisticated, steam-power was much more widely used[17], firms and factories were larger, productivity was higher[18], costs were lower. Certainly continental Europeans had the advantage of price and quality for luxury and fancy goods[19], but these articles were the product of traditional craftsmanship, profiting from a labour-force that was at once skilled and cheap, and not the product of mechanized large-scale industry. In the latter sphere British superiority was almost complete. She was, with some exaggeration but also with much truth, 'the Workshop of the World'[20].

This workshop indeed dominated international trade. Having been the first to achieve a technological break-through and having thus considerably lowered her costs and prices thanks to increased productivity and mass production, British industry's prices were cheaper than those of traditional artisan producers and the less advanced factories of the rest of the world, even though the level of wages abroad was much lower. Furthermore, at a time when the purchasing power of the vast majority of mankind was so low that it had to concentrate on basic necessities – food, housing and, among manufactured goods, clothing – Britain surpassed other countries in the production of cheap textiles, especially cotton goods. She surpassed them also in the manufacture of metal products (iron, rails, machinery, locomotives) which were necessary for the production and transport of staple commodities as well as for the 'modernization' upon which various

---

[17] In 1850, GB probably boasted steam-engines and locomotives totalling 1,290,000 hp against 700,000 hp for the five countries of western Europe. In 1860, the UK possessed steam-engines whose power was half that of all stationary steam-engines in Europe; Crouzet, 'Western Europe', p. 107; Bairoch, *Commerce extérieur*, p. 171 (table 53).

[18] Bairoch, *Commerce extérieur*, p. 175, reckons that, about 1860, total productivity in British industry (including mining) was 2.5 times greater than in the most advanced continental countries, and three times as great as that of Europe as a whole.

[19] Silks, certain worsted materials, French gloves, German toys, Swiss watches, etc. Moreover, at the Great Exhibition of 1851, it was noted that the Americans had perfected some machine-tools for the mass production of interchangeable parts, e.g. for firearms, and some new machines, e.g. harvesters and sewing-machines; but this was a narrow field, which did not compete directly with English industry.

[20] In 'Magnanimous Albion: free trade and British national income, 1841–1881', *Explorations in Economic History* , XVII (3), July 1980, 317 (note 7), D.N. McCloskey has made a calculation, which is simple but interesting. About 1870, Great Britain supplied one-third of world industrial production and exported roughly one-quarter of her own output. So these exports amounted to only one-eighth of the total consumption of manufactured goods in the rest of the world.

countries embarked in imitation of England and under her influence. The industries which she had transformed first of all – cotton and iron – were precisely those which were most likely to conquer wide markets at home and abroad. This concentration was one of the secrets of England's growth and her domination of world trade. The attainment of this domination had furthermore been enhanced by the Napoleonic wars, during which England's mastery of the seas had assured her a virtual monopoly of markets outside Europe. It was a position which she had largely been able to maintain after 1815, thanks to the low prices of her goods, the excellence of her trade networks and the habits acquired by consumers. Moreover she did not hesitate to resort to diplomacy or war or the exercise of her sea-power in order to widen her markets, for example in the opium war against China. It is estimated that around 1850 she had not only sole control of 20 per cent of the world's total trade, but also more than 40 per cent of the trade in manufactured goods. Around 1860 she was responsible for 30 per cent of Europe's commerce with outside countries, but 43 per cent of European exports of manufactured goods[21].

In addition, at a time when whole continents were almost empty or at a stage of extreme underdevelopment, awaiting immigrants, capital and equipment, Britain was almost the only country capable of supplying capital and capital goods, and the world economy tended to develop in a fashion which complemented the British economy. The 'new' or underdeveloped countries were developed thanks to English capital and equipment, and they became economic satellites of England (whether or not they belonged to the formal colonial empire, to which was added an informal empire). These new countries and even a number of European countries (especially among the smaller ones), supplied themselves with manufactured goods mostly from Britain and sent her their primary produce in exchange[22]. Furthermore she gave credit to the whole world, thanks to her abundant capital, the strength of her currency and a sophisticated banking system; but she did not demand credit in return. She sold her exports on credit but paid cash

[21]   Mathias, *The First Industrial Nation*, p. 251; S. Kuznets, *Modern Economic Growth; Rate, Structure and Spread* (New Haven and London, 1966), p. 306 (table 6.3) (the UK's share in total world trade was to reach its peak at 25 per cent in the decade 1860–70; as early as 1820–30 it probably exceeded 20 per cent); Bairoch, *Commerce extérieur*, p. 171. It is true that Switzerland led in terms of exports per head. In 1876–80, the UK still enjoyed 38 per cent of world trade in manufactured goods.

[22]   A tendency that was reinforced by GB's growing import-needs, because of her inadequate natural resources (except coal) and a rapid increase in her population. It was facilitated by her conversion to free trade (1842–6) which opened her to the products of all countries, but mainly to primary produce, because where manufactured goods were concerned her industry at first had no competition to fear, except in a few specialities.

for imports. World trade was dominated by the 'bill on London', almost an international currency, and it was largely financed by the City.

So between the end of the eighteenth and the middle of the nineteenth century Britain became the dominant economic power. This position was certainly the result of a unique combination of historical circumstances but was destined to be transitory. Although the Victorian era saw the zenith of British economic power and its predominance, it also saw the beginning of a relative decline which was to be no temporary phenomenon but was to continue and intensify right up to our own times.

This change of fortune started, as we shall see, with the slowing-down of British growth in the last decades of the nineteenth century, while other industrial powers progressed faster, and it is an essential theme of the present study. However, we must emphasize at once that the erosion of Britain's dominant position was slow and partial up to the end of Victoria's reign, and even up to the first world war[23].

Certainly Britain conceded first place among the industrial powers to the United States around 1880, the latter going ahead a little before 1880 on total GNP, and a little after on GNP per head. Bairoch reckons that the United States became the greatest economic power in the developed world in 1880, but he points out that this advance derived above all from the high productivity of their agriculture and that, as far as industrial production per head was concerned, the United States only surpassed the United Kingdom at the beginning of the twentieth century[24]. Then, from about 1905, Germany raised herself into second place among industrial powers, though in 1913 she was only slightly ahead of the United Kingdom on total GNP and far behind on GNP per head. None the less, on the eve of the first world war, Britain still kept first position as regards the textile industry[25] and her level of industrialization certainly remained the highest in the world[26]. It is

---

[23] This problem will be analysed in detail in Chapter 12.

[24] Bairoch, *Commerce extérieur*, pp. 19, 177.

[25] See Bairoch, *Commerce extérieur*, p. 138 (table 43), for 1913:

	Production of pig-iron	Consumption of raw cotton (kg. per inhabitant)
United Kindgom	228	22
Continental Europe	82	4
Germany	250	7

[26] Bairoch, *Commerce extérieur*, p. 137, has calculated an index of the level of industrialization (based on the ratio between industrial production volume and population) in 1898/1902. On a base of 100 for the whole of Europe we have:

United Kingdom	254
Belgium	230
Germany	177
Switzerland	150
France	140

true – indeed a more serious feature – that Britain had lost her technological superiority and had even fallen behind in several important spheres where her productivity stagnated. But of course her decline as an industrial power was only relative and her production continued to increase, although more slowly than that of several other countries.

But in all other spheres – foreign trade, services, finance – Britain held first place in 1901 and even in 1913. She remained the most important commercial power of Europe (with 24 per cent of total European exports in 1913[27], a reduced share since the zenith in 1860 when the proportion was 30 per cent) and also the first commercial power of the world. According to various estimates, Britain in 1913 accounted for 14 or 15.5 per cent of total world trade, which had enormously increased in the previous half-century. She was closely followed by the United States and by Germany, who had almost caught her up in exports[28].

Besides this, the British merchant fleet remained the largest in the world with a third of total tonnage in 1913, and it handled a large proportion of international traffic between non-British ports. British insurance companies and the commodity exchanges in London and Liverpool played a world role. London remained the world's most powerful financial centre and Great Britain the main source of long-term capital for other countries. She was also the first creditor nation, who had invested enormous sums abroad and continued to do so thanks to the permanent surplus in her balance of payments. Conversely, large sums were placed on short term in the City by foreigners. Sterling was the only reserve currency, and it was the currency in which international transactions were normally billed. The international gold standard was in fact a sterling standard regulated by the Bank of England, which wielded enormous power over world conditions of credit and whose discount rate controlled the policy of other central banks. Moreover most overseas countries and several European countries remained economic satellites of England. The latter's supremacy as exporter and importer, as shipowner, intermediary, commission agent and banker, her position at the centre of the delicate and complex international system of trade and multilateral payments, guaranteed the unity of the world economy in

---

[27]   Domestic exports. If re-exports were added, the percentage would be higher, as GB preserved a fair-sized entrepôt trade.

[28]   Kuznets, pp. 307–8 (table 6.3). The UK's share was 13 per cent of world traded exports and 15 per cent for imports. But the value of manufactured exports from GB was more than twice that of the US.

the Indian summer of liberal capitalism just before the first world war, and it ensured the smooth running and relative stability of the system[29].

Even if the British economy showed certain signs of weakness at the beginning of the twentieth century, she still remained the predominant economy, although less markedly than half a century earlier. In any case these few pages must have demonstrated that the supremacy enjoyed by England in the world economy was a most important factor not only in the economic history of the nineteenth century, but in the general history of that period. Furthermore it was a vital formative influence in the economy of Britain herself and its development.

A FEW MAIN TRENDS

We shall now outline the main trends of this development during the Victorian era, which is the main subject of this book. On the economic level, in any case, they remain straightforward and boil down very roughly to the continuation of a rate of economic growth which was rapid compared with the centuries of traditional economy (but rather slow in absolute terms as we shall see) and of the process of industrialization which had been launched by the Industrial Revolution at the end of the eighteenth century. Although in fact at Queen Victoria's accession Britain was already an 'industrial nation' for whom industry had become the prime activity, one must avoid anachronism, clearly seeing the limits within which industrialization developed, and remaining aware of everything that had not changed[30]. Certainly agriculture had given way to industry, from the standpoint both of labour employed and of contribution to national product, but it remained an important sector of the economy (not to mention its dominant political influence), and the British still for the most part lived in rural areas. Even within industry the new forms of production and organization created by the Industrial Revolution (i.e. large-scale industry mechanized and based on factories) for all their rapid and spectacular rise remained in a minority as compared with small-scale industry and artisan production that were largely traditional.

[29] Yet the financial predominance of London had become precarious, for it no longer corresponded with some fundamental realities of the world economy.
[30] Some very pertinent remarks on this subject are made by E.A.Wrigley in his review of R.M.Reeve, *The Industrial Revolution, 1750–1850* (London, 1971), in *Economic History Review*, 2nd series, XXVI (4), Nov. 1973, p. 703. He underlines the slowness of change up to 1850 as shown in this work and suggests that 'the Industrial Revolution was more a loose federation of associated changes than a unitary phenomenon until well into the nineteenth century'.

Although the first railway line of more than local interest, the Liverpool and Manchester Railway, had been solemnly inaugurated in 1830, and although from 1833 to 1837 England experienced her first boom of railway promotions, there were only 540 miles of railway track in service at the end of 1837. And, similarly, although the United Kingdom possessed 624 steam vessels in 1837 there were 19,912 sailing ships still in use.

The following decades saw the conclusion of the Industrial Revolution in the usually accepted, limited sense of the word; for in a broader sense the nature of this irreversible process is that it has never stopped and still goes on under our eyes. There then followed a whole series of technological and structural changes, always interdependent, which responded to the pressure of factors such as technical progress, capital accumulation and the evolution of the international context. They were changes which were certainly less dramatic and spectacular than those of the preceding period, the time of economic revolution strictly speaking, and their rhythm varied, especially in terms of the important phenomenon already mentioned – the slowing-down of growth at the end of the nineteenth century; but they were changes which in the end would profoundly transform Great Britain by the time the inconsolable Widow of Windsor departed this world.

Agriculture, which went into a speedy and continuous relative decline and also ran into serious difficulties in the last quarter of the nineteenth century, was to become a minor and almost insignificant sector of the British economy by the beginning of the twentieth. Then, a minority of the population remained in the rural areas while more than three-quarters piled into the towns and especially into the very large towns. The output of industry and the services sector was to grow enormously, and furthermore industrial processes became almost entirely of a modern type, carried out by machines that were themselves driven by steam and also, though on a limited scale, by electricity. A dense network of railways covered the whole country, and in the ports steamships now far outnumbered sailing-ships. A large share of the national wealth consisted of overseas investments, from which a sizeable percentage of the national income was derived.

British society was also changing. The Industrial Revolution did not simply lead to technological and economic change, it touched off a social revolution – cumulative, relatively slow, without violent rifts (at least in Great Britain), sometimes hardly noticeable, but always profound. As ever, these two revolutions, so intimately linked that they can be regarded as one phenomenon, were both destructive and creative. They disorganized, dissolved and even demolished the old social structures, a process which was already at work in Britain just after Waterloo when, according to Harold Perkin, the class society with its horizontal divisions and alliances permanently succeeded the society of the eighteenth century with its vertical links of dependence and patronage, where class divisions were only latent[31]. *A fortiori* the same process was at work in 1837. These silent revolutions led to a redistribution of the population, both occupationally and geographically, particularly as the result of rapid urbanization. As the development of towns in Britain was anarchic and haphazard, social change posed formidable new problems in the fields of housing, hygiene, health, law and order, and education – not to mention the problems which resulted from new work-conditions in factories. They were problems which caught contemporaries unawares and overwhelmed them. Government and voluntary effort only tried to find solutions late in the day, and even then only partially. The problems were all the greater because English society was very lightly policed and it had 'a cruel, primitive background' (G. Kitson Clark). The brutality, the violence, the drunkenness, the physical and moral degradation that were widespread in traditional societies were on the whole aggravated by industrialization, and it was only slowly that this society acquired humanity and became less cruel for the poor and the weak.

Furthermore, industrialization tended to weaken relatively, and even sometimes to eliminate, certain traditional social groups, while it gave birth to new groups and classes. There was the industrial proletariat of factory workers, which formed a growing part of the lower classes, and on the other side there arose the industrial bourgeoisie in the general framework of the rising middle classes. So industrialization brought with it a profound change in the balance of power within society, and led to serious tensions, given at the start the inadequacy of the institutions available to cope with the new social structure and also the violent contrast between the wealth of a minority and the poverty of the masses. Poverty had been inherited by industrial society from the traditional economy, but for a fairly long time it received little remedy from economic growth. It is true that, for all sorts of reasons (but this is no place to unravel them), England escaped the violent revolutions which these tensions and class conflicts might have provoked, and which were experienced by other nations.

---

[31] Even though these links survived in some parts of society, notably in the country. But on the whole there was an end to the stability of the eighteenth century, when the middle and lower echelons of society accepted as natural and just the exclusive government by the aristocracy.

Steadily and peacefully reforms of every sort adapted institutions to social changes and tackled some of the problems which were posed. The new 'counter-society' of 'black' England, which was created by the Industrial Revolution, developed outside an institutional framework that was almost unchanged since the seventeenth century. This led to strong protests from traditional élites and also from the poverty-stricken and disorderly masses, so that the 'counter-society' was only slowly admitted to the established community. Nevertheless, because of the slow-moving stolidity of social structures, political institutions and mentalities, a time-lag developed between economic change and other types of change, leading to the continued survival of the old social order. In particular, there was the paradox that in a country that was becoming more and more industrialized, the ruling class remained, until almost the end of Victoria's reign, the great landowners.

Yet technical progress and economic growth amassed wealth, created employment and led to such an increase in productivity that the goods and services available per head of population multiplied several times over (not a fractional growth such as had been achieved in the most favourable phases of traditional society's development); and all this in spite of an unprecedented rate of population growth. From this followed a very noticeable rise in the average standard of living and, in spite of an extremely unequal distribution of wealth and income, a progressive spread of affluence in the middle and lower strata of society. Ancestral poverty, which still burdened the mass of the population at the beginning of the nineteenth century, retreated (though it certainly did not disappear) and the living standards of the working classes made real progress, especially in the second half of the nineteenth century.

Furthermore, the more elaborate division of labour, which, as taught by Adam Smith, is an essential aspect of economic progress, multiplied the range of specialized occupations and created new forms of labour. This induced a diversification and elaboration of the social structure and occupational hierarchy, partly as a result of the development of the middle classes but also partly from a less elementary stratification of the working classes, which ceased to be an indeterminate mass of 'labouring poor' – their designation at the outset of the nineteenth century. Finally a limited but growing intervention on the part of the state brought the beginnings of a solution to the grave problems created by industrialization and urbanization.

Yet, as Harold Perkin has justly claimed, Victorian industrial capitalism was a half-way house, a transitional stage between the traditional society of the eighteenth century and that of the present day[32]. As in the economic sphere, a study which is balanced and avoids anachronism must give due emphasis to the aspects of both permanence and change. In particular, although a new balance of power had become established in politics, Victorian society remained extremely hierarchical and inegalitarian, with enormous differences of income and living standards between the base and the summit of the social pyramid. Although Victorian society displayed a mainly bourgeois complexion as the result of the progress of the middle classes and the influence of their values both on the upper classes and on the more prosperous stratum of the working class, it preserved many of the aristocratic traits of eighteenth-century England[33].

---

[32] H. Perkin, *The Origins of Modern English Society, 1780–1880* (London, 1969), p. 1, also pp. 3–5 for preceding points.
[33] The aristocracy absorbed and gradually integrated the top layer of the middle class. But, in addition, an organized workers' movement developed; and there was progress towards political democracy. This had for long seemed to be synonymous with social revolution, but in fact it integrated the working class into the body politic. So there was never a complete preponderance of the middle classes.

Part 1
A macroeconomic survey

1 The demographic boom

During the seven centuries that separated the Norman conquest from the Declaration of Independence by the United States, the population of England probably multiplied by six or seven, growing from a little more than 1 million to more than 7 million inhabitants. But the progression was irregular, consisting not only of many short-term fluctuations but also of two long cycles – an increase up to the Black Death, slump, then prolonged stagnation, sharp recovery from the end of the fifteenth century and growth up to around 1640-50, stagnation or slow growth at the end of the seventeenth century and beginning of the eighteenth, finally a fresh jump leading to the fastest rate of growth ever known in Britain, that of the nineteenth century. In only 110 years, from 1801, the year of the first census, to 1911, her population almost quadrupled, and within the span of Victoria's reign it rather more than doubled, with a continuous rise as demonstrated by table 3[1].

This fast and continuous growth, though with certain variations in its rhythm, was without precedent, and it has sometimes been described as the Demographic Revolution, because it constituted a decisive change both in the development and the size of the British population.

The beginnings of this growth are still obscure for lack of satisfactory statistical data for the eighteenth century, but it seems that the increase in population started in the middle of that century. Then there was a marked acceleration in the 1780s[2], which went on

---

[1] Taken from B.R. Mitchell and P. Deane, *Abstract of British Historical Statistics* (Cambridge, 1962), p. 6. This basic collection of statistics is quoted hereafter as *Abstract*. In 1837 the population of GB has been estimated as 17.6 million (ibid., p. 8). The author warmly thanks J.P. Poussou for his suggestions and remarks on this chapter.

[2] M. Drake (ed.), *Population in Industrialization* (London, 1969), p. 1: the mean rate of growth of the English population was probably 0.2 per cent per year in the first half of the eighteenth century and 0.9 per cent in the second half.

Table 3　Population of Great Britain

Mid-year	Millions of inhabitants
1801	10.5
1831	16.3
1841	18.5
1851	20.8
1871	26.1
1881	29.7
1901	37.0
1911	40.8

N.B. The first censuses were imperfect and several historians think that they underestimate the total population (by 5 per cent in 1801, by 1 per cent in 1831), which would mean a slight reduction in the growth for the first decades.

into the beginning of the nineteenth century. Between 1811 and 1821 the percentage increase per decade of British population was at its peak, reaching 17 per cent[3]. Then we observe a distinct slowing-down, caused by several years of high mortality. The increase between 1851 and 1861 was only 11 per cent, but then there was a recovery[4] which led to a new maximum of 13.9 per cent between 1871 and 1881. It is true that from 1881 onwards, there occurred a fairly noticeable decline and this time it was more permanent, becoming even more pronounced between the two world wars. The increase from 1901 to 1911 was only 10.3 per cent, still quite an impressive percentage, and between 1881 and 1911 Britain acquired 11 million new inhabitants[5]. Altogether the annual average growth-rate of British population between 1801 and 1911 was 1.26 per cent, and from 1841 to 1901 it was 1.16 per cent. Between one census and another the increase was always higher than 10 per cent, and substantially more in several decades[6].

It is true that this expansion was not peculiar to Britain and was part of a general movement which affected all European countries, but Britain showed a growth-rate in the course of the nineteenth century (and especially during the first half) which was notably higher than

[3]　P. Deane and W.A. Cole, *British Economic Growth, 1688–1959* (Cambridge, 2nd edn., 1967), p. 172: the annual rate of growth reached a maximum of 1.5 per cent between 1801 and 1831, then fell to 1.3 per cent between 1821 and 1851 and 1.2 per cent thereafter.

[4]　ibid., where this recovery is attributed to the effects of the Irish immigration after the famine (cf. p. 23.)

[5]　ibid., p. 288 (table 75).

[6]　Rate of 1.38 per cent between 1801 and 1851, and 1.13 per cent between 1851 and 1911.

that of most other countries, and of Europe as a whole[7]. On the other hand this advance was much less rapid than the demographic explosion of the underdeveloped countries in the twentieth century. The overall population of the latter has increased by more than 2 per cent per annum, and the growth of some countries has been at the rate of more than 3 per cent, the difference with Victorian Britain being explained mainly by the persistence of a relatively high death-rate.

The increase in population would have been greater but for the considerable emigration, mainly to the United States, followed by the new countries of the British empire – Canada, Australia, New Zealand, South Africa (the latter's share becoming preponderant at the beginning of the twentieth century)[8]. This emigration, which was on an individual, unorganized basis, consisted mostly of young adult males, so that in addition to the direct loss of this human capital there was added the subsequent absence of the children and descendants which these emigrants would have had in Britain if they had stayed. It is true that emigration was a safety valve which eased some economic and social tensions, that it brought some remedy to pauperism and unemployment[9] and that it opened up opportunities for the ambitious emigrants, for it included a fair percentage of educated and skilled men, which proves that the process was not simply a flight from penury[10]. What is more, this emigration, by contributing to the peopling and development of the new countries, opened up markets and sources of supply of primary products for Britain[11]. It was the result (in varying proportions according to periods) of the difficulty of finding jobs in Britain and of the attraction of overseas countries[12]. It showed clear fluctuations, in which Brinley Thomas has identified

[7] According to P. Bairoch, *Commerce extérieur et développement économique de l'Europe au XIXe siècle* (Paris – The Hague, 1976), p. 13, the rate of growth of Europe's population between 1820 and 1913 was 0.8 per cent per annum.

[8] 36 per cent of Europeans who emigrated overseas in the nineteenth century were British (including Irish); Bairoch, *Commerce extérieur*, p. 112.

[9] Whence various schemes, official or private, to encourage it.

[10] F. Bédarida, *A Social History of England 1851–1975* (London, 1979), p. 16.

[11] Yet Bairoch, *Commerce extérieur*, p. 122, weighs up its net result as negative, for it constituted a real transfer of factors of production. This helped on the industrialization of the United States, where England lost markets for her own industry, and the development of farm production in the new countries, which did serious harm to English agriculture at the end of the nineteenth century.

[12] It is the debate (on which we will not linger here) on the role of the 'push' and 'pull' factors, i.e. repulsion and attraction. See, for example, L.E. Gallaway and R.K. Vedder, 'Emigration from the United Kingdom to the United States, 1860–1913', *Journal of Economic History*, XXI (4), Dec. 1971, 885–97, which favours the preponderant influence of the 'pull' effect, i.e. the attraction of the United States and notably of opportunities for employment there.

'long cycles' lasting twenty years, linked to the differing conditions –
particularly as regards capital investment and house-building–on
both sides of the Atlantic, with 'an inverse relation between the
fluctuations of internal migration and home investment on the one
hand and those of emigration (and capital exports) on the other'[13].

Emigration was insignificant at the beginning of the nineteenth
century. It gathered pace in the 1830s and 1840s,[14] and even more so
later, being aided and indeed stimulated by the progress of sea-transport and the lowering of fares. Its great booms were in the 1850s, very
much in the 1880s, and even more so in the years which just preceded
the first world war, a period that was marked by a stagnation and even
a fall in investment and real wages in Britain[15].

Unfortunately statistics on emigration are defective. From 1860 to
1913 the net total (i.e. after deducting emigrants who returned) of
British subjects who left British ports bound for overseas countries
(excluding Europe) was 6,964,000, of whom 2,324,000 left during the
years 1900-13 alone. But these figures include Irish emigrants who
were particularly numerous (3.6–3.8 million between 1850 and
1910).[16] Furthermore, N. Tranter has calculated that between 1841
and 1915 England and Wales alone suffered a net loss by emigration of
9.6 million people, of whom more than 2.5 million left between 1911
and 1915[17]. On the other hand, according to Deane and Cole, the
negative balance on foreign migration for England during the second
half of the nineteenth century was probably only one million people;
but it was well over half a million between 1901 and the first world
war[18].

It seems impossible to decide between such different results, but it

[13] B. Thomas, *Migration and Economic Growth: A Study of Britain and the Atlantic Economy* (Cambridge, 1954), p. 126; passage cited by Deane and Cole, p. 289. See also B. Thomas, *Migration and Urban Development* (London, 1972). These views have been severely criticized.

[14] But, for England, it was more than offset by Scottish and Irish immigration before the middle of the nineteenth century. Between 1841 and 1851 there would have been a net gain of 294,000 people by migratory movements; Deane and Cole, p. 10 (table 4).

[15] The peak years were: 1851–5, 1881–5, 1896–1905, 1911–15.

[16] P. Mathias, *The First Industrial Nation: An Economic History of Britain, 1700–1914* (London, 1969), p. 452; *Abstract*, pp. 47–9; C.O'Grada, 'A note on nineteenth-century Irish emigration statistics', *Population Studies*, XXIX, 1975, 143–9. Bédarida, p. 30, mentions more than 3 million definitive departures from GB between 1850 and 1880.

[17] N. Tranter, *Population Since the Industrial Revolution: The Case of England and Wales* (London, 1973), p. 53 (table III). This figure was calculated from the figures of total population set against the excess of births over deaths. Yet it does seem enormous.

[18] Deane and Cole, pp. 10 (table 4), 289 (after A.K. Cairncross, 'Internal migration in England', in *Home and Foreign Investment, 1850–1913: Studies in Capital Accumulation* (Cambridge, 1953), p. 71 (table 14)).

must be emphasized that Great Britain also took in immigrants, mainly Irish (about a million from 1850 to 1910), and endured the backlash of her neighbour's demographic evolution, which was extraordinary and very different. The population of Ireland also increased rapidly after the late eighteenth century, roughly doubling in sixty years to pass 8.2 million at the beginning of the 1840s. But in 1845 there occurred the catastrophe of the potato blight, for the potato was the basic food of the Irish. The economic and social structure of Ireland, an unindustrialized country largely inhabited by indigent peasants growing potatoes on small patches of land, made her vulnerable to a 'Malthusian' crisis, so that she endured a terrible famine, accompanied by epidemics, which lasted up to 1848. This disaster killed between 500,000 and 700,000 people and forced one million Irishmen to emigrate between 1846 and 1851[19]. Between the censuses of 1841 and 1851 the population of the island dropped from 8.2 to 6.6 million. It was destined never to recover from this disaster and numbers continued to decline because of low fertility resulting from late marriage and permanent celibacy for many adults, and also from continued emigration in large numbers. By 1911 the population had fallen to 4.4 million, which made Ireland a unique case among European countries in the nineteenth century[20]. The influx across the Irish Channel, which in fact started well before the famine, consisted of poor, unskilled labourers and had important social consequences, influencing the labour market, reinforcing the ranks of the subproletariat and intensifying the overcrowding in the poorest quarters of the larger towns. Finally, at the end of the nineteenth and beginning of the twentieth century, a far from negligible immigration of Jews from eastern Europe took place, notably to certain quarters of London's East End. In spite of these additions to her population Great Britain suffered a net loss from emigration, and the demographic advance was therefore entirely the result of natural growth. For want of statistics there has been much controversy about the causes of the demographic 'take-off' in the eighteenth century and of the break in the equilibrium which kept the population of traditional societies stable in the long term. Some attribute the change to a fall in death-rate, others to a rise in fertility and the birth rate, others to a combination of the two

---

[19] C. Woodham-Smith, *The Great Hunger: Ireland 1845–9* (London, 1964), pp. 411–12 gives the excessively high figure of 1.5 million deaths. But there was certainly also a deficiency in births.

[20] The population of Ireland therefore fell from being 30 per cent of that of the UK in 1841 to 10 per cent in 1911.

phenomena[21]. Fortunately, the situation is clear and simple for the nineteenth century, especially from the start of civil registration of births, marriages and deaths, thanks to which these variables are well known for England from 1838 onwards. The country benefited from a strong natural increase because of the prolonged continuation of a high birth-rate, which was markedly higher than the death-rate: roughly three births occurred for two deaths throughout the period. The excess of births over deaths remained considerable even when the birth-rate dropped significantly at the end of the nineteenth century.

From 1841 to 1880, the five-year average of the birth-rate in *England* remained remarkably stable, oscillating imperceptibly between 35.2 and 35.8 per thousand and falling only once, in 1846–50, below 35 per thousand – and then only to 34.8![22] It is probable that the birth-rate was about the same level at the beginning of the nineteenth century, and it may sometimes have been even higher. A crude birth-rate of 42 per thousand has been mentioned for the 1811–21 decade, which saw the biggest percentage jump of the total population. Consequently the net reproducton rate remained high; even rising somewhat from 1.3 for the decade 1841/50 to 1.5 for 1871/80[23].

England and Wales experienced a high fertility-rate because of the restricted use of contraception and also because of the extent of available economic opportunities and the widening of 'work horizons'. Although the question of the Industrial Revolution's influence on population is a thorny and controversial one, it would seem that by creating wider job opportunities the Industrial Revolution led to a lowering of the age of marriage and so caused an increase in fertility[24].

---

[21] Thus Deane and Cole, pp. 286–8, who notice regional variations in the pattern of demographic growth. In industrial regions births went up; in London deaths went down. From the beginning of the nineteenth century these regional variations became less marked. On these discussions, see: Drake; M.W. Flinn, *British Population Growth, 1700–1850* (London, 1970); R. Mitchison, *British Population Change Since 1860* (London, 1977); E.A. Wrigley and R.S. Schofield, *The Population History of England: A Reconstruction* (London, 1981).

[22] See Tranter, p. 53 (table III).

[23] This rate is the ratio of female children being born to women at present in the child-bearing age-group and who are expected to survive to child-bearing age, if the rates of fertility and mortality by age remain unchanged; cf. E.A. Wrigley, *Population and History* (London, 1969), p. 195 (table 5.16); Bédarida, p. 113.

[24] But it is absurd to assert that the employment of children on a large scale in industry (which was nothing new) encouraged couples to have as many as possible, in order to increase the family income. They had to be fed for several years before they could work! The role played by age at marriage has been challenged by N.F.R. Crafts and N.J. Ireland, 'A simulation of the impact of changes in age at marriage before and during the advent of industrialization in England', *Population Studies*, XXX (3), 1976, 495–511.

In fact, fertility was higher and the age of marriages lower in industrial regions than in the parts of the country that had remained purely agricultural, although, of course, internal migration and the age structure of a younger population in the industrial districts were also contributing factors[25].

After 1880 the birth-rate suddenly showed a distinct decline, although this fall occurred gradually:

1881/85	33.5 per cent
1896/1900	29.3 per cent
1906/10	26.3 per cent
1911/13	24.1 per cent

The net reproduction-rate fell to 1.2 for 1901/10, and on the eve of the first world war the replacement of the generations was only just assured. The birth-rate certainly remained high, especially as compared wih France in the same period, but the downward tendency was destined to last during the interwar period and finally brought the birth-rate down to a very low level.

This change can be partly explained by later marriage, which led to a lower marriage-rate[26]. In 1911 the percentage of married individuals aged between 20 and 24 was one-third less than it had been in 1881. But the principal factor was the tendency of married couples to have fewer children. Table 4 shows that this decline in births began after 1860 and became very pronounced after the marriage cohort of 1871[27].

Add to this that out of 100 women married between 1870 and 1879, 61 had at least five children (and 17 had more than ten), and only 21 had fewer than three. For those married between 1900 and 1909, the corresponding figures were 28, 1 and 45.

There is absolutely no doubt that deliberate voluntary limitation of births was being practised – though much more by the old *coitus interruptus* method than by the new contraceptives which technical progress had made safer and handier. Although mass manufacture at low prices began at the end of the nineteenth century, their use remained limited. This 'prudence' was not entirely new. It had appeared among the nobility at the beginning of the nineteenth

---

[25]   Furthermore, industrial regions contain a growing percentage of total population.
[26]   An additional factor was an abnormal disproportion between the sexes, to the women's advantage, connected probably with large-scale emigration, which was essentially male.
[27]   Wrigley, *Population and History*, p. 197 (table 5.17); Tranter, p. 98 (table IV). This is the average number of children born of marriages contracted when the wife was less than 45 years old.

Table 4   Diminution of the number of children
per family by marriage cohorts in England and
Wales

Year of marriage	Number of children
1861/69	6.16
1871	5.94
1876	5.62
1886	4.81
1890/99	4.13
1900/09	3.30

century, especially noticeable in the postponement of marriage, then it
had spread into the middle classes (particularly the professions) and
into the households of some skilled working men (for instance, in the
textile industry during the 1850s) to such an extent that, even before
1880, marked differences were to be observed in the fertility of various
social groups. The decline in fertility after that date was similarly
variable according to class, being more pronounced in well-to-do circles
and less so among labourers, miners and agricultural workers[28]. On
the whole, however, birth-control became much more common at the
end of the nineteenth century, and this general move makes an
important turning-point around 1880 in the demographic behaviour of
the British people[29].

The explanation of this change, however, is debatable and remains
uncertain. A number of historians quote the simultaneous lowering of
infantile and child mortality – a topic to which we shall return [30]. The
survival of more children, according to this theory, led people to avoid
new births in order to balance family budgets. This attitude was
encouraged by the increase in the cost of bringing up children,
resulting from the limitation of child labour and the establishment of
compulsory schooling up to 13 years (1880). For the middle classes,
there was the growing concern of parents to send their sons to good
schools which would give them a better chance of successful careers
and social promotion, but whose fees were not compatible with large
families. Working in the same direction among the middle classes and
the better paid among the working classes was the desire to maintain
or improve living standards at a time when real incomes were rising
and the range of consumer articles widening. Anxiety about the future

[28] Wrigley, *Population and History*, p. 186–7 (table 5.13).
[29] Bédarida, p. 113.
[30] E.A. Wrigley, in *Economic History Review* 2nd series, XXVI (4), Nov. 1973, 726–7,
strongly criticizes the idea that this fall resulted in parents, who needed to have
fewer children in all so that a given number should survive, limiting their offspring.

arising from Britain's economic difficulties were also increasing at the end of the nineteenth century. Finally, one must take into account neo-Malthusian propaganda and the decline of the churches' influence, or at least that of the Anglican Church which remained hostile to birth control for a long time, while the Nonconformists supported it much earlier[31].

Despite the fall in the birth-rate, the population of Britain continued to increase after 1880, although more slowly than before, thanks to the decline in the death-rate.

It is probable, but by no means certain, that the death-rate had fallen in the second half of the eighteenth century. Around 1800 the crude rate was probably around 25 per thousand, and is likely to have diminished a little during the decades that followed. But from the 1830s to the 1870s, although there were short-term fluctuations with a few peaks in years of economic depression or epidemics (such as 1847 and 1849), the death-rate was constant in the long term at about 22 per thousand. For *England*, five-year averages from 1841/45 to 1876/80 oscillated between 20.8 and 23.3 per thousand. After 1880, however, the death-rate dropped, as did the birth-rate (but less rapidly, hence the slowing-down of population growth after 1880), falling below 20 per thousand:

1881/85	19.4 per thousand
1896/1900	17.7 per thousand
1906/10	14.7 per thousand
1911/13	14.0 per thousand

Thus a large excess of births over deaths, more than 10 per thousand inhabitants or even more, persisted throughout the nineteenth century, only to narrow at the beginning of the twentieth century.

One should note that the long-term fall in the death-rate started at various dates according to age-groups[32]. The 5–34 years age-group was the first to benefit at mid-century, then the 35–54 group, and finally the over-54s in the 1880s. Children's mortality was an important factor in the high level of general mortality, and this began to drop in the 1860s for children between the ages of 1 and 4 years. But infant mortality in the strict sense of the word – the number of children dying between 0 and 1 year per 1000 live births – remained unchanged at a high average level[33] (over 150 per 1000) right to the end of the nineteenth century. It only fell at the beginning of the twentieth

---

[31] See Tranter, ch. 4, pp. 97ff. But these various explanations do not carry conviction.
[32] Wrigley, *Population and History*, pp. 166–7 (fig. 5.3); Tranter, pp. 57–8.
[33] Yet it may have declined a little at the beginning of the nineteenth century, and it was then doubtless lower than on the continent.

century, and then sharply, thanks to the new weapons in the fight against infectious diseases. The figures were 156 per 1000 in England in 1896/1900, 109 per 1000 in 1909/13. Of course this infant death-rate varied, with sharp differences according to social class and income level, and also according to locality. In 1840, for example, the expectation of life at birth was twice as high for a native of Surrey as it was for a native of Manchester.

It is surprising how late in the nineteenth century the big drop in mortality came. Recent analyses have suggested that its diminution in the eighteenth century (which is the subject of controversy) resulted mainly from the disappearance of exceptional mortality caused by famine[34], due to agricultural development (which also led to food of a higher quality), and from a chance reduction in the virulence of serious epidemics. However, these were once-and-for-all gains. In the nineteenth century, the potential factors for reducing mortality had a limited effect for many years, and other forces worked in the opposite direction. Medicine remained helpless in the face of many infectious diseases whose causes were unknown[35]. Although Jenner's discovery of vaccination in 1798 was important, its spread was slow and its effects remain debatable[36]. There were serious outbreaks of cholera in 1832, in 1849 and as late as 1866. Tuberculosis was endemic, being encouraged by a damp climate and by overcrowded housing and unhealthy places of work. The number of doctors and hospitals was quite inadequate for the size of the population; the standard of living of the working classes was very low at the beginning of the nineteenth century and improved only slowly up to mid-century; and even at the end of the century a large section of the population remained in poverty. Hygiene and housing conditions in the towns were deplorable for a long time, and the mortality in the slums (which were themselves extensive) was appalling. So it was only at the end of the nineteenth century that gradual progress in these areas (for instance in the provision of clean drinking-water and the construction of drains), together with improvements in nutrition, personal hygiene and child-care, were advanced enough to reduce the ever-present menace of death.

[34]   It is true that the last nation-wide famine in England was in 1597, or at the latest in the 1690s. But things were different in Scotland and Ireland.
[35]   Let us not forget that Prince Albert died of typhoid.
[36]   Most historians maintain that its role must not be overestimated. But P. Razzell, *The Conquest of Smallpox: The Impact of Inoculation on Smallpox Mortality in Eighteenth-Century Britain* (Firle, Sussex, 1977), affirms the profound effect of the disappearance of smallpox, without which the death-rate would have been much higher in the nineteenth century, especially among children.

It seems that the factors explaining the rapid increase of British population from the end of the eighteenth to the beginning of the twentieth century were not constant nor did they always apply with the same force. The factors which sparked off the demographic 'take-off' at the end of the eighteenth century were doubtless different from those that led later to a swift and continuous increase in population[37]. In any case, the nineteenth century was for a long time a period of transition for the British people, revealing at the same time certain traditional demographic aspects (e.g. high birth-rate and mortality, especially infant mortality) and other, modern aspects (e.g. swift growth, without the intervening periods of stagnation or decline suffered by traditional societies, and also, in the later stages, a notable reduction in the death-rate). When finally this growth slowed down, it was not explained, as in earlier historical experience, by the Malthusian scourge of famines and epidemics (except in Ireland), but by a voluntary reduction in fertility[38]. So the end of the Victorian period saw the change to a new demographic situation – indeed some talk once again of a 'revolution' which affected most advanced countries simultaneously. It was a situation marked by low fertility and low death-rates, leading to slow growth.

Another trait which endured a long time was an age-structure in which the majority of the population was young.

Table 5 Distribution of the population of England and Wales by age-groups (as percentages of total population)[39]

	0–19 years	20–59 years	60 years and over
1821	49.0	43.4	7.3
1871	45.7	46.9	7.4
1911	39.9	52.0	8.0

In 1871 the age-pyramid was still little different from what it seems to have been at the end of the seventeenth century, according to Gregory King's data. This was normal, in spite of a hundred years of economic and social transformation, so long as the birth-and death-

---

[37] See Tranter, ch.3, pp.63ff.
[38] The high level of emigration in the 1880s and in the prewar period also contributed.
[39] After Tranter, p. 174 (table VIII). See also the data of Mathias, *The First Industrial Nation*, p. 450 (percentage of total population):

	0–14 years	15–64 years	65 years and over
1821	39	56	5
1851	35	60	5
1901	32	63	5

rates remained high. The decrease in the percentage of children in the population and the increase of the active age-group's percentage only occurred slowly, and the change was not noticeable until the end of the nineteenth and the beginning of the twentieth century[40]. The population then tended to get older, and the human wastage characteristic of traditional demography and of the Industrial Revolution decreased. Fewer men died in their prime, fewer children disappeared in infancy, and fewer women were exhausted by the effects of repeated pregnancies. The average expectation of life at birth remained low for a long time. In England it was only 40 years for men and 42 years for women born between 1838 and 1854. There was only slight improvement before 1880, but the expectation of life became 52 years and 55 years respectively for the cohort born between 1901 and 1912.

This new phenomenon, the rapid increase in population, worried a large section of British enlightened opinion, which took to heart the views expressed by Thomas Malthus in his *First Essay on the Principle of Population* (1798). This thesis maintained that population tended to grow by geometric progression, while the production of foodstuffs only increased by arithmetic progression. This meant that population growth could finally be halted by a catastrophic death-rate, unless births were voluntarily limited by the postponement of marriage and the strict continence of married couples. To the richer classes the demographic boom also seemed to be an agent of social revolution or at least of pauperism. These ideas had hardly any influence on demographic behaviour, but they did inspire certain policies destined to restrict the reproduction of the poorer classes, notably the reform of the Poor Law in 1834. In fact, Malthus was a prophet from the past who had admirably analysed the dilemma of traditional economies, but his model was only valid in terms of a static technology. It ignored the Industrial Revolution which was being played out under his very eyes and which was going to allow a rapidly increasing population to live and to enjoy a higher standard of living thanks to higher rates of economic growth[41].

[40]　Tranter, p. 175.
[41]　We shall analyse later, in Chapter 4, the question of internal migration and urbanization and, in Chapter 5, the influence of population on economic growth. On the problems raised here, see particularly, J.F.C. Harrison, *The Early Victorians, 1832–51* (London, Panther, 1973), ch.1, pp.23ff.

2 Economic growth

The Industrial Revolution – the Great Discontinuity, to use R.M. Hartwell's happy phrase – had snatched Great Britain at the end of the eighteenth century from a traditional economy, in which the growth of total production was slow and irregular, and that of production per head at best very small. It substituted an era of modern economic growth, which was relatively fast and sustained, and which affected not only total production but also (much more important) production per head of population[1]. This growth, whose pace had probably doubled during the last twenty or thirty years of the eighteenth century, continued throughout the nineteenth, and it is important to measure it. For a long time, historians were content to use a few isolated indicators (like the production of coal or pig-iron, consumption of raw cotton, value of exports), but their high rate of increase led people to overestimate the growth of the British economy. More recently several economists and statisticians, applying modern national accounting methods to past periods, have worked out some national income series for Great Britain or the United Kingdom which give a more satisfactory picture of total growth. But the primary statistical data available for these calculations, although they are more abundant and

---

[1] 'Growth' is increase in production over a *long* period. It should be distinguished from 'expansion', which is a temporary increase (usually in the course of a business cycle) and reversible. Sustained growth implies changes in the structure of economy and of society, and is often called 'development'. In the nineteenth century the two concepts are more or less identical. Economic growth, which was the darling of the quarter century after the second world war, is no longer fashionable. It must be admitted that it has its negative aspects and external costs, e.g. in the deterioration of the environment (nineteenth-century towns, like those of the twentieth, suffered from pollution that was different, but more dangerous), in the 'quality of life', in erosion of moral values and in human consequences of technological progress. Economists tend to think naively that an increase in available material goods is a good thing *per se*. It is not the task of this book to discuss the problem of growth as it is posed in our day, but we should emphasize that, in spite of its 'evils' and 'horrors' (frequent expressions of some authors), in the end the Industrial Revolution did assure a decent standard of living to most Britons and the inhabitants of other advanced countries.

reliable than for other countries, are still not as complete or certain as one could wish. Consequently, the series which we present must be treated with caution, especially for the first decades of the nineteenth century. They are approximations, including an element of speculation and sizeable margins of error in spite of the ingenuity and care with which they were calculated; for their authors were obliged, for want of data, to make many adjustments, interpolations and extrapolations. So one should not attach too much importance to decimals. Nevertheless the calculations give orders of magnitude which we consider valid, all the more so because the different scholars who carried out these exercises have arrived at results which correspond fairly closely.

LONG-TERM GROWTH OF NATIONAL PRODUCT[2]

(a) In 1962, Phyllis Deane and W.A. Cole, in their pioneering work *British Economic Growth*, produced the following estimates of Great Britain's GNP at constant prices, in millions of £:[3]

1801	138
1841	394
1901	1948

So real national product seems to have been multiplied fourteen-fold in a century and five-fold during Victoria's reign, with an average annual growth-rate of 2.7 per cent both for the century, 1801–1901, and for the 'Victorian' period, 1841–1901.

This series has the advantage of being the only one which covers the

[2] GNP=Gross National Product. GDP=Gross Domestic Product, which includes only the product generated on the country's territory; GNP includes in addition the net income coming from abroad. The difference is not very important (see Chapter 11, p.367). Gross Product includes maintaining and replacing physical capital. By deducting this, one obtains the Net National Product (NNP) or National Income.
(a) These various aggregates can be expressed at market prices or at factor cost (in the latter case one deducts indirect taxes so that the sum total is lower).
(b) Calculations and estimates can be made either from production, or from incomes, or from the side of expenditure.
(c) These aggregates are usually calculated first at current prices, but because of fluctuations in prices and changes in the value of money, it is generally preferable to convert the 'current prices' series into 'constant prices' series, in order to obtain a series of 'real' product or volume. But this deflation is a delicate operation, which can introduce distortions.
[3] P. Deane and W.A. Cole, *British Economic Growth, 1688–1959* (Cambridge, 2nd edn, 1967), p.282 (table 72). Constant prices are the average of those of 1865 and 1885, according to Rousseaux's index.

entire nineteenth century, but Phyllis Deane has since admitted, as certain critics suggested, that it overestimated somewhat the speed of growth[4].

(b) In 1968, Phyllis Deane published a new series of the United Kingdom's GNP, year-by-year this time, at factor cost and constant prices (1900), but it covers only the period 1830–1914[5]. The calculations were made by estimating expenditure (while the 1962 figures had been made on the income side), and the deflation method for obtaining GNP at constant prices was also different from what had been used previously. Triennial averages were as follows, in millions of £:

1830/2	408
1836/8	477
1900/2	1914
1911/13	2238

According to these figures the GNP of the United Kingdom exactly quadrupled during Victoria's reign, and it multiplied by 5.5 between the beginning of the 1830s and the eve of the first world war. As for the rates of average growth per year they were:[6]

from 1830–2 to 1911–13	2.1 per cent
from 1836–8 to 1900–02	2.2 per cent

We must emphasize that these figures apply to Great Britain and Ireland combined. As the growth of the latter was much slower than her neighbour's[7], the rates for the United Kingdom were markedly reduced for part of the period 1830–80. Phyllis Deane gives an estimate of the growth-rates of GNP for Great Britain alone by ten-year periods[8], from which we can reckon that it must have been multiplied by 6.3 between 1830 and 1910 (and by 4.4 between 1840 and

---

[4] Notably by the use as deflator of Rousseaux's index, which is inadequate, with the result that figures for the end of the century are too high. As for those of the beginning of the century, they are uncertain. N.F.R. Crafts, 'National income estimates and the British standard of living debate: reappraisal of 1801–1838', *Explorations in Economic History, 17(2)*, Apr. 1980, 176–88.

[5] P.Deane, 'New estimates of gross national product for the United Kingdom,1830–1914', *The Review of Income and Wealth*, series 14(2) June 1968, 95–112; see 106–7 (table B).

[6] Calculating them between ten-year averages, one would get:
   from 1830/9 to 1890/9: 2.3 per cent;
   from 1830/9 to 1905/14: 2.1 per cent.

[7] And almost nil for a period after the disaster of the famine.

[8] Deane, 'New estimates', 98 (table 2), and Chapter 3 see p. 51 (table 13). The two series only differ noticeably for 1830–50 and 1870–80. At most the decade rate of growth for the UK is 28 per cent less than that of GB.

1900), which corresponds to average growth-rates per year of 2.5 per cent between 1830 and 1900 (the same for 1840–1900) and of 2.3 per cent for 1830–1910[9].

(c) The most recent, complete and meticulous work of retrospective national accounting is that of Charles Feinstein[10]. Unfortunately, his point of departure is only 1855. From this work we will quote the indices (three-year averages) of gross domestic product at constant factor cost, on the basis of 1913=100[11].

	United Kingdom	Great Britain
1855/7	33.8	31.1
1900/2	83.0	79.6
1911/13	97.0	96.4

So GDP tripled in rather over fifty years. As for the average rates of growth per year, they were as follows:[12]

	United Kingdom	Great Britain
from 1855/7 to 1911/13	2.0 per cent	2.1 per cent
from 1855/7 to 1900/2	2.0 per cent	2.1 per cent

[9]   See N.G. Butlin's 'A new plea for the separation of Ireland', *Journal of Economic History*. XXVIII (2) June 1968, 274–91. This writer maintains that the growth of the GNP of GB was distinctly faster than that of the UK between 1860 and 1890; but it slowed down more between 1890 and 1914. The size of the difference, where per-capita product is concerned, depends on the ratio between the Irish and the British per-capita products, and on Ireland's rate of growth. The higher the former and the slower the latter, the more considerable the difference will be; but it cannot be more than a few tenths of a percentage point at most.

[10] C.H.Feinstein, *National Income, Expenditure and Output of the United Kingdom, 1855–1965* (Cambridge, 1972).

[11] From tables 6, col.4 and 54 col. 5, T.18–19, 118–9 in Feinstein, *National Income*, The series for the UK is a 'compromise estimate' between those based on production, income and expenditure. The one for GB is only based on production. The corresponding series for the UK (tables 6, col.1, and 8, col.5,T.18-19,24–5) would give rates of growth of 1.9 per cent per annum for the two periods indicated below. Feinstein does not give figures before 1870 for GNP at constant prices. Yet one finds a series established from his data (but a composite one – at factor cost before 1870, at market prices after) in B.R. Mitchell, *European Historical Statistics, 1750–1970* (London,1975), pp. 782,790. One can draw from it the following figure for the UK:

	£m	Rate of growth (percentage per annum)
1855/7	738 ⎫	
1900/2	2090 ⎬	2.3 ⎫ 2.2
1911/13	2430	⎭

[12] From p.214 (table 10.4) in Feinstein, *National Income*, giving ten-year averages of real product (GDP), at constant factor cost, one can reckon the following growth-rates (percentage per annum):

	UK	GB
1857/66–1908/13	1.80	1.99
1857/66–1891/1900	1.84	2.04

The figures for Great Britain are less than those of Phyllis Deane (1968), but one must remember that Gross Domestic Product is somewhat lower than GNP, because it excludes income from foreign investment, which increased greatly during this period; but the maximum divergence between GNP and GDP, just before 1914, was less than 10 per cent. Furthermore, the growth of the British economy slowed up considerably at the end of the nineteenth and beginning of the twentieth century, and it is normal that Feinstein's rates, whose starting-point was later, should be lower.

In addition, comparing the Phyllis Deane series (1968) with one of his own (also based on expenditure) for the period 1856–1913, Feinstein reveals compound rates of growth of 2.0 and 2.1 per cent per annum respectively for the United Kingdom's GNP at constant factor cost[13].

(d) Finally Paul Bairoch has calculated the rates of growth of GNP's volume at constant market prices, based on the data of Deane and Feinstein, as follows:[14]

from 1830 to 1913, for the United Kingdom within the boundaries it then had (i.e. including the whole of Ireland): 2.01 per cent per annum;
from 1830 to 1913, for the United Kingdom within its boundaries of 1970 (i.e. excluding Eire and including Great Britain and Northern Ireland): 2.26 per cent per annum.

The differences between these various estimates are ultimately pretty small and we can conclude with some confidence that, in round figures, the rate of average growth per year of the *United Kingdom's* GNP during Queen Victoria's reign was 2 per cent. The rate for *Great Britain* alone for the same period was slightly higher, but it remained below 2.5 per cent. The latter rate may well have been reached for the period 1800–1900.

These rates may well appear modest[15], but we must remember that, by compound interest, a growth of 2 per cent per annum multiplies the national product by 3.3 in sixty years and by 7.5 in a century, and an

[13] Feinstein, p.11 (table 1.5). See also the new figures of Feinsteins 'Capital formation in Great Britain', in P. Mathias and M.M.Postan (eds), *The Cambridge Economic History of Europe*, VII, part I (Cambridge, 1978), pp.86 (table 26), 87: the growth-rate of the GDP of *Great Britain* at constant factor cost between 1801 and 1860 was 2.6 per cent per annum (2.8 and 2.5 per cent for the sub-periods 1801–30 and 1830–60) and that of real per-capita product 1.3 per cent.
[14] Bairoch, 'Europe's gross national product, 1800–1975', *Journal of European Economic History*, V(2), Autumn 1976, 283, 305 (tables 5 and 17).
[15] P.Deane, 'New estimates', 97, emphasizes that for no period of at least ten years, even between a cyclical minimum and maximum, did the rate of GNP growth reach 3 per cent.

increase of 2.5 per cent multiplies it by 4.4 in sixty years and by 12 in a century. So Britain really enjoyed an increase in wealth that was considerable and unprecedented, but we must guard against talking about dramatic or spectacular growth, as some people do. The British case is a perfect illustration of Paul Bairoch's remarks on the 'myth of rapid economic growth' in the nineteenth century[16].

Nor was British growth anything exceptional. During the period 1830–1913 several European countries[17]. not to mention the United States, saw their national product grow at rates that were similar and even superior. This parallel experience is even truer if you look at the growth of these countries when they were at a stage of industrialization comparable to that of Britain in Victorian times – in other words with a certain time-lag arising out of the early start of the Industrial Revolution in England[18]. Finally, it is clear that British economic growth in the nineteenth century was far slower than that achieved by many advanced countries in the twentieth, and particularly in its third quarter, though it seems now that the 'miracle' growth-rates of the 1950s and 1960s will not persist as long as the more modest ones of Victoria's time.

THE GROWTH OF PRODUCT PER CAPITA

Considered in isolation the growth of national product has only limited significance and only attains its full meaning if it is matched with the growth of population to calculate the development of the average product per head; this must be the true criterion of economic progress and the condition for social advance[19]. As we have seen earlier that the British population's rate of growth in the nineteenth century was slightly over 1 per cent per annum, it is at once clear that national product increased about twice as fast and that per-capita product progressed too, but in an even less spectacular way than GNP.

We will re-examine the series already studied, but this time from the viewpoint of per-capita product.

[16] P.Bairoch, 'Le mythe de la croissance économique rapide au XIXe siècle', *Revue de l'Institut de Sociologie*, 1962 (2) 337ff.
[17] Belgium, Switzerland, Germany and the Scandinavian countries.
[18] Bairoch, 'Europe's gross national product',281–2;P.Bairoch, *Commerce extérieur et développement économique de l'Europe au XIXe siècle* (Paris–The Hague, 1976) pp. 151,156 (tables 48 and 51).
[19] This growth does not, *a priori*, imply anything about the distribution of its fruits among social classes, although it would be unusual for them all not to profit from it, though not equally. See pp.39–41.

(a) Deane and Cole give the following figures for Great Britain's national product per inhabitant at constant prices:[20]

1801	£12.45
1841	£21.15
1901	£52.25

This product would seem to have rather more than quadrupled in the century from 1801 to 1901, with an annual average rate of growth of 1.45 per cent. Between 1841 and 1901 it seems to have been multiplied by 2.5, an annual rate of 1.5 per cent. On the other hand, the rate for 1801–41 would seem to have been only 1.3 per cent.

(b) Using Phyllis Deane's 1968 series one gets the following figures for per-capita GNP in the *United Kingdom* at constant 1900 prices:[21]

1830/2	£16.98
1836/8	£18.60
1900/2	£46.17
1911/13	£49.26

This product per capita seems almost to have tripled between the early 1830s and the eve of the first world war, and was multiplied by 2.5 during Victoria's reign. The annual average rates of growth were:

from 1830/2 to 1911/13	1.33 per cent
from 1836/8 to 1900/2	1.44 per cent

Using the rates calculated by Phyllis Deane between ten-year averages of GNP per head, one finds between 1830/9 and 1890/9 a very similar figure of 1.4 per cent per annum.

(c) Feinstein has constructed a series for gross domestic product per capita at constant factor cost (1913) for the United Kingdom, whose three-year averages are:[22]

1855/7	£26.7
1900/2	£44.7
1911/13	£47.7

From this the following rates of annual average growth are derived:

from 1855/7 to 1911/13	1.1 per cent
from 1855/7 to 1900/2	1.15 per cent

[20] Deane and Cole, p.282 (table 72).
[21] For GNP we have taken three-year averages centred on the years 1831, 1837, 1901 and 1912; for population, the figures of the 1831 and 1901 censuses, and the estimates of B.R.Mitchell and P.Deane, *Abstract of British Historical Statistics* (Cambridge, 1962) (quoted hereafter as *Abstract*), pp. 8 and 10, for 1837 and 1912.
[22] Feinstein, *National Income*, table 17, col.4, T.42.

Feinstein has also calculated indices for ten-year averages of real product per head at constant factor cost for the United Kingdom, Great Britain and Ireland, on the basis 1913=100:[23]

	United Kingdom	Great Britain
1857/66	60.3	62.3
1891/1900	83.1	83.3
1908/13	93.9	93.7

Whence average annual growth rates of growth are:

From 1857 to 1908/13	0.91 per cent	0.83 per cent
From 1857/66 to 1891/1900	0.95 per cent	0.86 per cent

So, while the exclusion of Ireland makes the total product's rate of growth greater for Great Britain than for the United Kingdom, the reverse is the case for the product per capita. Feinstein, indeed, admits that the difference is small and within the possible margin of error, but still the result seems to him plausible, given the stagnant population of the Emerald Isle, the declining importance in the overall United Kingdom picture and the low level of the average income at the beginning of the period, as compared with Great Britain.

(d) As for Bairoch, his calculations of per-capita GNP's volume reach the following conclusions:[24]

from 1830 to 1910, a rate of growth for the United Kingdom, including Ireland: 1.21 per cent per annum

from 1830 to 1913, for Great Britain and Northern Ireland: 1.23 per cent.

On the whole there is fair agreement between the different estimates, if we bear in mind that Feinstein's series must normally grow more slowly given their late starting-point. These estimates give a bracket between 1 and 1.4 per cent per annum for the per-capita product's long-term growth-rate of Great Britain and the United Kingdom between the beginning of the nineteenth century and the first world war. The probable rate for Great Britain was near to 1.2 per cent, but it was slightly higher for the Victorian period than for the longer period because of the very small increase in per-capita product at the beginning of the twentieth century[25].

These figures call for several observations. Firstly, they confirm the idea of a very slow economic growth, at least by the criteria of our own times. Nowadays a growth rate of real GNP per inhabitant of 1 or even 2 per cent per annum is considered virtual stagnation. From 1953 to 1970, the volume of per-capita GNP in western Europe grew by 3.8 per cent per annum[26]. This slow nineteenth-century growth is confirmed

23 ibid.,p.214, table 10.4. It is in fact the per-capita GDP.
24 Bairoch, 'Europe's gross national product', 213 and 309 (tables 5 and 9).
25 Cf. Chapter 3, pp.52,62.
26 Bairoch, *Commerce extérieur*, p.148 (note 5).

by all we know from other data, both quantitative and qualitative, about the slow improvement in living standards of the bulk of the British population, especially during the first half of the nineteenth century. Conversely, this progress in per-capita product during the nineteenth century was swift compared with the very slow increase achieved by England over a long period in the pre-industrial era. It was also greater than what was achieved at the beginning of the Industrial Revolution towards the end of the eighteenth century. Furthermore, let us not forget that an annual average growth-rate of 1.2 per cent means a doubling of GNP in sixty years, which is far from negligible.

As in the case of total product, British growth was not exceptional, but even rather mediocre[27]. According to Bairoch's calculations – admittedly often the result of guesswork – during the period 1830– 1910 five European countries had rates of per-capita growth distinctly higher than the United Kindom's: Belgium, Germany, Switzerland, Sweden and Denmark. And several other countries appear to have had growth-rates not much different from the United Kingdom's[28].

Furthermore, if one ceases to look at the growth-rates and considers simply the *levels* of per-capita product, we must remember that, during the whole of the nineteenth century, the United Kingdom enjoyed the highest per-capita GNP in Europe, and also held the top place in the world up to around 1880; but this superiority was attributable to her early start in industrialization and not to an especially rapid growth[29]. However the income level per capita remained very low in Great Britain for a long time. Deane and Cole's figure for 1841 was £24 at current prices, very roughly equivalent to £300 in 1980. Even if national income had been evenly distributed, the average income enjoyed by each Briton would have given only very modest comfort. In fact the distribution was extremely inegalitarian. In 1867, according to Dudley Baxter's data, adjusted by Perkin[30], the shares of the three main social classes in England and Wales were as set out in table 6.

[27] ibid., pp.16 and 149, estimates the per-capita GNP growth at 1.3 per cent per annum between 1850 and 1913 for developed countries, and 0.9 per cent between 1830 and 1910 for the whole of Europe.
[28] Bairoch, 'Europe's gross national product', 276, 283–4, 298,309; Bairoch, *Commerce extérieur* p.156 (table 51). The last four of these countries might have had rates of per-capita GNP-growth 15 per cent higher than that of GB. For the period 1860– 1910, Germany, Switzerland, Sweden, Denmark and France (because of her demographic stagnation) show rates at least 15 per cent higher than that of the UK, which is no higher than for the per-capita GNP of the whole of Europe.
[29] See Introduction,pp.5–6.
[30] H.Perkin, *The Origins of Modern English Society, 1780–1880* (London, 1969), p.420 . (table 6).

Table 6   Distribution of national income between families in England and Wales, 1867

	Percentage of total no. of families	Percentage of national income received	Average income per family
Upper class (over £1000 a year)	0.5	26	£6079
Middle class (£100 to £1000 a year)	25.0	35	£154
Working class	74.5	39	£58
National average			£111

It is often thought that social inequality became more marked in the first half of the nineteenth century, with the affluent classes increasing their share of national income somewhat, to the detriment of the wage-earning classes, but not in such a way that the transfer cancelled the effects of the rise in per-capita income. However, from 1867 to 1914, the upper-class share seems to have lessened slightly, while the share of the other classes rose a little[31]. But there were no fundamental changes in the social structure, and enormous inequalities persisted. In 1905 5 million Britons shared half the national income, while the other half went to their 39 million less favoured compatriots[32]. Thus the great majority of the population enjoyed per-capita incomes much inferior to the national average. Yet average real wages did increase – modestly and irregularly in the first half of the nineteenth century (by 15 to 25 per cent between 1815 and 1850) and substantially in the second half (by about 80 per cent)[33]. So the common people's standard of living improved notably and had become satisfactory for the upper working class by about 1900. Yet a sizeable sector of the population (25–30 per cent) remained in poverty at the end of Victoria's reign. The researches of Charles Booth in London (1889) and of Seebohm Rowntree in York (1899) showed that nearly 10 per cent of the families in these towns had incomes that did not allow them to keep their members in good health ('primary poverty'). Another group, from 15 to 20 per cent, were at the 'vital minimum', being just able to survive, but with no margin of security and without

[31]   ibid.,pp.135–7, 140–1, 413–27. According to Bowley's data, quoted by S.Kuznets, *Modern Economic Growth: Rate, Structure and Spread* (New Haven and London, 1966) p.208 (table 4.5) the share in national income of the richest 5 per cent of population fell from 48 per cent in 1880 to 43 per cent in 1913.

[32]   Bédarida, p.151.

[33]   On the other hand, they fell slightly at the beginning of the twentieth century. For all this, see particularly S.Pollard and D.W.Crossley, *The Wealth of Britain, 1085–1966*(London,1968),pp.200–22, 234–47; Deane and Cole, p.26.

being able to save against penury occasioned by unemployment, illness or old age ('secondary poverty'). The situation had certainly been worse around 1860, and *a fortiori* in the 1830s and 1840s, and of course at the beginning of the century when a larger section of the population had been plunged in poverty more abject than that described in later researches, with employment even more irregular and casual. But one should underline the fact that living conditions had been no less miserable before the Industrial Revolution. At the end of the seventeenth century, according to Gregory King's data, which are generally accepted, half of England's population lived in poverty and could only survive with the help of private or public charity; this was mostly the result of the extreme irregularity of employment. Even from the poorer classes' standpoint the Industrial Revolution and Victorian growth brought positive improvement.

An essential factor in per-capita growth was the increase in labour-productivity. Unfortunately the only satisfactory series is Feinstein's (see table 7), which only covers the United Kingdom and starts in 1855[34].

Table 7   Labour-productivity (UK) 1855–1913

	Index of output per worker (1913=100)	*Annual average rates of growth*
1855/7	57	
1900/2	93	1.1%
1911/13	99	1.0%

If one takes into account the productivity of capital, whose growth was slower[35], one can work out an approximate index of total factor productivity (output per unit of total inputs); its rate of growth was 0.9 per cent per year from 1855/7 to 1900/2, and 0.8 per cent if you push the limit to 1911/13[36].

[34] Feinstein, *National Income*, table 20, col. 5, T.51–2 Production is of course at constant prices. Its divisor is the total labour-force employed each year. For the previous period we only have growth-rate of GB's total real product per head of population employed, from Deane and Cole, p.172 (table 39). They seem too high, at least for the end of the nineteenth century. For the period 1811/21 to 1841/51, the growth-rate is 1.4 per cent per annum. In fact, according to Feinstein, 'Capital formation', the growth of labour productivity in GB was probably faster in the first decades of the nineteenth century than after 1830.

[35] Cf. Chapter 5, pp. 129ff.

[36] We have given equal weight to the indices of productivity of labour and of capital, because of the nearly constant equality of labour and capital (despite a slight increase in the former's share) in income factors between 1855 and 1913, according to Feinstein, *National Income*, table 20,T.51–2. It seems again that the growth of total productivity in GB was faster from 1800 to 1830 than later.

THE GROWTH OF THE ECONOMY'S MAIN SECTORS

We will end with the long-term growth of the main sectors of the economy. For industrial production we have W. Hoffmann's index (see table 8). Although old and much criticized, it remains valid[37].

Table 8   Growth of total industrial production in Great Britain (according to Hoffmann)

1) *Indices (1913=100)*

1800/2	6.6
1836/8	18.5
1855/7	34.1
1900/2	93.1
1911/13	100.3

2) *Rates of growth (%)*

1 From 1800/2 to 1911/13 (a)	2.5
2 From 1836/8 to 1900/2	2.5
3 From 1855/7 to 1900/2	2.3
4 From 1855/7 to 1911/13	2.0

(a) The rate of growth would be the same if 1814/16 were the starting-point.

These rates of growth are modest and imply a slowing-down towards the end of the Victorian period, to which we shall return later[38]; moreover from 1800/2 to 1836/8 the rate appears to have been 2.9 per cent per annum. Nevertheless, the volume of industrial production was multiplied by fifteen between the beginning of the nineteenth century and 1913, and exactly quintupled during Victoria's reign.

We are less well provided with data for the other sectors of the economy. Deane and Cole (who overestimate, as we have seen, the growth at the end of the nineteenth century) only give growth-rates between ten-year averages for a succession of thirty-year periods (see table 9).

[37]   W.Hoffmann, *British Industry, 1700–1850* (Oxford, 1955;trans. from the German by W.H.Chaloner and W.O.Henderson), table 54. See K.X.Lomax, 'Growth and productivity in the United Kingdom', in D.H.Aldcroft and P.Fearon, *Economic Growth in 20th Century Britain* (London,1966), pp.10–11.Lomax had published in 1959 a new index starting in 1900. He has extended it up to 1960, but arrives at very few differences from Hoffmann's. The index used in table 8 includes building, to allow comparisons with the authors quoted later (the same applies to the use of the period 1855/7). The index excluding building would have a higher growth-rate for line 1 and a slightly lower one for line 3.

[38]   Which is only partly due to a possible underestimation of growth from 1860 or 1870 onward, for it takes no account of the growing complexity of the goods manufactured.

Table 9   Annual average rates of growth in real product of Great Britain (%)

	Agriculture (a)	Industry (b)	Trade and transport
1801/11–1831/41	1.2	4.7	3.0
1831/41–1861/71	1.3	3.0	2.0
1861/71–1891/1901	0.7	3.5	3.6

(a) Forestry and fisheries included.
(b) Mining and building included.

On the other hand, Feinstein gives more reliable series, which only start in 1855 (see Table 10)[40].

Table 10   Output at constant factor cost, Great Britain

	Agriculture (a)	Industrial production (b)	Transport	Distribution and other services
1) Indices (1931=100)				
1855/7	98	25	21	31
1900/2	97	80	72	79
1911/13	101	95	96	97
2) Rates of growth (%)				
1855/7–1900/2	−0.02	2.6	2.8	2.1
1855/7–1911/13	0.07	2.5	2.8	2.1

(a) & (b) as in table 9.

These various data reveal, on the one hand, variations in the pace of national product's growth, and on the other hand differences in the growth of the main sectors of the economy, involving structural change. These are two problems which must now be examined.

[39]   Deane and Cole, p.170 (table 38).
[40]   Feinstein, *National Income,* table 54, T.118–9. The rates of growth for the UK (table 8,T.24–5) would be a little lower for industry and distribution.

3 The periodization of growth

The mere measuring of long-term growth can never satisfy the historian. Growth does not evolve at a uniform pace and cannot be charted on a graph by a straight line. The history of an economy is punctuated by fluctuations, especially by the alternation of years of prosperity with years of depression, with crises at the point of change from one to the other. Broadly speaking, in nineteenth-century Britain, these 'Juglar cycles' are 'intradecennial', as the length of time separating two successive maxima or minima was less than ten years. But in addition to these short-term fluctuations, many scholars have identified longer cycles in the medium term, covering roughly a half-century. These cycles were first identified in the movement of prices (where long rises and long falls alternate) by Kondratiev, hence the name 'Kondratiev cycles' or simply 'Kondratievs'. Then J.A. Schumpeter and S. Kuznets worked out the concept of a series of 'long swings' in the total economy (sometimes called 'Kuznets cycles'). In the course of each of these, and also beyond the intradecennial movements, one may see a long phase of fast growth followed by a phase of deceleration and slower growth. Using these concepts, many scholars since W.W. Rostow in 1948[1] have established a periodization in British

---

[1]   W.W.Rostow, *British Economy of the Nineteenth Century* (Oxford, 1948), notably pp. 7ff. In fact the views of Rostow are far less clearcut than those of his successors. His table I (p.8) gives the following mean rates of growth (or decline) per year, between averages of five-year periods, centred on the indicated years, which are near to peaks of business cyles.

	Total industrial production %	Volume of exports %	General prices %	Real wages %
1793–1815	2.1	4.1	1.8	−0.5
1815–47	3.5	2.8	−1.4	0.7
1847–73	3.2	4.9	0.6	0.6
1873–1900	1.7	1.7	−1.5	1.2
1900–12	1.5	2.7	1.5	−0.5
1793–1912	2.6	3.3		

economic history between 1815 and 1814, which has become more or
less classic; and all the more so because the idea has the advantage of
corresponding with the breaks that have been brought to light in the
social, political and even cultural evolution of Great Britain. We will
first set out this standard view, and then see to what extent recent
research supports it.

A SIMPLE PICTURE

This scheme divides the history of the British economy betwen 1815
and 1914 into four phases, each corresponding to half a 'long swing'.
    The first phase stretches from the end of the Napoleonic wars to the
end of the 1840s, encompassing what is known as the early Victorian
period. It was characterized first of all by a steep and prolonged fall in
prices – 43 per cent between 1815 and 1850 according to the most
satisfactory index[2] – and by a fall in interest rates. The fall in prices
weighed both on the profit margins of firms and on money-wages,
which fell notably. It also struck agriculture a hard blow, bringing on a
depression at least up to the 1830s. A second characteristic was the
violence of short-term cyclical fluctuations, with very pronounced
booms, as in 1818, 1825, 1836 and 1845, followed by violent slumps and
long depression. These slumps and depressions often combined traditional aspects (i.e. high food prices due to bad harvests) with a modern
look (i.e. over-production and unemployment). They plunged the
working classes into utter penury and unleashed a wave of business
bankruptcies.
    It is true that these fluctuations did not prevent economic growth
over the whole period from being relatively rapid. Rostow has pointed
out that the growth-rate of British industrial production was higher
between 1815 and 1847 not only than it had been during the war years
that preceded Waterloo[3], but also than during any of the three phases
that followed. Furthermore, it is generally considered that this period
saw the end of the Industrial Revolution in Britain in its strict sense.
Most of the fundamental technical innovations which characterized it

---

[2]   It is the index of A.D.Gayer, W.W.Rostow and A.J. Schwartz, *The Growth and
      Fluctuation of the British Economy, 1790–1850* (2 vols.,Oxford, 1953;I,2nd ed.,New
      York, 1975), pp.12–13, 15–16, 468; synthesised in B.R.Mitchell and P.Deane,
      Abstract of British Historical Statistics (Cambridge, 1962) (quoted hereafter as
      Abstract), p.470; see P.Deane and W.A.Cole, *British Economic Growth, 1688–1959*
      (Cambridge, 2nd edn, 1967). There exists no general index of British prices for the
      nineteenth century which is really satisfactory.
[3]   Which probably had a braking effect here, as well as on the growth of real per-capita
      product.

had been made before 1830. It only remained to exploit and perfect these techniques, to enlarge the Revolution's base and follow up its achievements which in 1815 had still been fairly limited. So the Industrial Revolution expanded in scope and depth, with mechanization and the factory system penetrating new sectors and the transport system being transformed then by the rapid advance of railways. Certainly there remained at the mid-century extensive old-fashioned areas of activity, but the factory system had became preponderant and by the 1830s Great Britain was in fact an industrial nation.

However, this rapid transformation of economic structures undermined the social structure, causing acute tensions and class conflicts. The result was a society that was under great stress and unstable, and a troubled period in which three classes opposed each other – the landowning aristocracy, the industrial and commercial bourgeoisie and the working class – the second allying itself sometimes with the first and sometimes with the third in temporary partnership. These conflicts were exacerbated by the violent economic fluctuations, which punctuated the rise and fall of the popular movements – radical, owenite, chartist, etc. These sometimes took on a revolutionary aspect and became a threat, or so it seemed, to the established order. Industrialization, and the type of working conditions and society which it engendered, did in fact arouse serious resistance in the working classes, and all the more so because, in spite of economic growth, their standard of living improved very little. Some historians even maintain that it deteriorated, which is only true for certain groups, more particularly workers in the old domestic system[4].

However, with England remaining sheltered from the European revolutions of 1848, the year in which the country only saw the final fiasco of chartism, and with the Great Exhibition of 1851, a symbol at once of industrialism's triumph and of refound social peace[5], a quite

---

[4]   A.J.Taylor, (ed.) *The Standard of Living in the Industrial Revolution* (London, 1975), gives the most important articles in this debate and a useful synthesis. Also M.W.Flinn, 'Trends in real wages, 1750–1850', *Economic History Review* 2nd series, XXVII (3), Aug. 1974, 395–413, which locates most of the improvement in real wages at the beginning of the period, between 1813 and 1820, and also insists on their fluctuations. G.N.Von Tunzelmann, 'Trends in real wages, 1750–1850, revisited', *Economic History Review*, 2nd series, XXXII (1), Feb. 1979, 33–49; N.F.R. Crafts, 'National income estimates and the British standard of living debate: a reappraisal of 1801–1831', *Explorations in Economic History*, 17 (2), Apr. 1980, 176–88.

[5]   Excellent pages on this subject are to be found in Bédarida, pp. 3–8.

different era began, extending as far as 1873 – the era of the Great Victorian (or rather Mid-Victorian) Boom. Prices, profits and wages rose instead of falling. The economy showed a remarkable dynamism and achieved a striking expansion in production, investment and exports. The growth of national product, both total and per capita, gained speed and reached its highest levels for the nineteenth century. Although the growth of industrial production seems to have been slightly lower than in the preceding period (which has been denied), agriculture prospered again and the services sector developed rapidly. Inflation created a climate of optimism among businessmen, in clear contrast to the gloom which they had known during their long fight against deflation in the preceding decades, and which they would experience again after 1873. Above all, the mass of the population began at last to enjoy the benefits of industrialization. Real wages increased markedly and wealth spread in a way never before known. This period has been talked of as a 'golden age', 'a great leap forward' in the capacity to create and consume wealth, 'an economic miracle' and 'a fabulous enrichment'. This progress on all fronts brought a release of social tensions, and a truce to the bitter conflicts of the years before. It removed fears of revolution. It was W.L. Burn's[6] 'age of equipoise', Harold Perkin's 'rise of a viable class society', in which polarization gave way to 'mutual accommodation', and menace of violence to collective bargaining. As the quarrel between agrarian and industrial interests had been settled in 1846 by the repeal of the Corn Laws, the aristocracy and the middle classes were brought together by reconciliation and power-sharing. The painful birth-pangs of a new economy and society were now over. There was no more rejection of the industrial society, but only efforts, often successful, to adapt to it, to adjust institutions to its needs, and to master its dangers. Economic prosperity brought calm and stability to the social and political spheres, while the middle classes imposed their scale of values on much of society[7]. Finally, although the rest of the western world was also enjoying growth and prosperity, the industrial and commercial supremacy of Great Britain remained unthreatened.

However, the crisis of 1873 opened a third and much less favourable phase, which was to last to the end of the nineteenth century (1896, according to many historians) and which we call, as did the people of the time, the Great Depression. Again it was marked by a fall in prices,

---

[6] W.L.Burn, *The Age of Equipoise: A Study of the Mid-Victorian Generation* (London, 1964).
[7] These lines are inspired by H.Perkin, *The Origins of Modern English Society, 1780-1880* (London, 1969).

interest rates and profit margins. It is true that money remained
steady, so that real wages showed a distinct improvement, but the
working classes suffered an increase in unemployment. As far as
production and trade are concerned, the term 'depression' is misleading. In spite of many years of recession, the long-term trend remained
a rising one, but there was a very real slowing-down of the British
economy's growth in comparison with the first three-quarters of the
century. In agriculture, which was particularly hit by the fall in prices,
growth was non-existent or negative. Furthermore, Britain's supremacy was challenged by the faster growth of new industrial powers,
who were worrying competitors in international markets and she had
to yield first place to the United States among industrialized countries.
This produced an atmosphere of unease and anxiety among businessmen. There was also a return of social tension, and trade-union
activity took new directions. Socialist ideas had some success, as part
of the widespread questioning of Victorian certitudes, especially the
shibboleth of the liberal ideal.

Finally, a fourth phase began at the very end of the nineteenth
century and extended to the first world war. It was part and parcel of an
expansion of the whole world economy, which pulled out of the Great
Depression (which had been world-wide) to enter the prosperous times
of the Belle Époque. But this phase was far from being cloudless. Prices
and rates of interest certainly did tend to rise. British exports expanded
again, and capital investment abroad was considerable. But, as we shall
see later, there were other worrying tendencies – slow growth and a
slight lowering of real wages. The latter helps to explain the acute social
tension on the eve of the war, leading to outbreaks of violence. The
Victorian cultural system showed signs of breaking up. Indeed the calm
and prosperity of the Edwardian age was largely superficial.

This periodization of British economic growth – and in fact of British
history in general – is a convenient and attractive scheme. However, it
must be compared to the results of recent quantitative research,
without forgetting that the bases for the various statistical series that
have been worked out are not equally reliable.

QUANTITATIVE DATA

Using Hoffmann's index[8], Deane and Cole have calculated the
percentage increases set out in table 11 for the United Kingdom's

---

[8]   Up to 1900. Then the index of Lomax is used. Cf. Chapter 2, p. 42, (note 37); (also note
38), on the possible bias of Hoffmann's index. Even if it is biased, the incidence can
only be limited.

Table 11   Growth of UK industrial production

	Percentage increase per decade	Annual average rate of growth (%)
1810/19–1820/9	38.6	3.4
1820/9–1830/9	47.2	3.9
1830/9–1840/9	37.4	3.2
1840/9–1850/9	39.3	3.4
1850/9–1860/9	27.8	2.5
1860/9–1870/9	33.2	2.9
1870/9–1880/9	20.8	1.9
1880/9–1890/9	17.4	1.6
1890/9–1900/9	17.9	1.7

industrial production (construction excluded) between successive decades[9].

Clearly the most rapid growth was achieved in the 1820s and still more in the 1830s. There was a marked slowing-down in the 1840s, a revival in the 1850s, then a fresh slackening which was interrupted by a boom around 1870, the increase from 1855/64 to 1865/74 being 35 per cent, a rate of 3 per cent per annum; but the decline became very evident at the end of the 1870s and during the 1880s. It stopped from the mid-1890s, and there was even a very slight recovery, but this stabilization occurred with a growth-rate that was less than half the rates of the period before 1860.

For his part, K.X. Lomax, combining Hoffmann's index with his own (table 12), has worked out the growth-rates between the different cyclical peaks, in order to make more valid comparisons[10].

The contrast is very clear between the rates of 3 per cent and more

Table 12   Annual average rates of growth of UK industrial production (including construction) (%)

1792–1811	2.6
1811–39	3.1
1839–60	3.2
1860–77	3.0
1877–83	0.5
1883–91	1.6
1891–1902	2.4
1902–13	1.6

[9]   Deane and Cole, p. 297 (table 77).
[10]   K.X. Lomax, 'Growth and productivity in the United Kingdom', in Aldcroft and Fearon, *Economic Growth in 20th Century Britain,* (London, 1969), pp.11–2 (table 2).

up to 1877 (with an acceleration up to 1869) and the period which followed for which, from 1877 to 1913, the average rate was only 1.6 per cent. One must add that, if rates of growth of the Hoffmann index (building excluded this time) are calculated by exponential adjustment (i.e. by taking all years into account), the figures are 3.7 per cent per annum for the period 1814–46 (and 4 per cent for 1820–39, a phase suggested by the deviations from trend as being that of most rapid growth) and only 2.9 per cent for 1846–73[11].

For the second half of the century, Coppock, again using Hoffmann, has calculated rates of growth for industrial production (construction excluded) between averages of successive periods corresponding to business cycles (1847/53–1854/60 and so on), so as to eliminate the incidence of these cyclical movements. In addition, as output in the cotton industry (which weighs heavily in the Hoffmann index) slumped dramatically during the American civil war (so that the general index fell), but recovered sharply afterwards, giving rise to a big abnormal upsurge in the total index around 1870, Coppock has made a calculation which excludes this industry[12]. It appears then that the slowing-down of industrial growth began in the mid-1860s. Later, whether cotton is included or not, slow growth was particularly pronounced between the cycles 1875/83 and 1884/9, when the growth-rate (1.6 per cent) did not reach one half of earlier maxima. There was a slight recovery due to a high cyclical peak in 1897–1900, but this was ephemeral and there was renewed slow-down on the eve of the first world war. Coppock has also worked out the growth-rates of industrial production per capita, which are even more significant, showing a real collapse between the early 1870s and the late 1880s, and finally a negative growth on the eve of the war[13].

In spite of their tentative character these data show clear-cut trends: first of all, the great fact of the slow-down of British industrial growth which seems to have started in the 1860s, and secondly divergences from traditional turning-points.

---

[11] Hoffmann himself (*British Industry, 1700–1850* (Oxford, 1955; trans. from the German by H.Chaloner and D.Henderson), pp. 30–1), considered that the period of most rapid growth, with annual rates of 3 to 4 per cent, was between 1818 and 1855. Then there was a drop to below 3 per cent, and after 1876 to below 2 per cent.

[12] D.J.Coppock, 'The climacteric of the 1890s: a critical note', *Manchester School*, XXIV, 1956. Quoted from S.B.Saul, *The Myth of the Great Depression, 1873–96* (London, 1969), p. 37 (table IV).

[13] ibid. Annual average real growth-rates of per-capita industrial production (cotton industry included):

1861/5–1866/74	2.4 per cent
1875/83–1884/9	0.2 per cent
1900/7–1908/13	−0.2 per cent

As for the growth in national product, data are more uncertain and conclusions less clear. In 1962, Deane and Cole proposed the following periodization, valid both for real national product and for product per capita in Great Britain: high rates of growth (near to 3 per cent per annum for GNP) between 1811 and 1831, then a slower growth at mid-century (partly they thought a reaction to the Irish famine) reaching a nadir between 1851 and 1861, followed by a vigorous recovery, which brings the rates of growth to their highest figure in the nineteenth century, between 1871/81 and 1881/91. So there would have been a tendency towards an acceleration of growth up to the end of the century with a mere interruption around 1850, and it was only in the 1890s that there was a real slowing-down[14]. There would also have been a time-lag in relation to the development of industrial production, which could be explained by changes in the economic structure and notably rapid progress in the service sector at the end of the century[15], and a very marked difference from traditional periodization. But, as Phyllis Deane has more recently admitted[16], the use of an inadequate price index as a deflator led to the rate of growth between 1873 and the end of the century being overestimated; so one should probably dismiss the idea of a climacteric, or high point of British growth-rates and the start of her decline, in the 1890s[17].

Actually the new series of GNP for the United Kingdom published by Phyllis Deane in 1968 (table 13) gives rather different results[18].

Table 13   Annual average rate of growth of real GNP (%)

	United Kingdom	Great Britain
1830–40	2.31	2.77
1840–50	1.74	2.30
1850–60	2.54	2.76
1860–70	2.62	2.83
1870–80	2.00	2.77
1880–90	1.91	2.03
1890–1900	2.39	2.47
1900–10	1.19	1.20

[14]   Deane and Cole, pp. 282–4, 311 (tables 72, 73, 74, 83).
[15]   Which is in fact not certain.
[16]   P.Deane, 'New estimates of gross national product for the United Kingdom, 1830–1914', *The Review of Income and Wealth,* series 14 (2), June 1968, 99. This index of Rousseaux is based on the prices of primary products, which fell much faster at the end of the nineteenth century than those of manufactured goods.
[17]   A view notably advanced by E.H.Phelps Brown and S.J.Handfield-Jones in an article of 1951. However, it rises partly out of an 'optical illusion' caused by the temporary but violent boom at the end of the decade.
[18]   Deane, 'New estimates', 98 (table 2); also 96 (table 1). As indicated above, the growth-rate of total product was higher for GB than for the UK until about 1880.

We find again a marked slowing-down in the 1840s, but the fastest phase of growth is the third quarter of the century; the longest period of continuous expansion, and the highest rate, would seem to have been between 1858 and 1875, with a rate of 2.8 per cent per annum for the GNP of the United Kingdom and 2 per cent for product per capita. Then came a slowing-down, interrupted only in the 1890s, but (as with industrial production) it was probably due only to the exceptional boom of 1900. It led to an extremely low growth-rate at the beginning of the twentieth century, inferior by over 50 per cent to the maximum of 1860–70. The development of product per capita of the United Kingdom was comparable and its growth-rates between ten-year averages were as follows:

1830/9–1860/9	1.61 per cent
1835/44–1865/74	1.85 per cent
1860/9–1890/9	1.17 per cent
1865/74–1905/14	1.00 per cent

These results appear to be valid and fairly close to those reached more recently by Feinstein[19]. Table 14 gives his calculations of growth-rates for periods stretching between the peaks of successive business cycles[20].

We find a high rate of growth for the years 1850 to 1873, then a deceleration that is admittedly less marked than with Deane. It is interrupted in the 1890s but starts again and becomes worse at the beginning of the twentieth century[21].

Unfortunately, this Feinstein series has 1855 as its starting-point, but some figures, published subsequently, show a rapid growth of gross domestic product of Great Britain (about 3 per cent per annum) in the 1820s and 1830s, then an obvious slowing-down in the 1840s, followed by a swift recovery in the following decade.

Although we must always approach all estimates of aggregates for the nineteenth century with caution, the best of them seem to suggest the following periodization:

[19]   The small differences in the comparable series of these two writers are noted by C.H.Feinstein, *National Income, Expenditure and Output of the United Kingdom, 1855–1965* (Cambridge, 1972), p. 11 (table 1.5)

[20]   ibid., p. 19 (table 7). As before, we give the rates of his 'compromise estimate', in which the margin of proportional error is ± 25 per cent (p. 20 (table 1.8)).

[21]   It is true that if one calculates the rates of growth between the averages of Feinstein's indices of real production, total and per head, for *Great Britain*, in each of the periods from one cyclical peak to the next (ibid., p.214 (table 10.4)), there is little variation, except for the period 1901/7–1908/13, when the two rates are clearly less than those of the second half of the nineteenth century. We will come back to these problems in Chapter 12.

Table 14 Annual average rates of growth of
UK GNP (at constant factor cost) (%)

1857–66	1.85
1866–73	2.4
1873–82	1.9
1882–90	2.0
1890–1900	2.1
1900–07	1.5
1907–13	1.6
1857–73	2.1
1873–90	1.9
1890–1913	1.8

1. rapid growth (by nineteenth-century standards) of the British economy, with perhaps a tendency to accelerate, after the years of depression following Waterloo, up to the 1830s;
2. a slowing-down during the 1840s;
3. a new phase of rapid growth from 1850 to the boom of 1873, though there was probably a tendency for industrial production to slow down from the early 1860s;
4. a long phase of deceleration and distinctly slower growth than before from the early 1870s, with some recovery in the 1890s[22] but renewed slowing-down at the beginning of the twentieth century.

Speaking very roughly and taking no account of the short-lived slow-down of the 1840s, we are led to distinguish only two important phases in British growth between 1815 and 1913:

1. a phase of rapid growth up to 1873 with a rate near to 2.5 per cent per annum for total product, and well above 1 per cent for per-capita product;
2. a second phase of slow growth and even of deceleration from the 1870s to 1913, with an annual rate of 2 per cent for total product, and at best 1 per cent for per-capita product.

In any case, quantitative studies seem to put in doubt the traditional picture, as well as the homogeneity of the four phases which have been mentioned earlier.

As for the period 1815–50 the 'high' speed of the industrialization and growth-process seems confirmed, but we must take into account a probable slowing-down in the 1840s. Furthermore, if the long-term trend of prices was downward, it was particularly sharp at the

[22] The boom which reached its peak in 1900 and was responsible for this recovery is considered by several writers to have been an untypical accident. Cf. p. 61.

beginning of the period, just after the Napoleonic wars, and prices were relatively stable in the 1820s and 1830s before a new drop in the 1840s[23]. On the other hand this fall mostly reflected – especially for industrial products – a lowering of real costs of manufacture, thanks to technical progress and improvements in productivity. As for the crisis in agriculture, which contributed to the gloomy reputation of this period, it was less serious than has long been thought. It occurred mostly before the 1830s and was far from being universal, as some sectors and regions were little affected. Finally, although the acute social problems and tensions during this period should in no way be underestimated, one must make distinctions and not let the sombre tones used to describe the social scene necessarily darken the economic picture. This is particularly important where myths are concerned, like that of the Hungry Forties, which W.H. Chaloner has dispelled. The difficult years for the working classes, because of unemployment and high prices, were from 1838 to 1842. Afterwards there was steady, sometimes intense, activity, and the cost of living came down[24].

However it is the two subsequent phases of British growth according to traditional views – 'the Great Victorian Boom' and 'the Great Depression' – whose unity and even reality have been more seriously challenged by the recent penetrating analyses of R.A. Church and S.B. Saul[25].

THE MID-VICTORIAN BOOM

Church first attacked the idea that the period 1850–73 saw a continuous and general rise in prices, and showed that in fact there were two strong but brief bouts of inflation in 1853–5 and 1870–3, separated by a period during which general price indices remained at a relatively high but stable level, with even a tendency to fall after the end of the American civil war. This view of things resembles that of David Landes, who maintains that the period 1817–97 was characterized, thanks to a constant flow of cost-cutting innovations, by a long-term fall in prices only interrupted by a plateau during the mid-Victorian years.

The traditional interpretation of inflation in the early 1850s is based on a simple form of the quantity theory of money. According to this there is a direct relationship between the supply of money and the level of prices, so much so that the long-term movements of prices are

[23] Saul, *The Myth,* p.13, maintains that 'we can create almost any trend we like to 1850, depending on the choice of dates.'
[24] W.H.Chaloner, *The Hungry Forties: A Re-Examination* (London, 1957).
[25] R.A.Church, *The Great Victorian Boom, 1850–1873* ; Saul, *The Myth;* R.A.Church (ed.), *The Dynamics of Victorian business* (London, 1980).

determined by the changes in the production of precious metals. This bout of inflation is therefore to be explained by the discovery of rich gold fields in California (1848) and Australia (1851), and by their exploitation which in a short time caused the world stock of gold to swell massively. Since much of this new gold came to Britain, the metal reserves of the Bank of England increased considerably. The Bank reduced its rate of interest and increased its discounts, and the rest of the banking system followed suit.

The increase in the money supply made prices rise to very high levels during the upswing which followed the depression of 1848. To these undeniable monetary consequences of the gold discoveries are added their effects on incomes, arising from the demand for goods and services as well as the investment which those discoveries engendered[26]. What remains unexplained is why, once the influx of gold was stemmed in 1856–8, the general level of prices stayed high while interest rates remained stable. For this one must adduce a combination of factors. The development of the banking system facilitated some inflation of credit, but there was also military expenditure. Unlike the preceding period, the mid-Victorian years were marked by a series of serious conflicts. Even though Britain was herself only involved in one, the Crimean war, she suffered seriously from the American civil war, which caused the price not only of cotton but of other textile fibres to rise. There were also the indirect inflationary effects of other conflicts – the war in Italy in 1859, the 1866 war and, above all, the Franco-Prussian war. Furthermore these conflicts revealed another factor – the inelasticity of supply of many raw materials in a period of high demand.

It is true that the plateau of the general price indices masked sharp but not synchronous fluctuations in the prices of various commodities, as well as differences between raw materials and finished goods. This made for uneven profitability in different branches of industry, particularly in textiles.

As far as production is concerned, Church points out that according to Hoffmann's index the growth of industrial production was faster in the 1820s and 1830s than during the mid-Victorian period, but he admits that according to Deane's 1968 series the latter period saw the rate of growth of national product reach its highest point in the nineteenth century. On the other hand, he underlines that although this rate was high according to nineteenth-century criteria it was not

---

[26] We will return later to Rostow's model, which emphasizes among other things the unproductive and so inflationary character of expenditure on gold-mining.

spectacular, and it was not much higher, especially for Britain, than the rates in the periods before 1850 and after 1870. Further, it did not justify the attribution of real unity to the years 1850–73, all the more because the expansion was irregular, as we shall shortly stress. 'Neither in terms of growth nor price trends does the mid-Victorian period possess a unity.'

Nor can one say that fixed-capital formation in Great Britain reached very high levels at that time. In fact its ratio to GNP remained almost unchanged from the 1840s to the 1870s. Yet overseas investment showed a strong expansion, both absolutely and as a percentage of GNP[27]. This was an important factor in the growth of foreign trade. In this respect, the traditional concept of a mid-Victorian boom remains valid. Exports and imports increased very rapidly in value. Exports rose markedly in relation to national product, making Great Britain an export economy, and their contribution to growth was considerable, which was an original feature of the period. We must however make one reservation – the acceleration of growth applies to the *value* of overseas trade and not to its *volume*, whose rate of growth was hardly higher than that of the preceding period[28].

It is equally untrue to say that after 1850 the economy passed from spasmodic to regular growth. Between 1846 and 1874 the years of recession were nearly as numerous as those of expansion, and the slumps of 1857, 1862 and 1868 were hardly less severe than those of 1826, 1837 or 1842[29]. The British economy was still characterized by extreme instability. To the usual factors of this condition were added the chance shocks of war, which accentuated fluctuations in some industries such as iron and steel and shipbuilding.

It would be surprising if, in an economy which was at the same time so dynamic and so unstable, businessmen lived in such a constant state of euphoria and smugness as has been made out. Certainly there were years of optimism, speculation and expansion, but these were matched by others of uncertainty and anxiety, such as those of the American civil war for all textile industries. It is not true that firms earned money easily through 'profit inflation'. This idea of a sharp rise in profits thanks to wages lagging behind prices and of a stimulus to investment and expansion brought on by the expectation of new rises in prices has been discredited for the sixteenth and eighteenth

---

[27] See Church, *The Great Victorian Boom*, pp. 27 (table 3), 36–7; and Chapter 5.
[28] See Chapter 5, p. 116–17. This is explained by the fall in export prices before 1850, their rise and then their stabilization later at a high level.
[29] It is true that the effects of earlier depressions were made more serious by the high price of bread; Perkin, p. 334.

centuries, and it seems no more valid for the middle of the nineteenth century[30]. There is no proof that profit margins widened or that the profitability of firms was exceptional and clearly superior to that of the previous period or of the Great Depression. Several industries even experienced pressure on profit margins. Some firms responded by innovation and expansion, which assured them of good profits, but others were unsuccessful and the failure-rate remained high. There were also changes in the location of industries, with the decline of some regions (such as the Black Country) and of some activities. What is certain is that the boom was neither permanent nor general.

Furthermore, the challenges to British industrial supremacy were becoming more numerous, and even if foreign competition remained limited, internal competition was fierce and any let-up was fraught with danger. Victorian entrepreneurs were not at all resistant to innovation, and it was rapid in the textile and steel industries. According to Hughes, in the 1850s these sectors manifested a spirit of risk and speculation that was very striking. There was certainly no permanent state of euphoria in business circles.

As for the rest of the British scene, it seems that the numbers and incomes of the middle classes increased more than total population on the one hand and national income on the other, but more noticeably after 1860 than before. Wage-earners derived less benefit from the general prosperity. The available estimates of real wages show that they went up faster during the third quarter of the nineteenth century (an average of 36 per cent from 1850 to 1874) than during the second, but it was only from the mid-1860s that a marked upward trend became evident, especially for skilled workers. Little information exists on the incidence of unemployment, but it was serious during the depressions of 1858, 1862 and 1868[31]. Improvement in the standard of living for many workers was certain, if belated, but there is little proof of change in the underemployment and poverty from which the subproletariat suffered. Moreover, although no more violent agitation of the chartist type occurred, the mid-Victorian period was not one of cloudless social peace, especially round 1870 when prosperity stimulated rather than damped down the claims of the working classes.

[30] While wages lagged at the beginning behind prices, the prices of raw materials rose faster than those of finished goods.

[31] Church, *The Great Victorian Boom*, pp. 71–4; Saul, *The Myth*, p. 32; Deane and Cole, pp. 25–6; G.Best, *Mid-Victorian Britain, 1851–75* (London, Panther, 1973), pp. 93, 111, 148, 150, shares these rather pessimistic views. Church thinks that the average level of unemployment was nearly as high as after 1873, but Saul thinks otherwise. Anyhow, it is hard to understand why the real incomes of the bulk of the population did not increase substantially before the end of this period.

Finally one can question the general unity of the period. Several indices suggest that a turning–point, a climacteric, can be identified in the middle of the 1860s rather than after the boom of 1869–73, which was a bubble caused by exogenous factors such as the Franco-Prussian war. It was then in fact that a long-term decline in prices and interest rates began. The cotton famine caused serious interruptions in industrial production. Coppock has tried to exclude these by building an index which excludes the cotton industry, and he came to the conclusion that the slowing-down in the growth of industrial production and productivity started between 1861/5 and 1866/74, and not between 1866/74 and 1875/83. The origins of several long-term changes – and notably the beginnings of the slowing–down of British growth-rates – would therefore seem to date from the 1860s, so that the crisis of 1866 could constitute an important break[32].

Church observed, it is true, that the mid-Victorian period was marked by structural changes that could not be ignored. The relative contribution of industry to national product increased after having been stable for two decades. On the other hand, in agriculture a rapid fall of the labour-force started. The use of machinery and steam-engines spread to new industries. In brief, the industrial and urban society came to maturity; but its bases had already been firmly established during the preceding decades, and the process was to continue after 1873.

Summing up, Church, after having first written that his reply to the question Is it correct to talk of a Great Victorian Boom? would be 'a severely qualified affirmative', so as to avoid 'distortion in historical perspective', concluded that, apart from marked but unspectacular growth, 'the conception of a distinctive historical unity for 1850–73 is a myth'[33].

THE GREAT DEPRESSION

S.B. Saul is more outspoken in voicing similar reservations where the subsequent period is concerned. His book entitled *The Myth of the Great Depression* asserts that recent research has once and for all destroyed the idea that the period 1873–96 had a well-established unity which could be summed up by the words Great Depression[34].

---

[32] It is true that the slow-down came later for the GDP. See Chapter 3, p. 53 (table 14).

[33] Church, *The Great Victorian Boom*, pp. 76–8.

[34] Moreover, there is disagreement on the starting-point of the depression; Bairoch, *Commerce extérieur et développement économique de l'Europe au XIX siècle*, (Paris– The Hague, 1976), pp. 203–4, who relies on Deane and Feinstein's series, places it around 1875–7. For a thorough study of this period, the best work is W.Ashworth, *An Economic History of England, 1870–1939* (London, 1960), first part.

As far as prices are concerned it is true that after 1873[35] they fell continuously (apart from a slight recovery in 1880) and markedly for fourteen years, which was exceptional. However the downward trend became weaker after 1887. Prices then rose until 1891 and, despite a fresh dip which reached its lowest point in 1896, the fall was slower. Furthermore, the deviations of various commodities' prices from the general trend became greater. After 1896, a modest recovery took place up to 1914. Apart from short-term fluctuations, the five-year averages in Table 15 show these facts quite clearly.

Table 15   Board of Trade wholesale-price index[36]

1871/5	100
1876/80	92
1881/5	84
1886/90	71
1891/5	68
1896/1900	65
1901/5	67
1906/10	73
1909/13	77

As for the preceding period, recent work has restored credibility to the monetarist interpretation and has given a major role to the currency as a factor in price movements (which were much the same in all industrialized countries). No new discoveries of gold occurred between the mid-century and the late 1880s (when it was found in Australia, the Transvaal and then the Klondike). The increase in the world stock of gold was slow up to 1887, then it became faster – and it was the same for the money supply in Britain. This prevents us from regarding the period 1873-96 as a single entity; also, in so far as the fall in prices continues, though more slowly, after 1887, the monetary factor no longer appears to be responsible. In 1948 Rostow proposed an attractive explanation of long price-swings by changes in the balance between different types of investment and variations in their gestation periods. He argued that from 1850 to 1873 resources had been diverted to unproductive uses, e.g. the working of goldmines and financing of wars, and to massive investment in railways, notably overseas, whose gestation period was long. After 1873 there were no important wars, with inflationary effects, for a long time[37]. Furthermore British capital switched from foreign to home investment which had a short period of

[35] We have seen that some prices began to fall in the 1860s.
[36] Saul, *The Myth*, p. 14 (table I), completed by *Abstract*, p. 476.
[37] Saul admits that this absence of wars may have played a part.

gestation and brought in quicker returns in the way of final goods and a lowering of costs. This dynamic analysis was a great step forward, but Saul, like Church, now considers it hardly convincing. It is based on a view of the movement of prices which is not accurate, while the changing nature of investment which it postulates is too dramatic and does not tally with a detailed analysis of facts. As for the reduction in transport-costs, and notably sea-freight, which had also been invoked as explanation, this became evident in real terms only after 1880[38], continuing up to 1914, and it accounts for only a small part of the fall in prices of imported goods. And even if the costs of production of some articles (e.g. steel, tin-plate, soda) were reduced by technical innovations, there is nothing to prove that these innovations were more numerous or important in the 1870s and 1880s than before and after. On the other hand, given the key role played by Britain in international trade, the slowing-down in the growth of her industrial production influenced the prices of primary products, all the more because world productive capacity of the latter was tending to grow.

Altogether the fall in prices was the result of a complex combination of circumstances which gradually became cumulative. It was the same with their recovery. This began during the rising phase of a business cycle, whose vigour was stimulated by the inflationary influence of the Boer war. Its upward trend at a steady rate was sustained by the swelling of the money supply which followed new discoveries of gold, by a resumption of unproductive expenditure (e.g. naval armaments) and the recovery of world industrial production, at a time when the growth of the supply of primary products was slowing down. So the dates traditionally given to the beginning and end of the Great Depression have no significance in the long term. They represent the end of a strong boom and the beginning of another, not the sudden reversal of a long trend. For the downward trend of prices, which has been considered the dominant trait of the Great Depression, began in the 1860s and in some respects ended around 1887.

The movements of another significant factor – the terms of trade – do not agree with the traditional turning-points. For they show, after certain corrections, a plateau up to the middle of the 1880s, then a continuous improvement up to 1913, showing thus a turning-point in the middle of the Great Depression, and following their new trend well beyond 1896.

Employment is an essential element for determining if there was a

[38] Very sharp in the 1830s and 1840s, it was interrupted during the decades that followed. Saul, *The Myth*, p. 22 (table II).

'real' depression in addition to a fall in prices. Unfortunately, statistics are lacking, except as far as the members of trade unions are concerned. For the latter, unemployment was on average higher (7.2 per cent of members) between 1874 and 1895 than between 1851 and 1873 (5 per cent) and between 1896 and 1913 (5.4 per cent). But this rather high average was the result of bad figures for a few years only (1879, 1884–7 and 1892–5), and the situation was distinctly better for the rest of the period.

As for real wages, their average increase (about a third) was exactly the same during the two periods of twenty years on either side of 1873, so the Great Depression had 'no particular meaning' where they were concerned. This fairly regular progress was, of course, the result of the fall in prices and the improvement in the terms of trade, but it was also aided by the stability of money-wages which declined somewhat from 1873 to 1876, but were afterwards stable up to 1888, then rose by stages during the 1890s. There is no doubt that this stability was partly the result of the growing strength of trade unions. One consequence was a pressure on profit margins, particularly during bad years, and a marked increase in the share of the national income going to wages at the expense of profits[39].

On the production side, contemporaries were struck by the crisis affecting British agriculture and by its stagnating output. We shall see later that some sectors of agriculture suffered seriously, but that others escaped comparatively lightly. Furthermore the prevailing tendencies – e.g. the relative decline of agriculture in the country's economy, its loss of manpower, a changeover from cereal production to stock farming – were nothing new and had already emerged during the so-called Golden Age of agriculture in mid-Victorian times. As for industrial production, there is no doubt that its growth slowed down considerably during the last quarter of the nineteenth century (see tables 11 and 12) and that the slackening was even more evident in per-capita production. Few industries enjoyed a rapid growth during this period and the growth-rates of aggregate indices were very modest. However, according to Coppock's calculations (whose validity is admitted by Saul), which exclude the distortions caused by the American civil war, the slowing-down does seem to have started in the mid-1860s and not in the mid-1870s.

On the other hand, after the 1897-1900 boom, which several historians have tended to consider as a flash in the pan, the Edwardian

---

[39] Wages made up 52 per cent of the sum of wages plus profits in 1870/4, 62 per cent in 1890/4.

period seems no different from the end of Victoria's reign, whatever people may think because of the rise in prices. No acceleration of growth in industrial production or national product is discernible. Some historians indeed see this period as even more unfavourable than the Great Depression because of the near stagnation of labour-productivity and total factor productivity[40]. Furthermore money-wages did not keep up with rising prices, so that real wages dropped slightly just before the first world war because of difficulties in several industries and the rapid increase of the *adult* population. None the less, profits did not rise accordingly and home investment was inadequate. The prewar period, however, must not be seen in too dark a light, for in its last years an adaptation of industrial structures and a serious effort to remedy technological deficiencies were set in train[41].

To sum up, and to come back to the Great Depression, Saul considers that the period 1873–96 does not display any trends which were continuously and markedly different from those of the preceding or following periods in the matter of prices, terms of trade, wages, profits or growth-rates. The expression Great Depression is misleading because it gives this period a significance and unity which it does not deserve. Consequently, according to Saul, 'The sooner the "Great Depression"is banished from the literature, the better'[42].

A harsh judgement. Saul admits that the last quarter of the nineteenth century was a new and important stage in Britain's economic history because of the slowing-down of growth, the emergence of new great industrial powers which put an end to the unrivalled economic supremacy which England had enjoyed up to about 1870, and the growing competition which she was encountering. Moreover, during these decades Great Britain, like other countries, experienced economic difficulties and dislocations which were acutely felt by people at the time. They referred to these difficulties as the Great Depression and in any case the expression remains valid as a contemporary interpretation of what was experienced.

However, when all is said and done, what is challenged, both by Saul and Church, is the concept of fifty-year 'long swings', which were said to have given nineteenth-century economic history its pattern. One should stop putting the British economy into the traditional straight-jacket of four periods. D. Robertson has written that it would be wise to wait several centuries before asserting the existence of 'long swings'!

[40]   See, for example, Aldcroft and Fearon, pp. 40 (table 5), 56, 81–2.
[41]   See T.C.Barker, 'History: economic and social', in C.B. Cox and A.E.Dyson (eds.), *The Twentieth-Century Mind*, I: *1900–1918* (London, 1972), pp. 51ff.
[42]   Saul, *The Myth*, p. 55.

For Saul they are nothing but an illusion brought about by high cyclical peaks of prices and activity such as occurred in 1813 and 1873 (and also 1900), followed, probably by pure chance, two or three decades later by a severe depression, as in the 1840s and 1880s. These violent ups and downs give the intervening periods an appearance of unity, but careful examination shows it to be illusory.

Without taking sides on this point, one must admit that the periodization of British growth in the nineteenth century is certainly more complex than has long been asserted. Conversely, if one wants to simplify drastically, as already suggested, one can say that there were only two long phases, on each side of a watershed situated around 1865–75 – one of 'rapid' growth and one of 'slower' growth.

BUSINESS CYCLES

One should perhaps also take more account than has been done recently of the short-term fluctuations from which the long-term trends derived, at least in part[43]. For the growth-rate over several decades depended largely on the strength and duration of the booms they experienced[44].

The cyclical pattern has a 'solid reality' (Rostow) in nineteenth-century England. We can identify eighteen business cycles between 1815 and 1914, of which ten occurred during Victoria's reign. But only eleven of these fluctuations (seven under Victoria) were major cycles, according to the classification of Gayer, Rostow and Schwartz, i.e. at the end of their phase of expansion considerable investments were made, including investment abroad, and a state of full employment for the labour-force was almost reached[45]. Their average length (with very few variations) was nine years, from one peak to the next or from one trough to the next one. But to these major cycles were added minor cycles up to about 1860, and these lasted a shorter time (four years) and were not as violent. They derived essentially from foreign trade, with alternating bouts of massive exports, often speculative, which flooded overseas markets, and the subsequent contraction of these shipments once the news of the glut reached England. The increased speed of communications and the improved organization of trade

---

[43] ibid., pp. 9–11, 54.
[44] Church, *The Great Victorian Boom*, pp. 53–5; J.R.T. Hughes, *Fluctuations in Trade, Industry and Finance: A Study of British Economic Development, 1850–1860* (Oxford, 1960), pp. 288–9.
[45] See Rostow, p. 33 (table II). The peaks of these major cycles occurred in 1818, 1825, 1836, 1845, 1854, 1866, 1873, 1883, 1890, 1900, 1913. Some of these years also saw the beginning of a crisis.

tended to make these inventory cycles disappear in the second half of the nineteenth century. But the advance of industrialization tended to give a growing and finally dominant role to investment cycles, i.e. to the major cycles mentioned above. However, the two types of cycles were linked, and more especially the beginnings of a recovery from depression were nearly always touched off by a jump in exports, although the latter did not necessarily unleash an investment boom.

We will not linger on the mechanism of these fluctuations which resulted from forces inherent in liberal capitalism's economy as it functioned in the nineteenth century; but they were also influenced by external factors such as political crises, so that each cycle had its own individuality. We will only remark that, up to the middle of the nineteenth century and even beyond, harvests played an important part, not so much by altering the home demand for goods, other than food (according to Labrousse's model of an 'old style' crisis), as by reacting on credit conditions. In particular, a bad harvest led to large imports of cereals. These were largely paid for in gold, so that the Bank of England protected its reserves by putting up its interest rate and even rationing credit. All lenders followed and a financial crisis was liable to occur. A good harvest had the opposite effect and favoured expansion. However, the relative decline of British agriculture and the regular import of cereals were to reduce the role of harvests more and more. We have already pointed out the influence of export fluctuations, which were most important for those staple industries which exported a high proportion of their production but which were at the mercy of economic fluctuations overseas. It only remains to insist on the growing role of investment. Decisions to increase productive capacity were spasmodic and were mostly bunched at the end of a major cycle's phase of expansion when existing capacity became inadequate. However, this concentration, which went hand in hand with speculation (including the worst of its kind), was apt to cause rises in prices, wages and rates of interest. Tension in the money market made some businessmen seek liquidity, refuse credit and get rid of stock. Thus one went from boom to recession and sometimes to panic, usually the consequence of excessive speculation, when it was said of businessmen that they gambled not only on the future, but on the hereafter.

It remains to be considered if the amplitude and intensity of cycles and particularly major cycles changed in the course of the nineteenth century. Rostow, drawing on the researches of the team to which he had belonged, thinks that there was no significant change, except that a growing percentage of the population was directly affected by these fluctuations[46]. However, Church points out that the 1866 crisis was doubtless the last which resulted from one of those investment manias which ended in disaster, but not without having increased productive capacity and encouraged innovation. Furthermore Saul observes that up to 1873 investment booms in Britain herself and overseas roughly coincided, but after that date they did not synchronize. This flattened cyclical peaks and resulted in the economy never working at full intensity[47]. For these reasons changes in short-term fluctuations may have contributed to the slowing-down of long-term growth during the last third of the nineteenth century.

---

[46]   Rostow, pp. 44-5.
[47]   Church, *The Great Victorian Boom*, pp. 53-4; Saul, *The Myth*, p. 21, Chapter 2 of S.G.Checkland, *The Rise of Industrial Society In England, 1815–1885* (London, 1964), pp. 6ff, skilfully combines analysis in the short and in the medium term. And see W.A.Lewis, *Growth and Fluctuations, 1870–1913* (London, 1978).

4   Structural change

Sustained economic growth of the kind experienced by Britain in the nineteenth century inevitably implies profound changes in economic structures, especially when, as in this case, growth was based on industrialization. As the production of industry and the services or 'tertiary' sector increased much more rapidly than the output of agriculture, both the distribution of labour between the three main sectors of the economy and the structure of national product were transformed. Changes similarly came about, on the microeconomic scale, in the very structure of these sectors and of the firms. Finally, a process of rapid urbanization took place.

AGRICULTURE, INDUSTRY AND SERVICES

The basic tendencies of the changes in the structure of the British economy show up clearly in tables 16 and 17. But we must not forget that they indicate *relative* movements in the framework of an occupied population and a GNP that were both strongly on the increase[1].

The most striking tendency is the very pronounced *relative* decline of agriculture. It is true that this was the continuation and strengthening of a process that was already well advanced. This decline had started in the eighteenth century, probably even in the seventeenth century, for at the end of the latter the role of agriculture in England's economy was abnormally modest for a pre-industrial society. However, the decline was slow and was interrupted during the Napoleonic wars, a period of high prices and prosperity for the agricultural sector; but it became rapid again between 1815 and 1831, and at the beginning of Victoria's reign agriculture employed less than a quarter of the total

---

[1]   We must also take into account the increased percentage of the total population which was employed regularly and full time, as a result of the decline in begging, vagrancy and casual work, which were characteristic of traditional economies and still widespread during much of the nineteenth century.

Table 16 Distribution of the British labour-force (as percentages of the total occupied population)

	1801	1831	1841	1851	1871	1901	1911
Agriculture (a)	36	25	22	22	15	9	8
Industry, mining and construction	30	41	41	43	44	46	46
Trade and transport	11	12	14	16	20	21	22
Domestic and personal	12	13	15	13	15	14	14
Public, professional all other	12	10	9	7	7	10	10

After Deane and Cole p. 142 (table 30).
(a) Including forestry and fishing.

Table 17 The industrial distribution of the national income of Great Britain (as percentages of total national income at current prices in each year)

	1801	1831	1841	1851	1871	1901	1907
Agriculture (a)	33	23	22	20	14	6	6
Industry, mining and construction	23	34	34	34	38	40	40
Trade and transport	17	17	18	19	22	23	28
Domestic and personal	6	6	6	5	5	5	3
Housing	5	7	8	8	8	8	6
Income from abroad	–	1	1	2	4	7	5
Public, professional and all other	16	12	10	11	9	11	14

After Deane and Cole, p. 166 (table 37) and p. 175 (table 40) (for 1907: figures are not entirely in line with those of other years).
(a) as in table 16.
N.B. Percentages are approximate, especially at the beginning of the nineteenth century. Percentages are rounded.

labour-force and provided less than a quarter of national income. Its decline eased from 1831 to 1851 and even 1861, but reasserted itself after that, for agricultural production practically ceased to increase after the 1870s[2], and in 1881 agriculture provided only 10 per cent of national income. Finally, at the beginning of the twentieth century, the role of British agriculture as an employer and its contribution to the national income had become very small, reaching a level that was quite exceptional at the time among the most advanced and industrial-

---

[2] Between 1861 and 1901, agriculture's share in national income fell by two-thirds, whereas it had only gone down by 50 per cent since 1801 or 1811.

ized nations. It is true that in actual numbers, and thanks to the increase in population, the labour-force in agriculture had continued to grow up to around 1860, but it fell back afterwards, from 2.1 million in 1851 to 1.6 million in 1911[3]. As a percentage of the total, employment in agriculture was consistently a little higher than its contribution to national income, which shows, as one might expect, that labour-productivity was lower on the land than in the other sectors. In any case the redistribution of resources in the national economy was carried out to the detriment of agriculture.

Of course the counterpart of agricultural decline was that the role of industry (including mining and construction) increased strongly[4]. The respective positions of the two sectors were almost exactly reversed – between 1801 and 1831 as regards their contribution to national income and between 1801 and 1821 as employers of labour. At Victoria's accession industry employed two-fifths of the total labour-force and contributed more than one-third of the national income. It is true that after the 1830s its relative progress was only slow[5], for at the beginning of the twentieth century industry employed 46 per cent of the labour-force and provided two-fifths of the national income. Of course, in actual numbers, the labour-force of industry continued to increase greatly, jumping from 3 million in 1831 to 8.6 million in 1911. However, to carry the analysis further, we notice a slight retreat of the part played by manufacturing industry, notably on the employment side. Although the relative advance of the industrial sector continued, it was because of the sustained expansion of the mining branch (essentially coalmining), whose labour-force rose from 200,000 in 1841 to 900,000 in 1901 and 1,200,000 in 1911, and which provided 6 per cent of the national income in 1907[6].

We must not jump to the conclusion that the industrialization of Great Britain ceased from the 1830s onwards. We must first take into account the fact that a large proportion of the workers in industry (particularly domestic workers, who were then still very numerous)

[3]   Figures for the labour-force, as well as those cited later, are taken from P. Deane and W.A. Cole, *British Economic Growth, 1688–1959* (Cambridge, 2nd edn, 1967), p. 143 (table 31).
[4]   But not symmetrically, for the decisive change in favour of industry occurred between 1815 and 1831, while the decline of agriculture was gradual with a speed-up at the end of the century.
[5]   However, with a definite increase in its contribution to national income between 1851 and 1871. This suggests a considerable rise in labour productivity, since the percentage of manpower employed in industry hardly increased.
[6]   Of course the industrial sector itself changed in structure, as we shall see later on, with a notable growth of production-goods industries at the expense of those supplying consumer goods.

were partly occupied by transport and distribution duties, whereas later on there were more and more workers engaged full-time in industry. But in any case it is normal that at the advanced stages of industrialization – and it is even an essential part of the process as work becomes increasingly specialized – the tertiary sector should grow more rapidly than the industrial sector itself. Furthermore certain tertiary branches, e.g. transport, banking, insurance, were directly at the service of industry, keeping up supplies of raw materials, exporting manufactured goods, financing, production and so on. Given the growing complexity of the economy, these services would develop rapidly. In fact, at the beginning of the twentieth century, Great Britain was more industrialized than at Victoria's accession, for a higher percentage of available goods were of industrial origin, industry dominated economic life, and a few staple industries were the engine of growth. However, services added to the final value of industrial products a higher percentage than before; for, in the technical and commercial conditions of the second half of the nineteenth century, there had to be a greater increase in transport and distribution services to promote industrial production.

In any case there was a notable increase in the importance of services in the British economy during the Victorian period. During the preceding decades a confusing element had been introduced as a result of the hostilities at the beginning of the nineteenth century, which had swollen the numbers of the army and navy and so distorted the distribution of manpower and the structure of national income to the advantage of government and the services-sector generally. Once the war was over, and the armed forces and state expenditure had been reduced, the part played by the services-sector diminished, both from the employment and the national-income standpoint. But after its lowest point in 1821, it went up again, slowly at first, then faster from mid-century, as is shown by table 18.

However, these global percentages mask different developments among the various services. The percentage of manpower employed in trade and transport increased greatly, doubling between 1801 and 1911 and expanding by 50 per cent between 1841 and 1901 (with a big jump in the 1850s and 1860s), notably because of the development of railways and the expansion of the British merchant navy[7]. But, from the standpoint of contribution to national income, the relative progress of this sector, although real, was less impressive (especially after

[7] In absolute figures the labour-force of this sector went up from 1.2 million in 1841 to 4 million in 1911. It was the transport branch that played the largest role in the growth.

Table 18   Services as percentage of total occupied population and of national income

	Total occupied population	National income
1801	35	44
1811	37	44
1821	33	42
1831	35	42
1841	37	44
1851	36	45
1871	42	48
1901	45	54
1911	45	–

1870), and was outshone by the very rapid increase of income flowing in from abroad as the result of Great Britain's growing exports of capital. This overseas income, unimportant at the beginning of the Victorian era, made up 7 per cent of national income at the beginning of the twentieth century, and its expansion played a part equal to that of trade and transport in the growing importance of services in national income.

The contribution of housing to national income was stable from the 1830s onwards, while that of domestic and personal services drifted downward. As for the proportion of the labour-force employed in the latter services, it increased at the beginning of the nineteenth century but remained stable thereafter, with a moderate peak in 1891; but it should be underlined that it was considerable, reaching 15 per cent of the total, and also that such stability meant that in absolute numbers this labour-force (mostly female) increased markedly, going up from 600,000 persons in 1801 to 1.2 million in 1841 and 2.6 million in 1911. The large number of servants, whose employment by a family was an important sign of membership of the middle class, was an essential fact in the social structure of Great Britain in the nineteenth century. Clapham points out quite correctly that in 1831 there were 670,000 female servants, i.e. three times as many as the total number of men, women and children employed in cotton mills in 1834. He also added that 'in the England and Wales of the Reform Bill, there were more tailors, and many more shoemakers, than there were coalminers'[8].

---

[8]   J.H. Clapham, *An Economic History of Britain* (3 vols, Cambridge, 1926–38), I, pp. 72–3. The importance of domestic service, which had low productivity and was badly paid, slowed down the increase of productivity. A considerable proportion of women who worked were employed as domestic servants. Many of them came from the country, and it was this sector, as well as textiles and clothing, which benefited mainly from the redistribution of female labour.

As for the so-called unproductive services – central government (including defence), local government, the social services (e.g. education and health) as well as the small numbers engaged in the professions and various activities such as the leisure industries – their relative importance diminished during the first half of the nineteenth century, at first because of the end of the French wars and later because of the policy of strict economy and reduction of public expenditure, which meant that the latter increased more slowly than national income. On the other hand this sector increased notably from the 1870s onwards because of the development of government intervention (e.g. in education) and the growth in military expenditure. This meant a strong increase in the number of people employed in these activities, which rose fivefold from 1841 to 1911.

The observations just made on the connection between the secondary and the tertiary sector should not blind us to the fact that Britain increasingly directed her energies to the supply (and sale abroad) of services rather than goods – a consequence of, and perhaps a factor in, her relative industrial decline at the end of the nineteenth century. At the same time there was a slight decrease in the percentage of manual workers in the occupied population, particularly if account is taken of the reduction in the agricultural labour-force, while the white-collar sector – business and bank personnel, civil servants, teachers, professional men, etc. – showed an increase. The structural changes in the economy swelled the urban working classes during the first half of the nineteenth century, and later the middle classes.

On the whole, the decisive change in the structure of the British economy took place between the 1780s and the 1830s, with some pause at the beginning of the nineteenth century during the Napoleonic wars only for added vigour to be brought to the movement when peace returned. That was the time when industry, whose growth had speeded up, strongly enlarged its share of the occupied population and its contribution to national product, outstripping agriculture which had fallen back, but only relatively. At Victoria's accession Britain was already an industrial country, i.e. industry was the dominant and dynamic force in her economy.

During Victoria's reign, changes were much less spectacular. It appears that they were limited during the first fifteen years, increased during the third quarter of the nineteenth century, and tapered off again at the end of the century and the beginning of the twentieth. The most striking features in the structural developments that took place between the 1830s and the start of the twentieth century were agriculture's collapse in importance on the one hand and the increase in the relative weight of trade, transport and mining on the other.

The redistribution of manpower and capital resources, to the detriment of agriculture and to the advantage of industry and services, was a characteristic phenomenon of the Industrial Revolution and of industrialization generally. Firstly, because the occupied population and the national stock of capital increased, as they did in Great Britain in the nineteenth century, this transfer did not necessarily involve a reduction in absolute terms of the output, manpower and capital engaged in agriculture. In fact total farm production continued to grow up to the 1870s, the labour-force employed in agriculture only decreased after mid-century, and the utilized capital much later. The redistribution of resources came about mainly by the transfer of manpower and surplus capital which were to be found in the countryside. It was not rural depopulation (a later and rather limited phenomenon) which provided manpower for the other sectors[9] but the overall growth of the population. This growth of course occurred in rural areas which yielded their population surplus to the industrial areas, but also in the latter areas themselves, as in both kinds of districts natural increase was high. To a great extent, industry generated its own manpower.

As for the factors and mechanism of this redistribution of productive forces, agriculture as a general rule is subject to diminishing returns, while industry and transport, once the latter were mechanized by the introduction of the steam-engine, enjoyed increasing returns. In fact, in a long-occupied and cultivated country like Britain, there is an absolute shortage of workable land, which cannot be extended. On the other hand in the nineteenth century technological progress offered industry and transport increases in productivity that were far superior to those available to English agriculture, although the latter were not negligible. Finally, the demand for agricultural commodities grew more slowly than the demand for manufactured goods and services – which is far more elastic in relation to incomes. Moreover, British agriculture was exposed early on to the shock of foreign competition, which captured a growing share of her potential market. So the demand for farm labour was stable or slowly increasing up to the middle of the nineteenth century, and then began to decline, in contrast to a rapidly growing demand on the part of industry and services.

One result of these trends was a difference in earnings, which was the prime motive prompting the redistribution of labour from agriculture towards the other sectors and from the country towards the towns.

---

[9]   For a long time wrongly attributed to the enclosures, whereas the latter were in fact accompanied by an increase in rural population, and in any case they were almost over by 1820. Cf. Chapter 6.

There is no doubt that the wages of farm workers were markedly inferior not only to those of the limited number of skilled operatives who were the 'aristocracy of labour' but also to the wages of the semi-skilled 'hands' who formed the mass of factory-workers, and even of ordinary town labourers. It was the same story with real wages and standards of living. Furthermore, during the first half of the nineteenth century, farm wages themselves were higher in regions close to industrial centres (roughly north of a line passing through Birmingham to the Wash) than in the regions away from them (roughly the south of England)[10]. So it was the drawing power of better-paid industrial work, backed up by non-economic motives, which led to the transfer of labour away from agriculture towards industry. An element of compulsion was also present, however, for in some overpopulated rural areas, with no possibility of work or access to land, the choice for many was to starve or leave for the town[11].

Changes similar to those just analysed affected the structure of Britain's national capital[12]. At the beginning of the nineteenth century, according to Deane and Cole, land accounted for more than half this capital[13], but this share diminished rapidly, at least after 1830, dropping to one-third in the 1860s and to less than a fifth in 1885. If we exclude land from the calculations, which is preferable for an industrial economy, and consider only reproducible capital, we have Deane and Cole's opinion that its structure changed little and the economy remained non-capital-intensive until around 1830; but later, it changed radically, especially between 1830 and 1870[14]. So farmers'

[10] Cf. E.H. Hunt, *Regional Wage Variations in Britain, 1850–1914* (Oxford, 1973). These regional differences in wages, which were considerable, seem to have increased until about 1860.

[11] The nature of rural society encouraged emigration, given the reluctance of landlords to divide holdings. As the number of families increased, the surplus population had to find non-agricultural work, either locally or by emigrating.

[12] This passage is based on Deane and Cole, p. 271 (table 70), 304–7 (table 81). See also P. Deane, 'The role of capital in the industrial revolution', *Explorations in Economic History*, 10 (4), Summer 1973, 349–64, esp. 357ff. It is true that C.H. Feinstein has since produced some estimates that are certainly more solid (*National Income, Expenditure and Output of the United Kingdom 1855–1965* (Cambridge, 1972), table 43 and 46,T.96–7, 103–4), but they only start in 1860. His most recent work ('Capital formation in Great Britain', in P. Mathias and M.M. Postan (eds), *The Cambridge Economic History of Europe*, VII, part I (Cambridge, 1978)) covers the period 1760–1860, but arrives at very different figures for the capital stock in 1860 from those in his earlier book. So with some reservations, we use the estimates of Deane and Cole, mentioning in certain cases significant differences from those of Feinstein. The former are at current prices and the latter at constant prices.

[13] Feinstein gives only one-third for 1800 and 1830.

[14] According to Feinstein, *National Income*, the structure of reproducible capital did not change very much from 1860 or 1880 to 1913, apart from a noticeable increase in the share of the transport and communications sector.

capital probably fell from 20 per cent of the total around 1830 to 16 per cent in 1865, to 7 per cent in 1885 and to 2 per cent in 1913[15]. The share of building and public property probably dropped slightly, from more than a third at the beginning of the nineteenth century and around 1830 to a little less than a third in 1913. On the other hand, commercial (including transport), industrial and financial capital increased vigorously, both absolutely and relatively, being 45 per cent of the total around 1830, 61 per cent in 1885 and 66 per cent in 1913. As for the structure of this group, circulating capital (stocks, work in progress) made up over one-half in the early nineteenth century and as late as 1830, but its share declined fast after the latter date, while the share of fixed capital (industrial and commercial buildings, machinery, railways, etc.) became dominant, owing to massive mechanization in industry and to railway building[16]. Railways made up 12 per cent of total reproducible capital in 1865 and 14 per cent in 1885, but this percentage later fell. As for foreign assets, they were unimportant in the early nineteenth century – 6 per cent of reproducible capital around 1830 – but rose to 10 per cent as early as 1865, 18 per cent in 1885 and 25 per cent in 1913.

Deane and Cole reckoned that reproducible capital increased noticeably faster than production in the second and third quarters of the nineteenth century, whence an increase in the capital/output ratio. In other words the economy became more capital-intensive as a result of the mechanization of industry and transport. Yet from about 1880 onwards production seems to have increased faster than capital, and the capital/output ratio decreased. On the other hand, the more recent and exhaustive work of Feinstein shows a slow but regular diminution of the capital/output ratio, not only from 1885 onwards but also from the beginning of the nineteenth century and right up to the first world war[17]. This suggests a constant improvement and better use of capital.

This question touches on another important problem of structure – the use of national product and particularly its distribution between capital formation and consumption. However this will be tackled in Chapter 5.

There remains the question of the structure of the national product by factors. It presents serious difficulties, for available data is only –

[15]   In the opinion of Feinstein, 'Capital formation', the fall was less sharp, but he includes the fixed reproducible capital of agriculture.
[16]   The 1978 estimates of Feinstein ('Capital formation') give a smaller share to commercial and industrial capital, but within this sector he assigns at an earlier date a larger share to fixed capital in relation to circulating capital – and particularly to machinery and other industrial equipment.
[17]   Feinstein, *National Income*, table 20,T.51.

and hardly – valid from 1870 onwards. Furthermore it is impossible to distinguish the role of capital from that of labour in mixed incomes, i.e. in the incomes of the self-employed and the owners of businesses, great or small, who were also in effect the managers of those businesses. This concerns a category that was important, but whose relative importance in the occupied population certainly diminished in the course of the nineteenth century (from about 20 per cent to 11 or 12 per cent). However, Deane and Cole have provided certain estimates (see table 19)[18].

The only notable trend is the marked fall in the share of rents, which is normal given the relative decline in agriculture's contribution to national income, and given also the reduction of the share of rents in the net factor incomes earned in agriculture. As for dwellings' rents, their share seems to have increased right up to the 1880s, and then it fell back.

The stability of the other two sectors is fairly surprising. It would seem to show that the share of wages (in the broadest sense, salaries included) on the one hand and the share of income from capital on the other in the national product hardly changed at all, in spite of the considerable structural changes in the various sectors and the variations in the wage-fraction (i.e. the share of wages in costs) between one industry and another and within the same industry. Deane and Cole conclude from this that most of the transition to a system of unmixed incomes from employment must have occurred in the eighteenth century, being nearly complete by the beginning of the nineteenth. The specialization of the factors of production, leading to clearly distinct categories of incomes, was already an obvious feature of their distribution at the beginning of the nineteenth century.

Table 19 Distribution of income by factor shares (as percentage of total national income)

	Employment incomes	Rents	Profits, interest, mixed incomes
c. 1801: Great Britain	44	20	37
1860/9: United Kingdom	49	14	38
1890/9: United Kingdom	50	12	38
1900/9: United Kingdom	48	11	40

[18] Deane and Cole, pp. 299ff, 301 (table 80), also pp. 302–3. The same conclusions appear in S. Kuznets, *Modern Economic Growth: Rate, Structure and Spread* (New Haven and London, 1966), p. 168 (table 4.2). A. Offer, 'Ricardo's Paradox and the movement of rents in England, c. 1870–1910', *Economic History Review* 2nd series, XXXIII(2), May 1980, 236–52.

It is true that Feinstein reaches different results for the second half of the nineteenth century, with a marked rise (from 49 to 54 per cent) of the share of wages between 1860/9 and 1900/09, a drop of the same magnitude for profits (from 37 to 33 per cent) and a slight decline of rents (from 14 to 13 per cent)[19].

LARGE AND SMALL FIRMS

While the macroeconomic structures of Britain were evolving in the way just described, the organization and structure of the various sectors were undergoing a similar transformation at the microeconomic level. The exception was agriculture, which had long since been characterized by the predominance of both large estates and relatively large farms, and where changes were slight. The essential feature was what Harold Perkin has described as the change of 'scale' of nearly all human organizations, particularly in industry.

Traditional industry, and notably the textile industry, which was far the most important in England during the seventeenth and eighteenth centuries, had been on a small scale, consisting of craftsmen working at home with simple tools or machines, helped by the members of their families, sometimes with one or more journeymen. Of course, many of these artisans were not independent and worked as virtual wage-earners for 'merchant-manufacturers', who might employ hundreds or indeed thousands of them. But this commercial capitalism remained within the framework of the 'domestic system', small family workshops being the actual units of production and also usually dispersed over the countryside. Only a few branches of industry, because of their nature and by the exigencies of their technology, were organized in centralized larger undertakings, e.g. blast-furnaces, forges, foundries for non-ferrous metal, glassworks, bleaching and dyeing businesses, etc., but their size remained modest.

The Industrial Revolution brought large-scale industry into being – the factory system, mechanized and concentrated. The factory, the typical unit of the new economy, was the grouping in one building, or cluster of neighbouring buildings, of a large number of workers and machines (or other powerful and complex pieces of equipment), using a source of energy other than human. In the nineteenth century this was usually the steam-engine. The whole would belong to one owner – an individual or a company – and would make up a production unit that

[19]   Feinstein, *National Income*, table 1,T.4.

was altogether novel by its size, its complexity and the combination of its elements into a 'system'[20].

The general tendency of the structural change under review was simple. First came the development of the factory system at the expense of the traditional domestic system, as a consequence of the swift and continuous technological progress set in train by the Industrial Revolution. In addition, within the factory sector itself, there was a tendency for the size of firms and of fixed capital to grow.

The reasons for this development were equally simple. Some of the inventions at the beginning of the Industrial Revolution (notably the flying-shuttle and, among spinning machines, the jenny and the mule) were perfectly compatible with the domestic system and could be used in small workshops. But others were not – in particular Richard Arkwright's water-frame, for it was heavy, bulky and demanded water-power, and as a consequence required a concentration of workmen and machiney. This was why the first factories (in the strict sense) were set up, if one excludes the water-powered silk-throwing mills which antedated them but which were limited in number by the undynamic character of the silk industry in England. Furthermore, technical progress increased the size of machines like the mule so fast that they had to be worked by steam and so be set up in factories[21].

The new machines – or in industries other than textiles, the new manufacturing processes – led to increases in productivity and to economies in labour or raw materials which were often enormous. Hence a lowering of costs, shortly followed by the retail price thanks to competition, which made untenable the position of traditional producers and particularly domestic workers. Despite this, in certain branches, where the advantage of the machine was at first limited, the latter managed to conduct a long rearguard action, by resigning themselves to lower and lower wages. This led to the elimination, sometimes fast (as in spinning) and sometimes slow (as in weaving) of domestic workers.

[20] But not every large firm was a factory, a *machinofacture*. It could remain a *manufacture stricto sensu*. For example, this was the case up to the mid-nineteenth century for the making of pins, which was concentrated in the hands of a small number of big makers, who employed hundreds of workers within the same buildings. But in spite of the very advanced division of labour, which had struck Adam Smith, everything was done by hand; S.R. Jones, 'Price association and competition in the British pin industry, 1814–40', *Economic History Review* 2nd series, XXVI(2) May 1973, 238.

[21] Although prime importance has generally been paid to the use of power in the birth of the factory system, some historians emphasize the advantages gained from increased supervision and discipline among a concentrated labour-force, not to mention the possibilities of more intensive specialization.

Furthermore, industrialists who took up new machinery or new processes benefited from large profit margins, at least for a while until competition developed. They nearly always reinvested most of the profits at once to enlarge their firms, so that the size of these increased rapidly. In the climate of intense competition which prevailed from the beginning of the nineteenth century, the largest firms were in a better position than the rest, so long of course as they were well managed. They benefited from economies of scale, as costs per unit of output were lower when the equipment was powerful and mass production achieved. Thanks to their financial resources they were better able to keep to the forefront of technical progress and to withstand crises and cyclical depressions which depleted the ranks of smaller firms. Although the last advantage appears to be true, this elementary theoretical reasoning needs to be modified in the light of empirical data. In fact success was not the sole prerogative of giant firms, nor was sheer size a guarantee of efficiency. V.A.C. Gatrell has maintained recently that, during the first half of the nineteenth century, economies of scale were not evident in the cotton industry, which showed no marked tendency to concentrate between 1815 and 1850. Management problems limited the workforce of a cotton factory to a maximum of 1000, 1200, or at most 1400 people, and small and medium-sized firms could enjoy prosperity[22].

Finally, modernized industries, thanks to continuously improving productivity and to the lower prices that resulted, were in a position to widen their markets and profit more than old-fashioned firms from the expansion of internal and external demand. The growth of their production, therefore, was swifter.

Yet this triple development was relatively slow, much slower than has often been thought. It only affected the different branches of industry one after the other, so that for a long time traditional ways of working and organization, as well as transitional methods survived, and they even held the field at the beginning of the nineteenth century. The victory of the factory system over the domestic system was only gradual and, for a period, the two systems expanded simultaneously; moreover, for a long time very large firms remained the exception.

The Industrial Revolution started in cotton-spinning in the 1770s,

---

[22] V.A.C. Gatrell, 'Labour, power and the size of firms in Lancashire cotton in the second quarter of the nineteenth century', *Economic History Review* 2nd series, XXX(1), Feb. 1977, 95–139, especially 95, 97, 107, 109, 116, 125. R. Lloyd-Jones and A.A. Le Roux, 'The size of firms in the cotton industry: Manchester, 1815–41', *Economic History Review*, 2nd series, XXXIII(1), Feb. 1980, 32–82.

then it took over the spinning of wool and flax. The factory system triumphed in these branches and had almost completely eliminated domestic manual work by the beginning of the nineteenth century, with one important exception: wool-combing was only mechanized at mid-century. However, change was much slower and later in weaving. Although power-weaving had been tried at the end of the eighteenth century, it only really developed after 1820, or more exactly 1826. It progressed rapidly in the 1830s and 1840s, first, for cotton, then more slowly for the other fibres; but in 1850 the mechanization of weaving, apart from cotton, was still very incomplete. So the beginnings of Victoria's reign saw an important stage in this revolution (not only economic but social too) which led to the elimination of the handloom-weavers, who had been the most typical and numerous representatives of traditional domestic industry.

Elsewhere, several inventions of the eighteenth century – coke smelting, puddling and rolling, the use of steam-engines to drive the blowers [or blowing machinery] of blast-furnaces and the rolling-mills – had transformed the iron industry, leading to the creation of large integrated works (producing pig-iron, bar-iron and half-finished goods, and much larger in size than the traditional small works) and eliminating the old charcoal iron industry. It was in this branch that were to be found the giant concerns of the first half of the nineteenth century such as the Dowlais works in South Wales which in 1849 had eighteen blast-furnaces, employed 7000 workmen and were the largest in the world at that time. This was an exceptional case, but many iron-works had more than a thousand hands. However, the secondary metal industries, notably in their two great centres, Birmingham and Sheffield, for a long time remained the almost exclusive preserve of the small and even the very small firm. The typical manufacturer, of whom there were thousands, was a small employer, a 'garret master', with a tiny capital, say £100, and very simple equipment, employing fewer than ten workmen[23]. Although some factories did appear in this branch at the beginning of the nineteenth century (but the first cutlery-factory in Sheffield only dated from 1832), they were the exception for a long time. London, with an entirely different range of activities, was also a town of small masters and domestic workers. Even in an entirely new branch, engineering – the building of machines and machine-tools, whose development was the necessary condition and base of the spread of mechanization – most

---

[23] In the 1830s, Sheffield is said to have had 500 small furnaces for making steel.

firms were small and were workshops rather than true factories, executing individual orders and not making standardized articles[24].

Certainly in the branches where technical imperatives had given rise to 'proto-factories' and centralized work even before the Industrial Revolution, as already shown, e.g. in iron, non-ferrous metals, glass, ceramics, paper and chemicals (an almost new industry), the large or fairly large concerns progressed rapidly from the first decades of the nineteenth century. Side by side with these, at the beginning of Victoria's reign, one found industries where a few large firms emerged from a crowd of small ones, while several others remained hardly touched by technical progress, long faithful to craftmanship and domestic work, more or less associated with commercial capitalism. It was only in the second half of the nineteenth century, and sometimes only at the end of it, that mechanization and concentration in factories penetrated branches like the food industries. An exception to this was brewing where, in London at least, large firms had appeared at the beginning of the eighteenth century[25], whereas the manufacture of biscuits by machinery began only in 1846 thanks to the invention of George Palmer[26]. The second half of the nineteenth century also saw the factory system taking over hosiery (first factory 1851), clothing and shoemaking[27], as well as a whole series of consumer-goods industries. As for luxury articles, they remained a craft sector for the whole of the nineteenth century. Finally, there were sectors where technical progress was very limited and where structures remained traditional, in particular one as important as the building trade, where the small business was general[28], and even public works where, although a few very large firms existed, specializing mostly in railway-building, they generally made use of much smaller subcontractors. Historians tend to be too fascinated by the changes arising from mechanization in a few branches, and they forget that it was absent from vast areas where all the work was assured by sheer muscular effort, e.g. in everything to do with the handling of goods,

[24] The average personnel of machine-building firms in 1871 was only eighty-five workers; but there were some very large enterprises.
[25] Nevertheless many small breweries survived in the provinces and even in London.
[26] The adoption from 1877 onwards of steel rollers to grind grain (a Hungarian invention) produced large flour-mills powered by steam, and caused the disappearance of old water-mills and windmills using mill-stones.
[27] On these two industries where the factory system had not yet prevailed around 1900, see Chapter 7.
[28] And where traditional techniques predominated, in spite of the adoption of iron frames for certain types of building (e.g. factories and railway stations) and the growing use of cement.

which were far more often humped on men's backs than moved mechanically.

In any case it was estimated in 1851 that 'modern' industries employed 1,750,000 workers (of whom more than 500,000 were in the cotton industry alone), while industries which remained traditional employed 2,500,000[29]. So at the beginning of Victoria's reign most industrial workers remained outside factories. Most British workmen were not factory workers, but operated in small workshops or at home. This was all the more so because a considerable part of the labour-force in textile factories consisted of women and children. Just as the cotton mill was the typical factory of the Industrial Revolution, the typical factory worker was, one might say, the factory girl.

Certainly the advance of the factory speeded up in the second half of the nineteenth century. In 1871, 23,346 factories existed in the United Kingdom, employing 2 million workers, as opposed to 106,988 'workshops', which were manned by only 535,000 workers[30]. The domestic system was gradually eliminated from most branches where it had remained the rule in the mid-nineteenth century, and was reduced to a shadow. However it did not disappear, and indeed seems even to have picked up at the turn of the century in the clothing, shoe and hat trades and in other sweated trades in the East End of London, which saw a centrifugal tendency, a 'defactorization' in favour of work at home, with conditions and wages that were very poor indeed[31].

Despite this general trend, industrial firms of very large size remained relatively few, not to say exceptional, during the whole Victorian period and beyond up to 1914, and around them were to be found a mass of factories that were medium-sized or even small. So, in the first decades of the nineteenth century, a factory of more than 200 workers was considered large, and one that employed 1000 gigantic. In cotton-spinning, though it was the pioneer branch of industry in terms of concentration, there was only a handful of factories employing more than 500 people. In 1816 the average number employed by forty-one spinning-mills in Glasgow was 244, and by forty-three in the

---

[29] According to H.D. Fong, quoted by H. Perkin, *The Origins of Modern English Society, 1780–1880* (London, 1969), p. 114, the factory system had become predominant in industries which included about half of the total work force of industry in *England*.

[30] Perkin, pp. 109 and 115. But this statistic does not include the domestic workers who survived, and factories only had half the total labour-force of industry.

[31] Cf. J.A. Schmiechen, 'State reform and the local economy: an aspect of industrialization in late Victorian and Edwardian London', *Economic History Review*, 2nd series, XXVIII (3), Aug. 1975, 413–28; G. Stedman Jones, *Outcast London: A Study in Relationship between Classes in Victorian Society* (Oxford, 1971); also Chapter 7, p. 185. D. Bythell, *The Sweated Trades: Outwork in Nineteenth-Century Britain* (London, 1978).

Manchester area 300 – figures that were certainly higher than the national average. In all the cotton-mills inspected in 1838, the average number was 137[32], and at the time of a more complete enquiry in 1871 it was only 171. Furthermore, at that date, the 23,346 factories of the United Kingdom only employed an average of eighty-six people each[33].

Fierce competition at the end of the nineteenth century led to the elimination of many small concerns through the trend towards reorganization and concentration, from 1880 to 1890 onwards. Thus, in the Lancashire cotton-spinning industry, the average number of spindles per factory nearly doubled between 1884 and 1911. In coal and steel the average capital of limited companies rose by 45 per cent between 1885 and 1915. One even saw the appearance of giant firms or combines, equivalent to the American trusts or the German *Konzerne*. Such were the Salt Union which amalgamated sixty-four producers of salt in 1888, and United Alkali which in 1891 brought together all the firms that manufactured soda according to the Leblanc process. In 1897 a combine was formed which practically had the monopoly of cotton sewing-thread on the British market, and in 1906 Lever Brothers established a 'soap trust'. The motives behind these creations were often defensive, for instance most tobacco firms merged in 1901 to create the Imperial Tobacco Company, so as to resist the menace of an invasion of the English market by the American Tobacco Company of J.B. Duke. Most of these concentrations were horizontal, but there were cases of vertical integration. Some of these giant enterprises failed, others lasted and secured a very strong position in their market, but it was very rare that they achieved a real monopoly position eliminating all competition. In any case, concentration (as well as the trade agreements and cartels) went much less far than in Germany and the United States, and in fact the 'giants' just mentioned were

[32]   S.D. Chapman, *The Cotton Industry in the Industrial Revolution* (London, 1972), pp. 26, 29, 32; and 'Financial restraints on the Growth of Firms in the cotton industry: 1790–1840', *Economic History Review*, 2nd series, XXXII(1), Feb. 1979, 50–69. Gatrell, pp. 98, 125, 127; Chapter 7. According to Chapman, the representative cotton mill in 1822 had 100 to 200 workers in Manchester, and fewer elsewhere. The few giants were surrounded by a crowd of small firms. According to Gatrell, in 1841, the staff of the cotton-spinning and weaving mills in Lancashire averaged 193 people, and 260 in Manchester, where firms were larger. Out of 975 firms surveyed, 25 only had 1000 workers and more. It has often been said that in 1851 two-thirds of the workers in cotton mills were in firms that had fewer than 50 employees, but we have not been able to verify whether this assertion is true.

[33]   Perkin, pp. 110–11. Average numbers in mills: woollen, 71; worsted, 175; hosiery, 71; flax, 202; jute, 291; ceramics, 84. In the leather industry, the tanneries, where the largest firms were to be found, had on average fewer than 20 workers in 1871; R.A. Church, 'The British leather industry and foreign competition, 1870–1914', *Economic History Review*, 2nd series, XXIX(4), Nov. 1971, 545.

exceptions[34]. Even in an industry where the tendency to concentration was naturally strong, e.g. iron and steel, the number of firms remained high in 1914 – probably too high, as we shall see – and many of the firms were only medium-sized for that branch of industry. In coal-mining, which was the vital basis of all large-scale industry, but where technical change was slow few collieries in the middle of the nineteenth century employed more than eighty workers[35]. In 1914, next to some large mines that were well organized and equipped, one still found a mass of small or even very small pits.

For these reasons it is important not to overestimate the speed and extent of large-scale industry's progress, and one must understand too that its advance was the outcome of technical progress. The factory system triumphed only in the branches of industry where and when a new technology allowed mechanized production to lead to economies of scale congenial to large firms, when an industry can become capital-intensive by substituting capital for labour. One more example: right up to mid-century, shipyards, apart from the Royal Navy's dockyards and some yards on the Thames which built large East Indiamen, were very small firms. The innovation of iron hulls meant that in 1871 iron ship-building was the British industry that had the highest average number of workers per firm, i.e. 571[36].

So the restructuring of industry was relatively slow, even in textiles, although this industry had been the first to be transformed by technological progress and had set the example to the rest of industry. At Victoria's accession the use of machinery and the factory system had penetrated deeply, but their success had been variable between the different branches of this sector. Apart from the primary iron industry, the development of modern forms of production and organization was much less advanced in nearly all other industries. On the other hand, the long-term trend favoured modernization and in the second half of the century the factory system gained much ground and took over almost completely. In particular, in many of the branches

---

[34] P. Mathias, *The First Industrial Nation: An Economic History of Britain, 1700–1914* (London, 1969), pp. 390–5; B.W.E. Alford, *W.D. and H.O. Wills and the Development of the UK Tobacco Industry, 1786–1965* (London, 1973), Ch. 11, pp. 247ff and Ch. 14, pp. 309ff. Note also, in 1900, the amalgamation of twenty-four cement firms to form Associated Portland Cement Manufacturers Ltd. which reorganized this industry and, especially, introduced rotary kilns (article by W.H. Chaloner, *Manchester Guardian*, 11 Mar. 1959).

[35] And for a long time the archaic system of subcontracting was practised, whereby subcontractors came to an agreement with the owner or his manager to deliver coal at a fixed price, hired and paid the miners, and organized the working in their own way.

[36] Perkin, p. 111.

which had remained craft industries, handtools and simple manually-operated machines were replaced by more sophisticated and steam-powered equipment. But the triumph of the factory was not attended by extensive concentration. At the beginning of the twentieth century it was still the medium-sized firm which dominated in most branches, and in addition there survived a large number of small firms which were little more than workshops[37].

However, the contribution of a sector to the national product and its dynamic role in the economy were not strictly proportionate to the share of the labour-force which it employed, because of wide differences in productivity and capital-intensity. So, even if large-scale industry for a long time employed a minority of workers only, it never ceased to spread; it was the most powerful element bringing the rest of the economy under its influence. Even if a high proportion of the population was not in the immediate orbit of large-scale industry, all were more or less affected by it. Furthermore the development of the iron and coal industries created the base that was necessary for the furtherance of industrialization. It was large-scale industry which took the initiative in determining the general expansion and redeployment of productive resources, thanks to the considerable gains in productivity made possible by the use of machinery and steam-power.

Indeed one must underline the crucial role played by the steam-engine, undoubtedly the most revolutionary invention of the Industrial Revolution, which alone made possible the massive use of other machinery of all sorts. It is true that at the beginning of the Industrial Revolution water-power was widely used, but although this had the advantage of being free of current costs once the necessary installation had been set up, it had the serious inconvenience of being irregular according to the seasons, only available along stretches of water and of limited total potential, especially in a small country like England. The steam-engine on the other hand was independent of seasons and relatively inexpensive to use in a country where coal abounded. By increasing its size or installing several engines one could bring all the power which was needed to a given location. The steam-engine facilitated concentration and also had the advantage that it could be used wherever coal could be brought. In brief, it freed industry from troublesome bottlenecks.

However, the role of the steam-engine up to the middle of the century or even to about 1870 must not be overestimated. Around

[37] See also Chapter 5, p. 107, and Chapter 10, pp. 337–41.

1800, when J.R. Harris estimates that a good thousand of these machines were at work in Great Britain, they were mainly to be found in mining, for which they had been originally intended (but coal was the lifeblood of industry). As for manufacturing industry, steam-engines were almost only found in cotton-spinning and iron-making[38]. They then made rapid progress in textiles, particularly from the 1830s onwards, but mostly in the cotton industry which was at the heart of the 'steam revolution'. In 1838, 1850 and 1856, 64–65 per cent of the total power used in the textile industries, which rose from 74,000 to 108,000 and 138,000 hp respectively, was used by cotton mills.

In addition water-power remained important for a long time, benefiting from important progress in the construction of water wheels, built of iron and attaining impressive sizes as well as considerable power. In 1838, water provided 36 per cent of the power used by the textile industries, although this industry was the biggest user of steam, and it was still 19 per cent in 1850. It continued to remain important afterwards in small-scale metal industry, ceramics, etc.

A.E. Musson reckons that the total power of stationary engines in Great Britain, which had been less than 20,000 hp about 1800, rose to about 100,000 hp in 1824, with 5000 engines, including those in mining. In 1850, for manufacturing industry alone, 300,000 hp were reached and in 1870 977,000 hp. At these two dates the textile industries accounted for slightly more than half this power (513,000 hp or 52.5 per cent of the total in 1870) and the cotton industry for nearly one-third (300,000 hp). Then came the primary and secondary iron industries with 330,000 hp (34 per cent of the total) in 1870, but all the other industries (excluding mining) only disposed altogether of 134,000 (14 per cent of the total). Musson estimates that in 1850 and again in 1870 the steam-engine only played a very minor role in all these various industries, with a few exceptions, e.g. paper. Only a minority of British workers were employed in factories powered by steam. The massive expansion of the latter only occurred during the last decades of the nineteenth century, and in 1907 British industry boasted of steam-engines with a total of 9,650,000 hp. This is yet further proof of the slow triumph of the factory system, for the spread of the steam-engine went hand in hand with that of machinery in general, to which it supplied the motive power. There were few

---

[38] J.R. Harris, 'The employment of steam power in the eighteenth century', *History* LII, 1967, 147–8.

factories in the nineteenth century to be seen without one or more tall brick chimneys spouting thick black smoke[39].

The development of large firms was not confined to industry, and indeed it was in transport that the change of scale went furthest. The railway brought a revolution in the structure of transport that was at least comparable to the advent of the factory system. At the beginning there was a proliferation of small companies each running just one line, but they were already larger in all respects than the turnpike trusts or even the canal companies. Furthermore, mergers soon occurred which created large networks resulting in organizations of unprecedented size and complexity, employing a staff far more numerous than that of the largest industrial firms. Twenty-seven railway companies operating between 1830 and 1853 had an average of 2500 employees each, and from the 1850s onwards there were companies with over 10,000 employees. It is true that many small railway companies survived up to the first world war, and all short-distance transport[40] was supplied by horse-drawn vehicles, mostly belonging to very modest firms. In a brilliant article F.M.L. Thompson has recalled the horse's very important role in the nineteenth-century economy and its capacity to pollute[41].

In sea-transport the owners of wooden sailing-ships had seldom owned more than a small number of vessels, rarely displacing more than a few hundred tons each. The steamship, especially when it was built of iron, gave birth to large shipping companies owning true fleets, with ships of growing size, reaching giant proportions as was indicated by the name of the most celebrated and unlucky of the transatlantic liners – the *Titanic* (1912).

In the banking sector, the proliferation of small country banks, nearly always with just one office, of which there were nearly one

---

[39] A.E. Musson, 'Industrial motive power in the United Kingdom, 1800–70 *Economic History Review* 2nd series, XXIX(3), Aug. 1976, 415–39, notably 416–7, 420–4, 434–9. This article re-emphasizes the importance of cotton in the Industrial Revolution, which seems fully justified. The progress of the steam-engine was helped at the beginning of the nineteenth century by the invention of high-pressure engines – simpler, less bulky, cheaper and using less coal than the lower-pressure Watt engines – and later by compound engines, as well as by many improvements in detail. G.N. Von Tunzelmann, *Steam-Power and British Industrialization to 1860* (Oxford, 1978); J.W. Kanefsky, 'Motive-power in British industry and the accuracy of the 1870 factory return', *Economic History Review*, 2nd series, XXXII(3), Aug. 1979, 360–75 (discussion of Musson's article).

[40] Apart from urban passenger transport after the appearance of electric tramways in the 1890s, then motor-cars and motor-buses a little later.

[41] F.M.L. Thompson, 'Nineteenth-century horse sense', *Economic History Review*, 2nd series XXIX(1), Feb. 1976, 60–81.

thousand at the beginning of the nineteenth century, gave way gradually to a handful of large banks whose networks of branches (more than 7700 in 1913) spread over the whole country. The retail trade remained a chosen preserve of the very small firm, but besides the corner shops emerged the department stores and the multiple or chain stores, like Boots the chemists. However, in 1910 department and multiple stores together accounted for less than 10 per cent of total retail trade.

Finally, there developed a parallel process of concentration and specialization in the location of industrial activities. The old industrial picture had been a nebulous affair with its small workshops spread widely over the countryside. Its 'furnace' undertakings, notably blast-furnaces and forges, had to keep their distances from one another to be sure of their supply of wood and water-power. It is true that the different regions of England were already very unequal in their degree of industrialization and that each 'manufacturing district' had a given speciality arising from its resources and traditions. This situation hardly altered at the beginning of the Industrial Revolution. There was even at first a tendency to a wider diffusion of industry, either by the exploitation of resources hardly used before (e.g. the use of coal in the iron industry), or by attempts to bring new industries into new localities (where industrial activity rarely lasted), or also because the first factory masters had to look for the water-power and sometimes the labour-power they required in remote areas; and in any case they had to scatter their mills along stretches of water. But matters changed from the last years of the eighteenth century, when steam-engines came to be used in textile factories. We have long ceased to believe that steam led to the concentration of the textile industry on the coal-fields, so that it disappeared from traditional centres far from coal, e.g. the west country and Norwich. Many other factors contributed to this decline, which had started in the eighteenth century. Furthermore coal was only a small item in the costs of the textile industry. Lancashire and the West Riding of Yorkshire were important textile areas before their coal-seams were of any use to industry. The steam-engine's role was rather to free textile factories from their dependence on rivers and streams and to allow them to be set up in large numbers in towns where they found labour easily and where they enjoyed external economies, thanks to the presence of ancillary activities, either industrial (e.g. machine-building and chemicals) or services (e.g. merchants and banks). In any case the geography of the British textile industries took at the beginning of Victoria's reign a form which hardly changed subsequently. The cotton industry, which had been established in a variety of localities at the beginning of its big leap forward, concentrated itself in south Lancashire and the neighbouring area of Cheshire with some far less important centres near Glasgow and in the east Midlands. The West Riding accounted for nearly half the woollen industry, and nearly all the worsted industry. The counties of Leicester, Derby and Nottingham were the domain of hosiery.

The situation was different with iron and steel, for siting of these plants depended strictly on the position of iron-ore and coking-coal resources. Furthermore, given the bulky nature of these raw materials, iron-works had to be close to mineral deposits; so the geography of this industry changed as a result of some fields being exhausted and others being discovered. This led to the decline of several iron-making districts (notably in the Midlands) and the rise of new ones (notably Cleveland and Cumberland). In addition the iron and steel industry did not see the same movement towards existing towns as in textiles, but the concentration of large works on the same site encouraged the birth of important new towns – e.g. Merthyr Tydfil in South Wales at the end of the eighteenth century, Middlesborough and Barrow-in-Furness later. Other industries often developed in their traditional centres – hence small-scale metal trades in Birmingham and surrounding towns and in Sheffield, and also in all the large industrialized cities.

Contemporaries were struck from the second quarter of the nineteenth century onwards by the contrast between *North and South* (the title of Mrs Gaskell's famous novel). Most of British industry had concentrated on the coalfields of the north of England (above a line from the Severn estuary to the Wash) with annexes in South Wales and the Scottish Lowlands, whereas southern England, except for London, which had the gamut of industries to be expected in a great port and a metropolis, was almost purely agricultural and had even deindustrialized since the eighteenth century. This contrast was roughly true, but it had already appeared in the eighteenth century, when industry had developed faster in the north than in the south, and when population had increased more rapidly in the former than in the latter, apart from London. The Industrial Revolution certainly accentuated this contrast because of the increasing use of coal, whose reserves lay in the north, but it was not the sole cause. It was to last right up to the interwar period, when industrialization spread southward. However, this contrast does not tally with the difference that has often been made between 'Black' England and 'Green' England. Maps which show industrial districts as enormous blots spreading over nearly all the centre and north of England are misleading. The 'black' countries, of industry and mining, with their monotonous rows of small uniform terrace-houses, dominated by pit-head frames, tall mills with their long lines of windows, or the leaping smoke and flames of blast-furnaces, were of limited extent, and in the midst of these northern regions there were to be found 'wide open spaces', farming country or desolate moors. As J.B. Priestley wrote about Bradford at the beginning of the twentieth century, a hiker lost on the moors could die of exposure a few hundred yards from a tram terminus. Besides, despite the birth of new industrial areas, there was a certain tightening of the industrial fabric in the nineteenth century and further concentration in the towns.

The specialization of various industrial centres should also not be exaggerated. Doubtless each main region had a dominant industry – cotton in Lancashire, wool in Yorkshire, metal-processing in Birmingham – but a total commitment to a single industry occurred only at the level of narrowly defined localities. Hence some towns in Lancashire specialized in cotton-spinning, others in weaving (but Dundee, the jute town, made marmalade as well), and some regions, such as South Wales, concentrated on coal and iron. However, developments in the course of the nineteenth century tended to diversify the activities of each region, by giving rise to industries ancillary to the main one, or to activities which were more or less connected with it. Thus Sheffield, the cutlery town, also became a centre for steelworks and engineering. Specialization did exist and made for serious inconveniences when a slump struck the staple industry of a region. It also led to serious inequalities in development between regions.

URBANIZATION

A dramatic consequence of Great Britain's industrialization was the rapid growth of the towns. Their population increased much faster than that of the country as a whole, and they tended to absorb a growing proportion, and finally a great majority, of that population. It is true that this process of urbanization affected every western country in the nineteenth century, but it started earlier and was more marked in Great Britain than elsewhere. Furthermore this phenomenon was not only quantitative, in the demographic and economic order of things, but also qualitative, socially and culturally, turning British mentalities and conditions of life upside down. As Bédarida put it, 'in the course of this urbanization a new visual scheme emerged together

Table 20   Rural and urban population (as percentage of
the total population of England and Wales)

	Rural population	*Urban population*
1801	66	34
1841	52	48
1851	46	54
1871	35	65
1901	22	78
1911	21	79

with a new system of social relations and a new life style – in brief a
new civilization came into being'[42].

Table 20 shows *for England and Wales* the relative position of the
rural and the urban population (the latter defined as people living in
concentrations of more than 2500 inhabitants)[43].

Thus in one century the urban population passed from one-third to
nearly four-fifths of total population. It was around 1845 that
town-dwellers seem to have become the majority, and the census of
1851 revealed an event of great importance. For the first time in the
history not only of Great Britain but of any state of any note, the towns
numbered more inhabitants than the countryside. Furthermore, 38 per
cent of the total population lived in towns of more than 20,000
inhabitants, and this percentage rose to 53 per cent in 1881. As time
went on, the imbalance became more marked. Before 1900 no other
state was to reach a level of urbanization equal to that of Great Britain
in 1851, and she was the first country to experience a predominantly
urban way of life.

Given the increase in total population, which quadrupled between
1801 and 1911, and doubled between 1841 and 1901, this large
percentage increase of the urban population represented a prodigious
growth in absolute numbers. For Great Britain the growth was from
3.5 million in 1801 to 8.9 million in 1841, to 29 million in 1901 and 32
million in 1911. So the urban population almost multiplied by a factor
of ten in 110 years, and by more than three during Victoria's reign.
One guesses at once what formidable problems this 'galloping
urbanization' (Bédarida) must have imposed. And all the more so
seeing that the growth of urban population was fastest during the first
half of the nineteenth century – an average of 27 per cent every decade,

[42] Bédarida, p. 17.
[43] Taken from ibid., p. 17 (table 2). See also Deane and Cole, p. 7; Perkin, p. 117. For GB,
     the percentages of urban population would be a little lower.

the movement accelerating after 1820 and reaching its peak between 1841 and 1851, when it was accentuated by the influx of Irish immigrants. The increase then slowed down, remaining however over 20 per cent each decade up to 1881 and little less thereafter, only declining between 1901 and 1911[44]. In all, towns (still defined as concentrations of more than 2500 inhabitants) absorbed 67 per cent of the total increase of England's population between 1801 and 1841. Between 1841 and 1901 the increase in their population was nearly 18 million, more than 6 per cent higher than the growth of the country's total population. In the whole period 1801–1911 the towns gained more than 25 million inhabitants, or 94 per cent of the total growth of English population[45].

Although rural population did not cease to decline relatively in a spectacular way[46], in absolute figures it continued to grow slowly during the first half of the nineteenth century, passing in England from about 6 million in 1801 to 8.3 million in 1841[47]. But at the 1851 census a drop in population since 1841 was observed in a small number of purely agricultural counties, such as Wiltshire and Montgomery-shire, while the population of other counties remained stable. Then the movement affected East Anglia, Cornwall and most of the Welsh counties. By 1901 rural population had fallen to 7.2 million, but it recovered a little to 7.6 million in 1911. So it remained higher than had been the case at the beginning of the nineteenth century. Its fall between 1841 and 1901 was only 13 per cent (and 8 per cent between 1841 and 1911). Thus the depopulation of the countryside was very limited, the only regions seriously affected being some Welsh counties[48] and above all the Highlands of north-west Scotland which suffered as much as Ireland from the potato famine in the 1840s, following the clearances, i.e. the eviction of small tenants by landlords, so that the latter's estates could be transformed into sheep-pastures or shooting-reserves[49].

---

[44] Especially as the result of heavy emigration overseas at the beginning of the twentieth century, which particularly affected the growth of towns in the north of England (and already in the 1880s too), so that the net migratory flow was outward.

[45] Figures would be very little different for GB. Two-thirds of the 20 million inhabitants who were added to the population of England between 1801 and 1891 were to be found in towns of over 20,000 inhabitants; Perkin, p. 117.

[46] Its share of total population is constantly higher than the percentage of employed population working in agriculture.

[47] But between 1841 and 1861 the fall in rural population was very small.

[48] The industrialization of South Wales caused Glamorgan to have 10 per cent of the total population of Wales in 1851, but half in 1901; Bédarida, p. 13.

[49] Cf. Chapter 6, p. 177 (note 107). Rural population of GB fell by 16 per cent between 1841 and 1901, but only 10 per cent between 1841 and 1911.

This slight decline of the rural population was closely connected with the advance of the urban population. The causes and the process were the same – migration from country areas towards urban centres. In fact the rural regions continued to have a large excess of births over deaths, but from the mid-nineteenth century onwards departures to the towns, which previously had already been considerable, became greater than the natural increase. We have already broached the question of the causes of these migrations when looking at the transfer of labour from agriculture towards industry and services. These were the clear inferiority of wages for farm workers as compared with wages for industrial workers, and the sluggishness in the demand for labour in the countryside (and even decline after mid-century)[50], as opposed to the expansion of job opportunities that was assured by the growth of industry and services in the towns.

Furthermore, industry, which remained scattered over the country-side at the beginning of the Industrial Revolution, tended to concentrate itself in the towns, which in the eighteenth century had had a function that was more commercial than industrial. This concentration was due to the expansion of large-scale industry, the increasing use of the steam-engine, railway-building (which facilitated the supply of foodstuffs and raw materials to large centres), the external economies resulting from the development of industries and services ancillary to the staple industry of each centre, as well as from the existence of a labour-force both numerous and skilled. Hence a cumulative process – once industrial activities had taken root in a town, conditions developed favourable to new growth and advantages that strengthened the town's power of attraction, giving rise to additional activities.

Moreover, in some cases industry and transport developments created entirely new towns around one or more great works. Hence the railway towns like Crewe and Swindon, born at the site of important junctions or railway workshops. There were also towns resulting from the working of new ore-deposits and the iron-works which were set up near them, e.g. Barrow-in-Furness and Middlesborough, the latter a hamlet of 40 inhabitants in 1801, becoming a port for the export of coal and rising to 5500 inhabitants in 1841, then a great iron-making centre, which counted 91,000 inhabitants in 1901. These were, it is

---

[50]   The flight from the land was not influenced by the economic situation of agriculture. It was very considerable during its 'Golden Age', in the third quarter of the century; cf. A.K. Cairncross, 'Internal Migration in Victorian England', in *Home and Foreign Investment, 1870–1913: Studies in Capital Accumulation* (Cambridge, 1953), pp. 65–83, see p. 75.

true, exceptional cases. On the whole, it was usually existing towns which developed, and those which had the largest population at the beginning of the nineteenth century remained at the top.

Besides the economic attractions of the town for the surplus population of the countryside, there were motivations of a non-pecuniary kind – the lure of the 'city lights' (in spite of the gloom and unhealthiness of Victorian towns, and the horror which poor folk felt for the monotony of work and the hard discipline that reigned in factories), the opportunities for young people to lead a more independent life and to have more choice in their search for a mate, the hope of success for adventurous spirits, and for rebels and offenders the advantages of anonymity[51].

Rural exodus had started long ago (it had caused the growth of London in the seventeenth and eighteenth centuries), but it gathered momentum in the 1830s and 1840s[52], and remained very active up to about 1880, and then slowed down as the reproduction-rate and surplus population in the countryside were reduced by the very extent of the departures. After 1880 the movements of population were rather from one industrial region to another as the result of variations in their prosperity and employment prospects[53]. In addition, inhabitants concentrated in the towns began to spill out over districts that were previously rural, from which resulted the slight recovery in rural population at the beginning of the twentieth century. The great redistribution of the population unleashed by the Industrial Revolution and related to industrialization had finished by the end of the nineteenth century. It has been estimated that between 1841 and 1901 the rural areas of England and Wales lost more than 4 million people by internal migration, conceding 3 million to the towns and half a million to the mining districts[54], at the rate of more than 500,000 per decade (of whom nearly half went to London), except during the 1880s, which saw an important emigration overseas[55].

Despite this, immigration from the countryside was not the only or

---

[51]   ibid., gives an important role to railway-building, which created non-agricultural jobs and increased the mobility of labour.

[52]   According to ibid., p. 74, it speeded up earlier in the north than in the south.

[53]   In the 1890s the London conurbation absorbed four times as many immigrants as the industrial towns of the north, which were facing various difficulties. It has been mentioned earlier that after 1901 the extent of emigration overseas caused a migratory deficit for these towns; Cairncross, p. 68.

[54]   It was these mining districts which had the fastest expansion. Their population quadrupled between 1841 and 1911, when it reached 5 million; and it increased on average by 100,000 inhabitants every year. But, because of the high fertility in miners' families, the excess of births over deaths was responsible for five-sixths of the total increase; Cairncross, p. 77.

[55]   Cairncross, pp. 68, 71–2, 74–5, 77–9; Deane and Cole, p. 289.

even the main factor in the enormous increase of population in the towns, which had ceased (especially London) in the eighteenth century being graveyards and enjoyed a strong natural increase in spite of the persistence of a high infant-mortality rate.

It is unfortunately difficult to be precise about the respective parts played by this natural increase and by immigration in the growth of the towns. In any case they varied from one place to another. In 1851, more than half the adult inhabitants of Leeds, Sheffield and Norwich were born in the town, but this percentage fell to a quarter in Manchester, Bradford and Glasgow, and was even smaller in Liverpool. In London, between the 1840s and the 1880s, immigration seems to have been directly responsible for about half the total increase in population. In certain neighbourhoods its cumulative effect caused a situation in which less than half the inhabitants had been born in the town[56]. This gave rise to serious problems of integration and assimilation for the many newcomers, particularly the Irish colonies who lived turned in on themselves, a prey to the contempt and hostility of the 'natives'.

The nature of the migration from country to town was not a matter of long-distance moves, if one excludes the case, certainly important, of the Irish, who particularly after the disaster of the famine flooded not only into the regions closest to the Emerald Isle (e.g. Lancashire and Glasgow), but anywhere work was to be found, notably London. In 1871 567,000 people were to be found in England and Wales who had been born in Ireland, and 105,000 who had come from Scotland[57]. Within England itself no large-scale inter-regional migrations (and in particular no considerable movement from the agricultural south to the industrial north, as some have thought) had taken place, but a complex of small local movements in a series of concentric circles. The towns attracted inhabitants from the neighbouring countryside where they were replaced by migrants who came from somewhat more remote areas. Also small and medium-sized towns were often temporary staging-posts for country folk between the country and the large town[58]. Thus in London about one-quarter of immigrants came from the

---

[56] Cairncross, p. 79, estimates that between 1841 and 1911, in London and eight large towns of the north of England, the ratio between net gain by immigration and natural increase was 33 per cent; but he adds that this figure may be too low.

[57] These colonies of Irish, Scots – and foreigners – attracted more attention by their accents, their way of life, than their real numbers warranted.

[58] E.J.T. Collins, 'Migrant labour in British agriculture in the nineteenth century', *Economic History Review*, 2nd series, XXIX(1), Feb. 1976, 38–59, has drawn attention to the seasonal migrations of agricultural labour, from backward regions towards advanced ones (and also partly from towns to country). In rapid and continuous expansion up to the mid-nineteenth century, they afterwards fell away and had practically disappeared by 1914.

four neighbouring counties and another quarter from the counties that surrounded the latter, for the capital absorbed the surplus of south-east England's rural population. The northern industrial towns recruited their immigrants from the surrounding country districts, and they also had a strong natural increase due to high fertility. Industrial regions produced their own labour-force as has already been pointed out, which became an essential factor in the change of demographic balance between north and south. This had started in the eighteenth century and became more marked during most of the nineteenth. However, after 1880, the growth of northern towns slowed down or even halted, while the growth of southern towns, especially London, persisted[59].

Of course, the rate of growth varied very much according to types of towns. The population of small country or market towns, which were often sleepy and without industries of importance, increased more slowly than total urban population. The localities of 2500–20,000 inhabitants accounted for 14.5 per cent of the total population of England and Wales in 1801 and 15.3 per cent in 1841. This percentage reached its peak at 17.4 per cent in 1881, then dropped slightly, i.e. roughly speaking their total population quadrupled between 1801 and 1901, while the population of towns of more than 20,000 inhabitants was multiplied by a factor of eleven, and for the period 1841–1901 the multiples were two and four respectively. Similarly towns that were ancient but had no industry (e.g. Cambridge or Chester) or whose industry was in decline (e.g. Norwich or Exeter) experienced only mediocre expansion.

On the other hand, in addition to the very special case of the seaside resorts and spas, which had the fastest growth (proof of the spread of wealth and the boom in leisure activities), remarkable progress was registered by many industrial localities, which had only been glorified villages at the beginning of the nineteenth century and became important towns of 50,000–100,000 inhabitants. Such were the cotton towns of Lancashire (Oldham had 12,000 inhabitants in 1801, 43,000 in 1841 and 147,000 in 1911), mining towns like Wigan, and iron-making or -processing towns, like Wolverhampton. Table 21 shows the impressive growth of many medium-sized towns[60].

The most important phenomenon was the growth of large and very large towns, which played a crucial role in urbanization.

Largest of all was the London area, which, at the beginning of the

[59] Cairncross, p. 71. But over the whole of the nineteenth century the population of the north of England increased more than that of the south.

[60] According to Bédarida, p. 17 (table 2). Scotland had no town over 100,000 inhabitants in 1801, two in 1841, three in 1871, four in 1901 and 1911.

Table 21   Growth in urban population

	Number of towns in England and Wales by size of population				
	1801	*1841*	*1871*	*1901*	*1911*
20,000 to 100,000 inhabitants	16	48	88	141	165
More than 100,000 inhabitants	1	7	17	33	36
	Percentages of total population living in towns of more than 100,000 inhabitants				
	1801	*1841*	*1871*	*1901*	*1911*
	11	21	33	44	44

Table 22   Population of Greater London

	000s of inhabitants	*Percentage of the total population of Great Britain*
1801	1117	11
1841	2239	12
1871	3890	15
1901	6586	18
1911	7256	18

nineteenth century, had by a long way overflowed the limits of the two cities of London and Westminster and had passed one million inhabitants. The development of the population of what was later to be called Greater London is shown in table 22[61].

Right up to the beginning of the twentieth century when she was surpassed by New York, London was by far the largest town in the western world. Paris, which was for a long time second, only passed the 2 million mark after 1870 (though its suburbs are excluded). However, as Asa Briggs has remarked, this growth had no clearly defined causes. Industrial development was an important factor, for in 1861, with nearly half a million workers in industry, the capital was the country's main manufacturing centre; but this was not decisive[62]. One must add

[61]   Figures from *Abstract*, p. 19. This Greater London (corresponding to the Metropolitan Police Area) spread wider than what was to become the County of London (created in 1888) which had slightly under 1 million inhabitants in 1801, 1.9 million in 1841 and 4.5 million in 1901, which was its maximum figure.
[62]   Some of these industries declined later, as the large firms of the capital could not stand up to the competition from the north. From this developed the sweated trades, based on cheap labour and the maintenance of the domestic system, as already mentioned.

the various other activities of the metropolis – political capital, residence (at least seasonal) of 'society', premier port, main commercial and financial centre of Britain, her empire and the world in general. However, although London attracted to herself a growing proportion of the country's population, this was not true of the countrys' total *urban* population. Actually London's growth was distinctly slower than that of the latter, particularly in the first decades of the century[63].

An even more remarkable phenomenon was the growth of the large provincial towns, and above all of the great regional capitals. They had already shown much vitality at the beginning of the Industrial Revolution and even before, but they had then fairly modest populations, for in 1801 no provincial town had possessed more than 83,000 inhabitants. But their growth was very rapid, and in 1911 Great Britain boasted seven towns, besides London, with more than 400,000 inhabitants. With the sole exception of the one town amongst them – Edinburgh – which was neither industrial nor a great port, their population had roughly multiplied by ten since 1801[64].

Nine other towns in 1911 had between 200,000 and 400,000 inhabitants, whereas only four in all exceeded 200,000 in 1841.

Furthermore the end of the nineteenth century saw the appearance of the conurbation phenomenon, i.e. zones where towns, separate but neighbouring, had grown so much that their tentacles joined up and they tended to fuse into one vast agglomeration, loosely joined but

Table 23   Population of the main British towns (in 000s of inhabitants)

	1801	1841	1901	1911
Glasgow	77	287	953	1000
Birmingham	71	202	781	840
Liverpool	82	299	704	746
Manchester	75	252	645	714
Sheffield	46	111	409	455
Leeds	53	152	429	446
Edinburgh	83	166	395	401

[63] Between 1841 and 1911, the eight largest towns in the north of England saw their populations increase a little more than that of London; Cairncross, p. 78 (table 16). In total, the increase in London's population represents one-quarter of that of the total urban population of England, from 1801 to 1911, or from 1841 to 1901. For an excellent account of various aspects of the metropolis, see Bédarida, pp. 20–5.

[64] From *Abstract*, pp. 24–7. Except for 1801, these figures add to each town's official population that of the neighbouring localities which were later incorporated with it. But one could also add to the population of Manchester that of its sister-town Salford; 14,000 inhabitants in 1801; 53,000 in 1841; 221,000 in 1901; 231,000 in 1911. By 1891 GB had, in addition to London, four towns of more than 500,000 inhabitants out of a world total of twenty.

Table 24   Population of conurbations (in 000s of inhabitants)

	1871	1901	1911
Lancashire (Manchester)	1386	2117	2328
West Midlands (Birmingham)	969	1483	1634
West Yorkshire (Leeds)	1064	1524	1590
Merseyside (Liverpool)	690	1030	1157
Tyneside (Newcastle)	346	678	761
Clydeside (Glasgow)	?	1343	1461
Total	4455	6832	7470

practically continuous. One could pick out six main conurbations, in addition to the monster that was London, each centred on one regional capital (shown in brackets in table 24)[65].

The total of these urban clusters comfortably exceeded the population of Greater London. Their appearance was the result of an important phenomenon – the development of suburbs[66]. In spite of their demographic growth and the predominance of houses over tenements (except in Scotland), British towns in the nineteenth century did not, relatively speaking, sprawl, so they showed a very high density and a concentration of inhabitants that contributed largely to their unhealthy character.

The suburb results from a process of urban decentralization, but remains closely linked to the urban core. It is residential or industrial according to the nature of the activities, whether of consumption or production, that are transferred to it. It ministers to the desire to escape the pollution and other nuisances of the old central areas, and to the psychological need of the British family to have its own separate house (if not garden). It also solves the difficulty of industrialists in extending their factories in the centre of towns, given the shortage and high price of land. But the development of suburbs was largely dependent on the progress of transport facilities, which for a long time only advanced in tentacle fashion along roads, canals and later railways. Indeed, before the last quarter of the nineteenth century, public transport was not only inadequate but also much too expensive for the working class and even the lower-middle classes, who had to live within walking distance of their place of work, although people who were poor or of modest means were ready to walk long distances every day. So the expansion of towns took place for a long time through

[65] *Abstract* p. 19.
[66] See especially H.J. Dyos, *Victorian Suburb: A Study of the Growth of Camberwell* (Leicester, 1961); F.M.L. Thompson, *Hampstead: Building a Borough, 1650–1964* (London, 1974).

the addition of new districts of small houses in direct continuity with the urban centres[67]. The only people who were really able to escape from the towns, to flee their pollution and unhealthiness and settle at some distance in a more agreeable, semi-rural setting, were rich businessmen with their own means of transport, who were able to travel to their factories or offices every day on horseback or in their own carriages. Not until the last quarter of the nineteenth century did the proliferation of suburban trains and railway stations (formerly rather rare, but whose early examples became centres of growth for new suburbs), the appearance and extension of horse-drawn and later electric trams with relatively low fares and finally buses and the London Underground, allow the residential suburbs, fairly far from towns' centres, to be 'democratized' and spread very rapidly. It was then that the middle classes could satisfy their desire to escape by emigrating to the outer suburbs, often leaving the older inner suburbs (like Camberwell) to the working classes. But, on the whole, the daily migration of commuters over fairly long distances was a limited phenomenon for many years, and only reached massive proportions at the end of the nineteenth century, especially for manual workers. Furthermore, the development of suburbs was a factor of increased social segregation, for they were distinctly either residential and middle-class or industrial and working-class. The counterpart of this expansion and specialization, where urban life was concerned, was the depopulation of the old central areas from the middle of the nineteenth century onwards, and this was all the more so because some of the worst slums, where the poor were crammed together, gave way to public buildings, offices, shops and railway stations. The most striking case was the City of London. Its population had been stable at about 130,000 inhabitants between 1801 and 1851, but it then dropped rapidly to no more than 27,000 in 1901. On the other hand, more than 300,000 people came to work there in daytime. The City entirely lost its residential function to become solely a business centre.

British towns of the nineteenth century have a bad name. Too rapid, unplanned growth gave them a chaotic character[68] – ugly and

[67] The case of London was special because of the enormous growth of its population in absolute figures, whence an earlier development of suburbs than elsewhere. The population of Camberwell quadrupled between 1801 and 1831, and grew from 40,000 in 1841 to 200,000 in 1901; the influx of the middle classes had started in the 1820s and growth became faster after 1870. There was also an earlier growth of the suburban railway system. These brief remarks can be supplemented by T.C. Barker and M. Collins, *A History of London Transport* (2 vols, London, 1963 and 1974).

[68] We refer again to Bédarida, pp. 18–20, on the conditions in which building developed, and to his excellent remarks on the existence of a private system of town planning, which mitigated the chaotic character of urban growth.

monotonous buildings, dirt and pollution, a large part of the population packed into hideous slums, with extreme social contrasts and
segregation. The Improvement Boards, which in fact appeared as early
as the eighteenth century, and the new town councils resulting from
the 1835 reform, achieved some improvement in the quality of life but
only very slowly. These towns, and above all the largest – Manchester,
symbol of the new industrial age where Disraeli's 'two nations' faced
each other in particularly stark contrast, and London with its immense
size and its disparity between opulence and indigence[69] – fascinated
and at the same time frightened contemporaries, leading to judgements that were both passionate and contradictory.

However, an enormous effort in construction went with urban
growth, and one tends nowadays to think better even of Victorian
architecture. Finally we must emphasize that these towns were very
different from one another. Industrialization, far from making them
all look alike, differentiated them according to their dominant
industries, the scale of their firms, social mobility and relations
between classes, their vulnerability to economic fluctuations, and
finally the politics adopted by their town councils in the face of the
formidable problems caused by rapid growth. Each town, and in
particular each regional capital, had its own economic and social
structure, its own political tradition, and even its own 'culture'. Their
inhabitants also manifested a lively patriotism, a civic pride, reflected,
for example, in the building of imposing public buildings, neo-Gothic
town halls, neo-classical exchanges and, in Manchester, the Free
Trade Hall (1856), in the Lombardo-Venetian style.

At the beginning of the nineteenth century, most Britons were
farmworkers and rural craftsmen. A century later, they were factory-
and office-workers, living in towns and more and more in suburbs.
Mass civilization, industrial and urban, was born. However, among the
lower classes, a strong sense of local solidarity – of street and
neighbourhood – saved families and individuals from losing themselves in the anonymity of far-flung conurbations.

[69] Magnificently rendered in the 174 wood engravings of Gustave Doré for Louis
Enault, *Londres* (1876, 2 vols, Paris). For a survey of urban problems, see especially:
Asa Briggs, *Victorian Cities* (London, 1963); H.J. Dyos and M. Wolf (eds), *The
Victorian City: Images and Realities* (1973, 2 vols, London).

5 Problems of growth

It is most unfashionable in economic history to draw up laundry lists, i.e. to enumerate all sorts of factors, some 'favourable', others 'unfavourable', to the growth of an economy. The 'new' method is to resort to econometrics, in order to measure precisely the role in growth of certain variables. This task unfortunately remains to be completed for nineteenth-century Britain by practitioners of the New Economic History. So we have to make do with a traditional approach, despite its conceptual weaknesses.

One must state at the outset that the problem is to explain Great Britain's economic growth in the nineteenth century, and it is *a priori* absolutely different from the problem of the causes and origins of the Industrial Revolution, which began in the eighteenth century. But then is this not a false problem? After all, modern economic growth, which the Industrial Revolution set in motion, is self-sustained growth – a growth which supports and nourishes itself by its own momentum over a long period. Indeed, the basic result of many technical innovations that made up the Industrial Revolution was to achieve labour savings and productivity gains, which were sometimes enormous. Spinning machines offered the most spectacular examples: Hargreaves's first jenny (1770) enabled a worker to produce as much yarn in a day as eight handwheel spinners. Roberts' self-acting mule (1825) was at least 370-times more productive (in terms of hours of work necessary to treat 100 lb. of raw cotton) than hand-spinning and 15-times more productive than Crompton's mule (1779), a machine that was already advanced[1]. Hence a sharp fall of labour costs embodied in each unit of output. In other cases, particularly in the iron industry, innovations tended rather to reduce the costs of raw

---

[1] S.D.Chapman, *The Cotton Industry in the Industrial Revolution* (London, 1972), p.20 (table 2). Also H. Perkin, *The Origins of Modern English Society 1780–1880* (London, 1969), p. 112. One reckoned in 1827 that 750 skilled workmen operating in a factory produced as much yarn as 200,000 hand-spinners.

materials, either by replacing a costly material by a cheaper one (e.g. charcoal by coal) or by reducing the quantity of raw materials, especially fuel, that were required to produce a finished article. Thus, in South Wales, 8 tons of coal were needed to make 1 ton of pig-iron around 1790, but only 3.5 tons in 1830. These increases in productivity led to a rapid and enduring reduction in costs and in selling prices, especially as, after the end of the Napoleonic wars, there was a fall in the prices of raw materials and transport. The price index of No. 100 cotton yarn fell from 252 in 1795/7 to 85 in 1830/2; wrought iron cost £18 a ton in 1750, and £5 in 1843[2].

This fall in costs and prices had two important consequences. On the one hand it speeded up the progress and spread of technology by encouraging the discovery and adoption of improvements that would again reduce costs and safeguard profit margins menaced by competition. It also forced manufacturers to choose between innovation and extinction. It helped to give the Industrial Revolution its cumulative character and chain-reaction aspect. On the other hand, the reduction in the prices of manufactured goods (demand for which was often very elastic in relation to price) made them available to an increasing number of less and less wealthy consumers. So cotton goods, which had been luxury articles at the beginning of the eighteenth century, became standard working-class wear in the nineteenth. Cheaper prices assured a continuous widening of the market – in itself a factor in specialization and technical progress. They tended to create mass consumption and a mass market for a growing range of products.

Under such circumstances, growth became the normal condition of the economy, despite cyclical fluctuations, whose crises moreover contributed in the end to growth by eliminating the less efficient producers. It became a built-in part of economic structures, so that great changes followed one another at a fast pace, for the Industrial Revolution had broken the vicious circles that paralysed traditional economies and limited them to fitful bursts of expansion. Moreover, as growth up to our own times has been an irreversible process, one may ask whether it is necessary to 'explain' British growth in the nineteenth century, especially as it was not unusually fast. Is not the crucial problem rather to explain the slowing-down of British growth

2   A year of very low prices; in 1839 iron had been at £10 (B.R.Mitchell and P.Deane, *Abstract of British Historical Statistics* (Cambridge, 1962) (quoted hereafter as *Abstract*), p. 492); D.S.Landes, *The Unbound Prometheus: Technological Change and Industrial Development in Western Europe, 1750 to the Present* (Cambridge, 1969), p. 92. The index of yarn prices is taken from T.S. Ashton, 'Some statistics of the Industrial Revolution in Britain', in E.M.Carus-Wilson (ed.), *Essays in Economic History* (London, 1962), III, p.249 (table III).

at the end of the nineteenth century? It is indeed, but that question will be discussed as an epilogue to this book.

As for the decades which preceded this deceleration, one might ask whether the real problem is not to explain why the rate of growth of British national product was not higher then, as one might have expected, given the trump cards held by Great Britain – which need to be recalled in simple terms.

Natural advantages? A country whose soil is often very fertile and which, thanks to its small size, does not suffer from the handicap of long distances; where internal communications are easy, with mountainous regions confined to the fringes. A country which exploited such advantages by constructing a dense system of roads, canals and, after 1830, railways. An island which has easy relations with the outside world, anchored off the most developed region of continental Europe, at the focal point of sea-routes to distant countries. An island whose elongated shape meant that no part of it was far from the coast, where many sites for good harbours existed and were developed early on. Above all an enormous store of underground riches – deposits of iron-ore and non-ferrous metals, and many extensive coal-fields. It is true that by the mid-nineteenth century the former would either become inadequate or be worked out, but coal-reserves were almost inexhaustible, and moreover they were often of excellent quality, while extraction was easy and cheap. Certainly coal did not generate the Industrial Revolution, although the early development of a coal-fuel technology, starting in the sixteenth century, was a factor in it, as J.R. Harris has demonstrated[3]. However, coal was a necessary condition for the further spread of industrialization. After having concentrated on capital and labour as factors, economists nowadays remember land, i.e. natural resources. From that point of view, Great Britain was not very well endowed, except for coal, the importance of which well deserves to be stressed again; but this shortcoming, added to historical circumstances, led her on to build a special economic structure, based upon the international division of labour.

Great Britain also enjoyed political and institutional advantages. First of all, there was the long period of peace from 1815 to 1914 during which she only took part in one European war, the Crimean. She carried on innumerable colonial wars, but only one of them, the Boer war, was of any importance. Other European countries and the United States (with their long civil war) were less fortunate. The situation

[3]   J.R.Harris, *Industry and Technology in the Eighteenth Century* (Birmingham, 1972); J.R. Harris, 'Skills, coal and British industry in the eighteenth century', *History* LXI (202), June 1976, 167–82.

was the same at home. England endured periods of agitation and strife – mostly between 1815 and 1848 – but she escaped revolution. And in the political sphere, as Mr Podsnap said in *Our Mutual Friend*, thanks to 'the Constitution Britannique, which was as liberal in economics as in politics', *laissez-faire*, backed up by a hallowed respect for private property and by the wealthy classes' feeling of security, created conditions eminently suitable for enterprise and innovation.

Above all, on the purely economic plane, as has already been emphasized, England had been the first country to achieve its industrial revolution, spontaneously and without outside precedent or help, and so had gained from 1780 onwards a lead of several decades over her potential rivals and a crushing superiority that was at once qualitative (in technology) and quantitative (as far as the volume of industrial production was concerned). Moreover, historical circumstances, more particularly her command of the seas and her victories during the Napoleonic wars, had assured her supremacy in overseas markets, and she was the best placed to grasp the glittering prizes offered by the rapid expansion of international trade in the nineteenth century. Her early economic take-off gave her other comparative advantages: a labour-force trained early on to factory work, some occupational groups being highly skilled and productive; considerable acquired wealth and abundant capital, which had accumulated in a country which had long since dominated international trade, which had escaped defeats and revolutions, and where social inequality favoured accumulation; rates of interest which fell to modest levels after 1815; a banking and credit system that was also well in advance of other countries and which was able to transfer capital rather efficiently. Finally, Britain had numerous groups of entrepreneurs who were active, dynamic and bold, ready to seize every profit opportunity, open to technological progress, passionately seeking quick riches in the favourable atmosphere of a society which placed high value on material success and in which status in due course – though rather slowly – followed wealth. Nor should one forget the unrivalled experience of merchants and financiers, who knew foreign markets intimately and had long experience of the delicate mechanism of international trade.

In these circumstances, one can wonder why Britain's economic growth was not faster. But we will not try to answer this question for the moment, and the following pages will only analyse the effect upon growth of a number of factors, starting with the institutional factor of economic liberalism.

ABOUT *LAISSEZ-FAIRE*

If one had asked a well-informed Englishman of the mid-Victorian era – whether politician, businessman, or economist – what, in his view, was the main cause of Britain's prosperity, and of her economic superiority over other nations, it is highly probable that he would have pointed to the economic freedom which prevailed in his country to a higher degree than anywhere else, apart from the United States. As for historians, whether they have been favourable or hostile to the system, they have often regarded the Victorian era as the high noon of economic liberalism (or individualism), as the 'age of *laissez-faire*', especially after the victory at mid-century of free trade, which was a crucial aspect of liberalism. However, this idea has been challenged by recent writers, so that it will be useful to examine whether the Victorian era was really a period of *laissez-faire* and then, if the answer is in the affirmative, to enquire what the consequences of this system may have been for the development of the British economy[4]. *Laissez-faire* is both an economic doctrine and the policies which actually enforce it. The basic principle is that the welfare of both the community and individuals is best served when markets for goods, capital, land, labour and so on are left to the free play of supply and demand, and when the state interferes as little as possible, in both the economic and the social sphere.

It is beyond doubt that these ideas gained a strong hold on all influential circles in nineteenth-century England (though they lost some influence in the last quarter) and it has been maintained that *laissez-faire* was the 'philosophy in office'[5]. It is true that none of the great classical economists preached it as gospel, and all of them allowed infringements to the principle, on the understanding that the necessity for such exceptions should be justified in every case. However, the popularizers, journalists and politicians who effected the spread of these thinkers' ideas let these qualifications drop and proclaimed the ideology of *laissez-faire* pure and simple. It served of course the interests and aspirations of many important groups, including the business world and especially manufacturers. Furthermore, the influence of *laissez-faire* is part and parcel of the predomi-

[4] The pages that follow owe much to A.J.Taylor's treatment of the subject, *Laissez-faire and State Intervention in Nineteenth-Century Britain* (London, 1972). A lively criticism of this work is to be found in: C.J. Holmes, '*Laissez-faire* in theory and practice: Britain, 1800–1875', *Journal of European Economic History*, v(3), Winter 1976, 671–88.

[5] Holmes denies, on his side, that this 'philosophy' was a dominant factor in policy making by governments.

nance of the liberal ideal, in its broadest sense, over nineteenth-century England.

However, what counted was the actual practices of government and civil servants. From this point of view, matters become more complicated, for the respect for principles was tempered by considerations of opportunity and by the influence of circumstances and of pressure groups. On the one hand, the successive victories of *laissez-faire* must be underlined. At the beginning of the nineteenth century, the statute books were crammed with a great many laws, some of them dating from the middle ages, which authorized or prescribed the intervention of government in countless economic and social problems. Of course, since the end of the seventeenth century, the state had no longer bothered to enforce these laws and had left the field clear to private enterprise, so that most of those acts – apart from the protectionist control of overseas trade – had fallen into disuse. However, they remained legally in force, and from time to time a pressure group, e.g. workers whose trade was regulated by one of these laws, tried to revive it and have it enforced, in order to protect their interests. In fact such attempts nearly always achieved the opposite result to what had been hoped, i.e. the abolition of obsolete laws by a Parliament converted to *laissez-faire*. This happened with the whole battery of regulations applying to the woollen industry, the acts which allowed magistrates to fix wages, the system of apprenticeship (1814), etc. This liquidation, more or less completed by 1830, was in principle unfavourable to workers and gave a free hand to their employers, but one must remember that these laws had not in fact been enforced for a long time.

Far more serious for the lower orders was the new Poor Law of 1834, which made the conditions in which the poor received relief harsher and more restrictive; but it was a compromise measure, for the most doctrinaire economists wanted the complete abolition of the Poor Laws. Conversely, the Combination Laws, which severely punished combinations between workmen, were repealed in 1824 and 1825, thus opening the way to the legal development of trade unions and making strikes no longer unlawful[6]. Furthermore, the East India Company lost its monopoly of trade with India (1813) and then with China (1833). On the other hand, protectionism, defended as it was by powerful landed interests, proved more durable, but finally it too was dismantled from 1842 onwards. Its cornerstone and symbol, the Corn Laws, disappeared

[6]   But it was only the Acts of 1867, 1871 and 1875 which granted trade unions full legal recognition and broad opportunities for industrial action.

in 1846, and the long sacrosanct Navigation Acts, as well as other survivals of mercantilism, did not long outlive them[7]. Finally, restrictions on the creation of limited-liability, joint-stock companies, which had been imposed by the Bubble Act of 1720, were gradually abolished. In 1825 it became possible to float a joint-stock company without first obtaining the authority of Parliament or a charter. In 1844, a public company could be set up simply by registering it with the Board of Trade; but to benefit from limited liability still required the authority of Parliament. In 1856, an important Act allowed any firm that wished to do so to form itself into a limited-liability company as long as its trade name was followed by the abbreviation 'Ltd'. This measure was extended in 1858 to banks, which had been excluded from it at first, and in 1862 an all-embracing statute codified these various reforms of company legislation[8]. But these various measures were not unambiguous, because, while they made the creation of public companies much easier than before, they imposed a degree of regulation on them, so that some historians interpret them as an increase in state intervention.

Through such measures the Victorian era saw the completion of a liberalization of the economy that had started long ago. However, one can argue that even before it was complete, a reverse process was set in train. The point of departure was the Factory Act of 1833 which regulated the work of children in textile factories (earlier laws of 1802 and 1819 had had a much more limited scope and were not seriously enforced). It was to be followed in the course of the nineteenth century by a whole series of similar measures which in fact[9] violated the principle of freedom of contract between employer and worker – an essential aspect of *laissez-faire*. However, the latter's supporters managed to put a brake on the development of labour legislation for a long time. So it came about that, starting with an Act of 1842, which forbade women and small children to work underground in coalmines, the coal industry gradually became the most regulated and supervised of all. However only piecemeal measures were instituted at first, and it was not until 1908 and 1911 that laws of a new type were passed on the

---

[7] Yet the victory of free trade was anything but a simple application of liberal ideology. It resulted from a mixture of many forces and circumstances. The abolition of laws which forbade the emigration of skilled workers (1824) and the export of many types of machines (1843) can also be mentioned.

[8] See Chapter 10 on the special legislation on banks.

[9] These measures applied legally only to the work of women and children, which could be considered a special case of individuals deserving protection for reasons of humanity, and they made no regulations for adult men; but in practice the length of working hours for men was *ipso facto* equally limited.

length of working hours and on wages for miners, amounting to the first intervention of the state in the internal economy of a large industry.

Meanwhile, the 1830s had also seen the beginnings of a tendency to intervene in another sphere, thanks to the Municipal Reform Act of 1835. This opened the way to sporadic but sometimes vigorous action on the part of the new municipal corporations, with some stimulus from Whitehall, to improve the shocking state of public health in towns. The scope of these interventions in the urban ecosystem was to widen progressively during the nineteenth century, ending with 'municipal socialism' – notably the ownership and management by the corporation, of water-supply, gas, tramways, etc.

However, this type of intervention applied to the purely social sphere, and labour legislation was situated on the borderline between the economic and the social[10]. In both cases, restrictions on *laissez-faire* were based on humanitarian and moral considerations, which, in the eyes of public opinion and government, were more important than respect for economic principles, especially the principle that labour was nothing but another commodity. They were imposed by the urgency of the human problems caused by industrialization and urbanization.

None the less, even in the almost purely economic sphere, a similar pressure of new conditions arising from industrialization brought about interventions – in railway affairs, for instance. From the very start, the creation of railway companies, all organized on a joint-stock, limited-liability basis, was subject, as were formerly the canal companies and turnpike trusts, to the authorization of Parliament, which also virtually traced out the lines by granting powers for land expropriation. But the development of the railway system posed new problems – such as the establishment of safety-standards and the approval of company mergers. On the latter point, a conflict arose between two principles of liberalism – respect for freedom of enterprise and condemnation of monopolies – which produced an inconsistent policy towards mergers. Finally, when the nineteenth century ended, railways were submitted to thorough regulation, even though state intervention in this sphere remained considerably less in Britain than it was in nearly all other countries, including territories of the British empire like India[11]. In addition, Parliament continued to legislate in

---

[10]   Like the measures intended to improve the safety of crews and passengers on merchant ships, particularly the prohibition in 1876 of excessive loading (the Plimsoll Line).

[11]   Cf Chapter 9, pp. 287–8, 295–6. An eventual nationalization of railways was proposed by Gladstone himself, when he was President of the Board of Trade in 1844.

traditional fields, such as weights and measures, patents, bankruptcies, and of course currency and banking problems[12].

This is why some historians have maintained that *laissez-faire* was
on the decline from the 1830s onwards, and that the Victorian era was
not the age of *laissez-faire*. This is the view of scholars who are
concerned with administrative history and who are naturally im-
pressed by the development of nineteenth-century interventionist
institutions, such as the inspectorate of factories and mines, the Poor
Law Board, the bodies dealing with public health, and in a more
general way by the increase in number of the civil service and of local
government, with their growing professionalism. There has even been
talk of the appearance of collectivist tendencies as early as the 1830s,
and David Roberts has asserted that the origins of the welfare state
should be sought in the Victorian age[13]. Other more circumspect
historians have simply observed that, from the 1870s onwards, the
hold of liberal dogmas on public opinion lessened, including the dogma
of free trade which some businessmen and politicians were criticizing
as a result of growing foreign competition and difficulties during the
Great Depression. Meanwhile, the gradual accumulation of interventionist legislation and the growing power of trade unions were in
practice limiting *laissez-faire* and individualism.

Actually, as the victory of free trade was so important and the first
measure in social legislation were so limited in character, it would be
wise to place the high noon of *laissez-faire* in the mid-Victorian period,
and one can admit that it experienced some decline after 1870. But, as
a matter of hard fact, this decline was very limited and, even in the
social sphere where state intervention was most active, its limits were
very obvious. It was essentially negative, i.e. it outlawed certain
practices like child labour. Only during the Edwardian period, when
the Liberals were in power from 1905 onwards, were the first
foundations of the welfare state laid. As for the strictly economic
sphere, where humanitarian considerations were not as important,
laissez-faire won the day easily and continued to do so, in spite of a few
reverses in special cases, where the advantages of intervention
outweighed its inconveniences or the consequences of inaction.

A complementary factor, but an important one which supports this

---

[12] Sir Robert Peel, a determined supporter of *laissez-faire*, still managed to pass the
Bank Charter Act of 1844, which regulated the banking system very strictly.

[13] D.Roberts, *Victorian Origins of the British Welfare State* (New Haven, 1960). On the
extension of the powers of the state (the nature of its action being the important
point), the most recent works are O.MacDonagh, *Early Victorian Government 1830–
1870* (London, 1977) and W.R.Q.Henriques, *Before the Welfare State: Social
Administration in Early Industrial Britain* (London, 1979).

conclusion, was financial policy. All governments of the Victorian era (and those too which preceded them since 1815), helped by the absence of large-scale wars, adopted a policy of strict budgetary economy, in accordance with Gladstone's principle that money ought to be left to fructify in the pockets of the people. They balanced the state's accounts at the lowest possible level and reduced taxes, which had certainly been heavy just after the wars with France. Consequently, government expenditure increased much less fast up to 1870 than GNP, to such an extent that its ratio to the latter, which was probably 20 per cent in 1820[14] was not more than 6.6 per cent for the decade 1830/9, according to Phyllis Deane. It went up to 7.4 per cent for 1850/9 as a result of the Crimean war, but fell to a minimum of 5.3 per cent for 1865/74. However, it then rose gradually and reached over 8 per cent at the beginning of the twentieth century, because of the Boer war, the naval armaments race and the growth of social expenditure, which meant that budgetary expenditure increased faster than GNP[15]. Furthermore, a large proportion of these disbursements (89 per cent in 1820, 88 per cent in 1850, and still 45 per cent in 1890) was made up of military expenditure and the servicing of the National Debt, itself incurred during periods of war (mostly between 1793 and 1815). Central government spending on social services of every kind, was very low (21 per cent of total spending in 1890), but there was also spending of this kind by local government, which was far larger in total. The two categories increased substantially from 1870 to 1890 and very sharply at the beginning of the twentieth century[16].

British governments of the nineteenth century deliberately – and successfully – sought to minimize the state's unavoidable role in the economy as consumer and tax-gatherer. Generally, they were convinced, more or less consciously, that the prosperity of the economy

[14]   P.Mathias, *The First Industrial Nation: An Economic History of Britain 1700–1914* (London, 1969), p. 41 (table II). This percentage is not strictly comparable with those that follow.

[15]   P.Deane, 'New estimates of gross national product for the United Kingdom 1836–1914', *The Review of Income and Wealth*, series 14(2), June 1968, 99 (table 3). On the other hand, Taylor, p. 62, using the older work of Peacock and Wiseman, gives higher figures for the ratio government expenditure/national product: 16 per cent in 1831, 9 per cent in 1870, stability at that level up to the beginning of the Boer war in 1899, and a rise up to 12.4 per cent in 1913.

[16]   In spite of free trade and the restoration of income tax (non-progressive, 1842), the fiscal system was clearly regressive, i.e. it penalized low incomes more heavily than the rest. The state drew the bulk of its revenue from excise or customs duties on goods that were widely consumed: beer, tobacco, tea, etc. There is little point in emphasizing that public expenditure has grown much faster since 1914 than GNP; but it also rose strongly from the end of the seventeenth century to 1815, which shows the exceptional character of the nineteenth century.

was best guaranteed when market forces were given free play and each individual was allowed to find his own way to riches; so they abstained from all effort to control the economy and they indulged in the minimum of action. Even short-term fluctuations were accepted as inevitable, and little was done to prevent and moderate them or to mitigate their consequences. The commitment to *laissez-faire*, without being doctrinaire or total, was certainly positive.

Thus it seems right to conclude that the nineteenth century in England was indeed, in the economic field, the 'age of *laissez-faire*', especially by comparison with the periods which came before and after, and also compared with the policies of continental states in the same epoch. Granted that total economic freedom or a perfectly competitive market belong to the imagination of economists, as near an approximation as was practically possible in a modern state was achieved in mid-Victorian Britain.

For a long time, only the workers in a number of crafts were organized in trade unions; while combinations between manufacturers, which had been fairly common in some industries, e.g. iron, in the eighteenth century for fixing prices and sometimes production quotas (without, it is true, much success), became rarer[17] and were generally limited to temporary agreements for lowering wages or resisting workers' claims. Things did, of course, change during the Great Depression. The fall in prices and the fierce competition revived efforts to make producers' agreements; 'trade associations' came into being, trying to fix minimum prices, to mark out spheres of influence, and sometimes to restrict output. These associations were to be found in nearly all branches of industry during the 1880s, but as 'voluntary' groups they never gathered in all the manufacturers of the branch concerned and they could not penalize rule-breakers. It only required a few rebels to cut prices to cause a general collapse. The effect of these associations seems to have been only momentary. After 1890 another system, more formal and institutionalized, made its appearance – the cartel, on the German model. Its aims were more ambitious, notably to fix quotas of production with sanctions against offenders. A large number were started and they were horizontal in character, e.g. in the bleaching and dyeing of cottons. The most successful attempt was the system of 'conferences' in merchant shipping, of which the first was instituted in 1879 in the China tea-trade. These conferences fixed freight charges, but a rebate was granted to customers who undertook to use exclusively the ships of conference members. At the beginning of

[17] See for example S.R.Jones, 'Price association and competition in the British pin industry, 1814–40', *Economic History Review* 2nd series, XXXVI(2), May 1973, 238.

the twentieth century this system was in operation on most of the long-distance sea-routes for the liners regularly plying these routes. But in industry cartels were ineffective, chiefly because they lacked customs-protection, which alone makes it possible to sell dear on the home market, and practise 'dumping' overseas. British capitalism remained competitive and, as we have seen, it was made up of small units[18].

A last question concerns the economic consequences of this reign of *laissez-faire*[19]. A thorny problem and partly insoluble, for the reply will depend on the historian's personal philosophy. Liberals will insist on the stimulus to growth brought on by the abolition of obsolete regulations and obstacles to free enterprise; but, apart from customs protections, these hindrances had long since fallen into disuse and in any case had not prevented or even curbed the take-off of the Industrial Revolution. Liberals will also regard the state's abstention and the low level of taxation as positive benefits[20]. Socialists, on the other hand, will imagine that a social policy, which would have raised the people's purchasing power, and also some counter-cyclical measures, could have assured faster and more regular economic growth. It is for the reader to make up his mind. However, there is an area which can escape from subjective views, chiefly because it lends itself to quantification: that is the question of the economic consequences of free trade, an issue linked, however, to the broader problem of the role of overseas trade in the growth of the British economy.

OVERSEAS TRADE AND GROWTH

It has always been tempting to regard overseas trade as a major factor in Britain's economic growth. The position of premier trading power which she assumed at the beginning of the eighteenth century and

[18] Which was probably a better thing! Although German cartels could assist rationalization and technical progress, they seem in England to have been mainly concerned with fixing prices, which allowed the least efficient firms to survive. For all this, see Mathias, *The First Industrial Nation*, pp.386ff. Yet some British firms did take part in international agreements or cartels, e.g. in the glass industry.

[19] They were quite clear on the social level. Refusal by the state to intervene was in itself an intervention, generally to the advantage of employers and to the detriment of workers. However, it was in the social sphere that most violence was done to the principle of *laissez-faire*, so as to remedy social evils which shocked the consciences of the time.

[20] Which was lighter, in relation to GNP, than in other European countries. Deane, 'New estimates', 100, points out that economic growth was more rapid in the decades when the weight of public expenditure diminished. According to an article in *The Economist*, 10 Apr. 1976, the *real* weight of taxes diminished by two-thirds between 1815 and 1881.

which she kept up to the first world war; her long-standing superiority in technology, which gave her comparative advantages for supplying the rest of the world both with cheap consumer goods and with capital goods; the enormous increase in her exports during the nineteenth century (at constant prices, i.e. by volume, they were multiplied by a factor of thirty-five between 1814/16 and 1911/13); the presence of her ships, her merchants and her manufactures all over the world; the vastness of an empire which traded mostly with its mother-country; the undoubted importance of foreign markets for several staple industries, notably cotton. All these facts encouraged the belief in this assumption without much discussion.

This view has however been challenged by recent research[21], using simple quantitative methods. A convenient way of measuring the importance of overseas trade to an economy is to calculate the 'export proportion', i.e. the percentage of the value of exports in relation to national product[22]. This calculation can be made not only at current but also at constant prices so as to eliminate the influence of price movements, which can be appreciable. It is also possible to work out for successive periods the ratio between the value (and volume) of additional exports and increases in national product[23], which can be called, statistically at least, the contribution of exports to economic growth – without forgetting that exports are not income, but a part of national product which is withdrawn from home consumption[24]. Of course, such calculations only give orders of magnitude, given the

---

[21] Notably P.Bairoch, 'Commerce international et genèse de la révolution industrielle anglaise', *Annales E.S.C.*, XXVIII(2)mars-avril 1972, 541–71; F. Crouzet, 'Towards an export economy: British exports during the Industrial Revolution', *Explorations in Economic History* 17(1), Jan. 1980, 48–93; R.Davis, *The Industrial Revolution and British Overseas Trade* (Leicester, 1979).

[22] Of course, domestic exports of British goods are alone considered, and re-exports of foreign products excluded. S.Kuznets, *Modern Economic Growth: Rate, Structure and Spread* (New Haven and London,1966), pp. 312–3 (tab.6.4), gives the ratio of foreign trade (imports plus exports) to the GNP of the UK. At current prices they are:

1837/45	22 per cent
1909/13	44 per cent

But, for a study of growth, one can consider exports only.

[23] If X stands for exports and P for national product, this ratio (r), from year to year, is obtained by the formula:

$$r = \frac{Xtl - Xto}{Ptl - Pto} \times 100$$

[24] These methods are preferable to the simple comparison of rates of growth of exports and of national product, which is often used. The progress of the former, which is generally faster, can give a false impression of their role in economic growth, when their total value is small at the start: when exports amount to only 10 per cent of national product, their doubling in a given period will only give a rise of 10 per cent in national product.

uncertainty of national-product figures in the eighteenth and at the beginning of the nineteenth century. However, attempts have been made to calculate them, and the results may be found in tables 25 and 26.

It seems established that the progress of British exports between about 1700 and 1780 (which was indeed fairly slow and irregular) only played a minor part in the growth of the economy during that period, which included the first stages of the Industrial Revolution, so that this growth gained most of its momentum from domestic demand. On the other hand, from the end of the American war of independence up to 1802, exports enjoyed a growth of unprecedented speed, far superior to that of national product. Hence the export proportion increased sharply, climbing from about 8 per cent around 1783 to 18 per cent or even more around 1801. Furthermore, the increase in the value of exports was equivalent to 40 per cent of the increase in national product. So exports were a most important engine of growth for the British economy, which at the turn of the eighteenth and nineteenth century was tending to become an export economy.

However, tables 25 and 26 show that this development did not proceed in a regular fashion during the nineteenth century, and that there were important changes in the export proportion and in the contribution of exports to growth. Changes in these proportions depend actually not only on the growth in volume of exports and national product, but also on price movements, the latter being responsible for the differences in tables 25 and 26 between percentages at current and at constant prices.

After 1802, the increase in British exports was definitely slower than during the preceding twenty years, as a consequence of the wars against France and the post-war crises. Their *volume* certainly remained on an upward trend (though slowly till 1826), with an average growth-rate of 4.3 per cent between 1814 and 1846, which was high[25]. But export *values* fell between 1815 and the end of the 1820s, and they only resumed a clear upward trend ten years or so later, so that their growth-rate from 1814 to 1846 was only 1.1 per cent.

This contrast results from the very sharp fall in British export prices during the first half of the nineteenth century. Imlah's price index for exports drops by 60 per cent between 1801 and 1831, and by 74 per cent

[25]   This rate is calculated, as are several others in the pages that follow, according to the method of exponential adjustment, which takes into account all the values of the series, and not simply between two years or groups of years, as is the case generally in this book.

Table 25   UK (a) exports as percentage of GNP (at factor cost)

	1	2	3	4	5	6
	At current prices			At constant prices		
	Deane and Cole	Deane 1968	Feinstein	Deane and Cole	Deane 1968	Feinstein
1783	8					
1801	18			8		
1831	11	9		8	7	
1841	11	10		10	9	
1851	14	14	(17)(b)	15	13	
1871	25	20	22	24	19	19
1901	17	15	16	17	19	18
1912		21	22		25	25

(a) Except for the Deane and Cole figures which compare exports from the United Kingdom and Great Britain GNP hence slightly higher percentages than for the other series. Furthermore this series overestimates the GNP at the end of the nineteenth century.
(b) 1856.
Values used for the calculation of percentages (except for GNP columns 1 and 4) are three-year averages centred on the year specified.
Source
Exports: at current prices, *Abstract*, pp. 282–3; at constant prices, Imlah, pp. 94–98 (table 8). This series (which is at 1880 prices) has been recalculated at 1900 prices for columns 5 and 6, as the corresponding GNP series are at 1900 prices.

GNP: Deane and Cole, pp. 166 and 282 (tables 37 and 72); Deane, 'New estimates', 104–7 (tables A and B); Feinstein, *National Income*, tables 1 (col. 11) and 5 (col. 13), T.4–5, 14–15.
N.B. Bairoch, *Commerce extérieur*, p. 79 (table 20), gives a calculation of the same kind, but uses GNP at current market prices, and gives slightly lower percentages (18 percent in 1870), but with the same trend.

Table 26   Ratio between additional exports and increases in UK GNP (%)

	1	2	3	4	5	6
	At current prices			At constant prices		
	Deane and Cole	Deane 1968	Feinstein	Deane and Cole	Deane 1968	Feinstein
1801–41	4			12		
1841–71	38	27		37	28	
1856–71			31			
1871–1901	8	8	8	12	18	18
1901–12		46	44		65	63

Sources: as for table 25. See also its note (a).
These percentages are calculated between three-year averages centred on the year specified (except for GNP in columns 1 and 4).

between 1801 and 1851[26]. The fall was particularly sharp for cotton goods and yarn, at a time when the share of these articles in total exports was high and increasing. It was mainly the result of progress in mechanization and so in productivity and was not an unfavourable symptom; but it did mean that the value of exports increased much more slowly than their volume. Furthermore, national product at current prices was also affected by the fall in price of manufactured goods, but the prices of many other goods and services did not show the steep decline in price of cotton goods; at current prices, its growth-rate was higher than that of exports.

Consequently, the export proportion, calculated at current prices, fell markedly and regularly between 1801 and 1831, and from the end of the Napoleonic wars to the start of Victoria's reign it was roughly 10 per cent. On the other hand, at constant prices it remained roughly stable, or showed a slight increase, over the same period. As for the ratio between the increase in exports and that of national product between 1801 and 1841, it was insignificant at current prices and small at constant prices. Exports, in fact, contributed only little to growth[27]. It is a remarkable fact that, during a period which showed a very high rate of growth in industrial output and when in addition England had no serious rivals, the export sector of the economy made little relative progress in real terms and distinctly lost ground at current prices[28].

However, from 1852 onwards the average prices of exports started to rise (according to Imlah by 23 per cent between 1851 and 1871). The result was the disappearance of the difference between growth of volume (which was slightly faster between 1846 and 1873 than from 1814 to 1846) and growth of values (which greatly speeded up from 1848 onwards). Values grew even faster than volume, i.e. 5.6 per cent per annum against 4.7 per cent between 1846 and 1873, and both increased at least twice as fast as national product[29].

Consequently export ratios, both at current and at constant prices, increased sharply from the 1840s onwards. They at least doubled in thirty years, and around 1870 they reached and even exceeded 20 per

---

[26] A.H.Imlah, *Economic Elements in the Pax Britannica: Studies in British Foreign Trade in the Nineteenth Century* (Cambridge,Mass.,1958), pp. 94–8 (table 8). These falls are calculated from three-year averages centred on the year indicated.

[27] Yet, from both points of view, this ratio was definitely higher between 1831 and 1841 than it had been during the three preceding decades.

[28] P.Deane and W.A.Cole, *British Economic Growth, 1688–1959* (Cambridge, 2nd edn, 1967), p.311, think that the home market developed faster than exports during the first thirty years of the nineteenth century.

[29] See for example Deane and Cole,p. 83 (table 11).

cent according to the different GNP series which are used, but which give roughly the same results. As for the contribution of exports to total growth, this too increased strongly from the 1840s onwards, and between 1841 and 1871 it was in the 27–38 per cent bracket depending on the series used[30]. So it seems that, during the mid-Victorian period, the growth of exports gave a major stimulus to total growth, and they were even a leading sector, contributing decisively to the redistribution in factors of production, away from sectors where productivity was low and into more productive ones[31]. So, about 1870, Great Britain became as 'export economy', with a high exports proportion, much higher than continental Europe's[32]. Foreign trade, by its sheer relative weight in the country's economy, played a very important role, even a dominant one according to some historians[33]. But it must be stressed that this special situation was only reached late in the period.

According to S.B. Saul, this export economy was to continue to prevail in Britain up to 1914, and the period 1871–1914 had a unique character because it saw the maximum influence of foreign trade over the economy, at least in a purely statistical sense[34], i.e. the ratio of the

[30] This conclusion would be confirmed if one used a less rough method consisting of calculating for the whole of a period the sums of the additions to exports and to GNP in relation to the year (or groups of years) at the beginning of the period. You then calculate the ratio of these two aggregates. So, by taking Deane's GNP series of 1968, the sum of the extra exports amounts to 12 per cent of the sum of additions to GNP between 1830 and 1849, but 29 per cent between 1850 and 1873. This is the method used by Bairoch, *Commerce extérieur et développement économique de l'Europe en XIXe siècle* (Paris–The Hague, 1976), p. 209 (table 61); also p. 193. This direct contribution of additional exports to additional GNP reached its peak (attributable according to Bairoch to the adoption of free trade) in the period 1843/7 to 1857/61 (31 per cent in volume against 10 per cent between 1800 and 1830; 25 per cent in value), but it is not much less for the period 1857/61 to 1873/77 (27 per cent in volume, 24 per cent in value). Similarly, our conclusions are confirmed if one calculates the ratio between *total* cumulative exports and the sum of total GNPs for the periods in question.

[31] The opinion of R.A.Church, *The Great Victorian Boom, 1850–1873* (London, 1975), pp.27–8, who sees an export-led boom in the 1850s and a persisting influence of foreign trade in the 1860s. Bairoch, *Commerce extérieur*, pp. 160, 309, shares this view.

[32] See Bairoch, *Commerce extérieur*, p. 20 (table 3). Yet the British rate is lower than that of the small advanced countries (Belgium, Switzerland, Holland and Denmark) and is not much higher than that of Germany and even of France at the beginning of the twentieth century.

[33] Deane and Cole, pp. 28, 309, 312, who assert that, from the middle of the nineteenth century, foreign trade controlled the rhythm and structure of growth, and that there is a close relationship between changes in the volume of GB's international trade and those of its rate of growth.

[34] For it is not certain (the opposite has even been maintained) that exports formed the leading sector for the perfecting of new techniques and new products. S.B.Saul, 'The export economy, 1870–1914', *Yorkshire Bulletin of Economic and Social Research*, 17(1), May 1965, 5.

value of trade to national income reached its highest point in the 1870s and 1880s and diminished only slightly in the years that followed.

As far as exports on their own were concerned[35], things were in fact rather more complex. During the period which, for convenience, will be called the Great Depression, the growth of British exports did slow down most noticeably; in volume, between 1870/2 and 1900/2 (years of cyclical peaks), it was only 2.2 per cent per annum. Furthermore, as average prices of exports had fallen, according to Imlah, by 29 per cent between these dates, their growth in value was even smaller, only 0.8 per cent per annum[36]. On the other hand, the growth rate of national product settled at 2 per cent at constant prices and at 1.7 or 1.8 per cent at current prices[37]. Consequently the export ratio, calculated at current prices, fell from 20 per cent or more around 1871 to 15 or 16 per cent around 1901, while at constant prices it remained stable, close to 20 per cent. The contribution of exports to the growth of national product remained quite small (8 per cent) at current prices, larger at constant prices, but nevertheless much inferior to the contribution during the period 1841–71[38]. So demand on the home market increased faster than external demand (it has been pointed out earlier that there was a marked improvement in real wages during the last quarter of the nineteenth century).

But in the early twentieth century British exports recovered vigorously. Between 1900/2 and 1911/13, their growth rate was 4.3 per cent by volume and 5.1 per cent by value (their prices having increased by 6 per cent). This was well above the growth-rate of national product (2 per cent at current prices, 1.4 per cent at constant prices). So the export proportion rose notably, exceeding 20 per cent at current prices and reaching 25 per cent at constant prices, i.e. record levels, on the eve of the first world war. Table 26 also shows high and unprecedented percentages for the contribution of exports to growth[39].

[35] Saul quotes a series of ratios between averages of net imports plus exports, and national income, which are necessarily higher (the value of imports into the UK being higher than that of exports and more stable; Deane and Cole, p. 28) than the export proportion which we use.

[36] And only 0.1 per cent between 1873/7 and 1893/7. From Bairoch, *Commerce extérieur*, p. 205 (table 58).

[37] From data of Deane, 'New estimates', and of C.H. Feinstein, *National Income, Expenditure and Output of the United Kingdom, 1855–1965* (Cambridge, 1972). According to Bairoch, *Commerce extérieur*, p. 208, the implicit index of GDP prices only goes down 15 per cent during the period mentioned in the preceding note, and there is a deterioration of 23 per cent in the 'terms of trade of national production'.

[38] With a different method, Bairoch, *Commerce extérieur*, pp. 208–9 (table 61), also observes a very small contribution in value during the Great Depression, but little change in volume.

[39] This fits with the stagnation of real per-capita incomes during this period.

These remarks show that the demand from foreign markets was an engine of growth during fairly short periods only – from the end of the American War of Independence up to 1802, from the end of the 1840s to the beginning of the 1870s, and lastly during the Edwardian era. Even here demand from the home market was always larger than exports by a long way. The influence of exports on growth was small at the beginning of the nineteenth century and during the Great Depression. This was the trend in the long run; in the short term foreign demand was always an important factor in business cycles.

As British exports were made up mostly of manufactured goods, their development ought to have had a relatively stronger impact on the growth of industrial output than on total national product. Unfortunately, available data on the value of industrial production (i.e. added value) bear no comparison with the values of exports, which are final, and we have no accurate idea of the share of industrial output which was exported, nor of its changes. It may have been near to a third at the beginning of the nineteenth century; it was probably about 40 per cent around 1870, and somewhat more at the beginning of the twentieth century[40]; but it is most likely that it fluctuated, as did the contribution of exports to industrial growth, roughly parallel with the export/national-product ratio, which has just been examined. It doubtless fell in the first decades of the nineteenth centry (even in volume), went up noticeably from the 1840s onwards, stagnated or lost ground during the Great Depression, and recovered at least in the early twentieth century. We do indeed have data about the export/output ratio in some important industries, but they will be considered later. Roughly speaking they would confirm the movements which have just been suggested, and all we want to point out for the moment is that from the beginning of the nineteenth century only the cotton industry consistently exported more than half of its output, usually much more, and that foreign demand was undoubtedly the dominant factor in its growth. For the woollen and iron industries (and *a fortiori* for lesser industries), the share of exports in production and their role in growth were less important and not decisive.

However, an exhaustive analysis ought also to take account of the terms of trade, the gains from trade[41], the multiplier effects and the backward linkages of export industries, the influence which the widening of the market could have had on industries which would have

---

[40] Bairoch, *Commerce extérieur*, p. 204.
[41] See Imlah, ch. 5, pp. 82ff.

functioned less efficiently in a purely national market. All this would have to be considered from the standpoints of the division of labour, of innovation, of the spread of machine and mass-production methods and of the transfer of resources towards high-productivity sectors. Conversely, British industry, which depended to a relatively high degree on external demand, was sensitive to all the hazards of the economic and political situation abroad, a fact which helped to make fluctuations within business cycles sharper, even though the diversity of Britain's markets, which were truly worldwide, often cushioned the effects. In all, the rise of exports was certainly an important factor, though less than is often thought, in the growth of the British economy in the nineteenth century (and notably in Victoria's reign) and in changes in its rate of growth[42].

However, exports are not an independent variable, and there remains the vexed question of the sources of their growth. For some writers, they appear to be a random variable, foreign demand for British goods being exogenous, determined independently of Britain by factors peculiar to her various markets. This position seems hardly tenable, except to explain some short-term fluctuations. Of course, a progress of exports such as Britain experienced in the nineteenth century cannot be imagined without development of the world economy as a whole, but the latter evolution was not independent of Britain, because she occupied such a dominant position. Therefore, according to other experts, the source of exports growth should be looked for 'at home rather than abroad' (Deane and Cole), i.e. first of all in the increase of British demand for foreign products, itself caused by the growth of population and the rise in per-capita incomes in Britain. Indeed, increased imports provided foreign countries with extra purchasing power, which enabled them to buy more British goods. Furthermore, the development of overseas countries, notably the 'new' or colonial countries, geared to supply the primary-produce needs of England and other industrialized countries, was often achieved thanks to British capital, which provided them with the means of payment they needed and led to the sale of British capital goods. In any case, every boom in exports of capital went hand in hand with a rise in British merchandise exports[43]. Moreover, Britain's internal economic

---

[42] Of course, in addition to the changes we have just mentioned in the balance between home and foreign demand, there were also changes in the role of the main industries in the expansion of exports, and also in the relative importance of the various foreign markets. Cf. Chapter 11, pp.349ff.

[43] Bairoch, *Commerce extérieur*, pp. 103 and 200. The coefficient of linear correlation in between net exports of capital by GB and the volume of her exports for the period 1830–1913 is positive and high: 0.918.

growth, which had taken off without much help from foreign trade, led in itself to higher productivity in industries capable of exporting or already exporting, and therefore to a fall in prices and a widening of external markets. Finally, at some moments in the first half of the nineteenth century at least, foreign markets were a sort of dumping ground for goods that the home market could not absorb, for manufacturers increased their exports to keep their factories busy.

THE PROBLEM OF FREE TRADE

One special aspect, but an important one, of the problem of the relationship between foreign trade and the growth of the economy (but which is also linked to the issue of institutional factors) is the question of the influence of free trade[44].

The adoption of free trade by Great Britain was an epoch-making event of the early Victorian era, but its application arrived relatively late in the nineteenth century. It had of course been demanded for a long time (the London merchants' petition of 1820 is an important step in this connection) by liberal economists and by powerful pressure groups in business circles, but other interests (especially the landowners) fiercely resisted these moves. Of course the rigorous protectionism that had been traditional in Britain and had been reinforced during the Napoleonic wars and again by the Corn Law of 1815 (which aimed at closing the British market to foreign cereals) had been slightly mitigated and simplified in the 1820s. Still, at the beginning of Victoria's reign, the protectionist system remained intact in its essentials. In 1840, 1146 articles attracted customs duties, even though only a handful of them provided the bulk of the customs revenue, which was equivalent to one-third of the value of net imports. It was in the 1840s that the break came, caused by a whole complex of factors. Amongst these were the action of a remarkably well-organized and influential lobby, the Anti-Corn Law League, the pressure of a difficult economic situation (in particular the famine in Ireland) and the initiative of a courageous and intelligent statesman, Sir Robert Peel. The latter, particularly by his budgets of 1842 and 1845, completely abolished customs duties on more than 700 articles, mostly raw materials, as well as the prohibitions on imports and exports which persisted, and he much reduced the duties that were imposed on many other goods, including many manufactured articles. Then in

[44] We shall not deal here with the history of its establishment, and we will come back later (Chapter 6, p.154) to the Corn Laws themselves. See B.Hilton, *Corn, Cash, Commerce: The Economic Policies of the Tory Governments, 1817–1830* (Oxford, 1977).

1846 he abolished the Corn Laws though it was political suicide for him. The antique and long sacrosanct Navigation Acts were abolished in 1849, and the last traces of protectionism and the 'old Colonial system', notably 'imperial preferences' in favour of sugar, coffee and timber coming from British possessions, were eliminated in the 1850s. Henceforth Great Britain opened herself up freely and on an equal footing to the goods of all nations, and she maintained customs duties, for purely fiscal ends, only on a small number of articles (forty-eight in 1860) which she did not produce herself (e.g. tea, coffee, wine, tobacco), or which she did produce but subjected to equivalent excise duties (e.g. beer and spirits).

Supporters of free trade had reckoned that the example set by England would be followed and imitated by her commercial partners in Europe, which were nearly all resolutely protectionist. These hopes were realized, but not at once. It was not until the Anglo-French treaty of commerce of 1860, and the network of treaties between France and many other countries that followed, whereby the same customs concessions were granted to Britain as to France, that a general liberalization of trade in Europe and a widespread low tariff area were established. It was liberalization rather than free trade in its strict sense (for no country went so far as England along the road of customs disarmament), but it nevertheless developed on a scale that had no equivalent before the third quarter of the twentieth century. So to the long period of universal protectionism there succeeded, according to Bairoch's happy expression, a phase of 'unilateral free trade' on Britain's part (from Peel's reforms to 1860), then another period of 'widely shared' free trade, starting in 1860. But this period was relatively short, for it ended between 1879 and 1892, the respective dates at which Germany and France (as well as other countries) returned to a protectionism that was often very strict. Consequently, after these years of transition, England, who remained faithful to free trade, found herself again in a position of 'unilateral free trade'[45].

The consequences for the British economy of the adoption of free trade have given rise to the liveliest discussions, both at the time and since, but a broad consensus of opinion has been reached by economic historians. It was expounded with particular brilliance some years ago by A.H. Imlah and can be summarized in the titles of two of his

---

[45]   Bairoch, *Commerce extérieur* pp. 39–54, 73–4, also C.P. Kindleberger, 'The rise of free trade in western Europe, 1820–1875', *Journal of Economic History*, XXXV(1), Mar. 1975, 20–55. Some historians make the mistake of considering British customs policy without taking into account this international context.

chapters: 'The failure of the British protectionist system' and 'The success of British free trade policy'[46].

According to these views, protectionism slowed up the growth of British exports and industrial production during the first decades of the nineteenth century. The Corn Laws restricted the widening of the home market for manufactured goods by keeping the cost of basic foodstuffs at a high level[47]. They also limited the purchasing power of foreign countries, notably those of northern Europe, which were exporters of cereals. Furthermore, imports of cereals, which were only called upon when scarcity menaced, were made most irregular. The extra purchasing power which accrued to the supplying countries did not lead to an immediate and equivalent rise in the purchase of British goods, because these imports were to a large extent paid in gold, so that the fall in English export prices was aggravated in years of poor harvests. The customs duties on many raw materials, which were imposed right up to Peel's reforms, were also a charge on industry. Broadly speaking, in the trade with many regions, British exports were the dependent variable in relation to imports, and the limits set on these by the protectionist policy could only be harmful to industry.

Theoretically this reasoning is faultless, but we often neglect to check whether facts agree with theory. Sir John Clapham emphasized in 1925[48] the fact that, up to the 1840s, Great Britain had no need to import grain regularly in large quantities. As for other goods, the import of which was prevented or limited by protectionism, it was mainly a question of foreign timber, sugar and coffee, silks and wine from France, linen from Germany, but even if they could have entered more freely, they would not have been imported in such increased quantities as to be capable of influencing seriously the level of British exports. Finally – and it is an important fact neglected by Imlah – most European countries (France, Austria and Russia in particular) had

---

[46] Imlah, Chs 5 and 6, pp. 114ff. Recently, Bairoch too (*Commerce extérieur* pp. 151, 163, 196–8, 200–1) has supported the view that the adoption of free trade had favourable results for England, at least until about 1880. But his standpoint is basically different from that of Imlah and the free-traders. Convinced that protectionism is necessary for the development of backward countries, he sees the period of trade-liberalization in the nineteenth century as a confrontation between a country that was already highly industrialized (Britain) and neighbours who were in the process of industrializing. This confrontation could only be advantageous to the former and harmful to the latter, and, according to Bairoch, caused a widening of the gap between England and the rest of Europe.

[47] Manufacturers who were free-traders also complained that the high cost of living in GB forced them to pay high wages, which, by raising their costs, restricted their outlets.

[48] J.H.Clapham, *An Economic History of Modern Britain* (3 vols, Cambridge, 1926–38), I pp. 479–81.

since 1815 adopted a resolutely protectionist policy (there has sometimes been talk of a 'Second Continental Blockade'), while on the other hand, English goods could fairly easily penetrate some parts of Europe through the Netherlands and several German states; 'no amount of tariff manipulation or reciprocity could have opened European markets very much wider'.

However, one must admit that protectionism had some negative effects upon the British economy, but it cannot have been serious. Furthermore, the *volume* of British exports rose between 1814 and 1846 at an annual average rate of 4.3 per cent, which was quite fast, and very little below the rate achieved after the establishment of free trade, i.e. 4.7 per cent for the period 1846–73. A detailed analysis of trade statistics, using the deviations from the long-term trend, shows up a phase of fairly slow growth from 1815 to 1826, then a period of acceleration and very rapid growth at a rate of 5.6 per cent, which lasted till 1856, and finally, after this date, a slowing-down (only 3.8 per cent from 1856 to 1873), despite the boom that ended in 1873. So the changes of rhythm in the growth of export volumes seem to be independent of tariff policy, and the small difference between the rates for the periods 1814–46 and 1846–73 does not conform to Imlah's thesis that the establishment of free trade powerfully stimulated British exports and gave them phenomenal and unprecedented growth, thus confirming the forecasting of the economists who had preached free trade[49]. None the less, there was phenomenal growth after 1845 (the exact turning-point was 1848) in the *value* of exports; its rate jumped from 1.1 per cent per annum for 1814–46 to 5.7 per cent for 1846–73; but this change is to be explained by the reversed trend in export prices, which had fallen during the first half of the nineteenth century, but rose from 1852 onwards. This reversal had various causes, the most important of them being monetary, and it does not seem to have been linked to the establishment of free trade[50].

In any case, it would be unwise to take only aggregates into account and not to explore by a more detailed analysis how far the advantages

[49]   Imlah has moreover made a serious error in the calculations on which his judgement is based. For his rates of growth are underestimated for 1816–42 and overestimated for 1842–73. As before, the rates of growth are calculated by the method of exponential adjustment. For support of our conclusions, see Church, *The Great Victorian Boom*, p. 61, and p. 311 (table 83), in Deane and Cole.

[50]   Doubtless the same was true of the boom in the early 1850s. Bairoch, *Commerce extérieur*, pp. 190–3, 195, 201, 296–8, 300–1, 310) attributes it to 'unilateral free trade', but recognizes that it was exports to the British empire and especially to Australia (as the result of the discovery of gold), which were mainly responsible for the increase of total exports.

which were expected by the supporters of free trade were in fact obtained, as has been very effectively done by R. Church[51]. The free-traders' calculation was that the increase in imports into Britain thanks to free trade – and above all in the import of grain, the only important commodity that was likely to be imported in greatly increased quantities from abroad – would widen the home and foreign markets for British industry.

In the first place lower price of foodstuffs would increase the domestic demand for other products, i.e. manufactured goods. However, this fall did not in fact come about before the 1870s, for various reasons. There was the breakdown in exports from Russia and the United States caused by the Crimean war and the American civil war, the absence of large cereal surpluses in the world, and excessive transport costs for grain coming from distant countries. Free trade did not start an era of cheap food, and so it was not in a position to stimulate domestic demand for manufactured articles. On the other hand, given the continuous increase in Britain's population, cereal prices might have risen sharply if the Corn Laws had not been repealed, a situation which would have reduced the consumption of non-food articles. In fact, wheat imports increased considerably and covered an increasing percentage of consumption, so that overall the repeal of the Corn Laws was not without importance for the home market[52].

Free-traders had also gambled on the multiplier-effect of increased imports of cereals and other foodstuffs, which would give rising purchasing power to countries supplying Britain, thus stimulating her exports[53]. In fact one does not observe any spectacular jump in English exports to the three main suppliers of cereals – Russia, Prussia and the United States – in spite of the increase in grain purchases from these countries. But it is possible that Britain benefited indirectly, within the multilateral trading framework[54].

As for the liberalization of commerce in Europe following on the 1860

---

[51] Church, *The Great Victorian Boom*, pp. 58–65.

[52] In addition, the crisis for British agriculture which had been anticipated did not occur until the 1870s. Bairoch reckons that, before then, a cost-benefit analysis of the repeal shows that British GNP was slightly increased by it.

[53] Moreover, according to Imlah, the reduction (following the abolition of customs duties) of the gap between British domestic prices and the export prices of the suppliers, benefited mainly the latter. The grain trade lost its spasmodic character, which assured more stable markets in the grain-supplying countries.

[54] Church (*The Great Victorian Boom* p. 66) thinks that the liberalization of trade in Europe may have raised the global level of international commerce, and through multilateral mechanisms may have contributed to the expansion of English trade with overseas countries.

treaty with France, its effects should not be overestimated. Exports to France did, indeed, increase sharply at first, but this rise soon slowed down. The tariff concessions granted by the treaties between France and other countries only became effective about 1865. Though British trade with Europe increased, continental products did not flood the English market nor vice versa. Judging from the structure of British exports to Europe (coal, semi-finished goods, machinery), their increase resulted mostly from the industrialization of continental countries. There is no proof that this increase was stimulated by that of imports into Britain. On the contrary, the latter seem to have become a variable dependent on the sale of goods and services by England.

There is also the jump in British trade with the Middle East, Asia and Australia, which in each case had specific causes not directly linked with free trade[55]. We must also remember the influence on trade expansion of the railways and of steam-navigation, which reduced transport costs, opened up new markets and created an increased demand for British capital goods.

Church concludes that in the matter of free trade's influence on British growth in the mid-Victorian era 'all we can say is that on the basis of empirical evidence a positive judgement seems to be unwarranted'[56]. This is an opinion which this writer is inclined to accept, with the reservation that a positive judgement does not seem to him out of the question[57]. However, we have only dealt so far with the medium-run effects of free trade, up to the beginning of the 1870s, and its possible influence in the long run must also be considered. The most obvious effect was the arrival of the cheap food era which had been promised by free-traders, but in fact was postponed by a quarter of a century until the times when low-priced foodstuffs from the 'new' countries overseas invaded the unprotected British market in the 1870s. The results were twofold. On one side – and this was the positive aspect – the cost of food fell sharply, and from then onwards was at a lower level than in other countries, for Great Britain continued until very recently to feed herself from world markets at the lowest prices. Real wages also rose, in spite of the Great Depression. On the other side, the nation's agriculture, or at least its cereal sector, was

[55] Yet see the preceding note.
[56] Church, *The Great Victorian Boom*, p. 65.
[57] As for the views of Bairoch (see note 45), according to which the period of generalized free trade was more unfavourable to continental countries than to England, just because of this zenith of liberalism, they seem to be open to challenge. Although there was a general slow-down in growth in the 1860s, his figures do not prove that it was more marked on the continent than in Britain, and the crisis of agriculture only appeared in the 1870s.

sacrificed. As, even before the crisis, agriculture had become of minor importance in the economy, it is generally considered that the balance of these developments was mostly in England's favour, though Bairoch has recently argued that the fall in agricultural incomes, and consequently in rural demand for manufactured goods, was not without importance.

In other respects, the consequences of England's loyalty to free trade, at a time when most other countries from 1879 onwards were returning to protectionism and when many were industrializing, are not altogether clear (for, once again, the international context is important). In theory, results ought to have been favourable. British industry, subjected to growing competition at home and abroad, gave up activities for which it was not properly endowed and the continuance of which, in the shelter of a protective wall, would have been expensive for the community, while her traditional staple industries, which were certainly very competitive around 1870, were forced to keep in the forefront of progress. Meanwhile, the increase in imports and the export of capital opened up ever-widening foreign markets, which again improved British competitiveness.

But in actual fact this model was far from working. The British staple industries did not remain in the forefront of technical progress, and the British did not develop, or did not develop fast enough, new industries with a future – which would probably have required protection. On the other hand, new industrial powers enjoyed faster growth than England and caught up with her technically – and it is not impossible that, as Bairoch maintains, protectionism contributed to their progress. Their exports, which grew decidedly faster than England's, competed dangerously with British goods in world markets. These countries rapidly increased their sales of manufactured articles to Britain herself, while at the same time restraining their purchases of British goods, so that England's balance of trade in manufactured goods with industrialized and protectionist countries showed a heavy deficit. Bairoch maintains that the asymmetry of tariff policies between the United Kingdom (unilaterally free-trading) and other countries (more and more protectionist) was a major factor in the slowing-down of British growth during the Great Depression and at the beginning of the twentieth century[58]. According to this argument free trade would seem to have been harmful to Great Britain. This

[58] See Bairoch, *Commerce extérieur*, pp. 51, 53–4 (table 16), 151, 162, 201–17, 301. He reckons that between 1873/7 and 1893/7, the direct losses of outlets in industrialized countries might have slowed down the growth of English industry by 0.4 per cent per annum.

problem will be considered again later, but Imlah himself admits that, during the Great Depression, the advantages of free trade were less evident than in the preceding period. Furthermore, this was the opinion of a fair number of industrialists at the time, who were increasingly worried from the 1880s onwards by the stiffening of foreign competition and who lost sympathy for free trade. Some politicians felt the same, notably Joseph Chamberlain, who in 1903 was to launch a crusade, abortive as it turned out, in favour of tariff reform, i.e. a disguised protectionism. Anyway, one of the chief conditions that had assured the triumph of free trade, England's uncontested industrial superiority, had vanished at the end of Victoria's reign. But, because of the electors' attachment to the policy of cheap food, and also because of the recovery in exports at the beginning of the twentieth century, free trade was to prevail until 1914, and in practice until 1931.

To sum up, when Britain chose free trade, she gave up quite consciously the last remnants of the mercantilist imperial policy that she had pursued since the end of the seventeenth century, but that policy was in fact doomed following the independence of the Thirteen Colonies and the beginnings of the Industrial Revolution, in favour of accepting imports from the cheapest sources anywhere in the world; this contributed to strengthening the original character of her economic structure. For she had an economy that was open and specialized, pushing very far the international division of labour, abandoning primary production (except for coal), concentrating on industry (with special emphasis on a few staple industries), services and on an international trade founded on the exchange of manufactured goods against foodstuffs and raw materials. Free trade can be seen as a factor both of mid-Victorian prosperity and of late Victorian depression, but one can also believe that changes in tariff policy had only minor direct effects, and that on the whole free trade had little importance for the growth of the British economy[59].

---

[59]   This is D.N.McCloskey's opinion, in 'Magnanimous Albion: free trade and British national income, 1841–1881', *Explorations in Economic History*, 17(3), July 1980, 303–20. Using econometric methods, he comes to the conclusion that because of England's dominance in world trade in the middle of the nineteenth century, the demand for her exports and the supply of goods which she imported were inelastic; the growth of her imports was liable to turn the terms of trade against her, cancelling the advantages of her increased trade. Free trade may have reduced her national product by 6 per cent between 1846 and 1880, which, he says, is neither negligible nor disastrous. He concludes that free trade did not favour England, but the damage was limited. At any rate it was not one of the causes of her growth.

CAPITAL FORMATION

Capital formation means investment in physical assets (including stocks of goods, but excluding securities)[60]; its most important component in a modern economy is the formation of fixed capital, i.e. the addition of assets which are used for production over a period longer than the year in which they have been acquired. It includes the improvement of such assets but not their maintenance and repairs. In addition, by an extension of the meaning of the terms 'production' and 'productive', one includes investment in houses and buildings of every kind, but neither household durables, such as motor-cars today, which are regarded as consumer goods, nor military material and buildings. In general one considers mostly *gross* fixed-capital formation, which includes, besides new additions, expenditure incurred in replacing equipment that is scrapped or destroyed. To the formation of fixed capital is added the increase in stocks and work in progress; the total produces domestic capital formation[61]. But account must also be taken of *net* investment abroad[62] to obtain total capital formation.

This, and especially the fixed-capital formation, was an important factor (even though there is argument about its precise importance) in the growth of modern economies that arose out of the Industrial Revolution. One of the reasons for the rise in productivity and living standards in these economies was that the labour-force had at its disposal a growing stock of capital, and particularly machinery and other tools, to support its physical effort. Besides, it is investment which embodies technological progress and puts it into practice[63]. Moreover, capital and its accumulation have played a central role in the theories of economic development of the classical theorists, beginning with Adam Smith, and also of Karl Marx. More recently, after the second world war, economists who concentrated their attention on problems of long-term growth revived classical theory, and again attributed a central role in the growth-process to the accumulation of capital. In particular, according to a simple Harrod-

---

[60] Except where foreign investment is concerned, which includes both physical assets and portfolio investments.

[61] That is to say productive goods situated in the country in question. But it includes ships belonging to the residents of that country; Feinstein, *National Income*, p. 182.

[62] Or the balance of exports and imports of capital.

[63] But the two phenomena are not necessarily linked. One can replace or increase existing capital without improving productivity. D.H.Aldcroft, in D.H.Aldcroft and P.Fearon, *Economic Growth in 20th Century Britain* (London, 1969), p. 43 thinks that this is just what happened in the British staple industries at the end of the nineteenth and beginning of the twentieth century, when investment was made in unchanged technology.

Domar model, the increase in the rate of capital formation, i.e. of the share of national product devoted to investment, was considered to be the central phenomenon of the Industrial Revolution[64]. Arthur Lewis in 1954 and above all W.W. Rostow in 1956 and 1961 asserted that this Revolution had been a 'sudden acceleration' in the rate of capital formation, which was indispensable to the increase in real income per head. This rate roughly doubled, climbing from the 4 per cent or 5 per cent characteristic of traditional economies to 10 per cent and more, which is the level in modern industrial economies[65].

This hypothesis, or rather intuition–for in the case of Britain it rested on no precise quantitative data–was roughly true, but Rostow's mistake was to think that this doubling had occurred in a dramatic fashion during a short period of twenty years or so between 1783 and 1802[66]. As was demonstrated by his critics, and notably Phyllis Deane whose views have long gained wide acceptance, the change was much slower and more gradual.

The annual average rate of capital formation would seem to have risen from 3 per cent, at the end of the seventeenth century and beginning of the eighteenth, to 5 or 6 per cent in the 1770s. It certainly showed an increase in the next two decades, but a moderate one, going no higher than the 6–7 per cent bracket around 1800. It probably dropped at the end of the French wars and during the depression which followed. It was only in the middle of the 1830s that a genuine change in the level of investment took place, resulting from railway-building, which demanded heavy investment (including outlays in sectors which had links with railways, such as the iron industry), from the spread of machinery and from urbanization. The rate of capital formation increased considerably and reached a permanent level of over 10 per cent after 1850[67].

These views tallied with the results of other empirical studies dealing with various advanced countries in the nineteenth century,

[64] The abundance of capital in England, and the speed of its accumulation were considered as decisive factors explaining the early start of the Industrial Revolution in England, as a number of historians had already suggested.

[65] The debates on this problem are summarized in the introduction to F.Crouzet (ed.), *Capital Formation in the Industrial Revolution* (London, 1972), to which the reader is referred. Detailed references to quoted works will be found there. See also P.Deane, 'The role of capital in the Industrial Revolution', *Explorations in Economic History*, 10(4), Summer 1973, 350–4; on the methodological difficulties in studying these problems. (We have not been able to take into account the important chapter by C.H. Feinstein, 'Capital formation in Great Britain', in P.Mathias and M.M.Postan (eds), *The Cambridge Economic History of Europe*, VII, part I (Cambridge 1978), pp.28–96.

[66] It is the celebrated 'take-off', whose reality is rarely accepted nowadays.

[67] Reaching only then the level which had been considered necessary for the take-off.

where the rates of capital formation had also increased very gradually. They also agreed with the econometric analysis of the recent growth of advanced economies (of which only a limited fraction resulted from the increase in physical capital) and with the new views of theoreticians who put in question the central role of capital formation in growth and rather underlined the importance of improving capital's quality and efficiency[68]. Moreover, the technical and structural changes associated with the Industrial Revolution, which rendered industry more capital-intensive, had long been concentrated in a small number of branches (e.g. cotton-spinning, iron-making) and they could not have had a sizeable impact on the total rate of investment[69]. This was all the more so given the nature of technology at the beginning of the Industrial Revolution, when fixed equipment was relatively simple and cheap, and various expedients enabled expenditure to be limited in this area. Moreover it was sectors other than manufacturing industry, notably agriculture and transport, which absorbed the largest share of investment, and even within industry the need for working capital was greater than for fixed capital. So the Industrial Revolution in England would seem to have been realized with investments that were neither massive nor suddenly increased as a percentage of the national income. They did, indeed, increase strongly in absolute terms, notably those in fixed capital, but so did production, and they only absorbed a modest proportion of national product[70].

Yet the debate is by no means closed. In 1965, S. Pollard had strongly criticized the sources and methods of Phyllis Deane and had presented some 'orders of magnitude' for gross formation of capital in

[68] The increase of capital was certainly *one* of the sources of growth, but there has been a recent tendency to insist on other sources and especially on the 'residual', i.e. technical and scientific progress and the development of education. In any case, the relationship between *levels* of capital formation and *rates* of growth of production is not simple, direct or uniform.

[69] It is true that in these branches investment increased very rapidly – at rates which may have been 5 or 6 per cent per annum. Now economists have recently underlined the importance of the growth of the stock of capital which embodies innovations. So we have probably been wrong to concentrate on global rates of capital formation and not to examine it in the main industries; but there is work in progress on this subject. See J.P. Higgins and S.Pollard, *Aspects of Capital Investment in Britain, 1750–1850: A Preliminary Survey* (London, 1971); D.T.Jenkins, *The West Riding Wool Textile Industry, 1770–1835: A Study of Fixed-Capital Formation* (Edington, 1975).

[70] The Industrial Revolution would not be the result of an acceleration in capital accumulation. The opposite was rather the case. But one must also take account (Deane and Cole, p. 304) of the more effective and productive use of savings, which can have more influence on growth than a stronger propensity to save. In the substitution of the factory system for the domestic system, a better use of capital, an elimination of under-used capacity and a growing efficiency of production goods were inherent.

Britain which implied percentages relative to gross national income distinctly higher than those of Phyllis Deane – 6.5 per cent around 1770, 9 per cent around 1790/3, 8 per cent around 1815 and 11 per cent at the beginning of the 1830s[71]. Although some of these figures seem inflated, they admittedly make one think that Phyllis Deane's are too low. Indeed, Charles Feinstein has recently expressed the same conclusion, starting from estimates and calculations whose meticulousness cannot fail to impress[72]. In his view the proportion of total investment to gross domestic product in Britain (ten-year averages) probably rose from 8 per cent in 1761/70 to 14 per cent in the 1790s, so increasing sharply during the beginnings of the Industrial Revolution. It then remained stable at 13 or 14 per cent up to the 1850s[73]. During the last thirty years of the eighteenth century, the rate of gross fixed-capital formation rose from 7 to 11 per cent, to stabilize itself then at 10 or 11 per cent[74], without being affected by the railway booms of the 1840s and 1850s.

So the level of capital formation at the beginning of the Victorian era remains uncertain, and it may have been either relatively low, as Deane suggests, or fairly high, if one follows Pollard and Feinstein[75]. However, the main problem for the study of the Victorian period is the variation in this level. In this respect, we have annual series, some calculated by Phyllis Deane (from 1830 onwards), others by Charles Feinstein (from 1856 onwards). The average rates of capital formation by decades that result from these calculations are presented in table 27[76]. But these averages must not hide the fact that investment underwent sharp cyclical fluctuations both in absolute figures and as

[71]   Which gives for fixed-capital formation respective rates of 5, 7.5, 7 and 8.5 per cent. Cf. S.Pollard, 'The growth and distribution of capital in Great Britain, c.1770–1870', *Troisième conférence internationale d'histoire économique, Munich 1965*, (Paris–The Hague, 1968), I, pp. 335–65.
[72]   Feinstein, 'Capital formation', p. 31 (table 28).
[73]   These calculations are made at constant prices of 1851/60, while those of Deane and Pollard were at current prices. But the ratios to GNP would be little less. Feinstein puts forward these figures with commendable prudence.
[74]   Apart from a fall during the first wartime decade of the nineteenth century. Yet the stability of the rate during the 'railway era' is surprising – unless there was a sharp fall of investment in other sectors.
[75]   This difference has important consequences for social history. It has often been argued that one cause of widespread poverty during the first half of the nineteenth century was the high level of investment, which forced restrictions on consumption. This hypothesis seemed to have been destroyed by the work of Phyllis Deane. Perhaps it deserves renewed attention.
[76]   Let us refer for the record to the older calculations of Deane and Cole, p. 308 (table 82), and Kuznets, p. 236 (table 5.3) (which only starts in 1860–9). They both give rates of fixed-capital and total-capital formation much higher than those of Deane.

Table 27   Gross capital formation in the UK (ten-year averages as percentages of GNP)

	1	2	3	4	5	6
	After Deane			After Feinstein		
	Gross fixed capital formation	Net investment abroad	Total 1 + 2	Gross fixed capital formation	Net investment abroad	Total 4 + 5[(a)]
1830–9	4.1	0.9	5.0			
1840–9	6.0	0.7	6.7			
1850–9[(b)]	5.4	2.2	7.6			
1860–9	5.8	2.9	8.7	7.5		
1870–9	6.5	3.9	10.4	7.6	4.1	11.7 (13.0)
1880–9	5.6	4.9	10.5	6.0	4.8	10.8 (12.0)
1890–9	6.0	3.2	9.2	6.9	3.4	10.3 (11.6)
1900–9	6.4	4.0	10.4	8.0	3.8	11.8 (12.1)
1905–14	5.2	6.8	12.0	6.1	6.7	12.8 (13.7)

(a) Figures in brackets include the increase in stocks and work in progress (which varies between 0.3 per cent and 1.3 per cent of GNP) and are therefore those of total capital formation. Deane has not calculated an annual series of this type, but reckons (p. 99) that investment in stock would increase the rates in column 3 by 1 or 2 per cent.
(b) For 1856–9, the rate of fixed-capital formation was 5.3 per cent according to Deane's data, 5.5 per cent according to Feinstein's.
N. B. These rates are those of investment-expenditure in relation to GNP at current prices. If one calculates the rate of fixed-capital formation in relation to GNP at constant prices (1900) (from Feinstein, *National Income,* table 5, T. 14–15, cols. 5 and 10), one gets marginally higher percentages, the difference being under 10 per cent.
Sources
Columns 1 and 2: Deane, 'New estimates', 99 (table 3), 'Disposition of expenditure generating gross national product at market price'; she points out that the rates would be slightly higher (1 per cent maximum) if GNP at factor cost was used.

Column 4: Feinstein, *National Income,* table 39, T. 85–6, col. 6 (same data, table 3, T. 8, col. 3).

Column 5: ibid., table 15, T. 37–8, col. 16.
In these tables, Feinstein gives annual totals of investment (as well as, in table 2, col. 4, the increase in stocks). The percentages of their ten-year averages in relation to those of GNP have been calculated from Feinstein's series in his tables 1, T. 4, col. 11, for 1856–70, and 3, T. 10, col. 7, from 1870 onwards. This choice is based on B. R. Mitchell, *European Historical Statistics* (London, 1975) pp. 782, 790. But the first part of the series is at factor-cost, the second at market prices.

percentage of GNP[77]. Furthermore, some writers have identified long cycles in the growth of capital stock, which are to be found also in the United States, e.g. from 1895 to 1914, with a maximum in 1900–3[78].

There are obvious differences between the rates of fixed-capital

[77] See Chapter 3, p. 63, on the distinction between 'major' cycles – at the peaks of which investment decisions were taken – and 'minor' cycles.
[78] R.C.O. Matthews, 'Some aspects of post-war growth in the British economy in relation to historical experience', in Aldcroft and Fearon, p. 85.

formation given by Deane and those given by Feinstein, the latter (which seem more reliable) being noticeably and consistently higher than the former[79]. None the less, the share of national product devoted to fixed investment seems 'astonishingly low'[80], which can partly explain why the growth of British national product during the nineteenth century, although sustained, was relatively slow[81]. Furthermore, it showed no tendency to increase, except, if we follow Deane, for a leap in the 1830s and 1840s as a result of the railway boom. This share seems to have diminished slightly later, before reaching a maximum in the 1870s[82]. There was a distinct drop in the 1880s and at the beginning of the 1890s (probably in connection with the slow-down in growth); then a record level was reached at the turn of the century (7 per cent according to Deane for 1895–1904, 8 per cent according to Feinstein for 1900–9), but a renewed reduction on the eve of the first world war[83]. Deane observes that, even if one takes into account the increase of stocks, which she estimates at between 1 and 2 per cent of national product, gross domestic investment in the United Kingdom never passed (or even reached) 10 per cent of national product in any decade before 1914[84]. As Feinstein, in his calculation of this increase of stocks, reckons that it never exceeded 1.3 per cent of national product (ten-year average), the broad conclusion is the same, in spite of higher percentages for the formation of fixed capital.

It is true that foreign investment, whose increase was very rapid,

[79]   A detailed analysis of these differences by Feinstein, pp. 191–5. They result both from estimates of investment and from series of GNP which are used. Deane seems to have very much underestimated investment in industry and trade; but she does include investment for defence, particularly in warships.

[80]   Subject to a probable revision of Feinstein's data. In 'Capital formation', he presents estimates of capital formation which are not only much higher than those of Deane ('New estimates') for the 1830s, but also higher for the years 1856–60 than those which appear in his work of 1972. As he has kindly told us, this implies an upward revision of his series used for table 27, col.4.

[81]   Since the second world war, the gross formation of fixed capital in advanced countries has been of the order of 20 to 25 per cent of GNP.

[82]   We have seen above (according to Church, *The Great Victorian Boom*, pp. 36–8) that investment proportions in the so-called mid-Victorian boom were not very different from those of the periods before and after. On the other hand, Bairoch, *Commerce extérieur*, pp. 195, 199, 202, sees very rapid progress in domestic formation of capital, but he takes into account mostly short-term changes.

[83]   According to Feinstein, *National Income*, table 48.T.108, col.5, net fixed-capital formation, at constant prices of 1900, fluctuated violently as follows (annual averages):

	£m		£m
1860/9	15	1890/9	57
1870/9	39	1900/9	92
1880/9	27	1905/13	48

[84]   Deane, 'New estimates', 99–100.

complemented domestic investment; this was insignificant in relation to national product up to the middle of the nineteenth century, but it formed a large part of total investment after 1870. This share roughly fluctuated in inverse proportion to the rate of domestic capital formation, but eventually it surpassed the latter. The problems raised by these massive outflows of capital will be examined later; it has been pointed out already that they were a stimulus to the export of British goods, but on the other hand it is possible that they restricted the amount of domestic investment, notably in industry[85].

In any case, because of the additional and growing rate of savings, total gross capital formation increased during the Victorian era. Deane estimates it at about 8 per cent of gross GNP in the 1830s, at 10 per cent in the 1850s and at a maximum of more than 13 per cent in the decade 1869–78[86]. Feinstein arrives at a similar rate for this decade. Then, his rate falls (as does Deane's) and is under 12 per cent for the 1890s, but it rises to a peak close to 14 per cent in the last ten years before the war; however, more than half of total investment at that time was devoted to investment abroad.

Altogether, these proportions are far from high, and they remained pretty stable from mid-century onwards. Whenever a transfer from consumption to investment occurred (a characteristic of the Industrial Revolution), whether it was at the end of the eighteenth century or at the beginning of the railway era, this transfer from unproductive to productive purposes was limited in scale. The economic growth of Victorian England was achieved with a low and stable level of savings and investment, as well as with a slow growth in capital stock. The rate of the latter, according to Feinstein's data, was on average only 1.4 per cent per annum between 1855/7 and 1900/2, and 1.5 per cent between 1855/7 and 1911/13[87].

But there were appreciable inter-sectoral transfers in the allocation of invested capital and the structure of capital formation. Firstly, as compared with the period at the beginning of the Industrial Revolution, a fairly big relative reduction of investment in stocks and work in progress was possible, because of acceleration in the production process (due mainly to the disappearance of the domestic system) and improvements in transport; but this investment still represented 10

---

[85] Cf. Chapter 11. It is true that interest and dividends of earlier foreign investments were more than enough to cover new overseas investment.

[86] P. Deane, *The Industrial Revolution in England, 1700–1914* (London, 1969), pp. 51–2.

[87] From the index (at constant prices, of course) of Feinstein, *National Income*, table 20, T.51–2, col.3. See also Matthews (table 1), which gives a rate of growth of capital stock of 1.3 per cent per annum between 1856 and 1899.

per cent of total capital formation in the 1870s and 7 per cent in 1905/14. Conversely, foreign investment, which had only exceeded 10 per cent of the total during short periods in the first half of the nineteenth century, saw its share then increase sharply, though irregularly. It exceeded 20 per cent in the 1850s, came near to one-third in the 1870s and, after a sudden jump, passed the half-way mark on the eve of the first world war.

As far as the structure of gross domestic fixed capital was concerned, investment in transport and communication[88] consistently took the lion's share, according to Deane's data, from the 1840s onwards. Its percentage of the total, which had previously been fairly stable, increased sharply after 1830. In the 1840s, 1850s and 1860s this sector absorbed more than half of fixed-capital investment. Its share later diminished with the completion of the railway system, but it was still 39 per cent in 1905/14[89].

The second largest component was 'social capital', i.e. mainly housing[90]. It had the largest share up to the 1830s, but it then passed to second position and oscillated between 21 and 31 per cent of the total. So more than three-quarters of expenditures in fixed-capital formation during the Victorian era went to the building of the basic infra-structure of a highly industrialized and urbanized economy. On the other hand, a fairly small proportion, only exceeding one-quarter very occasionally and sometimes dropping below one-fifth, was devoted to directly productive investment in industry[91].

This conclusion has been strongly challenged by Feinstein. His figures for investment in industry and trade are much higher than Deane's, reaching 35 per cent of the total in 1882–9 and passing 45 per cent at the beginning of the twentieth century[92]. In particular, he has calculated expenditure on plant and machinery which is high, and, as

---

[88] Roads, canals, railways, port installations, ships, vehicles of all kinds, telegraph and telephones.

[89] Deane, 'New estimates', 101 (table 4). Before 1830, the share of this sector was probably 20 to 30 per cent. It rose to 37 per cent for 1830/9 and 59 per cent for 1840/9. Pollard (p. 362 (table IV)), and Feinstein, *National Income*, give lower percentages for the transport sector in the 1830s.

[90] But also public buildings, such as schools, hospitals, asylums and drainage systems.

[91] Deane, 'New estimates', 101–2. She includes state expenditure for military and administrative establishments, but this did not become considerable until after 1900.

[92] Feinstein, *National Income*, tables 39 and 41, T.85–6, 91–2; also pp. 194–5. He includes in this sector investment in agriculture (e.g. buildings, land improvement) which Deane neglected. It is true that it had been constantly declining in percentage terms since the end of the eighteenth century and in the end became very small. We have included in these percentages investment in water, gas and electricity systems. Feinstein, 'Capital formation', and Pollard give high percentages for this industrial and commercial sector at the beginning of the nineteenth century and in the 1830s.

a percentage of total fixed-capital formation, generally over 25 per cent from the 1850s onwards[93]. Conversely, in his view, the share of transport and communications, although it roughly doubled after the 1830s, was about 10 per cent less than Deane's figures – 39 per cent in the 1880s against Deane's 49 per cent, 29 per cent for 1905/14 against 39 per cent. On the other hand, his percentages for social capital, and notably housing, are fairly close to Deane's[94].

To sum up, it was just before and at the beginning of the Victorian era that important changes occurred in the structure and formation of fixed capital, with the increasing share of investment in industry (and notably in plant and machinery), then the steep rise in transport investment during the 1840s as the result of massive railway-building and a compensatory retreat of social capital. These conclusions seem incontrovertible, but beyond that, given the disagreements between experts[95], it is difficult to make any firm assertions. Certainly there is broad agreement that structural changes were small, but the big question mark is the relative importance of investment in industry, which was small according to Deane and large according to Feinstein. Thus Deane gives most weight to the transport sector and Feinstein to the industrial and commercial sector (apart from the 1840s). On the other hand, if we consider the overall rate of capital formation, the main undoubted fact is the very marked increase in foreign investment, which is the great change that came about during the Victorian age.

Be that as it may[96], the relatively low level of capital formation in England during the nineteenth century must be stressed[97]. As it has already been remarked, this could be one of the reasons for the relatively low rate of actual growth in national product. But this role must probably not be overestimated, because of the continuous fall (as pointed out above) in the capital/output ratio in the course of the

[93] But his 'Capital formation' does not confirm these high percentages, although it shows a relative rise of investment in machinery from the end of the eighteenth century.

[94] More than a quarter from 1880 onwards (Feinstein, *National Income*, table 41,T.91–2) for the whole 'social capital', 15 to 20 per cent for housing alone from the 1850s to the beginning of the twentieth century.

[95] And, what is more, between the views of Feinstein in 1972 and 1978 (i.e. between *National Income* and 'Capital formation'). And for the 1830s there are also serious divergences between him, Deane and Pollard!

[96] But, we repeat, contingent on the eventual publication of a completely new series by Feinstein.

[97] Which surprises Deane and Cole themselves, pp. 305–6, 308, who point out that, in spite of this, the basic capital of the British economy was completely transformed in the thirty or forty years after 1830.

nineteenth century, i.e. the percentage of national product that had to be invested to increase production by a given fraction never ceased to diminish. It is a mistake to think that the Industrial Revolution was dominated by innovations that required large amounts of capital. The falling price of machinery and other equipment tended towards a saving of capital[98]. To the reduction in price of plant was added continuous improvement in its quality, which meant that the produc-tivity of the capital stock improved progressively over time, for new capital and a large proportion of replacement capital embodied technological progress. Many experts nowadays tend to think that the essential characteristic of the nineteenth century was the constant flow of every type of innovation; gains in productivity and production stemmed more from the improvement in the *quality* than the quantity of inputs, and capital formation was less important than the way capital was used[99].

DEMOGRAPHY AND ECONOMIC GROWTH

To what extent could the large increase in Great Britain's population during the nineteenth century have been a major factor in her economic growth? The annual average rate of demographic increase, about 1 per cent, could account for roughly half the growth rate of GNP, which ran at about 2 per cent. Increase in population does in fact boost both effective domestic demand and available manpower. It also brings economies of scale, e.g. in transport, and facilitates the division of labour.

It is generally thought nowadays that the outset of the demographic upsurge in England (around 1750) predated the real beginnings of the Industrial Revolution, which came twenty or thirty years later; thus disconnecting demographic change from the Economic Revolution, all the more so seeing that the most likely cause of this demographic change was the lowering of the death-rate, which was probably not the result of economic changes linked to the Industrial Revolution. On the other hand, the onset of rapid population growth must have been one of

[98]   See the article by M.Blaug, 'The productivity of capital in the Lancashire cotton industry during the nineteenth century', *Economic History Review*, 2nd series, XII(3), Apr. 1961, 358–81, which shows that innovations increase real capital per worker, but not per unit of production. Also Deane, 'The role of capital', 364.

[99]   See Matthews, p. 81 (table 1). From 1856 to 1899 the growth of gross domestic product per worker was 1.1 per cent per annum. Out of this, only 0.2 per cent resulted from the increase of capital at the disposal of each worker, and 0.9 per cent from the 'residual', i.e. from technical progress. N.B. A special but important aspect of capital formation – railway investment – will be studied in Chapter 9. The financing of investments will be dealt with in Chapter 10.

the factors (a) in the modest but real progress in economic activity between 1750 and 1780, and (b) in the speeding-up of economic growth at the end of the eighteenth century and of the changes which made up the Industrial Revolution. The latter was given an external stimulus by the demographic boom; but, on the other side, without the increase in employment opportunities and the availability of foodstuffs thanks to the Industrial and Agricultural Revolutions, the population increase would soon have come up against the Malthusian check[100].

In the nineteenth century, the acceleration of demographic growth and later the maintenance of a high rate of population-growth would have exercised the same stimulating effect, with the additional help of urbanization. The inhabitant of towns, which absorbed nearly the whole of the increase in population, normally has a higher propensity to consume than the country-dweller; and the redistribution of population stimulated building and its ancillary activities in every region which benefited from it. Moreover, the sharp increase in Britain's population, which could not be fed by British agriculture, while industry needed increasing quantities of imported raw materials, led to a large rise in the purchase of primary produce abroad, and notably in the new countries overseas. The latter were thus provided with increased purchasing power which guaranteed the growth of British exports. Furthermore, the import of cheap foodstuffs contributed to the rise in real incomes and so to the widening of the domestic market for manufactured goods. The British demographic boom would have contributed to the formation of a world economy that was unified under British domination, and it also brought optimism to industrialists, by offering the prospect of a domestic market in constant expansion.[101]

In fact things were probably much more complex, and indeed, both on the theoretical and empirical plane, the causal relationship between demographic development and economic change remains a subject for discussion. It depends on the structure both of the population and of the economy of the country concerned, and it certainly does not work in only one direction.

It may be that in the eighteenth century the British economy, and notably industry, suffered from a shortage of labour in relation to capital and that this situation, by creating bottlenecks, contributed to the search for and the adoption of labour-saving innovations. But this shortage had certainly disappeared after 1815, and Sir John Habak-

---

[100] Perkin, p. 102.
[101] See especially N.Tranter, *Population Since the Industrial Revolution: The Case of England and Wales* (London, 1973), Ch.5, 'Population and the economy', pp.133ff.

kuk, in a famous book, has maintained that after this date there was an excess of skilled labour in England, which in the long run did harm to her industry, particularly as compared with the United States. Indeed, on the other side of the Atlantic there existed in the nineteenth century a shortage of labour (leading to its high cost) relative to other factors of production, capital and still more land. Because of the existence of the 'frontier', where fertile farmland was available at cheap prices, manufacturers had to pay their workmen wages that were high enough to keep them in their factories and discourage them from taking their chance as pioneers. The supply of labour was inelastic and the marginal cost to get it was well above the average. But in these conditions, a powerful stimulus existed to the invention and the rapid adoption of machines and methods which made it possible to save manpower that was scarce, expensive, unstable and mostly unskilled, and to obtain from it a high and growing productivity. In addition, there was the long-term fall in the prices of machinery, which moreover Americans made lighter and less durable. All this led to the 'American system of manufactures', as it was known to contemporaries, i.e. systematic mechanization, with mass production of standardized and interchangeable parts, and finally assembly-line methods. In Britain, on the other hand, the supply of labour was abundant and elastic, even with considerable chronic underemployment. In the short term, this was a favourable factor, for it reduced wage-costs, kept up profit margins, facilitated the accumulation of capital, and allowed increase in capacity – especially the rapid growth of the most dynamic sectors. But in the long run this situation tended to discourage the invention and adoption of labour-saving techniques, for the stimulus to look for them had lost some of its momentum. It encouraged the spread and improvement of existing techniques rather than the discovery of more advanced methods. Habakkuk, who thinks that the most favourable conditions for technological progress are obtained when there is an abundance of capital relative to labour, therefore believes that the oversupply of labour in Britain resulted in her industry becoming, as early as the middle of the nineteenth century, technically inferior to American industry in certain branches (e.g. the mass production of firearms), and that this inferiority continuously spread to other manufactures during the following half-century[102].

[102] H.J.Habakkuk, *American and British Technology in the Nineteenth Century* (Cambridge, 1962). The gross participation – i.e. the ratio between population employed and total population – hardly varied between 1861 and 1911, increasing a little for men and falling a little for women; Matthews, p.83.

This has been an attractive thesis – and remains one for the present author; but it has been challenged so often and so spiritedly, in such a sophisticated, not to say Byzantine, way, that it would be impossible to summarize the arguments here[103]. Let us only point out that England's technical inferiority became really marked only in a period later than the one mentioned by Habakkuk; for many writers, it is not proved that the labour factor was responsible for this inferiority, which could rather derive, for example, from the size and nature of the market. It has even been denied that American industry tended to save labour more than English industry, or that its capital intensity owed something to labour costs. In any case, the labour factor could not explain the technological superiority reached by Germany in various fields at the end of the nineteenth century, for that country certainly did not suffer from a labour scarcity, and the cost of labour was far lower than that current in England at the time. Probably one should push the analysis further, bringing new variables into the model, especially by distinguishing between skilled and unskilled labour. A recent article brings support to Habakkuk's view, although it deals with a period (the beginning of the twentieth century) later than the one he had studied. It suggests that Britain, by reason of her traditions and industrial structures, then had an abundance of highly skilled labour, compared with her American and German competitors. The latter largely used automatic machines and assembly-lines, which were appropriate to the unskilled labour which was available to them in abundance. British industry, on the other hand, was 'intensive in skills' and tended to neglect new methods of mass production[104]. In any case, the American example proves that a supply of abundant cheap labour was not indispensable for rapid economic growth.

Another assumption that needs qualifying concerns the influence of the demographic boom on the domestic market. Of course, in theory, the increase of a country's population does not guarantee a rise in the level of aggregate demand. If the increase is more rapid than the growth of production, it can lead to a drop in average real income, such as one has observed in a number of underdeveloped countries. It is true

[103] See notably the collection of articles, S.B.Saul (ed.), *Technological Change: The United States and Britain in the 19th Century* (London, 1970), with an excellent introduction by Saul.

[104] C.K.Harley, 'Skilled labour and the choice of techniques in Edwardian industry', *Explorations in Economic History* 11(4), Summer 1974, 3911–414. Skilled English workers were strongly unionized and so in a position to resist innovations which threatened their positions. D.L.Brito and J.G.Williamson, 'Skilled labour and nineteenth-century Anglo-American managerial behavior', in ibid., 10(3), Spring 1973, 235–52, present a different point of view.

that nineteenth-century Britain did not experience a demographic explosion of the same order as that of many Third World countries in the twentieth century, which has been so dramatic that it has prevented any rise in per-capita income. Nevertheless Harold Perkin seems too optimistic, when he asserts that, thanks to a 'very delicate adjustment', British population grew fast enough to ensure the growth of internal demand and avoid an excessive rise in wages, but slowly enough to avoid the Malthusian trap and not to reduce the cost of labour to a level which would have discouraged all labour-saving innovations[105]. We believe that Britain did not entirely escape this trap during the first half of the nineteenth century, and perhaps even later. Signs of overpopulation were then only too evident, especially the existence of a large subproletariat, deprived of any skill, only working casually, and living largely on public or private charity, or on crime. This 'reserve army of labour', swollen by an invasion of indigent Irish, which depressed wages, this 'unlimited supply of labour at subsistence wages' (W.A.Lewis) became an essential factor in the low standard of living of the working classes during that period, and in the slow rate at which it improved. Furthermore, though there was a redistribution of labour from low-productivity to modern, high-productivity sectors, this transfer was relatively slow and incomplete, with large numbers continuing in archaic branches, which were condemned to disappear because of technological progress and which paid miserable wages (especially handloom-weaving), or moving to the low-productivity sector of domestic service. In all, the level of effective demand per capita among the lower classes increased only marginally between 1815 and mid-century. It is legitimate to think that mass-market purchasing-power for manufactured goods, and so the overall size of the domestic market, would have been greater if the growth of the population had been somewhat slower. On the other hand, after 1850 or 1860, when the real incomes of workers increased perceptibly, the widening of the domestic market resulting from the demographic boom was strengthened. It is true that the growth of population slowed down markedly after 1880, but it seems ill-considered to see in this a factor for deceleration of economic growth and for delays in innovation during the same period, as has sometimes been suggested.

In spite of these qualifications, and even though the population-variable certainly had less influence on the economic development of the

---

[105] Perkin, pp.6, 101–2.

country in the nineteenth than in the eighteenth century[106], there can be no doubt that the high rate of British demographic growth was an important factor in the growth of total national product. On the other hand, its effect on productivity and on output per capita may have been negative, at least during part of the century[107].

It is too early, before the sectoral studies which follow, to try and answer the two fundamental questions which were posed at the beginning of this chapter – why was the growth of the British economy not faster in the first decades of the nineteenth century? And why did it slow down later, say from about 1873? Yet, briefly anticipating later chapters, one can say that the modern or advanced industries – especially cotton and iron – enjoyed a very fast growth up to mid-century, but their weight in the economy was not sufficient to boost national product at a faster pace, for many other sectors, mainly because of their old-fashioned methods, only advanced slowly or even stagnated. Furthermore, much of the labour-force was underemployed, and the demographic boom was probably excessive[108]. Finally, up to the 1840s the demand from overseas markets made only a modest contribution to growth.

The slow-down at the end of the century was particularly obvious in the staple industries – cotton and iron – which had previously put up such brilliant performances. Although other industries fared better, they could not take up the leading role of these branches, and few new substitution activities were found to back them up. As for exports, their contribution to growth, which had been very large in the third quarter of the century, later diminished. However, these are just observations and not explanations, which we shall try to explore in the sectoral chapters which make up most of Part 2, and draw together in the conclusion.

---

[106] For Deane and Cole, p.289, the changes in the growth-rates of population are less important from the point of view of economic growth than the fluctuations of migratory movements.

[107] P.Bairoch, 'Europe's gross national product: 1800–1975', *Journal of European Economic History*, V(2), Autumn 1976, p.285, notes that, at the European level, there is no significant correlation between the rate of demographic growth and that of the growth of per-capita GNP.

[108] It is often thought that the disaster in Ireland had a depressing effect on the economy of GB herself.

Part 2
Sectoral studies

6 Agriculture

The importance of the agricultural sector in the British economy declined irreversibly between the end of the Napoleonic wars and the beginning of the twentieth century[1]. About 1820, agriculture was outstripped by the industrial sector both as regards its contribution to national product and as a source of employment. However, compared with individual industries, agriculture remained, as Clapham wrote, 'the first British industry'. Only at the end of the nineteenth century did the decline of British agriculture reach a point where it came to occupy a minor position. Furthermore, this decline was only relative, and up to the crisis that struck agriculture in the last quarter of the nineteenth century, its production had gone on increasing – admittedly more slowly than the output of other sectors, but fast enough for its contribution to overall growth to be far from negligible[2]. From a purely economic point of view, agriculture remained therefore an important activity for a long time, while the political and social influence of the great landowners continued to be enormous.

Moreover, contrary to what is often claimed, natural conditions in Great Britain are far from militating against a prosperous agriculture. Only the west and north of the island, especially in their mountainous areas, have poor soil and a climate that is too damp and cold for cereal culture; but even these regions offer good possibilities for stock-farming. On the other hand the south, the east and the Midlands (plus the Scottish Lowlands) have land that is often very fertile, with a high proportion of soil that is now classed as first grade, and their climate is relatively dry. This basic contrast between 'grazing counties' and 'corn counties' must not, however, conceal the fact that geographical and historical factors gave rise to a large number of agricultural regions, very different from each other, with several patterns of farming in

[1] Cf. Chapter 4, p.67 (tables 16 and 17).
[2] P.Deane and W.A.Cole, *British Economic Growth, 1688–1959* (Cambridge, 2nd edn, 1967), p.171; see also their tables 38 and 39, pp.170 and 172.

competition. This is a fact that is too often forgotten by those who generalize about the history of British agriculture.

At the beginning of the nineteenth century, Great Britain was ahead of other countries in agricultural development as in other spheres, and the Industrial Revolution had its equivalent in agriculture[3]. Of course, the term Agricultural Revolution can be regarded as even more unsuitable and misleading than Industrial Revolution, inasmuch as it suggests a sudden and radical upheaval, which is almost ruled out in a sector where development is bound to be gradual and where changes which are usually covered by that expression stretched over a very long period, indeed a far longer time-span than was formerly thought. By tradition, the Agricultural Revolution had been centred on the eighteenth century, but recent research has shown that it had been prepared gradually and that some fundamental innovations were introduced, albeit in a small way, into English agriculture as early as the seventeenth century; indeed their origins dated back to the sixteenth century, and even to the middle ages. Moreover, although innovations came in faster and were more widespread in the eighteenth century, the Agricultural Revolution certainly did not end in 1800 or even in 1815. It continued without any break after these dates, and some of the most noteworthy advances occurred in the mid-nineteenth century. However, it is better to retain the term Agricultural Revolution because of the prime importance of the changes which took place during this long process. In particular they were the necessary precondition of the Industrial Revolution itself[4].

It is not part of the scope of this work to analyse the origins of the

---

[3]   The best recent survey is J.D.Chambers and G.E.Mingay. *The Agricultural Revolution, 1750–1880* (London, 1966), on which we have drawn freely. See also two useful collections of articles: W.E.Minchinton (ed.), *Essays in Agrarian History* (2 vols, Newton Abbot, 1968); E.L.Jones, *Agriculture and Economic Growth in England. 1650–1815* (London, 1967).

[4]   Indeed the Agricultural Revolution put an end to the famines and food shortages which periodically blocked demographic and economic growth. Furthermore, the increase in agricultural productivity was the one means of feeding a population that was growing and in which a rapidly rising proportion of families were in non-agricultural work, particularly in industry (which meant a *relative* decrease in the agricultural labour-force). This was all the more so because, before the middle of the nineteenth century, it was not possible to have recourse to large and regular imports of foodstuffs, for there were no large surpluses at the world level and transport costs were too high. On the relationship of the two 'Revolutions', see especially P.Bairoch, *Révolution industrielle et sous-développement* (Paris, 1963); E.L.Jones, *Agriculture and the Industrial Revolution* (Oxford, 1974).

revolution, and we will only recall two key factors arising out of England's peculiar economic and social structure. The first was the early commercialization of English agriculture. Farmers adopted a commercial outlook at an early date. Producing as they were for the market, thanks chiefly to the large demand from London and the industrial districts, they sought to increase their production and adapt output to demand so as to maximize their incomes, and this led them to improve their techniques. The second was the structure of landowner-ship and farming, i.e. the predominance of large estates, which was such a key fact in the history of England. Landlordism does not necessarily favour progress in agriculture[5], but in the particular socioeconomic context of modern England it certainly exerted a positive influence[6]. Deprived of their feudal rights, English land-owners drew most of their income from rents paid by their tenants, so it was in their interest that their tenants' profits should increase, and for that reason they looked for efficient tenant-farmers and helped them to increase their production through technical improvements. The landlord-tenant leasehold relationship also helped this support. The landowner provided the fixed capital (land, buildings, fences, ditches, access roads) and paid, at least in part, for its upkeep. The tenant supplied the working capital – livestock, implements, seeds, fertilizers, and cash to pay wages. British historians believe that this distinction between two types of capital was economically very healthy, arguing that large estates, such as existed in England, were much preferable to a peasantry of smallowners of the French type, inevitably poor and ignorant, having neither the means to make improvements, nor even the idea of so doing. In England, the heaviest expenses for carrying out improvements fell to the landowner, who had the required means, including the ability to borrow money, if necessary. As for the tenant, he was not tempted to economize with a view to buying more land (this was beyond his means), so he invested his savings in increasing and improving his livestock and imple-

---

[5] Although growing concentration of landed property was a different phenomenon from changes in land use and in techniques, there was a fundamental link in England between large estates and technical progress.

[6] Although nowadays there is not much support for the 'heroic' idea, which exaggerated the pioneer role of a few big landowners who were keen agronomists. The prime movers of agricultural progress were rather members of the gentry, prosperous yeomen, large-scale tenant-farmers, and the agents of great estates. But the big landowners helped to create the conditions of agricultural progress by their investment and indirectly in various other ways, e.g. by their role in the improvement of transport.

ments[7]. And although most farms in the nineteenth century were let on a year-to-year basis despite the advice of agronomists who recommended long leases to encourage improvements, leases were usually renewed, tenants enjoyed real security, and farms often passed from father to son. So an economic, social and institutional climate was created that was favourable to experiment, innovation and investment.

The main innovations by which the Agricultural Revolution broke the vicious circle that condemned traditional agriculture to poor and irregular yields per worker, per unit of time and per unit of space, were purely empirical, as 'scientific agriculture' only appeared much later[8]. The essential feature was the introduction of new crops – artificial grasses (clover, sainfoin, lucerne, etc.) or roots, especially turnips. These preserved the soil's fertility and so abolished the necessity for fallow periods, replacing the old simple, two- or three-year rotations with new complex rotations, which varied according to regions but were continuous[9]. Also, more forage was made available so that a larger number of livestock could be maintained, which produced more organic manure and ensured a higher yield for the crops. So British agriculture became animal-intensive[10], with mixed farming, even in the corn countries. Moreover, the quality of livestock was improved by the application of techniques first used for racehorses and foxhounds.

[7] We will return at the end of this chapter to the structure of landed property in the nineteenth century. Anyhow, in the eighteenth and nineteenth centuries landlords devoted an important, if variable, part of their gross rental to maintenance works and new investment.

[8] Based at first on the chemistry of soils, scientific agriculture made its first shy appearance with Rothamsted Experimental Station, founded in 1842, but agricultural research and education only really developed in GB at the very end of the nineteenth century.

[9] The well-known Norfolk crop-rotation (whose importance has perhaps been overestimated) alternated turnips, barley, lucerne and spring wheat. In addition, large flocks of sheep were pastured in the fields to manure them. The system suited the light and dry soils of East Anglia. On the wet clay soils of the Midlands, ley farming was practised: fields were cropped in successive periods of three or four years, sometimes in cereals, sometimes in artificial forage. Note also the development of water-meadows, flooded or irrigated, which gave high yields of hay. But one must emphasize the very wide variety of crop-rotations.

[10] P.K.O'Brien and C.K.Keyderz, *Economic Growth in Britain and France, 1780–1914: Two paths to the Twentieth Century* (London, 1978), pp.102ff., show particularly that the superior productivity of British agriculture as compared with French agriculture arose from the fact that the British devoted a larger share of the land and other resources to stock-farming, which led to higher yields (in added value per surface unit) than raising crops. In 1815/24 already, animal produce made up 42 per cent of the net production of British agriculture, a share that was to rise to 59 per cent in 1865/74 and 68 per cent in 1905/13 (p.113). See also P.K.O'Brien, 'Agriculture and the Industrial Revolution', *Economic History Review*, 2nd series. XXX, (1), Feb.1977, 166–81, esp. 169.

Animals with the required qualities were chosen, then systematically crossed, and their offspring after them, so as to develop these qualities. Thus new breeds of animals were obtained – larger, heavier and more robust, and specialized in providing either meat or milk or wool. Created in the eighteenth century, but still limited in numbers, these new breeds were to be perfected, with the system of herd-books started in 1822, and to multiply in the nineteenth century.

Another important aspect was the transformation of the rural landscape through the enclosures movement. Enclosure was a redistribution of land, which abolished the open fields and their countless long, unenclosed strips, and reorganized the countryside into a much smaller number of large, compact fields, which were then enclosed by fences or hedges. The owner had absolute rights, for the rights of common disappeared, and enjoyed complete freedom to select his crops. At the same time commons were brought into cultivation, enclosed and divided up for individual ownership. In the eighteenth and beginning of the nineteenth century, enclosure was usually carried out by private Act of Parliament, being authorized for a locality, with commissioners being appointed to put the award into effect. Of course, enclosures were not limited to the eighteenth and nineteenth centuries. The movement spread over many centuries, with a first peak in the fifteenth and sixteenth, to be followed by dramatic decline in the seventeenth century and at the beginning of the eighteenth. After 1760 the movement started up again with growing vigour, reaching its peak during the Napoleonic wars[11], with the result that nearly all land under the open-field system had been enclosed by about 1820, so that the number of new enclosures diminished rapidly after 1815[12].

The role of enclosures as a precondition for agricultural progress, and their influence on yields and output should not be overestimated,

[11] Under the stimulus of the high price of cereals during this period (cf.p.154). This idea is confirmed by the recent econometric article of N.F.R.Crafts, 'Determinants of the rate of parliamentary enclosure', *Explorations in Economic History*, 14 (3), July 1977, 227–49 (also some later articles in the same journal). On the controversial problem of the profitability of the enclosures, see the same article and D.N.McCloskey 'The enclosure of open fields: preface to a study of its impact on the efficiency of English agriculture in the eighteenth century', *Journal of Economic History*, XXII(1), March 1972, 15–35 who reckons that this profitability was very high. This enclosure movement then affected mainly the regions which had escaped it earlier, notably the Midlands, eastern and north-eastern England. But the west of England and Wales, which had never known open-field farming, were not touched.

[12] The number of Enclosure Bills, which had amounted to 983 for 1805–14, fell to 368 between 1815 and 1824, and to 177 between 1825 and 1834; Deane and Cole, p.95 (note 1). Between 1816 and 1845, only 200,000 acres were enclosed, as against about 7 million in England between 1760 and 1815. By 1820 England had only half a dozen counties where open fields covered more than 3 per cent of land under cultivation.

which has been the case for many years[13]. However, they indubitably helped on and speeded up the spread of innovations, e.g. by way of the consolidation of land into large farms with a single tenant. Moreover, from the social point of view, in spite of some unfortunate effects on the poorest inhabitants of the countryside, who suffered from the loss of their rights of use over land, enclosures did not lead to the general expropriation of smallowners and small tenants, and to their transformation into an indigent rural proletariat. The 'disappearance of the English peasant' too was a phenomenon of ancient origin, which was spread over a long period, and the enclosures did no more than reinforce this tendency. Nor did they lead to the depopulation of the countryside, for the new agriculture was more labour-intensive than the old[14].

Furthermore – and here was a major difference between Industrial and the Agricultural Revolutions – the latter was in no way based on the use of machinery and the steam-engine[15]. Certainly there were inventions (e.g. the seed-drill) and improvements to traditional implements, notably the plough itself. The scythe was perfected and gradually replaced the sickle, so that the cost of harvesting was reduced; but these changes were limited and their diffusion was slow[16]. The chief novelty was undoubtedly the substitution of iron or cast-iron for wood in agricultural implements, and their manufacture, from the end of the eighteenth century onwards, in engineering workshops and not by rural craftsmen. However, primitive threshing machines were invented in Scotland about 1800, and appeared in England soon

---

[13]   The open-field system was less rigid than historians used to think, and a number of technical innovations were made in its framework.

[14]   Because of continuous rotations, with crops that required a lot of labour (e.g. root-crops), and the increased number of animals; H.Perkin, *The Origins of Modern English Society, 1780–1880* (London, 1969), p. 120. Moreover it is not certain that the concentration of property was intensified to the benefit of large estates in the eighteenth century. E.E.Turner, 'Parliamentary enclosure and landownership in Buckinghamshire, *Economic History Review*, 2nd series, XXVIII (4), Nov. 1975, 565–81, finds very few changes in the *structure* of property during the enclosures, but that much land changed hands.

[15]   Particularly because of the differing nature of work on the land and of industrial processes. Agricultural machinery must be specialized, therefore varied, and mobile; but it is only used part of the time, which diminishes its profitability; O'Brien, 'Agriculture', 171.

[16]   E.J.T.Collins, 'Harvest technology and labour supply in Britain, 1790–1870', *Economic History Review*, 2nd series, XXII, (3), Dec. 1969, 453–73, insists on the importance of this progress in 'intermediary technology' of hand-tools, that were simple and cheap. But the substitution of the scythe for the sickle spread over several decades and only came to an end about 1870. Right in the middle of the nineteenth century, broadcast sowing was usual.

afterwards[17], but they aroused the fury of the farmworkers, who were deprived of employment, and caused the so-called Captain Swing riots, during the summer of 1830, in which 387 of these machines were destroyed. The terrified farmers therefore gave up their use for some time[18]. Similarly, after 1820, attempts were made to use harvesters, but without success[19]. As for the steam-engine, its use in agriculture really only started at mid-century.

So, in spite of the slowness of changes and of their limited penetration on medium-sized and small farms and in poor, isolated regions[20], British agriculture gradually achieved considerable technical progress, becoming the most advanced and productive agriculture in Europe, with output greatly increased[21]. During the Napoleonic wars landowners and farmers enjoyed great prosperity. Monetary inflation during this period, the frequency of bad harvests, the difficulty of importing grain and the rise in transport costs dramatically speeded up the rise in agricultural prices, which had started in the mid-eighteenth century, and which was greater than the rise in cultivation-costs. Hence high profits for farmers and rapidly rising rents for landlords, which stimulated investment, notably for more enclosures, and favoured innovation[22].

However, even before the end of the wars, this situation was

[17] But slowly in the south, given low wages there and also the imperfections of these machines.

[18] E.J.Hobsbawm and F.Rudé, *Captain Swing* (London, 1969; 2nd edn. 1973).

[19] For instance the invention of Patrick Bell (1826–8), which, according to P.David, 'The landscape and the machine:technical interrelatedness, land tenure and the mechanization of the corn harvest in Victorian Britain', in D.N.McCloskey (ed) *Essays on a Mature Economy: Britain After 1840* (London, 1971), pp.145–214, and 152–3, could not be used because of obstacles arising from the nature of the rural landscape. David's essay is reviewed by J.D.Gould in *Economic History Review*, 2nd series, XXVII (3). Aug. 1974, 455–60.

[20] For a long time changes only really affected the eastern regions of GB.

[21] According to Deane and Cole, production nearly doubled in volume between 1700 and 1820; p.65 (table 17). But O'Brien, 'Agriculture', 173–5, 179, reckons that the performance of British agriculture during this period and up to 1850, was not outstanding, as it just succeeded in satisfying the needs of the country, although there was a small but growing deficit in cereals.

[22] Recent articles by G.Hueckel challenge some accepted ideas on this period, for instance the abnormal frequency of bad harvests and the steep rise in tenant-farmers' profits. In his view, farmers did much less well out of the war than landlords. He has also worked out an index of agricultural prices, which goes up from 88 in 1792 to 206 in 1812, and he insists on the movement of the domestic terms of trade in favour of agriculture; 'War and the British Economy, 1793–1815: a general equilibrium analysis', *Explorations in Economic History,* 10(4), Summer 1973, 365–96; 'English farming profits during the Napoleonic wars, 1793–1815', ibid., 13 (3), July 1976, 331–45. Also S.Macdonald, 'Agricultural response to a changing market during the Napoleonic wars', *Economic History Review*, 2nd series, XXXIII, (1), Feb. 1980, 59–71.

reversed, which opened up the first of the three great phases which are traditionally perceived in the development of British agriculture during the nineteenth century. First, from about 1815 to 1850, came a difficult period, even a depression, ending in a recovery that started in the 1830s; then, in the third quarter of the century, there was a period of prosperity, a golden age; finally, from the 1870s onwards, a profound crisis developed, which was not fully offset by the slight improvement at the beginning of the twentieth century. This classic periodization is roughly accurate, but recent research leads us to qualify, at many points, the contrasts implied and to underline the persistence of broad, general, long-term trends.

DEPRESSION AND RECOVERY

The average price of wheat in the United Kingdom reached 127 shillings per quarter[23] in 1812, but it then dropped rapidly, falling to 74 shillings as early as 1814 as the result of good harvests, the return to normal peacetime conditions for imports, and the threat of an influx of cheap grain from eastern Europe. This collapse of prices put farmers in a dangerous position. They had contracted leases involving rent-levels that were calculated on the basis of high wartime agricultural prices. These rents would leave them no profits if prices fell sharply, or would produce actual losses. The great landowners, whose incomes were in danger from this situation, obtained from Parliament (which they controlled) the passing of the 1815 Corn Law[24], which was intended to give British farmers complete protection from foreign competition. Foreign wheat would only be allowed to enter the country when the average wholesale price at home reached 80 shillings per quarter, a price which was considered profitable for farmers and which was, in fact, very high. This system was made more flexible and less drastic by the sliding scale which William Huskisson introduced in 1828: when the domestic price of wheat reached 73 shillings a quarter, foreign wheat was admitted and paid a nominal duty of 1 shilling; but under that threshold the duty increased in proportion as the domestic level of prices fell, and all imports stopped when the domestic price was less than 52 shillings[25]. However,

[23] Wheat prices quoted are those from B.R.Mitchell and P.Deane, *Abstract of British Historical Statistics* (Cambridge, 1962) (quoted hereafter as *Abstract*) pp.488–9.

[24] Thiscontinued, but brought to its peak, a tradition of protection of agriculture going back to the end of the seventeenth century, which had been recently expressed in Acts of 1791 and 1804.

[25] The sliding scale aimed at reducing imports of cereals, without causing a shortage, and stabilizing the prices.

protectionism, which also applied to other agricultural products, remained rigorous and intact up to Sir Robert Peel's reforms between 1842 and 1846, culminating in the repeal of the Corn Laws.

This system harmed consumers (i.e. most of the population) and probably also industry[26], to the profit of the landed interest, which held political power. Besides, protectionism was ineffective and irrelevant, and did not supply the protection that had been sought. Certainly, the imports of cereals were only sizeable after poor harvests, their average quantity was small up to the 1840s (see table 28), and they only covered a small fraction of British consumption – about 5 per cent for wheat in the 1820s[27]. But annual average prices of wheat in the United Kingdom, although they were probably higher than they would have been without protection, fluctuated quite sharply[28]; they only passed 80 shillings a quarter in 1817 and 1818, then showed a long-run tendency to fall up to 1835 (when the price dropped to 39 shillings) and on the whole were distinctly lower than during the wars. From 1820 to 1849, five-year averages fluctuated between 54 and 62 shillings, against 102 shillings for 1810/14[29].

This situation may seem surprising, given the growing demand from a population that was increasing particularly fast and eating more and more white, wheaten bread[30]. It is generally thought that the reclamations, enclosures and various improvements effected during the wars had created a productive capacity that outstripped demand; but an abnormal and accidental number of bad seasons prevented production from reaching its potential level. Bad harvests became less frequent after 1812 and, demand for bread being inelastic, Britain had

[26] Cf. Chapter 5 pp. 121–4.
[27] 7 per cent of English consumption between 1829 and 1846. The percentage was less for all types of cereals; S.Fairlie, 'The Corn Laws and British Wheat Production, 1829–76', *Economic History Review,* 2nd series, XXII, (1), Apr. 1969, 88–116, at 103 (table 2); R.A.Church, *The Great Victorian Boom, 1850–1873* (London, 1975), p.62; W.Vamplew, 'The protection of English cereal producers: the Corn Laws reassessed', *Economic History Review,* 2nd series, XXXIII (3), Aug. 1980, 382–950
[28] It is often thought that the Corn Laws made these fluctuations sharper. In any case, the average price of wheat in the UK fell from 95s 11d in 1817 to 44s 7d in 1822.
[29] P.Mathias, *The First Industrial Nation: An Economic History of Britain 1700–1914* (London, 1969), p.474 (table 23). See also the graphs of Chambers and Mingay, p.110, and Fairlie, 105. F.M.L.Thompson, *English Landed Society in the Nineteenth Century* (London, 1963), p.232, estimates that the normal price of wheat in the 1820s and 1830's was two-thirds of the price in the period 1800–15.
[30] Although its predominance came later than has been thought. Bread made of rye or even barley continued to be eaten for a long time. In the North of England and in Scotland oats, in the form of porridge or oatcakes, remained an important form of food up to the end of the 19th century.

an excess capacity for cereal production, which was only gradually absorbed by the growth of population, all the more so because agricultural output continued to grow. As soon as the annual harvest turned out to be good or even average, there was overproduction and a fall in prices, in spite of the Corn Laws. Susan Fairlie has put forward a different interpretation of these trends, and it is a very plausible one. True enough, imports of grain were small on average, but Great Britain had a genuine deficit, which was tending to grow. Furthermore, as the demand for cereals was inelastic, imports of modest size could have a disproportionate effect on British domestic prices, which were in no way sheltered from the influence of foreign prices. In fact, British prices fluctuated in step with the harvests and prices of northern Europe. As the latter suffered from overproduction of wheat in the 1820s and 1830s, the prices there were markedly lower than English prices and had a depressing effect on them, especially when the continental harvest was good. Susan Fairlie further admits that protection made possible and even encouraged an increase in British wheat-production (and also in productivity), which made no sense economically[31].

Neither interpretation denies that, in the post-war years and in the 1820s, many British farmers were hard-hit by the fall in prices. Some tenants were ruined and landlords had often to accept the waiving and lowering of rents. Marginal lands which had been tilled during the wars, e.g. hillsides or moorland, were abandoned or restored to grass. However, the loud, alarming, partisan complaints about the 'distress' of agriculture and the depopulation of the countryside have been taken too seriously by many historians[32], who have extrapolated, for the country and the period as a whole, the situation of the regions that were most stricken during the most critical periods[33].

A first error is to overestimate the importance of wheat, the price of which fell more than that of other agricultural products. The depression especially affected arable farming. The dairying and stock-raising regions (especially those which were near large urban

[31] Fairlie *passim*.
[32] Especially Lord Ernle in his classic work of 1912, which is now completely out of date. We have seen (Chapter 4, p. 68) that labour employed in agriculture continued to increase, although slowly, up to 1851. Despite migrations, which were indeed traditional, from the countryside to the towns, there was no drop in the population of rural areas before mid-century. Indeed, they suffered from overpopulation during the first decades, leading to serious poverty (Deane and Cole, p.9).
[33] For what follows, see particularly E.L.Jones, *The Development of British Agriculture, 1815–1873* (London, 1968), pp.10–17; Thompson, *English Landed Society*, pp.230–7; Mathias, *The First Industrial Nation*, pp. 337ff.

markets, like the towns of Lancashire) hardly suffered at all, except at the beginning of the 1820s, for the price of cattle, meat, butter and cheese fell far less than that of grain. Even in the regions of cereal cultivation, the crisis was far from being general and constant. Rather, there was a succession of short crises, when good harvests forced prices down; and account must be taken of the basic difference between regions of light soils (most of eastern and southern England), and those of heavy, wet clays (notably in the Midlands). The latter were expensive to work, requiring teams of three or four horses for ploughing[34]; they were also unsuitable for fodder crops such as turnips, and thus for the new rotations. Farmers in these localities kept to the three-year rotation and their cash crop was wheat, which produced disastrous commercial results after 1815, all the more so because the sowing was late, the maturing season short, the percentage of poor harvests (in rainy years) high, making yields irregular. These were therefore the areas of real distress[35], which suffered acutely from the competition of regions with soils that were dry, sandy or chalky, where the crisis was much less serious, even though the cultivation of some very thin soils on the Downs had to be abandoned. The costs of farming in these areas were less, and technical innovations, particularly in the matter of new crops and new rotations, were already widely in use there.

These regions also showed a vigorous response to the pressures arising from the fall in prices. Landlords came to the rescue of their tenants, e.g. by lowering rents[36] and especially by making new investments[37]. Now, in the virtuous circle of the new agriculture, an investment at a given point was liable to ensure a general expansion of

---

[34] Against one or two in Norfolk.

[35] It also seems that more or less everywhere small owner-occupiers and small tenant-farmers, who had been for a long time in decline, but who had regained ground during the wars, suffered badly from the crisis (see p. 181 (note 116)). The tenants of landowners who could not borrow to invest, because of legal obstacles or because their estates were already too heavily mortgaged, were in the same position.

[36] Which on certain estates fell by 10 to 25 per cent, or even more, between 1816 and 1835. But in other cases they remained stable or even went up slightly, which clearly shows that the depression was not universal. Some landowners also took over the expense of repairing buildings, which they had left to the tenants' responsibility during the wars.

[37] R.A.Holderness, 'Landlord's capital formation in East Anglia, 1750–1870', *Economic History Review*, 2nd series, XXV (3), Aug. 1972, 434–47, reckons that expenditure by large landowners on repairs and new work, as a percentage of their gross rental, reached its maximum between 1806 and 1825, and diminished after 1830. Such investment was a help to tenants in the 1820s (see especially 439 and 441). Much building was done at that time, and one could talk of a real reconstruction of rural England.

output. The farmers reduced their costs, not only by lowering the wages of agricultural workers[38] but also, and above all, by developing innovations, e.g. generalizing and perfecting new rotations, selecting seeds and livestock (with an increase in numbers which led to more manure for fertilizer), using light ploughs made of iron, which could be pulled by only one or two horses, and above all resorting more and more to fertilizers 'imported' from outside to supplement the farm manure – night-soil from the towns, oil-cake and powdered bone, then, after 1840, guano[39]. Investment and innovation enabled farmers to produce more at lower cost and thus restore the profitability of agriculture[40]. Furthermore, these regions produced barley, demand for which increased considerably after the abolition of excise duty on beer in 1830. They also had large flocks of sheep, and the price of wool recovered earlier than prices of other agricultural products.

So these areas of light soils were the first to surmount the difficulties resulting from the falling prices – in fact, as early as the beginning of the 1830s. This recovery was confirmed after 1836 when there was a sharp cyclical rise in the price of cereals: wheat rose from 39 shillings in 1835 to 71 shillings in 1839[41]. This rise also benefited the heavy-soil regions[42], for it attracted capital to them, which was invested in drainage. This was the only technical solution to their problems, and new methods for it were devised. In the Fens (especially in Cambridgeshire) windmills for pumping were replaced by steam-engines, which allowed the cultivation of wheat and potatoes to be substituted for oats. In the Midland clays, huge 'mole-ploughs' were used which dug trenches for earthenware pipes, produced cheaply by machinery, and these ensured efficient subsoil drainage[43].

[38]   Hence the poverty of these workers.
[39]   Thompson attaches such importance to this phenomenon, which was to expand on a growing scale in the following decades, that he has called it 'the second Agricultural Revolution': 'The second Agricultural Revolution, 1825–1880', *Economic History Review*, 2nd series, XXI, (1), Apr. 1968, 62–7.
[40]   Worsening, on the other hand, by increased competition, the situation of the farmers who were not 'progressive'. But Jones emphasizes that, for reasons of physical geography, investment was not profitable everywhere.
[41]   Which of course stimulated chartist agitation and the campaign against the Corn Laws. Although the years 1837–42 were very good for the growers of cereals, the rest of the population suffered seriously. Fairlie, 107, thinks that Europe had passed from overproduction to shortage of cereals and that this was the fundamental cause of the repeal of the Corn Laws.
[42]   Whose representatives had been the only ones to renew their complaints when there was an enquiry in 1833.
[43]   In 1846, Parliament voted a law authorizing the lending of money to farmers for draining their lands. Later, private companies were formed for the same purpose. But the total of loans was modest at first, and although it increased later, most of the land which ought to have been drained, was not in fact improved.

Thus, at Victoria's accession, British agriculture had surmounted the depression (the gravity of which, once more, must not be exaggerated), and its situation had improved and stabilized. Thanks to better productivity (average yields of wheat increased by 16 per cent between 1815/19 and 1832/6), agriculture's profitability had been restored. Also, despite the fall in prices, agricultural production had increased considerably[44], but mostly thanks to progress achieved in the regions of light soils. For want of statistics[45], this increase in output cannot be quantified accurately; but the country's agriculture had succeeded, almost unaided, in feeding (and at a level of consumption per head that remained stable) a population which increased in Great Britain from 13 million in 1815 to nearly 18 million in 1837[46]. Wheat production would seem to have gone up from 11 million quarters a year on average for 1801/11 to 16 million in 1831/41 and to 18 or 20 million in 1841/51. In England alone, according to a new statistical series of Fairlie, wheat-production rose from 13.8 million quarters a year in 1829/36 to 15.6 million in 1837/46. Deane and Cole estimate the annual average growth-rate of real agricultural production at 1.5 per cent per annum between 1811/21 and 1841/51[47].

THE GOLDEN AGE

The thunderclap of the repeal of the Corn Laws in 1846 burst upon an agriculture that had become prosperous again and very progressive[48]. The reform was forced upon a Tory government, albeit allied to the landed interest, by the bad harvests of 1845 and 1846, and by the disaster in Ireland. Deprived of customs protection, landlords and farmers feared the worse, i.e. an invasion by foreign produce followed by a collapse of prices. However, these sombre predictions were only fulfilled in the long run, and for more than twenty years British agriculture knew prosperity and growth, so that the third quarter of

[44] With some acceleration at the very beginning of Victoria's reign.
[45] The annual censuses of agriculture only started in 1867.
[46] But Thompson, *English Landed Society,* pp.233 and 238, thinks that by this date demand had caught up with production and that GB henceforward had a large, permanent deficit.
[47] Deane and Cole, pp.170, 172 (tables 38 and 39); Fairlie, 102, (table 1).
[48] It was an important event, less for its immediate economic consequences, which were limited (as we shall see), than as a symbol of the victory of industrial over agrarian interests, of 'Black' England over 'Green' England. However, protectionism had already been seriously breached by the first customs reforms of Peel (1842), such as reduction of the sliding scale and free entry for imperial wheat. Jones (pp.27–8) does not accept the idea held by other historians that Peel had an overall plan to help the modernization of agriculture.

the nineteenth century is generally considered to have been its 'golden age', even though its calm was not entirely undisturbed.

Yet the imports of cereals, and notably of wheat, became considerable from the 1840s onwards (see table 28), their total annual average tripling in twenty years[49]. None the less, prices remained firm. Although they showed strong fluctuations in the short run, these cancelled themselves out over thirty years, and five-year averages between 1845/9 and 1870/4 oscillated between 49 and 59 shillings a quarter (with a slight tendency to fall), i.e. at a level that was slightly lower than between 1820 and 1846. However, they would very probably have been higher if the Corn Laws had not been abolished. The prices of animal products, in contrast, rose noticeably, and after 1853 the general index of agricultural products took an upward turn[50].

How can we explain this situation that was so very different from the big fall in prices hoped for by the free-traders and feared by the protectionists, but which reconciled the latter to free trade?

Population growth and the improvement in the real incomes of the working classes explain the rise in grain imports, and in part the increase in livestock and meat prices (since these products were difficult and expensive to import, foreign competition did not count), but they do not explain the strength of cereal prices.

In actual fact, there was no large world surplus of cheap grain that could flood the British market and compete ruinously with home

Table 28   Net imports of wheat and flour into the UK[51]

Annual average	Millions of cwt
1820/9	1.6
1830/9	3.7
1840/9	10.7
1850/9	19.3
1860/9	33.7
1870/9	50.4
1880/9	70.3
1890/9	85.9
1900/9	102.6

[49]   Imports covered 27 per cent of wheat consumption in England from 1849 to 1859 against 7 per cent from 1829 to 1846) and 40 per cent from 1860 to 1868; Fairlie, 103 (table 2). Nevertheless, in 1868, the UK still produced 80 per cent of the foodstuffs which she consumed (90 per cent for animal products).

[50]   For all this, see especially: Jones, pp. 17–34; Church, *The Great Victorian Boom*, pp. 28–30, 38; Thompson, *English Landed Society*, p. 238–68.

[51]   From Mathias, *The First Industrial Nation* p.472 (table 21). Imports of barley and oats increased as fast as those of wheat between 1840/9 and 1860/9, more slowly later.

producers. This was particularly the position in Europe which then supplied the bulk of grain imports into Great Britain[52] and where population expansion led to some hardening of the cereal market. In addition, the Crimean war stopped exports of Russian wheat and gave British wheat-growers their best years in the period. At the same time, American competition also remained limited by the still-high cost of transporting grain from the inland regions to the ports, while after the civil war domestic demand increased sharply in the United States[53]. In response to strong and growing demand, the increase in supplies available slowed down and sometimes stopped altogether. Furthermore, discoveries of gold in California and Australia unleashed a bout of inflation, and various factors, among them the wars of the 1850s and 1860s, later tended to keep the general level of prices relatively high.

For these reasons British wheat growers benefited from a quarter-of-a-century's respite, with prices which, without being high, guaranteed good profits to those who ran their farms efficiently on the soils that were best suited to that crop, i.e. mostly the light soils of the south and east. But wheat was less rewarding to farmers who were not so well situated, and its cultivation lost ground after the repeal of the Corn Laws, though this happened only gradually[54].

It was the rise in price of animal products and the development of stock-farming, not the prosperity of the cereal sector, which explained the 'golden age' of British agriculture. In fact cereals fell in price relative to livestock products, which clearly became the most profitable sector. In addition, the extension of the railway system enabled animals to be transported rapidly without losing weight, as previously happened when they had to travel on the hoof. Meat, too, and perishable goods such as milk, could be carried over a distance[55]. This being so, there was a clear move away from cereals towards stock-farming, and animal production made big strides, with beef output increasing by at least 50 per cent. The traditionally pastoral

---

[52] 87 per cent of wheat imports in 1840/9, against 13 per cent from North America. In 1860/9, the percentages were 61 and 27 per cent respectively; Mathias, *The First Industrial Nation* p. 473 (table 22).

[53] During the war itself wheat exports to England increased through the diversion of grain that was formerly sent to the south. But the shortage of cotton made the price of wool rise. A different view is taken by P.Bairoch, *Commerce extérieur et développement économique de l'Europe au XIXe siècle* (Paris – The Hague, 1976), p.304, who believes that the American civil war slowed down by about ten years the flow of American cereals to Europe.

[54] To be exact, after the 1845 harvest, according to Fairlie 98 and 102 (table 1), which gives the following annual averages of wheat production in England: 1837/46: 15.6m quarters; 1847/56: 13.4; 1857/64: 13.3; 1867/76: 10.8.

[55] As well as fertilizers and cattle feed in the opposite direction.

regions of the north and west specialized increasingly in animal production and became quite prosperous. As for the regions of mixed farming in the south and east, where cereal farming was allied to stock-fattening, the balance between these two joint activities changed gradually to stock-farming's advantage. Furthermore, this system became more intensive by the growing use of fertilizers bought by the farmers (guano, superphosphates, nitrates, potassium salts) and of animal feed also bought from outside (cereals other than wheat, oil-cake), which enabled farmers to increase their herds and their yields without being limited by their farms' resources in forage and manure. According to E.L.Jones, while in the mixed farming of the 1830s and 1840s animals were rather a sideline to crops, intended to provide them with manure, towards 1870 they were becoming dominant and supplying farmers with a large part of their income[56]. Moreover, in clay regions, the progress of drainage was also often accompanied by the conversion of arable land to grass, and so to the furtherance of stock-farming.

In all, the preponderance of stock-farming over arable farming was well established before the crisis of the Great Depression, as is shown by the following figures (percentage proportion in brackets) of agricultural output in the United Kingdom, in millions of pounds[57]:

	1867/9	*1870/6*
Vegetable products	104 (45)	95 (38)
Animal products	127 (55)	155 (62)

One can even ask why this trend was not pushed further. Both contemporaries and historians have criticized British farmers, and particularly those practising mixed farming, for not having profited from this favourable period to transform agriculture more thoroughly, a failure that was to cost them dear when the situation was reversed. So what were the rigidities which discouraged the response to price-movements that favoured animal production? One can put forward psychological reasons – the deep-rooted conservatism of farmers, the prestige attaching to wheat-production, a devotion to the harmonious and well-balanced system of mixed farming[58], and a confusion between technical and economic efficiency, with farmers

---

[56] An opinion challenged by P.J.Perry, *British Farming in the Great Depression, 1876–1914* (London, 1974).

[57] Jones, p.22, quoting T.W.Fletcher.

[58] Jones points out that also, by chance, during this period low prices of grain often coincided with high cattle prices. The cattle could be fed with cereals so that total receipts remained stable. And farmers did not have accounting systems which enabled them to isolate the decreasing profitability of wheat farming.

trying to produce as much as possible of cereals and livestock at the same time. In addition, there were technical obstacles. Specializations in intensive stock-farming would have involved techniques of forage production which were not perfected, as well as smaller farms than were needed when the accent was on cereals. Landowners shrank from the division of tenancies and the construction of the new buildings which would be necessary; they were even against putting up new cattle-sheds on existing farms to house more livestock[59].

Despite these inhibitions, British agriculture changed noticeably during this golden age. Indeed it promoted and diffused earlier innovations, while a new trend was the mechanization of harvesting, notably by the introduction of the mechanical reaper, especially the model invented by the American McCormick. This had been presented at the 1851 Exhibition and was much superior to machines of that kind that had previously been tried out in Britain[60]. However, the spread of this machine was slow. In 1874 only 47 per cent of the cereal harvest was carried out by machine in Britain against 78 per cent in the United States in 1870. This is a question that has been minutely analysed through econometric methods by Paul David[61]. According to this author, the relative failure of the harvester in Great Britain was only partly due to the conservatism of farmers, or to the low cost of a superabundant labour. The basic reason was that the harvester was not suited to a rural landscape inherited from the past, except in a few regions of north-eastern England and the Scottish Lowlands, where there were large tracts of land with well-levelled soil. Elsewhere, not to mention the rocky ground that put the machines out of order, there were many traditional ridge-and-furrow fields, designed to assist drainage, in which harvesters bogged down, or fields intersected by drainage ditches. There were also too many small and irregular fields, which meant loss of time in turning the machines and taking them from one field to another. Country lanes were often too narrow, and the access to fields and farms sometimes too small for the passage of this type of machinery. Here one touches on a problem which is to be found in other branches of the economy – the close and necessary interrelat-

---

[59] R.Perren, 'The meat and livestock trade in Britain, 1850–70', *Economic History Review,* 2nd series, XXVIII, (3) Aug. 1975, 385–400, shows that the system for marketing meat, especially in London, was defective and led to bottlenecks; R.Perren, *The Meat Trade in Britain, 1840–1914* (London, 1978).

[60] Note also the use of transportable steam-engines – particularly on the large farms of the Scottish Lowlands – for powering threshing machines, and also for pulling large ploughs by a system of cables. But steam-farming was only profitable on very large farms.

[61] David; see note 19, p. 153.

edness between various capital goods (in the broadest sense of the term) which are in use, and the incompatibility of some innovations with the existing infrastructure. Given the situation of agriculture in the mid-nineteenth century, the profitability of the harvester was limited, except on very large and well-equipped farms, and their costs of operation and maintenance were higher than those of manual labour. For the harvester to have become a paying proposition on most farms, it would have been necessary to transform the infrastructure, especially by levelling the fields, establishing subsoil-drainage and widening the approaches. But such works required large investment which reduced the profitability of mechanization.

David, parting company with British historians, who always insist on the advantages of the large estate and of the leasehold system, believes that the division of responsibilities and decisions between landlord and tenant created obstacles to this type of investment, which could involve the tenant in an increase in rent without the certainty that the landlord would benefit[62]. Much depended, of course, on the profitability of the 'mix' of mechanization and related investment. David has worked out that it would have been highest on farms with about 100 acres bearing wheat or oats, i.e. on the largest farms of 200 acres or more, which were relatively few. Overall the yield on these investments for a landlord could not have exceeded 4 per cent at any moment during the period 1851–71. At the end of that period, the purchase of a mechanical reaper and the preparation of the ground, so that it could be used efficiently, was not profitable if it was necessary to borrow the funds required, normal interest rates being 3.5 per cent, or 6.5 to 7 per cent including the amortization charges to pay off the principal[63]. Later on, the collapse in the price of cereals was to preclude investment in the improvement of terrain, but it also led to a contraction of wheat-growing, especially on land least suitable for the harvester, so that the percentage of harvesting by machinery increased, all the more because the machines were improved (the reaper-binder appeared in England about 1880) and could be used in more difficult conditions than before.

During the mid-Victorian period investment by landlords in agriculture had been considerable, and it was even the basis of the so-called 'high farming' system[64], which is often considered to have been

[62] This idea was challenged during the discussion of David's paper.
[63] The situation might have been a little more favourable in the 1850s. Later on the minimum size of farms where the harvester was paying its way rose, as did the cost of preparatory work, in view of the increase in wages.
[64] An expression specially applied to a form of mixed farming, intensive and integrated cereal cultivation and stock-rearing, as has been described earlier.

characteristic of this period[65]. This heavy expenditure was at first 'defensive' – a reply to the low price of wheat, which prevailed from 1848 to 1852, and to the loss of protection, which nearly all landowners knew to be final. They looked for an increase in production and a reduction in costs so as not to have to lower rents or lose good tenants. When prices hardened, they hoped that productive investment would enable rents to be raised. But several pieces of research have shown that the yield on these investments – often, it is true, badly costed without taking into account geographical factors that were poorly understood – was extremely low and disappointing, far inferior to what the enclosures had brought in. F.M.L. Thompson has calculated that, on a group of large estates which he has studied, the gross yield on improvement-expenditure was at most 3.6 per cent per annum, and even then only for a few years at the end of the period. If these sums had been invested in Consols, they would have brought in 3.2 per cent regularly, without any worry to their possessors. From 1847 to 1878, the Duke of Northumberland invested £992,000 in his estates, which only gave him a yield of 2.5 per cent in the years 1876/9. In brief, the great improving landlords subsidized agriculture, but over-capitalized it. Their motives, it is true, were perhaps not purely economic but involved reasons of prestige and *noblesse oblige*[66].

None the less rents rose in the period 1850–73 between 10 and 30 per cent in individual cases, and their average in England rose by 16 per cent. However, this increase was not only out of proportion to the scale of investment, it was also inferior to the rise of farm prices and of the general index of prices. So the real income of landlords diminished, and behind the façade of the golden age of agriculture came deterioration in the economic position of great landowners. Furthermore, a large part of the capital thus invested was lost, when the crisis at the end of the century removed all hope of getting a return, especially in the regions of cereal cultivation, where a large proportion of these improvements had been concentrated. Even earlier, the price of cereals was not high enough to justify the continuation of improvements destined to increase grain yields.

[65] Not strictly true. The expression was invented by James Caird in 1848, after the repeal of the Corn Laws. He recommended investment so as to obtain higher production at lower unit-costs, as an antidote to the fall in prices which would result from the repeal. In fact, the period in question did not see any noticeable fall in prices. Furthermore, the characteristic innovations of high farming had appeared before 1846.

[66] Thompson, *English Landed Society*, pp.239–40, 250. Landowners who borrowed money to invest broke even at best. According to Holderness, 435,439 (table 2), 446, there was a recovery in investment by East Anglian landlords after 1850, but it was substantial only on the very largest estates (see p. 157 (note 37)).

On the other hand, it seems that farmers, or at least some of them, derived more advantage from mid-Victorian prosperity than landlords. As for farmworkers, it is an important fact that for the first time their number noticeably diminished, for the pull of the towns intensified the flight from the land. Between 1851 and 1871, the labour-force in agriculture diminished by 300,000 people, or one-seventh – which implies a sharp increase in labour-productivity, at a rate which was probably unprecedented. It is generally thought that some shortage of labour resulted in certain regions, particularly during the peak summer demand, which gave that social group, so long disadvantaged, an improvement in real wages and conditions[67].

Feinstein's index for the volume of agricultural production in Great Britain goes up from 98 in 1855 to 112 in 1874, i.e. an increase of 14 per cent, which was modest (0.7 per cent per annum), especially as the peak of 1874 and 1875 was exceptional. Deane and Cole suggest a higher rate of growth of real agricultural production for the mid-Victorian period, but it remains inferior to their rate for the preceding period[68].

During the three decades that followed the repeal of the Corn Laws, British farmers showed enough flexibility and initiative to transform agriculture in part and achieve a rise in their incomes and real prosperity. The term 'golden age of British agriculture' is therefore not unjustified for the mid-Victorian period, but especially if the latter is compared to the difficulties of the following decades[69]. Such prosperity was unequally shared between the various agricultural systems and the various social groups involved. Finally, one must underline the fragility of the system of high farming, whose profitability was already mediocre, except on the very big farms, and which was soon to collapse owing to the excessive, not to say central, role given to cereal production[70].

THE DEPRESSION

The situation changed sharply for British agriculture at the end of the 1870s and it entered a long period of difficulties, even of crisis, and of

[67] Jones, pp. 32–4.
[68] C.H.Feinstein, *National Income, Expenditure and Output of the United Kingdom, 1855–1965* (Cambridge, 1972), table 54, T.118, col. 1; Deane and Cole, p.170 (table 39). See Bairoch, *Commerce extérieur,* p.205 (table 58); and also above (note 54).
[69] Let us not forget the much faster growth of other sectors, which led to a marked diminution of agriculture's share in the employed population and in the structure of national product; nor the *absolute* fall in its labour force.
[70] David, pp.176, 178–9.

structural change, which lasted up to the end of the century and was succeeded by only a slight improvement at the beginning of the twentieth century. Agriculture is considered to have been the main victim of the Great Depression, but it would be excessive to talk of a catastrophe[71].

The direct cause of the crisis was the fall in agricultural prices, and above all of cereal prices. The end of the 1870s was marked by a series of bad harvests, notaby in 1879, but the farmers saw with despair that prices fell at the same time. The annual average price of wheat in the United Kingdom, which had reached a peak in 1873 at 58 shillings a quarter and got near to that again in 1877 at 56 shillings, fell to 46 shillings in 1877, and permanently below 40 shillings after 1883. It reached a minimum of 22 shillings in 1894, followed by a slight recovery; but the peak reached before 1915 was only 37 shillings (in 1909)[72]. Table 29 sums up this development[73].

Table 29 Annual average price of wheat in the UK (shillings per quarter)	
1870/4	55
1875/9	48
1880/4	42
1885/9	32
1890/4	30
1895/9	28
1900/4	27
1905/9	31
1910/14	33

Over a span of thirty years the five-year average price dropped by exactly half. On the other hand, the price of animal products, except for wool, kept up better, falling later and less dramatically, notably for meat. There was even a rise in the price of eggs (see table 30).

Foreign competition was the basic cause of the fall in prices, and especially of the collapse in wheat prices. The British market, totally

---

[71] See particularly on this period: C.S.Orwin and E.H.Whetham, *History of British Agriculture, 1846–1914* (London, 1964); Perry, *British Farming*; P.J.Perry(ed.), *British Agriculture, 1875–1914* (London, 1973); S.B.Saul, *The Myth of the Great Depression 1873–96* (London, 1969) pp.34–5; Mathias, *The First Industrial Nation*, pp. 343–9; Thompson, *English Landed Society*, pp.308–26; W.Ashworth, *An Economic History of England, 1870–1939* (London, 1969) pp.46ff.

[72] *Abstract*, p.489.

[73] Mathias, *The First Industrial Nation*, pp.474–5.

Table 30 Board of Trade wholesale-price indices for cereals and animal products[74]

	Cereals	Animal products	General price index
1881/5	84	99	84
1886/90	68	85	71
1891/5	66	85	68

unprotected by customs barriers, was invaded by agricultural produce coming from the 'new countries', where vast stretches of fertile virgin land had just been put under cultivation – the central plains of the United States, then the Canadian prairies, the Argentinian pampas, and certain regions of Australia[75]. Farming there was extensive and often mechanized, so that production costs were lower than they were for Britain's capital-intensive agriculture. In addition, transport costs came down, notably in the 1880s, thanks to the construction of railways in those new countries (and to the lowering of their rates), aided by the progress of steam-navigation which brought a reduction in ocean-freight charges. However, this downward trend in freight-rates had been in train for a long time, and its effect should not be overestimated[76]. None the less, the 'freight factor', i.e. the share of freight in the total cost of goods delivered to British ports, came down considerably[77]. In all, from the end of the 1860s to the beginning of the 1900s, the cost of transporting wheat from Chicago to Liverpool fell by 72 per cent, or a sum equal to half the fall in the price of wheat on the English market[78]. However, foreign competition was much more intense in the cereal market than in the market for animal products, in spite of the appearance of cold-storage transport (the first cargo of

[74] Saul, *The Myth*, p.14 (table 1).
[75] Mathias, *The First Industrial Nation*, p.473 (table 22), gives the main sources of wheat imports. North America provided more than half during the three last decades of the nineteenth century, but her share dropped thereafter to the advantage of Australia and South America. Purchases in Europe (especially Russia) remained stable in quantity, but fell back from 61 per cent of the total for 1860/9 to 16 per cent for 1900/9. There were also sizeable imports from India (16 per cent of total imports in 1880/9).
[76] Index of freight from the United States to Great Britain (1830=100).

1875/9	50
1880/4	33
1905/9	22

[77] For Black Sea wheat arriving at Liverpool, this factor fell from 18 per cent in 1864 to 8 per cent in 1886.
[78] Perry, *British Agriculture*, p. xiv.

frozen meat arrived in London from Australia in 1880)[79]. Wheat was a standardized commodity with a genuine world price; besides, English wheat did not give flour of as high a quality as American Middle West 'hard' wheat. Hence the very sharp rise in British imports (table 28), which tripled between 1860/9 and 1900/9. They covered an ever-rising percentage of consumption, passing the three-quarters mark by the 1890s[80]. On the other hand, meat produced in Great Britain was of a quality superior to what was imported, and in fact intended for a different market, that of the well-to-do classes, so that it remained, in effect, protected from competition. Between 1870 and 1895, 'best English beef' only dropped 11 per cent in price, and 'best English mutton' 8 per cent, against 23 and 30 per cent for imported beef and mutton. Also, although imports of butter and cheese increased greatly, the transport of milk by sea was practically impossible. But the disparity in the trends of cereal and animal-product prices stemmed also from a change in the pattern of demand for foodstuffs. This demand continued to progress, given the increase in population and the rise in real wages (which was considerable during the Great Depression). However, this rise brought Engel's Law into play. Starting from a certain income level (which was at that time being reached by a large number of British people), per-capita demand for basic foodstuffs was no longer elastic in relation to income: it does not increase in proportion to income and even tends to diminish. The new purchasing power tends to be used for buying foods which were formerly luxuries – meat and other animal products, and fruit and vegetables, whose consumption per head remained elastic in relation to income. In fact, this type of consumption increased, which meant that the domestic price of such products resisted foreign competition effectively. When the working classes stopped living mainly on bread and potatoes, and varied their diet, the per-capita consumption of potatoes in Great Britain, which had reached its peak in 1871, went down by one-third between that year and 1900, and that of wheat, which had gone up since the 1840s, stabilized after 1870.

In these conditions the crisis did not strike the different types of production and the different agricultural regions to an equal extent[81]; for British agriculture, once again, was not homogeneous and displayed great variety.

[79] Imports of chilled (*not* frozen) meat of good quality coming from North America, as well as live cattle, had started in 1875; R.Perren, 'The North American beef and cattle trade with Great Britain, 1870–1914', *Economic History Review*, 2nd series, XXV (3), Aug. 1971, 430–44.
[80] 50 per cent in 1875/7, 77 per cent in 1893/5; cf. p.160 note 49.
[81] The intensity of the depression also varied in the period; Perry, *British Agriculture*, p. xix.

The producers of cereals, and above all of wheat, were the worst hit by foreign competition. Wheat-growing, which was no longer profitable on many farms, lost much ground, and the area devoted to it was reduced by half between 1872 and 1913. The cultivation of other cereals kept up much better despite the fall in prices (less serious, it is true, than for wheat), for farmers needed them to provide themselves with forage and straw. Furthermore, as the consumption of beer went up, reaching its peak in 1899, and as English barley and malt were superior in quality to others, the growing of barley remained rewarding. Green and root crops fell away also[82] and, in total, the arable surface of Great Britain diminished by 24 per cent between 1872 and 1913, falling from 44 to 31 per cent of the total land used for agriculture. But the acreage of pasture and grasslands rose by 26 per cent, and with this their share of the total from 56 to 69 per cent, as is shown in table 31.

Table 31   Crop acreage in Great Britain[83]

	Millions of acres			Percentage of the total		
	1872	1895	1913	1872	1895	1913
Wheat	3.6	1.4	1.8	12	4	5.5
Other corn	6.0	6.0	5.2	19	18	16
Cereals total	9.6	7.4	7.0	31	22	21.5
Green and root crops	3.6	3.2	3.0	12	10	9
Market gardening	0.2	0.3	0.4	0.8	1	1
Surface cultivated	13.4	10.9	10.4	44	33	31
Fallow grass, pasture	17.3	21.8	21.9	56	67	69

In 1867/9, vegetable products amounted to 45 per cent of the gross value of British agricultural output, and animal products to 55 per cent, and for England alone in 1867/71 the two sectors were exactly equal. In 1894/1903, however, animal production represented 70 per cent of the gross total, and crops only 30 per cent; and in England in 1894/8, the percentages were 63 and 37 per cent respectively[84].

The retreat of cereal-production, which was not only relative but absolute, both in volume and in value, applied above all to wheat-pro-

---

[82]   In the same way turnips, which are labour-intensive, lost ground because of the shortage of hands.

[83]   From Mathias, *The First Industrial Nation*, p. 476 (table 24), also p.344 (fig.16).

[84]   T.W.Fletcher, in Perry, *British Agriculture*, p.54.

duction, which in England amounted in 1867/71 to 43 per cent of the gross value of all crops and 22 per cent of total agricultural production, but had fallen to 18 and 7 per cent respectively in 1894/8[85]. In volume, England's arable output diminished by 5 or 9 per cent (according to the index chosen) between these two periods, and animal production rose by 20 or 18 per cent[86]. We may add that the number of cattle in Great Britain increased by 24 per cent between 1872 and 1913 (from 5.6 to 7.0 million), but the number of sheep fell from 28 to 24 million[87].

With such price and output trends, it was to be expected that the regions worst hit by the crisis should be the 'corn counties' of the south and east of England, and among them, as after 1815, the districts with wet, heavy soils[88]. Those with light soils fared better, thanks, for instance, to the cultivation of barley in East Anglia. Indeed, the production of cereals tended to be concentrated along the east coast, a region that is relatively dry. But, in the aggregate, farmers who went in for mixed farming (and especially the cereals–sheep combination) suffered badly. It was an elegant, well-balanced system, which was able to even out small variations in comparative prices of cereals and livestock, but was quite incapable of adapting to a sudden and drastic drop in cereal prices. Furthermore, many farmers attributed their misfortune at first simply to bad weather, and took time to understand that vast imports of wheat and low prices were there to stay. Finally, mixed farming had high costs in labour, artificial fertilizers and animal feed. The forced reduction in wheat-growing destroyed its precarious equilibrium, and reorganization was difficult. Many farmers (e.g. in Essex, the richest of the corn counties) hung on to cereals, ruined themselves and were replaced by Scottish or Welsh cattle-farmers who, used to working hard and living frugally, went in for extensive cattle-raising[89].

Against this, the grass counties of the north and west and part of the Midlands, which had specialized for a long time in stock-farming on permanent pastures, had far less difficulty, because prices of animal products kept firm and the cost of animal feed was low (from the 1870s

[85] ibid., pp.37,54. For the UK as a whole, percentages were lower, and in 1894/1903 wheat only accounted for 4 per cent of total gross production, against 15 per cent in 1870/6. See also Mathias, *The First Industrial Nation*, p.345; Saul, *The Myth*, p.34. In 1867/71 in England, the value of wheat production was equal to that of beef and mutton combined. In 1894/8, each of the following products exceeded wheat: milk, beef, mutton, pork, eggs and poultry.

[86] Perry, *British Agriculture*, pp.36–7.

[87] Partly, it is true, as the result of epizootic disease. Mathias, *The First Industrial Nation*, p.477 (table 25).

[88] Where symptons of crisis appeared as early as 1873; Perry, *British Agriculture*, p. xix.

[89] Jones, pp.21, 23–4; Perry, *British Agriculture*, p.xxviii.

onwards much maize was imported for animals). These differing fortunes led to disparities in the movements of wages, profits and rents. However, the basic contrast between corn and grass counties should be qualified. The latter did not entirely escape trouble, as stock-farming and particularly cattle-fattening involved serious risks[90]. The most favoured regions were those of dairying, as imports of milk were impossible, and per-capita consumption rose, especially in large towns, to which refrigerated transport by railway (1872) facilitated access; and milk prices held up. Certainly this redeployment to dairying posed some problems and required the learning of new skills, as well as initial investment for the purchase of milch cows; but from then onwards running costs were low and tended to fall further. The factor which made many farmers decide to specialize in liquid milk was the fall in price of English cheese after 1870 owing to foreign competition. Cheese-making became unprofitable and shrank by two-thirds from 1860 to 1910. English herds of dairy cows increased by 43 per cent between 1866/70 and 1906/10, and milk-production by 61 per cent, thanks to an improvement in yields (14 per cent between 1860/80 and 1896/1910). Milk production became the largest branch of English agriculture, providing 12 per cent of gross agricultural product in 1867/71 and 18 per cent in 1894/8, but a growing proportion (rising from one-third to three-quarters) went to the direct sale of liquid milk, while the percentage that went to the making of butter and cheese declined. Dairy farming was profitable and saved the outlay of many farmers[91].

Another prosperous branch was specialized and intensive market-gardening and fruit-growing, which progressed around large towns – for instance in northern Kent, where it supplied cheap jam-making in Bermondsey – and in the Vale of Evesham. The commercial horticultural acreage in Great Britain rose from 64,000 acres in 1867 to 365,000 in 1913, but the latter figure was only 1 per cent of total acreage.

However, the dominant fact was the part conversion of arable land to more or less permanent pasture devoted to stock-farming. This only continued a trend that had begun in the preceding decades through the spread of mixed farming and the structural changes in it which we have noted. The depression speeded up this trend, and indeed one can only again be surprised, given the market pressures, that this redeployment was not pushed further. There has been criticism of

[90] Perry, *British Agriculture*, pp.xvi, xxxviii, xlii.
[91] D.Taylor, 'The English dairy industry, 1860–1930', *Economic History Review*, 2nd series, XXIX (4), Nov.1976, 585–601.

British farmers for not adapting better to the new situation, as happened for example in Denmark. Always remembering the innate conservatism of farmers (and, according to Perry, most of them hesitated before making the effort required for conversion), we should note that in several regions natural conditions were not propitious for such a change, which called for capital that was simply not available[92]. In fact, for the first time, an agricultural depression did not lead to new investment by the large landowners, who were pessimistic about the future of agriculture and thought that this traditional remedy would be ineffective for surmounting such a serious crisis. Whenever they had disposable funds, they preferred to invest them in stocks and shares whose yield was higher than that of real estate. In fact there was net disinvestment and a deterioration in the physical capital of agriculture. Marginal land and a number of farms were abandoned, and the rural landscape was less well-maintained[93].

In the end, however, thanks to a redeployment which varied according to natural conditions and commercial opportunities, but which involved important structural changes (carried out without help from the state, which unlike the governments of nearly all the European countries, refused to return to protectionism), the crisis was less severe than has often been thought, and a modest prosperity returned at the beginning of the twentieth century. In the long term agricultural production did not diminish much in volume, the decline in cereals (and above all wheat) being compensated by the progress of stock-farming. The Ojala index shows a rise of 12 per cent in the United Kingdom's gross output at constant prices from 1867/9 to 1911/13. It is true that net product – after deducting the purchase of goods and services which were inputs to agriculture – diminished, at constant prices, by 7 per cent between 1867/9 and 1894/1903, and only went up by 3 per cent between that decade and 1911/13, when it settled at a level slightly below that of the end of the 'golden age'[94].

Feinstein has also calculated *Great Britain's* gross and net agricultural production at constant prices. Gross production was practically stable on trend from 1870 to 1885, then it rose slightly and ended in 1911/13 at 9 per cent higher than in 1870/6. On the other hand, as in the Ojala calculation, net production declined by 9 per cent between

[92] At the beginning of the depression a good number of landowners and tenant farmers, had exhausted their financial reserves, so that they did not have the means to put through changes.

[93] Perry, *British Agriculture,* pp.xxi, xxx, xxiv.

[94] Ashworth, p.69; also Mathias, *The First Industrial Nation,* p.348.

1870/6 and 1894/1903, then rose by 4 per cent in 1911/13, remaining a little under the pre-depression level[95].

With these trends in output, the productivity of the labour-force in agriculture improved markedly, for the exodus of farm-labourers continued. Their number fell from 962,000 in 1871 to 621,000 in 1911, and the total workforce in agriculture from 1.6 million in 1871 to 1.3 million in 1901. So the added value per farmworker at constant prices grew by 15 per cent between 1867/9 and 1886/95[96]. On the other hand, yields per acre did not improve, a sign that agriculture had become less intensive, commercial considerations having sometimes done harm to technical standards. English agriculture was no longer a model, even though it remained one of the most efficient in the world.

With production stagnating and a shrinking labour-force, British agriculture could only see its weight in the growing national economy dwindling rapidly to a minimal figure. Conversely, as this weight was already small at the beginning of the Great Depression, the decline in agriculture did not have as serious an effect on the national economy as in other countries, which, though industrialized, had a larger agricultural sector – e.g. France but also the United States and Germany. Its multiplier effects were limited, and the drop in foodstuff prices, which benefited the masses, even stimulated demand for other products[97]. As for the consequences of this depression for rural society, it has been reckoned that from 1873/7 to 1893/7, farm incomes dropped by 42 per cent at current prices and by 32 per cent in real terms[98], which seems an overestimate.

Yet the great landowners were seriously affected. They found it difficult to engage and keep tenants and, under the threat of seeing their farms abandoned, they had to consent to reductions in rent,

[95]   Feinstein, *National Income,* p.213 (table 10.3). At current prices the fall between the 1870s and the 1890s would of course be much steeper; Bairoch, *Commerce extérieur,* p.205 (table 58).

[96]   But in industry it grew by 25 per cent. A controversy about the productivity of agricultural labour between 1850 and 1914 broke out between E.H.Hunt, P.David and D.Metcalf; see *Economic History Review,* 2nd series, XX (2), Aug.1967, 280–92; XXII (1), Apr. 1969, 117–19; XXIII (3) Dec.1970, 504–19. It emerged from this that productivity (measured by David in bushels of grain harvested per unit of labour input) varied markedly (roughly 1:2) from one region to another, being low in the south and in East Anglia, although their husbandry was highly capitalistic, and high in the north. Hunt has explained these differences by variations in wage-rates. Where these were low, labourers, who were badly fed, had a mediocre productivity, because their bodies were not strong enough. Consequently, these differences in productivity did not cause noticeable divergences in unit-costs. However some uncertainties remain, for conclusions have been drawn from the exceptional wages paid at harvest times.

[97]   Bairoch, *Commerce extérieur,* pp.204, 211ff, indeed holds a different opinion.

[98]   Mathias, *The First Industrial Nation,* p.343; Bairoch, *Commerce extérieur,* p.211.

which amounted to one-quarter on average in England between 1874/8 and 1894/8. Furthermore the capital represented by their land lost value. Even so, at the beginning of the twentieth century, they only enjoyed an average yield of 3 per cent on agricultural property. But averages mask important variations. The more an estate produced cereals, the more severely the landlord was affected by the crisis, but thanks to the general fall in prices, the real value of rents was maintained on estates which grew little grain[99]. People at the time thought that the very large estates came off better than those of the gentry; but it is not true that the latter faced ruin and sold their properties. In any case, they would not have found buyers, as investment in land was no longer profitable. Only from 1910 onwards did large-scale sales of land begin for reasons that were largely political – the anti-landlord legislation of the Liberal government, especially its budget of 1909. The buyers were often the sitting tenants. It was the beginning of the break-up of the large estates and of the liquidation of the landed interest[100]. But, as early as the 1880s the economic position and, as a corollary, the social and political influence of the landlords, had become distinctly weaker[101].

On their side, many tenant-farmers were ruined at the beginning of the depression. Others gave up their farms and retired; but those who survived and the incoming tenants succeeded in maintaining real incomes that were quite satisfactory, to the extent that they could adapt to new conditions, concentrating on the most profitable activities (above all stock-farming) and lowering costs. Thus one saw a new type of farmer appear, with a purely commercial outlook and a concern for strict economy[102]. In addition, several legislative measures improved their legal status and guaranteed them more independence and security. The number of farmers only diminished slightly[103], but there were many varieties of experience resulting from differing geographical conditions, ease of access to markets, and the attitudes of landlords towards their tenants.

The numbers of agricultural labourers declined dramatically, as we

---

[99] The fall in rents was from 10 to 50 per cent according to districts, bringing them back to the level of the 1840s; but there were cases of rises, e.g. on the estates of Lord Derby in Lancashire; see Thompson, *English Landed Society*, pp.303, 310; Perry, *British Agriculture*, pp. xxvi–xxvii, 30, 36; also Deane and Cole, p.301, on the fall of rents' share in the net factor incomes earned in agriculture.

[100] Thompson, *English Landed Society*, pp.317, 321–2.

[101] The electoral reform of 1884 and the creation in 1888 of elected county councils contributed to this loss of influence.

[102] Perry, *British Agriculture*, p. xiii.

[103] The decline in the labour-force employed in agriculture was almost entirely due to the drop in the number of agricultural workers; Deane and Cole, p.143.

have seen, but not only as a result of the depression. Certainly the latter limited employment opportunities (owing to mechanization and less intensive farming), but the flight from the countryside was in part due to the attraction of the towns, and it was as massive in the regions of the north and west that had been spared as in the rest of the country. Furthermore, the money wages of day-labourers did not fall, and their real wages definitely increased.

LANDOWNING AND FARMING

Curiously enough, no document gives a general view of the distribution of landowning in Great Britain before a survey carried out in 1873 which was called *The New Domesday Book,* for it was the first – and last – enquiry of this sort since 1086. Despite various shortcomings, it revealed some striking results.

Admittedly, in the whole of the United Kingdom, more than one million people were owners of land, but for the vast majority of them it was only a question of having tiny plots; because 7000 persons owned four-fifths of the land, making up roughly the class of landowners. In England and Wales, there were 210,000 owners of land, but 122,000 of them possessed less than 10 acres. For England alone, the distribution of land was as set out in table 32.[104]

Table 32   Distribution of landed property in England in 1873

	No. of owners	Percentage of the total land surface held by each group
Owners of more than 10,000 acres	363	24
Owners of 3000–10,000 acres	1000	17
Owners of 1000– 3000 acres	2000	12.5
Owners of 300– 1000 acres	?	14
Owners of 1–300 acres	?	24.5

N.B. Waste lands are not included.

[104] From Thompson, *English Landed Society,* pp.27, 28, 32, 113, 116, 117 (notably tables II to VI). See also for what follows, pp.14–15, 25, 112. The total of these percentages is 92 per cent. According to G.E.Mingay, *The Gentry* (London, 1976), p.59 (table 3.1), the Crown and the Church of England owned 10 per cent of the land in England. Perkin, p.431, gives a higher number of large (and very large) landowners.

The landed aristocracy (F.M.L.Thompson), consisting of fewer than 400 very large landowners with rent-rolls above £10,000 a year[105], owned almost exactly one-quarter of the land in England. Half of them were peers of the realm. Within this group one found a few dozen 'super-magnates', possessing several tens, not to say hundreds, of thousands of acres. It is true that the largest estates were to be found in Scotland (several exceeding 200,000 acres) and consisted largely of mountains and moors, so that they were not the most lucrative[106]. The biggest landowner in the United Kingdom was the Duke of Sutherland with a regular 'little kingdom' of 1,358,000 acres[107]. The Duke of Buccleuch owned 460,000 acres and had the highest rent-roll in the country, £267,000. But several English magnates with less extensive properties received from them annual incomes of more than £100,000[108].

Next came about 3000 landowners in England (4000 in the whole United Kingdom) owning 1000 to 10,000 acres, drawing annual incomes from land of £1,000 to £10,000. One found there a number of 'poor' lords, but mostly the gentry, divided into higher gentry and simple village squires, with 3000 acres as the dividing line. This group owned 29.5 per cent of England's soil, i.e. more than the aristocracy.

[105] One assumes that in the nineteenth century on average rents produced one pound per acre.

[106] See Bédarida, p.47: 24 magnates owned one-quarter of Scotland and 350 landowners two-thirds.

[107] See E.Richards, *The Leviathan of Wealth* (London, 1973); also E.Richards, 'Structural change in a regional economy: Sutherland and the Industrial Revolution, 1780–1830', *Economic History Review,* 2nd series, XXVI (1), Feb.1973, 63–76. George Granville Leveson-Gower (1758–1833) became Marquis of Stafford in 1803 and a great landowner in England. He was also the heir of the famous Duke of Bridgewater, hence of his mines and canals. In 1785 he had married the Countess of Sutherland, who brought him nearly 1 million acres. So he possessed an enormous fortune, his rents amounting to £142,000 per annum, and his total income to £200,000 per annum. He was made Duke of Sutherland, but his eldest son, the second Duke, did not inherit the Bridgewater interests.

In the first decades of the nineteenth century, and again in the 1840s and 1850s, the estates of the Sutherlands and many other large landowners in the Highlands were systematically reorganized by clearances, i.e. the eviction of small tenants who tilled a modest patch, so that the land could be let to large-scale sheep-farmers, which was more profitable. The evicted peasants were reinstated on the coast, to become fishermen or factory workers, which involved heavy investment. But these industrial enterprises failed and finally many Highlanders emigrated, although a number of crofters succeeded in holding on.

[108] But a part of these very large incomes was of non-agricultural origin (urban rents, mining royalties, etc.). See A.S.Turberville, *The House of Lords in the Age of Reform, 1784–1837* (London, 1958), pp. 374–6, 407–10; Bédarida, p.63. In 1873, 874 people in England and Wales owned more than 5000 acres each; 525 members of the peerage owned more than half the UK. 49 peers had more than 50,000 acres, and 15 more than 100,000 each.

Finally one came to medium and small landowners, with less than 1000 acres, who possessed in total 38.5 per cent of English land. The wealthier ones, in fact, belonged to the lesser gentry, so that overall the gentry held more than half the land[109]. Many others were men of independent means who let their land to tenants, for in 1873 the owner-occupiers or yeomen only held a little more than 10 per cent of all land.

In total, *The New Domesday Book* revealed a very strong concentration of landed property in England, and in the whole United Kingdom, the greater part of the soil fit for cultivation belonging to a few thousand large landowners, and 53.5 per cent of English soil to fewer than 4000 people with more than 1000 acres each. Experts in the period believe that the situation had scarcely changed in the half-century before 1873, and that it continued until 1910 at least. Furthermore this concentration was an ancient phenomenon, as was its tendency to increase, with small yeoman property and even the estates of the lesser gentry giving way to the great estates. The trend dated back several centuries, to the end of the middle ages. It is true that a whole battery of laws prevented the break-up of large domains, except in the case of financial catastrophe, as happened to the Duke of Buckingham, who had to sell 50,000 acres between 1844 and 1857. This system ensured the consolidation of estates and their transmission intact to a single heir from one generation to another. Primogeniture was very often reinforced by entail and strict settlement, which gave the heir to an estate a simple life-interest and meant that he could not sell off land. The laws applying to mortgages protected the debtor, so that, although many estates were mortgaged, this situation was not necessarily a danger to the estate and was sometimes a stimulus to investment, which was indeed facilitated by these borrowings. Furthermore, from the 1830s onwards, a serious effort was made on many estates to practise careful and profitable management; indeed several causes of excessive expense and indebtedness which had jeopardized landed fortunes during the preceding century (e.g. country-house building, electoral expenses) were much less in evidence[110].

[109] Mingay, *The Gentry*, p.59 (table 3.1); also Thompson in his review of Mingay, *Times Lit.Sup.*, 11 Feb. 1977. But he emphasizes the gulf which separates the gentry from the 'magnates'. In any case, the proportion of land belonging either to the aristocracy or to the gentry varied very much from one county to another, the share of the very large landowners and the concentration of land ownership being generally bigger in the north and west of England than in the rest of the country.

[110] See Thompson, *English Landed Society*, ch. 6, pp.151ff. D.Cannadine, 'Aristocratic indebtedness in the nineteenth century: The case reopened, *Economic History Review*, 2nd series, XXX, (4), Nov.1977, 624–50, does indeed maintain that the indebtedness of the great estates persisted and even worsened – for the expenses of

On the whole, during the decades before 1873, the great estates remained intact. When they changed hands as the result of bankruptcy or the disappearance of a family (which was rarer than in the eighteenth century), they did so usually *en bloc,* preserving their unity[111]. There was even a tendency towards greater concentration, which had been interrupted during the wars against France, when all farmers were able to prosper. This concentration revived as a result of the postwar difficulties which were felt more harshly by yeomen and small squires than by big landowners[112], so that some had to sell their land to a rich neighbour. Besides, although yeomen were still quite numerous at the beginning of the nineteenth century (perhaps 160,000 in England and Wales in 1803), they even then owned a small proportion of the land – 15 per cent or a little more. After 1815, their numbers fell again and their share of English soil was only 10 per cent in 1873[113]. But it was a minor movement and on the whole the distribution of landed property in Victorian Britain remained stable.

The preceding pages have shown that, despite their wealth, the large landowners were not immune to economic fluctuations. Many of them suffered from the two periods of low farm prices and rents – after 1815 and above all during the Great Depression. But one must remember that there was a simultaneous general fall in prices which tended to keep up real incomes. On the other hand, during the prosperity of the third quarter-century, the economic position of landlords became relatively weaker, and the Great Depression did them undoubted harm. Indeed these traditional masters of rural England, who had largely succeeded in safeguarding and increasing their capital and income (especially the very big landowners), became painfully aware of their decline.

These generalizations hide some stark differences in the evolving fortunes of individual landowners. Much depended on the extent of their properties, their geographical situation, the type of crops chosen,

---

the aristocracy remained high; but this indebtedness was not ruinous, although it aggravated the effect of the depression at the end of the century and widened the gap between the very rich landlords and those who were less so.

[111] On the other hand, few new large estates were created during the nineteenth century. Some rich bankers built up a few at the beginning, but during the 'Golden Age' the price of land went up so much and the yield on investment in land was so low that the new rich held off, apart from the purchase of a fine country-house with a few acres around it.

[112] It is often thought that they also suffered more from the depression at the end of the century.

[113] Mingay, *The Gentry*, p.59 (table 3.1).These small owners were especially to be found in districts where fruit and vegetables were grown, e.g. Kent, or in poor, isolated regions like Wales.

the quality of management, the investments made, the level of debt and finally the size of the non-agricultural incomes which they had at their disposal. The main category of these extra incomes were those derived from mining for in English law (unlike on the continent) the owner of land was also the owner of what lay beneath its surface. Of course, few landlords themselves directly exploited the mines on their estates (through agents or managers), and most leased mineral rights against royalties. However, because of the extent of coal fields in Great Britain and the impressive growth of coal-extraction in the nineteenth century, this was a source of large incomes for many landowners (and particularly the bigger ones) in the north of England, in South Wales and in the Scottish Lowlands. Another important source of income was the leasing of land on the edge of growing towns, particularly Greater London, to developers, for building there on long-term leases. A few large landowners even played a more active part, launching themselves into industrial enterprises, the construction of ports, and real-estate speculation. Finally, from the mid-century, and even more after 1870, many members of the aristocracy lent their noble names to the joint-stock companies, thus inspiring confidence among savers, in exchange for lucrative sinecures on their boards. In most cases, the landlords were rentiers and not active agents of industrialization and urbanization, but these developments brought to many of them an extra income, often of substantial size, which offset the relative decline of their landed wealth[114]. This contributed to the fusion into one plutocracy of big-business leaders and landed magnates, a process which got under way at the end of Victoria's reign and triumphed during the reign of her son[115].

When considering the question of land use, it is important to note that the greater part of British soil was cultivated by tenant-farmers.

[114] See J.T.Ward and R.G.Wilson (eds.), *Land and Industry* (Newton Abbot, 1971); Bédarida, p.62, who nevertheless reckons with good reason that, between 1850 and 1880, four-fifths of the nobility's incomes were derived from agriculture. Before 1850, only a handful of big landowners drew half or more of their incomes from non-agricultural sources. A striking, but exceptional, case is that of the earls of Dudley, who obtained enormous sums from estates which were not large, but were located at the the heart of the Black Country, by leasing or directly working mines and ironworks; T.J.Raybould, *The Economic Emergence of the Black Country: A Study of the Dudley Estate* (Newton Abbot, 1973). Yet, in the same region, E.Richards concludes that after 1820 many aristocrats retired from industry, becoming rentiers instead of entrepreneurs; 'The industrial face of a great estate: Trentham and Lilleshall, 1780–1860', *Economic History Review*, 2nd series, XXVII, (3), Aug. 1974, 414–30. Also G.Mee, *Aristocratic Enterprise: The Fitzwilliam Industrial Undertakings, 1795–1857* (Glasgow and London, 1975); D.Cannadine, *Lords and Landlords: The Aristocracy and the Towns, 1774–1967* (Leicester, 1980).
[115] Perkin, pp.434–7, 453–4.

The great estate was in effect a unit of property and consumption, but not of exploitation, being divided into farms which were let out to tenants. Indeed the largest estates were not composed geographically of a single block but were spread over several localities or even several counties. Furthermore, the direct management of his acres was not considered dignified for a gentleman, still less for a nobleman. Apart from the home farm, whose role was to keep the country house in fresh food, or perhaps a few model farms, farms were rarely worked by the owner through a bailiff. On the great estates, the management was entrusted to one or more agents, who received a full-time salary. On the other hand, several small estates could be run by a single agent. Becoming more and more professional during the nineteenth century, these agents played a key role, selecting tenants, fixing the conditions of leases, and supervising the working of the land and the investment projects; but of course the division of responsibilities and decisions between owner and agent varied according to the interest of the former in agriculture.

As for the farms, which were thus the working units, one of the original features of British agriculture was that they were relatively large. Again, this structure went far back in time, but it was accentuated by the consolidation of farms during the enclosures movement in the eighteenth and beginning of the nineteenth centuries, and by the landlords' preference for negotiating with a small number of substantial tenants who would pay their rents regularly and with whom it was more convenient to deal. Yet one should not overestimate this concentration[116].

In 1851, the average size of farms in England and Wales was 115 acres, and in Great Britain 102 acres. Two-thirds of the 215,000 farms had less than 100 acres[117], but these covered less than a quarter of the area cultivated. Although they were few in number (a quarter of the total), the farms of 100 to 300 acres extended over 45 per cent of the area cultivated. Then 16,840 very large farms of 300 acres or more, which amounted to only 8 per cent of all farms, occupied 30 per cent of

[116] J.R.Wordie, 'Social change on the Leveson-Gower estates, 1714–1832' *Economic History Review,* 2nd series, XXVII, (4) Nov. 1974, 593–609, reacting against ideas which he considers too optimistic, see a distinct decline of the small farmer (20 to 200 acres) and the yeoman between 1813 and 1832 (and probably later) and a tendency to consolidation in large farms. S.W.Martins, *A Great Estate at Work: The Holkham Estate and its Inhabitants in the Nineteenth Century* (Cambridge, 1980).

[117] Less than 50 acres if one adds Scotland. In England, small farms of 5 to 50 acres made up 42 per cent of the total number, but only covered 9 per cent of the surface cultivated. Many of these small farms were in marginal regions, or in Scotland and Wales.

the land cultivated. A little more than 800 of them extended to more than 1000 acres[118]. This structure hardly changed over the country as a whole during the second half of the nineteenth century. There were amalgamations of small farms of less than 40 acres, which increased the average size of farms in the regions of grain-growing and stock-breeding, but the development of small market-gardens worked in the opposite direction, and the sector of very large farms did not increase.

Thus the family farm remained important. In 1831, out of 961,000 families employed in agriculture in Great Britain, 131,000 were cultivators' families who employed no outside labour, 145,000 others employed labour, and there were 686,000 families of agricultural labourers. So, on average, one farming family existed for 2.5 families of labourers, a little less than 5 of the latter on average being employed on each farm using outside labour. By 1851 the situation had hardly changed, in spite of a slight drop in purely family farms; but later the number of farm-labourers dropped sharply.

The essential feature of British rural society, as the enclosures had simplified it, was in fact its pyramidal structure in three tiers, i.e. three classes very clearly distinct[119]. At the top, a few thousand large landowners; beneath them, a middle class of working farmers – about 300,000 in number. The most prosperous were the medium- and large-scale tenant farmers, real capitalist entrepreneurs, often possessed of extensive capital, on which they normally obtained a yield of 10 per cent; but there were also a fair number of small tenant farmers and yeomen, particularly in remote and isolated areas, who were poorer and more backward technically. Finally, at the base of the pyramid, came the large proletariat of farm labourers, of which there were 1,483,000 at the 1851 census. Of these, 128,000 were servants housed by their employers, most of them being women. Used to hard work, but employed irregularly, with long periods of unemployment in winter, receiving very low wages, this proletariat made up one of the poorest categories of the British population. This was particularly true between 1815 and the middle of the nineteenth century, and in the corn counties of the south, which had a permanent surplus of labour.

[118] Bédarida, p.48; Chambers and Mingay, p.173; David, p.178.
[119] Very good pages in Bédarida, pp.45ff. The most recent study is G.E.Mingay, *Rural Life in Victorian England* (London, 1977). But in Wales, in the Highlands of Scotland, in some parts of the north of England, as well as Ireland, only two layers were to be found:landlords and a peasantry of small farmers, plus a few yeomen. Elsewhere, there were no 'peasants'. On the other hand, one must take into account the artisans, small traders, and members of the professions in villages and country towns. D.W.Howell, *Land and People in Nineteenth-Century Wales* (London, 1978).

Such an overstocked labour market depressed wages by 30 per cent[120], so that many families only survived thanks to help from the parish. This miserable, illiterate mass on several occasions gave way to outbreaks of violence and direct action, notably the riots of 1816 and the summer of 1830 and the Rebecca Riots in Wales in 1839–43 (which were of a different type). Even peaceful times were marked by a chronic tendency to protest by organized poaching, arson, mutilation of cattle and other rural crimes[121]. However, in the second half of the century, as the rural exodus gradually absorbed the surplus labour, real wages and work conditions among farmworkers improved; but poverty persisted in this group, which was badly housed, badly fed and generally despised[122].

Despite all this, British rural society showed strong cohesion because of identity of interests between landowners and tenants, and also thanks to the deference that was nearly always prevalent, i.e. the respect and obedience shown by the lower orders towards their betters, the landowners. This deference was largely voluntary, but it was strengthened by the administrative powers of the justices of the peace, who were appointed mostly from the ranks of the landlords. The traditional leadership of the latter was virtually unchallenged up to 1914.

Should one conclude that, by abolishing the Corn Laws, Great Britain sacrificed her agriculture – in the long term? It would certainly be too much to say this, for, in spite of the Great Depression, agricultural production did not flag noticeably after the 1870s, and the history of English agriculture is not identical with that of grain-culti-vation. In any case, as population had increased rapidly in a small island where the acreage of land suitable for cultivation was limited, it would have been impossible for the nation's agriculture to provide the necessary extra foodstuffs on her own. Even nowadays, Great Britain is not self-sufficient in food in spite of remarkable technical progress and government support. At the beginning of the twentieth century,

---

[120] Deane and Cole, p.26.
[121] See J.P.Dunbairn (ed.), *Rural Discontent in Nineteenth-Century Britain* (London, 1974). From the 1860s onwards and particularly in 1872–4, there appeared unions of agricultural workers who had recourse to peaceful methods, but they barely withstood the depression. The tradition of direct action persisted for a long time in the Highlands, and organized poaching went on nearly everywhere.
[122] Jones, pp.31–2; Perry, *British Agriculture* pp.xxxii to xxxiii. The recent work of Pamela Horn, *Labouring Life in the Victorian Countryside* (London, 1976), emphas-izes the persistence of poverty among agricultural workers at the end of the nineteenth century.

British agriculture only fed the nation for three days a week, but with very different proportions for the various foodstuffs[123]. Foreigners often saw in this a serious weakness in the British economy, but these views reflected an obstinately peasant mentality among the continentals. Certainly the deficiency in the country's agricultural production in relation to its consumption was a serious handicap for Britain during the two world wars, but one must not confuse the military and the economic point of view, and from the latter the development just described gave England important advantages[124].

Foreign competition forced British agriculture to abandon the less profitable forms of production (wheat in particular) in order to specialize in stock-farming, which was most favoured by geographical and economic conditions. Moreover, the relative decline of agricultrue, a sector with relatively low productivity, and the redeployment of resources, notably in manpower, to the benefit of other more productive sectors, helped to raised labour-productivity and average per-capita income. Furthermore, as Great Britain supplied herself from world markets at the lowest prices, the cost of living was cheaper than in other countries which protected their agriculture. This had favourable consequences for the British standard of living, and also for the competitivity of industry. Finally, the massive demand for foodstuffs coming from abroad, and especially from the new countries, increased those countries' purchasing power and widened the outlets for British industry.

---

[123] One-third for butter, 40 per cent for cereals, less than 60 per cent for meat, 100 per cent for milk. See for example Bairoch, *Commerce extérieur,* p.299 (note 5), also p.211. From 1873/7 to 1893/7 the volume of net imports of foodstuffs increased by 90 per cent.

[124] See, however, the different views on the effect of free trade expressed by Bairoch and McCloskey, Chapter 5, pp.126–8.

7 The textile industries

The importance of the industrial sector – including mining and construction – in the British economy made dramatic progress between the end of the Napoleonic wars and the 1830s, so that industry rose to take precedence over other activities. After that period its relative importance only increased slowly. However this stabilization should not hide the dynamism of the industrial sector and the considerable transformation it experienced. This showed three main tendencies.

THE STRUCTURE OF BRITISH INDUSTRY

In the first place, industrial production grew at a speed which was not very impressive (2.5 per cent a year on average between 1800 and 1913, and also between 1837 and 1901) and which slowed down after the middle of the nineteenth century. However, this growth, maintained over such a long period, meant that the volume of production was multiplied by five during Victoria's reign. Certainly industrial growth was the engine of overall growth for the economy.

Secondly, there was the sustained diffusion of technological progress, which was not confined to a few spectacular inventions, but consisted of an almost continuous flow of detailed improvements in the equipment and organization of industries, including those which did not undergo radical innovation. One knows that modern forms of production and organization, born in the Industrial Revolution, never ceased to advance at the expense of more archaic methods, and that the factory system and the steam-engine spread gradually to new industries to the detriment of traditional crafts. Power-driven machinery tended to become the central element in a growing number of industries, though one should not exaggerate the speed of this process[1].

[1] See A.E.Musson, 'Industrial motive-power in the United Kingdom, 1800–70', *Economic History Review*, 2nd series, XXIX(3), Aug. 1976, 415–390.

Machines became more complicated, more precise, more rapid and more completely automated. New manufactured goods appeared (e.g. electrical apparatus, bicycles, motor-cars) and existing products changed. A steamship of 1901 was very different from a 'steamer' of 1837. Certainly one can see a slowing-down of innovation in some industries in the last quarter of the century, especially as compared with other countries. Yet the technological basis of British industry changed profoundly and continuously, even if some opportunities for technical innovation were not sufficiently exploited[2].

Finally the structure of industry, i.e. the relative importance of its different branches, changed considerably, while retaining its essential character. Unfortunately it is not easy to follow these changes closely, for the first 'industrial census' dates from 1907, and the available data for earlier years are much less satisfactory. So we will start with the situation in 1907 (table 33) and will try to sketch out the changes which may have occurred during the preceding decades.

One is at once struck by the size of the three main branches – mining (mostly coal), the iron industry in all its forms and the textile industries (swollen of course by the clothing and footwear trades, etc.). By themselves these three branches provided exactly 60 per cent of the net value of industrial production. Furthermore, in 1911 they were to employ 49 per cent of the industrial labour-force and 25 per cent of the total employed population of Britain;[3] and in 1911/13 they were to supply more than two-thirds of British exports by value. After them came the food industries and construction each of which accounted for more than 10 per cent of the value of total production; but the size of the other industrial branches was really very small, since together they only provided 18.2 per cent of total output by value. If one considers manufacturing industry on its own, without mining, building and utilities, the value of its total output was split up as follows:

Production and processing of metals	32.0 per cent
Textiles and clothing	31.1 per cent
Food industries	16.7 per cent
Other industries	20.2 per cent

In fact, this concentration of British industrial activity on a small number of large staples, giving it a relatively narrow base, dated back a long time and was already a feature at the beginning of Victoria's reign. One can see it reflected in the data in table 34, based on the

[2] See W.Ashworth, *An Economic History of England, 1870–1939*(London, 1969), ch. 2, pp. 25ff.
[3] See table 34.

Table 33   Structure of British industry in 1907

Industries	Net value of output in £m	Percentages of national income	of total value of industrial output
1 Mines and quarries	119	6.0	16.2
2 Building and contracting	74	3.7	10.1
3 Gas, electricity, water	31	1.6	4.2
4 Engineering and metals manufactures	164	8.2	22.3
5 Textiles and clothing	160	8.0	21.6
6 Food, drink, tobacco	86	4.3	11.6
7 Paper and printing	33	1.6	4.4
8 Chemicals	21	1.1	2.8
9 Wood industries	21	1.1	2.8
10 Various	29	1.5	4.0
Total	738	37.1	100.0

After Deane and Cole p. 175 (table 40). Using *Abstract*, p. 270, one can add the following details, but they relate to the United Kingdom, which explains the slight differences:

	Net value of output £m	Percentage of total value of industrial output
Metal manufacture	45	6.3
Engineering	112	15.7
Textiles	95	13.3
Clothing and leather	46	6.4

census, which show the distribution of manpower between the various branches of industry. The information is far from reliable, but it gives a good idea of orders of magnitude[4].

It is striking that the three main branches – mines, metals and textiles – seem to have absorbed constantly the same percentage of industry's labour-force, i.e. 49 per cent in 1814 and in 1911, with minimal fluctuations (50 per cent in 1851, 46 per cent in 1901) in the interval. If one adds clothing, the percentage exceeds 60 per cent, but with a tendency to decline – from 70 per cent in 1851 to 62 per cent in

[4]   See B.R.Mitchell and P.Dean,*Abstract of British Historical Statistics* (quoted hereafter as *Abstract)*, on the difficulties of extracting data of this kind from the census and on the lack of homogeneity in the series. The data of 1841 are particularly unreliable and difficult to compare with those that follow. The fairly large residual category 'All others occupied' include no doubt workers in industry. On the other hand the group 'Clothing' embraces all sorts of people like cobblers who repair shoes but do not make them.

1911[5]. However, the essential fact was the stability of the whole group, and it is beyond dispute that, during the Victorian era and up to 1914, British industry was dominated by three great basic industries, whose activity was the dynamic factor in economic growth and fluctuations dictating prosperity or depression for the whole country – coal, iron and steel (primary and secondary), and textiles with their ancillaries. This special structure is explained by the traditional pre-eminence of the textile industries, by the early rise of iron manufactures in Great Britain and by her richness in coal; but it was also due to the large proportion of the output of these industries that was exported (except, for a long time, coal) and that led to a more rapid expansion after the end of the eighteenth century than was the case with the minor branches that worked mainly for the home market[6].

However, inside this group of basic industries, there occurred readjustments of some importance between 1841 and 1911, and changes in the relative importance of different branches, as is shown in table 34.

In the long run, the share of the building and food industries remained stable. But there was an increase, very marked in absolute figures (five-fold) and important relatively, in the labour-force employed in mining (which rose from 7 to 13 per cent of total industrial manpower between 1841 and 1911), corresponding to the rapid growth of the coal industry. The labour-force working in the various metal industries expanded a little less rapidly, but the important fact is that this group, which was far behind textiles in 1841, passed it in 1901 and in 1911 employed 20 per cent of the industrial labour-force. Table 33 has already shown that in 1907 metals supplied 22 per cent of the value of total industrial production and more than 8 per cent of national income. It is true that, if the labour-force in the clothing industry is added to that of the textile industry proper[7], the overall category remains in the top rank from the standpoint of numbers, but not by the value of its production. In any case, both the textile industry and its appendages had definitely lost ground since 1841–51. Textiles employed 29 per cent of the industrial labour-force in 1841, far outstripping the other branches, but only 16 per cent in 1901 and 1911, and it had to yield first place to metals[8]. Clothing's share also fell back

[5]   See also, for 1891 and 1911, P.Deane and W.A.Cole, *British Economic Growth, 1688–1959* (Cambridge, 2nd edn., 1967), p. 146 (table 32).
[6]   See W.Hoffmann, *British Industry, 1700–1850* (Oxford, 1955; trans. from the German by W.H. Chaloner and W.O.Henderson), pp. 83 and 85 (tables 19 and 20).
[7]   But see also p. 187 (note 4).
[8]   In actual figures the labour-force in textiles only increased by 16 per cent between 1851 and 1911.

Table 34 Distribution of industrial manpower in Great Britain

	1841	1851	1881	1901	1911
A. Manpower in the main industries (000s, of workers)					
1 Mines and quarries	225	394	612	937	1210
2 Building and construction	377	497	877	1219	1145
3 Metal manufacture and engineering (a)	410	572	1017	1569	1923
4 Textiles	883	1296	1299	1352	1509
5 Clothing (b)	558	909	1046	1215	1257
6 Food industries (c)	310	401	592	917	1114
7 Other industries (d)	296	441	725	1135	1320
Total	3059	4510	6168	8344	9478
B. Percentage of total industrial manpower employed in each industry					
1 Mines and quarries	7.4	8.7	9.9	11.2	12.8
2 Building and construction	12.9	11.0	14.2	14.6	12.1
3 Metals manufacture and engineering	12.9	12.7	16.5	18.8	20.3
4 Textiles	28.9	28.7	21.1	16.2	15.9
5 Clothing	18.2	20.2	17.0	14.6	13.3
6 Food industries	10.1	8.0	9.6	11.0	11.8
7 Other industries	9.7	9.8	11.8	13.6	13.9

Source: Abstract, p. 60. In each case, male and female workers have been included.
(a) Includes the building of vehicles and ships, even if they were not made of metal.
(b) Includes the footwear industry (including cobblers) and hairdressers.
(c) Not including the catering trade.
(d) Wood, building materials, ceramics, glass, chemicals, leather, paper, printing, water, gas and electricity.

from 20 per cent in 1851 to 13 per cent in 1911. Furthermore, the net output of the four main textile industries of the United Kingdom (cotton, wool, linen and silk) seems to have been 14 per cent of national income in 1821, 11 per cent in 1836, 10 per cent in 1850 and 9 per cent in 1870. The whole textile industry (clothing excluded) accounted for 10 per cent of British national income in 1881, but a little less than 5 per cent in 1907[9]. Finally, the proportion of the labour-force employed by 'various industries' increased perceptibly, from 10 per cent at mid-century to 14 per cent in 1911, which shows a

---

[9] Deane and Cole, pp. 174, 212 (table 52). See also table 2 in Hoffmann, pp. 18–19, giving the weight (out of 100 for all industry) which he atttributed, from the value added, to the various industries in the construction of his global index:

	1812	1850	1881	1907
Textiles	29	25	23	12
Metals	13	14	17	20
Mining	8	9	13	16

tendency to diversification, especially as their personnel more than quadrupled between 1841 and 1911.

Broadly, it was the heavy industries, complex in organization and usually capital-intensive, the makers of capital goods, which showed the fastest growth and so increased their share of the labour-force and the value of industrial production – mining, iron and steel, and several of the secondary metal trades (e.g. the manufacture of machinery, and shipbuilding). Against this, the light industries making consumer goods, above all the textile industries, which were by far the main sector of traditional industry and had been the first to be transformed by the Industrial Revolution, maintained their lead at the start (the other sector being very small at the end of the eighteenth and beginning of the nineteenth century), but later suffered a relative decline. According to Hoffmann's indices the rates of annual average growth from 1819 to 1913 were 3.4 per cent for producers' goods industries and 2.1 per cent for consumers' goods industries. For 1855–1913, the rates were 2.5 per cent and 1.6 per cent respectively[10].

In any case, given the relatively simple inter-sectoral structure of Victorian industry, analysis will be concentrated on the two main sectors: the textile industries and the metals industries[11].

The working of textile fibres had been by a long way the most important sector of traditional industry, especially in England with her powerful and venerable wool industry. It was also, after a technological stagnation lasting three centuries, the first to be transformed and indeed turned upside down by the Industrial Revolution; and it was the first to see the factory system take over by stages from the domestic system. Having been able to reduce dramatically both their costs and their selling prices, and benefiting from strong domestic and foreign demand at a time when textiles were the main manufactured goods consumed, the textile industries experienced a very rapid expansion from the end of the eighteenth to the middle of the nineteenth century, as is shown by an index (see table 35) worked out by Deane and Cole[12].

From this the following annual average rates of growth can be computed:

---

[10] Hoffmann, p. 74. Conclusion confirmed by the analysis of C.H.Feinstein's indices for 1855–1913: *National Income, Expenditure and Output of the United Kingdom 1855–1965*(Cambridge, 1972), tables 51 and 52, T. 111–2 and 114–5.

[11] With however a few words on coal and chemicals.

[12] Deane and Cole, p. 213 (table 53). These indices are those of five-year averages centring on the year indicated.

1800–37	4.2 per cent
1815–37	6.1 per cent
1837–57	4.2 per cent
1857–72	2.3 per cent

These figures reveal that growth was at its fastest between the end of the Napoleonic wars and the accession of Victoria. Then came deceleration, but the rate was still very high up to the accident of the American civil war, which broke the pace of growth of the textile sector. This recovered after the victory of the North, but much more slowly, as is shown by the following annual rates of growth (percentage) calculated from Feinstein's indices[13]:

	Textile industries	*Textiles, clothing, leather*
1857–73	2.3	1.9
1873–1900	0.7	1.0
1900–13	2.2	1.6

Under such circumstances, the textile industries reached their highest relative importance in the British economy between 1820 and 1840, and at the beginning of Victoria's reign they dominated the other industrial branches. On their own they employed nearly 30 per cent of the industrial labour-force and 14 per cent of all the population employed in Great Britain (1,300,000 in 1851) [14], contributing more than 10 per cent to national income and supplying 72 per cent of the total value of British exports in 1830 and still 63 per cent in 1850[15]. Textiles were the dominating activity and engine of growth of British industry, at least up to the 1840s, when, according to many writers, it

Table 35 Index of real net output of British textile industries (1800 = 100)

1770	76
1800	100
1815	127
1837	463
1857	1050
1862	863
1872	1481

[13] Feinstein, *National Income*, tables 51 and 52. His index of textile production increases from 45 in 1857 to 62 in 1873, 75 in 1900 and 100 in 1913.

[14] Not to mention the clothing branch.

[15] Up to 1840, exports of textiles increased definitely faster than those of other goods.

was replaced, as the result of railway-building, by iron and steel as the leading sector determining the pace of the economy's growth[16].

Textiles then went into a relative decline and, right at the end of Victoria's reign, were overtaken by iron and steel (in its widest sense), but only narrowly so. It was a decline that was only relative because total production continued to increase, although much more slowly than before 1860; and the textile industries kept an important position in the British and world economy. Although in 1911 they only employed 16 per cent of the industrial labour-force and 8 per cent of the employed population, that meant 1,500,000 people. And they remained the most important export industry providing in 1900/9 38 per cent of the total value of British exports.[17] These manufactures, which had been one of the most remarkable creations of the English industrial genius and an essential foundation of Britain's wealth in the nineteenth century, thus preserved a considerable importance at the beginning of the twentieth century.

However, there were several such industries, and not just *one* textile industry, each main branch corresponding to the fibre which it chiefly worked. Each branch had its own problems, and in particular the Industrial Revolution penetrated them at different dates and with varying effect. On the whole, however, the sequence developed in accordance with the law enunciated by Maurice Lévy-Leboyer, by which the modernization of British industry was carried out 'downstream', i.e. from spinning (intermediate goods) towards weaving (consumer goods). So it is proper to examine separately the history of each branch, whose relative importance is roughly revealed by the numbers of employees in Great Britain in 1851[18]:

> Cotton – 527,000
> Wool – 284,000
> Linen and hemp – 103,000
> Silk – 133,000
> Hosiery and lace – 129,000

[16] See Chapter 9, pp. 297ff, on this problem.

[17] P.Mathias, *The First Industrial Nation: An Economic History of Britain, 1700–1914* (London, 1969), p. 468 (table 17).

[18] Taken from data in Mathias, *The First Industrial Nation*, p.261 (table V); but these figures are higher than those in *Abstract*, p. 187. See also the figures in Musson, p. 437, for the power of steam-engines in these various branches in 1870, which, although this date is late, gives an idea of the level of modernization as well as the relative importance of each: cotton, 300,000; wool, 103,000; flax, hemp, jute, 63,000; silk, 7,600.

THE COTTON INDUSTRY

The cotton industry was insignificant up to the middle of the eighteenth century, and was not even autonomous, as cotton weft was nearly always mixed with other fibres' warp. However, it then grew very rapidly, and furthermore the spinning-process and its preparatory operations (notably carding) were completely transformed by technical innovations, so that they went over swiftly from the domestic to the factory system. Being the cradle of the Industrial Revolution, cotton has long received special attention from historians, and W.W.Rostow made it the leading sector in the 'take-off' of the British economy in the last twenty years of the eighteenth century. It is true that soon afterwards Deane and Cole maintained that too much importance had been attached to cotton in the industrialization process, and they underlined that, around 1805, the net or added value of this industry's production was only equivalent to 4 or 5 per cent of Great Britain's national income. This percentage probably went up to 7 or 8 per cent ten years later and remained at that level during the first half of the nineteenth century[19]. Even if we accept these estimates[20], a contribution of this order to national income is considerable, especially for a very young industry which overtook the old woollen and worsted industry around 1805 or 1806 from a value-added standpoint, and took first place among British industries – a supremacy which it was to keep for a very long time[21]. In any case, during the whole period under review, cotton was the largest of the textile industries.

Furthermore, this industry had a strategic importance as a living and practical example, showing the enormous advantages provided by mechanization. Also, the innovations which had first been carried out in cotton were imitated and adapted by the other textile industries, and were to a large extent the originating force for their modernization. As S.D.Chapman has written, even if cotton was not the leading sector of the British economy as a whole, it certainly played this part for all textile industries, in Great Britain and abroad, and its meteoric rise had consequences for several other branches of the economy[22].

---

[19] Deane and Cole, pp. 293–5. On this industry, see D.A.Farnie, *The English Cotton Industry and the World Market, 1815–96* (Oxford, 1979).

[20] S.D.Chapman, *The Cotton Industry in the Industrial Revolution* (London, 1972), p. 66, suggests à contribution to GNP of the order of 7 per cent from 1797 onwards.

[21] Naturally if one considers industries individually. For value added, cotton was still in the lead in 1871; but in 1907 it had fallen to third place.

[22] Chapman, pp. 66, 68, who mentions the appearance of iron-framed buildings, the development of gas lighting and, of course, machine-building.

Finally, the cotton industry played a leading role in British exports. It exported a large proportion (in value) of its production – possibly two-thirds as early as 1805–06. This proportion diminished later, but kept above 50 per cent up to the 1840s; then it increased again to reach 67 per cent of the final product's value in 1869/71, 79 per cent in 1899/1901 and 83 per cent in 1905/13[23]. The *volume* of cotton exports also increased very rapidly; for fabrics at an annual average rate of 5.5 per cent between 1814 and 1846, and again 4.0 per cent between 1846 and 1873, in spite of the accident of the cotton famine[24]. From the end of the eighteenth century the structure of British exports was turned upside down by the cotton industry's performance: as early as 1814/16, it supplied 40 per cent of the total value of the country's exports. This percentage reached its peak in 1830 at 51 per cent and, although it was to fall back slowly later, it was still at 40 per cent in 1850[25]. Exports of cotton goods were responsible for 46 per cent of the increase in value of total exports between 1814/16 and 1844/6, and still for 27 per cent between 1844/6 and 1871/3. Certainly protectionism in continental countries and the United States hindered the export of cotton fabrics, but several of them brought increasing quantities of yarn[26], and for fabrics the British managed to find ample compensation, overseas in underdeveloped countries with tropical climates and low purchasing-power, to which the light and cheap cotton goods were perfectly adapted – Latin America (notably Brazil), Africa and above all India. In the latter country the sales of English cotton goods were nil before the abolition of the East India Company's monopoly in 1813, but they then showed a lightning expansion, the products of mechanized English factories wiping out the old native craft industry by their low prices. In 1850 India was to take up 23 per cent of the exports of

[23]   Deane and Cole, p. 187 (table 43); R.E. Tyson, 'The cotton industry', in D.H.Aldcroft (ed.), *The Development of British Industry and Foreign Competition, 1875–1914: Studies in Industrial Enterprise* (London, 1968).

[24]   Rates calculated by exponential adjustment, taken from the volume series of A.H.Imlah, *Economic Elements in the Pax Britannica: Studies in British Foreign Trade in the Nineteenth Century* (Cambridge, Mass., 1958) pp. 208–10 (table II). The rate would be higher if yarn was included. For the period 1783–1814, it had reached the extraordinary figure of 12 per cent per annum. See also Mathias, *The First Industrial Nation,*, p. 485 (table 34).

[25]   It was to fall to 31 per cent in 1871/3. The share of other textiles in exports was much less and declining or stagnant between 1830 and 1850.

[26]   Imlah and M.Lévy-Leboyer, *Les Banques européennes et l'industrialisation internationale dans la première moitié du XIXe siècle* (Paris, 1964), have underlined the importance of the role played during the period 1815–50 by the growing exports of half-finished products, worsteds and linen yarns, plus semi-finished products and non-processed iron products. It was the consequence of continental protectionism, through which weaving, which was labour-intensive, enjoyed comparative advantages, so long as it was not mechanized in Britain.

English cotton goods, for which she had become the biggest single market since 1843, and then 31 per cent in 1860[27].

This boom in exports was a major factor in the cotton industry's rapid growth during the first half of the nineteenth century (in fact up to 1860) – a growth that was accompanied by fundamental technical and structural changes. Generally speaking, it was between 1830 and 1850 that cotton reached its zenith, as regards its importance in the British economy. After the American civil war crisis, things were never the same again. Growth was slow and changes were minor. So one must treat these two periods separately.

However, we must first tackle the reasons for the very swift increase in demand, both internal and overseas, for cotton goods. In essence they were very simple – the low price of cotton goods compared with fabrics made of other fibres, and the elasticity of demand for them. When their prices fell or when the incomes of consumers increased, demand went up more than proportionately. So, thanks to the laying down of vast expanses of land to cotton in the American southern states, which brought down the price of raw cotton, and thanks to the technological progress achieved in its manufacturing by British industry, from the 1790s onwards there was a real nosedive in the price of cotton yarn and fabrics, as is shown by the indices of T.S.Ashton in Table 36[28].

This fall began during the war period, when the general trend of prices was upward. It went on, of course, during the deflation after 1815, but for fabrics at least it was much more pronounced than for other prices. The fall was essentially attributable to the improvement in productivity, although it has been claimed that the fall in wages was a contributory factor, and that accompanying this went a considerable increase in profit margins. This is said to have allowed industrialists to finance the expansion and mechanization of production between 1815 and 1840 to the detriment of handloom-weavers on the one hand, and female and juvenile labour in factories on the other – an idea that does not seem justified[29].

Anyhow, the fall in the price of British cotton goods led to a

---

[27] Chapman, p. 52; also P.Bairoch, *Commerce extérieur et développement économique de l'Europe au XIXe siècle* (Paris – The Hague, 1976), pp. 83, 213; Lévy-Leboyer, pp. 180ff.

[28] T.S.Ashton, 'Some statistics of the Industrial Revolution in Britain', in E.M. Carus-Wilson (ed.), *Essays in Economic History* (London, 1962), III, p.249, (table III), also pp. 240–1.

[29] This is the opinion of Deane and Cole, pp. 189, 192, 295; Chapman is sceptical, remarking that recent histories of cotton firms show that, as people at the time complained, profit margins tended to fall for a quarter of a century after 1815.

Table 36   Indices of annual average cotton prices
(1829 = 100)

	Cotton yarn	Cotton cloth	General Index of Price
1795	252		134
1815	186	320	177
1837	118	89	109
1850	94	63	89

more-than-proportional expansion of demand[30]. Thanks to their cheapness, cottons were substituted for other fabrics (e.g. linen and even silk and wool materials) and for non-British cotton goods as well, as has been mentioned in the case of India. Furthermore, this fall in price created a new market, thanks to the increased total volume of demand for textiles, and cotton goods became the typical cheap, mass-produced articles which were within the means of ordinary people in England, and even in the poorest countries. There was no substitute for them so long as the cotton manufactures of other countries had not caught up with the British start, which was to take a very long time.

The growth of the industry can be measured satisfactorily by looking at the net imports of raw cotton. This can be considered as an index of the volume of production, with the one reserve that this method rather underestimates expansion at the end of the nineteenth century, because it does not take into account the improvement which took place in the quality of the articles manufactured. Table 37 presents data for several selected periods[31].

The growth of the industry was extremely fast from the end of the Napoleonic wars to the beginning of Victoria's reign, but it then slowed down, while remaining at a high level in the 1840s and 1850s. To be precise, the slower pace started in 1845, whereas there had been a tendency to acceleration from 1814 to 1845[32]. In fact, the rate of growth calculated by the method of exponential adjustment for the period 1814–46 was 6.6 per cent per annum[33]. Of course these rates were far

---

[30] Deane and Cole, p. 295. Between 1820 and 1845 the average price of cotton goods exported fell by two-thirds, but the volume of exports quintupled.

[31] Figures of Deane and Cole, p. 187(table 43), completed for 1911/13 by *Abstract*, p. 181. Figures for 1860/1 are abnormally high, but by taking those of 1858/60 the growth-rate since 1839/41 would only be reduced to 4.2 per cent.

[32] This emerges from the analysis of deviations from the long-term trends.

[33] This same rate is 5.5 per cent for 1783–1814 and 2.3 per cent for 1846–1873. Data taken from *Abstract*, pp. 177–9. See also Deane and Cole, pp. 187, 191–2, 194.

Table 37   UK consumption of raw cotton

	Annual average (millions of lb.)	Annual average rate of growth (%)
1819/21	141	6.0
1839/41	452	4.3
1859/61	1050	1.0
1869/71	1155	0.9
1899/1901	1510	2.5
1911/13	2038	3.0
1819/21 to 1899/1901 (or 1911/13)		

above those of total industrial production and output of all the other industries, with the exception of iron and steel.

It is true that, if looked at more closely, the pattern of growth was irregular, with several booms, involving strong bursts of investment which substantially increased productive capacity and rejuvenated equipment: 1823–5, 1833–6, 1843–5. Indeed, high rates of technical innovation and mechanization were other characteristics of the period before, as well as after Victoria's accession.

Spinning and its preparatory processes had been swiftly and completely mechanized and concentrated in factories during the 1770s and 1780s. There were then two different systems, one based on Arkwright's 'water-frame', and the other on the 'mule'. The latter had the advantage of being able to produce fine yarn, and although initially operated by hand, was soon assisted by steam-power during two of the movements of its four-stroke cycle. Mule-spinning technology conquered the field by the beginning of the nineteenth century, and after 1830 water-powered cotton mills using throstles were only to be found on the edge of the cotton areas. Meantime, a most important new invention, the self-acting mule of Richard Roberts, had been made in 1825, whose operating costs were 15 per cent lower than those of the traditional semi-manual mules. Its use spread widely after 1835 and, as it could carry many more spindles than the earlier machines, it tended to increase the size of spinning mills; but it only became general after the middle of the century, and the old mule was still used for the finest yarns up to the 1880s. The number of cotton spindles in the United Kingdom increased from 7 million in 1820 to 10 million in 1830, to 21 million in 1850 and to more than 30 million in 1861[34].

---

[34]   Chapman, p. 26; Deane and Cole, p. 191 (table 45). Production per spindle per day of No. 40 yarn grew from two hanks (of 768 m.) in 1820 to three in 1830 and four in 1834.

Of much greater importance than these developments in spinning was the technical revolution achieved in the cotton industry by the mechanization of weaving, which occurred much earlier than in the other branches of the textile industry. This technical revolution became also a human tragedy, which caused the disappearance of the handloom-weavers, the largest and most characteristic group in the traditional domestic industry[35]. The mechanization of weaving was distinctly slower than that of spinning, because the perfecting of a satisfactory power-loom took a long time, in the context of abundant low-wage labour which worked the handlooms[36]. Certainly the Revd Edmund Cartwright had patented a powerloom in 1785, but his attempts to exploit it commercially had failed. In the first years of the nineteenth century several improved versions had been built, but these powerlooms continued to suffer from shortcomings, and they were only suitable for the manufacture of coarse fabrics. Only 2400 of these looms were operating in Great Britain in 1813, and 14,000 in 1820, while there were more than 200,000 handloom-weavers in cotton alone. But the situation changed drastically in the 1820s. In 1822 Sharp and Roberts brought forward decisive improvements to the powerloom, and although not all problems were solved[37], the superiority of the powerloom over the handloom now became very clear. The former produced three or four times as much cloth per unit of time as the latter[38], and its triumph seemed inevitable after the 1826 depression. During the 1823–5, 1833–6 and 1843–5 booms, powerlooms were installed in large numbers by the great spinners, who found an outlet for their yarn in the weaving-sheds set up next to their mills, and hoped to compensate for the fall in prices and profit margins by spreading their overhead costs over a larger volume of production. Hence there was a rapid increase in the number of powerlooms, and an equivalent reduction in the number of handloom-weavers, who could

---

[35] The passages which follow drew much inspiration from D.Bythell's fundamental work, *The Handloom Weavers (Cambridge, 1969), which has dispelled many legends.*

[36] The rapid obsolescence of powerlooms and the fear of riots and machine-breaking also had a deterrent effect on manufacturers.

[37] Another important improvement was effected by W.Dickinson in 1828, but in the 1830s there were still fabrics that could not be woven on powerlooms.

[38] Bythell (p. 85) mentions that it is very difficult to calculate this ratio. Figures often quoted are open to argument because they do not take account of auxiliary labour in factories. So it is said that in 1826 a workman could mind two powerlooms and produce in a day fifteen times more cloth than a handloom-weaver. In 1833, two youngsters were able to look after four looms, which produced as much as twenty handloom-weavers; D.S.Landes, *The Unbound Prometheus: Technological Change and Industrial Development in Western Europe, 1750 to the Present* (Cambridge, 1969), p. 860.

Table 38   Powerlooms and handloom-weavers in
the British cotton industry[39]

	Powerlooms	Handloom-weavers
1795		75,000
1813	2,400	212,000
1820	14,150	240,000
1829	55,500	225,000
1833	100,000	213,000
1835	109,000	188,000
1845	225,000	60,000
1850	250,000	43,000
1861	400,000	7,000

not stand up to the competition in spite of the extremely low piecework
wages which they were ready to accept.

The figures in table 38 are not very reliable, for no official census of
powerlooms was taken before 1835. Bythell, while remaining sceptical
about all estimates made for the numbers of handloom-weavers at the
time, admits that at their peak the total was between 200,000 and
250,000; but he maintains that this peak was reached in 1826 and that
thereafter the number of handloom-weavers decreased continuously.
Others reckon that the peak was reached in 1833, with 250,000
handloom-weavers at work. So the disappearance of these weavers
started earlier than was thought. However, at the beginning of the
1830s, these domestic workers in the cotton industry were as
numerous as the factory workers (208,000 in 1833). The balance was
upset about 1835 and the number of handloom-weavers then diminished rapidly. In 1850 only about 40,000 of them remained, making
special, expensive fabrics. Fifteen years later, after the cotton famine
had dealt the death-blow, the species had disappeared where cotton
was concerned, and weaving had become completely integrated into
the factory system. The number of employees in cotton factories rose
from 110,000 in 1814 to 240,000 in 1837 and to 427,000 in 1860[40].

---

[39] This composite table has been drawn from the following sources: Bythell, pp. 54–7,
88, 90; Chapman, pp. 26, 60 (table 8); Deane and Cole, p. 191 (table 45); *Abstract*, pp.
185, 187.

[40] G.H.Wood's estimate, quoted in *Abstract*, p. 187. This increase is much less than the
rise in production, which demonstrates the gain in productivity. According to Deane
and Cole, labour costs per unit of output dropped by 50 per cent in spinning and more
than two-thirds in weaving between 1829/31 and 1859/61. Furthermore 125,000
people were enough to look after 250,000 powerlooms in 1850, so that the elimination
of the handloom-weavers brought about a small and temporary fall in the total
labour-force of the cotton industry, from the beginning of the 1830s to the beginning
of the 1850s.

The tragedy of the handloom-weavers' disappearance[41] has aroused much interest and controversy, both at the time (Parliament devoted several enquiries to it) and among historians. It has been seen as the typical example, on a massive scale, of skilled craftsmen who were independent, proud and prosperous at the end of the eighteenth century being reduced by the inexorable competition of machinery, first to the condition of a progressively pauperized and demoralized proletariat and ultimately to extinction[42]. It is often thought moreover that the handloom-weavers played an important role in popular agitation, notably in the chartist movement, which coincided with their agony[43].

It is certainly true that at the end of the eighteenth century the phenomenal boom of the cotton industry created a strong demand for labour and forced up piecework-wages for handloom-weavers, giving the most skilled of them a genuine prosperity and making the 1790s a kind of golden age. But this very prosperity soon upset the situation, for it attracted to handweaving a crowd of new recruits of very varied origins, including women, children and Irish immigrants. So, contrary to what has generally been thought, the weaver, apart from a minority making quality fabrics, was in no way a highly skilled worker, and his trade was easy to enter. Weaving could be learnt easily and speedily without any obligation of apprenticeship, and then one could set oneself up with little or no capital, for a loom was not expensive and in any case could be rented. This led to an influx and soon a surplus of labour which could only depress wages, especially in a period of violent fluctuations in demand, such as occurred during the French wars and their aftermath. But the fall in wages did not halt the influx before the 1820s, and this only worsened the situation. It must be emphasized that the fall in wages began before 1800, and so well before competition from powerlooms made itself felt, and during a period of inflation and general rise in wages. In fact competition from machinery, which did not come into effect until the 1820s, only dealt the *coup de grâce* to the incomes of the handloom-weavers. They had already found themselves in a marginal position and turned into a 'reserve army' of industry. They were the first to feel the impact of business depressions and the last to enjoy the effects of recoveries. Many

---

[41]   Of course the problem also arises for handloom-weavers working in other textile industries, but in a less acute way, for the change there was slower.

[42]   This is the view of E.P.Thompson's famous work, *The Making of the English Working Class* (London, 1963), ch. 9, pp. 297ff.

[43]   An opinion accepted by Bythell, but with some reservations, pp. 205ff. He sees political activism of the weavers rather as spasmodic.

manufacturers resorted to handloom-weavers for extra output in periods of rising cyclical demand, but they concentrated production on their own powerloom-sheds in times of depression[44]. According to Bythell's calculations, an index of piecework-wages for weaving muslins in Bolton fell from 144 in 1796 to 100 in 1805, to 56 in 1815 and to 40 in 1820. Another index, this time for calico-weaving in north-east Lancashire, fell from 100 in 1815, to 35 in 1830, and to 28 in 1841. Of course, the cost of living declined after 1813, but the collapse in weavers' earnings was much sharper, and they enjoyed no cyclical recovery after 1826[45]. There is no doubt that the standard of living of handloom-weavers deteriorated dramatically after the end of the 1790s. Also, especially after 1826, they were the poorest group amongst the working class, making a meagre living, at the cost of long hours at their looms,when there was work, and plunged into destitution in times of unemployment, when they became dependent on relief under the Poor Law or on private charity. Nor is there any doubt about the physical suffering and demoralization of this large group (about 800,000 people, including their families, around 1830), whose pauperization helps to explain the slow progress of the average standard of living of workers during the first half of the nineteenth century. Neither their sporadic attempts at organizing trade unions, which was made difficult by their dispersal, nor their rare outbreaks of violence[46], nor their repeated appeals to Parliament for a remedy for their troubles, met with any concrete result.

Bythell has emphasized that after 1815 a proportion of handloom-weavers were only casual workers, including a growing number of women and children, who obtained from weaving some extra money, taken up as opportunities occurred, but who generally worked elsewhere as well, mostly in agriculture. As for the final fate of the weavers made redundant by machinery, it is inaccurate to say that many died of hunger or finished in the workhouse. A number of them, devoted to their trade and repelled by the idea of factory work, were indeed unable to adapt and stuck to their looms, getting little work at dwindling wages. But Bythell points out that many weavers were easily and quickly absorbed by other employment, mainly in factories,

---

[44] This policy indeed contributed to the survival of handloom-weavers; but the spasmodic character of the adoption of power-weaving and its establishment outside the traditional areas of weaving helped to worsen their lot.

[45]. Bythell, pp. 99 (table 2), 105 (table 3), 118, 275–7, 280. Also Deane and Cole, pp. 26, 295. Bythell is sceptical about the classic estimate by G.H.Wood of average weekly weavers' earnings: about £1 between 1797 and 1806, 8s3d between 1818 and 1825, 6s or 6s3d in the 1830s.

[46] There was much machine-breaking in Lancashire in 1826.

particularly in powerweaving, but also in weaving other fibres (especially silk), and also in other sorts of occupation offering more security and often better remuneration. This at least was true in Manchester and in other large towns, where there was plentiful alternative work. But there was tragic unemployment and poverty in the remote villages of north-east Lancashire where no other opportunity existed. The agony of the handloom-weavers now appears shorter and less appalling than was once thought, and they had already endured much suffering before being hit by competition from power-looms in the 1820s. However, theirs was the most obvious and most important case of technological unemployment in the nineteenth century.

Another human problem of the Industrial Revolution, not peculiar to the cotton industry but especially notorious there, was female and child labour. This can only be dealt with cursorily here, but it must be mentioned. The development of the factory system in cotton had in fact been largely based on the employment of children and young women. This labour was of course cheaper and more docile than adult male labour, and in addition the latter's physical strength had become unnecessary for many jobs in a mechanized factory. Also men, to start with at least, revolted at the idea of submitting to the discipline of factory work. The feelings of twentieth-century people are often outraged by the long hours of work forced upon children sometimes only 5 or 6 years old during the Industrial Revolution. They are shocked by the harmful effects on their health and their intellectual development, and by the cruelties and dangers to which these very young workers were exposed (even though they have been somewhat exaggerated). But child labour was common in traditional domestic industry, and often in harsh conditions. The factory masters were only using it in their turn, without necessarily breaking up the family, for a father or mother often had their children as helpers. One can also maintain that they widened the work-opportunities for the least skilled elements in the population[47]. Despite such mitigating arguments, the pitiable condition of this infant and female labour-force aroused the protests of philanthropists at an early stage, and in the 1830s and 1840s the latter were supported after initial reluctance by many adult workers who appreciated that a limitation of children's working hours would of necessity lead to a reduction of hours for all the labour-force. Although the first Factory Acts (1802, 1819, 1831) were of limited scope and ineffective in practice, the Act of 1833, which

[47]   Opinion of Deane and Cole, p.294.

applied to all textile factories except silk, forbade the employment of children aged under 9, limited the hours of work of young people aged 9 to 13, and created a corps of inspectors to see that these rules were respected. During the following years, the powerful campaign of the Ten Hours Movement demanded a 10-hour day. Several laws (1844, 1847) increased restrictions on infant and female work; and finally in 1850 it was forbidden (but still only in textile factories) to make women and young persons under 18 years of age work more than 10.5 hours a day, and even then the work was restricted to between 6 a.m. and 7 p.m., so that the reduction in hours had in fact to be applied to the whole labour-force[48].

With this legislation the beginning of Victoria's reign saw a sharp decrease, both relative and absolute, in the employment of women and children in cotton factories.

After 1850 the percentage of children was to rise again, as high as 14 per cent in 1874, but they were no longer employed full-time, and further legislation later much reduced their employment. However, the percentage of female labour continued to increase slowly, so that it reached 61 per cent in 1901 and 1907. The disappearance of the handloom-weavers, who were mostly men, encouraged this characteristic switch to women in the cotton industry.

The final triumph of the factory system, which accompanied the rapid growth of this industry, brought with it massive investment. Chapman estimates that the industry's fixed capital increased six-fold during the forty years after 1815, and doubled between 1834 and 1856.

Table 39 Distribution of labour in UK cotton factories by age and sex[49]. As a percentage of the total labour-force

	1835	1847
Children under 13	13	6
Young people aged 13–18	30	30
Total of persons under 18	43	36
Females	54	58
Males	46	42
Adult men (over 18)	26	29 (in 1850)

[48] See J.T.Ward, *The Factory Movement, 1830–1855* (London, 1962); and the brief but convenient survey by U.R.Q.Henriques, *The Early Factory Acts and their Enforcement* (London, 1971).

[49] From *Abstract,* p. 188; also Deane and Cole, p. 190 (table 44).

He thinks, however, that this investment was used to enlarge and reconstruct existing factories so as to achieve an optimum size which had been much raised by technological progress, and that many small firms were eliminated. Indeed it was the large firms which achieved the integration of spinning and powerloom-weaving, and this led to concentration. From 1833/4 to 1850, the average consumption of cotton per spinning mill increased from 270,000 to 430,000 lb. These views have been challenged by V.A.C.Gatrell, who accepts that there was a slight tendency towards concentration and an increase in the average size of firms in Lancashire, but maintains that the structure of the cotton industry scarcely changed between 1815 and mid-century. 'Giant' firms certainly existed, but they were rare and their number did not increase. In 1841, Lancashire had no more than twenty-five cotton firms employing over 1000 workers, and only a further sixty employing between 500 and 1000. It is possible that management problems limited the desirable maximum to a thousand workers or a little more, the largest firm in 1841 having 1422 workers. Furthermore, Gatrell reckons that economies of scale were not obvious in the cotton industry, and that there was no clear correlation between size of firms and economies in labour per unit of output. In any case, in Manchester in 1841 the top ten firms (by power used) possessed 36 per cent of the steam horse-power and 31 per cent of the labour-force. And though nearly all the big firms were 'integrated' or 'mixed', this was equally true of a fair number of medium-sized undertakings, as the advantages of integration came from internal economies and not from technical economies of scale, while integration was not a necessary condition of success. In 1841, one-process firms made up two-thirds of the 975 cotton firms existing in Lancashire, and this proportion was hardly less in 1856. Indeed, among these, only 295 had 200 or more workers, and 680 had less, while nearly 400 used fewer than 20 h.p. In other words, small and medium-sized undertakings did not tend to disappear; they were very numerous and many of them were flourishing. As noted above, success was not the monopoly of the giants. In 1841 the average number of workers in Lancashire cotton factories was 193, ranging from 349 for integrated firms doing both spinning and weaving to 92 for simple powerloom establishments. In Manchester, where firms were larger than elsewhere, the average was 260. During the following two decades, no very perceptible change took place, and there was even a proliferation of small weaving firms in the 1850s[50].

[50]   Chapman, pp.30–4, 70; and A.J.Taylor's classic article, 'Concentration and specialization in the Lancashire cotton industry, 1825–1850', *Economic History Review*, 2nd

The use of the steam-engine made great strides in the 1830's, with even faster progress after this decade. By 1838 four-fifths of the cotton-mills were equipped with steam-engines, with a total of 46,000 h.p. (instead of perhaps 10,000 about 1811), whereas water-power in use amounted to 12,000 h.p. The power of steam-engines in the cotton industry rose to 71,000 h.p. in 1850 and to 281,000 in 1861[51].

At the same time, the process of geographical concentration of the industry reached its peak to the advantage of Lancashire – and especially its south-eastern part round Manchester – and the neighbouring areas of Cheshire, and to the detriment of the east Midlands, North Wales, Ulster and Scotland (even though the Glasgow-Paisley region remained a substantial centre, though technically behind Lancashire). At the end of the eighteenth century, Lancashire and its near neighbours embraced 70 per cent of the British cotton industry, while in 1835 the figure was 90 per cent[52]. This concentration did not derive so much from the existence of a coalfield in Lancashire (coal accounting for a small proportion of total costs), nor from the dampness of the climate and the softness of the water, as early historians maintained. It was mainly due to the technological advance of the county, which adopted new machinery earlier than the other regions, and to external economies resulting from the abundance of labour used to factory work, the presence of specialized ancillary industries (e.g. building and repair of machinery, and the chemical industry of Merseyside) and the transport facilities, notably the proximity of Liverpool, which at the beginning of the nineteenth century had become the first British port for cotton imports and where a very sophisticated cotton exchange had come into being around 1830. Between 1790 and 1830 Manchester had also snatched from London the international market for cotton yarn and goods, thus attracting many foreign traders (e.g. Friedrich Engels). So Lancashire brought together all sorts of activities, and even attracted other textiles, such as silk, to the detriment of London[53]. The mid-nineteenth century, at

---

series, I, (2 and 3), 1948–9; V.A.C. Gatrell, 'Labour, power, and the size of firms in Lancashire cotton in the second quarter of the nineteenth century', *Economic History Review*, 2nd series, XXX (1), Feb. 1977, 95–139, esp. pp. 95–9, 101, 116, 118, 120. In fact the views of Chapman and Gatrell converge, as the former seems to consider as typical the mixed factory of 20,000 spindles, 300 powerlooms and at least 300 workers, which is in fact a 'medium-sized' firm.

[51] *Abstract,* p. 185. The number of water-mills had continued to increase up to about 1830, and Chapman (pp. 18–21) thinks that there was more water-power than steam-power in use until then; but after 1838 total power of water-mills stagnated and even declined.

[52] Chapman, p. 20.

[53] Lévy-Leboyer, pp. 31ff, 42ff.

the time when her leaders had just played a decisive role in the battle of the Corn Laws, was undoubtedly her finest hour.

After a slowing-down of growth during the 1840s, the cotton industry, which was called 'the greatest manufacturing industry that has ever existed', then enjoyed a halcyon decade, with a big increase in cotton consumption and massive investment, which dramatically enlarged its productive capacity while at the same time improving productivity[54].

However, this boom was suddenly interrupted by the 'cotton famine' resulting from the American civil war[55]. On the eve of this conflict, 78 per cent of the raw cotton used in Great Britain came from the United States. The embargo imposed on exports of cotton by the Confederates, and then the progressively efficient blockade of the South's ports and coasts by the Northern navy, led to the collapse of American cotton imports[56]. It is true that at the beginning of the war Lancashire had ample stocks, as the result of very good harvests in the States in 1859 and 1860, and abnormally high imports during these years and again in 1861. Furthermore, new sources of supply[57] were sought and found, especially in India, where production was encouraged by the distribution of seeds and instructions to peasants. India supplied 55 per cent of total imports from 1862 to 1865 (two-thirds in 1864), but the quality of Indian raw cotton was mediocre[58]. Egypt and Brazil also supplied cotton. So the famine was far from being total. Certainly, gross imports into the United Kingdom fell from 1391 million lb. in 1860 to 524 million lb. in 1862, a drop of 62 per cent, but the shortage is exaggerated by using the exceptional consumption of 1860/1 as a base: the consumption of 1862/5 was only 53 per cent of the latter, but 70 per cent of the average consumption of 1850/9[59]. Furthermore, the beginning of the American civil war coincided with a crisis of

[54]   The number of spindles went up 50 per cent between 1850 and 1861, powerlooms by 60 per cent.

[55]   The classic work on this question is W.O.Henderson, *The Lancashire Cotton Famine, 1861–5* (Manchester, 1934; revised ed., 1969). More recent studies by D.A.Farnie, 'The cotton famine in Great Britain' , in B.M.Ratcliffe (ed.), *Great Britain and her World, 1750–1914: Essays in Honour of W.O.Henderson* (Manchester, 1975), pp. 153–78; N. Longmate, *The Hungry Mills* (London, 1978).

[56]   Direct imports from the United States were practically nil in 1862–4.

[57]   But there was a distinct inelasticity of supply, as other countries could not increase their production rapidly, or did not wish to, fearing the resumption of American exports.

[58]   Which forced the spinning-mills to modify their equipment.

[59]   Farnie, 'The cotton famine', p. 162; also *Abstract*, pp. 179–80. Similarly the Hoffmann index of the production of cotton yarns and fabrics (table 54B) for 1862–5 is slightly under 50 per cent of the maximum of 1860. See table 35 on the fall in total textile production.

overproduction in Lancashire's industry, which resulted from its intense activity and massive exports in the preceding years. This caused the reduction in activity by about a third, which occurred at the end of 1861.

Yet the price of raw cotton had started to rise in the summer of 1861 when the Confederate victory at Bull Run showed that the war might be a long one. Speculation then broke out, notably in 1862, when General Lee won his great victories while the North tightened the blockade. This rise would only give way to a fall in the summer of 1864, when it was obvious that the days of the Confederation were numbered. The average price of Upland cotton went up from 6 and two-thirds pence per lb. in 1858/60 to 27 and a half pence in 1864[60]. Speculation enriched many merchants and brokers in Liverpool, although there were bankruptcies when the trend went into reverse in 1864; and it also enriched the large spinners who had capital with which to speculate, and who invested massively in large modern factories in expectation of the forthcoming recovery. But the stocks on which the bulls and bears operated were in Liverpool's warehouses and not in the mills, which made Farnie suggest that speculation in the end did more harm to the industry, and especially to the small and medium-sized firms, who had neither stocks nor capital with which to speculate, than did the shortage and high price of cotton. On the other hand, many manufacturers could compensate for the increased cost of their raw material and their reduced production by raising their selling prices.

However this may be, the fall-off in activity in the cotton industry was severe. In 1862, mills were only working at 50 per cent or even 40 per cent of capacity; but from the end of that year onwards there were signs of recovery. During these years unemployment and distress were very serious in Lancashire, even though cotton was no longer the only industry in the county. But unemployed workers benefited not only from poor relief but also from large-scale private charity and from a programme of public works financed by government loans. It has also often been thought (but some historians have challenged this idea) that the workers of Lancashire, who were much interested in politics, had radical opinions, and were hostile to slavery, endured their sufferings stoically out of sympathy with the North's cause and the struggle for the abolition of slavery.

Recovery began even before the end of the war, and it was vigorous, despite a protracted slump beginning in 1866, and although it was not

---

[60] *Abstract,* p. 491.

before 1870 that Hoffmann's indices of production again reached their levels of 1860, and not until 1874 that they really overtook them. This revival soon flagged and the cotton industry never again knew the impetuous boom of the first decades of the nineteenth century. The famine was certainly the end of an era for this industry, which lost the hypnotic power it once exercised on men's imaginations[61].

Consumption of raw cotton, which had increased at an average rate of 5.2 per cent per year between 1819/21 and 1859/61, went up by only 0.9 per cent per annum between 1869/71 and 1899/1901, or 31 per cent in thirty years. Although the beginning of the twentieth century was more favourable, growth remained well below earlier records (see table 37). It is true that these figures slightly underestimate the advance in production, which went in more and more for fine yarns and fabrics; but during this whole period, right up to the boom of 1905-7, there were complaints of chronic overproduction and lower profit margins, especially for coarse yarns and goods[62]. What is more, spinning capacity hardly increased between 1878 and 1903[63].

This near stagnation can be explained by insufficient demand. As far as the domestic market was concerned, cotton goods were more and more used by the British people up to the cotton famine, but the latter induced a transfer of demand towards woollens, worsteds and linen, a demand which persisted. Consumption of cotton goods in Great Britain per capita was not to find its 1860 level again before the first world war. In fact, the proportion of production that was absorbed by the home market, already less than half in the mid-nineteenth century, diminished and reached a very low level at the beginning of the twentieth century[64]. Thus it was foreign demand that was responsible for the stagnation which the cotton industry suffered.

Cotton is often one of the first industries to develop in a country that is industrializing; for it requires neither skilled labour nor large amounts of capital, and it easily finds sales outlets. However, during the first half of the nineteenth century, the progress of this industry on the continent and in the United States had done no harm to Lancashire, which continued to export to these countries (especially yarn) and had above all opened up vast new markets in underdeveloped countries, notably in Asia, where little or no competition existed.

[61]   Farnie, 'The cotton famine', p. 174, who notes that the crisis in Lancashire did not prevent the rest of the country from being prosperous.

[62]   Tyson, pp. 100–27. We make wide use of this article in the pages that follow, without quoting references.

[63]   Deane and Cole, p. 191 (table 45). Against this, the number of powerlooms continued to grow fairly rapidly.

[64]   Cf. p. 194; Tyson, p. 103.

But the situation changed when a modern cotton industry emerged after 1870 in some of those countries themselves – India, Japan, China and Brazil, where wages were very low; the first two of them even became exporters[65]. This new competition affected mostly exports of British yarn, which were driven out of the Japanese and Chinese markets, and which fell markedly in volume from the 1880s onwards – except for fine yarns which continued to sell in Europe and even in India. Nevertheless, in 1913, England remained the first world exporter of cotton yarn, though closely followed by India. For cotton cloth, the situation was far more favourable. The volume of exports was stationary during the Great Depression while their value dropped a little, but after 1900 a strong upward swing developed, especially in export values – which rose by 59 per cent between 1900/4 and 1910/13. These developments stemmed mainly from the lowering of the price of primary produce in the 1880s and 1890s, which reduced the foreign purchasing-power of underdeveloped countries (and they were the main buyers of English cotton goods). The recovery of primary-produce prices and of world trade as a whole after 1900 then reversed this trend. The competition from foreign industries, both those of developed countries, which existed only for certain kinds of goods, and those of the new industries of Asia, turned out to be less dangerous and progressed less rapidly than had been feared at the end of the nineteenth century. The Indian industry was only able to supply a small share of its enormous potential market, and exports of British cotton goods to the subcontinent increased from a billion yards in 1870 to 2 billion around 1900 and to 3 billion in 1913. The loss of the Japanese market was off-set by a sharp jump in sales to the Dutch East Indies. In the same way, a drop-back in Brazil was made up by progress in the Argentine; and in China English exporters kept their end up very well. Furthermore, as in the case of yarns, competition only applied to coarse goods, and quality fabrics continued to penetrate European and American markets, despite customs protection and local production. Even though Great Britain's share of the international trade in cotton goods had diminished, she maintained her leading position in this business. In fact, danger came much less from foreign competition on third markets than from the growing ability of many countries to satisfy their own needs in cotton fabrics, usually behind high tariff walls. Though this was not yet a very serious threat, except

---

[65] In 1913, 20 per cent of the world cotton industry was outside Europe and the United States; Tyson, p. 101. Bairoch, *Commerce extérieur*, p. 83, points out that at first the substitution of British articles for the local craft production came to an end, then there was a reindustrialization of Asia.

for yarn and grey-cloth, some clear-headed businessmen saw the risks for the British cotton industry of a distribution of exports in which India, with a rapidly expanding industry of her own, received 43 per cent of total exports and China 10 per cent[66]. However, no one could foresee that, after the first world war, the volume of international trade in cotton goods would drop in absolute terms, plunging Lancashire into a crisis from which there would be no recovery.

The end of Victoria's reign were not great days for the English cotton industry, and the prosperity which it found in the Edwardian era was fragile. To the external factors, which have just been analysed, were added, according to many writers, some internal weaknesses. It has been pointed out that the labour-costs of British mills had become higher because of the rise in women's wages, which increased faster than for average wages, from a decline in the employment of infant and even juvenile labour (in 1907 only 26 per cent of the labour-force was less than 18 years old), and from a reduction in working hours. Also wage-costs (i.e. the proportion of wages in the total value added), which had fallen up to 1861, went up markedly in the last third of the century[67]. Yet, there is no doubt that workers in Lancashire factories had skills and efficiency which more than compensated in terms of wage-costs for the lower wages and longer hours of work in continental factories. Thus, around 1890, 3 people in Lancashire were enough to operate 1000 spindles, while 5.8 were required in Alsace, 6.2 in Switzerland and even more in other countries.

British cotton manufacturers have been accused of excessive conservatism, and even of routinism, in matters of technology, especially for not having widely adopted two American inventions – ring-spinning and the automatic loom – which would have led to higher labour-productivity. The ring frame, invented in the United States in 1844 and widely used across the Atlantic from 1860 onwards, was tried in England in 1867, but spread only slowly. In 1903 there were 37.6 million mule spindles and only 6.3 million spindles of the new type. In 1913 the latter made up 19 per cent of the total, against 86 per cent in the United States, 46 per cent in France, and 50 per cent in the world as a whole. The automatic loom, admittedly a much later development, being perfected in America in the 1890s, penetrated even less. In 1909 there were 200,000 in the United States against 8000 in England. Yet British machine-makers did embark on the manufacture

[66]   For all this, see Tyson, pp. 104–18, 125–6. The Dutch East Indies received 4 per cent of exports and the Middle East 8 per cent. Exports to these underveloped countries were subject to violent fluctuations, being especially dependent on the harvests there.
[67]   Deane and Cole, pp. 189–90.

of this new loom, but sold many more of them for export than on the home market. It has been deplored that these new machines, which were faster than the old ones and required less labour, should not have been adopted widely in Lancashire. The serious mistake was not so much the unwillingness to innovate during the stagnant years 1875–95, but the failure to profit from the recovery of exports and from the Edwardian prosperity (which led to an investment boom and to the building of many new mills, especially in 1905-8)[68], so as to re-equip with completely new machinery, instead of remaining faithful on the whole to traditional technology[69].

This view of the conservatism of British manufacturers has been challenged recently. If cotton masters remained faithful to the self-acting mule, this was from motives that were economically rational, linked to the pattern of costs and markets of English industry, because it was better adapted to their needs and especially better suited to produce medium and fine yarns, on which they were increasingly dependent. Also the English industry had at its disposal a skilled labour-force, which was useless for ring frames. By contrast the new technology was suited to conditions in the United States and in industrializing countries. Similarly, the automatic loom could only produce coarse fabrics, while it required yarn of good quality, because of the high speed of its movements; and it was expensive. None the less, the mule and the traditional powerloom, which had been considerably improved between the 1860s and the 1880s[70], had reached a state close to perfection at the end of the century, while the new machinery was open to improvement in many respects. The result of all this was that productivity in the British cotton industry, which had clearly increased from the middle of the century to about 1880, then lost its momentum. The real cost of making grey-cloth hardly fell from 1873 to 1910, as the saving from technical progress was absorbed by the rise in wages. On the other hand, an increase in productivity and a lowering of real costs were very noticeable in the United States. Yet Lancashire continued to produce more cheaply than the United States, and the danger to it came not from across the Atlantic, but from India and Japan, which combined ring-spinning and cheap labour[71].

---

[68] Between 1903 and 1914, the number of spindles went up from 48 million to 59 million, and powerlooms from 683,000 to 805,000.

[69] The opinion of Mathias, *The First Industrial Nation*, pp. 413, 415.

[70] A greater number of spindles per mule, higher working speed, etc. The quantity of yarn produced per worker had doubled between 1845 and 1880, and output of cloth had been multiplied by 2.5.

[71] Tyson, pp. 121–4; L.G.Sandberg, *Lancashire in Decline: A Study of Entrepreneurship, Technology and International Trade* (Colombus, Ohio, 1974), has asserted that there

In other ways British industrialists made efforts to improve the efficiency of their mills. They also conquered new markets, and as the severest competition was in low-grade yarn and coarse or grey-cloth, they tended to specialize in fine yarns and high-quality fabrics, dyed or printed[72]. Tyson maintains that their reaction to the difficulties which occurred at the end of the nineteenth century was generally vigorous, and that many of them were dynamic entrepreneurs. However, one cannot altogether discard the idea that cotton manufacturers could have done better, by giving up traditional products and technology, and by innovating more radically.

Another weakness of the industry, which has given rise to discussions, concerns its structure. The second quarter of the nineteenth century had been marked by a tendency towards vertical integration, by firms which carried out both spinning and weaving. After 1850, however, this trend was reversed, and a horizontal structure was attained, with thorough specialization and with physical and financial separation of the different stages of production – spinning, weaving, finishing – and marketing[73]. The latter was in the hands of Manchester merchants, who bought grey-cloth, had it bleached, dyed or printed, and then exported it[74]. This development was doubtless the consequence of the worldwide interests of the Lancashire cotton industry, which necessitated the production of a very wide range of yarns and fabrics. This made for the specialization of firms and also for the separation of manufacturing and marketing. Specialization was also geographical. Spinning was concentrated in south-eastern Lancashire and the neighbouring parts of Cheshire and Derbyshire. Weaving was spread almost all over the country, but it was, to the exclusion of spinning, dominant in its northern and eastern parts. Finishing was centred in Manchester, which had long been abandoned by the spinners, but had become the banking and warehousing centre, the commercial and financial capital of the cotton districts. This concentration had no equivalent in other countries, for France,

---

was distinct progress in productivity per worker and a fall in real costs between 1885 and 1914.

[72] A.J.Marrison, 'Great Britain and her rivals in the Latin American cotton piece-goods market, 1880–1914', in Ratcliffe, pp. 309–48, indeed shows that in countries where income levels were very low, it was hardly possible to improve the quality of cotton goods offered; at most the finish and appearance could be made better. Yet the British kept a large share of the South American market.

[73] Yet the firms combining spinning and weaving did not disappear. In 1884 they had 57 per cent of the looms and 39 per cent of the spindles in Lancashire, but in 1911 only 34 per cent and 21 per cent; Tyson, p. 119.

[74] A great number of these merchants were foreigners. Few manufacturers did export directly.

Germany and the United States each had several regions with cotton mills. It certainly made for external economies, but the extreme specialization which has just been described was not without its drawbacks. Cotton goods had to pass through a large number of hands, which could add to costs, and, what is more, many small, narrowly specialized firms were commercially weak[75].

C.D. Kindleberger wrote that in 1913 the British cotton industry was 'highly developed, technologically stagnant, competitively fragile'. Of course, because of its stagnation at the end of the nineteenth century, the industry no longer played the role in the economy that it did during the first half of the century. Its contribution to the national income of the United Kingdom was only 2 to 2.5 per cent. The net value of output in 1907 (£45 million out of a total of £94 million for the whole textile sector) was less than half that of the coal industry, and also exceeded by that of the engineering industry. Yet cotton remained a very large industry on the national and international level. Its mills employed 523,000 people in 1901 and 620,000 in 1912, i.e. about one-tenth of manufacturing industry's total labour-force. With more than four-fifths of production exported, cotton still accounted for 26 per cent of Great Britain's total exports. Furthermore, even though the industry consumed less raw cotton than the United States, it had more spindles because of its concentration on medium and fine yarns. Although enjoying a diminishing share of the world consumption of cotton and equipment, the British cotton industry still owned 39 per cent of the world's spindles (as against 54 per cent in 1880), and in 1909/13 it accounted for 70 per cent in weight of the world trade in cotton fabrics. Except for coarse fabrics, low-grade yarns and some special quality goods, the industry remained perfectly competitive. No other country provided such a wide range of products and exported to so many different markets. It remained the largest cotton industry in the world, and very self-confident[76]. No one could foresee that, because of high dependence on foreign markets and especially those of Asia, the first world war, by speeding up the rise of cotton industries in India, Japan and various underdeveloped countries, was to ruin this powerful industry – an industry whose very strength, based on an imported raw material and on outlandish markets, was something of a paradox[77].

[75] Tyson, pp. 119–20, 124–5.
[76] Tyson, pp. 100–1, 126; Deane and Cole, p. 294; *Abstract*, p. 188.
[77] Farnie, 'The cotton famine', p. 154.

THE WOOLLEN AND WORSTED INDUSTRIES

After being England's premier industry for centuries, the manufacture of wool had given way to the newcomer, cotton, at the beginning of the nineteenth century. The gap between the old and the new industry was to grow wider, and the relative decline of wool was to persist. Its contribution to British national product was between 4 and 5 per cent in the 1820s. This fell to about 3.5 per cent in the mid-nineteenth century and to 1.5 per cent at most at the beginning of the twentieth century[78]. Indeed the growth of the woollen industry was distinctly slower than that of its rival. This growth can be estimated through the consumption of raw materials, but for a long period can only be known approximately. Unlike cotton, which was imported and so fully recorded by the customs, 90 per cent of the wool consumed in the United Kingdom in 1810/19 and 62 per cent in 1850/9 (but only 29 per cent in 1890/9) was produced by British sheep. For a long time the national wool-clip total was not precisely known[79], so the figures in table 40 are put forward with some diffidence[80].

Table 40   UK consumption of wool

	Annual averages (millions of lb.)	Annual average growth rates (%)
1820/4	140	
1835/9	179	1.6
1870/4	454	2.7
1895/9	686	1.7
1909/13	846	1.5
1820/4 to 1909/13		2.0
1835/9 to 1895/9		2.3

From these figures it is clear that the growth of production was definitely slower (though less erratic) than in the cotton industry, even though, for the whole of the nineteenth century, the rate of growth of cotton was in the end only 3 per cent per annum.

[78] Deane and Cole, ɪp.199–200.
[79] Taken from data ɪn Mathias, *The First Industrial Industrial Nation,* p.487 (table 35). Wool production in the UK increased by 57 per cent between 1810/19 and 1870/9, but then went perceptibly down. Of course the greatest proportion of the growing wool imports came from Australia.
[80] Taken from Deane and Cole, p.196 (table 47); completed for 1909/13 by E.M.Sigsworth and J.M.Blackman, 'The woollen and worsted industries', in Aldcroft, *The Development,* p. 133 (table 33). We would get similar growth-rates, though generally lower, by comparing the ten-year averages of wool consumption in Mathias, *The First Industrial Nation,* quoted note 79.

Growth was slow right up to the beginning of Victoria's reign, especially as a result of the poor performance of exports which, from 1814 to 1846, were static in value and only grew by 1.5 per cent per annum in volume[81]. There was some acceleration from the end of the 1840s onwards, and the rate of growth was to reach its peak during and after the cotton famine, which made wool fabrics cheaper than cotton goods and obliged manufacturers, in order to lower their costs, to make all sorts of innovations in the composition of their products (e.g. mixtures of fibres, more frequent use of shoddy and other inferior raw materials), as well as to modernize their machinery[82]. However it was the great leap forward of the years 1860–74 which was responsible for the high growth-rate indicated by table 40 for the period 1835/9–1870/4. If one compared only 1835/9 to 1855/9, the rate would be no more than 2 per cent per annum, while it was 3.7 per cent between 1855/9 and 1870/4. Exports were the engine of this growth. Between 1846 and 1873 their volume increased by 4.6 per cent per annum and their value by 6.3 per cent[83], and the proportion of output that was exported passed 40 per cent in the early 1870s.

The end of the nineteenth century was, understandably, a less prosperous period. In particular British exports suffered from increased protectionism in many countries, notably in the United States, the largest buyer of British wool fabric, which imposed on them the heavy duties of the McKinley (1890) and Dingley (1897) tariffs. The woollen industry could scarcely find compensation, as did cotton, in tropical and colonial countries[84]. Exports of cloth fell sharply in volume after 1874, and in 1909/13 they had only risen again to their level of 1860/4, though there was expansion of exports in yarns and tops. On the other hand, domestic consumption grew thanks to the rise in real incomes and to the change in fashion in favour of wool and to the detriment of cotton fabrics, as has already been mentioned. As a

---

[81] This growth has been calculated by exponential adjustment. Worsted and woollen yarn contributed much more than cloth to this modest expansion. It seems that the share of production that was exported diminished sharply between the end of the eighteenth century and 1815, and it then settled at about 20 per cent. None the less, between 1830 and 1850, the wool industry provided 13 per cent–14 per cent of GB's total exports.

[82] R.A.Church, *The Great Victorian Boom, 1850–1873* (London, 1875), pp. 41–2, 45. The 1850s and 1860s saw great progress in mechanization and in the use of the steam-engine.

[83] Rate calculated by exponential adjustment. Exports were responsible for about 40 per cent of the increase in output between 1850/4 and 1870/4.

[84] Sigsworth and Blackman, pp. 135–6, 140–2. They estimate, it is true, that the performance of British exporters in 'neutral' markets was better than that of their French and even German competitors.

consequence and in spite of difficult moments in the 1870s and 1880s, and again in 1900–4, the woollen industry on the whole emerged quite well out of the Great Depression. If one takes into account the exceptional character of the 1860–74 boom, the slow-down was limited, and the rate of growth during the last quarter of the nineteenth century was superior to that of the cotton industry. Moreover, the last years of the prewar decade were to see a strong recovery[85].

At the same time, the woollen industry had largely overcome its considerable technical backwardness as compared with the cotton industry, which had persisted up to the mid-nineteenth century[86]. Labour employed in woollen and worsted mills increased from 55,000 people in 1835 to 154,000 in 1851, but there were then as many people working in their homes or in very small workshops[87]. In this connection one must, however, take account of the division of the woollen industry into two main branches, clearly separated and having a very different rate of technological progress – the worsted and the woollen. Roughly speaking, the former produced cloth of superior quality to that of the latter.

The manufacturing process for worsteds was technically similar to that of cottons and it followed in its wake. Furthermore, at the end of the eighteenth century, the putting-out system had triumphed in this branch of textiles, which was dominated by rich merchant-manufacturers. Several of these established spinning mills for worsted yarn from the 1790s onwards, using Arkwright-type machinery, which was easily adapted to working combed wool. This building of worsted mills, more and more of them powered by steam, intensified in the 1820s and 1830s, so that when Victoria came to the throne the spinning of worsted yarn was almost entirely carried out in mills. On the other hand, the essential preliminary operation of combing remained purely manual up to the invention of an effective combing machine by Lister and Donisthorpe in 1851. As this machine in a day treated as much wool as several dozen woolcombers, these highly skilled workers, renowned for their pugnacity, were quickly eliminated, and mechani-

---

[85] ibid., pp. 133–4. We shall see below that the two branches of the wool industry had very different fortunes at the time.

[86] This delay was caused by technical difficulties in the use of machines for working wool. Even when adapted and perfected, they worked more slowly than cotton machinery; Landes, *The Unbound Prometheus,* p. 88. Another hindrance was the weight of tradition and workers' resistance to mechanization, notably for the finishing of cloth. It was probably a reason for the slow growth of the industry, especially the woollen side, during the first half of the century, while the existence of a substantial margin of potential progress contributed to better performances later.

[87] Deane and Cole, p. 201; *Abstract,* p.199.

cal combing triumphed in a few years. Even though the superiority of the powerloom over the handloom was less obvious than in cotton, it spread fairly rapidly after the end of the 1830s. The West Riding of Yorkshire, the main centre of the worsted industry, had 2800 powerlooms in 1836, 19,000 in 1845 and 35,000 in 1856. At that date the last handloom-weavers were disappearing. Worsted was a factory industry, as mechanized as cotton, and with as much integration of spinning and weaving in large firms founded by merchant-manufacturers, who had become first 'spinners' and then 'weavers'[88].

The woollen industry proper remained very backward for a long time, in spite of the early appearance of a small number of 'factories' which remained in fact, largely *'manu*factories' and which, although quite untypical, have misled historians for a long time[89]. In fact work in factories – and very modest factories, often starting from a fulling mill[90] – was at first, from the 1790s onwards, limited to carding and slubbing, and factory processing spread to spinning strictly speaking only after about 1825. Before then, spinning was done on spinning-wheels or at best on a jenny worked by hand. In 1839, 36 per cent of woollen spinning-machines were steam-driven against 71 per cent in worsted; and in 1850 some machines were still worked by hand. In Yorkshire, where the manufacture of woollens was in the hands of independent master-craftsmen at the end of the eighteenth century, the 'clothiers', it was the most affluent and enterprising of the latter, plus some owners of carding and fulling mills, who developed their modest firms into real factories.

The weaving of woollens remained almost entirely manual up to the middle of the century. In 1850, there were no more than 9,400 powerlooms for woollens (and 33,000 for worsted, or a total of 42,000 in the wool industry, against 250,000 in cotton), while the number of handloom-weavers was estimated at 100,000. A strong upsurge of mechanization then ensued, which brought the number of powerlooms

---

[88] At the beginning, they kept their handloom-weavers and wool-combers working at home; then, like the cotton lords, they added weaving sheds to their spinning-mills. Thus John Foster, who started business in 1819 as a merchant-manufacturer in Queensbury near Bradford, built a large spinning-mill in 1834, added a weaving-shed in 1836 and made a fortune by using new fibres – alpaca and mohair. For the mixing of fibres was one of the characteristics of the worsted industry at this time and one of the factors in its success; cf. E.M.Sigsworth, *Black Dyke Mills: A History of John Foster and Son* (Liverpool, 1958).

[89] The largest and best known was that founded by Benjamin Gott near Leeds in 1792, but it was a hybrid factory, only partly mechanized.

[90] So water-powered; but there were fairly soon mills powered by steam. In Yorkshire numbers of these power mills (called 'company mills') were owned co-operatively by groups of clothiers. Others worked on commission.

for woollens up to 48,000 in 1870[91]; but handloom-weavers survived in Yorkshire right up to the 1880s, and much later in remote regions, producing specialities such as tweeds – e.g. Wales, the southern Highlands and the Hebrides[92].

The contrast between the two branches of woollen and worsted extended also to their structure. On the one hand firms were larger in the worsted than in the woollen industry. For a long time swarms of small (little more than workshops) businesses survived in the latter industry, many of which disappeared in the 1870s and 1880s. Against this, in the worsted industry, integrated firms, carrying out spinning, weaving and dyeing, were frequent. In woollens, however, there eventually emerged, especially after 1874, a horizontal structure as in the cotton industry, with specialist firms either carding, or spinning or weaving[93].

Finally, while the worsted industry was entirely concentrated in Yorkshire after expiring in Norwich, its old centre, around 1840, the woollen industry kept on in other centres, often not very dynamic, but which managed to survive, especially in the old broad-cloth district of the West Country[94]. The domination of the West Riding in the woollen industry was thus by no means as overwhelming as that of Lancashire in cotton[95].

---

[91]   Deane and Cole, pp. 200 (table 48), 201; *Abstract,* p. 198.

[92]   See J.G.Jenkins, *The Welsh Woollen Industry* (Cardiff, 1969), on the very backward 'peasant' industry (with very few exceptions) in central Wales. Old machines bought second-hand in England were used, and urine remained the main detergent; but it survived thanks to very low overheads.

On the other hand, a far from negligible tweed industry emerged from peasant origins in the Cheviots in the 1830s, thanks to a fashion for all things Scottish, bred of Romanticism and the works of Sir Walter Scott. It concentrated on quality goods for rich customers who went in for shooting and other sports; cf. C.Gulvin, *The Tweed-makers: A History of the Scottish Fancy Wool Industry, 1600–1914* (Newton Abbot, 1973).

[93]   As was the case with cotton, there was a reversal of the tendency to integration mentioned earlier. Sigsworth and Blackman, pp. 138–9, explain this specialization by the developing exports of worsted tops and yarns. Furthermore, firms were on average smaller than in cotton and almost entirely family businesses up to 1914.

[94]   The counties of Gloucestershire, Somerset and Wiltshire, which mainly made superfine woollen cloth. Their manufacturers made an effort to modernize, but generally they were behind the West Riding and depended on a market that was too narrow. The industry gradually shrank, especially after 1880, but did not disappear. Cf. J.de L.Mann, *The Cloth Industry in the West of England from 1640 to 1880* (Oxford, 1971); J.Tann, *Gloucestershire Woollen Mills* (Newton Abbot, 1967).

[95]   This region achieved its superiority over other districts as early as the eighteenth century. It probably accounted for half the labour-force of the wool industry around 1850, and three-quarters in 1913. The industrial region was not extensive, situated between the Aire and the Colne Calder Valleys. Worsted predominated in the west and north, woollens in the south of the district.

Curiously enough, the woollen industry, which had been limping along for years, overcame the difficulties of the late nineteenth century better than the worsted industry. The latter saw its exports continually declining (by more than a half between 1885/9 and 1909/13), particularly exports of mixed fabrics, which had once made Bradford rich and which feminine fashion now rejected for good and all. Furthermore, worsted met with stiff competition on the British home market from growing imports of French fabrics of pure wool. English manufacturers, not realizing that the change in fashion was definitive, were slow to adapt and re-equip their mills so as to resist this competition. But exports of worsted tops and yarns increased sharply. The manufacturers of woollen goods, who were not hit by such a violent change in fashion, managed to fight against customs barriers and foreign competition by reducing their costs through skilful mixtures of virgin wool with shoddy or cotton, with such effect that their exports picked up strongly at the beginning of the twentieth century[96].

So wool, before other industries, saw its foreign markets close and foreign competition make itself felt even on British soil. Yet it put up a good fight, though the proportion of output exported (41 per cent of cloth and 50 per cent of total yarn production in 1912) was far lower than in the cotton industry.[97] But, except during a brief period in the middle of the century, it was not too dynamic, and it is striking that, from the beginning of the Great Depression, both its labour-force and its plant stagnated or even declined[98].

OTHER TEXTILE INDUSTRIES

Two other branches of the textile industry – linen and silk – of much less importance, were also in decline.

The mechanization of flax-spinning had started in 1788 when John Marshall built a mill in Leeds that was to grow very large. The spread of machinery, which had been slow at first, led to a fairly rapid growth of the linen industry during the decades that followed, up to about 1830. Spinning was mostly done in England – and notably in Leeds – but linen yarn was sent to be woven in Scotland and Ireland, where labour-costs were much lower. But, after 1830, as a result of the competition from cotton fabrics, growth became very slow. There was

[96] Sigsworth and Blackman, pp. 136, 139, 142–57.
[97] ibid., p. 134. The wool industry only supplied 8 per cent of Britain's total exports in 1911/13, against 13 per cent in 1870.
[98] *Abstract,* pp. 198–9.

indeed a brisk recovery during the cotton famine, but it did not last and was followed by a decline in output at the end of the nineteenth and beginning of the twentieth century. Decline came first in England, then in Scotland, and at the same time the industry concentrated in Northern Ireland, a region which experienced expansion of production, and weaving, which had remained domestic and manual for a long time, was largely mechanized during the cotton famine. The number of powerlooms in the United Kingdom rose from fewer than 4,000 in 1850 to 31,000 in 1868. In Scotland the decline of linen was compensated by the rapid development of a new textile, jute, imported from Bengal, which replaced flax and hemp for making coarse material(e.g. packing, sacking, etc.); it absorbed much of the capital and labour previously used in the linen industry. The jute industry was born in the 1830s and was fairly soon mechanized in spite of the difficulties in handling this fibre; but it only became important after 1860. From the start, it was almost entirely concentrated in Dundee and its surroundings. However, total labour employed in the United Kingdom in flax, hemp and jute mills diminished after 1890, in spite of a fairly large expansion of the jute industry's output after 1870[99].

The silk industry was in the odd position of being one of the few sectors where British production was not competitive and had only survived behind tariff walls. While these lasted, expansion was rapid: consumption of raw materials was multiplied almost six-fold between 1819 and 1860, and it more than doubled between 1830 and 1860, i.e. annual average growth-rates of 4.3 per cent and 3.7 per cent respectively. Yet only the throwing and reeling of silk were done by machinery in factories while weaving remained almost entirely manual, at least up to 1850[100]. But in 1864, following the Cobden–Chevalier Treaty, protection was abolished. The French silk industry (i.e. Lyons) got its raw materials at better prices, paid lower wages, was superior in design and quality, and above all was a fashion-leader. Imports of foreign silks, especially French, rose from £2 million in 1854 to £7.3 million in 1875, then to £13.3 million in 1880. In the face of this invasion, the British industry contracted drastically. Between 1860 and 1907 its consumption of raw materials diminished by 33 per cent, the gross value of production by 78 per cent and the labour-force by 73 per cent (from 150,000 to 40,000 people)[101]. Some branches of the

---

[99]　ibid., pp. 203, 204; Deane and Cole, pp. 203–7.
[100] Moreover it attracted a section – and the most skilled one – of cotton handloom-weavers; and out of this developed the silk industry in Lancashire (cf. p. 205). But there was an effort made to mechanize weaving in the 1850s and 1860s.
[101] Deane and Cole, pp. 208–11.

industry, notably the manufacture of ribbons in Coventry, were wiped out, but a few firms learned how to adapt and survive, for example by making simple fabrics which could be woven on powerlooms. The most famous was Courtaulds, founded in Essex in 1828 by Samuel Courtauld, who came from a family of Huguenot origins. He made the firm prosper by specializing in black crêpe, which the Victorians used in vast quantities for mourning-wear. Courtaulds suffered from the Great Depression and from the decline in the use of crêpe, but managed at the end of the century to go over to coloured silks and then to launch into rayon, which was to make the firm a giant in artificial textiles[102].

There remain the branches that were allied to textiles. First of all hosiery, which was the main industry in the east Midlands[103]. Work there remained almost entirely manual up to mid-century. Various powered knitting-frames were tried, especially from 1845 onwards, but they were not satisfactory and had few advantages over hand-frames. The first steam-driven factory was established in 1851. Mechanization later made progress, but in 1875 hand-work still prevailed. The depression eliminated many of the small firms and helped the machine on, but in 1907 there were still 25,000 domestic hosiery workers. These framework-knitters met with as unfortunate a fate as the handloom-weavers, but without mechanization (which, as we have just seen, came late) influencing it. Their piecework wages never ceased to decline from the Napoleonic era up to the mid-nineteenth century, which explains the part they played in the Luddite riots of 1811–12 and 1816–17. It was a trade that was easy to learn, and that attracted many recruits in districts that had few other industries. Furthermore, the hosiery business was infested with middlemen who inflicted all sorts of exactions on the workers. Even though their condition was wretched, they kept going for a long time[104].

Another branch allied to the textile industry was the making of ready-to-wear clothes, to which the shoe industry should be added, for

---

[102] See D.C.Coleman, *Courtaulds, An Economic and Social History, The Nineteenth Century, Silk and Crape* (Oxford, 1969).

[103] Derbyshire, Leicestershire and Nottinghamshire. The latter also went in for the manufacture of lace, for which John Heathcoat had invented a machine in 1809. When its patent ran out in 1823, this machine was taken up widely, but the great majority of makers were small-scale entrepreneurs owning one or two of these machines (though of course they were complicated). In 1829 there were only about fifty steam-driven factories, but most of them were very small. The situation was almost unchanged in 1851, according to an unpublished thesis by K.Honeyman. A domestic and rural bobbin-lace industry, carried on by women and children, survived for a long time in Bedfordshire and Buckinghamshire.

[104] Chapman, p. 60 (table 8), gives a figure of 48,500 for these workers in 1833.

both were profoundly affected by the introduction from America of the Singer sewing-machine in the 1850s[105], and also the mechanical cutter for fabrics and various machines for working leather (thanks to the latter, the making of shoes could be entirely mechanized at the end of the nineteenth century). These machines were soon used in factories, powered by gas motors or small steam-engines, but these larger establishments, of which Leeds became the main centre for clothing, remained few and small for a long time[106], as sewing-machines could simply be worked by treadle. Also, in the shoe industry, side by side with factories, were many small workshops without power laid on, and a great number of domestic workers, employed on the lines of an eighteenth-century putting-out system, which used the cheap labour of women and children. Concentration into real mechanized factories, generally medium-sized, occurred slowly and was only achieved between 1895 and 1905[107]. In the clothing industry of London, J.A.Schmiechen has even observed, at the end of the nineteenth and beginning of the twentieth century, a centrifugal movement of 'defactorization', a rise of production in the workers' homes or in very small workshops (the notorious 'sweatshops'), thanks to machines such as the sewing-machine. Subdivision of work and subcontracting expanded, recalling the old domestic system, of which they were a survival or revival, with its low wages, bad conditions of work and seasonal irregularity of employment[108]. Clothing was still only partially a factory industry at the beginning of the twentieth century.

The vicissitudes of the different branches of the textile industry, which have just been examined, enable us to understand better the relative decline of the industry, after reaching its zenith in the British economy, shortly after the mid-nineteenth century. It was a zenith that followed on the very rapid growth of the cotton industry during the first decades of the century, and it related to cotton's growing weight in the textile sector. The impact of this rapid growth on the overall progress of the economy was bound to be strategic during this period, but above all during the two decades before Victoria's accession, when cotton's rate of growth was at its peak. Furthermore,

---

[105] In a sense, the sewing-machine created the clothing industry, considered as the mass production of ready-made garments.
[106] According to R.A.Church, 'Labour supply and innovation, 1850–1860: The boot and shoe industry', *Business History*, XII (1), 1970, this mechanization was only a means of replacing a skilled but restive labour-force by another that would be more docile.
[107] P.Head, 'Boots and shoes', in Aldcroft, pp. 158–85.
[108] J.A.Schmiechen, 'State reform and the local economy: an aspect of industrialization in late Victorian and Edwardian London', *Economic History Review*, 2nd series, XXVIII (3), Aug. 1975, 413–28.

between 1820 and 1860, the textile sector underwent considerable economic and social changes resulting from the mechanization of weaving and its integration into the factory system. Between 1835 and 1850, the number of workers in the cotton, wool, linen and silk mills rose from 338,000 to 596,000; but the famine broke the impetus of the cotton industry, and its growth was very slow during the Great Depression. The production of linen and silks actually diminished, so that these industries became almost negligible. It is possible that mechanization may have brought to the textile industry a massive increase in productivity once for all, and that progress could only be much slower after the middle of the nineteenth century[109]. None the less, from 1872 to 1907, the real output of the textile sector, according to Deane and Cole, increased by 80 per cent, which means a commendable rate of growth of 1.7 per cent per annum – due above all to the advance of the cotton industry, which at the beginning of the twentieth century dominated the whole of the textile sector to a much greater extent than a half-century earlier. The value of its output was double that of the wool industry and nearly half the value of the whole textile sector[110]. But we have seen how precarious its situation was in fact.

THE CHEMICAL INDUSTRY

There is nothing artificial about closing this study of textiles by tackling the problem of the chemical industry, for the latter industry developed to a great extent as a response to the demand of the textile industry for detergents, bleaches, mordants and dyes, though the needs of other industries, notably glass, ceramics, soap and leather played their part. Traditional processes (e.g. the use of sour milk to bleach linen, urine for scouring wool, and ashes for obtaining potassium and soda) would never have satisfied the growing requirements of industry. The solution was a series of innovations which enabled animal raw materials to be replaced by others, at first vegetable and then mineral. This freed production from an inelastic supply of raw materials, just as the iron industry freed itself from the restrictions imposed by the use of charcoal. In addition, the manufacture of chemicals was carried out with improved equipment and on a growing scale. Great Britain, at the beginning of the nineteenth century, acquired a basic chemical industry which employed only a

[109] D.C.Coleman, 'Textile Growth', in N.B.Harte and K.G.Ponting (eds.), *Textile History and Economic History* (Manchester, 1973), pp. 14–5.
[110] Deane and Cole, pp.211–4.

small labour-force, but which was none the less strategically important. Furthermore it led the world.

The basis of the chemical industry was the production of sulphuric
acid, obtainable in large quantities since 1746 by the lead-chamber
process. For bleaching linen and cotton, Charles Tennant, helped by
the chemist Macintosh, invented bleaching powder in 1797 and 1799,
obtaining it by using the action of chlorine on slaked lime. After
modest and difficult beginnings (twenty workers in 1814), Tennant's
factory at St Rollox near Glasgow was to become, at the beginning of
Victoria's reign, the largest chemical factory in the world and also to
boast the highest chimney stack in the world; the Tennant family
controlled an industrial empire during the nineteenth century. Soda
(more precisely carbonate of soda), which was used in many industries,
notably as a detergent for textiles, continued to be produced from the
ashes of barilla and other plants until the rather late adoption (1823)
in England of the process invented in 1787 by the Frenchman Nicholas
Leblanc. Salt was treated with sulphuric acid which gave sodium
sulphate; this was mixed with carbon and lime and then burnt. Black
carbonate of sodium was the result, which became white after
purification. The production of Leblanc soda developed rapidly,
reaching 140,000 tons in 1852, while its price fell substantially.
Needing bulky raw materials, such as salt, coal and lime, this heavy
chemical industry became quickly concentrated – in Glasgow, on
Merseyside (near to Cheshire salt, to coal, and to industries that were
large-scale users of chemicals) and on the Tyne, which in the
mid-nineteenth century was its biggest centre. Belching out clouds of
poisonous smoke and turning out dangerous waste-products, this
industry created moon-like landscapes around its works, until government intervention forced it to recover for use as much as it could of its
by-products, which turned into a source of profit[111].

The British chemical industry remained the largest in the world up
to the 1880s, and in 1876 it accounted for 46 per cent of the world
production of sulphuric acid. However it then quickly lost ground, even
though its production rose considerably, and in 1913 Great Britain was
only the third producer of chemicals (11 per cent of world total), far
behind the United States (34 per cent) and Germany (24 per cent)[112].
The chemical industry, which accounted for only 3 per cent of the net
value of total industrial production in 1907 and only employed in 1911
2.6 per cent of the industrial labour-force (against 1.7 per cent in 1881),

[111] See, for example, Landes, *The Unbound Prometheus*, pp. 108–14.

[112] H.W.Richardson, 'Chemicals', in Aldcroft, *The Development*, p. 278 (table 1), and, for
what follows, pp. 274–306; also Landes, *The Unbound Prometheus*, pp. 269–76.

played a more subordinate role in the national economy than in the United States and Germany, its two great rivals. It has often been considered one of the most striking examples of those branches where England fell behind at the end of the Victorian era, as a result, it is thought, of the manufacturers' conservatism and of their indifference to scientific research, which had become indispensable for success in such an industry.

This is a judgement that should probably be qualified, mainly because the respective positions of competing countries differed substantially according to products considered, and because England remained in the lead in some branches – paints, explosives[113], some fertilizers, intermediate products derived from coal-tar, and above all fats, with the remarkable progress of the soap-firm Lever Brothers, which was later to merge with a Dutch company to form the multinational Unilever[114].

However, the main charge against the British chemical industry is based on its technical backwardness and its weaknesses in three branches of great importance : soda, synthetic dyestuffs and sulphuric acid (and also all the new branches of organic chemistry and electrochemistry). This problem has given rise to some interesting debates[115].

In 1861, the Belgian Ernest Solvay had patented the new process for the manufacture of ammonia-soda, which was 'clean', leaving no waste, and less expensive than the old Leblanc process, even though the latter had recently benefited from many improvements in England. Within two or three decades the new method was to supersede the old one – except in Britain. Yet in 1872 Brunner Mond and Company (Ludwig Mond was a German chemist) had obtained from Solvay a licence to exploit the process (which in fact they found difficult to launch) in the British Isles, and on terms which in practice prevented other British firms from using it before 1886. However, very few firms tried it even then, in spite of the sharp fall in the price of soda, which caused the Leblanc process to be no longer profitable and

---

[113] Thanks to a subsidiary of Nobel.
[114] C.H.Wilson, *The History of Unilever: A Study in Economic Growth and Social Change* (2 vols., London, 1954). William Lever started his first soap factory in 1885 and within fifteen years had won a dominating position in the English market. GB also remained a big producer of soda (50 per cent of the world total of soda ash in 1904) and of sulphuric acid, but by archaic processes.
[115] In addition to Richardson's essay, see P.H.Lindert and K.Trace, 'Yardsticks for Victorian entrepreneurs', in D.N.McCloskey (ed.), *Essays on a Mature Economy: Britain After 1840* (London, 1971), pp. 239–83.

forced several works using it to close down[116]. The producers of Leblanc soda, whose reluctance to scrap plant which was good and 'modern' but suddenly obsolete, is understandable, tried to preserve their industry by modernizing and cutting costs. Then, in 1890, they amalgamated to form an enormous combine, the United Alkali Company, which was the largest chemical company in the world. This did not produce the profits hoped for[117]. The output of Leblanc soda fell from the 1890s onwards (although in 1894 it still represented two-thirds of total British production, while its share did not exceed 22 per cent in any other country) and it ceased during the first world war. H.W.Richardson, although he tends to defend the British chemical industry, considers that one cannot absolve the soda-makers from the 'sin of inertia'.

However, Lindert and Trace have recently attempted a rigorous analysis by measuring (as in other cases which will be mentioned later) profits forgone by British manufacturers owing to their non-optimal choice of techniques. They point out first of all that the cost-structure of the two processes was not the same in all countries, and it favoured the Leblanc process in England more than abroad. Up to 1886, as we have seen, Brunner Mond had, in effect, a monopoly of the Solvay process in Great Britain, and it is not certain that manufacturers, if they had adopted this process, would have made larger profits than with the Leblanc process, given the royalties they would have had to pay. Finally, these two writers have calculated that it was only after 1888 or 1890, perhaps even 1897, that substantial profits were forfeited because of loyalty to the Leblanc process, and that one can talk of 'entrepreneurial failure'[118]. If this was the case, the collapse of the Leblanc sector was so rapid that the efficiency of the chemical industry as a whole was hardly affected, and the mistake was 'buried' before it really slowed down growth. However, these historians admit that industrialists in this branch showed an 'early start' mentality, with an excessive attachment to tradition and a reluctance to admit that they had made a mistake. In the end they were certainly punished for their backwardness.

In another important branch of chemicals, the British were completely absent – the organic chemical industry, based on the distilla-

---

[116] While from the mid-1870s Brunner Mond declared annual dividends of over 25 per cent.

[117] In fact, in 1894, this company made an agreement with Brunner Mond to fix prices and share markets, an agreement which lasted up to 1914.

[118] But the terms 'soda' and 'alkali' in fact covered several products. For some of them, e.g. caustic soda, the Leblanc process long remained competitive.

tion of coal-tar, of which artificial dyes were the main products. Yet the fundamental discovery had been made by an Englishman, W.H.Perkin, with the first aniline dye in 1856. Furthermore, the raw material, tar, was abundant in England (Germany got her supplies there later) and the textile industry offered a huge market. Yet this industry did not take root in Great Britain, and Germany gained more and more a near monopoly, leaving a small share to Switzerland. In 1913 she supplied 85 per cent of world production, against 6 per cent for Switzerland and 3 per cent for England (nine-tenths of whose consumption was covered by imports) and 2 per cent for the United States. Lindert and Trace admit that in the 1870s and 1880s hardly any research was done in this field in Great Britain. Later, of course, as the Germans had carried out and exploited important innovations and had created powerful firms, it was difficult for the British to launch themselves in their wake. The large German firms could reply by dumping so as to nip competition in the bud, and a defective law of 1883 on patents allowed them to take out hundreds of vaguely worded patents in Britain without any obligation to work them or to grant licences to use them. These writers conclude by doubting whether one should 'revise the standard view of the dyestuffs example as a classic lost opportunity for Britain'.

Finally, for the production of sulphuric acid, Great Britain remained faithful to the old lead-chamber process and neglected at first the new contact process which was perfected in Germany about 1900; but the delay cost her nothing economically, for Germany herself in 1914 only produced 25 per cent of her sulphuric acid by this method, against 14 per cent in the United States and 11 per cent in Great Britain[119].

In these conditions, between 1880 and 1913, the imports of chemicals into Great Britain increased faster than both her total imports and national product, especially after 1900 when her competitiveness deteriorated noticeably. Yet her exports of chemicals shipped to imperial markets, remained higher than her imports, though the gap was narrowing.

Finally, Lindert and Trace, after showing that some of the missed opportunities of the British chemical industry were illusory, admit that there were genuine cases, where the loss had serious consequences. Although the laziness and amateurism of British industrialists have been overestimated, it does seem that the 'moderate performance' of the British chemical industry could mainly be explained by the inadequacy of scientific research, both pure and

[119] She also neglected the production of chlorine and caustic soda by electrolysis.

applied, not only in discovering new products and methods but also in perfecting old ones, while it had to face the resolute institutionalization of innovation which had taken root in Germany (even though research was often costly and only profitable in the long run), and the conviction of German and Swiss manufacturers that laboratories staffed with highly qualified chemists were indispensable, whereas such laboratories were very rare in England[120].

According to the free-trade outlook, which was still very influential, each country could not excel in all domains. Indeed, the United States had also been unable to build up an artificial dyestuffs industry, relying on imports from Germany. No one has thought of seeing here a proof of decline. One may add that the glass industry, near neighbour to the chemical industry which provided one of its raw materials (soda), had very early, in the 1850s, met with strong foreign competition and a flood of imports coming from Belgium. Around 1870, imports of window glass equalled total English output. However, the two main branches, hollow glass (bottles) and flat glass (window-panes, mirrors) showed a remarkable revival thanks to an effort of modernization, mechanization and improved management, particularly in the case of the great firm of St Helens (Lancashire), Pilkingtons, who clearly dominated the flat-glass sector from the end of the nineteenth century onwards[121].

---

[120] Richardson, pp. 286, 298, 302.
[121] T.C.Barker, 'The glass industry', in Aldcroft, *The Development*, pp. 307–25; and the new revised edition of his history of Pilkington: *The Glassmakers. Pilkington:The Rise of an International Company, 1826–1976* (London, 1977).

8 Iron, steel, coal

The production and working of metals, which had been much less considerable as an industry than the textile group at Victoria's accession, had overtaken it at the beginning of the twentieth century[1]. It is true that metals made up a very varied collection of industries, and we shall concentrate here on two strategic branches: first, iron and steel, later engineering, but it must be mentioned that, at the beginning of the nineteenth century, England was a large producer of copper, tin (mined in Devon and Cornwall)[2] and lead (Derbyshire) ores. Their production increased up to mid-century and even beyond, but then diminished or even ceased, owing to the exhaustion of deposits and the competition from abroad at lower prices.

IRON AND STEEL

The British iron industry, like cotton, had known a technological revolution at the end of the eighteenth century, thanks to the use of coke instead of charcoal in blast-furnaces (this process had been invented in 1709, but only became widespread after 1750), puddling and rolling (invented by Henry Cort in 1784 to turn pig-iron into bar-iron and quickly adopted by ironmasters in the 1790's), supported by the use of steam-engines to power blowers and rolling-mill[3]. The

---

[1] In 1870, the metals industries (primary and secondary) still only had 31 per cent of steam-power in industry, as against 52 per cent for textiles, according to P. Deane and W.A. Cole, *British Economic Growth, 1688–1959* (Cambridge, 2nd edn, 1967), pp.211, 266, and 34 per cent, as against 53 per cent according to A.E. Musson, 'Industrial motive-power in the United Kingdom, 1800–70', *Economic History Review*, 2nd series, XXIX(3), August 1976, pp. 437–80.

[2] Copper ore was smelted and refined in South Wales, especially in Swansea. This industry collapsed at the end of the nineteenth century.

[3] The most recent work on these problems is: C.K. Hyde, *Technological Change and the British Iron Industry, 1700–1800* (Princeton, 1977); earlier articles: 'Technological change and the development of the British iron industry, 1700–1870', *Journal of Economic History* XXIII (1), Mar. 1973, 312–12; also C.K. Hyde, 'Technological

transformation of this industry and its conversion to mineral fuel were completed by the beginning of the nineteenth century. This gave it unlimited possibilities of growth, whereas it had been handicapped for two centuries by the scarcity and high cost of wood in England. The half-century which followed was marked by the improvement of existing technology rather than by any new technical revolution. The size of blast-furnaces was increased, up to 15 or 20 metres, and from 1840 onwards their inside section was made circular. Puddling was improved, and the amount of iron lost in clinkers reduced (wastage being no more than 8 per cent around 1840, instead of 50 per cent half a century earlier). The Nasmyth steam-hammer (1839) enabled large blooms of iron to be forged. The most important innovation was James Neilson's hot-blast process (1829), which consisted of blowing pre-heated air into the blast-furnace. It meant that certain varieties of Scottish coal could be used directly in blast-furnaces without being transformed into coke beforehand; in such cases, it brought about a reduction of 60 per cent in the cost of fuel required for making a ton of pig-iron. It was the cause of the spectacular boom of the Scottish iron industry in the 1830s, but it was of less interest in England where qualities of coal were different, and it was adopted there less quickly[4]. These various improvements led to better productivity and, especially, to growing savings of fuel. However, new decisive innovations began to occur only in the 1850s, which have often been called the 'Steel Revolution' and which divide the history of the iron industry during the nineteenth century into two trends, especially as in the last decades of the century there was a clear slowing-down of growth-rates that had previously been very rapid.

It has generally been thought that the transformation and growth of the iron industry were stimulated by the wars against France. Certainly, the production of pig-iron quadrupled in twenty years, from 1791 to 1810. Against this, the peace brought on a long and serious depression, and growth only picked up again after 1820. Expansion

change in the British wrought-iron industry, 1750–1815: a reinterpretation', *Economic History Review*, 2nd series, XXVII(2), May 1974, 190–206. Hyde points out that the diffusion of new techniques was 'rationally' conditioned by relative costs. Half the iron was already produced with coal by the potting and stamping process before the invention of puddling. However, Hyde recognizes the importance of the latter, for it reduced prices and enabled blast-furnaces and forges to be integrated.

4   C.K.Hyde, 'The adoption of the hot blast by the British iron industry: a re-interpretation', *Explorations in Economic History*, X(3), 1973, which shows that the success of this process in Scotland came from fuel savings and not from the possibility of using blackband iron-ores; D.S. Landes, *The Unbound Prometheus: Technological Change and Industrial Development in Western Europe, 1750 to the Present* (Cambridge, 1969), pp.92–3.

was then very rapid (though also irregular), thanks to the economy's general momentum, and the many new uses to which cast and wrought iron could be put: machines of all sorts and in growing numbers[5], water- and gas-pipes, pillars and beams in buildings, (particularly in factories), iron bridges, the first iron ships, and finally railway demand – rails, locomotives, equipment of every sort. Though the role of railway demand should not be overestimated, it was considerable in the 1840s[6].

This expansion of domestic demand was the basis of the iron industry's growth; but the role of exports was far from negligible. It is true that at the beginning of the nineteenth century the bulk of iron and steel exports was made up of finished goods (ironmongery, cutlery, etc). But exports of semi-finished iron products (as well as machinery) definitely rose from the 1840s onwards, and especially when the building of railways abroad created a strong demand for rails, which local iron industries were not capable of satisfying, either in sufficient quantities, or at prices that competed with those of English goods. Exports of pig-iron, iron and steel doubled in weight every ten years, rising from 49,000 tons in 1815 to 194,000 tons in 1837 and to 783,000 tons in 1850. They passed the million tons mark in 1852 and reached 3,383,000 tons in 1872. From the late 1830s, these semi-finished articles made up the bulk of the total value of iron and steel exports, which had been only £3.3 million in 1814 and £4 million in 1837, but climbed to £53 million in 1873[7].The value of total exports of metals and metal goods[8] rose at an annual average rate of growth of 3.2 per cent between 1814 and 1846, and 5.7 per cent between 1846 and 1873. So the share of the metal industries in total British exports grew markedly, increasing from 9 per cent in 1815[9] to 11 per cent in 1830/9 and 18 per cent in 1850/9, and they made an important contribution to the growth of total exports. This being so, the proportion of net primary

[5] At the beginning of the Industrial Revolution many machines, notably textile machinery, had been built of wood.
[6] Cf. Chapter 9, pp. 300–1.
[7] B.R. Mitchell and P. Deane, *Abstract of British Historical Statistics* (Cambridge, 1962) (quoted hereafter as *Abstract*), pp. 146–7, 302–4; see also Mathias, *The First Industrial Nation: An Economic History of Britain, 1700–1914* (London, 1969), p.468 (table 17). The 1873 figures were exceptional, exports having doubled since 1866. A large proportion of iron exports, particularly rails, were destined for the United States, especially between 1848 and 1854. Later the continent and India took over as chief purchasers.
[8] This calculation, by exponential adjustment, includes non-ferrous metals and articles made from them, but their role was secondary and shrinking.
[9] In fact, according to Ralph Davis's calculations, the share of iron and iron goods in the current value of total exports was very small about 1815.

production of iron which was exported, either directly or indirectly (in the form of finished goods), after having settled at about 20 per cent between the beginning of the century and the 1830s, rose to nearly 30 per cent in the early 1840s, then to 40 per cent in the 1850s, and exceeded this percentage in the 1860s[10]. The contribution made by the increase in exports to the expansion of production seems to have been 43 per cent between 1835/9 and 1870/4. In spite of this clearly increased dependence on exports, it seems that the domestic market determined investment in the iron industry, which was made in periods of full-capacity working and so of rising prices. On the other hand, fluctuations in foreign demand reacted on the level of production; but the ironmasters, who had heavy fixed charges and so had to try and maintain production, sold large quantities abroad at low prices during bad years, so that exports had a counter-cyclical movement at certain times[11]. Indeed the iron industry, as with most capital goods, was very vulnerable to business cycles (e.g. from 1841 to 1842 production seems to have dropped by 28 per cent). These recessions posed serious problems for ironmasters. Should they reduce production, putting furnaces out of blast or should they keep it up? In the latter case, should they cut prices or accumulate stock? Ironmasters tried to agree on a common policy, at least at the regional level, but they never succeeded for any length of time. The large firms, having financial reserves, were able to retain stocks, but the smaller ones, lacking cash, were obliged eventually to sell at any price they could get[12].

In the long term, however, given the strength of domestic and foreign demand, the iron industry's production increased very rapidly after the postwar crisis, as can be seen from table 41[13].

[10] Deane and Cole, pp.224–5 (table 56); S. Engerman, 'The American tariff, British exports and American iron production, 1840–1860', in D.N. McCloskey (ed.), *Essays on a Mature Economy: Britain after 1840* (London, 1971), p.16, gives percentages that are different and a little higher.

[11] This is the opinion of J.R.T. Hughes, *Fluctuations in Trade, Industry and Finance: A Study of British Economic Development, 1850–1860* (Oxford, 1960), for the 1850s. See R.A. Church, *The Great Victorian Boom, 1850–1873* (London, 1975), p.43; Engerman, pp. 16–18, 21–2, 25, 34–5.

[12] See for example J.P. Addis, *The Crawshay Dynasty: A Study in Industrial Organization and Development* (Cardiff, 1957), ch. 3, pp.50ff.

[13] Up to 1854 the only figures for pig-iron output available are estimates. So we have given figures borrowed from Deane and Cole, p.225 (table 56) (completed by *Abstract*, p.132, for 1909/13) and others drawn from the recent series of annual estimates constructed by P. Ridden, 'The output of the British iron industry before 1870', *Economic History Review*, 2nd series, XXX (3), Aug. 1977, 455 (table 3). Fortunately, the rates of growth that one can reckon from them are very close to each other. Between the 1820s and the 1850s the production of pig-iron tended to triple every twenty years.

Table 41 Production of pig-iron in Great Britain

	Annual averages (000s of tons)			Annual average rates of growth (%)	
	Deane and Cole		Riden	Deane and Cole	Riden
1815/19			286		
1818	325				
1835/39	1150		1060		
1870/74		6378			
1895/99		8638			
1909/13		9616			
1818–1835/39				6.9	
1815/19–1835/39					6.8
1835/39–1870/74				5.0	5.3
1870/74–1895/99				1.2	
1895/99–1909/13				0.75	
1818–1910/14				3.6	
1815/19–1910/14					3.8
1835/39–1895/99				3.4	

The trend revealed is that of an extremely high rate of growth during the two decades preceding the beginning of Victoria's reign, and a slowing-down after that – but not at once. In fact, the peak rate, 7.2 per cent per annum, was reached between 1830/4 and 1850/4 when production quadrupled, but it fell to 4.3 per cent for 1850/4 – 1870/4[14]. The slowdown was to persist later without a break, but this disquieting symptom will be examined shortly.

Rapid growth was accompanied by important changes in the location of the iron industry, for the various iron-making districts (it was characteristic of Great Britain to have a relatively large number of them)[15] progressed at an uneven rate. During the period under review, the main development was the dramatic boom in the Scottish iron industry, centred on Glasgow, after 1830. Its output of pig-iron rose as follows:

1830	38,000 tons	(5 per cent of British production)
1840	241,000 tons	
1847·	540,000 tons	
1852	775,000 tons	(28 per cent of British production)

[14] According to Deane and Cole's figures. According to Riden's we would get 7.0 and 4.4 per cent respectively. The output of 1851 was 2.5 million tons of pig-iron.
[15] Thanks to the frequent coexistence of iron-ore and coal in the same fields.

At this point, the advance, which had reached 15 per cent per annum between 1830 and 1847, slowed down considerably, and Scotland's percentage in total British production definitely diminished. This boom can be explained by the rapid adoption of the hot-blast process, which brought down sharply the consumption of fuel in blast-furnaces. When the pioneers of this process had made fortunes within a few years, the industry attracted large speculative investment, often supplied by capitalists who came from outside the industry. Such investment made possible the expansion of existing works, between 1832 and 1837, and then the building of new ones, despite the depression which followed the crisis of 1837. This investment thus became counter-cyclical, and there was an enormous increase in productive capacity.

The other iron regions of England did not show such remarkable progress, but all increased their output of pig-iron up to mid-century, when the output of the old Midlands districts, e.g. Shropshire which had been one of the cradles of the Industrial Revolution, stabilized or declined. At the beginning of Victoria's reign, the two main areas were south Staffordshire (212,000 tons of pig-iron in 1830, 346,000 in 1839, 725,000 in 1852) and South Wales (278,000, 454,000 and 666,000 tons at the same dates)[16]. They displayed interesting contrasts. A 'new country', where the iron industry did not start on a large scale before the end of the eighteenth century, when mineral leases on large tracts of land had been granted to a few entrepreneurs by the local landowners, South Wales was the domain of a few large integrated enterprises with blast-furnaces, forges and rolling-mills, mainly situated, like the famous Cyfarthfa and Dowlais works, in the north-east of the coal-field, around Merthyr Tydfil, where there were outcrops of iron-ore and coal. When these firms were threatened in the 1830s by Scottish competition, they specialized in cheap rolled products, and especially rails, which brought them great prosperity[17]. South Staffordshire, which with some neighbouring parts of Shropshire and Worcestershire formed the Black Country[18], was also rich in minerals (with the famous 10-yard coal-seam), but its industrial activity went a long way back, and the ownership of the land was

[16]   *Abstract*, p.133.
[17]   M. Lévy-Leboyer, *Les Banques européennes et l'industrialisation internationale dans la première moitié du XIXe siècle* (Paris, 1964), pp.342–3, 345, observes that this vertical integration was not extended, any more than in most other centres of primary iron industry, up to the engineering industry, which developed in places where machinery was used.
[18]   This district is to the west of Birmingham, which does not form part of it.

usually much divided. Its ironmasters, sprung from the yeomanry, the lesser gentry or the craftsman class, were in charge of relatively small firms with a very varied output, custom-made and not mass-produced. Even the main (and untypical) industrial empire of the district, the firm of James Foster, was a conglomerate of separate units: mines, furnaces, forges, workshops, etc. With Scotland, these two regions accounted for three-quarters of the total production of pig-iron and bar-iron at the beginning of the Victorian era. But the Steel Revolution was going to lead, among other things, to the rise of new producing districts.

Up to the middle of the nineteenth century, the basic product of the iron industry – apart from foundry pig-iron – was puddled wrought iron, made at the cost of extremely arduous work on the part of the puddlers[19]. One could only make steel, which is both tougher and more flexible than iron, in small quantities (by the cementation or the crucible process) and at a high cost. Steel was a semi-precious metal, reserved for luxury objects. In 1854, Britain produced less than 100,000 tons of it. It was then that the need for armaments during the Crimean war led Henry Bessemer (1813-98), a professional inventor who had already amassed a fortune, to become interested in steel. He took out a series of patents between December 1855 and March 1856, and in August 1856 announced that he had discovered a process for producing steel 'without fuel'. He used a 'converter', filled with molten pig-iron, through which a violent current of air was blown by *tuyères*. The carbon in the pig-iron burnt quickly, and after adding some carbon and manganese one obtained steel which could then be cast. After some teething troubles caused by using impure iron, Bessemer perfected his invention within two years and in 1858 set up a steelworks in Sheffield, where the steel manufacturers had shown no interest in his process; but he at once undersold them by £10–£18 a ton. Bessemer made an immense fortune, helped by the sale of licences for his process, which many manufacturers took up eagerly from 1859–60 onwards[20].

The process was fast, the conversion of pig-iron into steel taking only a few minutes, but it was unsophisticated and difficult to control for

---

[19] Attempts at this time to mechanize puddling, either by rotating furnaces or by other devices, did not meet with much success.

[20] W.H. Chaloner, *People and Industries* (London, 1963), ch. 9, 'Sir Henry Bessemer (1813–98) and the coming of cheap steel', pp.74–85; Landes, *The Unbound Prometheus*, p.249ff; J.H.Clapham, *An Economic History of Modern Britain* (3 vols, Cambridge, 1926–38), II, pp. 53ff.

quality. In 1861 William Siemens invented a gas furnace giving high temperatures that could be regulated more exactly. In 1865 the brothers Martin, ironmasters at Sireuil in the Dordogne, made steel in a Siemens furnace, into which pig-iron and scrap-iron were put together. Soon afterwards, Siemens himself opened a steelworks in Birmingham, then another much bigger one in 1868 at Landore near Swansea. His methods there were a great improvement on those of the Martins and enabled exactly the required carbon content to be obtained, by the addition of pure ore and of manganese to molten pig-iron and by strict temperature control.

Yet one serious problem remained. These processes only gave a satisfactory product if the pig-iron used contained no phosphorus. This brought a rush to the non-phosphoric haematites of Cumberland, then to the equally pure ores of northern Spain, where British speculators hastened to obtain mining concessions. Imports of iron ores into Britain rose from 100,000 tons in 1865/9 to 3,060,000 tons in 1880. But the commonest ores in England, as elsewhere in Europe, were phosphoric. An amateur chemist, clerk in a London police court called Sidney Thomas, together with his cousin Percy Gilchrist who was employed in an iron works, embarked on research to discover a 'dephosphorization' process. They looked for an internal lining in the converter which would combine with phosphorus, and they found it, in 1879, in magnesian limestone, plus the addition of lime to the metal charge. There followed a rush to obtain licences from the two inventors, and Thomas made a fortune before dying young of tuberculosis.

These three processes, appearing within the span of about twenty years, enabled steel to be produced for the first time and cheaply in large quantities, so that it superseded puddled iron. This led to a real upheaval in the industry, though in Great Britain the change was more gradual than in some other countries.

The annual production of steel increased very rapidly, passing 500,000 tons in 1873, but time was needed before it was substituted for iron. The output of puddled iron continued to increase up to 1882, when it reached a peak of 2.8 million tons. Indeed, the high price of Bessemer's licences and the fact that steel-making remained at first costly slowed down the diffusion of the new technique; and although steel was more economic, being much more resistant and durable, several years were required to prove it. Furthermore, during the third quarter of the nineteenth century, the makers of puddled iron made enormous investments, at first to develop, and later to save, their industry: the number of puddling furnaces doubled between 1860 and 1870; this is an example of the slowing-down effect of large investment in traditional sectors. However, during the 1870s the superiority of steel was established beyond doubt, all the more so because its prices dropped sharply (e.g. by 60 per cent for rails between 1873 and 1883), as the result of competition, the fall in costs and the transfer of the steelworks from Sheffield and Birmingham to sites on the coast, where imported ores could easily be received. In the late 1870s the railway companies went over largely to steel rails, then shipbuilding, whose demand had supported the puddled iron industry up to 1882, also took up steel. After that date the production of iron declined and was passed by steel in 1886, but it was still 1.2 million tons in 1900 and 1913, mainly manufactured in the old districts of the Midlands.

Furthermore, the Bessemer process, which prevailed at first, was gradually supplanted by the Siemens or open-hearth process, which produced steel of higher quality. The production of Bessemer steel declined after 1890 and was overtaken by open-hearth steel in 1893. However, in 1910/14, 22 per cent of British steel output was still from Bessemer converters, whereas Germany had practically abandoned them.

The 'basic' Gilchrist–Thomas process had much more success abroad (and notably in France, where it was vital for Lorraine) than in its country of origin. Its percentage of steel output was only 16 per cent in 1895/9 and 27 per cent in 1910/14. So the large deposits of Jurassic phosphoric ores found in the eastern Midlands[21] were relatively neglected and were exploited rather late. In 1913 6.6 million tons of these ores were used, out of a national total of 16 million tons, to which were added 7.4 million tons of imported ores, although the latter, being of a higher grade, amounted to 61 per cent in value of ores used. England still had non-phosphoric ore resources, as well as a commercial organization and works located on the coast which favoured the import and use of foreign ores[22]. By this brief analysis one can glimpse delays in innovation and taking advantage of the Steel Revolution, a subject that has given rise to lively controversy, to which we shall return later.

In these ways technological change and geological factors altered the location of the iron and steel industry during the second half of the

[21] Leicestershire, Lincolnshire and Northamptonshire.
[22] *Abstract*, pp.129–30, 139. The production of iron-ore in GB reached its peak in the 1870s and then stabilized at a slightly lower tonnage. Two-thirds of imports came from Spain in 1913. Several iron and steel firms had interests in Spanish mines.

nineteenth century[23]. One natural condition that had favoured the growth of the iron industry ever since the Industrial Revolution had been the coexistence in the same basins, and sometimes in the same seams, of high-grade carboniferous iron-ores and of excellent coking coal, e.g. in the Black Country, on the northern boundary of the great South Wales coalfield, and around Glasgow. But from mid-century onwards, these iron-ore deposits, which were not very large and which had been worked intensively, began to be exhausted, as did occasionally the reserves of good coking coal. These districts ran into difficulties from the 1860s onwards, and sometimes even earlier. They were badly hit during the Great Depression, especially after 1880, and many ironworks, some of them famous, were closed and demolished. In the inland regions such as Staffordshire, Shropshire and south Yorkshire (Sheffield), the output of pig-iron declined and became generally quite small. They specialized in steelworks (while still continuing to puddle iron)[24], in making special steels, and finished products and steel-forging; some firms went over entirely to engineering[25]. Against this, the old iron-makers who were near the coast maintained their production better, because they could easily

---

[23]   In the following table are summarized the shares of the different districts in GB's total output at three successive dates (from *Abstract*, pp.131–2).

| | Pig-iron | | | Steel |
| | 1854 | 1880 | 1913 | 1913 |
	%	%	%	%
Scotland	26.0	13.5	13.3	18.4
North-east coast (a)	9.0	31.2	37.8	26.5
North-west coast (b)	1.7	20.6	13.3	
West Midlands (c)	31.7	9.0	8.3	4.8
East Midlands (d)	4.2	9.7	15.8	10.0
South Wales	24.4	11.5	8.7	23.6

(a) Durham, Northumberland, north Yorkshire.

(b) Cumberland, Lancashire, North Wales (an odd grouping whose important part was Cumberland and north Lancashire).

(c) Shropshire, Staffordshire, Warwickshire, Worcestershire.

(d) Derbyshire, Leicestershire, Northamptonshire, Lincolnshire.

Steel production in 1913 is taken from L.D. Stamp and S.H. Beaver, *The British Isles: A Geographic and Economic Survey* (London, 4th edn, 1956), p.374; but its classification for steel is not the same as for pig-iron! Hence a blank in this column. The north-west coast in its strict sense (Cumberland and Furness) made 11 per cent of pig-iron and 5.2 per cent of steel in 1913; Sheffield provided 11.4 per cent of steel.

[24]   In fact many ironmasters in these areas went over too late to steel, e.g. those in Wales to steel rails.

[25]   See for example G.J. Barnsey, 'The standard of living in the Black Country during the nineteenth century', *Economic History Review*, 2nd series, XXIV(2), May 1971, 220–9, who sees the zenith of this region in the 1850s and 1860s, but insists that the Great Depression there was 'very real'. Staffordshire supplied 30 per cent of the total output of pig-iron in 1850, 8 per cent in 1880. The industry of Shropshire collapsed after 1873.

obtain Cumberland haematite or foreign ores by sea. In South Wales the large works were concentrated in the Merthyr Tydfil area, and thus too far from the sea for receiving imported ores; they succumbed one after the other, or moved to the ports; but this redeployment was not completed by the beginning of the twentieth century. After 1872, South Wales fell well below the record production of pig-iron it had achieved in the third quarter of the nineteenth century[26]. In Scotland there was stagnation rather than retreat, but both regions lost ground, though much more in the production of pig-iron than of steel.

As well as decline in certain regions, the third quarter of the nineteenth century saw the birth of new iron and steel districts. In the 1850s, for example, blast-furnaces were set up at Middlesbrough to work the low-grade Liassic ore, of the Cleveland Hills and the nearby coal of Durham. This was the beginning of the north-east region, long renowned for the large size and modernity of its plants, whose production of pig-iron rose from 275,000 tons in 1854 to 2.4 million in 1880 and to 3.9 million in 1913, which puts it at the top both for pig-iron and for steel. In addition, in the 1860s, blast-furnaces and steelworks were established on the north-west coast close to the rich haematites of Cumberland and Furness, particularly near Barrow. This district reached its peak in the 1880s with one million tons of pig-iron produced in Cumberland alone in 1882, but it then lost ground relatively and even absolutely[27]. The phosphoric ores of the east Midlands attracted the establishment of a number of blast-furnaces in the area, but most of the ore extracted was sent elsewhere, and pig-iron was the main product.

In these ways the iron and steel industry moved in response to changes in the availability of its raw materials, but these shifts slowed down after the 1880s when the industry's geography was roughly settled up to the first world war, with most locations on the coasts, especially for blast-furnaces. But production also continued in many small centres, which had no justification apart from the existence of plant and skilled local labour.

It was not only the redeployment of the iron and steel industry which tailed off at the end of the nineteenth century. Growth also slowed

---

[26] Cf. W.E. Minchinton (ed.), *Industrial South Wales, 1750–1914: Essays in Welsh Economic History* (London, 1969), pp.XXII to XXV. The famous works at Cyfarthfa were sold in 1902 and closed just before the first world war. South Wales found compensation for the decline of her iron and steel industry in the rise of her coal-mining and of her tin-plate industry.

[27] The development of these two new mining areas involved heavy investment in the 1850s (twenty-seven blast-furnaces are said to have been built per year on average) and 1860s (thirty blast-furnaces were built in Cleveland between 1869 and 1874).

down. After regular but unspectacular progress in the 1850s and 1860s, the industry enjoyed a sharp boom between 1869 and 1873, largely due to enormous exports[28]. The industry's share of national product also reached its peak at that time. The proportion of its gross production (coal and imported ores being subtracted) to Britain's GNP, which had been only 3 to 4 per cent from 1818 to 1841, rose to 6 per cent in 1851 and reached 12 per cent in 1871; but it then began to fall back, being 5.8 per cent in 1901 and 5.4 per cent in 1907[29]. This was a clear sign of a serious slowing-down in growth during the last quarter of the nineteenth and the beginning of the twentieth century.

To appreciate the true nature of the decline in growth-rate, a distinction has to be made between the different branches of the iron and steel industry. It was the production of pig-iron that was most affected. Table 41 shows that this only increased by a third between 1870/4 and 1895/9, and by 51 per cent between 1870/4 and 1909/13 (an annual growth-rate over the last period of 1.1 per cent), whereas in the first part of the century it tended to triple every twenty years!

Against this, the production of steel increased very rapidly during the Great Depression (see table 42)[30].

From 1871/4 to 1909/13, the annual average rate of growth was 7 per cent. It is true that steel was substituted for wrought iron, whose production reached its peak in 1882 and then declined. Unfortunately, statistics for wrought iron output are only available from 1881 onwards; but this enables us to calculate the total production of iron and steel after that date (see table 43).

These rates appear modest, but they would be higher if one could take into account the 1870s when steel production increased very fast,

Table 42   Production of steel in the Great Depression

	Annual average output (000s of tons)	Annual average rate, of growth (%)
1871/4	486	
1895/9	4260	9.5
1909/13	6636	3.0

---

[28] Mostly made up of rails, intended especially for the United States.
[29] Deane and Cole, p.226 (table 57); also P.L. Payne, 'Iron and steel manufactures', in D.H. Aldcroft (ed.) *The Development of British Industry and Foreign Competition, 1875–1914: Studies in Industrial Enterprise* (London, 1968), p. 71.
[30] Mathias, *The First Industrial Nation*, p.474 (table 32); *Abstract*, pp.136–7. The output of 1913 was 7.7 million tons. Production of pig-iron was 10.3 million tons.

Table 43   Production of iron and steel after 1881

	Annual average output (000s of tons)	Annual average rates of growth (%)	
1881/5	4392	1.6 ⎱	
1895/9	5444		2.1
1909/13	7831	2.6 ⎰	

Table 44   UK metal production

	Index of metal production (1913 = 100)	Annual average rates of growth (%)	Index of ferrous metals production 1913 = 100)	Annual average rates of growth (%)
1857	24		19	
		3.4		4.2
1870	41	2.5	36	2.8
1900	80	1.7	75	2.2
1910	100		100	

expanding fivefold between 1872 and 1882, while the making of iron continued to rise.

Finally, table 44 shows Feinstein's indices for the production of metals, and the growth rates that can be derived from them[31]. These data confirm the slowing-down of the industry's overall production after 1875 and show that it continued at the beginning of the twentieth century.

As the output of iron and steel increased very rapidly in the United States and Germany in the same period, Britain's share of world output, which had been over 50 per cent for pig-iron and 40 per cent for steel in 1870, went into a rapid decline. The United States passed her in 1886 for steel, and in 1890 for pig-iron; Germany did the same for steel in 1893 and for pig-iron in 1904. By 1900 these two countries together were producing three times as much steel as Great Britain, and in 1913 the latter's output was only a quarter of the United States' and half Germany's (table 45)[32].

Britain's share of international trade in iron and steel, which she completely dominated around 1870, also declined after that date. In spite of an increase in her exports (but at a slower pace than was achieved by Germany, Belgium and the United States), she only supplied under a quarter of the steel entering the international market

---

[31]   C.H.Feinstein, *National income, Expenditure and Output of the United Kingdom, 1855–1965* (Cambridge, 1972) tables 51 and 52, T. 111–2, 114–5.
[32]   Payne, 'Iron and steel', pp.71–2, 75; Deane and Cole, p.227.

242   *The Victorian Economy*

Table 45 Shares of world production of pig-iron and steel (in percentages of the world total)

	Pig-iron			Steel		
	Great Britain	USA	Germany	Great Britain	USA	Germany
1875/9	46	16	13	36	26	17
1895/9	26	32	18	20	35	23
1910/13	14	40	21	10	42	23

in 1913[33]. Worse still, the British market itself was invaded by imports of foreign iron and steel, especially after 1895. Passing one million tons in 1902, these imports reached 2,231,000 tons in 1913 (i.e. 45 per cent of British exports of these products by weight), which made England the leading importer of steel in the world[34]!

As Payne has written, a superiority that was overwhelming at the start was completely and irremediably lost in forty years. The direct, undeniable cause of steel production's feeble growth and of England's decline in the league of steel-making countries was the relatively slow increase in the demand for British metal products, on both the domestic and the foreign market.

From 1876/80 to 1911/12 the consumption of pig-iron *per head* of population rose by only 12 per cent in the United Kingdom, but by 470 per cent in Germany and 633 per cent in the United States. It is true that these two countries, at the start, had absolute levels of consumption far lower than England's, and they only caught up at the beginning of the twentieth century; but these contrasts in growth are no less striking[35]. Of course, this near-stagnation of the domestic market is only one aspect of the slowing-down of the British economy's overall growth at the end of the nineteenth century – a problem which will be considered later; for the moment, it will be enough to record this fact.

If we turn to the foreign markets, which on average absorbed 40 per cent of British output during this period[36], we find that the main customers during the boom in the early 1870s were the United States

33   A third if one takes iron into account.
34   Payne, 'Iron and steel', pp. 75, 76 (graph III), 87; *Abstract*, pp. 141–3, 147. These imports had been insignificant in the 1870s.
35   Payne, 'Iron and steel', pp.76–7 (table III). If one compared 1876/80 to 1896/1900, the results would be hardly less unfavourable to England. From the late 1870s to the beginning of the twentieth century, steel consumption per capita quadrupled in the UK and was multiplied by ten in Germany and the United States.
36   Deane and Cole, p.225 (table 56).

and Germany; but these markets, which expanded rapidly, were soon closed to English products by tariff protection. Other markets had to be sought, often with success – in the British empire, in Latin America and in the Far East – but demand in these countries was not very buoyant, and British exporters ran up against dumping by the Germans (which must not be exaggerated) as well as untiring activity by Teutonic commercial travellers. However, the British put up a fine resistance and their alleged apathy has been much exaggerated. Furthermore, although the multiplicity of articles offered by them in response to their customers' very varied specifications (while German and the American works produced fewer and standardized goods) was probably a handicap from the technical and cost point of view, it was well adjusted commercially to the demand. Nonetheless, although supremacy in the empire markets was preserved, the British lost ground, especially after 1909. In 1912 and 1913, their exports of iron and steel were for the first time exceeded by German exports[37].

At the same time as British exports were under pressure in this way, the British market was invaded by foreign steel, which gives credence to the argument that production costs were higher in Britain than abroad[38]. Many historians have heavily criticized the British iron and steel industry for its loss of competitiveness. They admit that it would never have kept its leading position, especially against the United States, but argue that it would not have been overtaken so quickly, by the United States and also by Germany, if its leaders had shown more enterprise and energy. If they had not hesitated so long to innovate and invest, the technology of the British steel industry would not have fallen so much behind that of its great rivals[39].

One can indeed draw up an impressive list of examples of technical backwardness in Britain, e.g. in the recovery of the by-products of coking, in the improvement of blast-furnaces, in the adoption of engines burning gases from blast-furnaces, in factory-electrification, in the mechanical handling of raw materials, in fuel economy through the 'direct process', i.e. charging converters or open-hearth furnaces with liquid pig-iron coming straight out of the blast-furnaces[40]. And in

[37] Payne, 'Iron and steel', pp.75,77, 79–81, 84, 86–7.
[38] The costs of ore and fuel seem to have been very close in the three countries.
[39] Notably two classic works: D. Burn, *The Economic History of Steelmaking, 1867–1939* (Cambridge, 1940; 2nd edn, 1961); T.H. Burnham and G.O. Hoskins, *Iron and Steel in Britain, 1870–1930* (London, 1943); also Landes, *The Unbound Prometheus*, pp.263ff. Good discussion in Payne, 'Iron and steel', pp.88–99. Technological backwardness was worse in works using the Bessemer process, which were dying as early as the late nineteenth century, than in those with open hearths.
[40] It was in fact impossible in many cases where blast-furnaces and steel-works belonged to separate firms.

this connection the blame has been laid (as for the chemical industry) on the inadequacy of scientific and technical education in Great Britain, as compared with Germany, the relatively small number of qualified engineers, as well as the lack of authority they enjoyed in their firms.

This led to firms being criticized for not being interested in technical progress. Firstly, Great Britain had few large firms that were fully integrated (with blast-furnaces, steelworks and rolling-mills) and rationally organized. The move towards vertical integration which occurred at the beginning of the twentieth century was very limited. In 1907, Britain had 101 companies which owned blast-furnaces and 95 which made steel. These companies were too numerous and too small, inevitably poorly equipped and expensive to run[41]. The family character of most iron and steel firms has been considered responsible for this situation: they were run by men without scientific education, who were heirs to comfortable fortunes, also often elderly, or interested in many activities outside their works. This induced prudence, conservatism and undynamic responses. Furthermore they hated to lose complete control of their business, which would be the consequence of a merger effective enough to create large, efficient works. Ironmasters also often thought that weak home demand and foreign competition endangered the success of such enterprises, and even the reinvestment with modern equipment[42].

Peter Temin has tried to estimate exactly what would have happened if British ironmasters had not become demoralized in this way, and if they had made vigorous efforts to bring down their costs and their prices. He has come to the conclusion that, if this had happened, Britain, by reducing her imports and increasing her exports (at Germany's expense), could at best have lifted the annual average rate of growth of steel output between 1890 and 1913 from 3.4 per cent to 4.6 per cent and reduced Germany's from 9.6 per cent to 9 per cent. Even if British industry had brought down production costs below those of Germany, her rate of growth would only have been half and her production of steel two-thirds that of Germany. Temin also maintains that in no circumstances could the English iron and steel industry have equalled or even approached the growth-rates of her German and American rivals. Furthermore the very slowness of

---

[41] This dispersed structure was partly justified, especially at the semi-finished-goods level, by the variety of products required by the widely scattered markets of the English iron and steel industry.

[42] Deane and Cole, p.229, remark that at the beginning of the twentieth century few steelworks grew at all and no new ones were created.

growth led to technological backwardness and high costs, the latter being the consequence and not the cause of slow growth[43].

Payne regards these views as convincing[44], admitting, however, that a 'waning of entrepreneurial energy' probably played its part. But this idea is categorically rejected by Donald McCloskey's extreme 'revisionist' studies. He maintains that British ironmasters were not guilty of a routine outlook, lack of dynamism, or lethargy, claiming that their decisions were perfectly rational, and that the performance of the British iron and steel industry at the end of the nineteenth century was not at all bad. His arguments seem well based on one point. It has been asserted that the British made a great mistake in neglecting to exploit the deposits of phosphoric iron-ore in the east Midlands, thanks to which, cheap steel could have been produced by the Gilchrist–Thomas process. It seems no longer tenable to believe that the wider use of this process would have resulted in quick, substantial benefits in terms of productivity. McCloskey's other arguments and calculations seem more debatable, when he tries to demonstrate that productivity did not increase faster in America than in England (except to the extent that the United States started from a lower base), that total factor productivity in the two industries was about the same in 1907–9 (with a negligible superiority of the United States of 2–3 per cent) and that their technologies were little different, American works often remaining no less obsolete than British plants. If these assertions can be accepted, there was no entrepreneurial failure on the English side, and British industry would seem to have remained competitive up to 1914[45]. However McCloskey's methods have been severely criticized and some of his theses seem highly debatable, so the controversy is by no means over[46]. Indeed this question is part of a more general

[43] P. Temin, 'The relative decline of the British steel industry, 1880–1913', in H. Rosovsky (ed.) *Industrialization in Two Systems: Essays in Honor of Alexander Gerschenkron* (New York, 1966), pp. 148–9.

[44] Payne, 'Iron and steel', emphasizes that it was in the United States and Germany that the demand for steel products increased fastest; but the British were excluded from these markets by a high tariff wall. Given this situation, Britain's relative decline was inevitable. But P.H. Lindert and K. Trace, 'Yardsticks for Victorian entrepreneurs', in McCloskey, *Essays,* pp. 243, 270 criticize Temin for using an elementary model with a constant capital/output ratio and in fact returning, in a disguised fashion, to the 'poor entrepreneurship' thesis.

[45] D.N. McCloskey, *Economic Maturity and Entrepreneurial Decline: British Iron and Steel, 1870–1913* (Cambridge, Mass., 1973); D.N. McCloskey, 'International differences in productivity? Coal and steel in America and Britain before world war I', in McCloskey, *Essays,* pp. 295–9. See also some critical remarks, pp.305–6.

[46] See for example, in addition to technical criticisms, the excellent remarks by A.K Cairncross and W. Ashworth, in *Economic History Review,* 2nd series, XXV (3), Aug. 1972, 529, and XXVII (3), Aug. 1974, 491–2. Cairncross notes that wages in the iron and steel industry were twice as high in the US as they were in GB, but prices were not. Ashworth criticizes McCloskey for not having made a comparison with Germany

problem, which will be studied at the end of this book. However, what is important and beyond doubt, whatever the causes, is the sluggishness of the British iron and steel industry's growth after 1873, and its decline by comparison with the United States and Germany.

ENGINEERING AND THE SECONDARY METAL INDUSTRIES

The secondary metal industries consisted of a huge but ill-defined mass of varied undertakings, whose products ranged from pins to battleships; and there is no question of studying each one separately. However, these industries, considered as a whole, enjoyed faster growth than the others, and notably than the textile group (see table 46).

The general trend and the rates of growth remind one, as might be expected, of the primary iron and steel industry, but the slowdown at the end of the nineteenth century was less pronounced because the share of the iron and steel industry's output which was directly exported declined[48]. The rate of growth for Victoria's reign, as for the whole of the nineteenth century, was also distinctly higher than that of pig-iron output, at more than 4 per cent per annum.

Feinstein's indices of production for two main branches (table 47) give results which generally agree with those which have just been suggested[49].

Table 46 Hoffmann's index of production of iron and steel goods (including machines and tools)[47]

	Index (1913 = 100)	Annual average rates of growth (%)
1815/19	1.8	6.1
1835/9	5.8	5.0
1870/4	32.8	2.9
1895/9	66.6	2.1
1909/13	89.2	
1815/19–1909/13		4.2
1835/9–1895/9		4.1

and for having ignored several fields in which BC was undeniably backward. And if England's industrial performance was so good, why did she not match her rivals better in home and foreign markets? And see P.L. Payne, *Colvilles and the Scottish Steel Industry* (Oxford, 1979).

[47] Based on W. Hoffmann, *British Industry, 1700–1850* (Oxford, 1955; trans. from the German by W.H. Chaloner and W.O. Henderson), table 54A and B. This index does not include shipbuilding (in wood during the first part of the period) or the motor-car industry.

[48] Just as the rate of growth is lower than that of iron and steel up to 1870 because of the relative increase in exports of these semi-finished products.

[49] Feinstein, *National Income*, tables 51 and 62, T.111–2 and 114–5.

Table 47   Feinstein's indices of production in engineering and shipbuilding

	Engineering		Shipbuilding	
	Index (1913 = 100)	Annual average rates of growth (%)	Index 1913 = 100)	Annual average rates of growth (%)
1857	17		12	
1873	30	3.7	28	2.8
1900	67	3.0	71	3.5
1913	100	3.1	100	2.7

These industries have therefore played an increasingly important role in the British economy. The absolute and relative increase in the labour-force employed in the production and processing of metals has already been mentioned. The primary metals industries, intensive in capital but not in labour, only employed a small proportion of this manpower, and the large majority was employed in secondary activities. By 1907 the latter had over 1,600,000 workers against fewer than 300,000 in the primary industries[50]. Furthermore, in 1907 the single group 'engineering, shipbuilding, electrical equipment' provided 10 per cent of the net value of the United Kingdom's total industrial production; the figure would reach 16 per cent if other metal-processing branches were added[51].

An important factor, indeed an essential one, for the growth of these industries was the perfecting of machine-building, and especially of the manufacture of machine-tools for working metals. Eighteenth-century machinery, constructed largely of wood, had been built by hand individually, with the help of very simple tools. Moreover, the early factory-masters, and especially the cotton-spinners, often built their own machines. Yet a number of basic machine-tools had been invented in the eighteenth century, which were perfected and took their modern shape between 1820 and 1840, e.g. lathes with slide-rests, machines for planing, for gear- and screw-cutting, for boring cylinders and cutting metal for valves. These were used for making machines mechanically, including machine-tools, because of the increasing need for parts that were precision-turned and capable of working at a uniform and ever-increasing speed[52]. At the same time, specialized machine-

[50] It was an almost entirely male labour-force, with a high percentage of skilled workers. In 1870 the primary sector employed 26 per cent of labour in the metal industries; Musson, 438.

[51] Chapter 7, p.187, (table 33), based on *Abstract*, p.270.

[52] Whence the growing use of instruments for measuring very small dimensions so as to avoid time-consuming adjustments with files. In 1855 there appeared a tool measuring to one-millionth of an inch. On these questions, see Landes, *The Unbound Prometheus*, pp.105–7.

makers, who had been few at first, increased in number, especially in London and in Lancashire. It is true that they were mostly small firms, building machines to order and to measure. Only a few big manufacturers had standardized production and sold by means of a catalogue, such as William Fairbairn of Manchester, who in 1835 was able to supply the complete equipment for a cotton-mill[53]. Furthermore many machine-tools remained small, worked slowly and often imperfectly. But after 1850 many small improvements were developed which were cumulative and made machine-tools more powerful, more rapid, more precise and capable of carrying out more complex tasks. There were also important new inventions such as the turret lathe, the milling-machine, and grinding-machines. Hydraulic machines for piercing, riveting and folding iron and steel plates were also perfected, not to mention various lifting and handling machines, which were also powered hydraulically. The substitution of steel for iron, followed at the end of the century by the development of special, very hard steels, which allowed a 50 per cent increase in the speed of metal-cutting tools, brought new improvements[54]. As the progress of machine-tools has a leverage effect on productivity throughout an economy, this sequence brought about the general mechanization of industry after 1850 (and even more so after 1870, in spite of the depression), particularly in nearly all the metal processing industries.

These industries were fairly dispersed, but the bulk were clustered in six regional groups: the Glasgow area, with three powerful, interdependent sectors – iron and steel, heavy machinery (especially locomotives) and shipbuilding[55] ; the north-east coast, dominated by shipbuilding; Manchester and its region, the main centre for the making of textile machinery; the West Riding of Yorkshire, especially Sheffield and its surroundings, which at the end of the nineteenth century added armaments (armour-plates and guns) to its cutlery and steelworks; Birmingham and the neighbouring area; and finally London, whose supremacy, very clear at the beginning of the nineteenth century when the capital boasted several distinguished mechanical engineers, later went into decline. On the whole, small

---

[53]   At the same time there occurred some specialization in this or that type of machinery, but it was rarely pushed very far, and there were many general workshops who made whatever their customers ordered. S.B. Saul, 'The engineering industry', in Aldcroft, *The Development*, p.186.

[54]   See below on the problem of Britain's lagging behind the US in the matter of machine-tools.

[55]   See S.G. Checkland, *The Upas Tree, Glasgow, 1875–1975: A Study in Growth and Contraction* (Glasgow, 1976), which shows that this powerful centre showed signs of structural and technical obsolescence as early as the end of the nineteenth century; A. Slaven, *The Development of the West of Scotland, 1750–1960* (London, 1975), chs.5 and 7.

firms, often hardly specialized, predominated. But in some branches there were very large businesses, e.g. in the making of textile machinery, where six large firms employed three-quarters of the labour-force at the beginning of the twentieth century. The biggest of them, Platts of Oldham, which had 7000 workers in 1875, employed 12,000 in 1913[56].

We will not linger on the most traditional trades, such as cutlery in Sheffield, ironmongery, nails, the manufacture of firearms and all imaginable varieties of small metal articles, which were the speciality of Birmingham and neighbouring towns. They remained the domain of the small firm, but the introduction of automatic machines, often of American origin, after 1890, squeezed out many independent craftsmen. None the less, most firms remained quite small[57]. We will examine at greater length the engineering industry, which was one of the foundations of Victorian England's industrial strength. But one must distinguish between two types – on the one hand traditional products, which originated in the Industrial Revolution and had developed during the first half of the nineteenth century, and on the other new specialities born at the end of the nineteenth century. The central question is that of British competitiveness which, roughly speaking, remained good for traditional articles, but was poor in new products.

Table 48 shows the relative importance of several branches of engineering at the beginning of the twentieth century[58].

Table 48 Gross value of output of selected engineering industries in 1907

	£m
Textile machinery	13.0
Locomotives and rolling-stock (including repairs)	28.2
Steam-engines and boilers	11.0
Bicycles and motor-cycles	5.6
Motor-vehicles	5.2
Machine-tools	2.9
Agricultural machinery	2.4

[56] Saul, 'The engineering industry', pp.186–7, 191.
[57] At the beginning of the twentieth century in Sheffield, 8000 adult cutlers worked in 2800 different workshops. Factories, as in Birmingham and its region, often rose out of the progressive enlargement of firms who had started as modest workshops, e.g. the firms of Marsh and Kendrick.
[58] Saul, 'The engineering industry', p.192 (table 1); also S.B. Saul 'The market and the development of the mechanical engineering industries in Britain, 1860–1914', *Economic History Review*, 2nd series, XX(1), April. 1967, 112 (table 1). The pages that follow are to a great extent inspired by these two articles to which repeated references will not be made.

Among traditional activities, the construction of textile machinery held a special place, because of its early start, its size (it employed 40,000 workers at the beginning of the twentieth century), its concentration in the hands of half a dozen very large firms, and finally the unquestioned technical and commercial superiority which Great Britain kept in this field up to 1914. Its largest company, Platts, had an output equal to that of the whole American textile machinery industry, and in 1913 Britain's exports of these machines (nearly half her total production) were three times those of Germany[59].

In fact, the textile machinery industry would be the biggest branch of engineering if one separated the building of locomotives from that of railway trucks and carriages (in 1907 the value of the former was inferior to that of the two others), which were in fact rather different activities, but they had one feature which was important and peculiar to Great Britain – the division of production between railway-company workshops and private builders[60]. At the beginning of the railway age, a large number of engineering workshops undertook to make locomotives and rolling-stock, but with the increase in demand the advantages of large-scale production made themselves felt, and small builders were fairly soon eliminated. Furthermore, in the 1840s, railway companies, who at first had bought their engines from private industry, began to build them on an increasing scale, together with trucks and carriages, in their own workshops. A court decision of 1876 was to forbid them to sell to third parties, but the domestic market was seriously reduced for independent engine-builders. Several of them disappeared in the 1850s, so that by 1870 only nine or ten remained (and only six in 1907), with their activity dependent more and more on exports[61]. Of course they held sizeable markets, above all India, where they enjoyed a *de facto* monopoly, also South Africa and Latin America. In years of high demand they exported 600 locomotives

---

[59] Saul, 'The engineering industry', pp.191–5, and 'The market', pp. 112–13, which shows up certain weak points and the loss of the American market as the result of tariff protection.

[60] So much so that Saul ('The engineering industry', p.195) considers that there were in fact two separate industries. In 1907 the output of the company workshops was higher than that of the private sector.

[61] Glasgow became the main centre of the industry, having at the end of the nineteenth century three of the four largest firms, who merged in 1903 to form the North British Locomotive Co., which built 450 engines a year on average between 1904 and 1913. This was as much as the largest German firms, but much less than the American giant Baldwin of Philadelphia, who turned out 2700 locomotives a year. The other centres were Manchester, Leeds and Newcastle. There were as many builders specializing in small engines for industry, public works, etc. The private firms building railway-waggons and carriages had Birmingham as their centre and included large undertakings that early on adopted assembly-line methods.

(1890) and sometimes even over 900 (1908), i.e. much more than total French production at the time. But they came up against increasing competition from American[62] and, above all, German makers. In 1913 the exports of German engines almost equalled England's. Yet the latter enjoyed a boom from 1909 to 1913, despite their shrinking geographical base, and the division of the industry into two sectors was a disadvantage. The railway-company workshops were large establishments, and the main ones, the Great Western Railway works at Swindon with 14,000 workers in 1914, were the largest engineering undertaking in Great Britain; but some of the chief engineers who ran them were criticized for their conservative outlook. However, the British, whose workshops were nearly always very well equipped, remained unbeatable for quality[63].

Steam-engine manufacture was also, of course, a large traditional branch of engineering, although stationary engines, designed for a country where coal was cheap, had little success abroad. Yet England kept a very strong competitive position in world markets up to 1914, in certain lines:compound marine engines with double and triple expansion (whose construction made great strides after the 1860s), steam-turbines invented in 1884 by Charles Parsons (a most important innovation first used to power dynamos and so assisting the growth of electricity production, then used for liners and warships after 1892), boilers and small portable steam-engines, especially for agriculture. Likewise for machine-tools of traditional types, especially the heavy varieties, for which British constructors, despite some loss of impetus in the middle of the nineteenth century, were without rivals. From the end of the nineteenth century, Germany tended to pull ahead with some new machines that were complex and sophisticated; and the Americans, as early as the mid-nineteenth century, had perfected all sorts of medium-sized machine-tools, enabling standardized and so interchangeable parts to be made in long runs.

In general, these old branches of engineering, which were born during the Industrial Revolution and made up most of the industry up to the end of the nineteenth century[64], continued, according to Saul, to

---

[62] In fact British and American locomotives were very different articles. The former were built to order and according to the customers' precise specifications. They were high-quality products, made with great care. On the other hand the Americans mass-produced a few standard types for stock, which were cheaper, but did not last as long and were more expensive to run and service.

[63] Saul, 'The engineering industry', pp.195–205; 'The market', 114–7.

[64] Yet around 1860 the manufacture of agricultural machinery (dispersed through eastern England), of wood-working machinery, of plant for. paper mills and food-processing industries was not insignificant.

display much vitality and competitiveness. In spite of some weak points, they were ready to accept innovations. Of course, several of these industries were to see their markets shrink after the first world war, but one cannot reproach them for failing to foresee this disaster before 1914[65].

It was the same story with another large, but rather distinct, industry – shipbuilding. This was distinct because of the revolution which it underwent by the substitution of steamships built of iron, and later of steel, for the wooden sailing-ship. It is true that this contrast must be qualified, for almost up to mid-century steamships were still mostly built of wood, and from 1868 onwards the tonnage of new sailing ships built of iron exceeded the tonnage of those built of wood. Furthermore, the substitution of the new navy for the old was more gradual and came later than has often been thought. Iron definitely overtook wood in shipbuilding only between 1865 and 1874 and it was between 1870 and 1880 that a reversal of the same kind worked in favour of steam as against sail[66].

Sidney Pollard has shown that during these twenty years Britain succeeded in taking advantage of these technological changes to capture the lion's share of the new world-wide shipbuilding industry. The industry was new because it made a new product – the steamship built of iron, and after 1880 of steel. It was a successful coup because only England had the necessary resources to develop modern shipyards on a grand scale[67]. This industry, thanks to the replacement within twenty or thirty years of almost the whole of the world's merchant fleet, was one of the rare branches which escaped the Great Depression[68], and whose growth-rate between 1873 and 1900 was

[65]   Saul, 'The engineering industry', pp.205–9.
[66]   See the statistics of shipbuilding in *Abstract*, pp. 220–4, and below Chapter 9 on the transformation of the British merchant navy. C.K. Harley, 'On the persistence of old techniques: the case of the North American wooden shipbuilding', *Journal of Economic History*, XXXIII(2) June 1973, 373 (table 1), gives five-year averages of tonnage built in iron and wood in the UK showing that wooden construction was preponderant up to 1860/64 (68 per cent of total tonnage built, and much more earlier, of course – 95 per cent in 1850/54). The two were equal in 1865/9; then in 1870/4 iron ships made up 57 per cent of the total, and their share increased to 92 per cent in 1885/9.
[67]   S.Pollard, 'British and world shipbuilding, 1890–1914: a study in comparative costs', *Journal of Economic History*, XVII (3), Sept. 1957, 426–44, esp. p.433. We draw heavily on this article in the paragraphs that follow.S. Pollard and P. Robertson, *The British Shipbuilding Industry, 1870–1914* (Cambridge, Mass., 1979).
[68]   Except for a serious recession from 1884 to 1887. This industry reached its maximum relative importance in the economy between 1875 and 1884, contributing 1.6 per cent of national income against 1 per cent in the 1860s and 0.5 per cent in the first half of the nineteenth century; Deane and Cole, pp.235–6.

higher (3.5 per cent per annum) than during the preceding period (see table 47). The overwhelming superiority which England won and then maintained in this domain appears in the figures in table 49[69].

Great Britain's supremacy faltered in the 1890s, for several countries then made an effort, with some success, to develop their shipyards, but they ceased to gain ground at the beginning of the twentieth century. England's share of world shipbuilding settled at 60 per cent, which meant that by herself she built half as much again as the tonnage produced by all other countries. A sizeable proportion of these new ships were sold directly abroad: 12 per cent of the tonnage built between 1869 and 1883, and 24 percent for 1900/13. In these circumstances it was reckoned in 1902 that 70 per cent of the world fleet of steamships had been built in British yards[70].

What were the reasons for this superiority? It was all the more remarkable in that nearly all other countries tried to protect their shipyards against English competition by premiums, subsidies and other devices. The answer is simple: British yards built more cheaply (10 per cent less in 1901 than the Germans, their only serious rivals) and achieved better quality[71]. Indeed they had a large domestic market, i.e. the British merchant fleet (36 per cent of world tonnage in 1890, 34 per cent in 1913), to which were added substantial exports. The very size of this market was a major factor in the maintenance of English supremacy. It allowed different yards to specialize in certain types of ship, to apply mass production methods to some processes and

Table 49   UK share in world shipbuilding (annual averages)

	Tonnage launched in UK (000s)	*Percentage of tonnage launched worldwide*
	Merchant ships	
1892/6	1021	79
1901/5	1394	59
1910/14	1660	61
	Warships	
1892/1914	112	33

[69] Taken from Pollard, 'British and world shipbuilding', 427 (table 1). In 1880 GB built probably 80 per cent of world tonnage.

[70] Pollard, 'British and world shipbuilding', 428; Deane and Cole, p.235. In addition British shipowners sold a large proportion of their old ships second-hand abroad.

[71] We will see in Chapter 9, p.308 that they did not have this advantage in the first half of the nineteenth century when wooden construction prevailed, for the Americans and Scandinavians benefited from abundant reserves of high quality timber near their coasts and they built at lower cost. It was the steam and iron revolution which gave GB her advantage.

to use their capital assets to the maximum. Furthermore, as they absorbed a large percentage of the iron and steel industry's output, the yards required large quantities of identical semi-finished products and so got their steel more cheaply than did their rivals. They also benefited from external economies, as they obtained much accessory material from a great number of satellite firms situated nearby. Yet the equipment of British yards – except the very largest – was not particularly advanced: quite the contrary. They were behind their foreign rivals in the use of hydraulic, pneumatic and electrical power, new machines to drill and rivet, and gantries for handling[72]. But these shortcomings in fixed capital were more than outweighed by the skill and experience of workers and managers. The productivity of the labour-force was far superior to that of other countries[73]. Finally, tradition, prestige, the quality-label attached to a ship built on the Clyde or the Tyne, and the long-standing links with foreign ship-owners all helped to attract orders.

Shipbuilding was one of the few branches of engineering where British industrialists not only maintained but improved their position after the mid-nineteenth century, and in 1914 they had no more reason to fear foreign rivals than in 1890 or 1870.

There remain two points to mention. Firstly, the technical revolution in shipbuilding changed the size and siting of shipyards. For a long time these had been small and dispersed, but with an important centre in London for large ocean-going ships; they then concentrated on the banks of a few river estuaries in the north, near to the ironworks which supplied them. The two main centres were the north-east (Tyne, Wear and Tees), mainly building colliers and tramps, and the Clyde, renowned for its passenger liners and warships. Barrow-in-Furness, Birkenhead and Belfast were less important, but had large yards and built vessels of quality. The long-famous shipyards of the Thames nearly all closed down between 1860 and 1880.

In addition to merchant ships were the warships built for the premier navy in the world, and also for export. The Royal Navy also had its technical revolution, especially after the appearance of the iron-clad battleship (1859–60). The whole technology of armament, which had been pretty rudimentary, became progressively more

---

[72]   But Pollard, 'British and world shipbuilding', 436, maintains that this equipment, which was modern but expensive, did not pay in foreign shipyards.

[73]   Pollard, 'British and world shipbuilding', 438 (table 3), measures it according to the number of tons launched per worker per year: UK – 12.5; US – 6.8; Germany – 3.3; France – 1.8.

sophisticated and complex, especially after 1880. Up to the 1870s, warships and other armaments had been almost entirely built or manufactured in government dockyards and arsenals but then the state gave up its monopoly and awarded half its armaments' orders to the private sector from 1887 onwards, and two-thirds from 1900. This was done to economize on investment in its own establishments, and to create a reserve capacity that could be mobilized in time of war. Thus a private armaments industry began to develop, especially after 1880 and particularly for warships, which were the most elaborate products of industry at that time. A large firm like Vickers was able to deliver an entire battleship ready for commission. This industry enjoyed a great deal of activity thanks to England's massive naval programme at the end of the nineteenth and beginning of the twentieth century[74], and export orders from many foreign countries whose industries were not capable of producing armaments at an increasingly high level of technology. According to Clive Trebilcock, England was the world's leading exporter of armaments, especially warships, and was at the forefront of technological progress in many sectors of this industry. The development of arms-production created an élite of large firms, financially powerful, spending heavily on research, acquiring any innovations that they could use, perfecting them and then applying them to their civilian production. But the spin-off effect would seem to have been even more extensive. After 1880 the new products, e.g. special alloy steels, new manufacturing techniques perfected in the military sector were later used by a wide range of engineering firms in the civilian sector, particularly in shipyards, which were re-equipped and modernized after 1900[75].

Armaments was one of the new industries which appeared in Britain in the last decades of the nineteenth century. Few of these industries were British in origin, but that is less important than is often thought. What mattered was their adoption and success in the United Kingdom. In this respect, results were mixed. Some were successes. Sewing-machines, for instance, which have been called the first 'consumer durable'. The American firm of Singer introduced their manufacture, building a factory in Glasgow in 1867, which prospered and produced more in 1885 (10,000 machines a week) than the parent factory in New

[74] Warships totalling 193,000 tons were launched by British yards in 1913.
[75] See the works of C. Trebilcock, in particular 'Spin-off in British economic history: armaments and industry, 1760–1914', *Economic History Review*, 2nd series, XXII (3), Dec. 1969, 474–90; 'British armaments and European industrialization, 1890–1914', XXVI (2), May 1973, 254–72; *The Vickers Brothers: Armaments and Enterprise, 1854–1914* (London, 1977); also J.D. Scott, *Vickers: A History* (London, 1962). The private armaments industry had appeared at the time of the Crimean war.

Jersey. But the bicycle industry was much larger and, in addition, it saw the first large-scale penetration of American mass-production methods, with standardized and interchangeable parts. Patented in 1868, the bicycle established itself in Coventry, but remained a tiny industry up to the 1880s, when it benefited from various technical improvements, particularly pneumatic tyres and the making of steel tubes without welding. It also profited from a craze for cycling as a sport and relaxation among the middle classes. To deal with this boom, manufacturers installed modern automatic machines and reorganized their workshops. New firms were started and, after a crisis in 1897 caused by excessive speculation, prices fell and brought the bicycle within the means of workers and young people. In 1907, Great Britain produced 628,000 bicycles and in 1910 exported 150,000, completely dominating world markets. This success came partly from the fact that the making of bicycles fitted neatly into the framework of light engineering in the Midlands[76].

Against this, besides being ineffective in minor branches, such as watch and clock manufacture (which was almost annihilated in England by American and Swiss competition)[77], office machinery (for which the all-powerful Americans opened subsidiaries in Great Britain after 1900)[78], and harvesters (as might be expected from the slow spread of these machines)[79], British performance was not satisfactory in the two great fields of technological progress at the end of the nineteenth and beginning of the twentieth century: the internal-combustion engine and electricity. This relative failure was also apparent in their industrial applications, and the new sophisticated techniques and machine-tools which resulted from the development of these two really 'new' industries.

The internal combustion engine was a German invention, but the motor-car itself was a French innovation (1891), rather fortuitous because it resulted from the links of Panhard and Levassor and of Peugeot with Gottlieb Daimler. Exploiting its early start, the motor-

---

[76] Saul, 'The engineering industry', pp.189–90, 212–5; 'The market', 123–6.

[77] Cf. R.A. Church, 'Nineteenth-century clock technology in Britain, the United States and Switzerland', *Economic History Review*, 2nd series, XXVIII (4), Nov.1975, 616–30. Yet England was supreme in this field in the eighteenth century. However, in the nineteenth century, her technology stagnated, while the Americans and Swiss launched mass production with interchangeable parts, as for office machinery. D.S. Landes, 'Watchmaking: a case study in enterprise and change', *Business History Review*, LIII (1), Spring 1979, 1–39.

[78] Saul, 'The engineering industry', p.212.

[79] ibid., p.211 (and Chapter 6, p.163–4); 'The market', 118–20, which on the other hand insists on British successes in the manufacture of other agricultural machinery.

car industry developed rapidly in France, making her the leading European producer up to 1914[80].

In Great Britain, the manufacture of motor-cars began in 1896[81]. By 1900 there were 53 builders, though one of the largest, Daimler, only produced 150 cars in 1899. Then expansion speeded up: 221 firms were started between 1901 and 1905, and in 1907 Great Britain produced 11,700 vehicles and chassis. At that point a crisis carried off a number of firms. In 1914 only 113 of them remained (out of 393 started since 1896), which was a large number and showed that the industry was fragmented into small units, although in 1913 seven firms produced more than 1000 vehicles each. After a break, there was a vigorous recovery, and in 1913 total production reached 34,000 vehicles, of which 29,000 were private cars[82]. At this time England had partly caught up with France, from whom she had previously imported many cars (French production totalled 45,000 cars in 1913), and she was well ahead of Germany and Italy. Her motor-car industry had become a large one, employing nearly 100,000 workers, with four firms having more than 2500 each on their payrolls. Furthermore, one should take into account the production of motor-cycles and commercial vehicles, for which Britain was better placed. Motor-cycles, which had been manufactured since 1899 and were within the reach of modest purses, had a great success from 1908 onwards, and in 1913 they were not far short of private cars in number. In addition exports of motor-cycles were considerable. The number of lorries produced was also quite large, and in 1910 a satisfactory type of motor-bus was perfected, which very quickly drove the horse-drawn bus from London streets[83].

From this evidence T.C. Barker has been able to maintain that, on the eve of the first world war, the English motor industry was quickly catching up with France; since 1910 its exports had surpassed imports of vehicles in value[84]. Other historians, notably S.B. Saul, have been

[80] Cf., for what follows, S.B. Saul, 'The motor industry in Britain to 1914', *Business History*, V (1), Dec. 1962, 22–44; and in 'The engineering industry', pp.222–6; T.C. Barker and C.I. Savage, *An Economic History of Transport in Britain* (London,3rd edn, rev., 1974), pp.135–43; *Abstract*, p.230; Mathias, *The First Industrial Nation*, pp.424–5; K.Richardson, *The British Motor Industry, 1896–1939* (London, 1977); I. Lloyd, *Rolls-Royce: The Growth of a Firm* (London, 1978).

[81] According to Saul, one must not exaggerate the restricting role of the Red Flag Act (abolished in 1896) which limited the speed of power-propelled vehicles on the roads to 3 miles per hour and compelled them to be preceded by a man carrying a red flag.

[82] Feinstein's index of motor vehicle production (*National Income*, table 52, T.115, col.5) goes up from 27 in 1907 to 32 in 1910 and 100 in 1913.

[83] Just as taxis had eliminated cabs and other hired horse-vehicles between 1905 and 1913.

[84] In 1913 the total count of private cars was 125,000 in France, 106,000 in GB (307,000 for all motor vehicles, including motor-cycles), 93,000 in Germany.

more severe. They have underlined the technological backwardness in relation to France and Britain's dependence on her, at least at the beginning. Many English cars were only adaptations of French models, while many manufacturers confined themselves to assembling engines and spare parts imported from France, and 'dressing up' French chassis. Above all it has been emphasized that the English industry and the French too, were hopelessly behind the American automobile industry, both in numbers (the latter produced 469,000 cars in 1913) and in production methods, although these methods were known in England, because in 1911 Ford opened an assembly factory in Manchester, which sold cars much more cheaply per horse-power. It is true that this comparison with the United States can be challenged. The crushing superiority of numbers made in America was a recent fact, dating from 1910, when Ford began real mass production. This great rise in output achieved across the Atlantic between 1910 and 1914 was unattainable in a European country because of differences in the 'social depth of the market'. In Europe, where incomes were distinctly lower, the motor-car, even when it was cheap, remained a luxury article, confined to the rich and limited clientele which had previously owned horses and carriages[85]. However, Saul is justified in reproaching English – and French – motor-manufacturers for not having given up traditional ways so as to take up mass-production methods, e.g. interchangeable parts, assembly-lines, the Taylor system. They made too many models, changed them too often, manufactured nearly all spare parts themselves, which then had to be adjusted by hand. Finally, they were obsessed by perfectionism and concern for quality – what has been called the Rolls-Royce attitude – and preferred to produce luxury cars. It was only just before 1914 that the two future 'giants' of the English inter-war motor-car industry – Herbert Austin and then William Morris – launched the small, cheap motor-car.

Yet the new industry generally had leaders who were competent, enthusiastic and dynamic. They had come from very varied backgrounds (including the aristocracy, e.g. C.S. Rolls and Lord Talbot), but mostly from various secondary metal trades, especially the cycle industry; but it was often the firms founded by new men and strangers to manufacturing which succeeded best[86]. Nor did the industry lack skilled labour, and it found capital without difficulty. According to

[85] Doctors were an exception, but they too had owned carriages. However one can demonstrate that English industry did not exploit all market opportunities, for in 1914 a third of the vehicles in use had been imported.

[86] Also its location was largely the same as that of the bicycle industry, with many firms in the Coventry–Birmingham area.

Saul, its technical backwardness, as compared with the United States, can be explained by the fact that engineers, who had been trained in the traditional engineering industries. were not abreast of new methods, or did not understand their advantages. They were individualists, more interested in technical performance than in commercial success. Furthermore, the English machine-tool industry was not capable of supplying them with the necessary equipment. On the whole, however, in spite of a late start, the performance of the British motor industry, without being brilliant, was less poor than has often been said, but it showed certain worrying weaknesses[87].

What was certainly more serious was the slowness of electrification in Britain and the deficiencies of its electrical engineering industry[88]. The use of electricity for lighting became possible on a large scale thanks to the dynamos of Gramme (1870) and Siemens, and to the incandescent filament bulbs of Swan (1878) and Edison (1879). There was a small boom in the construction of small power-stations in England in 1882, but it was ephemeral, because electric lighting remained more expensive than gas lighting. A second boom occurred in 1889–91, but investment in electric lighting only became considerable about 1900. At that date gas still provided ten times as much light as electricity; but in 1903 all towns of more than 100,000 inhabitants, except two, enjoyed electricity. At the same time, the innovation of the electric tramway was introduced from the United States. Between 1897 and 1902, 2100 miles of tracks for these trams were installed, and horse-drawn trams disappeared. Also, under the inspiration of Charles T. Yerkes, a shady but dynamic financier from Chicago, a network of underground electric railways was built on a big scale in central London, and the bulk of it was completed within a few years, starting in 1900[89]. Electric motors for industrial use differed technically from the motor that drove vechicles and were not perfected before 1900. Their use spread fairly rapidly in Britain, especially in engineering and shipbuilding, but much less in mining and textiles. In 1912 one quarter of the power used in industry and mines was supplied by electric motors. So electrification and the demand for electrical

---

[87] See also Saul, 'The engineering industry', pp.217–22, on the mediocre achievements of the British in diesel engines (and in engines burning gas from blast-furnaces and coking-ovens), in which shipowners and shipbuilders were not interested.

[88] This study is very much inspired by I.C.R. Byatt, 'Electrical products', in Aldcroft, *The Development*, pp.238–73; I.C.R. Byatt, *The British Electrical Industry, 1875–1914: The Economic Return to a New Technology* (London, 1979).

[89] See T.C.Barker and M. Robbins, *A History of London Transport*, II: *The Twentieth Century to 1970* (London, 1974), chs 2–5. A very small number of railway lines were electrified before 1914.

equipment were limited in the 1880s and 1890s, then came a major boom about 1900, but after that progress was slower, and the use of electricity in industry had to compensate for the slower demand for material from tramways and the London Underground and for lighting. On the whole, the use of electricity spread more slowly in Great Britain than in the United States and Germany. The reasons for this were the structure of energy costs which often made the retention of gas or steam more profitable, the existence of a considerable infrastructure for gas lighting, and perhaps also, as Byatt has suggested, a slower growth at that time of towns and industrial production which caused electrification to be mainly a substitute for existing equipment. However, from the last years of the nineteenth century, investment in electrification was considerable and offered a large market to producers of electrical goods[90], which at that time consisted mostly of heavy equipment for power-stations, the distribution of current, propulsion of trams and trains and the electrification of factories[91].

The electrical engineering industry did have one peculiarity. It was quickly dominated by a few big firms coming from countries where most of technological progress had been achieved: General Electric and Westinghouse from the United States, AEG and Siemens from Germany[92]. 'Multinationals' before their time, these firms not only exported on a large scale to other countries, but they also set up subsidiaries, especially in Britain, thus tending to dominate the British market.

Several British firms had embarked on building electrical equipment in the 1880s, but few of them survived. The situation improved in the early 1890s, when there were five large firms and several small ones, and imports were low. But British engineers and manufacturers, apart from Ferranti, a brilliant inventor and innovator but a mediocre businessman who was to go bankrupt in 1903, achieved little technical progress. On the other hand, the boom in tramway-construction in the United States around 1890 had led to the perfecting of a new

[90]   See Byatt, 'Electrical products', p.239 (table 1): Fixed investment in power-stations, electric railways, in the distribution of electricity, in tramways and underground electric railways, went up from 4 per cent of gross UK investment in 1898 to 8 per cent in 1901 and 14 per cent in 1913; see also pp.238, 240–4.

[91]   A quite separate sector – the oldest, as telegraph saw the first practical use of electricity – was the manufacture of the relevant equipment, and especially submarine cables. In this field the British firms kept strong positions, although one of them, Siemens, was in fact German. The telephone remained insignificant, as there were only 360,000 subscribers in GB in 1911; Byatt, 'Electrical products', pp.240–1, 262–4, 273.

[92]   One could add Ganz of Hungary and Brown Boveri of Switzerland.

traction-motor and of other equipment, as well as to a sharp fall in prices thanks to economies of scale. When tramways in their turn spread widely in Britain and there was a strong demand for electrical equipment at the end of the 1890s, British manufacturers were unable to satisfy it. Hence a strong increase in imports from America and Germany, followed by the establishment in England of subsidiaries of large foreign firms – first of all British Thomson–Houston, who handled General Electric's patents and set up a factory at Rugby in 1902, while Westinghouse opened a big one in Manchester. In 1913 these two subsidiaries of American companies were to be among the four main producers of electrical material in Britain, one of the other two, Siemens, being German, but long established in England. Of course, some British firms did survive or emerge, such as the British General Electric, which was quite distinct from its American name-sake and set up a large factory in 1903. However, their financial situation was not always sound and they made a poor showing against the German and American giants.

Despite their questionable performance the setting-up of these firms very much reduced imports from the United States so that after 1903 Britain's exports increased rapidly and definitely exceeded imports. However, while exports were of simple equipment destined mainly for empire countries and Latin America and ordered by electricity and tramway companies controlled by English capital, imports, coming especially from Germany and again increasing after 1910, were made up of advanced, sophisticated apparatus which was not produced in England.

In all, the British did not succeed in establishing a viable national industry, especially for electric generators and motors[93]. The English electrical industry after 1895 was nothing but an offshoot of American and German giants, with a fair-sized fringe of British producers. But Byatt reckons that if English manufacturers had obtained the customs protection which they sought, in the absence of these foreign firms the process of electrification would have been delayed. However, he considers that the shortcomings of this industrial branch were not crucial for the British economy[94].

The preceding pages show how much variety there was, at the end of the nineteenth and beginning of the twentieth century, in the

---

[93] The English market in electric light-bulbs was almost entirely controlled by the Germans and Americans.

[94] Byatt, 'Electrical products', pp.239, 244–62, 266–73. In 1907 three-quarters of electrical generators were still powered by alternating steam-engines, whereas the superiority of turbines had been well established.

situation of different branches of engineering, and in their competi-tiveness in relation to the new industrial powers – which was of great importance, seeing that they exported a large proportion of their production. In certain branches, among them such an important one as shipbuilding, British superiority remained undisputed; in others, technological backwardness and a retreat in foreign markets were evident. A recent article on the import of agricultural machinery by the colony of Victoria (Australia) shows that, between 1870/4 and 1905/9, the share of British machines dropped from 93 to 14 per cent mainly, it seems, because England was not in a position to provide new types of material[95]. Yet overall Great Britain in 1914 continued to hold firmly on to empire markets, though the situation varied not only by products, but also by markets. Against this, Germany had the advantage in Europe, which was a serious matter because it was the world's largest single importing area for capital goods. In Latin America, the United States, England and Germany followed closely on each other[96].

With such contrasts Saul can describe a 'complex pattern of success and weakness' for British engineering. In a classic article, he has been at pains to point out that the nature of their market explained certain weaknesses in these industries, and that it was impossible for British firms, many of whom showed vigour and dynamism, to change their 'objective environmental conditions'[97]. British industry was mainly orientated towards heavy capital goods where possibilities of mass production were limited, but Saul has maintained that, when it was possible commercially to use American methods of mass production utilizing standardized and interchangeable parts, British manufactur-ers generally resorted to them[98]. However, he admits that English

---

[95] I.W. McLean, 'Anglo-American engineering competition, 1870–1914: some third-market evidence', *Economic History Review*, 2nd series, XXIX (3), Aug. 1976, 452–64, esp. 455 (table 1).

[96] Saul, 'The engineering industry', pp.227–30. His figures for exports of 'mechanical engineering products' in 1913 place the UK a little behind Germany; but motor-cars, bicycles, firearms, railway waggons and carriages and ships are left out. If these were included, England would probably go into the lead.

[97] Saul, 'The market', especially 111, 114–5, 117, 120, 122–3, 125, 127–30; also Saul, 'The engineering industry', pp.230–7. On the other hand Saul rejects the idea of a decline in entrepreneurship within family firms at the third generation, pointing out that few engineering firms went back further than 1850 and that entry into most branches was easy. He also scouts the idea that the new industries were short of capital.

[98] The first examples were the production of firearms with American machines and methods established by the state at the new arsenal at Enfield in 1854, and imitated by private industry. There were also isolated examples in Singer's and then in a few manufactures of small steam-engines and machine-tools.

industry, for a long time, did not know how to produce or use medium machine-tools, which would have made mass production possible. The breakthrough only came with the bicycle and then the motor-car, which necessitated a new generation of machine-tools; but there remained too many general engineering workshops equipped in the old style. This interpretation has been criticized by R.C. Floud. The reason why English manufacturers in the 1890s widely adopted new American machine-tools (imports of which had been minimal up to that date but then rose strongly, amounting to an 'invasion') was not that they had become less conservative, but that the prices of these machine-tools had fallen: they were now at last competitive and their use was now a paying proposition and rational[99]. In any case, Saul readily admits that the market does not explain everything, and he has also insisted on an 'overcommitment to the past', i.e. an excessive attachment to training methods for operatives and engineers, to systems of organization in workshops, and to types of machine-tools that were no longer suited to the needs of the end of the nineteenth and beginning of the twentieth century. Yet he remarks that on the eve of the first world war the grip of tradition was loosening, and adaptation to the new technology was in progress at an increasing pace.

COAL

This survey of the main British industries will end with the coal industry, which was the condition of existence of practically all the others at a time when coal was almost the only source of energy. Furthermore, its importance in the national economy did rise continuously. Its contribution to national income seems to have been less than 1 per cent at the beginning of the nineteenth century, and less than 2 per cent up to 1850, but it was 6 per cent from the end of the century onwards[100]. Great Britain owned enormous reserves of this combustible fossil, which were estimated in 1915 at 197 billion tons, which would have allowed continued extraction, at the very high level then current, for five centuries. In addition, coal was generally of good quality – sometimes excellent – and it was relatively easy to work.

Despite these advantages, the growth of production was not achieved at a particularly fast pace, partly, it is true, because many innovations,

[99] R.C.Floud, 'The adolescence of American engineering competition, 1860–1900', *Economic History Review*,2nd series, XXVII (1), Feb. 1974, 57–71. See also his book *The British Machine-tool Industry, 1850–1914* (London, 1976), which defends this industry against its critics.
[100] Deane and Cole, p.214

especially in the iron and steel industry or in steam-engine design, tended to economize on fuel. Official statistics of coal output only began in 1854, when the United Kingdom's coal production was 65 million tons. Before that we only have estimates, which suggest that production was about 10 million tons at the beginning of the nineteenth century, 16 million in 1816, 22 or 30 in 1830[101]. According to Deane and Cole, growth was slow from 1800 to 1830 because of high transport costs, but it then speeded up thanks to a reduction in such costs and in other charges, leading to a fall in retail prices. Growth was fastest in the nineteenth century between 1830 and 1865[102]. We can accept a mean annual rate of growth higher than 3 per cent[103] between 1816 and 1854, as well as between the beginning of Victoria's reign and 1854. After that we have reliable figures, which are shown in table 50[104].

It is apparent that the most rapid advance was achieved during the mid-Victorian period, the 1850s and 1860s and the boom at the beginning of the 1870s, when output doubled in twenty years[105]. But

Table 50   UK production and exports of coal

	Annual average production (in millions of tons)	Annual average rate of growth (%)	Annual average exports (in millions of tons)	Ratio of exports to production (%)
1855/9	67		6	9
1870/4	121	4.0	12	10
1895/9	202	2.1	35	17
1910/14	270	2.0	63	23
1855/9-1895/9		2.8		
1855/9-1910/14		2.5		

[101] The first figure is taken from ibid., p.216 (table 54); the second from Mathias, *The First Industrial Nation*, p.267. The growth-rates for the beginning of the Victorian era depend of course on the estimate made for 1830. They are (for the period from 1830 to 1854) 4.4 per cent per annum taking the first figure and 3.2 per cent with the second. S. Pollard, 'A new estimate of British coal production, 1750–1850', *Economic History Review* 2nd series, XXXIII (2) May 1980, 212–35.

[102] Deane and Cole, p.217. This rate would have been 4.4 per cent per annum. It is a fact that several important new coalfields were opened up during the 1830s.

[103] And perhaps even distinctly higher: 3.7 per cent between 1816 and 1854.

[104] Taken from Mathias, *The First Industrial Nation*, p.481 (table 29). Exports do not include bunker coal on ships leaving British ports, but it is included in figures on pp. 265–6.

[105] See Church, *The Great Victorian Boom*, p.44, on the interaction of the reduction in transport costs (which destroyed regional monopolies and widened markets), technical innovations, investment and price movements.

this period of prosperity came to an end in 1875, growth became definitely slower, reaching its lowest point between 1885 and 1895, bringing low prices and mediocre profits. On the other hand, after 1897, bad years were much rarer; prices, profits and wages all rose. Although the growth of output did not recover to its mid-century level, it was 2.5 per cent per annum from 1905 to 1913, bringing production in the last year before the 1914 war to its highest level ever, 287 million tons – a peak it has never achieved since. Although this prosperity, which was accompanied by excellent financial results, showed certain weaknesses to which we shall return, the general appearance of the industry was most impressive[106].

These changes in the rhythm of growth can partly be explained by serious changes in the nature and size of the various markets for coal. At the beginning of the nineteenth century, domestic consumption and small-scale industry probably absorbed most of the output. Then heavy industry (particularly iron and steel which were large customers, playing an important role in the expansion of demand during the second and third quarters of the century), railways and steamships, and the gas industry increased their share of consumption. But, at the end of the nineteenth and beginning of the twentieth century, the main factor in the growth of the coal industry was the export demand[107].

Exports of coal reached 500,000 tons, or a bit more than 2 per cent of total production, for the first time in 1830[108]. They then increased very rapidly during the following thirty years, at an annual average rate of more than 9 per cent passing 1 million tons in 1837, and 4 million tons in 1854. But it was only around 1860, when exports came near to 10 per cent of total production[109], at 7 million tons, that they became an important factor for the coal industry and for British exports as a whole. Although growth of exports was subsequently slower, i.e. 4.5 per cent per annum between 1855/9 and 1910/14, it was much faster than the growth of domestic consumption and production, of which

---

[106] A.J. Taylor, 'The coal industry', in Aldcroft, *The Development*, pp.37–8, 42–3. The net yield on capital invested in coal-mines rose from 3 per cent in the 1880s to 10 per cent 1910/13.

[107] Deane and Cole, pp.215–6, 218–20 (notably table 55); Mathias, *The First Industrial Nation*, p.480 (table 28). The iron and steel industry consumed 25 per cent of the coal used in the UK in 1840 and 30 per cent in 1869, but its share then fell sharply (11 per cent in 1913).

[108] Earlier they were much less. The reduction and then the abolition in 1834 of export duties on coal helped the growth of this trade. Of course coal then only amounted to a tiny proportion (0.5 per cent) of the value of total exports.

[109] Including this time (and in 1913) bunker coal on ships leaving British ports. In 1869 this reached 3 million tons, which brought total exports up to 13.2 million tons.

exports absorbed an increasing share; and they reached high figures, to culminate in 1913 at nearly 98 million tons, or nearly one-third of total output and more than one-tenth of the value of British exports[110].

The growth of coal exports was the result of industrialization in Europe and of the transport revolution – the development of railways and steam-navigation, plus the fact that many countries, among them some 'advanced' countries like France, were deficient in coal. France was England's biggest customer, her imports of British coal passing from 1 million tons in 1856 to 12 million tons in 1913 – which was more than one-fifth of the coal used in France[111]. Italy, Germany (English coal arriving in her ports more cheaply than coal from German mines) and the Scandinavian countries were also important customers. But, although the bulk of exports went to Europe, others reached more distant countries such as Egypt and South America, especially to supply bunkering coal for shipping. Though from the end of the nineteenth century England came up against competitors, particularly Germany, and her share of world coal-trade decreased, she still had 50 per cent of it in 1909–13, and she continued to dominate the most lucrative markets. This supremacy had a geographical basis – the proximity to the sea of several British coalfields, among them the two great districts of South Wales and the north-east[112] – whereas German and American mines were considerably further from the coasts. The fall in sea-freights in the nineteenth century, which was particularly steep after 1880, could only reinforce this key advantage enjoyed by British exporters of coal, and make the task of their competitors harder, especially in distant markets[113].

With world demand growing and foreign competition contained, the export trade in coal was more prosperous than ever during the prewar years. It played an important role in Great Britain's foreign trade and also in international trade. It contributed to the growth of the English merchant fleet by providing bulky outward cargoes[114], which foreign merchant fleets did not enjoy, and which helped to reduce freight-costs on imports. There were few people in Britain like Alfred Marshall who thought that these massive exports depleted a natural capital asset

[110] Taylor, p.39; Mathias, *The First Industrial Nation*, p.480; *Abstract*, p.121.

[111] English coal was predominant along the whole coastal fringe of France; see F. Crouzet, 'Le charbon anglais en France au XIXe siècle', in L. Trenard (ed.), *Charbon et sciences humaines* (Paris – The Hague, 1966), pp.173–206.

[112] These two coalfields provided 70 per cent of exports in 1913 (40 and 30 per cent respectively). In addition they had excellent coal, particularly the Welsh steam-coal which was ideal for bunkers.

[113] Taylor, pp.39–42

[114] Coal made up 80 per cent of the total weight of British exports.

that could not be replaced, or who were surprised that a growing proportion of exports from a highly industrialized country was made up of a raw mineral.

Furthermore, the size of exports helped to make the coal industry particularly sensitive to cyclical fluctuations. Foreign demand was highly irregular, whereas supply was very inelastic, because of the long period of gestation for investment. Months were needed for a new coalface to reach the production stage, and sometimes years for a new pit to do so. Hence strong fluctuations in prices, in the value of output, in employment and in wages, which contributed to a deterioration of industrial relations. Nor was this instability very favourable to technological progress.

Paradoxically, the coal industry, which was the basis of the whole modern sector of British industry, was never technically distinguished, apart from the use of the steam-engine from the moment it first became available, i.e. from the early eighteenth century, for pumping out water, or later for hauling coal to the surface. But apart from this, mining technique was singularly backward at the beginning of the nineteenth century and productivity low. Shafts were shallow, from which a narrow underground zone was worked with much wastage, especially where the roof-and-pillars system was used, which left a considerable amount of coal in position. Cutting was of course done with pick-axe, preceded if necessary by a charge of gunpowder. For transport underground, tramway lines and small trucks had been introduced in the eighteenth century, which children pushed by hand, although it was more usual to see them pull boxes or a sort of sledge loaded with coal. The latter was lifted to the surface in wicker-baskets by a winch or a steam-engine, but in the more backward regions it was the miners' wives who carried the coal to the surface on their backs, climbing ladders[115]. The miner himself went down or up on a knotted cable, putting his leg in one of the knots. After 1830, and even more after 1850, various technical improvements were indeed carried out – metal cages sliding on iron uprights to move personnel and material vertically in the shafts, use of metal cables to hold or haul these cages, underground haulage by ponies or endless cables powered by stationary steam-engines. Furthermore, the size and depth of mines increased (many went below 300 metres[116]), methods became more

[115] An act of 1842, which was strictly enforced, prohibited work underground for women of all ages and for boys less than 10 years old.
[116] Which increased the problem of security. These had been lessened for firedamp thanks to the invention of the safety-lamps by Humphry Davy (1813), but their use was not universal and some miners continued to work with candles. However, explosions due to coal-dust remained a hazard, so from the mid-century air-pumps and ventilators were adopted.

intensive and the working of the thinner seams was no longer neglected. The productivity of the labour-force (which formerly had often worked seasonally) showed an increase[117].

This latter tendency, however, was not destined to last, and this brings us to the difficulties, which were masked by the brilliant façade of the late Victorian and Edwardian coal industry. From 1880/4 to 1910/14 annual output per worker employed in the mines of the United Kingdom[118] fell from 313 to 247 tons, or 21 per cent. To take a local example, in the steam-coal or eastern zone of the South Wales coalfield the peak figure was 314 tons in 1883 and the minimum 228 tons in 1911, i.e. a drop of 27 per cent[119].

It is true that labour-productivity also declined after 1890–1900 in the mines of other west European countries, but definitely less than in Great Britain. Against this, it rose constantly in the United States. However output per man remained higher in England than in other countries, though with a diminishing margin[120]. The cost of coal at the pit-head was cheaper than anywhere else in Europe, even though the wages of miners in England were higher and working-hours shorter. Because of such falling productivity, the increase in output could only be obtained by a large expansion of the labour-force, so that this industry, whose efficiency was sagging, took up a growing share of the working population. The number of miners, which had been only 216,000 in 1851, rose to 496,000 in 1881, 807,000 in 1901 and to 1,128,000 in 1913[121].

It is possible to argue that this decline in productivity was inevitable. The mining industry is subject in the long run to the law of diminishing returns. The longer a field is worked, the deeper one has to sink the pits, the thinner the seams of coal which have to be exploited, and the further in each mine is the distance from the shaft to the coalface, which requires a higher percentage of miners for underground transport[122]. In England, coal had been mined for longer

---

[117] Church, *The Great Victorian Boom*, p.44; Taylor, p.48.

[118] It is unfortunately the only figure we have, and we cannot make a distinction between underground and surface workers. It seems that the latters' productivity also diminished (Taylor, p.50), in spite of improvements in equipment, but their percentage in the labour-force did not go up.

[119] Mathias, p.481 (table 28); R. Walters, 'Labour productivity in the South Wales steam-coal industry, 1870–1914', *Economic History Review*, 2nd series, XXVIII (2), May 1975, 280–303, esp. 281–2. In this coalfield the two periods of steep decline were at the end of the 1890s and after 1900. The figure of 1913 is a little higher than that of 1911.

[120] It had disappeared as regards Germany in 1913.

[121] Mathias, *The First Industrial Nation*, p.260 (table V); *Abstract*, pp.118–9; Taylor, pp.44–50 for this and what follows.

[122] Walters, 283, attaches importance to this rise in the percentage of non-productive workers underground.

than in any other country, and by wasteful methods that had creamed off the best deposits, so that the marginal cost of extraction had to rise. This view is confirmed by the varying performances of different British coalfields. The drop in productivity was earlier and more pronounced in the old fields (Durham, Lancashire, the Black Country) than in the new ones (south Yorkshire, east Midlands).

D.N. McCloskey thinks that this geological explanation is in fact sufficient to explain the difference between the productivity of British and American miners (who produced about twice as much per head) at the beginning of the twentieth century. In his view, natural conditions, or resource-endowment, determined productivity. Indeed, coal deposits were very different in quantity and quality between the two countries. In Britain, resources were on the way to exhaustion, mediocre and costly, at least in comparison with the United States, necessitating deep pits and long galleries, an input of land per worker that was only one-fifth of that on the other side of the Atlantic. In the United States reserves, only recently exploited, remained so enormous that their rate of exhaustion was negligible. McCloskey also emphasizes that, in the United States, the coal-seams were thicker, nearer to the surface and less faulted. The thickness of the seams, he thinks, explains about half the difference in productivity, the greater depth of British mines being responsible for the other half. Thus it would be superfluous to seek other explanations[123].

However, British scholars, while admitting the importance of the geological factor, maintain that other causes played their part. Coal-owners complained that miners worked less than before. In fact, given the rapid increase in numbers, there was at any moment a high percentage of inexperienced workers, and furthermore the Act of 1908, implemented in 1909, reduced the working day to eight hours. It cannot be denied that in years of prosperity and high *piecework* wages, the underground miner showed a leisure-preference by increased voluntary absenteeism and reduced individual effort. There was an inverse correlation between wage-levels and productivity[124]. Money-wages of miners increased by 50 per cent between 1880 and 1913, or more than the wages of any other workers' group, and in 1914 they were among the best-paid British workmen[125]. However, this was a

---

[123] McCloskey, 'International differences', pp.289–95. This article is a fierce criticism of Taylor's views. See ibid., pp.305–6, 308, for strictures on the views of McCloskey, who has been reproached, as in the case of the steel industry, for making comparisons with the US, where conditions were too different, and not with Germany.

[124] Taylor, pp.50–5; confirmed by Walters, 283, 285. The fall in productivity was not regular, but by stages, which confirms these views. Do not forget that labour-costs were a high percentage of total costs.

[125] Taylor, p.43. But their wages fluctuated much more than others.

recent state of affairs and during most of the nineteenth century their wages were relatively low for a job that was skilled, physically demanding and dangerous[126]. Long considered plain savages, they formed, together with their large families (which guaranteed recruitment), a mass of several million people, mostly living in large isolated villages, self-contained and introverted.

The miners (and various experts) blamed the coal-owners for not having profited from prewar prosperity to improve both the working and the management of the mines, and also the organization of the industry as a whole. On the first point, the most controversial problem is that of mechanization at the coalface, and especially the hewing of coal by coal-cutting machines. Almost nil in 1900 (actually 1 per cent), the proportion of coal that was cut mechanically was only 8 per cent in 1913, whereas it was 25 per cent in the United States in 1910. Of course, conditions were much less favourable than in America, especially given the irregularity of the coal-seams, their sloping nature and the frequency of faults. It would have required the guarantee of solid financial gains (which was not the case) for the coal companies to have undertaken the mechanization of cutting on a grand scale. It would also have involved the reorganization of the whole work-pattern underground, which would have been expensive and might have stirred up resistance among the miners, all this at a time when profits were good and not too much affected by the rise in wages. Taylor thinks that more general mechanization would hardly have slowed down the fall in productivity or the rise in costs. Its absence seems to him more serious as an indication of conservatism among the industry's leaders[127].

The coal industry was characterized by the large number of firms that composed it. In 1913 there were 3289 collieries worked by 1589 separate firms[128]. The average colliery had a workforce of 340, but variations were great. More than one-third of the collieries were worked by fewer than 50 miners, but these provided only a very small percentage of total output. The great majority employed from 50 to 2500 without their size having any influence on their efficiency. It was only in pits with above 2500 workers, and an output exceeding 600,000

---

[126] In addition to great disasters, there were a large number of small accidents (plus the constant danger of silicosis) and at the end of the nineteenth century an average of 1000 miners were killed a year. At the coalface the miner worked on his knees or even lying on his side in the narrow seams.

[127] *Abstract*, p.123; Taylor, pp.55–60, who thinks that too much attention has been paid to this question of mechanical coal-cutting. There were also other innovations which did not 'take' in England, e.g. electrical traction for coal-trains underground, steel props, etc. Walters, 296, points out the absence of technical progress in Wales.

[128] Their number had dropped a little, having been 1787 in 1900.

tons per annum, that economies of scale appeared; but there were relatively few instances of operations on this scale: several dozen very large mines (57 in 1914) and a few very large companies employing up to 10,000 miners and producing more than 2 million tons a year. Concentration was infinitely less advanced than in Germany[129] and the industry was dominated by small and medium-sized firms. It is tempting to see here, writes Taylor, proof of an individualistic conservatism responsible for the weaknesses of British industry. However, the leaders of the industry were not solely responsible – far from it – for this situation, though it must be recognized that, notably at the colliery-manager level, there were undoubted weaknesses[130]. The situation derived to a large extent from geological and geographical conditions, e.g. the large number of coalfields, each of which had its own market more or less protected by distance, which guaranteed the survival of inefficient mines. Also there was the institutional factor of private ownership of underground resources, which generally had not made for the leasing of large tracts of land and the creation of big mines, and which hampered rationalization[131]. Finally, there was the 'legacy of the past'. The growth of the industry had been irregular, with the bulk of investment concentrated during a few booms. The biggest of these booms had been in the early 1870s, and it weighed on the industry during the half-century which followed. More than half the coal extracted in 1914 came from mines that had been planned before 1875. Furthermore, it is too easy to criticize men before 1914 for errors of judgement, whose consequences would only appear in their full gravity after the impact of the first world war and other extraneous factors. However, one cannot exonerate the British coal industry from the charge of inefficiency. After all, its real costs increased by about 25 per cent between 1880 and 1914, or more than in any other country. One noted a slackening of effort, a reluctance to accept innovation and to adapt to new situations, and a deterioration in industrial relations which, although they were faults common to other British industries, were to create a difficult future for this great industry; and in view of its role in the nation's economy, these faults certainly had a widespread negative influence[132].

---

[129] Just like vertical integration in the steel industry. Attempts at creating cartels and trusts on a regional or national scale met with failure.

[130] Taylor, pp.60–2, remarks that up to 1870 colliery managers generally came out of the ranks and were sometimes almost illiterate. Then their qualifications and status improved, but their training was essentially empirical and pragmatic. Furthermore, as the profession was badly paid, it did not attract the best talents.

[131] In 1914 there were 3800 royalty owners.

[132] For all this, see Taylor, pp.63–70.

It would be fitting to conclude this study of British industry with a picture of 'industrial society' in the limited sense of the term, i.e. the section of the population directly dependent upon industry. But one can only evoke it very rapidly, just as earlier we evoked rural society. In any case, industrial society soon became larger and also more complex than rural society, for it would be simplistic to analyse industrial society in terms of two homogeneous and antagonistic classes – the capitalist bourgeoisie, controlling the means of production, and a uniformly wretched proletariat. It is the diversity of industrial society which must be stressed.

The Industrial Revolution had brought a new type of man into being – the industrialist, who was at the same time the creator and the product of this revolution. He was distinctly different from the leaders of traditional industry (which was 'an industry without industrialists' or at most with a small number of 'proto-industrialists'), who were mostly merchants and 'putters-out'. At once owner and manager of a factory, the industrialist took charge of the organization of production at every stage. At a time when nearly all firms were personal or family businesses, and remained so even when they dressed themselves up as public companies, the manufacturer was not a *rentier* living on dividends but an active head of a business, not sparing of his pains, often as hard on himself as he was on others. Of course, this new type of man only appeared by stages in British industry, as the factory system spread. Almost confined at first to the iron and cotton-spinning industries, he then appeared in other branches.

In spite of the inevitable advance of concentration, small and medium-sized firms remained very numerous in British industry up to the twentieth century. Although they were gradually eliminated from some sectors, new branches of industry appeared whose structure remained dispersed for a long time. As a result, the 'captains of industry', masters of great undertakings, founders or heirs of powerful dynasties, lording over a factory village or even a small district, should not take up too much attention. They were exceptional cases, limited to a small minority compared to those whom one might call the 'industrial bourgeoisie', i.e. heads of medium-sized firms, and the 'industrial rank and file', i.e. a crowd of small masters (in the metal trades, for example), employing a minute capital and a handful of workers, from whom they could hardly be distinguished by their external appearance or their style of life, and beside whom they very often worked. They lived a hand-to-mouth existence, sometimes passing several times in the course of their careers from the status of wage-earner to that of self-employed and vice versa. One finds manufacturers at all levels of the middle classes in the nineteenth century, and the group had little homogeneity, especially as there were strong regional variations in its structure, its behaviour and its ways of thinking. The towns of Lancashire were the domain of the 'cotton lords', for a long time the most typical industrialists. The Black Country was a region of many small ironmasters, while South Wales was dominated by a few great iron dynasties, such as the Guests and the Crawshays.

Apart from a few great captains of industry, such as the ones just mentioned, manufacturers did not acquire very large fortunes. Recent research shows that the millionaires who emerged from industry during the Industrial Revolution were few in number, and the same was true for a long time in the nineteenth century. Around 1800, seven-eighths of the holders of fortunes over £100,000 were land-owners, and in the 1880s half the richest men in Great Britain were still landlords. Among the rest, merchants and bankers (mostly Londoners) were far ahead of northern industrialists. The typical fortune left by a manufacturer at his death was £100,000 after 1850, and less before that date. It was not before the end of the nineteenth century that many fortunes were made in the provinces, which were capable of rivalling those of rich Londoners[133].

It was naturally among the richest manufacturers that there was the earliest and strongest tendency to draw near to the upper class and integrate more and more with it. Certainly, the development of joint-stock companies at the end of the nineteenth century enabled very rich businessmen to avoid having to retire completely in order to enjoy the aristocratic way of life, and to keep control of their firms' general policy while delegating the day-to-day running of the business to professional managers; but in doing so they deviated from the classic model of the entrepreneur, helping to diversify even more the manufacturing class[134].

This diversity reveals a difficult problem concerning these manufac-turers – the question of their origins and recruitment. It was long thought, on the word of nineteenth-century writers, like Samuel

---

[133] W.D. Rubinstein, 'The Victorian middle classes: wealth, occupation and geography', *Economic History Review*, 2nd series, XXX (4), Nov. 1977, 603–23, where there will be found reference to earlier works of this author. H. Perkin, *The Origins of Modern English Society, 1780–1880* (London, 1969), p.431, confirms that it was about 1880 that the number of businessmen having incomes, or rather declaring profits, higher than £10,000 equalled the number of landlords receiving rents in excess of this total.

[134] Perkin, pp.430–2. It was at this time, from 1880 onwards, that a number of leading industrialists, beginning with brewers, were raised to the peerage, which had been very rare before. Of course, the rising number and role of managers or senior executives, and the improvement in their social status, were important phenomena, which led to a certain renewal of the actual leaders of industry.

Smiles[135] that the pioneers of the Industrial Revolution and many nineteenth-century manufacturers were 'new' self-made men, of modest or even humble origins, sons of workmen or small farmers, who had started life labouring with their hands, but who, by hard work and thrift, had been able to set themselves up on their own account, develop their businesses and sometimes become great industrialists. Nowadays, historians do not deny that there were some self-made men of this type – e.g. Richard Arkwright, the creator of the factory system – but they regard these as spectacular exceptions among a majority of manufacturers whose social background lay in the middle class, though perhaps generally in the middle or even lower strata of that class, e.g. tenant-farmers, small merchant-manufacturers or dealers, who came from families who enjoyed some competence and were able to help their sons at the start of their careers. Against this, neither the traditional élites (the landowners, the professions and even the merchant-princes) nor the working classes (especially the very poor) provided recruits in significant numbers.

These views are surely well founded. Nineteenth-century manufacturers were 'heirs' rather than 'new men' and, what is more, by the Victorian era the age of the pioneers of modern industry was over, and in many industrial branches the growth in the size of firms considerably raised the threshold of entry into the business for a newcomer, and especially the minimum capital which he had to make available. But the lack of quantitative studies prevents us from drawing too precise conclusions[136]. Furthermore, one must distinguish between dramatic individual success stories that brought *one* man from rags to riches, and the gradual ascent, by stages, of families who achieved wealth only in the second or third generation. One can assert that, in the mid- and late Victorian periods, a high proportion of manufacturers (perhaps half or more) were inheritors in the literal sense, their families before them owning the firms which they ran. The newcomers were either men who emerged from the middle class (particularly from trade), or men of frankly modest origins (e.g. foremen and craftsmen), who made up a not inconsiderable minority. Social mobility in an upward direction had not disappeared, but it operated within limited groups. In any case, one should not forget that the death-rate of firms –

---

[135] Though this is not really the thesis of his best-seller, *Self-Help* (1859); but in nineteenth-century novels, manufacturers are self-made men.

[136] An exception is the important work of Charlotte Erickson, *British Industrialists: Steel and Hosiery, 1850–1950* (Cambridge, 1959), who reveals a more and more exclusive recruitment in the iron and steel industry and, as one might expect, more openings for newcomers in hosiery.

by bankruptcy, liquidation or dissolution of partnerships – was very high in the nineteenth century, a phenomenon which will have to be taken account of when dealing later with entrepreneurship[137].

A deep divide – but one that could be crossed – separated manual workers from the rest of society, and especially from their employers. But one should also underline the diversity of the working classes, which was no longer the undifferentiated mass of 'labouring poor', as they had been viewed at the beginning of the nineteenth century. Furthermore, this complexity survived the homogenization brought about by the development of work in factories. But one must underline the distinction between industrial workers and the rest of the lower classes, especially the teeming *lumpenproletariat* of casual workers. The latter had no fixed occupation, worked only irregularly and hardly ever in industry; attached to it were beggars, tramps and the underworld which lived off crime, delinquency and prostitution. This subproletariat was of course the most wretched section of the population, but examples of its degradation are sometimes quoted while referring to the industrial working class in its strictest sense[138].

At the beginning of the nineteenth century, factory operatives were only a small minority among industrial workers and, even after 1850, they only formed the majority in the main industrial regions of the Midlands and north. The biggest group was then the mass of people working at home within the framework of the domestic system, but the mechanization of weaving and of other production processes drastically reduced their numbers in painful, not to say tragic, circumstances. They were replaced by factory operatives (male or female), semi-skilled but employed more regularly and better paid. Most of this development was completed around the middle of the nineteenth century, and one can then distinguish three main strata in the working class, according to their members' qualifications, which determined the level of remuneration, whence flowed all the other variables – regularity of employment, type of housing, standard of living and education.

At the top was the 'aristocracy of labour', i.e. craftsmen who were highly skilled, relatively well paid and in comfortable circumstances. They turned up as much in large-scale industry or the new branches (especially engineering) as in traditional trades, e.g. carpenters,

[137] For all this, see P.L. Payne, *British Entrepreneurship in the Nineteenth Century* (London, 1974), pp.24–9.
[138] It is likely that this category of casual labourers tended to shrink at the end of the nineteenth century without actually disappearing. Many of them worked, when they could, in service activities and transport.

goldsmiths and silversmiths, etc. Contrary to what has generally been assumed, their relative importance was not lessened by the Industrial Revolution and by mechanization. Some skills, e.g. wool-combing, were of course rendered obsolete, but new ones were created, some quite rapidly. This group made up 10 to 15 per cent of the wage-earners, with a tendency to increase its share[139]. A barrier, which was not always clear-cut and which could be crossed, separated this group from the bottom layer of the lower-middle class, with whom it shared the yearning for respectability, i.e. for independence and respect for Victorian moral principles.

Below the skilled men came the much larger group of less qualified workers, including most factory workers. Their condition was relatively satisfactory in periods of full employment, but they did not enjoy the same safeguards as the highly skilled workers in times of adversity[140].

Finally, there were a great number of labourers without any skill, having only the strength of their muscles, condemned to hard jobs, badly paid and employed irregularly. Like the subproletariat, this group, even at the end of the nineteenth century, was permanently near or even below subsistence level.

It is impossible to deal here with the vast and difficult problem of the condition of the working class – and the changes in their standard of living – especially as it is made up of aspects at once qualitative and quantitative. Nor did money-wages move at the same rate in all industries – far from it. Indeed we have already dealt with this question briefly, and have stressed the mediocre progress of the *average* standard of living up to the mid-nineteenth century, and even beyond, though this did conceal both considerable improvement in some occupations and real pauperization for people like the handloom-weavers. After the 1840s came a marked rise in living standards during the 1860s and the Great Depression, followed by stagnation at the beginning of the twentieth century. It is true that by then the top layer of the working class had attained the 'basic material amenities' of civilized life, and the English workman had the highest standard of living in the world outside the United States. But before arriving at that point, the condition of the working class, however much it

[139] Perkin, p.143. This 'aristocracy' was the first to organize in trade unions and for a long time was the only part of the working class to be unionized. It has often been blamed for having betrayed the cause of the working class as a whole and ruined all chance of revolution.

[140] Miners would belong to this group, but their condition distinctly improved from the end of the nineteenth century onwards.

improved, remained undoubtedly bad for a long time, even for the top stratum of workers. However, the Industrial Revolution and capitalism were not responsible for this state of affairs. On the contrary, it was only this transformation that prevented a Malthusian disaster on the Irish pattern and eventually dragged the bulk of the population out of their age-long destitution.

9 Steam and the Transport Revolution

Although the Industrial Revolution was well under way when Queen Victoria came to the throne, the Transport Revolution caused by the use of the steam-engine, with the truly revolutionary innovations of the railway and the steamship, had only just begun. In this field, the Victorian era was to be the scene of some of the most spectacular achievements of the new technology and economy.

True enough, before 1830 great improvements had already been made in the transport system. Its inadequacy and costliness had been a serious bottleneck in the traditional economy; the Industrial Revolution and the process of urbanization could never have taken off and gathered speed had there not been substantial changes in transport, beginning in the seventeenth and swiftly gaining pace from the mid-eighteenth century. But these only amounted to a 'semi-revolution', improving the infrastructure and existing vehicles, without any qualitative change. To meet the deficiencies of the traditional system, which left to each parish the task of looking after the roads which crossed it, a great many toll or 'turnpike' roads had been constructed. Although built by private enterprise, they were not quite unplanned, starting with trunk roads branching out from London. There was little progress in road-making techniques, however, until after 1815, when the influence of J.L.McAdam in particular began to be felt. By 1838, 22,000 miles of turnpike roads were operating in England, which were of considerable help to short-distance goods transport and greatly speeded up passenger travel[1]. For heavy goods, the waterways provided the only means of transport that distance did not soon make impossibly expensive, but the navigability of many rivers had been

[1] T.C.Barker and C.I.Savage, *An Economic History of Transport in Britain*, (London, 3rd edn, rev., 1974), pp.45, 120. We have used this work a great deal as well as H.J.Dyos and D.H.Aldcroft, *British Transport: An Economic Survey from the Seventeenth Century to the Twentieth* (Leicester, 1969), without referring to them as often as we should. Turnpike roads have been taken up by W.Albert, *The Turnpike Road System in England, 1663–1840* (Cambridge, 1972) and E.Pawson, *Transport and Economy: The Turnpike Roads of Eighteenth-Century Britain* (London, 1977).

improved, and above all, beginning with the Duke of Bridgewater's famous canal (finished in 1776)[2], which linked Manchester with the Mersey, Great Britain was endowed with a network of canals. Most of these were in manufacturing and coalmining districts but canals linked London and the main sea-ports with the Midland towns, while there were also some in purely agricultural regions. By 1830 Great Britain had over 4000 miles of navigable waterways, of which two-thirds were canals. Water-transport costs were about half those of road transport, and by facilitating the supply of coal and raw materials to factories, canals played a very important part in the Industrial Revolution, and also helped in the progress of agriculture.

Thus, on the morrow of Waterloo, Britain already had a well-developed transport system[3], but the expansion of the economy at the beginning of the 1820s showed up some of its inadequacies. Traffic on the canals – many of which were narrow and could only be used by 'narrow boats' – was slow, with congestion on stretches that were heavily used or had flights of locks; it could be interrupted by frost, flood or drought; and users were complaining that the canal companies were exploiting their monopoly position to charge too much, without providing better facilities[4]. The maintenance of roads, particularly when they had to bear heavy traffic, remained an unsolved problem. So the incentive to use and develop a new means of transportation was strong, and the means for providing it – the railway – lay to hand. Railways had the decisive advantage of being at once cheap and speedy, and hence of serving simultaneously types of customers which previously had been dissociated: heavy goods that had relied on water transport, freight of high unit-value, and passengers who normally travelled by coach. Railways were superior to the other two forms of transport in speed, consistent time-keeping, capacity to carry heavy traffic, and in eliminating the need to break bulk and transship[5].

'THE EARLY RAILWAY AGE' (J.H.CLAPHAM)

As an innovation, the railway derived from two different inventions in combination: the iron track and haulage along it by steam-locomotive[6].

---

2 A few less important canals were built earlier.
3 One should never forget the considerable importance of coastal traffic.
4 Complaints that were often unjust, for the profits of the canal companies were not abnormally high.
5 Barker and Savage, p.15; P.Mathias, *The First Industrial Nation: An Economic History of Britain, 1700–1914* (London, 1969), pp.275–6.
6 In addition, experts believe that a true railway ought to be open to all, and not reserved for the use of its owner; that it ought to carry both passengers and goods; and that it ought to be submitted to some form of state control.

It emerged gradually, over two centuries. Of the two techniques, the first was the oldest and originally took the form of a double line of wooden beams set on sleepers. This was in use on the continent at the latest during the sixteenth century, and is known to have been used in England as early as 1603 or 1604. The 'Railway' or 'Tramroad' spread during the seventeenth and even more in the eighteenth century, especially in the coalmining area round Newcastle, as a link between the mines and the wharves on the Tyne. Moreover there were technical improvements during the eighteenth century. To save wear, tracks were reinforced with metal plates, the wooden beams were replaced by cast-iron rails, which from the start were very similar in section to the modern version. With these came waggon-wheels of cast-iron with a flange. There was actually a rival system, 'plateways', i.e. rails that had an L-shaped section and waggons with flat wheels; but standard rails eventually prevailed. To counter the brittleness of cast-iron rails, John Birkinshaw patented in 1821 a process of rolling wrought-iron rails. The advantage of iron trackways lay in the greatly reduced friction on a plane surface, which enabled far heavier loads to be moved by the same power than on an ordinary road: one horse alone could pull several loaded waggons. They came to be used more and more at the end of the eighteenth century and during the Napoleonic wars, owing to the expansion of mining and the iron industry and to the rise in the price of fodder, which in turn compelled economy in the use of horses. At the start lines were quite short, then longer ones were added, especially in the industrial regions of South Wales and north-east England[7], where the terrain was hilly and ill-served by waterways. Towards 1820 there were at least 400 miles of railways in Great Britain[8]. These were mostly mineral lines, connecting a mine or an ironworks to the nearest navigable waterway (so much so that the railway began as a series of antennae from the waterways, with a purely local interest), and they were used only privately. But in 1803 the first 'public railway' was opened on the outskirts of London, which carried goods for the general public. By the beginning of the nineteenth century some bold spirits dreamed of the construction of a national network of railways. Given that traction along railway lines could only be effected with horses, aided or replaced sometimes by gravity on downward slopes or by cables worked by stationary steam-engines, such ideas could only seem chimerical.

The locomotive, of course, provided the solution. It was a much later

[7]   But there were small isolated lines all over the country.
[8]   Barker and Savage, p.56; P.Deane and W.A.Cole, *British Economic Growth, 1688–1959* (Cambridge, 2nd edn, 1967), p. 229.

invention, only possible after Trevithick had invented the high-pressure steam-engine, for Watt's low-pressure machine was too cumbersome. The inventor of the locomotive was Trevithick, who tried out one model in South Wales in 1804 (which was too heavy and broke the track) and another in 1808, after which he gave up his experiments. Following this in 1812, Blenkinsop built the first machine to be used commercially on a mineral line near Leeds. In 1813 several locomotives appeared in the north-east, but they were heavy and slow and failed to generate enough steam.

At this point George Stephenson appeared, the true father of the railway engine and the railway. He was not of course the inventor of the locomotive, but he gave it several decisive finishing touches; and even more it was his energy, his determination, his unshakeable confidence in himself and the future of railways, and his demonstration that it actually worked, that drove public opinion into sharing his enthusiasm, and in the end, in spite of every sort of obstacle and prejudice, brought about the triumph of the new system of transport[9]. He was of working-class origin, starting quite young as a colliery worker, becoming a fireman, then an engine-wright, later a 'consulting engineer'. At the age of 18 he could neither read nor write, and he never learnt to write properly; but he was one of those self-educated men of genius who played such an important role in the Industrial Revolution. With no theoretical knowledge he had remarkable mechanical skills, and in addition a talent for organization and for inspiring others[10].

He built his first locomotive, the *Blucher,* in 1814 for a colliery company. Its use of the steam-blast made it an improvement on all previous engines; but the public remained sceptical as to the usefulness of these machines. Stephenson proved his case in two stages. In 1821 a syndicate directed by two Quaker bankers, Edmund and Joseph Pease, obtained the right to build a railway, to be known as the Stockton–Darlington, opening up the Auckland collieries to the sea. Stephenson was put in charge of the undertaking. He persuaded

---

[9]   It was thanks to him that the railway was the 'child of the north-east' and that almost everywhere else the traditional gauge of the old mining lines of this region was adopted, i.e. 4 feet 8½ inches, or 1.44 metres. The great engineer Isambard Kingdom Brunel wanted to substitute the broad gauge of 7 feet which he used on the London-Bristol line (1835) and which remained there up to 1892. However, in 1846, the building of new broad-gauge lines was prohibited.

Lancashire, the premier industrial region of the country, was the location of the first great railway enterprise, just as it had seen the beginning of the canal age.

[10] But he was more and more helped by his son Robert, who had received a fairly advanced education and had great talents as engineer and administrator.

the company's directors to use Birkinshaw's newly invented rails and his own locomotives, to build which he set up a factory at Newcastle in 1823. The opening of this line on 27 September 1825 is sometimes hailed as the opening of 'the Railway Age'. It was, indeed, the first 'public railway' to use a locomotive and to provide a service for passengers. The trains for the latter were, however, pulled by horses; locomotives were only used for coal-trains, and there were various other archaic features[11]. All the same, this line was of local interest only and not sufficient to demonstrate the value of the railway as a really important means of public transport[12].

This role was to belong to the Liverpool and Manchester Railway, which linked two great provincial centres. Those who used the Bridgewater Canal had for long complained about its delays and excessive rates. In 1824 a group of Liverpool businessmen, including some grain merchants, invited George Stephenson to draw up a plan for a railway line. This called for considerable construction works, and the whole project aroused opposition from both landowners and canal companies. The bill authorizing the line was thrown out by Parliament in 1825, but passed in 1826[13]. The company directors, though they had put Robert Stephenson in charge of the undertaking, were for long undecided on the method of traction to be used. Some of them were in favour of stationary steam-engines. Finally, they decided to hold a public competition to choose the best locomotive – the famous Rainhill trials in October 1829. The *Rocket* built by the two Stephensons, father and son, was a comfortable winner. They had continuously refined their machines, and the *Rocket* was light (4 tons), had a simple transmission system, and was fast and powerful, thanks to its tubular boiler. In 1830 they produced the *Planet,* the prototype of all later locomotives. The battle was won and the Liverpool–Manchester line was opened with great pomp on 15 September 1830, in the presence of the Prime Minister, the Duke of Wellington[14].

[11] The track could be used by private transport operators. There were two inclined planes with stationary steam-engines and cables.

[12] Some writers mention a first boom in railway promotion during the speculations of 1824–5 (Deane and Cole, p.230), but it was feeble and the achievements very limited.

[13] On the advice of his agent, J.Loch, the Marquis of Stafford, heir of the Duke of Bridgewater's estates (cf. Chapter 6, p.177 (note 107)), including his canal, had accepted in the meantime to subscribe for a large block of shares (for £102,500, at a discount), which was essential for the enterprise's success on the financial and parliamentary level.

[14] The ceremony was marred by the death of William Huskisson, Tory MP for Liverpool, who as President of the Board of Trade had followed a liberal policy. Falling out onto the track while his train was stationary he was run over by a locomotive – the first victim of a railway accident.

Now the 'prehistory' of the railway had ended and the Railway Age had really begun. The Liverpool–Manchester line was the first 'complete' railway, on which traction was provided solely by locomotives and run by the company itself with no subcontractors. The locomotive had triumphed and its monopoly was assured: there would be no more talk of horses or stationary steam-engines. Furthermore, the company quickly found that it had to cope with a large and quite unexpected number of passengers, proving that the railway was not just a means of transporting coal; and, although the cost of construction was far higher than expected, the Liverpool–Manchester was an obvious financial success, a profitable concern, seldom paying its shareholders less than 9 per cent dividend, while its shares doubled in value after a few years[15]. Such excellent results attracted people with capital to invest, and plans were quickly laid down for further lines; the movement gathered speed, the scale of building grew larger, and within twenty years Great Britain had acquired the arteries of its railway system[16].

The rhythm of construction gathered speed, but erratically and in cycles that depended on the general business context[17]. Railway-building needed much capital; it was therefore affected by the state of the capital market, the availability and cost of money, and the level of business confidence. In times of prosperity, when credit was easy and rates of interest low, plans for railway-construction abounded, new companies were started and there was a ready market for their shares. At their peaks, these waves of company-promotion became highly speculative, involving fanciful or shady projects. Even these could attract investors, deluded by over-optimistic estimates both of building-costs and of receipts from traffic. When a recession came, money became scarce and dear, many projects foundered, activity slackened and there were fewer new enterprises. Existing companies carried on building, but might be delayed through lack of funds. As a matter of fact, the period of gestation for railways would be lengthy – two to four years[18] between the setting up of a project and actually starting work

---

[15] See E.S.Richards, 'The finance of the Liverpool and Manchester Railway again', *Economic History Review*, 2nd series, XXV (2), May 1972, 284–92.

[16] A speed which contrasted with the slowness of the railway 'take-off', for the technical conditions had been created about ten years earlier.

[17] This connection and this cyclical character of investment were already apparent at the time of the construction of canals, which were started in years of prosperity and cheap credit.

[18] The length of this period, to which the slowness of parliamentary procedure contributed, tended to shorten, thanks to the growth of large public-works firms. It was three to four years in the 1830s, only two years in the 1840s. Also in the first instance, the peak years were 1836 for company promoting and 1840 for lines

Table 51   UK railway-construction (Length in miles)

	Sanctioned by Parliament	Opened	Total in service at end of each period
1833–7	1918	374	540
1838–43	243	1503	2044
1844–7	9461	1832	3876
1848–51	522	2925	6803

on it. Then, when the economic climate improved, more projects would be planned again. These phenomena appear clearly in table 51[19].

There were thus two main cycles of railway investment, the first in the 1830s, the second of much greater magnitude in the 1840s. The first began in 1833, when two companies were authorized[20] to construct the first 'trunk lines' along the country's most important transport axis – between London, the Midlands and Lancashire[21]. The Grand Junction Railway was to complete a link between Birmingham and the Liverpool–Manchester in 1837, the London and Birmingham was to connect the two cities in 1838. But numerous other smaller and less profitable projects were launched, especially in 1836 at the peak of the boom, when Parliament sanctioned the construction of 955 miles of rail[22]. This 'mania', which was accompanied by heavy speculation in railway shares, came to an end when a financial crisis (of outside origin), starting towards the end of 1836, turned into a serious general economic depression in 1837. There was a sharp fall in railway shares, company promoters could no longer raise capital and some companies failed. Up to 1841 and even 1843 the economic situation was mostly depressed, and there were very few new projects. Parliament passed only six Railway Acts between 1838 and 1841. But the well-established companies went on working and between them opened 528 miles

opening. In the following cycle the corresponding maxima were in 1846 and 1848; Mathias, *The First Industrial Nation*, pp.281–2.
[19] From Mathias, *The First Industrial Nation*, p. 280 (table VI). See also Deane and Cole, pp.231–2 (tables 59 and 60).
[20] We shall return to this procedure on p.287.
[21] Mathias, *The First Industrial Nation*, p. 284, notes that similar requirements by regional economies led to the same order of priority in the development of railways as it had done for canals. Up to 1835 railways remained of local interest, going from a port or waterway towards the interior. Then came the trunk-routes, linking regions along interior lines of communication. The first of these joined London to the Midlands and to Lancashire. Later the north-east was linked to the Midlands and then to London, and the Midlands and London to Bristol.
[22] Mathias, *The First Industrial Nation*, p.280 (table VI); G.R.Hawke and M.C.Reed, 'Railway capital in the United Kingdom in the nineteenth century', *Economic History Review*, 2nd series, XII (3), Aug. 1969, 270–1. In one year the paid-up capital of these companies grew from £7.5 million to £13 million.

in the year 1840 alone. It has been estimated that the first railway boom of 1833–7 produced 1400 miles of railway lines, and by the end of 1843 the United Kingdom had 2044 miles in service.

The economy picked up again in 1844, which was a very prosperous year, and so began the second railway boom, helped by very low rates of interest. The Bank of England increased its discounts[23], thus expanding the money supply and encouraging feverish speculation in railway stock. Expansion and speculation were not continuous, for a first cyclical peak in the summer of 1845 was followed by a financial crisis, then came a recovery in 1846, followed by a second crisis in the spring of 1847, which put an end to the boom. This railway boom was far more violent than the preceding one, reaching its highest pitch in 1846 when Parliament passed 225 Acts authorizing new railways with a total capital of £133,000,000. During the four years 1844/7, the construction of nearly 9500 miles of lines was sanctioned. Of these 4540 were in 1846 alone[24], a year in which prudence was cast to the winds and numbers of absurd projects – which were never carried out – were given Parliamentary sanction. Although there were successive and partial calls on shares, such massive issues tended to drain the resources of the market and to create a tension that had its role in the panic of spring 1847. This same year saw, on the one hand, the collapse of numerous new projects, but on the other hand feverish construction-activity. More than a quarter of a million men were said to be at work on the 6455 miles of line that were being laid in the middle of that year. Over £40 million were invested in railways that year, i.e. about 7 per cent of national income. This was, both absolutely and relatively, a peak figure, never to be surpassed, something which, as Hawke has pointed out, occurred very early on in the creation of the British rail network. Although activity declined abruptly in 1848, it was during this year that the biggest mileage of new lines – 1253 – was opened to traffic. Altogether, in the three years 1846–8, 2600 miles were opened, with another 1429 in the two years following, i.e. 4028 in five years. By the end of 1851 Great Britain had 6800 miles in service, or three times as much as in 1844. The combined capital raised by the railway

23   After the Bank Charter Act; see Chapter 10, p. 328.
24   A.D.Gayer, W.W.Rostow, and A.J.Schwartz, *The Growth and Fluctuation of the British Economy, 1790–1850*, 2 vols (Oxford, 1953; 2nd edn, New York 1975), I, pp. 304–6, 315–18. They believe that railways were the decisive factor in this cyclical fluctuation, but place its peak in 1845. Their railway-share index (1840=100) rises from 97 in July 1843 to 168 in July 1845, and then falls. On the other hand, the record number of Railway Acts was in 1846, but this was due to delays in parliamentary procedures, for the new projects were already falling off.

companies increased from £68,000,000 in 1843 to £239,000,000 in 1850[25]

Among the main achievements of these years we may mention two lines to Scotland (one along the eastern coast of England, the other along the west), the line to Holyhead for communication with Ireland, and the penetration of railways into the south-west of England and into East Anglia, which had so far been neglected. By the middle of the century Britain possessed a close-knit national rail network, with all its trunk lines completed – not merely those radiating from London, but also many cross-country lines. Only the north of Scotland and the centre of Wales were without a rail service. What is extraordinary is that this colossal achievement, unprecedented but for the building of the pyramids or the Great Wall of China, was completed within the brief period of two decades, and with almost equally primitive methods. The trackway on which iron railroads were laid was made with pick and shovel, and the occasional help from gunpowder, by armies of workmen, each man on average moving twenty tons of earth and rock daily, without any mechanical or power-driven aids. Much of the workforce was recruited from local farm-labourers, but there were also gangs of skilled workers who moved from one site to another, taking on the more difficult assignments. They were nicknamed 'navvies', the name given earlier to the canal-diggers ('navigators'). They were relatively well paid for their difficult and dangerous work. Living in wretched hutments, great eaters and heavy drinkers, picturesquely clad, violent and riotous, they terrorized the countryside, but considered themselves the aristocrats of the working class[26]. But, in celebrating the humble labour of the diggers of tunnels and cuttings, one should not forget the unfailing energy, boldness, inventiveness and exceptional talent for organization of the engineers, such as the Stephensons, or the promoters and directors of companies who, with no precedents to guide them, launched out on enormous projects, nor the contractors such as Morton Peto and Thomas Brassey, who carried out their schemes. No less remarkable was the daring, not without its element of greed, of investors and capitalists who risked their money in enterprises that at the outset could have seemed

[25] G.R.Hawke, *Railways and Economic Growth in England and Wales, 1840–1870* (Oxford, 1970), p.205; also Deane and Cole. p.232 (table 60), 296; Mathias, *The First Industrial Nation*, p. 280 (table VI); Barker and Savage, p.69; Hawke and Reed, 270–1.

[26] Cf. T.Coleman, *The Railway Navvies* (London, 1965; Pelican edn. 1968). Many navvies were Irishmen or Highlanders. They generally worked for subcontractors who themselves worked for great contractors who had been allotted various sections of a railway line.

extremely hazardous. The bourgeoisie of the nineteenth century were rarely so dashingly adventurers as were the British in building a railway system that gave them such a big lead in this as in many other fields. By the end of the year 1850, Great Britain possessed, in a far smaller area, a rail network equal in length to that of all the five countries of western Europe put together. In 1855, she had three times more miles of railway per square mile than Belgium, or New York State, or Pennsylvania, and seven times more than France and Germany[27].

It is especially remarkable that British railways were built by private enterprise and with private capital, unlike those of continental Europe and even the United States, where government intervened in route-planning and contributed to the costs of construction. In Britain, neither government nor Parliament initiated any schemes for railways; these originated from groups of individuals who formed companies, drew up plans, raised the capital needed, and supervised the execution of the work (all this bears witness, of course, to the abundance of capital and a vigorous spirit of enterprise). All they needed was to obtain the sanction of Parliament for a compulsory purchase of land, first demonstrating that their projected line met a genuine need. This sanction was also required for the formation of a limited-liability company. Such powers were granted by Parliament in private Acts, according to a procedure which had been elaborated at an earlier period and used for enclosures, turnpike trusts and canal companies[28]. This procedure for obtaining parliamentary sanction, which involved an *ad hoc* committee of enquiry, could be slow and costly, if there was opposition[29]. This could come from parties whose interests might be damaged by a railway, particularly canal companies, but mainly from large landowners, whose estates were to be invaded by machines belching out smoke and noise, which would frighten livestock and game. They had to be compensated, sometimes heavily. Landowners were said to have held the railway companies to ransom, but this was an exaggeration, save in a few cases. All the

---

[27] P.Bairoch, *Commerce extérieur et développement économique de l'Europe au XIXe siècle* (Paris – The Hague, 1976), p.173 (table 54), gives an index of the development of railways in 1860, which relates their length to the population and area of each country – forty-four for the UK, thirty for Belgium, twenty-one for Germany, eighteen for France, nine for the continent as a whole.

[28] These Acts specified the amount of capital for which subscription was authorized. They also fixed maximum fares, which in practice was not effective.

[29] And these could well make a bill fail, as was the case for the Liverpool–Manchester in 1825.

same, 10 to 20 per cent of the companies' capital expenditures were for the purchase of land, though payment was often made in shares[30].

Thus Great Britain got her railways with no cost to the taxpayer. In return there was hardly any state control[31], nor was any overall plan imposed. Much has been made of the resulting confusion and waste. It was not unusual for rival companies to serve almost identical routes, for one town to have several stations with no means of transferring from one to the other, and of course there was absolutely no standardization of equipment. But one must not exaggerate these peculiarities. There was a certain logic in the way the railways were built; they followed routes where there was likely to be the most traffic. As for the initial multiplicity of small companies, started with the express object of linking two neighbouring towns, the aim was to make sure of local support in the towns and areas concerned at a time when it was still uncertain if investors were ready to risk their money in such untried schemes. In any case a move towards amalgamations soon led to very large rail companies[32]. Moreover, to make traffic easier, companies started early on to co-operate. By the end of the 1830s tickets valid on several different lines were being issued and in 1842 the leading companies joined in forming the Railway Clearing House, in which accounts between them could be settled by a stroke of the pen.

Critics have alleged that the costs of constructing the British railway system were excessive – on average £40,000 per mile, distinctly higher than in France, Germany and above all America. This was accounted for by legal costs, the high price of land, the nature of the terrain, especially in the rugged north, and perfectionism on the

[30] More shares were distributed to ease the passage of bills. Committees for launching railway companies soon included a few MPs and peers. In 1865, 157 MPs and 49 peers were directors of railway companies, forming a powerful railway interest, which opposed, generally with great effect, any measures that were displeasing to the companies; but this pressure group declined at the end of the century. See G.Alderman, *The Railway Interest* (Leicester, 1972).

[31] An Act of 1840 created a railway department at the Board of Trade with powers of inspection which led to an improvement in security. But, in 1844, when company mergers provoked a fear of monopoly, Gladstone, then President of the Board of Trade, proposed a bill which would have allowed the government to enforce fare-reductions and to buy up lines eventually. However, the project was emasculated by Parliament under the railway interest's influence. There remained still the 'Parliamentary trains', i.e. the obligation for companies to run on each line at least once a day a train on which adult passengers would not pay more than one penny per mile. In 1846 the Railway Board was created, especially to control fares, but it was abolished in 1851.

[32] See pp.291–3.

part of the engineers which sometimes amounted to megalomania[33]. Nevertheless, with all their over-capitalization and heavy fixed charges, the British companies remained profitable right up to the first world war.

There remains the question of how construction was financed. Like canals, railways were built by joint-stock companies, the only bodies capable of assembling the considerable amount of capital required. Where this capital came from is a much discussed question. For the very first companies, the initiative, and a large share of the capital, came from small groups of local businessmen such as the Pease family of Darlington and a number of merchants and bankers from Liverpool. They invited their fellow citizens, particularly those whose business could benefit from the opening of a railway, to subscribe for shares. But even in the early days quite a lot of capital came from more distant sources. In 1829, of 4100 one-hundred-pound shares in the Liverpool and Manchester Railway, 2233 shares were owned in Liverpool, only 91 in Manchester, but 781 in London, and 995 elsewhere; in addition the Marquis of Stafford had 100 shares.[34] During the 1830s much of the capital seems to have continued to come from local sources, especially from businessmen in the towns served by the new lines and thus directly interested in them, e.g. those which were to be merged in the Lancashire and Yorkshire Railway. But in addition, the groups that had promoted the earliest lines, the Quakers of Darlington and still more the Liverpool Party,[35] played an important part in promoting and financing new companies, especially those running between London and Lancashire. Quite soon, however, the flow of external (notably from London) capital increased, without any special business interest in the projected lines: anonymous, 'blind' capital seeking a worthwhile return on its investment or speculative gains in times of boom. Companies would advertise in the press and in the 1840s capital was flowing in from nationwide sources. Shares changed hands quite often, and some sources of capital – London for example – were highly volatile. Contemporaries believed that large numbers of clergymen and widows were keen dabblers in railway shares. In fact, this 'rentier' capital, coming also from gentlemen and members of the professions, seems to have been largely invested in well-established companies with a good dividend record. Scottish and Irish railways were heavily

---

[33] Mathias, *The First Industrial Nation*, p. 282.
[34] Cf. H.Pollins, 'The finances of the Liverpool and Manchester Railway', *Economic History Review*, 2nd series, V (1), 1952, 90ff; Richards, 285; Barker and Savage, p.60. The distribution of the 4100 £25 shares was very much the same.
[35] Yet doubt has been cast on its existence!

dependent on external capital, mostly derived from London, local capital, less plentiful than in England, tending to be invested mainly in industry. Railway companies also had to borrow short-term, chiefly from banks and insurance companies – but little is known about this practice[36].

THE RAILWAYS FROM 1851 TO 1914

The middle of the nineteenth century marks the end of the heroic age for Britain's railways. The length of lines under construction, which was 6455 miles in the middle of 1847, after that date rarely exceeded 1000 miles at any given time (only in 1857, 1858 and 1860, and then by very little). The length of new lines opened, which averaged 806 miles annually from 1846 to 1850, fell to 397 miles from 1850 to 1859, and though a third, modest railway boom in the years 1864–6 raised it to 514 in 1860–9, the total annual increments fell steadily throughout the following decades (see table 52). Moreover, in the mid-1850s, the number of 'servants' employed in running the railways[37] exceeded for the first time the number of navvies and others employed in constructing new ones, while the sums earned from rail traffic were higher than the total of new investment[38]. Nevertheless the history of British railways after 1850 shows several interesting developments and is worth further study[39].

To begin with, the network continued to grow quite rapidly in the mid-Victorian period (the total length of lines doubled between 1850 and 1870), then decidedly more slowly; but new construction never stopped, and the increase in total mileage between 1869 and 1912 was quite large, if one takes into account its importance at the beginning of the period. It is often said that most of this increase consisted of secondary or branch lines of purely local interest, not to mention pointless duplication of existing track; this was over-investment,

---

[36]   Cf. especially: S.Broadbridge, *Studies in Railway Expansion and the Capital Market in England* (London, 1970); M.C.Reed, *Investment in Railways in Britain, 1820–44: A Study in the Development of the Capital Market* (London, 1975). The financing of railways might be compared, thanks to J.R. Ward, *The Finance of Canal-Building in Eighteenth-Century England* (London, 1974), to the financing of the canals, where local capital supplied by large landowners played an important role, but where the investing public was already pretty wide.

[37]   See p.300. At first these employees were recruited among old soldiers (and some executives among former officers), policemen or even navvies, as well as among mining engineers. The work and the discipline were hard and the pay moderate, but 'railway servants' had a stable job and some prestige.

[38]   Deane and Cole, pp. 232–3 (tables 60 and 61), 296.

[39]   On this period see Barker and Savage, ch.4, pp. 85ff.

Table 52   Development of the British railway network (in miles)[40]

	Annual average total of newly opened lines	Total length of line in service at end of period
1845/54	587	7,157
1850/9	397	8,737
1860/9	514	13,170
1870/9	255	15,411
1880/9	225	17,152
1890/9	176	18,038
1912		20,038

extravagant, unprofitable and likely to bring trouble later on. These criticisms are certainly valid for many branch lines, as well as for longer lines in Scotland and Wales, that were costly to build and bore little traffic; also for lengths of line that were strategic, built simply to keep a competitor out of a company's special preserve, or to break into that of a rival. The most obvious case of extravagance was the last of the main lines from London to the north, Marylebone to Sheffield by the Great Central, finished in 1899. But some investments were rational, particularly those made to shorten long routes, sometimes by spectacular masterpieces of technological skill like the Severn Tunnel (1886), and the Tay (1878 and 1887) and Forth (1890) bridges, or when heavy traffic made a second line worth while. Whatever the reasons, the total capital raised by British railway companies grew from £239 million in 1850 to £530 million in 1870, £1161 million in 1900 and £1318 million in 1912[41]. This growth did create problems. Once more profitable lines were finished, investors became more cautious, so that railways had more and more recourse to borrowing and issuing preference shares.

The expansion of the rail network led to a trend towards concentration and amalgamation through mergers or takeovers. The early companies had been formed to build single lines from one city to another which produced initially a multiplicity of companies, mostly very small (about 200 in 1843). But when several were merged, there could be savings in running costs and also easier traffic organization. With, moreover, a taste for power, a breed of empire-builders soon

[40]   Deane and Cole, p. 233 (table 61); B.R.Mitchell and P.Deane, *Abstract of British Historical Statistics* (Cambridge, 1962) (quoted hereafter as *Abstract*), pp.225–6.

[41]   Hawke and Reed, 270–1. But this fresh capital was not used only for building new lines. There was the enlargement and reconstruction of stations, and moreover companies invested heavily in hotels, docks and other port installations, and in steamers for services to the continent and Ireland.

appeared on the scene[42]. The first amalgamation of two companies took place in 1834, but the movement only really got under way during the railway boom of 1844–7, when there was a series of consolidations of separate local lines into genuine regional networks. Their promoters followed a quasi-military strategy, seeking to lay hands on the traffic that went through the area whose main lines they already controlled, and to stop the traffic that inclined towards their rivals. The most famous was George Hudson, the 'railway king', who started as a draper in York. In 1836, he launched the York and North Midland Railway; then in 1844, from a merger of three lines, he created the Midland Railway which radiated from Derby. With this as his base he aimed at controlling the traffic from London to the north-east, also pushing out a line to the south-west as far as Gloucester and Bristol, moving north into Scotland and penetrating into East Anglia. At his peak he controlled 1500 miles of line and a capital of £30 million; but he concealed losses, paid dividends out of capital and went bankrupt in 1849[43]. Still the Midland survived, reached London in 1857, and there built the splendid Victorian Gothic St Pancras Station in 1868. Following Hudson's example, the banker George C.Glyn set up the London and North Western Railway in 1846, a merger of the London and Birmingham with the Grand Junction, the latter having in 1845 absorbed the Liverpool and Manchester. The LNWR was eventually to become the most powerful British railway company[44]. After a pause came the formation in 1854 of the North Eastern Railway which a few years later controlled all lines between the Humber and the Tyne, acquiring the tightest regional monopoly of any company. In the 1860s the Great Eastern absorbed most of the lines in East Anglia, and in Scotland the Caledonian and the North British made many takeovers[45]. In addition to all these amalgamations, there were various agreements between independent companies – for example, allowing trains of one company to use the tracks of another, or pooling certain types of traffic.

In spite of all these mergers, there were still more than 100 railway companies in existence in 1904 (Parliament had sanctioned the creation of about a thousand), but they were very unequal in size. Fourteen of them owned 85 per cent of the total track between them,

---

[42] The amalgamation of companies required the authorization of Parliament, which was sometimes refused.

[43] His Florentine palace in Albert Gate is now the French embassy.

[44] With 1949 miles of line in 1912 and a paid-up capital of £125 million, i.e. several times larger than that of the biggest industrial companies.

[45] A government proposal to prohibit mergers had failed in 1854.

and the four giants (LNWR, Midland, GWR, North Eastern) had 43 per cent and earned two-thirds of total takings. Also many of the small companies were actually controlled by the big ones. Such concentration was normal, for in the running of railways economies of scale are large, and the small companies, which were generally inefficient and unprofitable, proved an easy prey for their powerful neighbours, who, however, also grew through their own resources, particularly by new construction[46]. These larger railway companies were, in respect of capitalization, numbers of employees and turnover, by far the largest concerns to appear in the nineteenth century. They soon became bureaucratic bodies with a complex staff hierarchy and detailed rules of operation necessitated by their widely dispersed activities and the demands of safety. Moreover, separation of ownership from management happened almost immediately, foreshadowing the big firms of the twentieth century. Responsibility was devolved onto salaried professional managers, whose conduct of affairs and motivations might be quite different from those of nineteenth-century classical entrepreneurs[47].

The performance of the railway companies is measured in table 53 which shows that the growth of traffic was very rapid up to the 1870s then slowed down sharply and became quite modest at the beginning of the twentieth century. This was due in small measure to the general deceleration of national economic growth at the end of the nineteenth century, but mainly to the fact that by 1870 railways had already diverted and captured practically all potential traffic; hence the very rapid growth after 1840, which was largely a substitution phenomenon[48]. The branch lines which were subsequently opened brought very little extra traffic, so that the difference between the rate of increase in railway activity and the growth-rate of the economy as a whole was bound to diminish[49].

[46] P.J.Cain, 'Railway combination and government, 1900–1914', *Economic History Review,* 2nd series XXV (4), Nov. 1972, 623. For 1912, Barker and Savage, pp.110 (table 4), 111, give eleven main companies controlling 68 per cent of railway lines.

[47] G.Channon, 'A nineteenth-century investment decision: the Midland Railway's London extension', *Economic History Review,* 2nd series, XXV (2), Aug. 1972, 448–70, suggests – about an isolated example of decision-making, it is true – that these managers were less interested in maximizing profits than in obtaining for their company a 'status of great independent power'. See also T.R.Gourvish, *Mark Huish and the London and North-Western Railway: A Study of Management* (Leicester, 1972).

[48] Although there was 'creation' of passenger traffic (see p.303 (note 81)). Growth at the end of the period is underestimated by the table, which does not include holders of season tickets, whose number grew dramatically with the development of suburbs.

[49] According to Deane and Cole, p.296, the net output of the railway industry grew faster, but less and less faster, than national income up to the end of the 1880s.

Table 53   Traffic on British railways[50]

	No. of passengers (in millions)	Weight of goods carried (millions of tons)	Annual average rate of growth (%)	
			Passengers	Goods
1843	22		14.0	
1856	121	64	7.9	6.6
1873	439	188	3.5	3.0
1900	1115	420	1.0	1.7
1912	1265	514		

This slowing-down of the increase in traffic was to cause problems, and the financial situation and profitability of the railway companies tended to deteriorate after 1870, though some other factors were involved. Total gross receipts increased more slowly than traffic (but the value of money was rising) and profits rose even more slowly[51]. The ratio of operating expenses to total receipts was increasing. Before 1870 it was under 50 per cent; it exceeded this after 1873, gradually grew to 57 per cent in 1893 and reached 62 per cent between 1900 and 1912[52]. Hence the return on invested capital and dividends diminished, although a number of companies continued to pay good dividends. What is the explanation of this decline, these diminishing returns, with moreover a very slight increase in productivity after 1880? There was no intense competition, though the railways never had the absolute monopoly imputed to them and had to compete with coastal shipping (especially for coal), with some canals, and for suburban passengers with the newly introduced tramways[53]. But the competitive fare-cutting that had gone on in the 1850s and the competition which had taken place in the 1860s for the best sites in towns for stations and depots had more or less ceased. After 1870, competition took different

[50]   Taken from *Abstract*, pp. 225–6. The rates of growth were probably higher (1.9 and 2.2 per cent) for the period 1900–13, but the figures for 1913 are not strictly comparable with the earlier ones. Unfortunately we have no statistics of the 'kilometric units' type, which are the most satisfactory, except for the first decades (and for England alone), taken from Hawke, pp. 48–9 and 62–3. The number of passenger/miles carried grew from 211 million in 1840 to 2780 million in 1870, i.e. a growth-rate of 8.9 per cent per annum. For the number of passengers alone from 1843 to 1873 the figure is 10.5 per cent. The number of tons/miles increased at a rate of 13 per cent per annum between 1846–7 and 1865, cattle not included.

[51]   According to Deane and Cole, p. 233 (table 61), this average annual operating profit doubled between 1855–64 and 1875–84, but only increased by 26 per cent from 1875–84 to 1890–9.

[52]   Barker and Savage, pp.100, 114. Cain, 624, gives the ratio between operating profits (or net receipts) and paid-up capital – 4.55 in 1871–5, 3.63 in 1896–1900.

[53]   Moreover, if they misused their position, they harmed the competitive position of the region they served and so, in the end, their own traffic.

forms. Railways competed for customers (who had become rather choosy), not by lowering fares, but by offering better service: improvements were made in the frequency, speed, safety[54] and above all comfort of passenger trains. Apart from this there developed a subtle mixture of competition and collaboration between companies, the latter becoming more common. As a large proportion of traffic involved more than one company, it necessitated agreements and occasionally combined provision of certain services. Competition did not disappear, and could always revive sharply if there was any chance of grabbing a new source of traffic – but it became 'reasonable'[55].

However, neither these factors nor the reduction in cost of materials used by the railways (as a result of the Great Depression) offset the increase in costs which resulted from improvements in services and from not always very judicious investment policies. An additional factor was the increasingly hostile attitude of railway users, particularly large numbers of businessmen. They complained that railway companies not only kept their rates unchanged when all other prices were falling but had a multiplicity of preferential rates and discriminatory practices according to various categories of custom. For a long time the companies had succeeded in keeping state control to a minimum, in spite of a growing tendency of government and Parliament to oppose discriminatory practices and the creation of monopolies by mergers. But in 1873 an Act of Parliament set up the Railway Commission, a three-member body charged with supervising the railways and seeing that they obeyed the law. Their powers were rather limited, but it was an important step. Then, following more clamorous protests from businessmen and chambers of commerce, Parliament (in which the railway interest had lost much of its influence) voted much harsher measures between 1888 and 1894. These virtually forbade the companies to raise their rates for goods traffic above the 1892 figures (but passenger fares remained uncontrolled), which, in this trough of the Great Depression, were pretty low. The idea of railways as a service to the public, rather than a way of making the highest possible profit, was gaining ground[56].

[54] Many companies abolished the second class and raised the third class to its standard, i.e. upholstered and not wooden seats. Also note the introduction of carriages with corridors and WCs, of sleepers, of dining-cars, etc.

[55] Cain, 624–6. Around 1900 most large towns were served by at least two companies. The market was duopolistic or oligopolistic.

[56] For all this, see Barker and Savage, pp. 85ff, 104ff. As we have already pointed out (Chapter 5, p.108), politicians were torn between their belief in free competition (which could well lead to monopolies), their hostility to monopolies, the knowledge that large companies were the most efficient, and the idea that the interests of the public had to be protected. Hence policies that were often incoherent, and a number of enquiries and draft legislation without much result.

During the Edwardian period, the railway companies found that, although they had lost the power to fix their own rates, they were faced with costs rising much more quickly than receipts, as a result of factors over which they had no control. Raw materials, especially coal, cost more, and so did labour: wages were higher, hours of work shorter, unions were getting stronger, finally organizing a general strike of railwaymen, though a rather short one, in 1911. Balance sheets started to suffer, dividends were cut and share-prices fell. In the face of these difficulties, further attempts were made to limit competition, with ambitious schemes for agreements, even mergers, between the principal companies, viewed favourably by the government but coming to nothing[57]. Some companies made serious attempts at cutting down their costs, particularly the Great Eastern. Here the prime mover was G.Gibb, who was inspired by the example of American railways to reorganize administration, set up a statistical office and increase the average load carried by goods trains, doubling it between 1902 and 1913, though he failed to improve productivity as much on passenger trains. He managed to pay good dividends. Most companies succeeded in achieving higher productivity in goods traffic, but not in passenger traffic, where they made the mistake of not increasing fares[58].

Opinions are divided on the state of the railways on the eve of the first world war. P.J.Cain sees them as being in a 'sorry state', and several historians such as Dyos and Aldcroft blame mediocre managements, wedded to old-fashioned modes of operating, over-investing but at the same time sticking to their habit of transporting coal in absurdly small 10-ton trucks. T.C.Barker, on the other hand, though aware of the companies' financial difficulties, emphasizes the efforts they made to solve them and the fact that, even if shareholders suffered, the public was given very good service[59].

The steam-locomotive may have been a symbol, perhaps *the* symbol of the Victorian age, but it did not monopolize all inland transport. Railways certainly very quickly killed the long-distance transport by road of passengers (by stagecoach) and goods, which was far more expensive. On the other hand, supported by the growth of the population and of the economy, short-distance road transport to and

---

[57] Cain reckons (p. 638) that it was only the war, by driving the railways to the verge of bankruptcy, that made possible the 1921 amalgamation into four large networks.

[58] R.J.Irving, *The North Eastern Railway Company, 1870–1914: An Economic History* (Leicester, 1975); Barker and Savage, pp.111–3.

[59] Cain, 637; Barker and Savage, p.118; Dyos and Aldcroft, pp. 182–6. R.J.Irving, 'The profitability and performance of British railways, 1870–1914', *Economic History Review*, 2nd series, XXXI (1), Feb. 1978, 46–66.

from railway stations increased enormously both in town and country. This traffic was entirely horse-drawn, until the appearance of the electric tramway in the 1890s and motor-vehicles a few years later. F.M.L.Thompson has calculated that the number of commercial vehicles on the roads in Great Britain increased from 100,000 or more in 1811 to 161,000 in 1851, 702,000 in 1901, and 832,000 in 1911, while the number of horses in non-agricultural use increased from 535,000 in 1851 to 1,766,000 in 1901 (overtaking the number of horses employed in agriculture), of which more than 1,000,000 were employed commercially. Thus the railway did not displace the horse, but created new jobs for it[60]. Canals, on the other hand, were killed by railways, but after a longer and more painful decline than is often realized. Initially, to combat their new rivals, they lowered their rates and improved their service, and their business increased[61]. But, after the 1840s, railway companies became more aggressive, buying up canals and, according to some critics, 'sterilizing' them. By 1865 they controlled one-third of all canals, more than half by 1883. Many canal companies remained independent, but the technical superiority of railways was so overwhelming that they monopolized long-haul traffic, and canals came to be used only for heavy loads over short distances. Even so, few of them were able to pay dividends to their shareholders after 1850.

RAILWAYS AND ECONOMIC GROWTH

This last point is only a minor aspect of a larger, more important and more controversial problem, that of the economic consequences of the railway revolution. Contemporaries were naturally struck by the stupendous effort put into the construction of the British railway system, and how it had improved inland transport, in ease, comfort, speed and cost. Historians on the whole see the advent of the railway as a crucial aspect of the economic growth of Victorian Britain, as a powerful, though intermittent, stimulus to investment and growth. Some have even maintained that railways practically saved the life of British capitalism which, in the 1830s and 1840s, was suffering from

[60] Barker and Savage, ch.5, pp.120ff; F.M.L.Thompson, 'Nineteenth-Century horse sense', *Economic History Review*, 2nd series, XXIX (1), Feb.1976, 60–81, esp. 64, 72 (table 1), 75–8, 80. The number of horses given above includes those for commercial vehicles, private carriages, and horse-riding. Thanks to the increase in road traffic, turnpike roads often remained commercially viable, but they were abolished at the end of the nineteenth-century, when roads became the responsibility of local authorities.

[61] In 1840, goods-traffic by water between Liverpool and Manchester remained double what it was by rail; Barker and Savage, p.63.

an internal crisis, as well as being threatened from outside by social protest. Once the first stage of the Industrial Revolution had passed, there was a shortage of profitable investments to absorb the capital that was accumulating constantly, and a danger of structural disruption. The railways provided the capitalist system with an answer, for they opened up vast opportunities for profitable investment. What is more, by creating a considerable demand for all sorts of capital goods, they made it possible for a still rather narrowly based large-scale industry to expand and diversify. They relaunched the Industrial Revolution into a new phase characterized by the predominance of heavy industry[62].

Curiously enough, no detailed analysis of this problem had been undertaken until the appearance of a pioneer article by B.R.Mitchell in 1964 and in 1970 of a book by G.R.Hawke who used the methods of the new economic history[63] and the approach of Robert Fogel and Albert Fishlow. These had shown that the traditional assumption that railroads had played a key role in the development of the American economy was incorrect.

The problem of the influence of the railway, or of any other means of transport, on economic growth is extremely complex. It is proper to distinguish between the effects attending the actual construction work of a rail network and the consequences of its existence and functioning after its completion. In both cases, there are both direct and indirect or secondary effects; and it is the latter that make it hard to evaluate accurately what the overall consequences of the invention of railways actually were.

To begin with, the cost of building the railway lines was high – much higher than the cost of digging the canals which had preceded them on the same routes. For the trunk lines cost several million pounds each, e.g. £3.7 million for the Liverpool–Manchester, and more than £6 million for the London–Birmingham[64]. Intermittent though it was, and subject to violent fluctuations, investment in railway building absorbed large amounts of capital. According to Mitchell's calculations,

---

[62] See for example, S.G.Checkland, *The Rise of Industrial Society in England, 1815–85* (London, 1964), pp. 24–5; E.J.Hobsbawm, *Industry and Empire* (London, 1968), p. 71–8 of the Penguin edn, 1969.

[63] B.R.Mitchell, 'The coming of the railway and United Kingdom economic growth', *Journal of Economic History*, XXIV (3), Sep. 1964, 315–36; Hawke; P.O'Brien, *The New Economic History of the Railways* (London, 1977).

[64] Barker and Savage, p.78.

gross capital investment in railways[65] amounted to an average of £9 million a year for the three years 1838–40, or just under 2 per cent of national income[66]. It was less in the years 1841–3, then jumped to an average of £27 million a year for 1845–8, i.e. 4.8 per cent of national income. In one of these years alone, 1847, when railway-building was at its peak, £37 million was invested, or 6.7 per cent of national income. This sum was nearly equal to the value of two-thirds of the country's total exports, and twice the highest value of the Bank of England's gold reserves during the 1840s. But that was the climax, for 1847 saw the high point of railway investment, whether in absolute value or as a share of national product, and it was never reached again. Throughout the 1850s (with the exception of 1854) railway capital formation was well below 2 per cent of national income, and did not exceed this percentage later, except during the years 1863–6. Railway-construction never again played such an important part in the British economy as it did at the end of the 1840s[67]. It would appear from the tables compiled by Deane in 1968 that railway investment represented 55 per cent of gross capital formation during 1845–9, but only 20–25 per cent in the 1850s and 1860s[68].

This large but very fluctuating share of railways in the formation of capital might incline one to suppose that, from the late 1830s to the end of the 1840s, they had been an engine of growth and a leading sector for the British economy; certainly no other innovation absorbed resources of men and money on such a scale or could provide such a stimulus[69]. Nevertheless the investment time-chart set out by Mitchell leads him to emphasize, 'the supporting rather than leading nature of the role of railway-building in the economic fluctuations of the time.

[65] Mitchell, 321, (table 1). They consist of expenditure for building the infrastructure and purchasing rolling-stock, i.e. expenditure that generated income. Unproductive and transfer payments (purchase of land, parliamentary costs) are not included; but they figure in the totals of capital formation (which are therefore a little higher than those which we quote), as given by Mitchell, 335–6, and in the figure quoted for 1847, p.285.
[66] Total investment for 1833–43 (in the sense of note 65) was about £50 million; Mathias, *The First Industrial Nation*, p.283.
[67] Deane and Cole, pp.231–2 (tables 59 and 60); Hawke, p.205. The gross formation of railway capital was £10 million per annum on average from 1851 to 1860.
[68] P.Deane, 'New estimates of gross national product for the United Kingdom, 1830–1914', *The Review of Income and Wealth*, series 14 (2), June 1968, 104–5 (table A); R.A.Church, *The Great Victorian Boom, 1850–1873* (London, 1975), p.32.
[69] Mathias, *The First Industrial Nation*, p.283, points out that the price of iron, bricks and other building materials fluctuated in sympathy with the number of railway projects. Deane and Cole, pp.295–6, see the railway as a new pacemaker, starting with the late 1830s.

Railway-building may have sustained, even at times accelerated, economic growth; but it did not lead it.' It attracted capital that was in search of investment or speculative gain, when conditions were favourable in financial markets and also, because the period of gestation between an investment decision and the completion of a project was so long, the latter often overlapped a period of recession and had a certain counter-cyclical effect[70].

There were also, undoubtedly, some strong side-effects, for instance on public works and on the production of building materials. In 1839 work on railways probably employed 50,000 men, or one-seventh of the total public-works and building manpower, and about 1 per cent of all occupied males. During the record year, 1847, on 1 May, there were 257,000 men at work on railway-construction – about 4 per cent of the total male labour-force then in employment[71]. Railway-building also used up in 1837 between a seventh and an eighth of all bricks produced in Britain, and a third in 1847.

However, the key problem concerns the effects of railway-construction on the iron industry, because of the close backward linkages with it and of the size of that industry. However, such effects appear to have been less important than was once thought. According to Mitchell, actual tracks-construction (mainly rails) used on average 7 per cent of the national output of pig-iron between 1835 and 1843, 18 per cent between 1844 and 1851, but only 8 to 9 per cent during the 1850s and 1860s. An addition to this was the much lower proportion used for stations, sheds, locomotives, rolling stock, etc. It was only for a short time that demand from the railways really mattered to the iron industry. Between 1839 and 1841 it only amounted to 150 to 200,000 tons, a considerable but not a vital quantity. It consumed the greatest part of the increase in pig-iron production between 1844 and 1847, but was only in a really commanding position in the years 1846 and 1847, when, in two years, it used the equivalent of a million tons of pig-iron. Later, the iron industry continued to expand in spite of a decline in demand from railways, which took less than 10 per cent of its production and ceased to have much significance after 1870[72].

The impact of demand from railway-builders was indeed felt unevenly in the various iron-making regions. In Scotland it was

[70] Mitchell, 320, 329–30. The same view is expressed in Hawke, pp.376, 378.
[71] Mitchell, 322–3, 329; but there was a drop to about 50,000 workers (and even less) in the 1850s.
[72] ibid., 325 (table 2), 326–7. Hawke, ch. 9, p.213ff, accepts Mitchell's figures while apparently regarding them as rather high, especially that of 1 million tons for 1846–7. His own percentages for railway demand in *England* in relation to the production of pig-iron in the *UK* are naturally lower; pp.240, 255, 259 (tables IX, 11, 13 and 15).

negligible, according to an article by W.Vamplew[73], but it was heavily concentrated on South Wales, where an early start was made on the production of rails (for export as well). South Wales soon came to dominate the market, of which it greatly enlarged its share, thereby giving a considerable boost to local ironworks[74].

Although the manufacture of rails used more iron than that of any other product, Hawke concluded that the role of the railways was not dominant and that the existence of railways was not essential for the development of an iron industry[75]. Moreover, both the iron and the engineering industries had begun to diversify before the advent of railways, and the shift of British industry away from the relatively declining textile trades towards production goods had appeared early on in the Victorian age, and was not entirely dependent on railway demand[76].

Hawke's description of the effects of the railways on the iron industry has been criticized by Peter Mathias[77]. He points out that to measure these effects simply by calculating the quantity of iron used by railways is to assume that, if the latter had not existed, all other economic flows would have been the same as they were with the railways (or else one would have to calculate the differences, which has never been done and is probably impossible). Further, if there had been no railways, less iron would have been produced and economies of scale smaller (but how much less?). So other outlets for the sale of iron would have been affected, though with a net result dependent on the elasticity of demand for such alternative products, while the necessity

---

[73] W.Vamplew, 'Railways and the transformation of the Scottish economy', *Economic History Review*, 2nd series, XXIV (1), Feb. 1971, 37–54, considers that the railway demand did not contribute to the expansion of the heavy Scottish industries, except late in the period.

[74] Hawke, pp.215ff.

[75] ibid., p.244. He also observes that railways brought no technical progress to this industry and had no role in the development of the steel industry before 1870. However, one must take into account F.Caron's remark (in P.Léon, F.Crouzet and R.Gascon (eds), *L'Industrialisation en Europe au XIXe siècle* (Paris, 1972), p.248), that the British iron industry already had much wider outlets than its equivalents in foreign countries, so it was normal that railway orders should be relatively less important for her. See also R.Fremdling, 'Railroads and German economic growth: a leading sector analysis with a comparison to the United States and Great Britain', *Journal of Economic History*, XXXVII (3), Sep. 1977, 583–604 (see 599–601), who underlines the importance of the demand from foreign railways for the British iron industry in the 1840s and 1850s.

[76] Barker and Savage, p.78; Church, *The Great Victorian Boom*, pp.31–2, 34; Mitchell, 328. During the boom of the 1840s, one-fifth of the production of the engineering industry was for the railways.

[77] In a detailed review of Hawke's book in *English Historical Review*, LXXXVII, No.CCCXLIV, July 1972, 582–9. On this point see p.585.

of developing other forms of transport would have had many interacting effects, all rather difficult to quantify!

There remains the second problem, the long-term gain to the economy as a whole from the services provided by railways. Here the critical question concerns the reduction in the cost of transport and its consequences. The usual estimate is that by the 1830s and 1840s the reduction on the routes served by railways was as much as 50 per cent and that it continued to increase later on. Hawke's estimate is that in 1865 the cost of transporting coal – the principal freight both for rail- and water-transport – was only 27 per cent of what it would have been by canal (without the lowering of rates forced on the canal companies by rail competition); but the amount thus saved was only a very small fraction of national product[78]. However, it has often been asserted that this reduction in the cost of transport and the speeding up of movement indirectly stimulated a number of other activities, opening up new markets (e.g. for perishable foodstuffs and for livestock), sharpening competition, helping industrialists and traders to reduce their stocks, and hence their circulating capital, providing a rapid and cheap mail service thanks to the penny post, and so on. Hence the widely held view that the railways and improvement in sea-transport played a considerable role in the growth of the economy.

To give a more precise idea of the size of this contribution, Hawke has used, following the methods of Fogel and Fishlow, the concept of 'social saving', that is the difference – in this case for the year 1865[79] – between the actual cost of transportation by rail and the hypothetical cost of the same volume of transport if railways had not existed, i.e. by canal for goods and by stagecoach for passengers. This difference, which can be expressed as a percentage of national product, measures the margin of gain resulting from the reduction in cost brought about by railways. After detailed calculation, Hawke concludes that the saving on the transport of goods (principally minerals) arising out of the use of railways in 1865 might have been 4.1 per cent of the national product of England and Wales. For passengers, it might have been between 2.6 and 7.1 per cent according to the value attached to the greater comfort of trains compared with stagecoaches. This means that, if England had not built her railways, her national product in 1865 would have been 7 to 11 per cent lower than it actually was, unless she had made other technological innovations which would

[78]   Hawke, p.173.
[79]   For which there exist many reliable statistics. Mitchell, 318, 320, thinks that it was only about this date that the British transport system was profoundly transformed by the railways.

have been substitutes for railways and devoted enough resources to developing them. In other words, English national product was at most 12 per cent greater in 1865 than it would have been without a rail network. This is by no means insignificant (Hawke comments that it is remarkable that 10 per cent of national product should be derived from a single innovation) and is far larger than similar figures for the United States (3 to 6 per cent). All the same it is lower than one might have expected. Furthermore, the saving of 11 per cent made in 1865 would have been less for earlier years, diminishing as one goes back in time. It is equivalent to the growth of national product over three or four years; so it is clear that the economy did not receive any decisive boost from the railways[80].

These conclusions have, of course, been disputed, firstly on technical points. Thus D.McCloskey has maintained that Hawke's calculations have an upward bias and overestimate the contribution of the railways, inasmuch as, basing his argument on the actual traffic in 1865, he does not take into account the elasticity of demand for transport; without railways traffic would have been much less, especially for passengers[81]. Peter Mathias has made more fundamental criticisms[82]. He considers that Hawke's calculations of 'social saving' rest on 'very arbitrary assumptions', which make them non-operational. Thus to base one's calculations of actual costs upon receipts and fares of railways in 1865 is to assume a perfectly competitive market. Moreover, it is unrealistic to suppose that the costs of transport by canal or coach would have been the same in 1865 as in 1830 if the railways had never been built. It is conceivable that the pressure of an increase in traffic would have produced a rise in unit-cost and monopoly profits might also have further increased freight-rates. Finally, it is arbitrary and subjective to quantify almost intangible qualitative changes such as greater comfort for passengers, which represents a considerable part of the 'social saving' calculated by Hawke[83]. So Mathias suggests that the figure of 10 per cent for the contribution made by the railways to English national product in 1865

---

[80] Hawke, p.6, ch.7, pp.187ff., p.401–2, 404–5, 410. Also pp.405ff. on the high internal social yield of railway investment between 1830 and 1870.

[81] D.N.McCloskey, review in *Economic History Review*, 2nd series, XXII (3), Aug. 1971, 493–5. In his own review (see note 77, p.588), P.Mathias has in effect made the same criticism, pointing out that the bulk of passengers went third class and made up a new clientele for transport, having moved on foot before the railways came – or stayed at home. Yet Hawke, p.405, had partly answered this criticism in advance.

[82] Review by Mathias, ibid., 586–8.

[83] Same remark by W.J.Baker, in *Journal of Economic History*, XXI (3), Sep.1971, 718–19.

is probably too low, inasmuch as one ought to take into consideration various secondary effects (in both meanings of the phrase), which the development of railways had on other activities and institutions, and which it is impossible to measure.

For example, railways created jobs. The enlistment of an army of navvies may have been a temporary phenomenon, but the permanent employees of the railway companies increased in number from 56,000 in 1850 to 250,000 towards 1875, 350,000 in 1890 and over 600,000 in 1910[84]. In addition, the railway companies and some independent manufacturers set up workshops, sometimes of great size, for building and repairing locomotives and rolling-stock; as mentioned earlier, these constituted an important section of the engineering industry and became active centres for the training of engineers and highly skilled mechanics.

Railways also brought about an enormous increase in human mobility. The promoters of the early lines had envisaged them as being used chiefly for transporting heavy goods and were surprised by the rush of passengers. In its very first year the Liverpool–Manchester carried 400,000 persons and the London–Birmingham 500,000. The process of urbanization has therefore been considered by many writers as being closely connected with extension of the rail network. The railways certainly broke down some of the limits to the growth of towns – by facilitating the supply of food, for instance. They also created new towns and gave a tremendous boost to seaside resorts. In London, the opening of the first underground railway (1863) and the obligation imposed on companies (1864) to provide 'parliamentary' workmen's trains with low fares, helped the growth of suburbs and the increase in house-building in the third quarter of the nineteenth century, leading to the boom of the 1870s. In the large provincial cities, however, improved transport facilities had less effect: rapid expansion of local industries, the resulting demand for labour and immigration were the main factors in an increased need for housing. Mitchell and Hawke show also that the railways did not bring about any sudden and drastic change in the location of industry, only a lot of small-scale movements over short distances; nor did they give rise to many new industries, apart from their own workshops and the exploitation of coal-deposits that had previously been isolated[85].

Moving to a different sphere, one finds general agreement that the large financial needs of railway companies had an invigorating effect

---

[84]   And see p.297 for the stimulus to horse-drawn road traffic.
[85]   Mitchell, 316–7; Hawke, pp. 392–5; also Vamplew, 'Railway', 54.

on the capital market. The London Stock Exchange ceased dealing almost exclusively in government stocks and other fixed-interest securities, and during the 'mania' of the 1840s dealings in ordinary shares predominated. In the provinces, the first railway boom led to the founding of the Liverpool and the Manchester stock exchanges: the boom of the 1840s gave rise to a dozen others in large provincial cities. The investing public grew (though in the early days the habit of issuing shares in denominations of £100 put them out of the reach of the small investor) and the idea of investing in transferable securities, particularly ordinary shares, began to spread; and so did the concept of limited liability[86].

Railways also influenced Britain's economic relations overseas. British capitalists were quick to invest in railways abroad. These were often constructed by British contractors, engineers and even navvies, e.g. the Paris–Rouen line, built in 1841–3), while British industry provided rails and locomotives. Indeed, the massive exports of capital that took place from the middle of the nineteenth century onwards were largely destined, directly or indirectly, to finance railway-construction, especially in the United States, Latin America and the British empire. It is well known that this export of capital helped the export of goods. Altogether, the railway was a potent factor in British economic growth, not only early in Victoria's reign but in the mid-Victorian period also. Mathias is right in stressing that the importance of railways for the economy as a whole was that they enabled all other economic sectors to expand[87], to such an extent that their influence pervaded the whole economy, even when their direct impact was much diminished. The direct and immediate effects of the actual construction of the railway network were only intense for a brief period during the 1840s. On the whole, however, the part played by the railways was less than has often been claimed, and their appearance on the scene was essential neither for the survival of the capitalist system – which in any case was not under threat – nor for the sustaining of economic growth, which was anyhow well under way[88].

---

[86] Mitchell, pp. 330–1, 333; Hawke, p.402 (who seems sceptical on this point); W.A. Thomas, *The Provincial Stock Exchanges* (London, 1973). These stock exchanges were so closely linked to railways that several of them disappeared when the boom foundered. The activity of the rest declined and did not pick up again until the 1870s when many industrial firms changed into joint-stock companies (see, Chapter 10, p.339).

[87] Mathias, *The First Industrial Nation*, p.281.

[88] In the formation of fixed capital, railway investment was the main element for a short period, but after 1850 it increased less fast than national product. Moreover, if one admits with P.Deane – and Hawke seems to confirm it – that railways caused a definite rise in the rate of capital formation, this means that it involved a reduction in consumption. If it had not occurred, consumption could have replaced part of the

THE TRIUMPH OF THE STEAMSHIP

The steam-engine, combined with the substitution of iron, and later steel, for wood in shipbuilding, was also to effect a revolution in sea-transport. This was a particularly important area for the British, who succeeded in exploiting this technical change to reinforce their already overwhelming predominance at sea.

This revolution at sea was more gradual and, above all, later in date than the upheaval in inland transport, as is shown in table 54[89].

This table illustrates first the development of the British merchant navy. Tonnage was quadrupled during Victoria's reign, but such figures are not very meaningful, for technical change led to a proportionately far greater increase in carrying capacity. Initially, this increase was an almost automatic reaction to the growth of international trade and intercontinental migration, together with Britain's own growing needs for shipping. However, the two factors worked reciprocally: the rapid growth of international trade was partly due to technical progress in shipping and the resulting reductions in freight-charges. These actually created some trade currents that hitherto had been unprofitable or physically impossible, such as the long-distance transport of heavy and bulky goods (e.g. coal, grain, etc.)[90].

The most interesting fact thrown up by the table is how long it took

Table 54　Shipping registered in UK (000 tons)

	Sailing ship tonnage	Steamship tonnage	Total	Steamship tonnage as % of total
1815	2477	1	2478	—
1837	2264	70	2334	3
1850	3397	168	3565	4.5
1860	4204	454	4659	10
1870	4578	1113	5691	20
1880	3851	2724	6575	41
1890	2936	5043	7979	63
1900	2096	7208	9304	77
1913	847	11273	12120	93

effective demand created by railways, while investment of a different nature would have been necessary to make up for railways; Church, *The Great Victorian Boom*, pp.33–4, 39.

[89] Taken from *Abstract*, pp.217–19. As for the number of ships, it varied little, rising from 21,869 in 1815 to a peak of 28,971 in 1866, and falling to 20,938 in 1913; but it tells very little, except in so far as its stability reflects the growing dimensions of vessels.

[90] Dyos and Aldcroft, pp.248–51.

for steam to outnumber sail in the British merchant navy – the year 1883 is the turning-point (by tonnage), though one ought to take an earlier date if one were to reckon by freight actually carried since, ton for ton, steamships had greater capacity, or if the building of new ships was considered. None the less, the technological revolution at sea was delayed until the second half of the century, and its victory was not assured until the 1870s[91].

Still, steamships were actually in existence and in commercial use at the beginning of the century. Robert Fulton's *Clermont* had steamed up the Hudson River in 1807; the first British steamship, the *Comet*, had cruised round the Clyde in 1812. But for a long time the steamship laboured under severe disadvantages in relation to sail – not to mention the bigoted hostility of merchants, shipowners and seamen. It was more expensive to build and to run; its engines were cumbersome and heavy like the paddle-wheels they drove and which moreover were fragile (they were not to be replaced by screws until the middle of the century). Worse still, a steamship had to carry its fuel (and its engine used a great deal), which took up valuable cargo-space, all the more on a long voyage, so that the cost of transport of cargo per unit of weight increased with the distance away from the coaling port, while sailing-ships' freight did not vary in proportion to distance. This was the main reason why the change from sail to steam took so long[92]. For years, steam's only advantages were greater speed and punctuality, so, at the start, it was only used for short crossings[93], and for carrying passengers, mail and goods of great value but small weight, for all of which speed and punctuality were paramount, compensating for higher freight-rates. Thus, by 1855, steamships monopolized the passenger traffic to Ireland and the Channel and North Sea ports, and had captured most of the import trade from ports between Brest and Hamburg, though English coal was still shipped there by sail. Steam had also penetrated the Mediterranean, where wind and weather are uncertain and from which came perishable foodstuffs (fruit), and by 1865 most English trade with that part of the world was steam-

---

[91] ibid., pp.247, 260. The classic article on this question is G.S.Graham, 'The ascendancy of the sailing ship, 1850–85', *Economic History Review*, 2nd series, IX (2), Aug. 1956, 74–88.

[92] C.K.Harley, 'Shift from sailing- to steamships, 1850–90', in D.N.McCloskey (ed.), *Essays on a Mature Economy: Britain after 1840* (London, 1971), pp.217–18 (a good study, but treating mainly heavy-goods traffic). He points out that coaling in foreign ports was not a solution as coal, usually imported from England, was more expensive there. It is worth noting that for a long time steamships remained equipped with auxiliary sails.

[93] In addition to passenger services in estuaries, and use as tugs.

propelled[94]. On the North Atlantic, the earliest steamship companies – such as that founded by Samuel Cunard in 1840 – only survived thanks to hidden subsidies in the shape of advantageous contracts with the Post Office for the carriage of mail[95]. But on this route sailing-ships prevailed, and everywhere else in the long-distance trades they won hands down by their cheap freights and kept their monopoly. This was helped by technical progress in sailing ships, which were made more efficient, with smaller crews and thus lower freight-charges. Early in the century, Americans had invented the clippers – long, streamlined ships, heavily canvassed and fast. They could cross the Atlantic in a fortnight and could reach Australia in three months. British shipbuilders, who for long had been badly behind in design, started to imitate them after 1837, building clippers for the Australia and China trades (the famous 'tea race' took place on the return journey from China). Later on, in the 1860s, iron was increasingly substituted for wood in building large sailing-ships[96]. By 1850, Britain had 168,000 tons under steam and nearly 3,400,000 under sail – roughly, one steamship for every twenty sailing-ships.

From 1815 to the 1840s, the British merchant fleet had not prospered, and its tonnage had actually diminished, failing to pass its 1816 level again until 1838. British shipbuilders were facing tough competition from the Americans and the Scandinavians, both of whom had plenty of good timber close to their coasts, and so were able to build more cheaply than the British, who had to import most of their ship timber. Moreover, as already stated, the Americans were better designers, they ran their ships more economically with smaller, harshly driven crews. American ships carried two-thirds of Anglo-American trade and three-quarters of the immigrant traffic from the United Kingdom[97]. Although the situation improved for Britain in the 1840s[98] and the fleet grew fairly rapidly thereafter, it is quite wrong to

[94] Harley, 'Shift from sailing', p. 221.
[95] On Cunard, see F.E.Hyde, *Cunard and the North Atlantic, 1840–1873: A History of Shipping and Financial Management* (London, 1975). The first crossing of the Atlantic entirely by steam dates from 1833. Even a ship which was technically a great leap forward, the *Great Britain* of I.K.Brunel (1843), built of iron and screw-driven, was not a success on the North Atlantic, and everyone knows the misfortunes of the *Great Eastern*, built by the same engineer and too much in advance of her time. In 1856, 96 per cent of passengers disembarking at New York had come by sail; Harley, p.263.
[96] There was an intermediary stage in the 1850s with composite ships – iron frames and wooden planking.
[97] Similarly the traffic with Scandinavia and the Baltic largely eluded British shipping.
[98] In the late 1840s the Cunard steam-liners (which were wooden) began to gain the upper hand on the North Atlantic over American clippers, who moved to the

say that the Navigation Acts were repealed in 1849 because Britain no longer had anything to fear from foreign competition, thanks to the lead she had won through the building of iron steamships. Before steamships could emerge victorious and establish British predominance, they needed new technological advances, achieved more rapidly than those on sailing-ships, and which reduced their running costs relative to those of sailing-ships – as the ratio between their costs determined the share of the traffic which fell to each type of ship[99]. The first of these technological changes was the substitution of screws for paddlewheels. The screw made its first appearance in 1838 but was not widely used until the 1850s. Next came the iron hull, which had been tried in the 1830s but was not much used until the 1850s, and then at first on transatlantic liners and on colliers plying between the north-east ports of England and London. But it was not until the late 1860s that the *total* tonnage of new construction in iron (both steam and sail) equalled that of wooden ships, and it did not exceed the latter until the early 1870s. The iron-ship was lighter and less expensive for the same tonnage, as well as being more durable. Above all, the use of iron eliminated the limitations on size imposed by the use of wood, so that ships of greater and greater tonnage could be built, with economies of scale, and lower unit building- and running-costs[100].

The use of iron gave Britain an important advantage over her foreign rivals, particularly the United States, since she could produce it more cheaply. Moreover, she had many ironworks near the coast and a workforce skilled in metal-working; in 1860, American ironships cost one-third more to build than British ones. In 1861 occurred the historic accident[101] of the American civil war, when Southern privateers preyed upon Northern merchant ships, so that they were sold to foreign owners in large numbers. The American merchant navy never recovered from this disaster, and by the end of the century, it had only a small number of ships.

However, iron hulls also gave sailing-ships a new lease of life[102], so

California route via Cape Horn. M.Lévy-Leboyer, *Les Banques européennes et l'industrialisation internationale dans la première moitié du XIXe siècle* (Paris, 1964), pp.214ff, 233, 238, points out the advantage gained from the growth of coal exports, notably to France.

[99] Harley, 'Shift from sailing', pp.215–16.

[100] The costs of building ships of iron, and then of steel, fell by one-third between c.1860 and c.1890; C.K.Harley, 'On the persistence of old techniques: the case of North American wooden shipbuilding', *Journal of Economic History*, XXXIII (2), June 1973. p.377. See also Chapter 8, pp.252–4.

[101] It seems that American competition had weakened even before the war.

[102] Although iron-building prevailed for steamships before 1850, but only after 1868 for sailing-ships.

that right up to 1870 they remained more profitable than steamships over most of the long-distance route[103]. Large numbers of them continued to be built, a record 272,500 tons in 1864, bringing the British merchant fleet under sail to its highest ever tonnage of 4,937,000 tons in 1865. After that tonnage under sail remained static, then declined, while steam tonnage increased rapidly; as early as 1870 the latter exceeded one million tons as against 168,000 twenty years earlier.

What finally gave steam the upper hand was the considerable improvement made in fuel economy in marine engines, which lowered running-costs and reduced the amount of space that had to be used on steam-ships for bunker coal. This was a gradual and continuous process, but one of the most important steps was the invention of the compound steam-engine which, after many experiments, appeared in 1854, was perfected during the 1860s and widely used after 1870. By 1890 the triple-expansion engine had appeared which proved to be the death warrant for the sailing-ship[104]. The consumption of coal per hour per horse-power, which had averaged 5 lb. in 1855, fell to 3.5 lb. in 1865, 2 lb. in 1872, and still less in 1890[105], with the result that steam could displace sail on longer and longer routes, even for bulky cargoes.

By the 1850s and 1860s steamships prevailed on short-haul trade with the continent and were getting a grip on the grain traffic with the Baltic and the Black Sea, as well as the coal trade from the north coast to London. After this came the winning of the North Atlantic about 1870, where the steamship had been acquiring an increasing share of passenger traffic since 1865, but now it also began to capture merchandise trade – first grain from New York, later cotton from New Orleans.

At the same time, the opening of the Suez canal in 1869 created a major breakthrough for the trade with India and the Far East. Sailing ships could, of course, be towed through the canal but the hazards of the Red Sea rendered it almost impassable for them. Only steamships could benefit from the reduction in length of the voyage to the east, and sailing ships soon disappeared from the East India trade; they even lost the China trade within ten years, in spite of the longer distance,

[103] In 1872 sailing-ships were still definitely preferable for carrying bulk cargoes more than 5000 miles; Harley, 'Shift from sailing', p.218.

[104] In a compound double-expansion engine, steam passes first into a high-pressure cylinder, and then into a low-pressure cylinder. In the triple-expansion engine a third cylinder is added. The use of these engines necessitated higher pressure in the boilers, which was achieved by making them of steel. The use of turbines (Parsons, 1897) was limited to passenger liners and warships. Oil-firing and the diesel-engine only appeared at the beginning of the twentieth century – and on a very small scale in British ships.

[105] Harley, 'Shift from sailing', p.220.

because of the high value of the goods carried (especially tea). Henceforward sail was only used on small coasting vessels, and on large ships for very long-distance trade round Cape Horn or the Cape of Good Hope, carrying nitrates from Chile, guano from Peru, wheat from California and wool from Australia. For such trades sailing-ships continued to be cheaper and profitable until the 1890s at least, and continued to operate at the beginning of the twentieth century[106]. Technical factors had gradually achieved the victory of steam over sail, just as at the same time steel gradually displaced iron in ship-building[107]. Table 55 illustrates these stages[108].

Both relatively and absolutely the building of steamships remained fairly insignificant up to the middle of the century. It increased in the 1850s and 1860s, and in 1863 for the first time more than 100,000 tons of steam tonnage was built, though very large numbers of sailing-ships were also constructed in 1868 and 1869, so that they made up almost two-thirds of total building for 1865–9. But an abrupt change came in the 1870s. From 1870 onwards – with the exception of 1875, 1876 and 1885 – the tonnage of new steamships exceeded that of sailing-ships, although quite large numbers of the latter continued to be built right up to the end of the century. In fact, in 1892 the almost record figure of 259,000 tons of sailing-ships launched was attained. But this proved to be the swan song of the sailing-ship, and by the beginning of the twentieth century the number built was insignificant (an annual average of 37,000 tons between 1900 and 1909). The technical revolution in merchant shipping took place, therefore, after 1870. In its wake came the rebuilding within three or four decades of practically the whole merchant fleet, which accounts for the substantial activity in the shipyards for the greater part of this period; so much so that at the beginning of the twentieth century Britain's merchant fleet was new and highly modernized. In 1913 44 per cent of all tonnage had been built since 1905[109].

Not surprisingly the proportion of sailing and steamships in this fleet had changed radically. Always remembering that, by reason of their higher speed and quicker turn-round, the cargo-carrying capacity of the steamship was, ton for ton, superior to that of the sailing-ship, it

[106] ibid., pp.222–5, 227.
[107] The first experiments took place in 1863–5; but steel was too expensive at that time, and shipbuilders, owners and insurers were distrustful. Steel began to prevail after 1875 and especially after 1880, when industry learnt how to roll plates of even quality and at low cost, made of mild steel, i.e. with a low carbon content. After 1890 there was no more building ships of iron.
[108] From Mathias, *The First Industrial Nation*, (table 37); *Abstract*, pp.220–2. The table includes ships built for British owners only.
[109] Dyos and Aldcroft, p.260.

Table 55   Steamships built in the UK

	Average annual output in thousands of tons	Percentage of total tonnage built
1820/9	3.0	4
1830/9	6.2	6
1840/9	11.8	9
1850/4	36.1	21
1855/9	59.0	24
1860/4	93.9	32
1865/9	121.9	36
1870/4	295.5	75
1875/9	221.7	55
1880/9	337.2	73
1890/9	500.9	83
1900/9	674.2	95
1909/13	751.9	96

is noteworthy that the former constituted only 10 per cent of the merchant fleet in 1860 and 20 per cent in 1870. But sailing-ship tonnage reached its peak in 1865 and then diminished. In 1883 it was overtaken by the rapidly rising level of steamship tonnage (at the world level, this turning-point came ten years later) and after dwindling to a quarter of total tonnage in 1900 the sailing-ship finally disappeared from the ocean-going merchant marine.

The primacy of the British merchant fleet throughout the nineteenth century is hardly surprising[110]. This position had been won in the eighteenth century and reinforced by the wars with France. England was after all the foremost commercial power, and, as an island, dependent on sea-transport for the whole of her foreign trade. However, the steam-cum-iron revolution that she was the first to undertake undoubtedly confirmed this primacy, and with the coincidental help of the civil war defeated the commercial challenge of America. Britain's share of world steamship tonnage was always larger than her share of total world shipping, steam and sail combined. It would appear that, from at least the middle of the nineteenth century, she possessed a third of the world's merchant fleet, with a rather higher percentage of ocean-going ships and a much higher percentage of steam ships – 50 per cent in 1880, 40 per cent in 1913[111].

[110] According to ibid., p.252, the US took first place in 1860, but only by including her Great Lakes fleet, amounting to 2.7 million tons.
[111] D.H.Aldcroft, 'The mercantile marine', in D.H.Aldcroft (ed.), *The Development of British Industry and Foreign Competition, 1875–1914: Studies in Industrial Enterprise* (London, 1968), p.327 (table 1), gives 35 per cent of the world ocean-going fleet in 1860, 36 per cent in 1890, 34 per cent in 1911.

This fleet was not only the largest but also the most modern and efficient in the world.

British ships not only carried more than half of the country's foreign trade; they also carried a large proportion of other countries' trade with non-British ports. Probably about a fifth to a quarter of all British merchant ships rarely entered British ports, especially many tramps. In 1912 British ships carried 55 per cent of the trade between the various territories of the British empire and foreign countries, and 30 per cent of all trade between foreign countries, carrying altogether about half of total world trade[112]. For example, they had almost a monopoly along the South American Pacific coast and a large share of the trade along the China coast and on the Yangtse Kiang[113] – all of which contributed greatly to Britain's invisible earnings[114].

It is remarkable how little British merchant shipping was affected from the late nineteenth century by the foreign competition that was hitting other parts of the economy. After 1880, as other countries were increasing and modernizing their merchant fleets, English ships did lose some of their share in the trade of many European and even some English ports; but on the long-distance routes the British flag remained unaffected, except in the Far East where it suffered – but at a late date – from Japanese competition[115] and on the North Atlantic, where it faced a German challenge.

Indeed, Germany was the only serious rival. Her merchant fleet grew from 1 million tons in 1870 to 3 million in 1911. It became the second largest in the world and the only one to increase its share of world tonnage, from 6 to 9 per cent. Nevertheless, on the eve of the first world war, its total tonnage, though consisting of modern ships, was only just over a quarter that of Britain. Contrary to a widespread belief, this expansion had not been helped on by state subsidies or other unfair practices, and the Germans had no economic advantage over the British. Aldcroft suggests simply that their shipping companies were fewer in number because of greater concentration, more willing to co-operate with one another, and led by a few talented

[112] Dyos and Aldcroft, pp.248, 250; Aldcroft, 'The mercantile marine', p.328. For example, 45 per cent of imports into France and 55 per cent into the US about 1900 were carried in British ships.
[113] See for example S.Marriner and F.E.Hyde, *The Senior: John Samuel Swire 1825–98. Management in Far Eastern Shipping Trades* (Liverpool, 1967), on the China Navigation Company, founded by John Swire, merchant in Shanghai; also F.E.Hyde, *Far Eastern Trade, 1860–1914* (London, 1973).
[114] Cf. Chapter 11, pp.359–60.
[115] The Japanese merchant navy was very small in 1900, but had become the third in the world by 1914. For all this, see Aldcroft, 'The mercantile marine', pp.328ff.

entrepreneurs, who were better managers, more skillful and unscrupulous tacticians than their British rivals, particularly in using the conferences system to effect an entry into a particular trade, and subsequently open the door wider[116]. By the end of the nineteenth century, the Germans had succeeded in getting a foothold in all the main sea-routes, but the only serious threat to Britain was for the North Atlantic passenger traffic made up chiefly of immigrants; there was a steep increase in their number at the end of the nineteenth and beginning of the twentieth century, and the fact that they came largely by now from eastern and southern Europe favoured German shipping. The British had enjoyed a short-lived monopoly of this traffic after the American civil war, but this was soon threatened by the Hamburg–Amerika and the Norddeutscher Lloyd liners. There followed a series of agreements to regulate and share this business (passengers pools), but they proved insufficient to prevent bouts of cut-throat and ruinous competition. The British lost ground at the end of the nineteenth century, but hit back by launching new giant liners, technically in advance of their rivals. In 1906, an agreement allotted them 37 per cent of all passenger traffic from Europe to America, and during the ten years prior to the war they seem to have maintained, even improved, their position. But this was the only sea-route on which the Germans gained the upper hand, and Aldcroft's conclusion is that British maritime industries (shipbuilding included) in 1914 had an invincible lead over all competitors. Neither owners nor builders had suffered any serious hurt from foreign competition and they were capable of meeting any that was offered[117].

A last question concerns the effects which the changes just described had on the structure and organization of the shipping industry. At the beginning of the nineteenth century, this consisted of many small businesses that usually combined trading with shipowning (though there were a few specialized firms), rarely owning more than two or three ships; moreover, to spread risks, the ownership of ships would often be divided up into numerous shares. Ships would rarely be over 200 or 300 tons, except those on the India and China trades. The appearance of steamships, which generally belonged to firms specializing in shipowning, brought about an increasingly clear distinction after the 1860s between shipowners and merchants. Compared with the use of iron, this encouraged an enormous increase in the size of ships. At the beginning of the twentieth century a typical freighter had

---

[116] On conferences, cf. Chapter 5, p.111.
[117] Aldcroft, 'The mercantile marine', pp.347ff, 361.

a capacity of 7500 tons, and several transatlantic liners exceeded 60,000 tons. Another result was the growth, often from modest beginnings, of the great shipping firms – Cunard, P & O, Royal Mail, etc. – that alone had the resources to build and operate large ships[118]. At the beginning of the twentieth century, after many mergers and takeovers, a third of all British tonnage was in the hands of twenty-four companies, several of which owned about a hundred ships. However, there were also a number of small tramp shipping companies, many of which often had only one or two vessels; for in 1914, tramp-ships made up from a third to two-fifths of the British merchant fleet. The shipping industry was a business that was susceptible to sharp and sudden fluctuations in activity, in freight-rates and in profits, not to mention the problem of keeping up with continuous technological change. 1815 had seen the start of a long depression, but from 1840 onwards shipowners seem to have been generally prosperous. The Great Depression hit them in certain respects, but they were compensated by a fall in running-expenses and in building-costs. The beginning of the twentieth century, however, proved to be a rather difficult period.

The results of the revolution in sea-transport have not been studied in such detail as the economic consequences of the railways. During the nineteenth century, as a result of technological improvements in both sailing and steamships, a heavy fall in freight-charges took place, which began long after the triumph of steam. In real terms this fall was halted in the mid-Victorian period, but it resumed rapidly after 1880 and continued steadily after 1900[119]. One should not exaggerate the importance of freight-rates, which principally affect heavy goods; but it was precisely this growth of heavy-goods transport that was a basic feature of nineteenth-century international trade, and was especially important for Britain, allowing her to get supplies of primary produce from distant countries and to export increasing quantities of coal. The technological breakthrough in sea-transport seems to have been a precondition for an increased international division of labour, for many changes in the world economy and for its unification under Britannia's trident. In addition, the shipping revolution, and especially the increasing size of ships, demanded considerable capital expenditure for the development and enlargement of ports – at least the major ones, as the smaller ones suffered a sharp decline.

[118] Though the cost of ships per ton burden declined. On this paragraph, see Dyos and Aldcroft, ch.9. pp.276–99.
[119] S.B.Saul, *The Myth of the Great Depression, 1873–96* (London, 1969), p.22 (table II).

To sum up, whatever small disagreements one may have with traditional views on the part played by railways, the Victorian era was the age of the Transport Revolution, clearly subsequent to the Industrial Revolution – as the latter alone was able to provide it with two essential ingredients, iron and the steam-engine. But this revolution proceeded by fits and starts – in the 1830s and 1840s for railways, after 1870 for sea-transport. There were times when it consumed a rather large portion of the nation's resources and clearly affected the rhythm of the economy, but these did not last[120]. It is undeniable that the development of new transport facilities on an unprecedented scale had all sorts of effects, both direct and indirect, both economic and social, though they are difficult to quantify accurately.

[120] Deane and Cole, pp.229, 238–40, 295–6, see a peak in transport investment at the beginning of the 1870s, with massive building of steamships and the substitution of steel for iron on the railways; but there was a relative decline after 1890.

10 Banks and credit

The expression Banking Revolution is used to describe the sudden and widespread appearance in the mid-nineteenth century of large joint-stock banks in continental Europe, but it is not applicable to Great Britain. The fact is that, ever since the beginning of the nineteenth century, and even the end of the eighteenth, she had a banking system that was much more advanced and sophisticated than that of any other country, which had evolved gradually since the end of the seventeenth century. It certainly underwent considerable changes in structure during the nineteenth century and many major innovations were introduced, while the system as a whole and the resources at its disposal enjoyed a massive expansion, unbroken by any sudden or dramatic upsets.

THE BANKING SYSTEM UP TO 1844

This study of the banking system starts at the beginning of the nineteenth century, or rather in 1821, when the normal convertibility of banknotes for gold, which the stress of war had obliged the government to suspend in 1797, was restored. The system comprised three different components, and may be compared to a three-storey pyramid[1].

At the top sat, enthroned, the Bank of England, already an institution of venerable age, having been founded in 1694. It was a private firm, but closely connected with the government, which had awarded it a number of privileges. Of these the most important was to be the only joint-stock bank *in England*, a monopoly that did not extend to Scotland, which had its own separate banking system, with –

---

[1] On the banking system in the eighteenth century and beginning of the nineteenth century, see especially P.Mathias, *The First Industrial Nation: An Economic History of Britain, 1700–1914* (London, 1969), pp.165ff.

ever since the eighteenth century – three joint-stock banks[2]. In England, as a consequence of the Bubble Act (1720), other banks could only function as ordinary partnerships, and with a maximum of six partners[3]. At first the Bank of England was primarily the government's banker, a function it has always retained. The major part of the liquid funds held by the government was deposited there, especially the proceeds of taxation. The Bank serviced the National Debt and it constantly gave the government short-term loans. But in the course of the eighteenth century the Bank developed its own private business, especially discounting bills of exchange, but also giving short-term loans in the form of overdrafts, for a large clientele of London merchants, manufacturers and even tradesmen. In fact, in its capacity as private bank, it was more the Bank of London than the Bank of England, and the notes it issued in advancing money to the government, or in its discounting business, though they constituted the chief medium of circulation in the capital, hardly spread into the provinces. Nevertheless, after the middle of the eighteenth century, the Bank tended, without any deliberate policy on the part of its directors, to acquire the functions of a genuine central bank. The strength of its resources, the volume of its notes in circulation, the size of its reserves in specie compared with those of other banks, taken with its privileged relations with the government, all contributed to this situation. Moreover, when between 1797 and 1821 the Bank was released from its obligation to exchange its notes for gold, these became the basis for notes issued by other banks, which thereby came under its control. Further, in times of financial crisis the Bank became the lender of last resort[4]. Other banks in London had opened accounts with it, and in difficult times used the Bank to rediscount bills they had accepted[5]. Although they continued for a long time to maintain that they were a private bank like any other, the Governor and the Court of Directors eventually admitted around 1815–33 that their primary obligation was not to maximize profits for their shareholders, but that, as a central bank, their responsibility was to ensure the

[2]   See the excellent work by S.G.Checkland, *Scottish Banking: A History, 1695–1973* (Glasgow and London, 1975). Scotland was the cradle of many innovations in banking practice.

[3]   Unless authorized specially by Act of Parliament or Royal Charter – which never happened.

[4]   It could act on the demand for credit not by varying the discount rate, on which the old Usury Laws imposed a ceiling of 5 per cent, but by being more or less strict on the quantity of the bills it discounted and sometimes by actual 'rationing'.

[5]   The classic work on the Bank is J.H.Clapham, *The Bank of England: A History* (2 vols, Cambridge, 1944). R.S.Sayers, *The Bank of England, 1891–1944* (3 vols, London, 1976).

stability and smooth running of the whole banking system and indeed of the national economy. However, their apprenticeship to this role was protracted and difficult[6].

The private banks in London formed the second layer of the pyramid. There were seventy-three in 1807 and about a hundred in the 1830s. Although they were all partnerships, mainly family businesses, they were often long established, rich, solid and carrying considerable prestige. A number of bankers were of foreign origin, and at the end of the Napoleonic wars Nathan Rothschild had risen to the forefront. Although private note issues were not prohibited, they had given up issuing their own banknotes in the eighteenth century, but their activities were varied and rather specialized. West End banks had their clientele among the nobility and gentry, often lending money on mortgages. The more numerous City banks engaged in short-term financing of business transactions, by discounting bills, or by very short-term loans, such as loans 'on call' to stockbrokers. Some specialized in financing foreign trade, overseas remittances, the acceptance of bills of exchange for smaller firms, and already in making investments overseas; in all this they were the forerunners of what would later be called merchant banks. Others specialized as agents in London for country banks, carrying out a variety of operations for them, such as cashing the bills of exchange on London that they had discounted ('bills on London' had become the medium of payment for most transactions that involved large sums of money), and transferring funds to other parts of the country.

The country banks formed the bottom layer of the pyramid. They were the most original aspect of the English system, but their rise had been rather recent. Up to the middle of the eighteenth century banks in the provinces had been few in number, but they increased rapidly, especially during the wars with France and after 1797, when convertibility was suspended and Britain was suffering from a severe spell of inflation. In their heyday, 1809–10, some 900 country banks flourished, and in spite of numerous bankruptcies thereafter, there were almost as many in the 1820s. They proliferated: every market-town had its bank, and every town of any size had several. Most of them, of course, remained quite small, without much capital and confined to a purely local clientele. Very few set up branch offices. None the less, since the Bank of England restricted its operations to the capital, they formed the only credit institutions for the greater part

---

[6] S.G.Checkland, *The Rise of Industrial Society in England, 1815–85* (London, 1964), pp.189, 196. We have drawn much inspiration from his ch.6, pp.189ff, and from Mathias, *The First Industrial Nation*, pp.350–61.

of the country, and so played an important part in the economy. They took deposits, made loans (nearly always short-term), but their principal business lay in discounting, supplying their clients with bills on London (which, as already shown, were a widely used means of payments, especially in industrial districts) and issuing banknotes, convertible on sight into gold or Bank of England notes[7]. These issues were a large component of the money supply, and in many areas the notes of local banks were almost the only means of payment, especially during the suspension of convertibility.

These various elements combined early on to form an integrated financial system on a national scale, thanks to the unifying activity of the Bank of England, and also to the appearance, around 1800, of bill-brokers. These dealt in bills of exchange, acting as intermediaries between bankers in industrial areas, who were constantly asked to discount bills, and bankers in agricultural areas with liquid funds for which they had no immediate use. The latter could invest those surpluses at short term by discounting bills coming from the industrial areas via the bill-brokers. London thus became 'the great junction' through which regions with a short-term capital surplus could supply those that were capital-hungry. 'The thrift of the South and West supported the enterprise of the Midlands and North.' This discount market, in conjunction with the system by which London bankers acted as agents for country banks, compensated for the fact that the Bank of England had no provincial branches and there were no large clearing banks with provincial branch networks. The bill-brokers were thus the principal intermediaries for inter-regional dealings and transfer of money. In addition, after 1825, bill-brokers, henceforward known as discount houses, started to receive a great deal of short-term funds from London banks (and hence from the country banks for which the latter acted as agents). This gave bill-brokers the means to discount bills at their own risk and not simply act as intermediaries. If they were short of cash, they could apply to the Bank of England[8].

Although this system had reached a high degree of sophistication and greatly helped the economy, it had various flaws. One was that it tended sharply to accentuate the impact of business cycles. It was in every banker's interest, especially one who issued his own banknotes, to build up his issue and discounting business, and in times of optimism and speculation many tended to forget the simple rules of prudence and the need to back their commitments with adequate

[7]   Anyone could set up as an issuer of bank-notes so long as he took out a licence, which did not cost much, and no law limited the value of his issues.
[8]   Mathias, *The First Industrial Nation*, pp. 354–5.

liquid reserves. Thus a period of prosperity could become a 'bubble', inasmuch as the Bank of England rarely intervened in time and used the fairly effective means at its disposal to halt inflation. Since most country banks had only a limited capital of their own, as soon as conditions became less favourable and *a fortiori* if a crisis broke out, many found themselves in very risky situations. In addition in such circumstances a panic was likely which would cause a 'run' on the banks, a sudden rush to exchange notes for cash, which could ruin the most solidly established firm. Consequently, every economic crisis was accompanied by numerous failures, both of country banks and of their London correspondents who were involved in their collapse[9]. In contrast, those which survived immediately restricted their note circulation and reduced their discount business at the very time when businessmen had greatest need of credit. The Bank of England, however, tended on such occasions to be more generous, lending its support to firms that were confidence-worthy, but at risk. As Mathias has stated, English laws on banking maximized instability by tightly controlling the structure of banks (limiting them to six partners, etc.), while leaving them complete freedom of operation – no control on the quantity of notes they issued, their cash ratio, their reserves, etc. W.H.B.Court considers that before the 1830s the organization of credit failed to keep up with that of industrial production, which suffered severely on several occasions from crises on the money market[10].

British public opinion – or rather that part of it involved in business and politics – was very conscious of these flaws and periodic failures of the banking system, and tended to hold it responsible for economic fluctuations and crises, as the mechanism of business cycles was hardly understood. Moreover, people tended to discuss monetary problems as if they belonged to the realm of physical sciences, in the belief that they might be subject to a set of general principles, a system of scientific laws that would guarantee stable growth, and that once this philosopher's stone had been discovered there would be no need for state interference. Hence brisk and incessant discussion of these banking and monetary problems, particularly between the years 1809 and 1844, which, Checkland suggests, were a distraction from rather more fundamental questions. These discussions usually also had a political tinge. Actually, where central banking was concerned, the

[9] The sufferers were not only their own clients but all holders of their notes, which suddenly lost all their value. The failure of the local bank could sow desolation over the whole of a small region.
[10] Mathias, *The First Industrial Nation*, p.38; W.H.B. Court, *A Concise Economic History of Britain, From 1750 to Recent Times* (Cambridge, 1954), p. 102.

dominant theme of banking history in nineteenth-century England was the search for a simple principle in the light of which currency and credit could be regulated[11]. The result was a series of legislative measures which, together with action taken by financiers, gradually but profoundly reformed and strengthened the English banking system.

The debate had started in 1809 at the height of the Napoleonic wars, when Bank of England notes had depreciated against precious metals and foreign currencies, and other symptoms of inflation were appearing. In an article, followed in 1809 by a pamphlet, David Ricardo and, following him, a House of Commons select committee known as the Bullion Committee asserted that the depreciation of banknotes was simply the result of excessive issues by the Bank of England, though in fact the Bank's role in inflation had been almost passive. The so-called bullionists proceeded to demand an early resumption of cash payments, i.e. convertibility of notes into gold, so as to preserve the value of the currency. The government of the day very sensibly refused to accept such utterly unrealistic proposals in the middle of a desperate war. They won their battle, but the bullionists were to prevail once peace returned. The Bullion Committee's 1810 report remained for a long time the tablets of the law of monetary orthodoxy, and inspired the Currency School, as we shall see later on[12].

After much discussion, convertibility was restored in 1821 at the prewar parity, which implied a fairly severe deflation in the preceding years, and meant that henceforward the Bank's note issues were to be regulated according to the rate of exchange and the price of gold, so as to maintain this parity. Nevertheless, the business cycle which ended in 1825 culminated in a speculative mania, followed by a panic in December 1825 and January 1826 and an acute crisis during which over seventy (perhaps a hundred) London and country banks failed[13]. This showed that convertibility was not such a panacea as was claimed, and resulted in the enacting of the first important measure of bank reform, an Act of 1826, which attempted to remove many of the faults of the existing system at one go.

Although the Bank of England shared in the responsibility for the

[11]   Checkland, *The Rise*, pp.190, 192.
[12]   Court, p.100. At this date the directors of the Bank of England refused to admit that there was a connection between the volume of their issues, on the one hand, and the price of gold and the exchange rate on the other; but their views changed rapidly later.
[13]   The subject of controversy; see Court, p.100; Mathias, *The First Industrial Nation*, p. 354; Checkland, *The Rise*, p.195. It is true that some banks only suspended their payments temporarily.

'mania' as well as the panic, the country banks took most of the blame: their rashness, speculations and over-issuing of notes were said to have led to disaster, none of which was strictly true. All the same the new Act forbade the issue of notes of less than £5, since the smaller notes of £1 and £2, which had been issued since 1797, were thought to be a cause of instability[14]. The Bank of England was authorized to set up provincial branches so as to increase the circulation of its own notes (and of gold) and thereby check that of country banknotes. But the most important provision was to authorize the formation of joint-stock banks, up till then forbidden except in Scotland, where existing ones had stood up well to the panic of 1825. They were permitted to issue banknotes. There was one important proviso: such banks were not allowed in London or within 65 miles of the capital, thus leaving the Bank of England its privileged domain. However, this restriction did not last long: a new Act of 1833 allowed joint-stock banks to set up in London, but not to issue notes there. This was symptomatic of a tendency of the authorities to restrict note-issuing by private banks and to concentrate it in the hands of one institution, the Bank of England. This tendency was to be strongly confirmed ten years later[15].

The appearance of the joint-stock banks was a new and important development, which was completely to transform the banking scene. More than a hundred were founded in ten years (seventy-two between 1834 and 1836) and this enormously increased the country's banking capacity. By 1841, in spite of failures, 115 were operating in England, and they were starting to take over smaller country banks and to open their own branches. As early as 1838, there were more branches of joint-stock banks in the provinces than private banks, which were steadily dwindling in number[16].

However, joint-stock banks met with opposition, especially those which, profiting by the Act of 1833, wanted to set up in London where the private banks were hostile. So was the Bank of England, which refused to let them open accounts, to provide cash when they were in

[14] This measure, which did not apply to Scotland, remained in force until 1914.
[15] See especially Mathias, *The First Industrial Nation*, pp.350ff; Court, pp.184ff. At the same time (1833) the notes of the Bank of England became legal tender, which aimed at avoiding runs on gold; and the Bank no longer had to respect the Usury Laws and could make discounts above 5 per cent.
[16] B.L.Anderson and P.L.Cottrell, 'Another Victorian capital market: a study of banking and bank investors on Merseyside', *Economic History Review*, 2nd series, XXVIII (4), Nov. 1975, 598–615, indicate two periods for launching joint-stock banks in Liverpool – the 1830s and the mid-1860s, separated by a period of little activity. Many of such banks established during the first period were in fact transformations of private banks that existed before. Their shareholders were concentrated in the localities they served.

difficulties, or to rediscount bills they had accepted. They were not admitted to the London Clearing House until 1854. The first-comer was the London and Westminster Bank, founded in 1834, but in the face of much resistance, by 1844 there were still only five joint-stock banks in London. However, the newcomers finally succeeded in overcoming the hostility of old-fashioned bankers.

The growth of joint-stock banks was a significant event of the early days of Queen Victoria's reign, during which they were gradually to eliminate private banks. They had in principle considerable advantages over them – and this was one reason for their legalization in 1826, when there was a revulsion against country banks. Their freedom to issue shares enabled them to build up far more capital than private banks with their maximum of six partners could possibly do, and this made them more powerful, more stable and likely to attract deposits from a wider clientele, which in turn increased their resources. But, contrary to optimistic predictions, they were not necessarily more cautious than private bankers. Rather less so, in fact. With greater resources of their own, they could take greater risks. They had also to bid for their clientele, offering better facilities than established banks – slightly higher interest on deposit accounts, sometimes even interest on current accounts. They would also accept more doubtful bills of exchange than the older banks, because they could rediscount them in quantities in London. They did as much business as they could, but on small profit margins, and they kept lower cash reserves than their rivals. The establishment of these banks not only enlarged the total capacity of the banking system. It also made it more dynamic, though not more stable, and it encouraged competition, putting an end to local monopolies and knocking out weak or badly run businesses. Joint-stock banks fostered the expansion of credit and helped to speed up the fall in interest rates that had been under way since the end of the wars[17].

However, the growth of these banks did not put an end to economic crises, and Great Britain suffered two in close succession in 1836 and 1839, the second being followed by a depression that lasted until 1843. These crises brought a renewal of accusations against the banks (once again many had failed) who, together with the Bank of England, were held responsible. They also brought to a head the bitter controversy between two groups of economists and financiers, heirs to the bullionists and anti-bullionists of 1810 – the Currency School and the Banking School. They were in rough agreement on the desirability of

[17]   The interest on 3 per cent Consols fell from 5.1 per cent in 1812 to a minimum of 3 per cent in 1844.

concentrating note-issue in the hands of one institution only – the Bank of England; but they disagreed deeply on how the Bank should conduct its business.

The Banking School, whose leading exponent was Thomas Tooke, generally wanted trust to be placed in the bankers, to whose 'discretion' – meaning their sagacity and judgement – it should be left to control the money supply (in terms of bank notes), which should be made available in constant proportion to 'the needs of trade' and of the economy. It took up again the idea of 'real bills', on which the directors of the Bank of England had based their defence before the Bullion Committee. No issue of banknotes could be excessive (and moreover fluctuations in the economy would be minimized) so long as the Bank only issued notes in discounting 'good' bills of exchange, bills that represented actual commercial transactions and matured in less than sixty days. No ill effects could result from such a policy; very much the contrary in fact. So the legislature should leave the bankers their freedom of action and impose no rigid rules[18].

The Currency School, championed by S.J.Loyd (later Lord Overstone) kept strictly to the quantitative theory of money and had as its prime objective the maintenance of the currency's stability. This, together with the convertibility of banknotes for gold, would be endangered if the banks were given a free hand in creating currency. The control of the latter was too important to be left to the bankers, even the directors of the Bank of England. What was needed was to draw up simple, widely understood, automatically functioning regulations, and thus insulate the currency from the control or influence of any individual, group, bank or government. A set of rules of this kind, which had been sought after for years, could only be based on the current liquidity of the central bank, on the ratio of its gold reserves to its obligations in the form of banknotes, which would be used as a barometer determining the management of the whole economy[19].

---

[18] Tooke, who published a monumental and still useful history of prices (and indeed of the English economy) from 1793 to 1856, had some original ideas foreshadowing Keynes. But the Banking School had an extremist wing, with men like the Birmingham banker Thomas Attwood, which was openly inflationist.

[19] Checkland, *The Rise*, pp. 198–9; D.K.Adie, 'English bank deposits before 1844', *Economic History Review*, 2nd series, XXIII (2), Aug.1970, 285–6. In an interesting review of the published correspondence of Lord Overstone, S.G. Checkland (*Economic History Review*, 2nd series, XXVII (1), Feb.1974, 129–30) notes in the latter an authoritarian tendency (e.g. a desire that the Bank of England should control the whole monetary system) and a moralizing attitude (e.g. to prevent inflation from disturbing creditor-debtor relations), but also much realism. There must be simple rules, as automatic as possible, so that the Bank of England can 'do its duty', and resist the pressure of businessmen, who are against any contraction of credit.

A parliamentary committee of enquiry accepted the simple, perhaps simplistic, ideas of the Currency School and took the view that the recent instability and financial crises were caused by over-issues of notes by the Bank of England, which encouraged similar over-issues by other banks. So its freedom of action had to be limited and its fiduciary note-issue kept in proportion with its gold reserves. These conclusions, which were accepted by the Prime Minister, Sir Robert Peel, were in line with the feelings of the directors of the Bank, who raised no objections to the Act of 1844. This was the Bank Charter Act, which amended the charter of the Bank of England and was the most famous and important piece of banking legislation of the nineteenth century.

One of the aims of this Act was to discourage and restrain the issue of banknotes by country banks. No bank which had not been a bank of issue could become one, nor of course could any new bank. Those which already had the right were encouraged to renounce it by the offer of privileges of 'accommodation' with branches of the Bank of England, and in any case their issues were not allowed to exceed the average of the beginning of 1844. Once a bank ceased to issue notes, it lost the right to start again. All this amounted to a statement that note-issue would eventually become the monopoly of the Bank of England, but without haste or harsh measures of coercion. Thus country banknotes, which at the beginning of the nineteenth century had been the basic means of monetary circulation outside London, were to die a slow and natural death. In fact, their circulation had already much diminished; by 1840, i.e. before the Act, Bank of England notes formed more than three-quarters of the fiduciary currency. By the beginning of the twentieth century 'country notes' had become a curiosity. In 1910 there were only £250,000 in circulation, though it was only in 1921 that the last 'country bank' ceased to issue notes[20].

Restrictions, however, were imposed on the Bank of England too. Its 'issue' and its 'banking' departments were henceforward to be strictly separated, and the specie reserves of the former, which covered the note-issue, could not be used by the latter in moments of need, for example at a time of strong demand for discounting bills and for loans[21]. Moreover the note-issue was limited to a sum of £14 million,

---

[20] Mathias, *The First Industrial Nation*, p.356; J.H.Clapham, *An Economic History of Modern Britain* (3 vols, Cambridge, 1926–38), II, p. 340. The number of private issuing banks fell from 207 in 1844 to 104 in 1880 and again to 74 in 1890.

[21] In fact, in moments of crisis, it was the Banking Department which felt strong pressure, for notes did not lose the confidence of the public, who did not ask to exchange them for gold.

said to be 'fiduciary' or 'uncovered', beyond which any further issue had to be covered 100 per cent in bullion. What is ironical about this 1844 Act is that it was so strict that quite soon some of its provisions had to be disregarded. During the crisis of 1846, the banking department almost exhausted its reserves, while the issue department had plenty of bullion covering its notes in circulation. The Treasury allowed the Bank to draw on this, but it turned out to be unnecessary. Permission was again granted – and used – during the crisis of 1857, and the same request was nearly repeated in 1866 and 1890. On the whole, however, it is remarkable how few these infractions were[22].

It could be argued in retrospect that the Bank Act of 1844 was rather anachronistic. The controversy that raged between the Currency and the Banking schools had concentrated on the question of note-issue, without realizing that its importance to the economy was already waning. They took no account of the great increase in bank deposits and overdrafts, and the use of cheques, which were substitutes for banknotes and caused them to be less used. D.K. Adie has shown that, as early as 1822, the total of deposits in all banks was as great in value as that of notes in circulation, and that henceforth it increased more rapidly than fiduciary currency. But the Act of 1844 said nothing about deposits, thus leaving the Bank the discretionary powers that had been withdrawn from it in the case of note-issues; in fact a completely free hand. The Bank very quickly realized how much influence it could exert on the money supply and on the other banks by its management of deposits. Adie reckons that the Currency School, which had attempted to contest the whole principle of central banking or at least to subject it to strict rules, had only won a hollow victory. The legal shell of the Act remained, but in practice its basic principle became a dead letter[23].

The Bank Charter Act, however, remained the statutory base of the British banking system up to 1914. Starting from unrealistic assumptions, it ended by playing a role quite unlike that for which it had been cast. It failed to provide the Bank with a code of conduct that would allow it, by closely relating its issues to its reserves, to cushion the impact of cyclical fluctuations, while the progressive concentration of note-issue in the Bank's hands did not bring about the hoped-for stability. Its importance lay in the fact that, on the one hand, it put an

[22] Mathias, *The First Industrial Nation*, pp.356–7.

[23] Adie, 285–7, 296; also Mathias, *The First Industrial Nation*, pp. 492–3 (table 39), taken from R. Cameron (ed.), *Banking in the Early Stages of Industrialization* (London, 1967), p.42; and see p.333 (table 57). Adie considers that the drafters of the Act thought that the volume of deposits was insignificant.

end to any risk of serious state intervention in the monetary system and, on the other, in the eyes of public opinion, and particularly that of the world of business and finance, the debate was closed, and the Act of 1844 taken as final[24].

BANKS AFTER 1844

British banking history is rather calmer after 1844, in the twofold sense of showing less legislation of any importance and of seeing the accession of a more stable and consistent system[25]. There were, however, several major trends which developed slowly and without serious interruption.

The first is the way the Bank assumed its role as a central bank and perfected a policy of control over the currency within the framework of the gold standard. It began by withdrawing from the discount market. Between 1826 and 1844 the Bank had not sought discount business, leaving this to the discount houses and the commercial banks. Although, on the morrow of the 1844 Act, it redoubled its discounting activity, this was only for a short time and after 1846 it adopted a stance above and outside the bill market, keeping bank rate, i.e. its own rate of discount, markedly above the prevailing rate, except at times of crisis[26]. It remained a private bank, but renounced some opportunities of profit, so as to avoid conflict with its public responsibility as a regulator and a lender of last resort.

The principles of acting as regulator were theoretically simple. If the Bank started to lose gold – indicating a deficit in the balance of payments, due to a boom causing prices in England to rise too fast or to external causes such as excessively heavy imports of grain – it raised the bank rate, i.e. the price at which it was prepared to help as lender of last resort. Actually, up to 1847, when faced with heavy demands for rediscounts from the discount houses, it adopted the harsh expedient of rationing credit quantitatively[27]. The raising of bank rate warned businessmen that loans were going to cost more, and made them draw

[24] Checkland, *The Rise*, pp.200–1, who considers, however, that, as a result of the Act, the ratio of issues to the gold reserves was higher than it otherwise would have been.
[25] Court, p.102, who reckons that the system of the early Victorian era remained 'disconnected and unreliable'.
[26] But, according to R.A. Church, *The Great Victorian Boom, 1850–1873* (London, 1975), p.54, in the 1850s and 1860s, the Bank of England let its rate follow the market rates, and refused to try to influence economic activity.
[27] It was a tradition of the period previous to the partial repeal of the Usury Laws (1833, see note 4); but there was recourse to it again in 1836, 1839, 1847; Mathias, *The First Industrial Nation*, p.354.

in their horns, causing occasional bankruptcies among the more venturesome. The rise in prices would thus be halted, perhaps reversed, exports would increase, imports be reduced, the drain on the gold reserves arrested; the rise in the rate could also attract foreign money. The gold reserve would be replenished, the Bank could resume lending, reduce bank rate and so revive economic activity. However, actually exercising this form of guidance was no easier after 1844 than before, since everything depended on the efficient management of the Bank's gold reserves. Techniques of control were fairly crude. In times of excessive speculation and boom, in order to get results, severe and sudden shocks had to be administered to the business world by sharp rises in bank rate. Often the resulting recession was allowed to go on too long, inflicting severe loss and damage on the economy – and on society at large. Checkland considers that the Bank's manipulation of affairs was not always wise, and that it committed a long series of mistakes in managing its reserves up to 1857. From then onwards it displayed increasing skill in foreseeing and coping with crises. The crisis of 1866 was the last of the bank and money-market scares[28], though far from the last experienced on the Stock Exchange. The Bank became bolder in its handling of the bank rate, so as to exert an overall influence on short-term rates, not only in London and Britain, but in the entire world, and to control the economy, much more effectively, in many cases, than by its adjustment of note-circulation, although the vast size of deposits in the large clearing banks helped them to become increasingly independent of the central bank. The Bank of England perfected other techniques of restraining the market when it was in danger of running wild, and if this proved impracticable it arranged for orderly settlements. After 1873 'open market' operations, which had been tried out for a long time, became current practice. The Bank bought or sold government stock with a view to decreasing or increasing the money supply, thus ensuring an orderly expansion or contraction in liquidity and credit and avoiding scares. In spite of the difficult economic conditions at the end of the nineteenth century, and of certain weaknesses in its banking department, the Bank of England, after its notably long apprenticeship, managed to make the gold standard work smoothly and effectively, and keep the pound steady, by using the bank rate to influence the international flow of capital. It was effective from the British point of view. When there was a shortage of money in London, a rise in the bank rate was enough to

---

[28] The development of a national network of large banks contributed to the disappearance of these panics.

draw in gold from all over the world and get business moving again. The consequences could be awkward for other countries, who willy-nilly lost gold and had to put the brake on economic activity. But such were the advantages of being the dominant economic power[29].

The second major trend in banking history after 1844 was the renewed expansion and the greatly increased role of the joint-stock banks, as well as their drive towards amalgamation. Some of the restrictions imposed by the Bank Charter Act had slowed down or even stopped the growth of this new kind of bank, but it started up again vigorously in the 1860s[30], thanks in part to an Act of 1858, extended in 1862, which gave banks the facilities of obtaining limited liability, which the Act of 1856 had awarded to other companies. Some banks were slow to take advantage of this concession for fear of alarming their clients[31]: others were less inhibited, and particularly the chief private banks in London, and many provincial ones converted to limited liability during the 1860s.

There was thus a noticeable shrinkage in the number of private banks, caused as much by conversion to joint-stock as by failure or mergers. Small country banks had to accept, or even seek, amalgamation with joint-stock banks, for these were attracting the major share of new clientele and new business and offered services the others could not match[32]. Later on, small joint-stock banks had to let themselves be absorbed by the larger ones, for the same reasons[33], with the result that, with some additional disappearances and failures, the total number of joint-stock banks remained unchanged at first and eventually became much smaller, as table 56 shows:

[29]　For all this, see Court, p. 188; Checkland, *The Rise*, pp.194–5, 200–2, 212; Mathias, *The First Industrial Nation*, pp.357–8; also F.W.Fetter, *Development of British Monetary Orthodoxy, 1797–1875* (Cambridge,Mass., 1965).

[30]　It is true that the boom in launching joint-stock banks in the 1860s (108 between 1863 and 1866 according to Anderson and Cottrell, 603) included a fair number of 'finance companies' (cf. p. 335), not to mention shady and ephemeral ventures.

[31]　These scruples disappeared after the fraudulent bankruptcy of the City of Glasgow Bank, an unlimited joint-stock company, had ruined in 1878 its many shareholders.

[32]　For all this and what follows, see Clapham, *An Economic History . . .* , II, pp.340–2, III, pp.278–82; Mathias, *The First Industrial Nation*, p.352 (who gives 172 as the number of private banks in the provinces in the 1880s); also P.Mathias, 'Capital and entrepreneurship as factor markets in British industry, 1750–1914', in K.Nakagawa (ed.), *Marketing and Finance in the Course of Industrialization: Proceedings of the Third Fuji Conference* (Tokyo, 1978), pp. 208–10; R.S.Sayers, *A History of Economic Change in England, 1880–1939* (London, 1967), pp.152–3; Anderson and Cottrell, 600, 602, according to whom the number of private banks in England and Wales fell from 273 in 1844 to 157 in 1857.

[33]　Between 1826 and 1865 joint-stock banks took over 129 private banks. Between 1865 and 1885 there were on average five amalgamations a year; Clapham, *An Economic History*, III, p.278.

Table 56 Banks in England and Wales[34]

	Private	Joint-stock
1841	321	115
1875	252	120
1886	251	117

Up to the middle of the 1880s, the decline of private banks and the process of amalgamation had not yet proceeded very far – in contrast to Scotland, which, with its long-established tradition of joint-stock banking, had no more private banks as early as 1864, and only thirteen joint-stock banks, falling to ten in 1886 and nine in 1914[35]. However, private banks were nearly all small, with few branches, while joint-stock banks held between them in 1886 over one-half of all deposits and dominated the banking scene. They varied in size, but about ten of them were very large, with more than fifty branches each. Few banks had had branches prior to 1830, but they had begun to spring up around that year in Lancashire and this process had been very active in the 1840s and 1850s. In 1864, there were 1016 head offices and branches in England[36], and 2712 in 1880.

After 1890, the move towards consolidation accelerated[37] as well as the increase in branches. The two developments are related: small banks became branches of the large ones, but there was also a deliberate policy on the part of 'alligators' (to use Mathias's expression) to expand and draw in more private savings. Between 1891 and 1902 as many as 114 bank amalgamations took place. The total number of independent banking firms fell from 168 in 1891 to 66 in 1914. Of these, 20 had more than 100 branches and 3 (Midland, Lloyds and Barclays) had more than 500 each[38]. Besides these giants, which operated nation-wide, there were a number of joint-stock banks with

[34] Limited to commercial banks dealing in strictly English business, writes Clapham so not including London institutions aiming their activity overseas (cf. p.333–5).

[35] And where also the density of branches in relation to population was definitely higher than in England. There were 1800 in 1914.

[36] 73 per cent of them belonging to joint-stock banks, some of whom already had more than 100 branches.

[37] Clapham, *An Economic History* . . . III, p. 280, sees the influence of the Baring crisis in 1890, when one of the most eminent private banks nearly crashed, which would have tarnished the prestige of private banking. Sayers, *A History*, p. 153, considers significant the creation in 1896 of Barclays Bank, by the merger of many private banks, most of them ancient, and often Quaker.

[38] Mathias, *The First Industrial Nation*, p. 352, adds to these three banks the District Bank and Martins Bank, which would have formed the Big Five. On the other hand, C. Kindleberger, *The Formation of Financial Centers: A Study in Comparative Economic History* (Princeton, 1974), pp.13–16, includes in these five the Westminster Bank and the National Provincial Bank. According to Sayers, *A History*, p.153, it was only during the first world war that the concept of the Big Five emerged.

local or regional branch networks, particularly in Lancashire, where quite a few remained independent, others without branches, and also a dozen private banks which were to disappear after the first world war[39]. But while the number of banks declined sharply, the number of branches increased, reaching the figure of 7747 in 1913. The biggest banks had branches all over the country, even in the smallest of towns.

Meanwhile, the larger provincial banks found it necessary to set up in London so as to make a more efficient and profitable use of their deposits. It was no longer enough to have a correspondent in the capital, an associated bank or a branch. Many of the largest banks had, in fact, started in the provinces. The founder of Lloyds Bank (which started in Birmingham in 1765) came from a family of Welsh ironmasters. Then, after having expanded considerably in the provinces after 1860, it took over two London banks in 1884 and set up a main office in London, but it did not transfer its headquarters there until 1910. The Midland Bank came to London in 1891, having also started in Birmingham, but as a joint-stock bank, in 1836. The National Provincial, as its name suggests, had been founded in 1833 specifically to operate outside the 65-mile radius round London, but it set up there in 1864, having already 122 branches. On the whole, it was through takeovers of London banks that these provincial newcomers, thrusting and ambitious, set themselves up in the metropolis and so acquired nation-wide status. There were also movements in the opposite direction, such as the formation of Barclays Bank in 1896[40].

It must be emphasized that all the banks we have been discussing were commercial or 'clearing banks', members of the London Clearing House. They took in deposits from their local clientele and used them for short-term loans to businesses, large and small, through discounts, advances on security and overdrafts. Some funds were invested in government securities, some in bills of exchange, but usually there was little direct contact with international transactions, though these banks had begun to take some interest in them on the eve of the first world war[41]. Nor did they indulge in long-term investment, e.g. taking up shares in other firms. On the whole their methods changed very little[42]. However, they profited without much exertion from the

---

[39] Again this concerns only commercial banks.

[40] Kindleberger, pp.13–16; Clapham, *An Economic History* ... III, p. 281; also R.S.Sayers, *Lloyds Bank in the History of English Banking* (Oxford, 1957), which is the best of the monographs on banks.

[41] Sayers, *A History*, pp.152–3. Lloyds opened a branch in Paris in 1913.

[42] The practices of the London clearing banks have been studied by G.A.E. Goodhart, *The Business of Banking, 1891–1914* (London, 1972), who does point out certain changes.

considerable changes in financial methods that occurred in the nineteenth century, particularly in its second half.

There was a decline in the use of 'inland' bills of exchange as a means of settling accounts and transferring money, and, on the other hand, a rapid increase in bank deposits, and in the use of cheques and credit transfers for making payments, as table 57 shows[43].

The figures reveal an enormous increase in deposit banking, the amount of bank deposits largely exceeding, in the last third of the century, the total value of cash, banknotes and bills of exchange. Savings were thus tapped by the banks on a massive scale and put to productive use, but, according to the rules of financial orthodoxy, on a short-term basis only.

Clearing banks were not, however, the only credit institutions in Great Britain – far from it. But the British banking system was characterized by specialization, with many different kinds of banks and financial institutions, each functioning in one particular sphere[44]. There were no mixed banks dealing both in short-term and long-term credit, such as figured prominently in other countries, especially Germany. The most important of these other banks were well established and continued to follow their own path, though with occasional deviation. Such were the merchant banks, which at the end of the nineteenth century were rather called accepting houses, since

Table 57 Money-stock and means of payment in England and Wales

	Bank deposits	Structure of means of payment (as percentages of total)			
	(£m)	Specie	Banknotes	Bank deposits	Other means (a)
1831	40	18	17	24	40
1844	81	16	13	37	34
1855	145	13	7	39	41
1875	409	18	6	70	6
1913	1075				

(a) Chiefly bills of exchange.

---

[43] Taken from Mathias, *The First Industrial Nation*, pp.492–3 (table 39), himself using Cameron *et al*. The passing away of the inland bill was accelerated by the crisis of 1866. But it was only in the 1870s that the banking habit prevailed in industrial districts; Anderson and Cottrell, p.615; Church, *The Great Victorian Boom*, p. 54.

[44] In this connection let us mention some more modest types of credit institution:
(a) trustee savings banks, which started *c*. 1804 and were aimed at encouraging saving in the working classes;
(b) building societies, which lent on mortgage to people who wanted to become house-owners. They were numerous at the end of the nineteenth century, but their business almost entirely local then;
(c) investment trusts, which appeared in the 1860s.

one of their principal activities was accepting bills of exchange drawn on or for a foreign house and undertaking thus to pay them on maturity. But they also dealt in long-term credit, by issuing on the London Stock Exchange the shares, bonds and any other form of security of British or foreign firms which operated abroad, and foreign or colonial governments[45]. Their activity was mostly at the international level. Curiously enough, the heads of these firms were the aristocracy of the city, a narrow but not exclusive élite, which included, from an early date, families of foreign origin, notably the Barings and the Rothschilds, who were the leaders, but also newcomers of the same provenance such as the Hambros, Morgans, Goschens, Oppenheims, Lazards and others. It was from this charmed circle that the Governor and directors of the Bank of England were normally chosen, rather than from the heads of the clearing banks[46].

There were also the discount houses. Having dominated the discount market for inland bills, which flourished exceedingly in the middle of the nineteenth century, they had to turn elsewhere for business when this means of transferring funds became obsolescent. They had also suffered in reputation with the spectacular collapse of the leading firm Overend and Gurney in 1866. So the London discount market started to move towards the financing of international trade, where the great majority of payments were made by bills on London, or at least drawn in sterling. Vast numbers of these 'foreign bills' were negotiated, discounted or rediscounted in London, whither foreign capital seeking short-term and profitable employment was also attracted. So the discount houses assumed on the international scene the same intermediary role as they had played at home when they first started, developing a call market for foreign funds[47].

Even since the Napoleonic wars, London had been the financial centre of the world, the mart where international transactions were financed and settled, and where foreigners could lend or borrow money freely. But this activity expanded enormously and took on a new dimension in the second half of the nineteenth century, and especially after 1880. In addition to foreign bankers who came and settled in London, many foreign and British colonial banks opened branches there. Especially after the Acts of 1858 and 1862, 'Anglo-Foreign' banks started to appear, i.e. banks that were registered and had their

[45] They are also sometimes called investment bankers or issuing houses.
[46] See Checkland, *The Rise*, pp.205–6, 209–11, who mentions the fears kindled by the 'money power' and fanned by antisemitism and xenophobia.
[47] Mathias, *The First Industrial Nation*, pp. 358–60.

head-office in London, and whose capital and management were mostly English, but which operated overseas. There were Anglo-Indian banks, the first of which dated from 1842, followed by others founded in the 1850s, whose activities also extended to China and which dealt largely in foreign exchange. Later, in the 1860s, came a crop of 'finance companies', i.e. investment banks rather on the lines of the French *Crédit mobilier*, with which or with other French groups they sometimes had links. Some of them had the backing of well-established banks, but others were just speculative, even rather dubious enterprises, e.g. those that dabbled in the Egyptian boom during the cotton famine to take advantage of the usurious rates of interest that prevailed there. Most of them collapsed in the crisis of 1866, but some survived to play a minor part on the British financial scene, where 'investment banking' never really took root[48].

The City gradually became the centre of international finance, and this helps to explain how it came to be accused of turning its back on its own country and British industry – a subject we shall tackle later[49].

THE FINANCING OF ECONOMIC GROWTH

Of course, the same accusation has been directed against the entire British banking system, which has been reproached for its rigid orthodoxy. A bank whose clients may have their deposits back on demand, or after only a brief delay, cannot afford to sink them in long-term investments, which are not quickly realizable and may even be risky, such as loans to industrial enterprises for creating fixed capital or a share in the equity of some other firm. Banks must at all times maintain a prudent degree of liquidity. Recent research has shown, however, that these rules of orthodoxy were not always observed, at any rate during the actual Industrial Revolution, in the eighteenth century and at the beginning of the nineteenth. It is true that banks (especially country banks) did not as a rule grant long-term loans to industrial firms, but so many exceptions to this rule have been found that the whole generalization seems in doubt. Cases have been

---

[48] Checkland, *The Rise*, pp.206–7. On the finance companies see, for example: D.S.Landes, *Bankers and Pashas: International Finance and Economic Imperialism in Egypt* (London, 1958), notably pp.52ff; P.L.Cottrell, 'London financiers and Austria, 1863–1875; The Anglo-Austrian Bank', *Business History* XI (2), July 1969, 106–19; ibid., 'Anglo-French financial co-operation, 1850–1880', *Journal of European Economic History* III (1), Spring 1974, 54–86.

[49] Mathias, *The First Industrial Nation*, p. 353.

found of straightforward loans by banks to businesses that needed capital for expansion, and cases, undoubtedly more numerous, of short-term loans which were renewed several times (not always willingly on the part of the bank, but the undesirable alternative was to bankrupt its debtors), so that they actually became long-term and were used for investment in fixed assets.

It was only gradually that orthodoxy and conservative principles over loans became general and that clearing banks abstained entirely from investment in industry. Mathias has drawn attention to this development, but dates the triumph of orthodoxy after 1850 or even 1860, though it would appear that links between banks and industry, as regards long-term loans, had been getting weaker during the preceding decades. Certainly a number of country banks had burnt their fingers in such ventures and even ended by going bankrupt. City banks on the other hand had always been more conservative than provincial ones, and the views of their chairmen and directors reported by the national press, by parliamentary enquiries, and by many pamphlets could not but influence opinion. Above all, even if the earliest joint-stock banks had not perforce behaved more cautiously than private banks, the rise of large banks with many branches and the consolidation of the banking system into a small number of very large firms had a lot to do with the triumph of orthodoxy. Branch managers had only limited freedom of action, while pressure from head offices was always in the direction of caution. Sayers' view is that initially these very large banks were over-centralized and not sufficiently flexible in meeting the needs of their clients[50]. Anyway, English banks of the late nineteenth century did not supply long-term financial support to industry comparable with that provided by their contemporaries, the German *Grosse Banken* (recently, however, doubt has been cast on the importance of the latter's role, which may have been overrated)[51].

All the same, it would be absurd to suggest that banks played only a very small part in the industrialization and economic growth of Victorian Britain. The banking system was highly efficient in

[50]   ibid., p. 352; P. Mathias, 'Capital, credit and enterprise in the Industrial Revolution', *Journal of European Economic History*, II (1), Spring 1973, 121–43, especially 135–9; Mathias, 'Capital and entrepreneurship', pp.209–11, F. Crouzet (ed.), *Capital Formation in the Industrial Revolution* (London, 1972) pp.46–8, 180–2; Sayers, *A History*, p. 153.

[51]   In his long review of the book by Cameron *et al.*, L.S.Pressnell, 'Money, finance and industrialization', *Business History* XI (2), July 1969, 128–33, see 131, is sceptical about the superiority of the German system.

providing short-term credit in the form of discounted bills, advances and overdrafts, the usefulness of which cannot be overemphasized. For industrialists it was an easy source of part of their circulating capital, which, in the early nineteenth century and even in large-scale industry, formed a high proportion of all capital employed; and this left them free to use their own funds for long-term investment in fixed capital. The indirect contribution of banks came from the credit they granted to merchants and the support they gave to the trade-credit system as a whole. This enabled manufacturers to get credit from the merchants that supplied their raw materials, and in turn to grant credit to their customers, as they could discount their bills upon the latter or obtain advances from the commission agents to whom they consigned their goods. Finally, deposit banks were the intermediaries through which the savings of all classes, rich or not so rich, were mobilized for the provision of credit and made productive, instead of being sterilized in hoards. Checkland has asserted that the renovation of the British economy in the nineteenth century was 'in one sense an act of continuous mobilization of capital', a process in which the banks played a vital part[52]. Moreover, in spite of fluctuations in interest rates, the nineteenth century was a period during which, on the whole, rates were low and credit cheap and readily available[53].

This brings us back to the question touched on earlier in these pages: how was long-term finance organized in the British economy, especially for investment in fixed capital? It is important to understand that the great majority of industrial and commercial enterprises in the nineteenth century belonged to a single owner, or to a few partners, who were often friends or relations[54]. Their initial capital would be contributed by the working partners, supplemented often by relatives or friends, who would be, in effect, sleeping partners, or who might grant loans. One might also obtain a loan on a mortgage or from a wealthy merchant with whom the new firm would deal. Expansion

---

[52] Checkland, *The Rise*, p. 189. And of course the money market in London continued to play an important role in the short-term financing of economic activity.

[53] It is true that this was a period when currency was stable and even appreciated in the long term, so that there was no lightening of the debt burden by inflation – quite the opposite in fact.

[54] See P.L.Payne, *British Entrepreneurship in the Nineteenth Century* (London, 1974), pp.17–19, on the advantages of the partnership, which minimized risks, was flexible and adaptable, 'kaleidoscopic' by nature, allowing a firm to accumulate the necessary capital and expertise. It answered the needs of most sectors of the economy during nearly the whole of the nineteenth century. But it sometimes became the arena for violent conflicts, not least among members of the same family.

would be self-financed[55], by ploughing back at once the major share of profits – actually an inadequate expression since such profits had never left the business. This form of reinvestment would not be so drastic as in the heroic days of the Industrial Revolution, when the founders of businesses paid themselves little more than the wage of a skilled worker, and for years reinvested all their profits, while leading a life of Spartan frugality. Times had changed, and convention imposed a certain standard of living on the middle classes. Besides, a number of businesses had prospered and grown so much that they had reached a size that their owners judged large enough; many of them, too, preferred not to have all their eggs in one basket, so that new profits were not reinvested in the firm but elsewhere – in the purchase of landed property (an old-established tradition) or in stocks and shares, especially after the 1830s and 1840s, in railway securities. At all events, partnerships displayed a remarkable ability to expand without having to change their mode of organization.

However, one significant aspect of economic development in the nineteenth century was the increase in the number of joint-stock and limited-liability companies, and their calls on a large public, not just small groups of friends and relations, to raise the capital they needed. Both public opinion and the law were for long opposed to those kinds of companies, and it was only in 1825 that parliamentary sanction ceased to be necessary for joint-stock companies, and in 1856 and 1862 that the last restriction on the formation of limited-liability companies was abolished. Still, one must not overestimate the effect of this legislation. Even before 1825 there were various legal devices, such as equitable trusts, which enabled joint-stock companies to be formed without legislative sanction[56].

The use to which these new dispensations were put varied very much in different sectors of the economy. It has been seen that the joint-stock company, which had been the usual form chosen by canals, was taken up almost without exception by the railway entrepreneurs, who needed vast quantities of capital. Although shareholders in the early companies were mostly local people, after 1840 capital poured in from all over the country, while in the boom of 1844–6 the City played a prominent part. We have already described how the appearance of railway shares widened the activity of the London Stock Exchange, which up till then

---

[55] With the traditional appeal to relatives, friends and business contacts in case of difficulties or need for heavy investment.

[56] But these procedures were little used, notably in industry (in spite of some cases in mining and metal-smelting companies at the beginning of the nineteenth century), which shows that the need for them was not acute.

had dealt almost exclusively in government stock, how it was responsible for the establishment of provincial stock exchanges, how it boosted the capital market and investment in stocks and shares. The joint-stock company, financed by the issue of shares or some other form of stock, became more common and even prevalent in those sectors where it had existed prior to 1825, e.g. docks, harbours, water- and gas-works; also among shipping, telegraph and insurance firms, and we have just seen how it spread through the banking system. But this was not the case in manufacturing industry. It is true that during speculative booms, such as that of 1836, industrial joint-stock companies were formed, but few of them succeeded and survived. For instance, several companies of this kind were founded in the South Wales iron industry, but nearly all of them disappeared quickly[57].

The legislation of 1856 and 1862 opened the way to the 'corporate economy' (Payne), but industrial firms were in no hurry to take advantage of it, neither to obtain limited liability nor to draw capital from the deep pockets of the British public via the Stock Exchange. It was only among industries undergoing rapid change, where technological progress demanded heavy capital investment in large-scale plant that many firms soon became public companies with limited liability: iron and steel, chemicals, shipbuilding, some food-processing industries and, for special reasons, brewing. On the other hand, the traditional family partnership continued heavily predominant in textiles, metal-working, ceramics and, of course, wholesale and retail trade. In 1885, only 5 to 10 per cent of the major industrial firms had converted to limited-liability companies, though admittedly these were usually the biggest in their particular branch.

The Stock Exchange for long dealt mainly in government and railway securities, British or foreign. In 1883, the total nominal value of these two categories represented 93 per cent of the total value of securities which were quoted on the London Stock Exchange. The remaining 7 per cent represented mainly stock in public utilities, with genuinely industrial shares only forming under 1 per cent of the total. This increased to 2.5 per cent in 1893 and 8 per cent in 1913, or £872 million out of a face value of £11,000 million for all securities quoted on the Stock Exchange. The percentage remains roughly the same if securities quoted in provincial stock exchanges are included[58]. On the

[57] For all this and what follows, see Mathias, *The First Industrial Nation*, pp.383–6; Mathias, 'Capital and entrepreneurship', pp. 211–16; Payne, *British Entrepreneurship*, pp. 19–23; Sayers, *A History*, pp.145–6, 150.
[58] Although there was a lull after the end of the railway booms, they came to life again after 1870–80, thanks to the conversion of industrial firms into public companies,

eve of the first world war, when there was a surge of new share-issues by industrial firms, it appears that the money thus subscribed amounted to only a fifth of total net investment in Great Britain. More than half of all investment in industry came from profits ploughed back. As for new firms, their capital was usually raised privately, from the founders' own pockets, and from their friends and wealthy relations. The role of the Stock Exchange and the official capital market was marginal; and was even more so, of course, in previous decades. As Mathias has justly remarked, these conditions were reminiscent of the eighteenth century[59]. It was unusual, moreover, for a new firm to be established from the start as a public company and raise capital by issuing shares through the Stock Exchange. That body had very strict rules concerning the minimum amount of capital to be raised; moreover, the procedure was expensive and apt to raise suspicions. Stock issues were usually made by large and well-known firms seeking more capital for expanding. In contrast, small savers did not invest in industrial companies, which were considered risky, but preferred government stocks and railway or public-utilities securities. Industrials were bought by the rich or by institutions.

Although after the 1880s there was a distinct rise in the number of industrial public companies and of their shares offered to the public, the heads of firms seeking external capital had no intention of risking the loss of control of their businesses. Very often, when a partnership turned into a joint-stock company, the partners would retain a majority of the shares, only allowing a minority to fall into the hands of the public. Or else they would issue debentures, or preference shares, which took precedence for dividend payment over ordinary shares, and had a kind of guaranteed fixed dividend, but carried no vote. Ordinary shares, which had the right to a vote, would be kept for the original partners and their families, thus perpetuating control by the founding dynasty. A much-used device, though it was only legalized in 1907, was that of the private company, which was not allowed to make a public issue of shares, but which did enjoy limited liability. Although it might have difficulty in raising fresh capital, it retained all the advantages of a partnership, e.g. secrecy and absolute family control, without any of its disadvantages, such as the need for reconstitution each time a partner died or retired, and *un*limited liability.

---

which was easier and less expensive than in London; but W.A.Thomas, *The Provincial Stock Exchanges* (London, 1973), thinks that none the less the role of the issues launched there was marginal.

[59]   Mathias, 'Capital and entrepreneurship', pp. 213–15.

So it was that the development of public limited companies at the turn of the nineteenth century does not seem to have triggered off any clear move towards a separation of the functions of owning and managing business firms. Both remained in the same hands and the same dynasties. The managerial revolution, which brought about their separation, had barely begun at the outbreak of the first world war, when a few big combines, huge but badly managed, were reorganized under the guidance of men who possessed only a fraction of their equity capital. Prior to this, changes in the corporate shape of firms had been purely cosmetic. The development of the public company, by making it easier to raise fresh capital, had simply reinforced the primacy of the large firms and of the families that controlled them.

To sum up: although railways and other public utilities got their funds from the capital market, neither the banks nor the Stock Exchange contributed very much towards long-term investment in British manufacturing industry. This has been seen as one of the causes of the latter's decline, and British industrialists have been blamed for not being more outward-looking in their search for the capital (and talent) they needed (a need which has yet to be substantiated). It must be borne in mind, however, that in every western country, with the possible exception of the United States, nineteenth-century industrial firms were family businesses[60].

---

[60] P.L.Cottrell, *Industrial Finance, 1830–1914: The Finance and Organization of English Manufacturing Industry* (London, 1980).

11 Foreign trade and the export of capital

Great Britain's foreign trade in the nineteenth century has often been described as a strategic factor in her economic growth, the changing rates of which are supposed to have been closely connected with those of the volume of trade. An analysis set out in an earlier chapter shows that this view needs to be considerably qualified, inasmuch as demand from overseas markets was only an engine of growth during short periods of Britain's economic history in the eighteenth and nineteenth centuries. It has been also shown that only the cotton industry depended on exports to dispose of the bulk of its production, though other industries gained in efficiency through having the wider outlets provided by foreign markets[1].

It would, however, be absurd to deny the great importance to Britain of her foreign trade, particularly after the 1840s, when the ratio (in value) of imports, as of exports, to national product increased appreciably and became really high. If one takes three-year averages of exports and retained imports, the ratio grows from 10 per cent of British national income for 1830/9 to 17 per cent for 1850/9, to 30 per cent for 1870/9, and is only slightly lower at 27 per cent in 1900/13[2]. As population increased a good deal more rapidly than agricultural production, which became static after the 1870s, Britain had to import

---

[1]   As this problem and some others relative to foreign trade, e.g. the effect of free trade, the exports of the main industries, etc., have been dealt with earlier, we will not touch on them again in this chapter.

[2]   S.B. Saul, 'The export economy, 1870–1914', *Yorkshire Bulletin of Economic and Social Research*, 17(1), May 1965, 5 (table 1). See Chapter 5, p.115 (table 25), for the ratio exports/GNP. As regards net imports, their ratio to national income rises from 12 per cent in 1820 to 18 per cent in 1850 and to 26 per cent in 1900; Mathias, *The First Industrial Nation: An Economic History of Britain, 1700–1914* (London, 1969), p.244 (table IV(d)). According to P.Deane and W.A. Cole, *British Economic Growth, 1688–1959* (Cambridge, 2nd edn, 1967), pp.310, 311 (note 1), this ratio reached its peak at 36 per cent in 1880/4 and fluctuated afterwards until 1914 between 29 and 32 per cent; but these figures seem to apply to *total* imports.

more and more foodstuffs, in fact over half her total consumption in 1913. She also depended more and more on imported raw materials, either because her own resources, such as metal ores and wool, had become inadequate, or because new technologies called for new raw materials that she did not produce, e.g. oil and rubber. In 1913 seven-eighths of the raw materials processed in Britain, apart from coal[3], were imported, and the life of the country depended on a huge and increasing volume of imports that had to be paid for by providing the world with goods and services. But it is anachronistic to regard exports as designed solely to pay for imports. They were the fruit of long-established usages in several staple industries, of vantage-points gained by virtue of Britain's early industrialization and preserved by her sustained and successful efforts. Her exports also provided employment to many of her working people.

Britain depended far more on foreign trade than other powers, with the exception of the smaller advanced countries such as Switzerland and Belgium, whose per-capita exports were even higher than Britain's[4]. In the middle of the nineteenth century she had established a very specialized and exceptional position in the world economy, selling manufactured goods to the world and importing primary produce on a massive scale. In 1850 she made over 40 per cent of the world's output of manufactured goods that entered international trade, and by 1876/80 she had 30 per cent of world trade in primary produce[5]. She was by far the greatest commercial power, with a quarter of all

[3]   Mathias, *The First Industrial Nation*, p.249.
[4]   P. Bairoch, 'European foreign trade in the 19th century: the development of the value and volume of exports (preliminary results)', *Journal of European Economic History*, II(1), Spring 1973, 5–36, see 17 (table 5), 18. In fact, Switzerland was always in the lead in this respect, but Belgium outstripped England at a late stage.
[5]   See some interesting remarks of Mathias, *The First Industrial Nation*, pp.250–1. It was often thought that the growth of world trade, particularly in the new conditions created by free trade, would lead to a strengthening of this specialization in favour of Great Britain. It was thought that the complementarity of the 'workshop of the world' and the economies supplying her with primary produce would grow. So the United States was seen, except by a few engineers who had observed American industry, as a great reservoir of cotton, grain and meat for England. In fact, some of these economies, complementary to and dependent on England, survived or emerged, with England as the main buyer of a few of their products – nitrates and copper from Chile, guano from Peru, wines from Portugal, then meat from Argentina, meat and dairy produce from Denmark and New Zealand, etc. P. Bairoch *(Commerce extérieur et développement économique de l'Europe au XIXe siècle* (Paris–The Hague, 1976), p.260) notes that small European countries had to opt for one or other of two possible strategies of development: to be complementary with England, the dominant economy, by selling her primary produce (Denmark, Portugal, Norway), or to compete with her by industrializing (Belgium, Switzerland, Sweden). But the vision outlined above did not come about, because England did not remain the only developed country and industrialization brought her serious rivals.

international trade passing through her ports, and retained this position, although by a steadily decreasing margin, up to 1914[6].

These questions have been dealt with elsewhere but there are three aspects of the history of British foreign trade that are worth further study: the various stages of its growth; its composition, i.e. what imports and exports consisted of; and its geographical distribution. But Britain's commercial dealings overseas were not confined to visible merchandise trade; there was also an important invisible trade, supplying services and capital. This is of particular importance since Britain was able to maintain her very strong position in this section, compensating for her setbacks in visible trade, so that by 1914 she continued to hold a central role in the world economy.

BRITAIN'S OVERSEAS TRADE

The increase in the *volume* of Britain's foreign trade, is the most significant fact, since in this index the influence of price movements has been eliminated so as to reveal *real* trends[7]. The result is shown in table 58 in two complementary forms.

There was a rapid growth in trade between the end of the Napoleonic wars and the early 1870s, with a marked acceleration in the case of exports. To be more precise, exports grew only slowly during the ten years following the wars[8], then they show a very rapid rise between 1826 and 1856, with a mean rate of increase of 5.6 per cent per year; then there was a slow-down, and in spite of the boom which reached its peak in 1873, the rate of growth between 1856 and that year was only 3.8 per cent[9]. The movement of imports was somewhat different, but taking total foreign trade, one finds that the most rapid growth was during the third quarter of the nineteenth century, between the 1840s

[6]   See Introduction, pp.7–9; also Bairoch, *Commerce extérieur*, pp.77 (table 18), 78; Bairoch, 'European foreign trade' p. 14 (table 3). He thinks that GB's share in Europe's total exports increased up to 1870.

[7]   We have seen in Chapter 5 how the sharp fall in the price of manufactured goods during the first half of the nineteenth century caused the value of exports to increase very slowly (1.1 per cent per annum between 1814 and 1846). Similarly, during the Great Depression, values grew much more slowly than volume. But the opposite was the case during the third quarter of the nineteenth century, a period of rising prices. For current values of trade see Mathias, *The First Industrial Nation*, pp.467–8; B.R. Mitchell and P. Deane, *Abstract of British Historical Statistics* (Cambridge, 1962), pp. 282–4.

[8]   From 1814/16 to 1825/7, the rate of growth was only 2 per cent per annum. Protectionism in continental states and the loss of purchasing power by primary producers at a time of falling prices probably contributed to their decline.

[9]   Unlike the others, these rates have been calculated by the method of exponential adjustment.

Table 58 UK foreign trade

	Exports	Net imports (a)		Total of exports and net imports
A. Annual average rates of growth in volume (%)				
1811–41	4.0			4.0
1821–51	4.7			4.4
1831–61	4.5			4.5
1841–71	4.9			4.6
1851–81	3.8			4.1
1861–91	3.1			3.5
1871–1901	2.3			2.9
1881–1911	2.7			2.5
B. Indices of volume (1880 = 100) and annual averages rates of growth				
1814/16	7		6	
		3.5%		4.8%
1836/8	15		17	
		4.9		4.3
1872/4	86		78	
		1.8		3.0
1900/2	143		177	
		4.4		1.9
1911/13	229		217	

Sources
A: Deane and Cole, p. 311 (table 83). The rates of growth are calculated between decade averages centring on the years specified. Table 8, p. 29, gives the same series of figures for the last column, except for a rate of 3.4 per cent for 1811–41. The data used by Deane and Cole come from Imlah.

B: Based on data from *Abstract,* pp. 328–9, using Imlah's indices.
The annual average rates of growth taken over a long period are the same for 1814/16 to 1911/13 as they are for 1836/8 to 1900/2, namely 3.5 per cent for exports, 3.7 percent for imports.
(a) That is after deduction of re-exports.

and the early 1870s; but it was scarcely less rapid in the previous decades, and there was a rate of growth of more than 4 per cent per year for the whole of the period 1811–81[10].

As already noticed, the Great Victorian Boom is only slightly reflected in the volume of foreign trade[11]; it is part of a long swing, extending from 1826 to 1873, during which conditions were, on the whole, very favourable to Britain. At the beginning of this period her

[10] So there is some discrepancy with the growth of industrial production, whose highest rates are thought to have been in the 1820s and 1830s. On the other hand there is agreement with the growth of real national product, which seems to have been highest in the third quarter of the nineteenth century. Nevertheless foreign trade grew distinctly faster, which led to its growing importance in relation to national product and to a large contribution of exports to the latter's growth.
[11] But where the *value* of trade was concerned there was an enormous expansion. Combined imports and exports quadrupled in the twenty-five years from 1848 to 1873. In the short run, trade was violently disturbed in the 1860s by the American civil war.

trade enjoyed unrivalled predominance thanks to the availability of goods for current consumption, which were mass produced, cheap, but durable, well finished, adapted to their various markets, and meeting with hardly any competition[12]. Towards the middle of the century several European countries, and the United States, had progressed with their own Industrial Revolutions but, except in the case of a few special products, they were unable to offer Britain any serious competition in third markets. On the other hand, their own incipient industrialization gave rise to a strong demand for machinery and plant, and of course coal, which Britain was particularly well placed to satisfy, inasmuch as a considerable liberation of trade from tariff restrictions was achieved[13]. At the same time improvements in sea- and rail-transport, the expansion of new countries and 'new frontiers', the opening up of underdeveloped countries (sometimes by gunboat diplomacy) created or enlarged new markets and new sources of supply in distant lands. Britain bought increasing amounts of primary products from these countries, and so provided them with the means of purchasing simple consumption goods, such as textiles, and some capital goods, for all of which she was undoubtedly the best supplier[14]. For a brief period, the growth of both the developed and the underdeveloped countries helped British trade.

The situation changed in the last quarter of the century when there was a sharp fall in the growth-rate of British foreign trade. Exports were particularly affected. Their decennial growth-rate, in volume, fell continuously, down to 1 per cent per annum between 1890 and 1900[15], while, owing to falling prices, their value stagnated until 1895. The growth of imports also slowed down, though less markedly, since larger imports of foodstuffs were needed to keep up with the growth in population and the higher real incomes resulting from improved terms

[12]   Remarks of M. Lévy-Leboyer, *Les Banques européennes et l'industrialisation internationale dans la première moitié du XIXe siècle* (Paris, 1964), pp.148ff.

[13]   But it came late on the continental side and probably had only a limited influence; cf. Chapter 5.

[14]   Just as she was in a position to buy most of their primary products. In 1881/4 still she was consuming most of the sugar imported into Europe.

[15]   Bairoch, 'European foreign trade', 25 (table 9); Bairoch, *Commerce extérieur*, p.76 (table 17). Percentage rates of annual average growth of exports by volume (between three-year averages, centring on year specified):

	United Kingdom	Germany
1860–70	3.8	6.7
1870–80	2.6	2.3
1880–90	2.7	2.2
1890–1900	1.0	4.2
1900–10	3.8	5.7

of trade and lower prices. This difference between the growth of exports and imports caused a large increase in the trade deficit. The rate of growth, in volume, of total foreign trade fell to below 3 per cent per year between 1871 and 1901, and was no more than 2.5 per cent during the three decades that preceded the first world war. However, after 1895, exports recovered vigorously in volume, and even more in value thanks to rising prices – altogether the most satisfactory feature of the Edwardian era. Meanwhile the volume of imports slowed down further, probably because average real incomes were stagnating.

It is not hard to find reasons for the slowing down of the growth of British exports at the end of the nineteenth century. One was the Great Depression, a world phenomenon which hit all branches of international trade. Another was the spread of industrialization which not only produced two industrial giants, Germany and the United States, but also affected many other countries to a lesser degree. We have already seen how industrialization in Asia reacted on British exports of cotton yarn and cloth. Another reason, not unrelated to this last phenomenon, was the return of many countries to protectionism, sometimes pursued vigorously, as in the United States, whose industry captured an increasing share of the home market and practically excluded several traditional imports from Britain. Finally, the more advanced countries, particularly Germany, were rapidly building up their foreign trade, not only in Europe where the Germans became the principal suppliers of manufactured goods to most of their neighbours, but also overseas, in the underdeveloped countries like those of Latin America or the Middle East, where German competition was becoming very keen. In the Canadian market, geographical proximity and a similar market-structure gave Americans a clear advantage[16]. It would be wrong, however, to see the movement of exports as purely dependent on exogenous conditions; for one cannot disregard the possibility of a decline in competitiveness or an inability to keep up with new patterns of international trade – a subject to which we shall return later.

Britain's share of international trade in manufactured goods was appreciably reduced, from 41 per cent in 1880 to less than 30 per cent in 1914; but this reduction came after 1890, while for France it began

[16] According to Bairoch, 'European foreign trade', p.25 (table 9), between 1860 and 1910, the growth-rates by volume of the exports of all industrial countries in Europe (except Italy) were higher than UK rates–and often considerably so. The same goes for exports per head of population, p.27. But according to the rates quoted in the preceding note, between 1870 and 1890, the volume of British exports grew a little faster than the volume of German exports, and it was only after 1890 that Germany gained a decisive advantage.

earlier. Both countries lost trade, relatively, to Germany and the United States all over the world, and to India and Japan in eastern Asia. However, if exports are broken down into categories, one finds that Britain kept her place in the principal sector, that of textiles, in spite of many countries having developed their own cotton industry; also, not surprisingly, for coal. There was actually an improvement in various finished goods such as furniture, leather and rubber goods, jewelry, drinks and tobacco products. But there was a sharp though relative fall in iron and steel, metal-manufactures, machinery and transport equipment. This was actually the sector in which the growth of international trade was most rapid, more than twice as great as for total international commerce between 1880 and 1913. Meanwhile, growth had been slow or non-existent in sectors in which Britain had done well and kept a large share of world trade, principally textiles. She was undoubtedly hit by the rise of iron and steel industries in advanced countries, like the United States, whom she had previously supplied – and still did in the boom of 1873 – with semi-finished or simple iron and steel products, such as rails. But in addition, she had failed to replace her traditional exports by 'new' and up-to-date products, the more sophisticated goods demanded by advanced countries, particularly in the field of mechanical engineering. Efforts in this direction were made, but inadequately; all the same Great Britain did continue to dominate world trade in a few important branches of capital equipment[17].

It is arguable also that the improvement in Britain's terms of trade during the Great Depression – the price of primary products falling more than that of manufactured goods[18] – was unfavourable to her exports by reducing the purchasing power of new or underdeveloped countries. On the other hand, the increase in the volume of these countries' exports and the fall in shipping costs could have reduced or compensated for this handicap.

However, this situation changed after 1896 when the terms of trade moved in favour of countries exporting primary products, and from 1899 to 1913 world exports of manufactured goods enjoyed their

[17] Saul, 'The export economy', 11–18 (esp. tables V and V1). For the problems of British overseas trade as a whole during this period, the basic work is the book by the same author, *Studies in British Overseas Trade, 1870–1914* (Liverpool, 1960). Saul considers that GB's weakness in the engineering sphere arose from the narrowness of her home market for many products of this kind, whose export could only develop from the springboard of a strong domestic market guaranteeing a high level of productivity. See Chapter 12, p.384, on the question of 'old' and 'new' products.

[18] Some have seen here a proof of the deterioration of GB's competitive position, for the price of her exports had fallen less than those of the goods sold by her competitors; Saul, 'The export economy', 10.

biggest expansion toward semi-industrialized countries such as Australia, New Zealand, South Africa and India. This was just the sort of trade in which, for historical reasons, Britain had the edge on her rivals. By contrast, trade between industrialized countries, for which she was not so well adapted, grew much more slowly. She benefited by this change in geographical distribution of world trade[19], and her export business picked up briskly. Moreover, the prewar period was one in which production and trade expanded so rapidly, when the growth of the 'new' countries and some colonial territories opened up such enormous potential markets that there was room for all to get their share of the cake; the development of these new regions compensated Britain for the loss of some of her former markets, but this shift toward underdeveloped countries could be interpreted as accepting defeat, since the main market for goods with a future, i.e. capital goods and machinery, was in the industrialized countries, especially Europe, where Germany now had the lead[20]. These variations in the rates of growth of British commerce, together with the changes in the structure of the British and world economies, brought about a change in the pattern of trade.

The structure of exports had undergone a spectacular change between the end of the American war of independence and Waterloo by reason of the enormous growth of cotton cloth and yarn exports (completely eclipsing that of woollens and worsteds, so long the staple of Britain's foreign trade), and in the years 1814/16 they represented 40 per cent of the total value of exports. This percentage was to increase and reach its maximum of 51 per cent in 1830, by which date cotton goods and yarn were responsible for half of the increase in value of all exports during the previous half-century. While during the eighteenth century British exports had diversified, the Industrial Revolution gave them a swift but unbalanced growth and an increasingly narrow base.

On the other hand, from the 1830s onwards, a new form of diversification emerged, as table 59 shows[21]. The cotton industry's

---

19 ibid., 14.
20 ibid., 17–18. Criticizing Kindleberger, Saul underlines the dangers of anachronism, i.e. reasoning based on our knowledge of subsequent events. One cannot blame the British for having continued to sell rails to Latin America or coal to Europe while these were both in strong demand on the grounds that this demand lessened or disappeared after the war.
21 Taken from Mathias, *The First Industrial Nation* (table 17). See also his simpler table, p.244 (table IV), and Deane and Cole, p.31 (table 9). Yet this diversification was fairly slow and irregular, and it was only from the 1840s to the early 1870s that there was a general advance along a broad front. Exports of all kinds increased at the same time, cotton goods alone lagging behind in the 1860s because of the famine.

Table 59   Structure of British exports (ten-year average)

	Percentages (in value) of total exports at current prices				
	Cotton cloth and yarn	All kinds of textiles (a)	Metals and metal goods (b)	Coal	Various goods
1830/39	48	72	12	1	15
1850/59	36	60	20	2	18
1870/79	33	55	20	4	21
1890/99	28	44	21	7	28
1900/09	26	38	24	10	28

(a) Cloth and yarn in cotton, wool, silk, flax, clothing, hats, etc.
(b) Iron, steel, non-ferrous metals unwrought or manufactured machines, vehicles and ships.

share of total exports steadily dwindled, the increase in its sales overseas having become lower (especially after the cotton famine) than that of total exports. It fell to 40 per cent of the latter in 1850, 36 per cent in 1870, 28 per cent in 1890 and 24 per cent in 1910[22]. The wool and the linen industries progressed a little, relatively, up to 1850, then again briefly during the famine, but declined thereafter. The woollen and worsted industries provided only 9 per cent of total exports in 1910 as opposed to 14 per cent in 1850. Thus textiles as a whole, which had represented nearly three-quarters of total exports around 1830, were falling back. This was due both to the more rapid increase in other categories of exports, and also to the fall in value of British textile exports at the end of the century, during the Great Depression. This fall in turn was due to the closure of markets in industrialized countries of Europe and America, except for top-quality cloths and yarns, and to the long-lasting stagnation in cottons exports to Asia[23]. None the less, textiles remained more than half total exports in the 1870s and more than one-third in 1913.

Against this the metal-making and manufacturing industries made relative progress. Their share in total exports was small, 6 per cent, in 1814/16. By 1830/9 it had doubled, but only to 12 per cent; it increased fairly rapidly in the 1850s to reach 20 per cent, where it remained, increasing somewhat at the beginning of the twentieth century. The proportion of machinery, insignificant at first, grew sharply, to 7 per cent of total exports in 1900/9; but it remained smaller than that of semi-finished iron and steel products and of old-established items like

---

[22] And their contribution to the increase of total exports, which had been predominant, suffered a sharp decline.

[23] Saul, 'The export economy', 9, insists on the long stagnation in cotton exports from 1888 onwards; but it was partly masked by the recovery in prices, and so the rise in value, at the beginning of the twentieth century.

hardware and cutlery, although these too lost some ground after 1890[24]. What is remarkable is that it was not until the beginning of the twentieth century that the metal industries' share of total exports reached a quarter, in spite of opportunities offered by railway-building in other countries (to which, in fact, Britain did sell large quantities of rails and locomotives), in spite also of Britain's large exports of capital, and the industrialization of Europe, America, plus, finally, some other countries.

The steadily increasing share of coal in total exports is significant. It was still very small in 1830 but was to reach 10 per cent at the beginning of the twentieth century. The reason was the growing demand from industry, railways and steamships in countries with few coal resources; but there is something paradoxical about these massive exports of a raw material by a highly industrialized country, to such an extent that the proportion of manufactured goods in total exports fell appreciably between 1850 and 1913. Finally, there was a distinct increase in the share of a variety of other merchandise, so confirming the diversification (possibly insufficient) in British exports[25].

The growth and structure of imports may be seen in table 60[26]. During the first half of the nineteenth century, and even beyond, by far the largest share of imports consisted of raw materials for industry (60 per cent in 1820), and among these textile fibres figured most

Table 60   Structure of British imports

	Percentages (in value) of total net imports at current prices		
	Foodstuffs (a)	Raw materials (b)	Manufactured goods (c)
1840	40	57	4
1860	38	57	6
1880	44	39	17
1900	42	33	25
1910	38	39	24

(a) Food, drink and tobacco.
(b) Including semi-finished goods.
(c) Including sundry merchandise.

[24] ibid. As the value of machinery exports increased sharply between 1880 and 1900, and as their share (and that of coal) in total exports expanded, while the share of textiles contracted, Saul sees an important change in the structure of exports during the 1890s.

[25] Bairoch, *Commerce extérieur*, p.94 (table 28), shows the differences in structure of British and German exports in 1913. Textiles were only 13 per cent of total German exports; metal goods had a slightly larger share than in British exports; chemicals made up 8 per cent of the total, against 4 per cent.

[26] Table from Deane and Cole, p.33 (table 10). See also those of Mathias, *The First Industrial Nation*, p.244 (table IV(f)), 467 (table 16).

prominently. The industrialization of Great Britain was broadly dependent on imported raw materials. It is surprising that this share declined appreciably after 1860, while Britain's own natural resources were becoming depleted and her dependence on foreign supplies was increasing – for example in wool, iron-ore, non-ferrous metals, not to mention new products such as rubber and petroleum. Moreover, the increase in imports of textile fibres became very slow towards the end of the century[27], but the main reason for this relative decrease stemmed from the development of two other large groups of imports.

During the years following 1815, the share of foodstuffs in imports had increased in spite of the Corn Laws, though only slowly. It went up more rapidly between 1860 and 1880, with an invasion of cheap foreign foods that pushed it higher than that of imported raw materials. After that the proportion diminished, though the absolute quantities imported became larger and larger, so that Britain became more and more dependent on imported food[28].

Ultimately the reasons for these variations must be sought in the third group of imports featuring in table 60, whose share of total imports shows the most marked change. Until the adoption of free trade, Britain imported very few manufactured goods[29]. Her own industry was unsurpassed for all important merchandise; she only imported a few specialities, and the chief of these, French silks, were subject to heavy customs duties until the treaty of 1860. But free trade allowed all such goods in, e.g. toys and German optical equipment, and naturally silks, for which a rising standard of living had increased demand, together with other sophisticated or luxury goods that Britain did not make, or did not make so well, e.g. French worsteds, already referred to above. At the end of the nineteenth century, a more disturbing phenomenon emerged: as some new industries had developed insufficiently or not at all in Britain, increasing quantities of their products had to be imported from countries that had achieved a commanding position in these branches – aniline dyes from Germany, various advanced electrical goods from Germany and the United States, new types of machine-tools and office machinery from the United States, motor-cars from France, margarine from Holland, etc.

[27] Their share of total imports, which had reached 32 per cent in 1850, fell regularly later and reached 17 per cent in 1913, a decline which was not compensated by the modest increase of the share held by imports of other raw materials.
[28] In these imports, between 1850/9 and 1900/9, the share of grain and flour remained stable; the share of 'groceries' (sugar, tea, wine, tobacco) diminished; that of cattle, meat, dairy produce increased considerably; Mathias, *The First Industrial Nation*, p.467 (table 16).
[29] And they were partly intended for re-export.

Furthermore, on the eve of the first world war, Britain became the largest importer of semi-finished steel, from Germany and Belgium. Hence the large rise in the proportion of manufactured goods to all imports: from 6 per cent in 1860 to 25 per cent at the end of the century. This was the principal change in the structure of imports. Panic reactions to this invasion of the British market by foreign manufacturers were overdone. These imports, looked at in the light of free trade and the international division of labour, were not excessive, and in the case of semi-finished steel benefited the steel-using industries. Nevertheless, it is difficult to dismiss the idea that they showed up a weakening of Britain's competitiveness and a reluctance to innovate in the design and production of 'new' goods, in which Britain's share of the international market was small and diminishing[30].

The distribution of British exports can only be described here on the basis of continents. Table 61 shows great stability in the main currents of trade over a long period, with only gradual change[31]. The eighteenth century and the period of the French wars had seen an 'Americanization' of British trade, which for various reasons, of which the final one was Napoleon's Continental System, turned away from Europe towards America: at first to the Thirteen Colonies and then the United States, where demand increased very rapidly, and later to Latin America, whose markets had been opened up from 1808 onwards as a result of the Peninsular war.

After the peace in 1815, British exporters, who were hoping for a restoration of trade with Europe, had their hopes dashed by a second blockade in the shape of the ultra-protectionist policies of many European states. The United States were and long remained Britain's chief customer, but their economy was subject to sharp cyclical fluctuations, which in turn caused Anglo-American trade to fluctuate widely, both absolutely and relatively, with dire results for British export industries[32]. In the face of these difficulties, they turned towards new markets, the opening up of which was a significant development in the decades following 1820: India after the abolition of the East India Company's monopoly and the discovery that it could be a huge market for cotton goods[33], the Middle East, Africa and Latin

---

[30] Deane and Cole, pp. 32–3; R.A. Church, *The Great Victorian Boom, 1850-1873* (London, 1975), p.58; Saul, 'The export economy', 16–17.

[31] See also Mathias, *The First Industrial Nation*, p.414 (fig. 23); Church, *The Great Victorian Boom*, p.64 (table 5).

[32] In 1837, a year of crisis, in the US, 16 per cent of British exports went to North America.

[33] Also China from 1842 onwards, although this outlet was limited for a long time. But, in 1895, 80 per cent of the external trade of China was with the British empire.

America. The winning of independence by the Latin American states raised the hopes of British exporters too high, and they were to be greatly disappointed: populations were small, impoverished and politically unstable, transport was difficult, there was a lack of return-cargoes and means of payment. Nevertheless this outlet was far from negligible[34]. It was these new markets which helped Britain to overcome the crisis in exports immediately after the war and were responsible for most of the increase in exports between 1815 and the 1840s. Table 61 shows that their share of total exports had appreciably increased during this period but remained less than those of Europe and the United States, even though these were falling at the time[35]. So Britain was partly switching her trade towards the less developed countries. The traditional explanation for this is that the warm climates, the low standards of living and the absence of tariffs made these countries a splendid outlet for cheap Lancashire cottons. It is now thought that exports to these countries were also stimulated from the 1820s onwards by increasing imports of tropical products by

Table 61 Geographical distribution of British trade, by continents (in percentages of the total value of imports or exports)

	Europe	Africa	Asia	America		Australasia
				North	South	
A. *Destinations of exports*						
1816/18	44.2	1.0	8.3	37.3	9.3	—
1836/8	41.1	3.6	11.3	21.2	20.7	2.2
1849/51	38.0	3.8	14.8	24.5	16.0	3.6
1869/71	41.6	6.2	17.6	17.9	11.2	5.5
1889/91	34.8	6.7	21.6	15.5	11.8	9.5
1899/1901	39.4	10.2	22.4	10.3	8.5	9.2
1911/13	35.0	10.2	23.3	11.2	11.3	9.1
B. *Sources of imports*						
1849/51	34.8	4.2	20.0	24.4	15.1	1.4
1869/71	42.3	7.6	16.4	19.3	10.0	4.5
1889/91	44.3	4.8	13.7	26.2	4.2	6.9
1899/1901	43.0	4.5	10.0	30.3	5.4	6.9
1911/13	40.6	6.4	13.0	22.3	9.7	8.0

After W. Schlote, *British Overseas Trade from 1700 to the 1930s* (Oxford, 1952), pp. 156–160 (tables 18 and 19).
N.B. There are no statistics for the current value of imports by country of origin prior to 1849.

[34] See also D.C.M. Platt, *Latin America and British Trade, 1806–1914* (London, 1972). Brazil was the most satisfactory market, especially for cotton goods.
[35] Exports to Europe fell in value between about 1815 and 1830, as did their share of total exports; but this share climbed back later to its former level.

Britain and other advanced countries, whose populations were growing and standards of living rising.

The third quarter of the nineteenth century saw a considerable increase in exports to Europe, especially north-west Europe, which by now was industrialized and converted to freer trade. Its share of total exports increased, but was later to fall slightly[36]. There was a more substantial fall in the case of North America, i.e. the United States, where the civil war brought about in 1864 severe protectionism, later to become severer still[37]. In both continents the relative decline of British exports was due to the same causes – protectionism, to which European countries returned gradually after 1879, and industrialization[38]. Moreover the new industrial powers started to break into Britain's special preserve, Latin America, which caused her exports there to fall[39].

Trade with Asia, Africa and Australasia, on the other hand, continued to improve. India was the largest of these distant markets, chiefly because she took 40 per cent of all cotton exports. However, trade expanded with China, Japan and the whole of the Far East (thanks to the entrepôts of Singapore and Hong Kong), together with South Africa, which became an Eldorado at the end of the nineteenth century, and some British colonies in West Africa.

This increasing tendency of Britain's exports to turn towards distant non-European markets, especially those of underdeveloped countries, was a unique feature of her economy, distinguishing it from those of continental countries, for whom intra-European trade was much more important[40]. As far as British imports are concerned, the proportion which came from Europe was large and did increase slightly, because of the rise in imports of manufactured goods, as mentioned earlier, and also of foodstuffs from the Netherlands, Denmark, etc.

Likewise, while North America's share of British exports was falling sharply, her share of Britain's imports remained fairly steady over a long period and reached a peak at the end of the nineteenth century.

[36] The 1899/1901 percentage is exceptionally high.
[37] Also, after 1880, the 'volatility' of American demand no longer had much influence on the economic situation in GB.
[38] Saul, 'The export economy', 6, reckons that the effects of protectionism were balanced by the demand for coal and machinery resulting from the industrialization of Europe.
[39] But Platt, *Latin America*, maintains, contrary to Saul, that the British held their position fairly well and remained competitive. They suffered at least as much from the protectionism by Latin American countries as from foreign competition.
[40] Underlined by P. Bairoch, 'Geographical structure and trade balance of European foreign trade from 1800 to 1970', *Journal of European Economic History*, III(3), Winter 1974, 557–608, esp. 570–2, 582, 592. The same difference was repeated in the case of imports, but in both cases it became rather less after 1890.

Britain imported, of course, increasing quantities of American food-stuffs and raw materials, and she succumbed to an invasion of American machinery and other manufactures in the late nineteenth century. Actually, the United States were consuming a growing share of their own agricultural production and exporting less, but they were replaced by Canada, which was by now developing rapidly, as a supplier of foodstuffs.

Apart from Australia and New Zealand, both of which supplied Britain with increasing quantities of wool, wheat, meat and dairy products, the distant lands in which British goods found expanding markets were not developing their own exports to Britain to the same extent, and their share in her imports actually diminished. There came to be marked disparities between the movements of imports from and exports to the main regions of the world, so that Britain's balance of trade with them was in surplus here, in deficit there.

Before dealing with this question, we must turn to that of Britain's commercial relations with her empire, since it is often thought that this was a principal factor in her flourishing trade[41]. However, in spite of the facts that the British empire grew enormously in the nineteenth century – 2.3 million square miles were added between 1880 and 1900 – that massive sums were invested in it, and that its great natural resources were actively exploited, its share in Britain's total trade was remarkably static and relatively small – a little over 25 per cent – between 1815 and 1913. If late nineteenth-century imperialism was actuated by mainly economic motives (which has not been quite demonstrated), the results were disappointing[42], which is hardly surprising since it generally led to the annexation of desert or very underdeveloped lands.

The commercial links between Britain and the empire differed significantly as between exports and imports. In the former, the share

---

[41] This problem has been touched on by F. Crouzet, 'Trade and empire: the British experience from the establishment of free trade until the first world war', in B.M. Ratcliffe (ed.), *Great Britain and her World, 1750–1914: Essays in Honour of W.O. Henderson* (Manchester, 1975), pp.209–35. It will only therefore be dealt with briefly here. However, this article was published originally in 1964 and much new work has since appeared about the economic aspects of British imperialism. See particularly D.C.M. Platt, *Finance, Trade and Politics in British Foreign Policy, 1814–1914* (Oxford, 1968); D.C.M. Platt (ed), *Business Imperialism, 1840–1930* (Oxford, 1977); D.K. Fieldhouse, *Economics and Empire, 1830–1914* (London, 1973); R.J. Cain and A.G. Hopkins, 'The political economy of British expansion overseas, 1750–1914', *Economic History Review*, 2nd series, XXXIII (4), Nov. 1980, 463–90 (with detailed bibliographical references).

[42] After 1870, foreign manufactured goods penetrated into the empire, especially from the US into Canada. There was also a slow-down in the demand for cotton goods.

of the empire was between 25 and 30 per cent before 1850. Subsequently there was a slight increase: 32 per cent in 1854/7, 35 per cent in 1909/13, an average of roughly one-third[43]. Half of these exports went to colonies of British settlement (the dominions to be), about a third to India. Some authorities consider that the possession of imperial markets was a source of weakness and of loss of competitiveness for the British economy. Her trade had no legal privileges in empire countries, except the 'imperial preference' granted to her goods by some of the future dominions; but, in fact, thanks to existing commercial networks, to contracts with colonial governments or companies under British control (especially railway companies), it was difficult for competitors from other countries to gain a foothold. Yet markets where there is no competition do no good to the country that enjoys them[44].

The empire's share of imports into Britain was smaller: a quarter of the whole, even a fifth if a deduction is made for re-exports, and it hardly changed in the long run. The pattern of imports, however, changed considerably. Consisting mainly for a long time of 'colonial produce', they contained an increasing amount of temperate-zone foodstuffs grown in colonies of European settlement, such as wheat, meat, butter, cheese, that had not existed in the mid-nineteenth century and were shipped in increasing quantities[45]. Goods from the dominions grew from a third to a half of Britain's total imports from the empire.

The importance of the empire for Britain's trade and economy can easily be exaggerated and the 'Imperialists' who, in the late nineteenth and early twentieth century, called for empire free trade or an imperial customs union to solve Britain's economic difficulties were rather unrealistic. There was, however, one imperial possession, India, the 'brightest jewel in the English crown', that did play a most important part, not only because it was the largest unprotected market for the British cotton industry from the mid-century onward, but also because of its role in Britain's balance of trade and balance of payments.

It is a surprising but well-established fact[46] that, throughout the nineteenth century, and already during the eighteenth, Britain's visible trade was in deficit. The margin of imports over exports grew

---

[43] Confirmed by Saul, 'The export economy', 5–6.

[44] Bairoch, 'Geographical structure', 570.

[45] But in 1913 Europe supplied a larger share (38 per cent) of imports of foodstuffs than the empire.

[46] In fact, if GB's balance of trade had been favourable, she would have drained away gold from other countries or she would have had to invest abroad more than she did.

vigorously, though irregularly in actual figures: on average £23 million for 1835/40, and £177 million for 1901/5. As a percentage of imports, which in the long run grew more rapidly than exports, this margin tended to increase, but there were considerable fluctuations. If one takes five-yearly averages, the margin was generally about a quarter or a fifth of the total value of imports before 1875, though for two quinquennia it was more than 30 per cent. It showed a sharp increase during the Great Depression – more than 33 per cent (except in 1886/90) and reaching 39 per cent in 1896/1900. However, it fell back relatively and absolutely in the ten years preceding the first world war, when it was no more than about 25 per cent[47].

Britain had a sizeable trade deficit with many countries or regions: the United States (£50 million in 1910), Canada, Argentina, South Africa, New Zealand and continental Europe (£45 million in 1910). Deficit with the latter area had increased considerably as a percentage of imports, exceeding 40 per cent after 1880[48].

On the other hand, Britain had a surplus with India – which was large (£60 million in 1910) – also with China, Japan, Australia and Turkey. Now, at the end of the nineteenth century, the United States and industrialized countries in Europe stepped up their imports of primary produce from underdeveloped countries, especially India, without increasing their own exports to these countries, partly because British exporters were already entrenched there. As a result they had large deficits with them. A system of multilateral settlements thus arose, through which Britain's surpluses, especially with India, were used to clear some of her deficit with her other trading partners. India thus occupied a key position in Britain's system of international payments. It was a rather worrying situation for Britain to have large deficits with advanced countries and surpluses with underdeveloped countries, which were accepting her traditional goods for partly political reasons[49].

All the same, world-wide, Britain's trade was in deficit. Fortunately the gap was more than covered by large invisible earnings.

---

[47] We use the series of Mathias, *The First Industrial Nation*, p.305 (table VII). See also Deane and Cole, p.36 (table 11); A.H. Imlah, pp.28 (table 2), 39 and 45 (figs 4 and 5), 70–5; Bairoch, 'Geographical structure', p. 586 (table 12).

[48] Bairoch, 'Geographical structure', 590 (note 42).

[49] Saul, *Studies*, ch.3, pp. 43–89; Crouzet, 'Trade and empire', pp.225–7; Mathias, *The First Industrial Nation*, p.317 (fig.14); E.J. Hobsbawm, *Industry and Empire* (London, 1968), p.149 of the Penguin edn, 1969, who insists on the importance of England's *political* domination of India for at the same time keeping the Indian market open to her cotton goods and preserving this system of multilateral payments.

INVISIBLE EARNINGS AND FOREIGN INVESTMENT

Invisible earnings played a growing part in British international operations in the nineteenth century, her comparative advantages probably becoming increasingly evident in the sectors in which they originated. It has been calculated that net invisible income amounted to 25 to 30 per cent of all receipts from abroad between 1800 and 1860, 35 to 40 per cent between 1870 and 1914[50]. Little is known about them unfortunately, in spite of the meticulous work of Imlah, whose series are the basic source in this field[51].

A distinction has to be made between income resulting from the sale of services to other countries, usually known as invisible exports, and income resulting from British capital invested abroad. Income from services grew considerably in the nineteenth century, and by itself it was generally enough or almost enough to cover the deficit in the balance of trade (table 62). Prior to 1891/5 it was, anyhow, larger than the receipts derived from foreign investment.

The largest earnings, roughly two-thirds of the total, came from shipping. This was hardly surprising as the British merchant fleet continued to be the largest in the world, by a particularly wide margin in the last third of the century. It lost a little ground after 1890, but this was negligible. Not only did British ships carry more than half of all Britain's trade, but they also carried a high proportion of other countries' trade, even between non-British ports. Net earnings from shipping grew more rapidly than those from merchandise exports between the 1830s and 1884 (with record growth during the 1850s and 1860s), and later at about the same pace. Deane and Cole reckon that shipping contributed between 4 and 5 per cent to national income from 1860 to 1910. It also brought about supplementary invisible earnings,

Table 62   Visible deficit and invisible earnings (UK) 1816–1910[52]

	Net income from services		Commodity trade deficit
1816/20	15	£m	− 9
1836/40	19		− 24
1851/5	24		− 28
1871/5	87		− 62
1896/1900	101		−161
1906/10	137		−142

[50]   Deane and Cole, p.35.
[51]   Saul, 'The export economy', 10, criticizes them severely.
[52]   Taken from Mathias, *The First Industrial Nation*, p.305 (table VII). Income from services is the total *net* income from shipping, insurance, banks, commissions on re-export trade, tourism and transfer of funds by emigrants or immigrants.

for when goods were carried in British ships, they were generally handled and insured by British firms[53]. The premiums earned by British insurers from foreign policy-holders provided substantial sums (£25 million in 1913). The large fire and life insurance companies operated on a world-wide scale, expanding their foreign business considerably at the end of the century[54], and almost every ship in the world was insured at Lloyds.

There were other forms of commercial activity that produced more invisible earnings, such as the old-established carrying and re-exporting trade, especially in colonial produce from the empire re-exported to Europe, such as tea, coffee, ivory, non-ferrous metals, rubber, and also wool and cotton. This trade brought commissions to British middlemen, but tended to contract over the years as other industrialized countries built up direct overseas connections. However, it had a period of revival and expansion in the 1850s and 1860s[55], and even at the beginning of the twentieth century re-exports accounted for 11 to 12 per cent of total exports.

As a direct result of this trade and, above all, of imports into Britain, important markets or 'exchanges' grew up in London and Liverpool, for wool, metals, colonial produce, cotton, etc. They had no direct contact with the commodities which were traded there, and of which large quantities were never even landed at a British port. However, they were so efficiently organized and turnover was so large that they provided the best prices and the quickest service. The brokers operating on these exchanges earned commission from the foreign businessmen for whom they acted.

In addition, many British trading houses had either established themselves in foreign countries or set up agencies or branches, particularly in the colonies or in underdeveloped countries. Typical cases were the great Far Eastern marts of Singapore, Hong Kong and

---

[53]   See Chapter 9, p.313; Deane and Cole, pp.36 (table 11), 234 (table 62), 236; Saul, 'The export economy', 11. Net income from shipping (annual averages in millions of £):

1836/40	11
1871/75	51
1906/10	89

[54]   See for example B. Supple, *The Royal Exchange Assurance: A History of British Insurance, 1729–1970* (Cambridge, 1970). This venerable institution launched into fire insurance business abroad from 1889 onwards, and in 1913 one-third of its receipts came from overseas. But the San Francisco earthquake (1906) cost it dear. Saul, 'The export economy', 10, thinks that Imlah's figures underestimate the rapid growth of income deriving from these insurance activities abroad.

[55]   Church, *The Great Victorian Boom*, pp.58, 63. This trade had reached its peak during the Napoleonic wars.

Shanghai. These firms dealt in the import and sale of British goods and the export of local products, but provided also all kinds of financial or other services. A proportion of their profits went back to the home country; and they arranged insurance, discounted bills, etc., in London[56].

The activities of British banks and the ubiquitous role of the City of London were another source of invisible earnings, for they provided short-term finance for much international trade, including trade between foreign countries, by discounting and rediscounting bills on London, drawn in sterling, which were the normal means of settlement in international transactions. Throughout the nineteenth century London was the principal money market for short-term credit and discounts. Competition from Paris which had developed under the Second Empire was cut off by the Franco-Prussian war.

Britain naturally had some 'invisible expenses'[57], but the balance was positive and almost equalled her trading deficit. When the increasing returns on foreign investment were added, the balance of payments was strongly in surplus[58].

Between 1815 and 1914 British investors exported capital in ever increasing amounts and invested it in foreign countries and in the empire[59]. These investments reaped an ever-rising return in interest and dividends[60]. What were the reasons for this growth in overseas investments? The chief inducement for most investors was that the foreign securities they bought held out the promise – which on the whole they kept – of a higher yield than they could get on British stock of the same category and involving a similar degree of risk. The

---

[56] See for example S. Marriner, *Rathbones of Liverpool, 1845–73* (Liverpool, 1961); F.E. Hyde, *Far Eastern Trade, 1860–1914* (London, 1973).

[57] Government expenditure on the diplomatic service and above all on the armed forces stationed abroad; expenditure (no small sum) by English tourists; funds taken away by emigrants.

[58] Whereas a large slice of invisible income was connected with England's visible trade, there was another independent source connected with the British merchant navy's predominance.

[59] References should be made to the works of Imlah and Cairncross already quoted, as well as to the classic books by J.A. Hobson, *Imperialism: A Study* (London, 1902 and 1938); H. Feis, *Europe, the World's Banker, 1870–1914* (New Haven, Conn., 1930); L.H. Jenks, *The Migration of British Capital to 1875* (London, 1927) and to an excellent recent survey by P.L. Cottrell, *British Overseas Investment in the Nineteenth Century* (London, 1975), quoted as Cottrell, *Investment*, with detailed critical bibliography. See also the collection of articles: A.R. Hall (ed.) *The Export of Capital from Britain, 1870–1914* (London, 1968); and Mathias, *The First Industrial Nation* pp.320–34.

[60] In fact, this meant portfolio investments by purchase of foreign securities. Direct investment was not large (cf. p.367). Furthermore it was investment by individuals or companies. There was no lending from state to state, as before 1815 and after 1914.

securities in question were mostly government stock, railway shares and debentures. A higher return could be had by buying shares of home-based industrial companies, but until the end of the nineteenth century there were not very many to be had, and in any case most investors rather distrusted them.

Why were higher returns available on overseas investment? The answer is simple. There was plenty of capital available in Great Britain, with rapid accumulation of savings, though in relatively few hands, since national income was very unequally divided. Thus rates of interest were low and their long-term trend downward. After 1820 the return on government stock was just 3 per cent, and mortgages offered the same. At the end of the century railway securities yielded no more[61]. Exports of capital were much increased after the middle of the century, and this is certainly connected with declining opportunities of getting a good return on publicly issued and quoted British stocks.

Many foreign countries, on the other hand, were short of capital, and rates of interest, especially on fixed-interest stock, were higher than in Britain. This was particularly true of the 'new' countries and the colonies, which needed a lot of capital for development and for creating the necessary infrastructure – especially railways. There were also impecunious governments that were ready to borrow money dearly. Foreign investment might have appeared hazardous, but in the nineteenth century it was most unusual for a state to default on its debts, and, even if it did, this was usually only a temporary lapse. Moreover British securities, apart from government gilt-edged, were not always totally foolproof, and many publicly quoted firms failed. In spite of some unfortunate experiences, British investors did not lose much money overseas, especially after the middle of the century, and the higher yields obtainable there did not involve any higher risk. But there was a great difference in yields. Taking a sample of 566 securities, Edelstein has estimated that the mean geometric annual yield 1870–1913 on British ones was 4.6 per cent, and on foreign 5.7 per cent. At a time when factors of production had complete liberty of movement, capital tended to be invested where it would get the highest return[62].

The search for this highest return was the main incentive for the

---

[61]   While gilt-edged securities enjoying a guarantee of interest by government such as Indian railway debentures, yielded interest of more than 5 per cent at the beginning of the twentieth century.

[62]   Cottrell, *Investment*, pp.27–9; Church, *The Great Victorian Boom*, pp. 68–9; M. Edelstein , 'Realized rates of return on UK home and overseas portfolio investment in the age of high imperialism', *Explorations in Economic History*, X111(3), July 1976, 283–329, esp. 294 (table 3), 321–2.

private investor[63]. However, those who organized and promoted the export of capital had different motives. After the middle of the century, more and more of these intermediaries flourished. Merchant banks had become more numerous and more powerful, and they played the main role, but new types of issuing houses appeared, particularly the Anglo-Foreign and Anglo-Colonial banks mentioned above, also investment trusts and other bodies. The market for issuing foreign securities was very imperfect prior to 1850 but was gradually improved. In any case, there were in the City and in the provinces (particularly in Scotland) numbers of banks and finance houses who specialized in draining savings toward overseas investment. During the second quarter of the century, which was a time when organizations and methods were being tried out, they perfected their techniques and they were constantly on the lookout for investment opportunities[64]. Issuing loans to foreign governments or placing shares in firms operating overseas brought to these firms good commissions and premiums; and the greater the risk, the greater the profit, though it was usually the shareholder who bore the risk. In different cases, exports of capital were made with a view to selling British goods abroad and with an eye on the resulting profits. Thus Great Britain became banker to the world, the main source of long-term capital for all developing countries.

Exports of capital proceeded at an irregular pace, with bursts of speculation followed by slack periods. During the first half of the century, these movements, which still involved relatively small sums of money, coincided roughly with business cycles in the economy as a whole, and so their periodicity was about ten years. But, in the second half of the century, several authors claim to identify specific investment cycles, lasting about eighteen years[65]. Moreover, during each boom in overseas investment, investors directed their attention towards a small number of regions and well defined types of investing. If they were disappointed in their hopes, which often happened, a long time had to elapse before public interest returned to the same fields.

After the Napoleonic wars, the British made loans to several

---

[63] As it was of the insurance companies or banks who also bought foreign securities.
[64] Cottrell, *Investment,* pp.24–5, 29–34. He points out that the reform of company law in GB, the adoption of the gold standard by many countries, etc., also helped the growth of foreign investment . Provincial and Scottish capital took part from before 1860.
[65] We cannot discuss here the complex question of these long swings, which is partly linked to the views of Brinley Thomas, mentioned in Chapter 1, pp. 21–2, on cycles of emigration to America, formation of capital and house-building in GB and the US. A good introduction to these problems and bibliographical references are to be found in Cottrell, *Investment,* pp.57ff.

European governments whose finances were in trouble, including France, to help her pay off the war indemnity to her conquerors. But the first explicitly speculative 'mania' for foreign investment took place in 1824/5 after the emancipation of the Spanish possessions in South America had been firmly secured. The new states borrowed heavily in London, while various companies were set up to operate in them, especially to reopen the gold and silver mines that had been abandoned during the wars of independence. But the Latin American governments soon defaulted on their interest payments and many investors, like the character in Dickens, had their hearts 'broken in the mines of Peru', or lost all their money, like Benjamin Disraeli.

The second wave of foreign investment, in the 1830s, which peaked in 1838, concentrated on the United States, with heavy buying of bonds issued by states' governments (not the federal authority) to finance public works and especially railways. British investors also bought shares in banks, railway or canal companies. But, once again, the results were disappointing. Several states defaulted on their interest payments during the 1840s, with the result that for some time all American securities were viewed with distrust.

There was a fresh change of direction in the 1840s, this time towards the continent of Europe, where a lot of British capital was invested in railway companies, particularly in France. but the crisis of 1847 and the 1848 revolutions put an end to these investments.

It has been calculated that between 1815 and 1830 Britain invested between £75 million and £88 million abroad, and that by 1854 her total accumulated overseas investment amounted to between £195 million and £235 million[66]. This was a modest sum, and the ensuing income – an average of £9½ million for the years 1846/50 – was also modest in comparison with visible and invisible exports, and with national product (though at 2 per cent it was not negligible).

1855 was the starting-point for a rapid but erratic rise in capital exports. Between 1856 and 1875 they averaged £41 million a year, as against £6 million since 1815, with a maximum of £75 million a year between 1870 and 1875. Even higher figures were to be attained later on. Within twenty years, therefore, the total of British assets abroad almost quadrupled, rising by £800 million and exceeding £1 billion in 1875.

At the same time, a new and permanent change of direction took place. Although British investors were still investing in European railways during the 1850s, they were beginning to turn away from

[66]　Cottrell, *Investment*, p.13. Estimates vary for calculating these sums according to the method used (ibid., pp.11–12). Reference should be made to this work (pp. 19–25, 35–40) for more detail on the chronological sequence of foreign investment.

Europe[67], leaving it to the French to help out financially embarrassed governments and build railways there. Instead, they were looking overseas, towards the colonies, as yet rather neglected, and other undeveloped countries, with whom there could be no progress of trade without some prior foreign investment, chiefly for building railways.

Three 'long waves' of foreign investment can be observed, with 1872, 1890 and 1913 the peak years. But upswings were not uniform, the first wave, for example, having been briefly interrupted by the crises of 1857 and 1866. It was remarkable for heavy investment in American railways – except during the civil war – and in railways in Canada and still more in India, where the mutiny had shown up the necessity of an effective railway network. This last was financed by issuing bonds bearing interest guaranteed by the government of India. At the end of this wave came the start of heavy investment in the Argentine.

After a lull at the beginning of the Great Depression, the second wave of capital exports began early in the 1880s and gathered momentum after 1886. Once again the flow was directed towards the United States, but also to Australia and the Argentine. But it was brought to a halt by the Baring crisis, when this famous bank faced collapse as a result of its unsound ventures in the Argentine. In the 1890s foreign investment was on a much reduced scale, except for capital involved in the development of gold and diamond mines in South Africa. After 1900 came a vigorous recovery and a huge wave of overseas investment that reached unprecedented figures: an annual average of £161 million from 1905 to 1913, and £224 million in 1913 itself. As we have already seen, net capital exports were higher than gross domestic capital formation in Britain. Investment in Canada was to the forefront, but other 'new' empire lands (Australia, South Africa), the United States and some European countries (including Russia) shared in this golden shower[68].

The cumulative net total of British assets abroad, which passed £1 billion in 1875, doubled in the following quarter-century, exceeded £2 billion in 1900, and reached £4 billion (a round sum on which all authorities agree) in 1914[69]. Britain was thus the leading creditor

---

[67] In 1850, two-thirds of British assets abroad were in Europe (mostly in government funds) and one-third in America; Church, *The Great Victorian Boom*, p.67.

[68] Edelstein, 321, notes that during this period the yield on British securities was especially low.

[69] Cottrell, *Investment*, p.15. See also C.H. Feinstein, *National Income, Expenditure and Output of the United Kingdom, 1855–1965* (Cambridge, 1972), tables 7, 15, 50, T.21–2, 37–8, 110; Bairoch, *Commerce extérieur*, p.99. D.C.M. Platt, 'British portfolio investment overseas before 1870: some doubts', *Economic History Review*, 2nd series, XXXIII (1), Feb. 1980, 1–16, suggests that these figures ought to be revised downwards – by one-third for 1914.

country, owning 41 per cent of total international investment and leaving France, which was second, far behind, with less than half Britain's assets. Table 63 shows the geographical distribution of these investments[70].

It is remarkable how little was invested in Europe, where two-thirds of foreign investment had been located in 1850; also how modest was the share of underdeveloped countries, especially in the empire. The latter received nearly half of all investment, of which three-quarters, however, went to the dominions; the colonies and even India, all tropical countries, did not receive very much. Moreover, the Argentine alone had 42 per cent of all the considerable investment in Latin America[71], from which one concludes that the 'new countries', i.e. the Argentine, the United States and the four white-populated dominions, had the lion's share. Furthermore 68 per cent of money subscribed between 1855 and 1914 for foreign securities issued in London was destined for 'temperate regions of recent settlement' – in other words, by a fairly obvious train of rational calculation, relatively or actually rich countries[72].

As for the use made of this capital, 41 per cent, perhaps even 44 per

Table 63   Geographical distribution of Britain's foreign investments in 1914 (or percentages of her total national investment abroad)

Europe		5.25
North America		35.25
USA	21	
Canada	14	
Latin America		18.50
Australia		11.00
India and Ceylon		9.25
Rest of Asia		8.50
S. Africa and Rhodesia		9.00
Rest of Africa		3.25

[70]   Calculated from Mathias, *The First Industrial Nation*, pp.469–70 (table 19). See also Bairoch, *Commerce extérieur*, p.104 (table 32), who makes a comparison with the distribution of French and German investment. For France, 52 per cent were in Europe, only 5.5 per cent in North America. But he notes (p.107) the marked discrepancy (although less than for France) between the geography of investment and the geography of trade. In 1913, 41 per cent of England's trade was with Europe and 19 per cent with North America.

[71]   Cottrell, *Investment*, pp.41, 43. It was Latin America who in all received most English capital between 1820 and 1914; but between 1865 and 1914 it was the US.

[72]   ibid., pp.27, 41.

cent, was invested in railway securities[73]. To this should be added the proportion earmarked for financing railway-construction by the foreign or colonial governments out of the loans made to them, such loans having by themselves absorbed 25 per cent of all foreign investment. Further large sums were invested in the development of other forms of transport, such as ports and canals, and of public services, such as gas-works. Altogether it has been reckoned that 69 per cent of funds subscribed in London for export overseas between 1855 and 1914 was used to build up the infrastructure of the countries for which it was destined[74]. On the other hand, relatively little capital was invested in industrial enterprises, mining, agriculture (e.g. plantations in the tropics, ranches in North America or the Argentine, etc.). In many such cases investment was direct, by British firms that set up subsidiaries abroad, so that very little capital was raised for these purposes by public issues.

Britain's foreign assets amounted to 10 per cent of national capital (not counting land) in 1865, 18 per cent in 1885, and 25 per cent in 1914[75]. Interest and dividends earned by these investments were quite modest, as we have seen, up to the middle of the nineteenth century, but subsequently grew very rapidly, as table 64 shows[76].

According to Feinstein's calculations, this net foreign income amounted to 24 per cent of Britain's gross domestic product in 1855/9, 5 per cent in 1870/9, 7 per cent in 1890/9, and 8.5 per cent in 1905/14

Table 64   Net income from foreign investment

Periods for which annual averages are calculated	£m
1816/20	1.7
1836/40	8.0
1851/5	11.7
1871/5	50.0
1896/1900	100.2
1911/13	187.9

[73] Of which 16 per cent was invested in American railways; but it was portfolio investment, particularly in debentures, which gave the British no control over American railway companies.

[74] Cottrell, *Investment*, pp.27, 40, 63.

[75] Deane and Cole, p.306 (table 81). According to Edelstein, 285, foreign securities made up 33 per cent of the face value of all securities held by British investors in 1870 and 45 per cent in 1913.

[76] Mathias, *The First Industrial Nation*, p.305 (table VII). Feinstein, *National Income*, table 7, T.21–2, col.6, gives an index of net income from abroad at constant prices, which, on the basis of 1913 = 100, rises from 20 for 1870/9 to 55 for 1890/9.

(roughly 10 per cent on the eve of the first world war)[77]. Receipts from dividends constituted the most dynamic component of invisible earnings, continuing to grow during the Great Depression and overtaking earnings from services from 1891/5. In the same period, they also grew more rapidly than merchandise exports, whose value was stagnating; a situation, however, which was reversed between 1900 and 1914[78].

Except during peak periods of capital exports (1856-75 and some years before 1914), income from existing overseas investments was equal to or even larger than the total of new investment. In other words, one may put it that the latter was financed out of income from earlier investment, without any need to call on fresh resources from domestic savings. The build-up of foreign assets was thus achieved almost automatically, without any strain on the economy[79].

Since invisible exports alone almost sufficed to make good the deficit in the balance of trade (except in the 1890s and up to 1905), income from foreign investment created a constant surplus in the balance of payments, which was available for further overseas investment and generated a constant flow of it. Table 65 shows two examples[80].

Thanks to a revival of exports which reduced the visible trade deficit, and to the growth of her invisible earnings, the position of Britain on the eve of the first world war had improved in relation to

Table 65   UK balance of payments

	Yearly averages	
	1896/1900	*1911/13*
	£m	
Balance of trade	−161	−134
Net income from services	101	153
Net income from foreign investment	100	188
Balance of payments on current account	40	207

[77] Feinstein, *National Income*, table 18, T.44–5, col.10. Cottrell, *Investment*, p.48, gives lower percentages, because they are calculated in relation to GNP: 7 per cent in 1910/14.

[78] Saul, 'The export economy', p. 11.

[79] Cottrell, *Investment*, p.45. Interest and dividends received by British investors from 1856 to 1913 were equal to 130 per cent of net investment abroad, which shows that the latter were successful and that there was no wastage of capital. Also Deane and Cole, p. 36.

[80] Taken from Mathias, *The First Industrial Nation*, p.305 (table VII); also Deane and Cole, pp.36, 37 (tables 11 and 12).

what it had been at the end of the Victorian era, when she seemed to be on the way to becoming a *rentier* country, compensating for a large trade deficit which showed up her inefficiency as an exporter, by the income from her foreign investments. On the contrary, in 1911–13, she lived entirely on what she earned – visible exports and invisible services.

There has been much discussion about the results of foreign investment by Britain and other wealthy countries. This is not the place for discussing the particularly controversial question of their effect on the receiving countries. We may, however, say that those who received the most (apart from the special case of the United States, for which imported capital only represented a fraction of total capital formation) were the future dominions, which, thanks to this capital, experienced remarkable economic development, though with some distortions. Besides this, without British exports of capital, which gave developing countries the power to purchase basic equipment, the rest of the world would have suffered from a sterling famine, which would have been crippling to world trade. British investment fuelled its expansion.

There remains the question of what effect the export of capital had on Britain herself. Some writers think it was entirely harmful, a hypothesis that will be discussed in the next chapter. We may limit ourselves here to mentioning a few indisputably positive effects. For one thing it encouraged the export of capital goods, especially rails and railway material[81]. On the whole, there was a fairly close correlation between export of capital and the export of goods, although it may have diminished after 1870 as a result of the increasingly multilateral pattern of trade relations: a loan from London did not directly result in orders for British industry, but it did none the less stimulate exports. Although, at the end of the nineteenth century, in the long term domestic investment fluctuated inversely to foreign investment, in the short term the latter helped to get the economy moving again after a depression[82].

Another positive effect resulted from the construction of railways

---

[81] In the case of India and the colonies, there were unofficial arrangements to 'buy British'; but in general a railway company which obtained its capital in London also bought its material in England.

[82] Cottrell, *Investment*, pp.47, 51–2; Bairoch, *Commerce extérieur*, pp.110–11, 199–200, 215. We have already mentioned in Chapter 5, p. 120, note 43, his calculations of the correlation between exports of capital and of goods from 1830 to 1913, which gives a high positive coefficient of 0.918. Before 1860, the 'inversity' of domestic and foreign investment did not exist, and their simultaneity was a factor in mid-Vicitorian prosperity; Church, *The Great Victorian Boom*, pp.67–70.

and harbours, and other investments in North America, the Argentine and Australia: they encouraged the output of primary products and their export to Britain; they brought down the real cost of Britain's imports, gave her cheaper food and raw materials, and so contributed to the widespread rise in the standard of living during the last quarter of the century.

Eric Hobsbawm has maintained that Britain got over the difficulties resulting from the slowing down of her growth at the end of the nineteenth century, not by modernizing her industry, but by exploiting certain aspects of her traditional superiority, i.e. by increasingly directing her export trade to the colonial and underdeveloped countries; by taking the utmost advantage of her own last great innovation – the iron steamship; finally, by developing her role as go-between, as insurer and banker, which reached its peak at this time. Paradoxically, the very factor that weakened British industry, competition from more progressive rival powers, strengthened British finance. The multilateral system of payments described earlier ensured that every thread of the world's commercial and financial networks passed through London, so that it was between 1870 and 1913 that the City was truly the economic heart of the world. This financial zenith would have compensated for industrial decline. But, in fact, did the British economy decline? And if so, why?

[83]   Hobsbawm, p.151.

12   The decline of the British economy?

In the course of the preceding chapters it became evident that the growth of several branches of the British economy slowed down, roughly from the 1870s onwards. It also became clear that in certain fields Britain lost the technological leadership which she formerly enjoyed. Finally, it was suggested right at the beginning of this work that the growth of the economy, taken as a whole, similarly lost impetus at the end of the nineteenth century. At that time, however, other advanced countries showed faster growth, so that the United States and Germany overtook England in industrial power, and the British lead in other spheres, e.g. income per head, was reduced. So one can consider the question of Britain's economic decline (a relative decline, of course, for her production and wealth continued to grow in absolute terms), from two points of view, i.e. in relation to her own rate of growth during earlier decades and in relation to that of other countries.

This 'decline', or retardation, poses a problem which is important and interesting in itself, but also extends beyond the period under discussion. One is led quite naturally to wonder whether the close of the Victorian era and the Edwardian decade were not only 'the end of an epoch'[1], that of English supremacy, but also the beginning of the long process of chronic economic difficulties, and deterioration of the British position in the international economy, which unfolded irregularly but inexorably right up to the present day. There is no question of dealing with this problem here, but, taking such a long view, the decades at the end of the the nineteenth century and the beginning of the twentieth and their economic problems assume an increased importance, appearing as a major turning-point in the history of England.

This 'decline', which was already anxiously perceived by a number of

---

[1]   S.Pollard and D.W.Crossley, *The Wealth of Britain, 1085–1966* (London, 1968), p.223.

contemporaries, has fascinated economists no less than historians for a
quarter of a century, and an abundant literature has already been
devoted to it. This literature is indeed as dispersed as it is abundant,
being essentially in the form of articles and has not yet been digested
in a major work[2]. The pages which follow will be able to give no more
than a summary, too often brief and oversimplified, of the opposing
theses and the main explanations that have been put forward to
account for the decline of the British economy. However, even the
reality of this decline has never been universally accepted, and
simplistic opinions, on a problem that has many sides to it, are in
danger of leading to serious mistakes.

THE SLOW-DOWN IN GROWTH

In the Preface of this book we emphasized that nineteenth-century
statistics and *a fortiori* the calculations of aggregates and other
refinements derived from them must be treated with reserve. Nevertheless, nearly all the data and calculations available confirm that
there was a slow-down in British growth-rates at the end of the
nineteenth century. The only matter in doubt is the exact moment of
the turning-point. Let us recall a few conclusions drawn from the
quantitative data presented earlier in this book.

For agriculture the story is simple: real output increased slightly
from about 1870 to 1913, but net output dropped between 1870 and
approximately 1900, and despite a slight recovery later, it was at a
lower level in 1913 than at the end of the 1860s.

The study of the main industries has shown that, on the whole, their
growth was markedly slower between 1873 (the reference date
generally used, being the peak of a major cycle) and the end of the
century, and even 1913, than during the early and mid-Victorian
periods. Of course differences existed between one industry and
another, and there was even one exception – shipbuilding, whose
growth-rate from 1873 to 1900, for special reasons that have been
analysed, was higher than for the previous period. Indeed, the
metal-manufacturing and engineering industries were, on the whole,
reasonably immune from the slow-down. Against this, the deceleration
was very clear in the primary-metal industry, where the output of
pig-iron and iron and steel increased only slowly after 1873 instead of
at a growth-rate of 5 per cent per annum as previously. This was

[2] D.H.Aldcroft and H.W.Richardson, *The British Economy 1870–1939* (London, 1969),
gives in Section D, pp.305–36, a very complete critical bibliography of works
previously published. We will attempt below to indicate the most important recent
contributions. Roland Marx, *Le Déclin de l'économie britannique* (Paris, 1972), is
useful for non-British students.

equally true of the textile industries, chiefly because of the large role played by the cotton industry. The impetus of the latter was broken by the cotton famine so that from the American civil war to the end of the century it experienced a miserable growth-rate of only 1 per cent per annum; but the woollen and worsted industry, which had prospered in mid-Victorian times, also endured a real slow-down in the last quarter of the century[3].

As for total industrial production, the Hoffmann index, as Lomax has emphasized, shows a striking contrast between a growth-rate of 3.1 per cent per annum from 1811 to 1877, and a rate of 1.6 per cent for the period 1877–1913, i.e. a sharp fall of nearly 50 per cent. Within the period of Victoria's reign, the rate was 3.14 per cent between 1836–8 and 1872–4, and 1.80 per cent between 1872–4 and 1900–2; but it showed no recovery, and even a fresh fall, during the Edwardian period[4]. One can even query whether the early 1870s is the real turning-point betwen 'rapid' growth and 'slow' growth. Coppock, through excluding the effects of the American civil war, found that the slow-down in industrial production began in the middle of the 1860s. He did, of course, show that it became more pronounced from 1875 onwards, and occurred again at the beginning of the twentieth century. But it does seem that the period of most rapid industrial growth is to be found much earlier in the nineteenth century, in the 1820s and 1830s – in other words before Victoria's accession! The Hoffmann index displays its highest growth-rate at 4 per cent per annum between 1830 and 1839[5]. During roughly the same period the cotton, iron and metal-manufacturing industries achieved growth rates of 6 or 7 per cent, which were never equalled subsequently. Performance in the early and mid-Victorian periods was already less striking. So would it not be true to say that the first stage in the deceleration of industrial growth occurred at about the time of Victoria's accession? This is true in a sense; but the problem has hardly been posed, let alone solved[6]. However, this phase of deceleration was

[3]   See tables 35, 36, 37, 40, 41, 44, 46 (pp. 191, 196, 197, 214, 233, 241, 246); also C.H.Feinstein, *National Income, Expenditure and Output of the United Kingdom, 1855–1965* (Cambridge, 1972), tables 51 and 52, T.111–15.

[4]   See also Chapter 3, p. 49 (tables 11 and 12). Feinstein's index of GB's industrial output at constant factor cost (table 54, T. 118–19) gives the following growth rates (percentage per annum):

1855/7 to 1872/4	3.24
1872/4 to 1900/2	2.24
1900/2 to 1911/13	1.59

[5]   Calculated by exponential adjustment.

[6]   Deane and Cole have drawn attention to the phenomenon in the 1840s and explained it by the famine in Ireland and the immigration coming from there. This slow-down is none the less surprising given stimuli such as railway-building and the large contribution of exports to growth from the 1840s onwards.

much less marked than that which occurred in the last quarter of the century. High growth-rates were maintained both for the main industries (except for cotton after 1861) and for the global index right up to the 1860s and 1870s.

Some writers dispute the validity of industrial-production indices based on the consumption of raw materials – a basis used both for the series put forward for measuring the growth of several industries, and for a great number of those from which Hoffmann's general index was constructed. We readily admit that such indices probably have a downward bias, in other words they underestimate growth towards the end of what was a long period, because of the growing complexity of the finished goods which were manufactured. But this bias can only explain a small percentage of the difference in rates of growth between the third and fourth quarters of the nineteenth century. Hoffmann has also been criticized for not having included in his index certain industries which expanded rapidly at the end of the nineteenth century, mostly those producing cheap articles of current consumption for which increased purchasing-power among the working classes and new patterns of consumption had created a mass market. Notable among these goods were convenience foods (e.g. tinned goods, jam, sauces, meat extracts and various concentrates, custard, chocolate and sweets), but also soap, toothpaste, cosmetics and other toiletries, cigarettes, not to mention boot-polish and postcards[7]. In fact a number of these were included in Hoffmann's index[8]. Furthermore, the analysis of industrial structure in 1907 has already shown how the share of 'various industries', some of them undoubtedly 'new', and their contribution to national product remained modest when compared with the great staple industries. The slowdown of the latter and of overall industrial production after, say, 1873 seems to be beyond dispute.

Let us admit at once that things are less clear as far as national product is concerned[9]. Certainly the series published in 1968 by Phyllis Deane shows a very clear slowdown. It makes it clear that the longest

[7] See Charles Wilson, 'Economy and society in late Victorian Britain', *Economic History Review*, 2nd series, XVIII (1), Aug. 1965, 183–98, esp. 187–8,191; P.Mathias, *The First Industrial Nation: An Economic History of Britain, 1700–1914* (London, 1969), p.405. These industries did not have advanced technologies destined to be 'strategic' for growth in the twentieth century. A good electrical engineering industry would have been more useful in the long run than sweets or chocolate manufacture. These industries were neglected in Chapter 7 and 8; but their rise was perhaps more important on the social than on the economic plane.

[8] Whose coverage rate – two-thirds of industry at this period – should be considered as good.

[9] Pages on this point in Chapter 2 may be rather too dogmatic.

and fastest period of expansion of the United Kingdom's real GNP in the period 1830–1914 was between 1858 and 1875, with an annual rate of growth of 2.8 per cent. The rate then fell to only 2 per cent between 1872–4 and 1900–2, and to 1.2 per cent between 1900 and 1910. R.A.Church concludes from this that British GNP reached its maximum long-term growth-rate during the nineteenth century between the 1840s and the 1870s[10].

Feinstein's series, on the other hand, are much less conclusive. Though the growth-rate of the United Kingdom's real gross domestic product fell from 2.1 per cent per annum between 1857 and 1873 to 1.9 per cent between 1873 and 1890, the decline was marginal. True, the calculation of growth-rates from one cyclical peak to the next shows a lower trend after the particularly high figure of 1866–73, but they remain stable up to the beginning of the twentieth century, when a distinct and undeniable slow-down occurs[11]. During the last quarter of the nineteenth century, there may have been simply a stabilization in the growth of gross domestic product. If, in the preceding period, the rate had tended to accelerate (which is by no means certain), that would be an unfavourable symptom. But these data could support D.McCloskey's thesis that the slow-down of British growth started in the Edwardian and not in the late Victorian period (when, on the contrary, there would have been a rapid growth of GDP). This would place the climacteric around 1900[12]. While he criticizes McCloskey on certain points, D.H.Aldcroft admits that there was no dramatic

[10] See Chapter 3, p.51 (table 13); also P.Deane, 'New estimates of gross national product for the United Kingdom, 1830–1914', *The Review of Income and Wealth*, series 14 (2), June 1968, 96 (table 1); R.A.Church, p.23. P.Bairoch, *Commerce extérieur et développement économique de l'Europe au XIXe siècle* (Paris–The Hague, 1976), pp.151 and 156 (tables 48 and 51), also shows a slow-down in growth of GNP volume before 1890 (and of product per head as well).
[11] See Chapter 3, p.53 (table 14), and Chapter 3, p.52 (note 19); also Feinstein, *National Income*, table 20, T.51–2, from which one can compute rates of growth that are only marginally smaller between 1872–4 and 1900–2 than between 1855–7 and 1872–4.
[12] D.N.McCloskey, 'Did Victorian Britain fail?', *Economic History Review*, 2nd series, XXIII (3), Dec.1970, 446–59; esp. 456–7 (table 2). This article does not use the Feinstein series (1972), but a rather heterogeneous GNP series. On the other hand Aldcroft and McCloskey use Feinstein in their 1974 articles, quoted below, pp.376, 387 (notes 13 and 47). See also R.C.O.Matthews, in D.H.Aldcroft and P.Fearon, *Economic Growth in 20th Century Britain* (London, 1969), p.81 (table 1): from 1899 to 1913 the growth-rate of real GDP was only 1.1 per cent. If the slow-down came after 1900, it is particularly serious as showing up a 'British disease', which McCloskey rebuts for the Victorian period, because the slow-down then coincides with a period of prosperity and vigorous growth in the world economy, and not with the Great Depression, which provided an excuse.

slowing-down of GDP before 1900. In spite of a few dips, he sees no break in the GDP's rising trend, but some slow-down only after 1890[13].

However this may be, there is a divergence, according to Feinstein's data on national product between the development of the latter and that of industrial production, just as there is between the growth-rates of these two aggregates during the last quarter of the nineteenth century. This has surprised some writers, but there is nothing abnormal about it[14]. It is a matter of personal judgement to choose between the turning-points indicated by these different series. However, the data on industrial production, including its global index, seem more reliable than the estimates of national product, in spite of the quality of Feinstein's calculations. Secondly, industry was the heart of British economic power. Retardation in industrial progress therefore seems to us more serious than stabilization in the growth of the national product, the index of industrial production being the most important for the long-term development of the economy, indeed the key sign of progress or decline[15]. As a result, we will locate the climacteric in the 1870s at the latest. Furthermore, one observes a simultaneous stabilization of the economic structure. The major changes brought about by the Industrial Revolution, especially the redistribution of labour and population at the expense of agriculture and the countryside, are nearly complete; and at all levels, in spite of many changes in detail (e.g. in technology or the siting of industries), stability appears to be the order of the day.

The British economy seems not to have found a second wind. Even if this is not strictly the case, several foreign countries were forcing the pace or were immune to any slow-down. The result is that Great Britain was outclassed as an industrial power.

GREAT BRITAIN OVERTAKEN

It was pointed out at the beginning of this book that the growth of Britain's GNP, either in aggregate or per capita, was not especially

[13] D.H.Aldcroft, 'McCloskey on Victorian growth: a comment', *Economic History Review,* 2nd series, XXVII (2), May 1974, 271–4, esp. his two tables at 272 and 273. This article revives the thesis held by Phelps Brown and Handfield-Jones, which placed the climacteric in the 1890s and which was rejected in Chapter 3 (p.51). However, Aldcroft and McCloskey ignore the view held by Saul and others that the boom, which reached its peak in 1900 creates a statistical freak, being an 'accident' or 'flash in the pan'.

[14] See McCloskey, 'Did Victorian Britain fail?', 47–8, 456. The Hoffmann index is gross and is not an index of income generated by industry. It is normal that it should grow more slowly than national income.

[15] Remark by S.B.Saul, *The Myth of the Great Depression, 1873–96* (London, 1969), p.38. Indeed, it is on the problems of British industry that discussions have been centred.

fast in comparison with other advanced countries over the whole span of the nineteenth century, and particularly between 1870 and 1913[16]. Although international comparisons in this domain present all sorts of difficulties and many uncertainties, we will quote Angus Maddison's growth-rates[17], which give valid orders of magnitude and have the advantage of being calculated for the particular period that interests us[18]. They concern twelve advanced western countries – ten in Europe[19], plus the United States and Canada. Table 66 is a summary of the essentials.

Where the growth of total output is concerned, Great Britain was in the eighth position, equal with the Netherlands and Norway. Only France and Italy came below her.

Table 66 Annual average rates of growth in several countries from 1870 to 1913 (%)

	Total output (a)	*Output per head*	*Output per man-hour*
United Kingdom	2.2	1.3	1.5
Germany	2.9	1.8	2.1
France	1.6	1.4	1.8
Sweden	3.0	2.3	2.7
Average of ten European countries (b)	2.4	1.4	1.8
United States	4.3	2.2	2.4
Average of twelve countries (b)	2.7	1.6	1.9

(a) Gross domestic product at constant prices.
(b) Not weighted.

[16] For industrial production, see the calculations by D.H.Aldcroft in D.H.Aldcroft (ed.), *The Development of British Industry and Foreign Competition, 1875–1914: Studies in Industrial Enterprise* (London, 1968), p.13 (table II):

	Long-term rates of growth per annum 1870/1–1918 (%)	
	Industrial production	Industrial productivity
UK	2.1	0.6
USA	4.7	1.5
Germany	4.1	2.6

[17] A.Maddison, *Economic Growth in the West: Comparative Experience in Europe and North America* (New York, 1964), pp.28, 30, 37 (table 1–1,1–7). These data have been used by S.Kuznets, *Modern Economic Growth: Rate, Structure and Spread* (New Haven and London, 1966) p. 352 (table 6.6).

[18] A drawback is that they are a-quarter-of-a-century old, so that the series used for certain countries have now been replaced by more satisfactory ones. But Bairoch's tables, *Commerce extérieur,* pp.139, 292–3 (tables 44, 79, 80), which are calculated by 'customs periods' and so less convenient from our point of view, generally confirm Maddison's figures.

[19] Belgium, Denmark, France, Germany, Italy, the Netherlands, Norway, Sweden, Switzerland, the United Kingdom. We do not reproduce figures for small European countries, giving Sweden, which had the most successful record, as the only example.

For per-capita output (as well as for labour-productivity) Britain's position was no better. Her growth-rate was ninth on the list, equal with Switzerland and only ahead of the Netherlands and Italy. Because of her stagnating population, France, which did badly in total output, caught up and just overtook England in per-capita output. Finally, in relation to productivity, England was tenth, again only ahead of the Netherlands and Italy. The result of all this was that the real per-capita output income of the United Kingdom, which was the highest in the world in 1870, was overtaken by the United States around 1880 and by Canada right at the end of the century; the gap with the most advanced continental countries was also considerably reduced[20].

Furthermore, as Great Britain's industrial production only doubled beween 1870 and 1913, while world production quadrupled, with particularly high growth-rates in the United States and Germany (roughly twice as high as the British rate), England's share in world industrial production fell back dramatically (table 67). She had to yield the position of first industrial power to the United States around 1880–5, and the position of runner up to Germany around 1905, though the gap with the latter remained small[21], while the gap with the United States had become huge by 1914.

The other old industrial countries – France and Belgium – also lost ground, but relatively less than England, while the share of the

Table 67 Shares of total world industrial production (%)[22]

	1870	1913
United Kingdom	31.8	14.0
Germany	13.2	15.7
France	10.3	6.4
United States	23.3	35.8

[20] According to Bairoch, *Commerce extérieur*, p.292, between 1890 and 1913 the gap between the per-capita product of the UK and of the continent diminished by 15 per cent. He seems also to prove that it was mainly after 1890 that the inferiority of GB's growth was marked, although it was already clear in relation to Germany for the period 1860–90; see pp.139, 151, 156, 290, (tables 44, 51, 58, 77). D.H.Aldcroft, in D.H.Aldcroft and P.Fearon, *Economic Growth in 20th Century Britain* (London, 1969), p.38 (table 4), shows a clear English inferiority in the growth of industrial production from 1901 to 1913.

[21] See C.P.Kindleberger, 'Germany's overtaking of England, 1806–1914, Part II', *Weltwirtschaftliches Archiv*, 111 (3), 1975 478–504, which concludes that, except in industrial power, Germany did not really outstrip England.

[22] Taken from P.Deane, in H.D.Habakkuk and M.Postan (eds), *The Cambridge Economic History of Europe*, VI: *The Industrial Revolution and After* (Cambridge, 1965), p.25. Saul, *The Myth*, p.39 (table V), gives rates of growth of industrial production *per head of population*, which are lamentable for England by comparison with the US and Germany.

newcomers to industrialization – Russia, Italy, Sweden and Canada – increased. England's decline was particularly striking in iron and steel, where she had formerly dominated. In 1913 she made 7.8 million tons of steel against Germany's 17.6 and the USA's 34[23]. Against this, she kept her leading position in textiles.

Britain was no longer 'the workshop of the world' in the sense of having a near monopoly of modern industry. She was only the world's third industrial power, and some would say that she was the weakest and least dynamic of the Big Three. Yet, however disagreeable this loss of status may have been for British pride, one should not exaggerate its significance and gravity[24]. On the contrary one should qualify it and avoid false problems. Thus it is obvious that, from the moment when industrialization spread, the share of the pioneer countries in world industrial production was bound to diminish. It was also unlikely that England would stay ahead in every field; new competitors with special comparative advantages could forge ahead in certain specialities and even trespass on traditional British preserves. Above all, when there was a country like the United States, which spread over half a continent, with immense natural resources, a large population that was energetic and educated, together with various other conditions that were favourable to growth, it was inevitable that she would become a great industrial power and finally overtake a small island. To a lesser degree the same reasoning applies to Germany.

So Peter Mathias was absolutely right to turn the usual question upside down. The surprising phenomenon, which is hard to explain, was the chain of circumstances which gave Great Britain a predominant position in the world economy during most of the nineteenth century, and not the fact that other countries caught her up at the end of that century. In other words, it is a mistake to think that England's supremacy was normal and her decline abnormal[25].

Of course, in this new international context, it was inevitable that

---

[23] In 1901, output of steel had been 5 million tons in the UK, 6.1 in Germany and 14.8 in the US. In 1880 GB had produced as much steel as all the rest of Europe, and twice as much coal as the US. In 1913 her coal production was only half the latter's, but it remained higher than Germany's.

[24] It does indeed show the mistake made by those who brand as a 'statistical illlusion' rates of growth such as those of table 61, pretending that it is easy for an economy to achieve very high rates when it begins to industrialize, but difficult to keep them up when it is 'advanced'. Even if it is valid in certain cases, e.g. for the Scandinavian countries, this reasoning cannot apply to the United States and Germany, whose economies in absolute terms were already in 1870 comparable to England's; Saul, *The Myth*, p.39; Mathias, *The First Industrial Nation*, p.406.

[25] Mathias, *The First Industrial Nation*, pp.251, 255, 406; P.L.Payne, 'Iron and Steel Manufactures', in Aldcroft, *The Development*, p.98.

Britain would encounter difficulties, particularly because of the peculiar, unbalanced structure of her industry, which has been described above. It was dominated by a few large staple industries which produced (for many years with great efficiency) a fairly narrow range of goods, for which there had been a vigorous demand in the decades before 1870. With the spread of industrialization to other countries, often relying after 1879 on the revival of protectionism, the great staple English industries like textiles and iron and steel were in danger of losing a part of their foreign markets. This was a fact which England had to accept and could not counteract, but it was perhaps not as significant as one might think[26]. Moreover, even if world industrialization brought problems of adaptation or even wholesale change for the pioneer economy, because it could not maintain growth by always making the same products, there was nothing insurmountable about these problems. It was a question of creating new industries, new products, and new skills to replace those which were suffering from new competition, of redeploying resources and innovating.

Furthermore, the situation of an old-established industrial country in a world that was becoming industrialized did have some favourable aspects. Industrialization increased and diversified demand from other countries – both from advanced countries[27], and before 1914 Germany was Britain's second-best customer, just as Britain was the *Reich's* best customer[28] – and from new or colonial countries which, thanks to the industrial world's growing demand for their primary produce, provided wider or even new markets for manufactured goods.

In addition, the expansion of international trade provided scope for increasing the provision of services to foreigners (opportunities that the British seized with success), so swelling invisible earnings. It must be stressed that, even if Great Britain lost her leading position as an industrial power, she kept it easily in shipping, insurance, brokerage

---

[26]   D.N.McCloskey, 'Britain's loss from foreign industrialization: a provisional estimate', *Explorations in Economic History*, VIII, Winter 1971, has maintained that the influence of the industrialization of Germany and other countries on the British national income was very small (a deficiency of the order of 4 per cent of the 1913 GNP). See also Mathias, *The First Industrial Nation*, p.407: none of the perturbations of foreign origin which occurred after 1870 ought necessarily to have affected growth, investment and innovation in GB.
We have seen that Bairoch puts forward a contrary thesis and makes 'unilateral free trade' responsible to a large extent for England's troubles, protectionism gave her rivals a growth in production and exports that was definitely more rapid, and also enabled them to catch up on the technical side; *Commerce extérieur*, pp.51, 53–4, 74–5, 151, 162, 201–17, 301.

[27]   Especially for coal and machinery which England was well placed to supply.

[28]   Mathias, *The First Industrial Nation*, p.255.

and commission services, as well as in international banking and provision of long-term capital, not to mention her position as the world's chief trading power. Her continued supremacy in these sectors very much made up for her 'decline' and certainly preserved her position as the dominant economy.

Britain's loss of position as an industrial power was, in certain respects, inevitable because of changes in the world economy, over which the British had no control – particularly over the rapid progress of American and German industry. In these circumstances it may be that some slow-down in British growth was normal[29]. On the other hand, one is inclined to regard the loss of lead in per-capita income and the reduced gap in this respect with several countries as more serious. A number of writers see here a proof that, in addition to external changes over which the British had no control, there were also internal weaknesses for which they were responsible. The really worrying symptom was that Britain had lost her technological leadership, had not improved her productivity sufficiently and so had seen her competitiveness reduced. The heart of the problem is thus identified as a failing in innovation[30].

TECHNOLOGY AND PRODUCTIVITY

We now embark on a subject where much ink has been spilt. One generally accepted idea strongly emphasizes the technological deficiencies of British industry during the period under review; but, as has been pointed out on several occasions in earlier chapters, there has recently been a reaction against this pessimism. Indeed, the very idea of a failure of late Victorian industry has been disputed and even completely rejected.

It appears that the most advanced continental countries, as well as the United States, reached England's technological level in the 1860s, and after 1870 at the latest she was certainly no longer the leading

[29] All the more so, it has been said, in that GB had arrived at a stage where the tertiary sector, in which gains in productivity are usually small, grows faster than the secondary sector. This is a change of structure that retards per-capita growth, but which J.R.T.Hughes, in D.N.McCloskey, *Essays in a Mature Economy: Britain After 1840* (London, 1971), p.389, considers normal, desirable and having been successfully achieved in a very advanced country like GB.

[30] See in Aldcroft and Fearon, p.119 (table 10) (in an article by J.Knapp and K.Lomax), a calculation of GB's annual average lag behind the weighted group USA-Germany-France-Sweden, between 1870 and 1913, according to Maddison's data. It shows negative rates (hence a growing lag) for wages–rates, labour productivity and competitive performance, but positive rates for unit labour-costs and export prices. So, on every count, there was deterioration in the British position.

centre of technical innovation[31]. Her inventive genius had doubtless not dried up and British inventions remained numerous and important; but some of these were adopted more speedily and on a larger scale in foreign countries than in their land of origin. Moreover, in the new fields that were decisive for future industrial development, that is chemistry, electricity, the internal-combustion engine and machine-tools, nearly all important inventions were made abroad[32]. This point would be of secondary importance and without economic significance if these new inventions had been swiftly and widely adopted by British industry. But that is just the question that is hotly argued.

In any case it is widely thought that the new industrial powers – the great ones like the United States and Germany, of course, but also some smaller ones like Sweden – overtook Britain in the technological field at the end of the nineteenth century. English industry did not succeed in adapting to the new conditions of the international economy, which were discussed above, in making the necessary and large-scale effort of innovation, which would have made up for those unfavourable conditions. On the one hand, traditional industries failed to sustain a high level of technology that would have kept them competitive. Thus the textile industries, notably cotton, shunned all important innovation. Ring-spinning and the automatic loom were only slowly adopted. The steel industry did not go in for integrated works; it remained faithful too long to the Bessemer process, and refused to use low-grade ores which would have led to the production of cheaper pig-iron than could be made from imported ores. Mechanization in coalmines was well behind other countries and the productivity of labour there tended to fall from the 1880s onwards. In many branches, anyway, productivity ceased to improve after 1880 and real costs did not fall. So these old industries did not accept innovation, which, by lowering prices, would have widened their markets and given them faster growth. On the other hand, the new industries, e.g. organic chemistry, electrical equipment and motor-cars, only developed at a modest rate, too modest to replace the old industries whose slow-down was probably inevitable and far slower than the pace of advance which was being achieved in the United States and Germany.

---

[31] Bairoch, *Commerce extérieur*, pp.28–9, 45, 141–5, 200–01, 288; especially his table 45, p.141, already quoted (Introduction, p.3), where he gives statistics of the main inventions listed by Derry and Williams: between 1870 and 1899 England only supplies twenty, the continent and the US fifty-three. He also notes a slow-down after 1877–9 in the increase of the number of patents issued in GB.

[32] H.Perkin, *The Origins of Modern English Society, 1780–1880* (London, 1969), p.412; Mathias, *The First Industrial Nation,* pp.415–17.

It has also been deplored that, in a number of industries, modern machinery and equipment were of foreign origin, either imported or made in England by subsidiaries of foreign firms[33]. In other cases, British manufacturers failed to adopt new machinery perfected abroad.

So one can paint a very gloomy picture of British industry at the end of the nineteenth century: it was backward, did not innovate any more itself and rejected innovation and best practice from abroad. It is a picture that is probably biased. Firstly, one can question whether it is reasonable to compare each aspect of British technology with the outstanding foreign success in the same sphere, especially as this best practice was often American. There has been too much comparison with the United States that is often crushing for England. For all sorts of reasons such as the extent of its home market, its endowment of natural resources and the very speed of growth, it was normal that, at the end of the nineteenth century and the beginning of the twentieth, American industry should have been the first to invent and develop certain industries with a future, using mass-production methods[34]. Therefore, in 1907, the United States had twice as much capital invested per worker and used twice as much energy as Britain; value added per worker was £500 a year as against £100 in Britain[35]. What was more devastating for England was the comparison with Germany, who between 1870 and 1900, established a very clear technological lead in industries like steel, electricity, precision machinery, and optical and chemical goods[36]. It appeared earlier, of course, that certain criticisms of British technology were hardly justified. Thus ring-spinning was less appropriate than traditional mules for the production of medium and fine yarns, then becoming the main products of the English cotton industry, which concentrated on quality articles, leaving coarse goods to developing countries. The use of iron-ores from the East Midlands would not have brought the advantages that have been assumed. In coalmines, mechanization encountered geological obstacles that were absent in the United States; and, although productivity fell, it was still higher than in other European countries.

---

[33] This was the case for some electrical apparatus, for machinery used in the dairy industry and in shoe-making, for typewriters, for sewing-machines, etc.

[34] T.C.Barker, 'History: economic and social', in C.B.Cox and A.E. Dyson (eds), *The Twentieth-Century Mind: History, Ideas and Literature in Britain*, I: *1900–1918* (London, 1972), p.63. However, contemporaries often went in for this sort of comparison.

[35] Mathias, *The First Industrial Nation*, pp.425–6.

[36] D.S.Landes, *The Unbound Prometheus: Technological Change and Industrial Development in Western Europe, 1750 to the Present* (Cambridge, 1969), pp.326ff.

However, rather than repeat these criticisms on specific points, we will mention the more general counter-offensives mounted against the ultra-pessimistic view.

First of all there is the 'moderate' case, which is also traditional in its methods, and which has been presented particularly by T.C.Barker. He does not deny that British industry was backward in some respects, especially (and inevitably) in comparison with the United States, but he insists that it was generally narrowing the gap fairly quickly, both by adopting new techniques and by designing new products with good sales prospects in the long-term[37]. His main point is that one must think in terms of *products* and not industries, 'new' or 'old', for some of the latter could manufacture 'new' articles[38]. He holds the view that this shift to new products with a future, for which England was in some cases strongly placed, and this tendency to diversify were on their way to fulfilment during the Edwardian era, e.g. the English motor-car industry, on the eve of the war, was on the point of catching up with its older French rival. However, hostilities interrupted this promising progress, which would have enabled British industry to adapt itself to changes in world demand – changes that were gradual in peacetime, but speeded up by war – by developing exports of new products to make up for the inevitable fall of several traditional exports. So the first world war alone was responsible for 'England's crisis' in the 1920s – and we can hardly blame the Victorians and Edwardians for having failed to foresee the war's consequences[39]!

S.B.Saul comes to much the same conclusions, when he considers the engineering industries in particular. First of all he shows that Britain in the late Victorian and Edwardian periods held a very clear lead in several branches of these industries. He admits that there were weaknesses, but maintains that, once the considerable advantages brought about by American machines and methods were understood, these were quickly adopted. He also asserts that the rhythm of change and adaptation speeded up on the eve of the war[40]. Putting it simply, the various articles in the book *The Development of British Industry and*

[37] Barker, 'History', pp.51–70.
[38] Among them the cotton industry, in so far as it produced more and more fine yarns and fabrics of quality.
[39] Barker, 'History', passim. Same opinion held by Hughes on the role of the war, in McCloskey, *Essays*, p.389. For Barker, the very mediocre growth of the Edwardian period is explained by external factors: repercussions of the 1907–8 American financial crisis on England, reduction in the hours of work, strikes; but he emphasizes that after 1910 stagnation gave way to a vigorous recovery.
[40] Cf. Chapter 8, p.262–3, and the conclusion of his contribution, 'The engineering industry' to Aldcroft, *The Development*, pp.236–7; also *The Myth*, p.46.

Foreign Competition, 1875-1914 testify to the wide diversity in British industry during this period, even within each branch and subsector[41]. For this reason one cannot talk of general technical backwardness and complete impotence in the face of foreign competition.

A more systematic, ambitious and devastating counter-attack – at least in appearance – has been mounted by some British and American authors, often using New Economic History methods, especially cost-benefit analysis. The most outspoken has been D.N.McCloskey, who, with quixotic generosity, has made himself the uncompromising champion of the late Victorian economy, particularly its entrepreneurs, against the common hypothesis, to which we shall return, that inadequate management explains England's supposed inferiority in technology. Basing his views on papers read at a colloquium held in 1970, he has asserted that the performance of the British economy was much better than has hitherto been supposed[42]. He admits the existence of weaknesses but points out that all economies, including those of Germany and the United States, suffered from some deficiencies. In a difficult period, when its predominance was waning, the British economy proved to be competitive and prosperous, even including the old industries, and the growth-rate or productivity was as high as in the United States up to about 1900. During this colloquium a number of participants, mostly American, took up the same point of view. In their technical choices and investment policies, British businessmen behaved 'rationally', in the economic sense of the term, and intelligently, given the conditions imposed on them. They responded adequately to technical changes and new commercial prospects, and they could not have done much better.

However, some British participants at the gathering were much more cautious. Sidney Pollard, supporting the traditional view, insisted that there was no excuse for the outdated equipment of industries that were crucial for exports, e.g. cotton and steel, nor for shortcomings in chemicals, electrical material and motor-cars. Summing up, Saul was more guarded. He recognized the validity of some of the arguments which had been put forward in support of the 'American' thesis, but he did not find them decisive. He stressed that it was a serious matter that Great Britain had ceased to engender new

---

[41] Remark by N.Rosenberg in his review, *Journal of Economic History*, XXXI (3) Sept.1971, 698–700. English performances appear to him better than to British writers.

[42] McCloskey, *Essays*, esp. pp.4–7 of his introduction; also the general discussion pp.389–92, and Saul's final comments, pp.393–7, in his 'Some thoughts on the papers and discussion on the performance of the late Victorian economy'. Most of the papers printed in this volume have been quoted earlier.

products and new processes. These had been the means by which she had established her pre-eminence during the Industrial Revolution, and by which the United States had overcome her handicaps and achieved supremacy in her turn. He also pointed out that American firms had lower productivity in their English subsidiaries than in their factories across the Atlantic[43].

True enough, the studies assembled in the *Essays* are on specific topics. Although they support the 'moderate' view on the technological performance of the late Victorian economy, they do not resolve the overall problem[44]. However, McCloskey has recourse to aggregates in calculating the productivity of the British economy, i.e. the proportion of the growth in GDP which was not attributable to the increase in inputs of capital and labour, or in other words the residual that arose roughly from technological progress. It emerges from these calculations that the growth of productivity was definitely inferior after 1870 to that of the decade 1860–70 (2.2 per cent annum), but that it progressed fairly steadily between 1870 and 1900 at an average rate of 1.2 per cent per annum, which was roughly the same as prevailed in the United States in the same period. On the other hand, there was a drastic slow-down after 1900, and from that year up to 1910, growth was negative at 0.4 per cent. So the cries of alarm about the slow growth of British productivity at the end of the nineteenth century, which would be the only valid proof of a 'failure' of the economy, seem to be absolutely unjustified[45].

These views have been criticized by D.H.Aldcroft, whose calculations (as in the case of real GNP) show a regular rise in 'residual' productivity up to 1890, then a deceleration; for his growth-rate, measured between cyclical peaks, never passes 0.5 per cent per annum after 1890, whereas it was nearly always over 1 per cent before that date[46]. Moreover, Aldcroft maintains that this decline was inevitable because of the economy's structure. There was no new sector with rapid growth and high investment leading to steep rises in productivity. As for traditional industries and the services sector, which was vigorously

[43]   ibid., pp.391, 393–6. See also the review by A.K.Cairncross, in *Economic History Review*, 2nd series, XXV (3), Aug. 1972, 528–9, who poses the problem of the sources of technological progress at the end of the nineteenth century, wondering whether they underwent a fundamental change that was unfavourable to GB. See on the other hand a favourable review by L.Sandberg, in *Journal of European Economic History*, II (2), Autumn 1973, 511–14.

[44]   At the purely methodological level, some of them are open to serious criticism.

[45]   McCloskey, 'Did Victorian Britain fail?', 458–9 (esp. table 3). Matthews, in Aldcroft and Fearon, p.81 (table 1), also discovers a 'residue' with negative growth between 1899 and 1913, using Feinstein's data.

[46]   Aldcroft, 'McCloskey on Victorian growth', 272–4 (esp. tables 1 and 2).

expanding, they knew no major innovations and even few improvements in technical detail. Growth was achieved solely by increasing and accumulating inputs of capital and labour and not by better use of these resources, which explains the drop in the residual. Aldcroft sees examples of this in coalmines and railways. So he concludes, 'The fact is that productivity did begin to decelerate in Victorian Britain.'

In reply McCloskey sticks to his guns, i.e. that 1900 was the turning-point in the growth of productivity. However he is cautious, confessing that a Student test only gives a slight preference to this date, and that 1873 and 1890 might be the climacteric dates[47]. One must recognize that McCloskey has always warned how tricky it is to measure productivity and how great is the margin of error[48]. Altogether one may wonder whether calculations of total or residual productivity for the whole of the economy have any validity for the period under consideration.

The calculations of labour-productivity, which are more traditional, are certainly more reliable. As far as industry is concerned all those which have been made show a clear fall in the growth-rate of this variable after the cycle 1866–74 or even, according to Coppock, after 1861–5. This fall continued uninterruptedly, bordering on a collapse, and ended in a negative rate at the beginning of the twentieth century (table 68)[49]. Similarly, if one calculates national product or domestic product per worker, one sees a steady decline in its growth-rate from 1865–74, when it was 1.4 per cent per annum according to Aldcroft, down to 0.9 per cent between 1890 and 1901 and 0.5 per cent between 1907 and 1913[50]. So it seems difficult to accept McCloskey's position which denies any real failure in productivity or negligence of 'modern' technology in Victorian times. He does indeed admit a sharp fall during the Edwardian era, but considers it too brief and late to be considered a climacteric[51].

---

[47] D.N.McCloskey, 'Victorian growth: a rejoinder', *Economic History Review*, 2nd series, XXVII (2) May 1974, 275–7.

[48] McCloskey,'Did Victorian Britain fail?', 455, 459: he pointed out that a change of 3 per cent in estimating the variables on which he calculated productivity is enough for its growth-rate between 1870 and 1900 to vary between 0.77 and 1.62 per cent per annum.

[49] Pollard and Crossley, p.226. The rate on line 1 is not exceptional, but typical of the earlier period; Saul, *The Myth*, p.37 (table 4), gives figures taken from Coppock, that are very close.

[50] Aldcroft, 'McCloskey on Victorian growth', 272–3 (tables 1 and 2). These are rates of growth between cyclical peaks.

[51] McCloskey, 'Did Victorian Britain fail?', pp.458–9. McCloskey, 'Victorian growth: a rejoinder', p.277. But this stagnation of productivity at the beginning of the twentieth century, which was serious (see p.375 (note 12)), has been explained neither by McCloskey nor by any other writer.

388   *The Victorian Economy*

Table 68 Annual average
rates of growth of labour-productivity in industry

1861/5–1866/74	2.2
1866/74–1875/83	1.0
1875/83–1884/9	0.5
1884/9–1890/9	0.1
1890/9–1900/7	0.2
1900/7–1908/13	−0.1

Moreover McCloskey has never denied that there was a slow-down in the growth of industrial production from the 1870s onwards. His aim was only to prove that this slow-down did not result from a similar trend in productivity, and so to exonerate British entrepreneurs from all responsibility for the 'decline' of Victorian England. Nor did this slow-down have its origins on the demand side and notably in exports; but rather in 'constraints of supply'. J.R.Meyer had calculated in 1955 that, if the growth-rate of British exports between 1852 and 1872 (4.8 per cent per annum) had been maintained between 1872 and 1907, the rate of growth of Hoffmann's index of industrial production during the latter period would have been 3.7 per cent per annum, when in fact it was only 1.7 per cent, and industrial output in 1907 would have been twice what it actually was. McCloskey takes the view that growth of this order of magnitude was just impossible, given the inelasticity of production factors. Where labour was concerned, unemployment was low in spite of the Great Depression[52] and the reserves of underemployed rural labour were nearly exhausted. The halt of emigration overseas would not have been much help. One could certainly have substituted capital for labour, but to achieve the rate of growth of 3.7 per cent, an increase in the stock of capital of 6 per cent per annum would have been required, i.e. four times what it in fact was at the end of the nineteenth century. Also the British would have had to save 42 per cent of their incomes. The ending of capital exports would only have made a small contribution, and capital would even have had to be imported on a massive scale. So it was the inadequacy of labour and capital resources and their inelasticity which prevented faster growth. Given these conditions, the British performance was reasonably satisfactory. This was an economy which grew 'as rapidly as permitted by the growth of its resources and the effective exploitation of the available technology'. On that last score, McCloskey considers that the

---

[52] Whereas it ought to have been considerable if it was the fall in exports which prevented rapid growth.

Victorians had little reason to reproach themselves, and other cliometricians, e.g. Paul David on the subject of the harvester, think that objective factors, particularly natural, geological and historical ones (or their combination, as in the English rural landscape) explain the technological weaknesses, which have to be admitted. They believe that the 'land' – or the natural-resources – factor ought to be restored to its proper place, in order to understand the economic history of the nineteenth century[53].

Aldcroft has criticized McCloskey for assuming an excessive rigidity and lack of room for manoeuvre in the British economy of late Victorian times. In particular, he doubts whether the supply of labour and capital was as elastic as McCloskey makes out. On the labour side, emigration, unemployment, underemployment and the inefficient use of much of the working population make one doubt the existence of a bottleneck. On the contrary, one could even argue that a relatively elastic and growing supply of labour and capital allowed a certain amount of growth up to the beginning of the twentieth century, without requiring the improvement in productivity, which could only have been brought about by an exogenous shock or strong upward pressure on costs[54].

On the whole, the views of McCloskey and other cliometricians have certainly been stimulating and useful. Firstly, from the point of view of historiography, they are almost completely opposed to those of the generation of American economic historians who had treated these problems before them. The latter, brought up in the optimistic atmosphere of pre-Vietnam America, had a Faustian or Promethean approach, according to which nothing is impossible for an economy if it is served by good entrepreneurs. But if the performance of an economy is mediocre, the responsibility rests above all with businessmen and their lack of entrepreneurship. The new generation has perhaps been influenced by a different economic climate and by the recent erosion of the United States' economic supremacy (rather reminiscent of late Victorian England's situation), and it has also been nurtured on neo-classicism, so that its vision is rather Panglossian: what is, is and on the whole it is the best possible. Moreover these scholars, who are often more economists or indeed econometricians than historians, have a strictly quantitative approach which makes them indifferent to

---

[53] McCloskey, 'Did Victorian Britain fail?', 446–51, 455, 459.

[54] Aldcroft, 'McCloskey on Victorian growth', 271–3; Church, *The Great Victorian Boom*, p.74. The discussion goes on: N.F.R. Crafts, 'Victorian Britain did fail', and D.N.McCloskey, 'No it did not: a reply to Crafts', *Economic History Review*, 2nd series, XXXII (4), Nov.1979, 533–41.

human factors – or at least, they would reduce the importance that used to be attached to the entrepreneur, and would exonerate him from responsibilities that now lie with endowment factors and with geographic and economic constraints. Has the energy crisis perhaps contributed to the rediscovery of land and natural resources?

These new views are equally useful when it comes to the question of substance. They confirm what was thought by a number of economic historians, i.e. that a uniformly dark picture of the British economy at the end of the nineteenth century was mistaken. As William Ashworth has suggested, this period was a combination of great achievements (e.g. after 1870 the use of the steam-engine spread widely in industry) and of missed opportunities to exploit new technical possibilities. Despite the vigour of the argument that all was well in the best of all possible worlds, the writer of these lines continues to think that, on the technological plane, the British economy showed up serious deficiencies, and that there was too little innovation. It is our task to seek an explanation of this failure and of the slow-down in the growth of industrial production from the 1870s onwards[55].

ECONOMIC INTERPRETATIONS

Explanations, as numerous as they are varied, have been advanced for the British 'decline', and many are unconvincing. Some of them point to one single cause and assert that it was overriding, but recent debates have clearly shown that the main causes were linked to one another and that the fundamental question is whether British failings were the result of circumstances which were objective and independent of human will, or of 'irrational' decisions made by entrepreneurs[56]. In short, whether the chief factors were economic or human.

Among economic explanations, one of the most popular relies on long-term economic fluctuations. It rests on the principle that total demand determines production, and it argues that production only increased slowly in Great Britain from the 1870s onwards because demand was inadequate, notably export demand which absorbed a large proportion of British production, especially in staple industries. This poor export record was itself the result of an exogenous factor – the unfavourable international economic situation during the Great Depression, when foreign demand grew more slowly than previously, while England ran more and more up against competition from new

---

[55]   W.Ashworth, *An Economic History of England, 1870–1939* (London, 1969) pp. 259–61, also 241, 253.
[56]   Remark by Feinstein, in McCloskey, *Essays*, p.390.

industrial powers and also against tariff barriers. But attention has also been drawn to the home market, which certainly expanded less fast than in America and Germany, and finally became narrower than either. Prominence has also been given to certain peculiar aspects of this home market which would have hampered the growth of strategic industries. Saul has suggested that the narrowness of the British market for certain new equipment, notably machine-tools, prevented England from developing a substantial export trade in a sector that had a good future. On the whole, he considers market conditions to have been a serious obstacle to growth[57].

It is true that the rate of growth of British exports slowed down at the end of the nineteenth century. In volume, it had been 4.9 per cent per annum between 1841 and 1871; it was only 2.3 per cent from 1871 to 1901 – a diminution of more than a half, and the lowest figure in the whole nineteenth century for a period of that duration[58]. We have also seen (table 26) that, during the second period the contribution of exports to economic growth was feeble, whereas it had been considerable in mid-Victorian times[59]. It seems beyond dispute that this situation contributed largely to the slow-down of industrial production, especially in the cases of the cotton, wool, and steel industries.

However, explanations based on the Great Depression forget that this was an international phenomenon from which all countries suffered, and it slowed down the growth of world trade as a whole. Now, the slow-down in growth and innovation was much more marked in Britain than in other countries, particularly the United States and Germany, though these two powers also had their difficulties. Why was there this difference in performance, which caused England's share in world production and trade to fall?

It has of course been said in reply that the Great Depression struck England more severely and for a greater length of time than it hit other countries, because her economy was more deeply involved in international trade. Furthermore, during the third quarter of the century, the British had profited from a very favourable conjunction of events – the rapid industrialization of advanced countries (though

[57] Saul, *The Myth*, pp.49–50; Saul, 'The engineering industry' pp.235–6.

[58] Figures from Deane and Cole, pp.311 (table 83) 312. These writers attribute the decline in overall growth to these stagnant exports. Saul, *The Myth*, p.49, gives rates of growth of the volume of exported *manufactured articles:* 4.8 per cent per annum from 1854 to 1872, 2.1 per cent from 1876 to 1910; and see Chapter 11, pp.342–59. But there was a slow-down in exports from the 1850s onwards, i.e. before the slow-down in industrial production: noted by Lomax, p.13.

[59] On the other hand it was very large at the beginning of the twentieth century (as in the mid-Victorian era), when there was a definite recovery in the growth of exports.

they were still unable to do without the capital goods supplied by England, and also unable to compete in third markets) and the opening-up of many new countries, thanks above all to British capital and equipment, especially in railways. But, after 1873, Britain had to face a new situation. On the one hand, advanced countries had developed their industries to a point where they had no more need of many British goods; indeed, after 1879 they closed their frontiers to these goods by raising tariffs, and finally they became dangerous competitors. On the other hand, thanks to improved transport, the new countries threw enormous quantities of primary products on the market, which led to a fall in prices. This meant that the terms of trade moved against these countries, and their power to purchase British goods was reduced, as well as their demand for capital and equipment, which usually came from Great Britain[60]. However, this does not take into account the fact that the purchasing power of primary producers does not depend solely on the price of their commodities and the elasticity of demand for them. The volume of exports, which was growing rapidly, also plays a part, and so does the cost of transport; the fall in the latter reduced the impact on the producers of the drop in prices on European markets.

Moreover, those who base their explanation on the Great Depression must recognize that the British economy, in which agriculture, from the 1870s onwards, was a minor sector, was only marginally affected by the agricultural crisis that had dramatic effects in other less industrialized countries. On the contrary, the British gained advantages from the influx of cheap primary products, which increased the real purchasing-power of the population. This orthodox view has recently been challenged by Bairoch, who asserts that, although only a small percentage of total population was employed in agriculture by the end of the nineteenth century, its loss of income still had a significant effect on the domestic demand for manufactured goods[61].

In any case, this explanation, based on the slow growth of British exports, suffers from one serious weakness. It calls mainly on exogenous factors, e.g. the Great Depression (and the causes that

---

[60]   A debatable point. In the 1870s it was GB's terms of trade which deteriorated.

[61]   Bairoch, *Commerce extérieur*, pp.211–2. He has not tried to calculate this effect, but puts forward the hypothesis that the agricultural crisis plus the loss of markets at home and abroad resulting from 'unilateral free trade', to which GB remained faithful, explains 60 to 70 per cent of the slow-down of British industrial growth in the last quarter of the nineteenth century; he seems, however, to attach more importance to the foreign-trade factor. Moreover, Bairoch (pp.122, 214–17) attributes a negative role of importance to emigration – both of men and of capital – which was a real transfer of production factors to the detriment of England and to the advantage of the receiving countries. It did substantial harm both to British agriculture and to British industry.

generated it, such as the falling production of gold), the rise of new
industrial powers, the revival of protectionism, etc. One must admit
that these were factors over which the British had no control.
However, it has already been emphasized that these changes in the
international scene also brought new opportunities, and that everything depended on the way the British reacted, adapted, innovated,
and tried to create new products and open new markets; for the latter
are not given once for all and resistant to all initiatives[62]. One can, of
course, argue that the slow-down in demand did not encourage
innovation and investment in new technology, for which there were,
moreover, few opportunities of self-financing in a period of falling
profits. Slow growth could of itself cause technical backwardness and
stagnant productivity, leading to a loss of competitiveness for Britain,
dragged down in a sort of vicious spiral. However, unless one supposes
an almost total passivity on the part of British entrepreneurs[63], which
involves a different type of causality, the explanation we are
discussing does not resolve the key problem of inadequate innovation.
Exports are not an independent variable in the growth process: they
can be a consequence as much as a cause.

Furthermore, some have suggested that England suffered less than
other countries from the Great Depression, and that the persistence of
her prosperity harmed her in the long run, because it did not force
fundamental changes. In the same way, the possession of soft and
virtually protected empire markets spared businessmen the necessary
effort of renovation and diversification[64]. Finally, there is general
agreement that the end of the Great Depression occurred in 1896 at the
latest. However, while other countries at the start of the twentieth
century enjoyed rapid growth during *la Belle Epoque,* England
certainly benefited from a recovery in exports, but this did not show up
in other key indices. On the contrary, productivity took a most
disquieting turn, as has been stressed by the very supporters of the late
Victorians.

There is a somewhat different explanation, which derives from
Schumpeter's ideas, and postulates long cycles in technological

[62] But P.Temin, 'The relative decline of the British steel industry, 1880–1913', in
H.Rosovsky (ed.) *Industrialization in Two Systems: Essays in Honor of Alexander
Gerschenkron* (New York, 1966) (see Chapter 8, p.244), has maintained that, in iron
and steel, whatever British industrialists had done, they could not have increased the
rate of growth of their output by more than 1.2 per cent per annum.
[63] Hobsbawm, p.182, writes that the British were not ready to adopt the new solutions
which would have been necessary; also Bairoch, *Commerce extérieur,* p.210; Saul, *The
Myth,* p.50, who points out that Englishmen were often at that time considered poor
salesmen.
[64] Saul, *The Myth,* p.50.

innovation. Britain's growth up to 1870 would have been based on the increasing application of the great basic inventions of the Industrial Revolution, e.g. the steam-engine, railways, textile machinery and the factory system. However, after 1870 this source of momentum was just about exhausted, especially in the country that had initiated it. These great innovations had lost their impetus and no longer produced increasing returns. Later, of course, a new group of innovations emerged connected with the use of electricity and the internal-combustion engine, and with the development of new industries like organic chemicals. These were the basis for a new leap forward in productivity and investment from the 1890s onwards. Meanwhile, there would have been a 'technological lull', a plateau which caused a slow-down in investment and growth. In fact, there is no sign of this lull, and technological development did not have the intermittent character suggested by this thesis. Moreover the 'steel revolution' and the spread of the steam-engine in industry were in full spate during the 1870s and 1880s, just when industrial growth was slowing down. Even if later there was a temporary lack of important inventions, it still has to be explained why England's competitors did not suffer from it as much, and why England was behind in innovation[65].

So one ought to exclude as a determining influence all exogenous factors coming from outside and linked to the international situation. Are more satisfactory interpretations to be found in domestic economic factors, peculiar to Great Britain, and notably in endowment in the factors of production, which some have maintained was unfavourable to the pursuit of swift technological progress?

One explanation, which is hardly tenable, supposes that at the end of the nineteenth century Britain suffered from worsening conditions as far as natural resources were concerned, owing to her growing dependence on imported raw materials, caused by increasing consumption and also by the complete or partial exhaustion of certain indigenous mineral deposits (ores of iron and non-ferrous metals). However, this theory positing a decline in natural resources would only apply in relation to the United States; for, compared with European countries, Britain was not in a position of inferiority, except perhaps for iron – certainly not as regards coal! Furthermore her traditional commercial supremacy had located the main raw material exchanges in her ports, where commodities like cotton and wool were a little cheaper than in continental ports[66].

---

[65]   See Mathias, *The First Industrial Nation*, pp.408–9; Saul, *The Myth*, pp.43–4.
[66]   Landes, *The Unbound Prometheus*, p.332.

A much more convincing thesis is the one advanced notably, with great brilliance, by Sir John Habakkuk. It is based on the difference between the costs of labour in England and in the United States. This thesis has been presented and briefly discussed above, and we shall not return to it now, except to recall that it can only explain Britain's technological backwardness in relation to the United States and not to Germany where, up to 1914, wages and labour-costs were distinctly lower than in England[67]. In addition, during the period in question, i.e. between 1873 and the end of the century, British manufacturers ought to have been especially inclined to look for savings in labour, for money-wages were stable, while prices of industrial products were falling, which endangered profit margins. Yet they do not, on the whole, seem to have tried very hard to improve the productivity of their workers, which made only slow progress. Americans, on the other hand, who no longer had the same pressing reasons to substitute capital for labour as in the early decades of the nineteenth century, thanks to the influx of cheap labour from the 'new immigration', continued to use and develop a more and more capital-intensive technology[68].

The problem concerning factors of production which has stimulated the liveliest discussions has certainly been the use of capital at the disposal of British investors. Indeed the slow rate of growth and technological progress has been attributed to inadequate investment in Britain herself, especially in industry. This deficiency would have resulted from excessive investment abroad. This arose from the imperfections and 'perversity' of the capital market, which channelled capital abroad to the detriment of national industry. This led to mediocre performances in industry, which was starved of funds, so that new investment tended to be diverted more and more towards foreign countries. Although some of these views had the support of J.M.Keynes, they do not seem incontrovertible. It has already been seen above (table 27) that, in the light of current research, the rate of fixed-capital formation in Britain does not seem to have been high at any moment in the nineteenth century. It also seems that, between 1875 and 1914, the net rate of domestic capital formation was definitely inferior to that of Germany and still more to that of the

---

[67] We mentioned above the migrations of labour in Germany, from agriculture to industry, which restrained the rise in wages.

[68] Saul, *The Myth*, pp. 50–1, also 39–40, where he points out, following an article by Ashworth, changes in the structure of the population of a working age (e.g. reduction in the percentage of non-productive people, fall in the work-force of low-productivity sectors like agriculture) and in working conditions. All these, except (possibly) for the reduction in working hours, ought to have contributed to a growth in productivity.

United States, though the causal relationship remains uncertain: did faster growth lead to a higher rate of investment, or was it the other way round[69]? However, though the rate of fixed-capital formation in Britain, whether calculated on Phyllis Deane's data or on Feinstein's, was lower during the 1880s than in the 1870s, it rose later and roughly equalled the latter level – even exceeded it; only between 1905 and 1914 did investment levels fall to a fairly low percentage, less anyhow than the ratio of net investment abroad to GNP. So it is difficult to share the view that the domestic investment proportion dropped after 1875 or 1885[70]. Ashworth, it is true, has emphasized that at two points in time – at the end of the 1870s and around 1900 – a large part of this domestic investment was spent on housing, in building new suburbs, that were comfortable and healthy, as well as seaside resorts, but this involved considerable expenditure on basic equipment that was largely unproductive and was underused, e.g. rolling-stock for suburban trains, which only functioned at rush-hours. A lot of money too was spent on public health (water-supply, main drainage, paving roads), which was excellent from a social point of view, but less so on the economic level. So there was probably some wastage of resources, and certainly a predominance of low-yielding investment, which did not stimulate the growth of national product and the efficiency of the economy[71]. Yet one can doubt whether this diversion of resources was large enough to affect those two variables seriously. Anyway, the bulk of domestic investment has always been devoted to transport, housing and other basic infrastructure-development, whereas a small proportion only has gone to directly productive ends, i.e. industrial plant. It is

[69] Saul, *The Myth*, pp.40–1 (table VI), 42, quoting Kuznets' calculations:

Net domestic capital formation
as percentage of net domestic product

	UK	Germany	USA
1855–74	7.0	8.5	13.9
1875–94	6.8	11.4	12.9
1895–1914	7.7	15.0	

[70] We have serious doubts about the figures of Pollard and Crossley, p.228, for the percentage increase in physical capital invested in industry per head of population, for they show a slow-down which is improbable:

1865–75	39
1875–85	14
1885–95	6
1895–1905	7

[71] W.Ashworth, 'The late Victorian economy', *Economica*, N.S., XXXIII (129), Feb.1966, 17–33; critical remarks by Saul, *The Myth*, p.43, advising not to overestimate the building booms. Ashworth also wonders whether the more and more complex equipment being installed at this period was used in the optimal way, given the shortening of the working day and the rarity of shift-work. Hence a poor return which discouraged new investment.

possible that the formation of fixed capital in industry diminished (available data do not allow us to be more specific), but this would be a consequence, much more than a cause, of inadequate innovation[72].

There still remains the question of capital exports, whose importance in the late Victorian and Edwardian periods has already been stressed, as well as their tendency to increase both in absolute figures and as percentages of national product, with fluctuations going counter to domestic investment, which they finally outstriped on the eve of the first world war[73].

A reaction has taken place recently against Keynes and writers like Rosenstein Rodan, who asserted that 'the City of London and its financial institution were the greatest single threat to the prosperity of England', because they diverted savings away from industry, showing no interest in it and preferring to invest money abroad (at which London was past-master). Many recent writers tend to think that there is no proof that exports of capital deprived British industry of the funds it needed to re-equip itself and adopt innovations. Nor do they believe that domestic interest rates were kept at a higher level than they should have been, an idea which supposes a shortage of capital, which was not the case[74]. The most one could accept is that investment in housing, especially just before 1914, and in public works undertaken by local authorities may have been somewhat affected. But it does not seem as if industry lacked capital or innovators were disappointed in their search for it. This was not the case, for instance, in the bicycle and motor-car industries. The problem of innovation and the alleged inadequate development of 'new' industries is much more complicated than a question of one or two percentage points more or less in the ratio of domestic investment to national income[75].

Moreover it has been emphasized that the sources of finance for home industries were different and separate from those for exports of

---

[72] Aldcroft, in Aldcroft and Fearon, *Economic Growth...*, pp.43–4, suggests that much investment in staple industries was made without changing techniques of production. There was only replacement or addition to existing equipment, and therefore little increase in productivity.

[73] Cf. Chapter 11, p.363ff. Shifts from one type of investment to another, to which Rostow attached much importance (see Chapter 3, p.59), cannot explain the slow-down in growth and innovation.

[74] See for example Barker, 'History', pp.55–6, 59. During the period 1870–1913 there were few defaults leading to serious losses on capital invested abroad. Domestic investment, on the other hand, was not immune from risk. The mortality of joint-stock companies was high; bankruptcies and even frauds were frequent.

[75] Yet at some periods, there were signs of a rise in unemployment in periods of heavy outflow of capital, for the rise in mechandise exports which resulted did not make up for the fall in domestic investment.

capital; so competition between these two types of investment was marginal. M.Edelstein has maintained that British financial institutions could cope perfectly well with every kind of loan, large or small, short-term or long-term, and notably for the financing of industry, but there was separation of functions. The great city houses specialized in big issues of state bonds or railway stock – which was perfectly rational as their unit costs were low. It would certainly have been costly for medium-sized industrial companies to issue securities on the London market, but provincial firms, which made up most of industry, had only modest capital needs. Access to the London Stock Exchange was not indispensable for such businesses, for they found many facilities for finance locally – solicitors, banks, provincial stock exchanges, etc.[76]. Indeed, when at the end of the century several large provincial firms made issues in London, they ran into no difficulties. Edelstein has calculated that between 1870 and 1913 the face value of foreign securities held in the United Kingdom increased from 33 to 45 per cent of total British portfolio investment, but at the same time the proportion of British company securities, other than railway stock, rose from 4 to 19 per cent. He has also denied that there was a distinct preference among investors for the 'big' issues by government and utility companies, and he estimates that on the contrary they tended after 1890 to concentrate on truly British securities. Hence the conclusion that there was no 'irrational bias' in the capital market, as had been said, in favour of foreign investment[77]. Defender as always of the late Victorian economy, McCloskey has gone even further, rejecting all idea of 'perversity' on the City's part in favour of exports of capital, and maintaining that imperfections of the capital market led only to a tiny reduction in national product's rate of growth. In his view, there is no proof that a reallocation of resources to the advantage of domestic investment would have speeded up this growth[78].

There has been no lack of criticism of such views. It has been observed that, even if the capital market functioned perfectly, it could none the less distribute resources in a way that was undesirable, economically and socially. Brinley Thomas has suggested that up to 1900 British capital exports were justified, for they made possible the

[76] P.L.Cottrell, *British Overseas Investment in the Nineteenth Century* (London, 1975), p.53 quoted as Cottrell, *Investment*), admits that this argument is valid and that the problem of access to the London Stock Exchange should not be exaggerated.

[77] M.Edelstein, 'Rigidity and bias in the British capital market, 1870–1913', in McCloskey, *Essays*, pp.83–105; see also M.Edelstein, 'Realized rates of return on UK home and overseas portfolio investment in the age of high imperialism', *Explorations in Economic History*, XIII (3), July 1976, 283–329.

[78] McCloskey, *Essays*, pp.451–5, 459.

influx of cheap primary produce into England, but after that date her suppliers possessed the necessary infrastructure. Yet between 1902 and 1913, exports of capital became enormous, at a time when various important technological innovations would have demanded massive investment by British industry for their effective exploitation[79]. An article by W.P.Kennedy, based on an econometric analysis, has criticized McCloskey's views severely, asserting that overall the distribution of savings which actually occurred, with a major part going to foreign investment, restricted the opportunities for growth and structural change in the British economy[80]. In the latest synthesis on these problems, P.L.Cottrell challenges McCloskey's idea that exported capital was not, in fact, a surplus available for the stimulation of economic growth; this ignores the effect that larger domestic investment would have had on the British economy's structure after 1870; and Cottrell writes that the debate is by no means closed[81].

Finally, S.B.Saul considers that the whole problem of the effects of foreign investment on industry remains obscure, but he suggests that it is not of cardinal importance. The main source of finance for industrial investment remained the ploughing-back of profits. The worrying fact was that profits stagnated at a low level after 1873, except during a few years. However, this financing difficulty does not itself explain why manufacturers did not react more energetically, if only to restore their profit margins. Saul emphasizes that many of them ran family firms, and they did not want to risk losing control of them. Having a tradition of self-financing, they were reluctant to borrow and resort to the capital market, particularly for equity capital[82].

One can also notice that the 'cushion' given to England and her balance of payments by the income from overseas investment was able to conceal certain serious defects in her industrial structure. Yet the sources of this income were less secure and flexible than a powerful, diversified and efficient home industry.

There remains one final problem connected with the financing of industry – banking systems and the different roles they might have played in England and Germany. There is no doubt that the former

[79] McCloskey, *Essays,* pp.106–11, 390.
[80] W.P.Kennedy, 'Foreign investment, trade and growth in the United Kingdom, 1870–1913', *Explorations in Economic History,* XI (4), Summer 1974, 415–44. British investors preferred foreign stock with fixed interest to British shares with variable yield.
[81] Cottrell, *Investment,* pp.54–5.
[82] Saul, *The Myth,* pp.40–2.

disposed of more capital than her rival, who had for a long time been a net importer of capital and whose industries greedily absorbed all available savings, only leaving a small portion for investment abroad, which was often government-inspired for political motives. Moreover, there was nearly always a revealing difference, of 1 or 2 per cent, between interest rates in Berlin and in other places, London in particular. However, it has often been argued that the economic growth of Germany was stimulated by the originality of her banking system, and particularly by the *Grosse Banken,* which combined the functions of commercial and investment banking. They undertook to issue industrial shares and often kept big allocations for themselves. But their participation was far from passive, for the banks watched the performances of the firms in which they held shares, through staffs of financial and technical experts and often by having representatives on company boards. So they could give well-informed advice and encourage growth, technological innovation and concentration. They were not content with just providing long-term capital: they also pressed for its most efficient use. Thus intimate collaboration sprang up between banks and industry. On the other hand, in Britain, the two sectors lived in a state of divorce. The banking system concentrated almost entirely on the provision of short-term credit and was passive rather than active, responding to demand rather than creating it, not troubling to encourage new enterprises or to direct capital into channels where it would help the spread of technological progress. As for the few banks that dealt in long-term credit, and the Stock Exchange too, they were orientated towards issues of government, railway and utilities stock, often, as we well know, syphoning off savings overseas. It has been asserted that this divorce was particularly disastrous at the end of the nineteenth and beginning of the twentieth century, when British industry went through a phase of concentration and the formation of combines. If English banks had followed the German model, they would have intervened, first of all to encourage this movement (which went less far than it did in Germany and the United States), and then to make sure that the new combines were rationally organized and well managed (which was far from always being the case). They would also have encouraged them to invest in technological innovation. The separation of the functions of industrial entrepreneur and mobilizer of capital had a harmful effect on growth.

Recent research suggests, however, that the role of the banks in the industrial success of Germany, which was connected with her late and sudden industrialization, should not be overestimated. Furthermore it may be that the British banking system was not interested in long-term financing of industry because industry never asked for such a service and did not suffer from the lack of investment banks. When capital is required, there are always lenders to supply it. This brings us back to the attitude of the industrialists themselves[83]. But before we deal with it, there remains one economic problem to examine.

THE BURDEN OF THE PAST

According to one attractive theory, Britain was handicapped by her 'early start' and paid the penalty for the pioneer role she played in the Industrial Revolution. This early start gave rise to some structures which, by the end of the nineteenth century, hindered the rapid pursuit of innovation.

In particular, Britain possessed an extensive infrastructure and intact operating plant which still worked effectively, so that people hesitated to replace machines even though they were often technically out of date. The weight of the past and the heritage of this old-fashioned equipment paralysed or delayed investment in new plant and processes. The soda industry has often been regarded as a perfect example of this delayed modernization. Early urbanization was also sometimes a handicap. The towns, which had grown up during the first half of the nineteenth century around factories of that period, imprisoned the latter, so to speak, when at the end of the century these enterprises needed space which could only be acquired at prohibitive cost or by a complete change of site. In this way, many steelworks found themselves on sites that were narrow and badly shaped, where it was difficult for them to integrate all the processes of steel-production, from blast-furnace to rolling-mill, and to resort to other new processes like burning gas from coke-ovens. Similarly, British railways, where the art of the engineer in this field had been perfected, often had curves that were too sharp and bridges that were not strong enough for the fast, heavy trains that could be introduced at the end of the nineteenth century. The wide use and cheapness of gas-lighting, which was supplied to all English towns, slowed down the adoption of electric lighting, and together with the continued use of the steam-engine, consequently hampered the growth of electricity production and the

[83] For all this, see Mathias, *The First Industrial Nation*, pp.419–20; Landes, *The Unbound Prometheus*, pp.333–4, 348-52; Saul, *The Myth*, p.41; McCloskey, *Essays*, pp.106–10, where there are criticisms of Edelstein's paper by Pollard and Mathias. Saul, p.305, accepts his analysis of the efficiency of the market and makes the remark (which links on to the next problem discussed) that historical factors gave British commercial banks only a limited role in the financing of industry; L.S.Pressnell, 'Money, finance and industrialization', *Business History*, XI (2), July 1969, 128–33.

manufacture of electrical machinery. It has even been maintained that the dense network of railways and tramways hindered the success of the motor-car.

Against this, the latecomers, countries which industrialized at the end of the nineteenth century, could adopt at once and in one 'package' all the most modern plant and techniques, benefiting from the experience, the inventions, and indeed the mistakes of the British, which had often been very costly. They could also launch out into new industries with bright prospects of long-term growth, while England remained over-committed to old industries, making rather simple articles with unsophisticated machinery, whose growth was to come to a halt in the twentieth century[84].

Saul remarks acutely that, theoretically, this reasoning is totally false. A pioneer country has accumulated capital (and England was certainly richer in this respect than Germany and even the United States) and it ought to have no difficulty in acquiring modern plant, even if its cost was increasing. The fact that it owns old factories ought to be no disadvantage: 'Capital invested is capital sunk, bygones are bygones.' If it pays a latecomer to install new plant, it should also pay an old industrial country to dismantle its outdated plant and replace with new. It is in no way handicapped in its choice of technology, and there is no reason why such a latecomer should be overtaken on the technical level by the newcomers. Let us not forget either, the expertise acquired by the British, from 'captains of industry' to humble workmen, the prestige of their products, their trade networks and their supremacy in many markets. It has often been emphasized in our own day how difficult it is for less developed countries to catch up with advanced countries, and how the difference between the two is growing. The freedom for newcomers to choose the best and most recent technology seems to be largely theoretical, and even if they adopt it, they may not succeed in using it efficiently. Recent experience, it is true, has shown that these pessimistic views were not always justified after all, for in several cases, newcomers have made gigantic strides at the technological level[85]. Also the situation was certainly different in the nineteenth century where competition from Germany and the United States was concerned, for their lag behind

---

[84] See p.384, and Saul, *The Myth*, p.46, on the danger of anachronism in this connection. The fact that some industries found themselves in a critical state after the first world war is not proof that they contributed to the slow-down of growth before 1914. So long as these industries paid, it was rational to continue to develop them.

[85] Japan, of course, but also South Korea, Singapore, Hong Kong, Taiwan, etc.

England was as nothing compared with the distance that nowadays separates industrial nations and the real Third World.

However, Saul admits that in practice the argument has more substance. As Landes has suggested, the effort of catching up in follower countries engenders reactions that favour innovation, both in individuals and institutions. These reactions become built-in habits and stimulate further growth and technical progress. In contrast, the pioneer country can have difficulty, for institutional and psychological reasons, in breaking with methods that have become traditional. The skills and work habits acquired by workers and managers in old industries can be not only inadequate but inimical to the development of new industries and new products. Thus makers of steam-engines are not interested in diesel-engines and cannot manage to build satisfactory ones. Engineers brought up in the tradition of quality, embodied in craftwork, do not know how to put mass-production methods into operation. As, in addition, the British seem to have had a sentimental attachment at every level to traditional technologies such as steam-engines and gas, one can see how manufacturers often confined themselves to perfecting machines with which they were familiar, simply replacing those that were worn out with the same models. However, it is also clear that the handicap of the pioneer role had nothing inevitable about it, and that the burden of the past made itself felt only to the extent that the British did not react to throw it off, by changing their equipment. So, in the end, one comes to a human factor – a traditionalist attitude.

Despite these considerations, a pioneer country can suffer from another structural disadvantage which seems to be more strictly economic[86]. This is the interconnection and interrelatedness of the various elements in an established technology. None of these elements functions in isolation from the others. So a steam-engine, the textile machinery driven by it, the shafts and belts transmitting power from the former to the latter, the buildings where this equipment was installed, were all planned to form a coherent whole. So it is hardly possible to change one of these elements without modifying the rest, and this will add to the cost of the operation, often drastically. Paul David, as mentioned earlier, has given a remarkable and convincing analysis of the incompatibility of an infrastructure inherited from the

---

[86] Certain 'institutional' structures, built into the economy at an earlier stage, also may have hindered adaptation to changes in techniques and markets. An example was the horizontal structure of the cotton industry, which deprived manufacturers of any direct contact with foreign markets, and might have made it harder for them to adapt to changes in demand; Mathias, *The First Industrial Nation*, p.419.

past and a technical innovation. His example was the English fields-system and the harvester, where the latter could not be viable without large investment beforehand to level fields, widen lanes, etc. He has generalized this analysis to industry, emphasizing that, at the end of the nineteenth century, because of slow productivity gains in the building industry and rising wages, it was expensive to alter or replace old factories. In the absence of a rapid expansion of the market, which would have encouraged the introduction of best-practice techniques, manufacturers confined themselves to replacing worn-out machines with ones that could be set up in existing buildings[87].

The most obvious example of interrelatedness was to be found in railways. Trucks for carrying coal were nearly all very small, i.e. 10 tons in capacity, but to substitute others of greater volume, it would have been necessary to alter many elements in railway infra-structure – tracks, bridges, tunnels, marshalling yards, equipment for loading and unloading coal. This would have involved considerable investment. There was also an institutional obstacle – most of these trucks were the property of the mining companies and not of the railways. Saul admits that such difficulties played a part when heavy investment was involved, but he cannot see why, in smaller industrial concerns, new firms should not have emerged, as in Germany, to shed the burden of the past and use the most advanced techniques. One can, of course, reply that the micro- and macroeconomic aspects are complementary, and that the modernization of an enterprise can depend on the co-operation of its equipment-suppliers and of its subcontractors.

David has argued that an industry which used the modern methods at the start can, if it is ruled by strict considerations of replacement and modernization costs in its plant, find itself caught in a vicious circle which will bring it fairly soon to a state of protracted technical backwardness. This model is probably too schematic, and several writers totally reject the idea that the dead wood of ancient equipment paralysed the modernization of the British economy. Nevertheless, it seems that Britain had to pay a price for the pioneer role she had played in the Industrial Revolution. The existence of massive quantities of plant installed at a technological stage antedating the end of the nineteenth century may have delayed the introduction of innovations during the latter period, for the cost of investing in the most advanced technology was high and the incentives light, even though such

---

[87] But, with this last point, David reintroduces the demand factor.

investments would have had a strong multiplier effect later[88]. The strength of Britain before 1870 may have created seeds of later weakness. Yet why did the British not manage to break cleanly with the past and shake off the inherited load of outdated equipment? We need now to turn to the human factor[89].

ABOUT ENTREPRENEURS

The preceding analyses all lead in the end to a sort of 'residue'. Objective handicaps do not completely explain the weakening of the British economy at the end of the nineteenth and beginning of the twentieth century. More exactly, they do not explain why British businessmen did not surmount the undoubted obstacles which they then encountered. McCloskey in fact was right when he maintained that all theories apart from his own (a denial that there was any failure of the Victorian economy, whose slow-down in growth was solely attributable to 'constraints of supply') boiled down finally to the old explanation of 'entrepreneurial failure', or the shortcomings and incapacity of businessmen, more particularly of manufacturers[90]. The present writer is not convinced of the validity of McCloskey's position and, although he has several times argued that economic historians ought to exhaust all strictly economic explanations before resorting to imponderables like outlook, attitudes and social values[91], he does think that in this case such factors played an important role and do supply the explanation of last resort. But he is fully aware that this

---

[88] For all this, see Landes, *The Unbound Prometheus,* pp.334–6; Mathias, *The First Industrial Nation* p.420; Saul, *The Myth,* pp.44–6; also 'Some thoughts', p.395, where he appears in favour of this idea of the burden of the past; P.David, 'The landscape and the machine: technical interrelatedness, land tenure and the mechanization of the corn harvest in Victorian Britain', in McCloskey, *Essays,* pp.158, 179–81. On the other hand, this thesis is rejected outright (except for the gas industry!) by Barker, 'History', p.89.

[89] Saul notes (in 'Some thoughts', p.395) that the farmers of East Lothian, whose fields were well suited to the harvester and who were among the first to adopt it, were in any case famed for their skill as agronomists. In a more general and theoretical way, P.H.Lindert and K.Trace, 'Yardsticks for Victorian entrepreneurs', in McCloskey, *Essays,* pp.239–40, maintain that the thesis of the early start (with its variants of overcommitment and complementarity) is only a form of explanation based on entrepreneurial failure. For entrepreneurs were the channel of transmission for the cramping effect of the heritage of the past, which would have been swept away but for their conservatism and their incapacity to maximize profits. Old equipment, as shown above, is a 'gift of the past', which a 'rational' entrepreneur will only keep as long as up-to-date plant does not offer opportunities for higher profits.

[90] McCloskey, 'Did Victorian Britain fail?', 446.

[91] And in general he tends to think that such attitudes are rather moulded by the objective environment in which entrepreneurs operate.

explanation should be qualified in the light of various pertinent criticisms levelled at it recently, which mean that this is not as widely accepted as it was some years ago[92].

Let us first present in simplified, not to say simplistic, form the 'traditional' thesis, which has been supported with great talent and persuasiveness by David Landes[93]. As Payne has written, British men of business let the sceptre of industrial pre-eminence fall from their grasp (the assumption being that the decline of a firm or an industry is the responsibility of its leaders). It is alleged that there was a weakening of entrepreneurship – that subtle blend of imagination and initiative, of boldness and energy, of flair for seizing opportunities and of organizing ability – among the leaders of British industry, especially in the old sectors that went back to the Industrial Revolution.

Nearly all firms, even when they were dressed up as public companies, were in fact family businesses. The almost inevitable changes in the abilities, attitudes and general behaviour of successive generations of the same family could have serious consequences for the management of the family business. At the end of the nineteenth century, firms which had been founded at the end of the eighteenth and beginning of the nineteenth century were usually run by third-generation men. The grandfather was long since dead: it was he who had created the business by ferociously hard work, often made possible by an exceptional physique, a drive for power, aggressiveness, and sometimes sharp practice and a parsimony that bordered on avarice, together with total dedication to his firm. The son, who had much expanded his inheritance but had often remained faithful to his father's methods, had handed over the reins to the third generation. These 'heirs', these 'children of affluence' (Landes), had not been

---

[92]   See McCloskey, *Essays,* pp.5, 391, 393; McCloskey, 'Did Victorian Britain fail?', 459, 466; Saul, *The Myth,* p.46; P.L.Payne, *British Entrepreneurship in the Nineteenth Century* (London, 1974), pp.45–6. Of course McCloskey maintains that the thesis which he is fighting has been completely discredited. Saul and Payne admit that it has received some rude shocks, but nothing decisive. Saul (in McCloskey, *Essays,* p.396, and *The Myth,* pp.48–9) rightly suggests that we ought also to take into account the effect of restrictive practices, imposed by trade unions, on technological progress and of their opposition to the adoption of new methods and new machinery. However, he adds that these hindrances must be viewed in the more general context of bad relations between employers and workers. One should also remember the influence of labour legislation, e.g. in the matter of security in mines.

[93]   Landes, *The Unbound Prometheus,* pp.336–9, 352–4; see also for example D.H.Aldcroft, 'The entrepreneur and the British economy, 1870–1914', *Economic History Review,* 2nd series, XVII (1), Aug. 1964, 113–34. Accusations were hurled against British businessmen for their failings as early as the end of the nineteenth century: they were the reaction of national pride when faced with England losing the economic race.

brought up the hard way like their grandfather, or even their father. They had often been educated in a public school where, to put it mildly (we will return to this later), the education they had received hardly prepared them for managing an industrial undertaking. They had hobnobbed with fellow schoolboys from the upper class, whose manners and tastes they had adopted and whose lifestyle they hoped to imitate. In a word, they had become 'gentlemen', that is enlightened and civilized amateurs who, in losing the harsh character and rough manners of their forefathers, had also lost much of their dynamism.

Once they took over the family spinning-mill or iron-works, they did not devote themselves to it with the same devouring passion as their predecessors, and the business was for them just a source of income which assured them the life of a gentleman. Their real interests were those of the gentry – foxhunting, grouse-shooting, a busy social life, politics and charitable activity. Some of them withdrew from effective direction of their businesses, leaving the day-to-day running to managers; but the latter were usually employees risen from the ranks, 'practical men', marked by the routine of subordinate jobs to which they had long been confined, and lacking in calibre[94]. As for those owners who remained effectively in control of their factories, their outside interests reduced their concentration and their dynamism. They ran their businesses in a repetitive or imitative manner and forgot the necessity of maximizing profits. Their way of life involving heavy expenses, they no longer reinvested almost automatically the bulk of their profits, a part of which they also used to buy land or speculate on the Stock Exchange, so that the firm was sometimes deprived of the capital necessary for its modernization. In certain cases these attitudes led to ruin, and one often heard the old Lancashire saying 'From clogs to clogs in three generations'; but more often there was 'gentrification', or a more or less complete integration of the industrial haute bourgeoisie into the upper class[95]. This bourgeoisie,

---

[94] It has already been noted (Chapter 8, p.273) (from Perkin, pp.430–2) that the spread of joint-stock limited-liability companies (combined with the transport facilities supplied by railways) allowed manufacturers who had made a fortune to avoid complete retirement on their country estates – a decision which previously the newly rich had to make sooner or later. Now they could combine an aristocratic lifestyle in the country with continued supervision over the running of their firm. So they remained at the head of the latter until an advanced age and did not make way for newcomers. This caused a decline in upward social mobility among leaders of industry (noted also by Payne, *British Entrepreneurship*, p.28), and also, according to Perkin, a decline in the traditional entrepreneurial ideal, that of the active capitalist with a total commitment. Let us add, however, that the internal promotion of managers is not a guarantee of their mediocrity.

[95] We have also mentioned in Chapter 8, p.273 (note 134), the accession to the peerage, from the 1880s onwards, of a number of leading industrialists.

which had a strong group identity at the beginning of the nineteenth century, had lost most of it by the end of that century. An exception were the families who remained faithful to the Nonconformist sects and did not aspire to join the Church of England, as did those who aspired to join the upper class. This integration did not make for dynamism in the economy, but a fair number of the industrial bourgeoisie ended by withdrawing completely from business and assimilating themselves entirely to the gentry. The economic difficulties of the Great Depression often contributed to this withdrawal.

It is true that this only affected the families of large industrialists; but they were the leaders who would have been best placed to innovate and extend their enterprises. More usual was the tendency of many businessmen to rest on their laurels and give way to self-satisfaction, complacency and an imperturbable confidence in their superiority over foreigners, and in traditional practices and techniques which had proved their worth[96]. They paid little attention to the changes taking place in the world economy, or to the progress made by their rivals, whom they despised and considered inferior. They often made no effort to resist the very competition that was in fact most dangerous[97]. This led to a conservatism and rigidity among manufacturers, which was damaging. They shrank from trying new machines and new methods, finding it easier and cheaper to make constant repairs or at best substitute similar equipment for the old, which, true enough, was solid and durable. Peter Mathias mentions six steam-engines installed in breweries before 1800 which were still going strong in 1900, and he writes that their long life was 'one of the finest tributes to British engineers and one of the worst indictments of British industrialists'[98]. This respect for tradition went hand in hand with the cult of practical experience, and with contempt or suspicion of scientific research and analysis. Rule of thumb was the general habit, both in technical matters and in management, where the new American methods

---

[96] Barker, 'History', p.69, admits the 'arrogance' of the Lancashire cotton lords at the beginning of the twentieth century. In support see D.C.Coleman's excellent quotation in his article, 'Gentlemen and players', *Economic History Review*, 2nd series, XXVI (1), Feb. 1973, 92–116.

[97] Reports from British consuls – a source which can, of course, be challenged – abound in complaints about the failings of British exporters, who make no attempt to adapt themselves to the needs and tastes of foreigners, who only write in English, etc. Similar lamentations were written at the time by French consuls about French businessmen.

[98] Mathias, *The First Industrial Nation*, p.418.

emerging at the end of the nineteenth century were ignored[99]. Moreover, forecasting and plans for expansion were nearly always undertaken with excessive caution and a very limited time-horizon, according to a narrow and strictly classical accounting rationality: new machinery was only acquired if it would bring in higher profits under existing conditions, and no account was taken of the prospects for growth.

It is an easy game to contrast these attitudes with the behaviour of American and German businessmen. Because the industrialization of their countries was recent and swift, these were often 'new men' of the first or second generation. Like English pioneers of the Industrial Revolution, they devoted themselves wholeheartedly to their firms, worked prodigiously hard, and showed themselves ingenious and aggressive, not to say unscrupulous. The Germans besides had the reputation of being ready to do anything to satisfy their clients. Furthermore, heads of firms and managers were often expert technicians, with a scientific education, and not amateurs – hence their passion for innovation. Of course, they did not constantly make major inventions, but every novelty they encountered was tried out and every success exploited. So American and German industry benefited from a continuous flow of minor improvements, which ended up by revolutionizing their technology, especially in chemistry and electricity[100]. Finally, the Germans had a different rationality from the British – it was technological and not financial. They looked first of all for technical efficiency, for more advanced mechanization, and for methods that were more scientific and capital-intensive. This was not necessarily 'rational' on the strictly financial level and in the short term; but as the general trend of technology was in this direction, this attitude paid off in the long run. In other words, German manufacturers had wider horizons and longer perspectives. Of course, these 'ideal' portraits of the English manufacturer and his German or American rival are stereotyped caricatures. We should now qualify them in view of criticisms that have been levelled at them, some of which are more valid than others.

Without denying that some businessmen showed signs of apathy, historians have pointed out that England at the end of the nineteenth

[99] D.H.Aldcroft, 'Investment in and utilization of manpower: Great Britain and her rivals, 1870–1914', in B.M.Ratcliffe (ed.), *Great Britain and her World, 1750–1914: Essays in Honour of W.O.Henderson* (Manchester, 1975), pp.287–307, mentions this in connection with the use and management of labour, which was rarely employed in a really efficient way.

[100] Between 1886 and 1900 the six main German firms which distilled coal-tar took out 948 patents. Their six British opposite numbers took out only 86.

century did have some bold, dynamic and innovating entrepreneurs, who proved themselves to be worthy successors of the pioneers of the Industrial Revolution. Charles Wilson has picked out several, particularly in the 'light' industries, e.g. food, pharmaceutical products, soap; and indeed one rarely comes across a captain of industry so aggressive and energetic as William H. Lever[101]. Saul has shown that many engineering firms reacted with vigour and imagination to foreign competition. The bicycle and motor-car industries also had gifted innovators such as William Morris. Stress has also been placed on the original innovations achieved in Britain at the end of the nineteenth century in distribution and retail trade, for which a new pattern was invented, with a high turnover and low margins of profit, using chainstores with many branches. Some of these firms were founded and developed by outstanding entrepreneurs such as Thomas Lipton for groceries and Jesse Boot for pharmaceutical products[102].

However, up till now, few such examples have been discovered in the old industries, which remained the big battalions of the British economy – coal, iron and steel, textiles. Routine habits may have been encouraged by the growing difficulty of entry into these branches (especially in heavy industry), and the increasing size and cost of the smallest viable units of production. Thus, in iron and steel, the spectrum of industrial traders came to be drawn from a narrower social group in the second half of the nineteenth century; they were recruited more and more from rich families. Landes maintains that talent was diverted away from these old industries, which no longer offered a 'new man' the possibility of making a fortune, because of the difficulty of entry and their low profitability. So talent went to the services, commerce, the professions, etc.[103].

A more penetrating criticism attacks the very idea that much of British industry at the end of the nineteenth century was controlled by

---

[101] He adopted marketing methods and high-pressure advertising, imported directly from the US, which led to a rapid and sensational expansion of his business.

[102] Wilson, 'Economy and society', 189ff; Mathias, *The First Industrial Nation,* p.405; S.D.Chapman, *Jesse Boot of Boots the Chemists* London, 1974). Lipton started his first shop in 1872. By 1898 he had 242. J.Boot started as a herbalist in Nottingham. His success was based on large-scale publicity for products sold much more cheaply than they were by ordinary chemists, who kept their prices up by agreements; on the manufacture of many patent medicines and other specialities; and on the sale of all sorts of goods. Having got properly started in the 1880s he had 181 shops in 1900 and 618 in 1920, plus factories where some of his goods were made. The frenzied, lonely work and the autocratic temperament of this self-made man recall the pioneers of the Industrial Revolution.

[103] Landes, *The Unbound Prometheus,* p.339; Payne, *British Entrepreneurship,* p.28, quoting C.Erickson.

third-generation men who were alleged to be mediocre entrepreneurs. In fact we have no age-pyramid for nineteenth-century industrial concerns. We only know that the mortality rate of firms was high – because of bankruptcy, of course widely sparked off by every cyclical crisis, voluntary liquidation and the dissolution of partnerships[104]. We also know that the death and renewal rates varied from one industry to another. Among the woollen and worsted firms of the West Riding, only 17 per cent of those existing in 1875 survived to 1912, which shows a drastic rejuvenation in the industry[105]. In engineering, at the beginning of the twentieth century, few firms had been founded before 1850, and the third generation had not yet taken control by 1914. So Payne notes quite correctly that it is impossible to estimate the percentage of firms that remained under the control of the same family for two or three generations, but he doubts whether there were many of them. Indeed one comes across fairly few great industrial dynasties that lasted. Some ruined themselves, others left their factory to pursue the life of the country gentleman. Conversely, we do know of family firms which developed progressively, making their most remarkable advances under the second or third generation, or even later. But, on the whole, the renewal of the employing class seems to have been fairly swift. Newcomers doubtless had the same varied and relatively modest origins (near the bottom of the middle class) as their predecessors during the Industrial Revolution, and there never seems to have been a shortage of potential entrepreneurs[106].

Be that as it may, these arguments leave the reader dissatisfied. Their supporters rely on a few case-studies, company histories, or biographies of businessmen, which can be used to back up different points of view. However, one does not know how representative they are, and it would be rash to draw firm conclusions, especially of a quantitative kind, seeing that the basis of most of them is qualitative and narrow. Even the widening of our knowledge, which is coming about by the accumulation of new monographs, will not solve the problem, especially as there is the additional task of isolating entrepreneurship and measuring it objectively. One can understand

[104] This was compulsory by law when one of the partners died. Many other liquidations resulted from disagreements between partners or from other causes.

[105] E.M.Sigsworth and J.M.Blackman, 'The woollen and worsted industries', in Aldcroft (ed.), *The development,* pp.130–2. As many small businesses disappeared between 1870 and 1875, there remained in 1912 only 9 per cent of the firms existing in 1870, but the survival of their trade-name does not imply the continuance of the same family at the head of the business.

[106] Payne, *British Entrepreneurship,* pp.27, 28, 35; Saul, 'The engineering industry', p.233.

the impatience of American 'new economic historians' at British empiricism, their efforts to work out a proper standard of comparison that would enable them to measure British performance beside the best American (or German) practice. They therefore resorted to econometric models and calculations, to compute either the total productivity of the economy or, in the case of individual industries, the profits that were lost by sticking to old methods. The assumption is that there was a 'failure' if the profits that were forfeited as the result of refusing to make specific investments were high[107]. Thanks to these methods, examples of which have been quoted, McCloskey and L.S.Sandberg thought that they had saved the Victorian entrepreneur from damnation and assured his redemption[108]. However, we agree with Payne in his doubts about these statistical manipulations, together with the assumptions and yardsticks used in such studies, which anyway are very few in number, and not generally convincing[109]. Perhaps the wisest solution lies somewhere halfway – leaving many late Victorian industrialists in some sort of Purgatory, undamned but still unredeemed[110]?

But might they not have found there many of their colleagues of earlier generations? Payne has pointed out that to assert that the entrepreneurs of the late nineteenth century did not have the qualities of their predecessors is to assume that a spirit of enterprise was previously much more potent and widespread. Yet, judgements on the Industrial Revolution period are based on a biased sample, i.e. a number of great entrepreneurs whose careers are well documented and who scored brilliant successes, but in circumstances that were often

---

[107] Payne, *British Entrepreneurship*, pp.12, 27, 46–52; Saul, *The Myth*, p.47; Lindert and Trace, pp.240–2; H.W.Richardson, in Aldcroft, *The Development*, pp.274–7. Lindert and Trace think that one cannot measure entrepreneurship, but only its economic consequences. Furthermore, they criticize severely, but often pertinently, the laxness of their predecessors for having believed all sorts of contemporary opinion of doubtful reliability and impartiality, and for having adopted a sort of worship of modern equipment without ascertaining whether it paid, etc.
    On the other hand, Coleman, 'Gentlemen and players', pp. 94–5 rejects international comparisons and adopts the criteria which businessmen of the time set themselves as proofs of success.

[108] D.N.McCloskey and L.S.Sandberg, 'From damnation to redemption: judgements on the late Victorian entrepreneur', *Explorations in Economic History*, IX, 1971.

[109] Payne, *British Entrepreneurship*, pp.12, 51–2, who emphasizes that these studies should be based on business records, for the quality of an entrepreneur is to be judged from his actions in a given set of conditions, within the framework of his firm. See also the review of this work by D.H.Aldcroft, in *Economic History Review*, 2nd series, XXVIII (2) May 1975, 337, which suggests other lines of research.

[110] Saul, *The Myth*, p.47, notes that in large sectors of industry there were many small firms run by ignorant, narrow-minded men. But there is no proof that they were relatively more numerous in England than in other countries.

exceptionally favourable[111]. The faceless crowd of men who failed is not taken into account. As for the period which followed, from 1830 to 1870, little is known about its entrepreneurs. Payne notes that it saw the decline of some great and old-established firms, like Marshall (flax-spinning) and Ashworth (cotton-spinning). It also saw the consolidation, not to say ossification, of the industrial structure, dominated by the medium-sized family firm, specializing in some product, often protected by a patent or a trade-mark, with limited horizons and few opportunities for rapid growth. However, he sees an important difference as compared with post-1870 industrialists: a sharp eye for appreciating the value of innovations, the ability to exploit all their possibilities, e.g. all the new equipment linked to the development of railways.

These remarks are interesting in that they disperse the impression left by some writers that the quality of British entrepreneurship suddenly changed in the 1870s, so that one asks oneself why suddenly 'pure gold was turned to vilest dross'. Payne also takes up the idea that the abnormal phenomenon was British supremacy at the beginning and middle of the nineteenth century, and not its later decline. He suggests that, in the new conditions of intense international competition at the end of the nineteenth century, some structural weaknesses and some errors or shortcomings on the part of businessmen, which had never been entirely absent even in the heroic age of the Industrial Revolution, had much more harmful consequences. He underlines particularly that American and German competition came mainly from very large firms, which were able to send swarms of commercial travellers abroad; moreover, they were often organized into cartels with centralized marketing. In order to compete with them, British industry ought to have been reorganized into larger units, with lower costs and better commercial methods. The move towards concentration at the end of the nineteenth century and beginning of the twentieth century was quite inadequate, for most firms remained purposely too small, refusing amalgamation. Therefore they could not support travellers abroad and depended for their exports on overseas importers and commission agents, from whom they could not expect such keenness as would have been shown by their own salesmen. So the trouble could have been not so much a general decline in entrepreneurship as the excessive individualism of a disaggregated industry. Payne of course ends by stressing that it is dangerous to generalize. There

---

[111] A hasty judgement in view of the crises and difficulties of the Napoleonic wars and post-1815 periods.

was no such thing as *the* British entrepreneur. There was too much diversity, not only between one industry and another, but within each industry[112]. But, again, some of the industrial studies in earlier chapters seem to have shown up a lack of entrepreneurship in several branches.

SCIENCE AND EDUCATION

Education is closely linked with the problem of entrepreneurship, as the kind of education which entrepreneurs received in their youth matters a great deal. It can help to explain not only the decline in entrepreneurship and the technological stagnation in old industries, but also the tardy and inadequate development of new industries and new products[113].

At the end of the nineteenth century, the conditions for innovation were becoming very different from those existing at the time of the Industrial Revolution, when the main inventions had been the work of practical men with little education, clever craftsmen or amateurs addicted to tinkering. Invention now depended more and more on the deliberate and systematic application of scientific knowledge to industrial technology – and of course science had made enormous strides in the meantime. This was particularly the case in the chemical and electrical industries which depended entirely on applied science; but there was, to a lesser degree, the same tendency in many other industries, where the use of scientific discoveries opened up great prospects for increased productivity and profit[114].

It does seem that Britain failed to achieve the marriage of science and industry, which was the strength of the German economy. She did not apply the scientific discoveries of the end of the nineteenth century as much as she might have done. There were certainly brilliant exceptions, but on the whole British inferiority was glaring. Much of the responsibility lies at the door of the education system which could

---

[112] For all this see Payne, *British Entrepreneurship*, pp.30–45, 48, 53–8. Very sensibly, Payne warns historians against judgements that are too categorical, and that benefit from hindsight, about the behaviour of businessmen nearly a century ago.

[113] For what follows, see especially Landes, *The Unbound Prometheus*, pp.339–48; Mathias, *The First Industrial Nation*, pp.421–4. The importance of these problems is admitted by Payne, *British Entrepreneurship*, p.53; Saul, *The Myth*, pp.47–8; but it is challenged by Barker, 'History', p.58.

[114] R.A.Church, 'The British leather industry and foreign competition, 1870–1914', *Economic History Review*, 2nd series, XXIX (4), Nov. 1971, 565, gives an example in an industry as ancient as tanning, where ignorance of chemistry prevented the English from adopting a new tanning process.

not give to entrepreneurs, managers, executives, foremen and operatives the scientific and technical training which they needed. For a clear appreciation, however, several levels of instruction must be distinguished – four, according to Landes – each of which has its special contribution to make to the performance of an economy; but, at every level, Germany, and to a lesser extent the United States, were far ahead of England[115].

The first level was elementary education – reading, writing and arithmetic. Its economic effect is not very clear, for at this stage, much industrial work could be done by illiterates, as during the Industrial Revolution. On the other hand, good and widespread instruction of this type gives clever children the minimum qualifications to advance further, thus increasing the stock of talent, and optimizing the distribution of human resources. In any case, the difference in this sector between England and Germany was considerable, and the Prussian schoolmasters, who were believed by many people to have (already) won the 1870 war against France, may have achieved a similar victory later in the industrial war against England! For a variety of religious and political reasons which cannot be detailed here, primary education only became compulsory in Britain by the Acts of 1870 and 1880. Of course, many children attended some sort of school before those dates (although probably not more than 50 per cent of all children of school age by 1860), but attendance was often irregular and for a short time only. The instruction was mediocre in quality in most schools and did not open the way to secondary studies[116]. In Prussia, compulsory education existed from 1763 onwards, and the other German states followed. By 1860, 97.5 per cent of all German children between 6 and 14 years went to school, receiving an education of high quality, which enabled a minority to go forward to secondary establishments.

The second level is technical education, which trains skilled workers and middle management; the third is the training of engineers (which combines theoretical science and its practical application) and also of managers and entrepreneurs. Their link with technological and economic progress is obvious and became very close at the end of the nineteenth century, when not only executives but also skilled workers needed a minimum knowledge of science.

---

[115] Except perhaps at the second level.

[116] E.G.West, *Education and the Industrial Revolution* (London, 1975), who wanted to rehabilitate primary teaching before state intervention (which in his opinion was useless), has been severely criticized, although some progress in literacy before 1870 probably occurred.

In technical education, the British tradition was 'on-the-job' training with, sometimes, a debased form of apprenticeship[117] – all of course left to be supplied by the firms themselves. The only national effort, in response to the Industrial Revolution, had been the Mechanics' Institutes movement, which started in 1824 and provided evening classes in a wide range of disciplines. They were designed to enable literate workers to acquire enough scientific knowledge to qualify as foremen, or even engineers. In practice, they abandoned their original aim and after 1850 provided mostly evening classes in general subjects and were not comparable to German or Swiss technical schools.

P.L.Robertson has maintained, it is true, that the lack of facilities for technical education in Britain did not have any harmful effects at least in the two related industries which he studied – shipbuilding and marine engineering. He admits that the leaders of industry refused to recognize the usefulness of applied science and to finance its diffusion (the government had the same attitude), but in the short term this policy was rational from an economic standpoint, for the need in these industries was for manual skills, and they could only be learned on the job, and 'by doing'. Besides, British labour in these industries had a better productivity record than that of other countries, which took much more trouble over technical education[118]. One cannot say whether this was the exception or the rule, but Saul considers that at the end of the nineteenth century engineering needed a new type of 'superior workmen trained to think, to devise and scheme and accommodate known principles to new ends'[119]. At the third level, that of the education of senior executives, there was a total void up to the middle of the nineteenth century, and it was only partially filled after that. For engineers, the training consisted usually of an apprenticeship, often involving long spells of manual routine work[120]. The result was that the social status of the engineer was low, far lower than it was on the continent. Indeed it is striking that in English the same word 'engineer' is used for both the educated expert and the engineering

---

[117] Apprenticeship was made too costly by the growing complexity of equipment.

[118] P.L.Robertson, 'Technical education in the British shipbuilding and marine-engineering industries, 1863–1914', *Economic History Review*, 2nd series, XXVII (2), May 1974, 222–35.

[119] Saul, 'The engineering industry', pp.232–3. He does indeed note that labour relations in most firms did not encourage initiative on the part of the workers. They received no incentive and feared that change would force them to work harder for the same wages.

[120] ibid., p.230.

workman[121]. This did not, of course, prevent England from having many first-class engineers, some of whom were also inventors.

What was probably more serious was the quality of secondary education. The tone there was set by the public schools (actually, private and expensive). There were about half a dozen of these – ancient and renowned – at the beginning of the nineteenth century. Many new ones were added from the 1840s onwards, but they copied their seniors slavishly. Rich industrialists had sent their sons to public schools early in the Industrial Revolution, but the influx of third-generation boys only became a torrent after 1850. A growing number of men who were to manage large firms in Britain at the end of the nineteenth and beginning of the twentieth century passed through these establishments[122], in order to improve their social status by obtaining a passport to the 'gentleman's club'. This was only normal, for the aim of the ambitious British businessman remained what it had been in the pre-industrial era. He did not solely seek to make his financial fortune – the maximization of profits was a means rather than an end in itself. His goal, as in the past, was to raise himself in the social hierarchy and, above all, to cross the only really important boundary in British society – the one that separated gentlemen from the common people, whom Coleman calls, in cricket parlance, 'players' – the professionals. It was the latter who had made the Industrial Revolution. A manufacturer, at the beginning of the nineteenth century, was certainly not a gentleman, but, once his fortune was made, his ambition was that his sons should cross the magic line. Coleman suggests, half ironically, that economic growth slowed down because manufacturers were 'too busy becoming gentlemen'.

The public schools were the instruments of this transformation, for the education given there was a liberal one, precisely planned to train gentlemen. The ideal gentleman had considerably altered in the course of the centuries, and had changed again recently under the influence of the religious revival, which led the reformed public schools of the middle and end of the nineteenth century to put the accent on a new model, 'the Christian gentleman'. The gentleman was an 'educated amateur', who was taught a good deal of Latin and Greek, a little of

---

[121] Coleman, 'Gentlemen and players', points out that in Brunner Mond, a go-ahead firm, there was a club for executives to which chemists with university degrees and men who had come from the professions were readily admitted, but where entry for engineers and members of the sales department was difficult.

[122] For all this, see the brilliant article by Coleman, 'Gentlemen and players'. The title is taken from the cricket matches which once a year, from 1806 to 1962, opposed a team of amateurs to a team of professionals – the 'players'.

divinity, some pure science in the form of mathematics, but no applied science, which would have been part of a vocational training and thus far beneath him[123]. Everyone knows that to these curricular activities were added games and particularly team games, and that the emphasis was put on character-building rather than on intellect.

The problem is, of course, to know what influence their attendance at public schools and the education they received there had on the business decisions of young men who later became heads of firms[124]. This is not a simple problem and does not boil down to the fact that they had learned no science, or that these schools turned their backs on the industrial world[125] and inculcated the ideal of the Christian gentleman, who was too virtuous for 'competitive industrialism' and unsuited for business success. On the other hand, this education bred social confidence and inculcated leadership. Coleman points out that the influence of the public school might have been insignificant after all, and that many public schoolboys were very successful in some branches, such as merchant banking and other City activities; but he maintains that the main result was to perpetuate the twin cults of the 'educated amateur' and the 'practical man', which went back at least to the eighteenth century. These were two distinct social types, but they complemented one another, and their partnership dominated British industry, or at least its large firms, at the end of the nineteenth century. Practical men were generally executives, but some of them rose to sit on company boards. Coleman thinks that this combination created or at least reinforced a certain hostility towards innovation. By their education gentlemen shared with the players a mistrust of theoretical knowledge and a belief in the 'mystique of practical experience'. They were both hostile to technical or scientific training for their subordinates. The men who had risen from the ranks were relatively old and therefore cautious, while gentlemen had been exposed to influences which depreciated the maximization of profits and unbridled competition, but stressed stability and tradition[126]. As for medium-sized and new firms, they remained the preserve of

---

[123] And only fit for 'players'.

[124] It is indeed probable that, in addition, they helped to turn many gifted young men away from business towards non-economic callings, which carried more prestige, e.g. the civil service, the army, the professions, the Church, not to mention the leisured life of the 'free and unconfined' gentleman. Those who went or rather returned into business had in fact come from families already in business.

[125] Coleman also notes ('Gentlemen and players', 106–7) that many industrialists hesitated to send their sons to these schools, but pressure in their favour went on increasing.

[126] ibid., 115. The external costs of American-style 'robber barons' could have been considerable.

'practical men' who were not gentlemen. This was not necessarily unfavourable to innovation, but these men had often been to secondary schools, which were of inferior quality but none the less aped the more famous public schools. Some of these schools may have given some place to scientific or commercial subjects, but it remained very limited. It is thus clear that the peculiarities of British secondary education, notably in public schools, had an important influence on economic and technological development.

As for the highest level – that of high-quality scientific teaching and research – the two ancient universities of Oxford and Cambridge almost ignored it up to the mid-nineteenth century, for they only taught the classics, theology, a little history, philosophy and political economy. It was only later that they created degrees in scientific disciplines, but these did not prove attractive. Cambridge in 1872 had only a dozen undergraduates reading for the science tripos, and most of them were destined for medical studies[127]. It is true that the University of London, which developed from 1828 onwards, and Scottish universities had a more modern outlook. There was also a movement in favour of developing genuine scientific education, of which some industrialists were for the first time feeling the need. This led to the foundation of several provincial universities – civic or redbrick[128] – and also of colleges for engineers[129]. Receiving no support from the state[130] and having no rich endowments like the ancient universities, these young rivals sought and obtained the financial assistance of rich businessmen in their district, and in return they made serious efforts to establish curricula and degrees suited to local economic needs. Much was accomplished, particularly in the quarter century before 1914. It seems that in the few years prior to the first world war the universities, far from failing to produce the graduates needed by industry, threw on the market more chemists and engineers than industry needed, so that many of these young people went in for teaching or else emigrated[131].

However, the British university system as a whole, in spite of the

<hr>

[127] ibid., 109. These universities attracted more and more the sons of businessmen – but for reading classics and other arts subjects.
[128] The starting-point was Owen's College, founded in 1851, which became the University of Manchester, the first of the redbrick universities.
[129] Royal College of Chemistry, 1845; Government School of Mines, 1851.
[130] It was only in 1890 that public funds were for the first time granted to help scientific education, and in 1901 total grants of government to universities were £27,000.
[131] See M.Sanderson, *The Universities and British Industry, 1850–1970* (London, 1972); M.Sanderson, 'The professor as industrial consultant: Oliver Arnold and the British steel industry, 1900–14', *Economic History Review*, 2nd series, XXXI (4) Nov. 1978, 584–600.

high quality of some of its professors and scientists, cut a poor figure with its total of 9000 students in 1913 compared with the 60,000 students[132] in the many large German universities, generously financed by the government, equipped with splendid laboratories and having a teaching staff which was the best in the world. In addition, in Germany academic scientists had close, institutionalized links with industrial research, forming a union of science and industry. This of course promoted technological progress and had no equivalent in Great Britain.

A society has the educational and scientific system which it desires, and the contrast which has just been underlined was the result of differences in demand, which arose out of Great Britain's early start in industrialization and the efforts of Germany to catch up. In England, the Industrial Revolution occurred spontaneously, at a time when there was no true educational system, apart from what was appropriate to a traditional society[133]. Innovations were then the work of practical men or else of amateurs. From this fact sprang a powerful tradition of indifference or even hostility to education, and to technical or scientific education in particular. Many manufacturers thought that all book knowledge was misleading and illusory, that technical training was an impossibility, and scientific instruction useless. The self-made men, no less than those who were the products of public schools, saw confirmation of these prejudices in their own careers and successes. Foremen and skilled workers, on their side, feared or despised those who had 'studied'. So even when industry became more and more science-based, the man who had been trained on the job continued to be preferred to the one who had received a theoretical education[134]. The usefulness of research was only recognized very late, almost on the eve of 1914. Firms which established laboratories before that date did so with reluctance, usually in some old shed, with a small, badly paid staff[135]. Finally, let us not forget the power of the gentlemanly ideal and the cult of the educated amateur, and also the state policy of parsimony and *laissez-faire* in the fields of education and research.

---

[132] Hobsbawm, p.182.

[133] However, the high level of literacy on the one hand, and the existence of educational establishments like the Nonconformist academies on the other, certainly favoured economic progress in the eighteenth century.

[134] Saul, *The Myth*, p.48; Payne, *British Entrepreneurship*, p.53. Saul notes that it would have been possible to make up for the deficiencies in research by acquiring foreign patents (like in the glass industry, as Barker has shown), but this was pretty rare.

[135] Hence the lack of job prospects for science graduates mentioned above.

Against this, the Germans discovered before the mid-nineteenth century that, if the economy was going to catch up with Britain's, a strong system of technical and scientific education was indispensable. Out of this arose a cult of science and technology, the foundation of educational establishments at every level, and of substantial laboratories within the big firms. Large and small companies alike were ready to entrust responsible, well-paid posts to science graduates. Germany created her education system with a view to serve not only the needs of the state, but also those of the economy and to prepare her for industrialization. It was naturally better adapted for her needs than the English system, which inherited its most prized institutions from a pre-industrial society and continued to preach aristocratic values. Some other institutions were created somewhat haphazardly, slowly and hesitatingly, during the nineteenth century, so that liberalism and pragmatism, which were England's strength, eventually worked against her[136]. As Saul remarks, with the passing of time we begin to see that, at some point near the end of the nineteenth or beginning of the twentieth century, fundamental changes ought to have been carried out in the English economy. The British were badly prepared for it in terms of education and training[137].

At the end of this long presentation of the different (and often contradictory) interpretations of the British economy's 'decline', the reader may understandably feel a certain bewilderment. Unfortunately we cannot entirely dispel it.

It is certainly legitimate to talk of 'decline' during the late Victorian and Edwardian periods, if comparisons are made with both the earlier performance of the English economy and the contemporary achievements of several foreign countries. The key signs of this decline were the slower growth of industrial production and productivity, and a good deal of backwardness in the technological field. However, it does seem that just before 1914 England made a serious effort to catch up. Moreover her position was much stronger in other sectors and particularly in the field of services. So we must stress that her decline was only limited; and the idea that it was only the first world war

[136] See Landes, *The Unbound Prometheus*, p.348, on the paradoxical contrast between England, that was liberal and becoming democratic, but had an educational system that could not be less egalitarian, and Germany, that was authoritarian and stratified, but developed a structure more open to talent.
[137] In McCloskey, *Essays*, p.391. A.D.Chandler, 'The growth of the transnational industrial firm in the United States and the United Kingdom: a comparative analysis', *Economic History Review*, 2nd series, XXXIII (3), Aug. 1980, 396–410, discusses the problems of the family firm and the education of managers.

which caused really serious damage to an economic fabric that had weakened but was not seriously sick, can reasonably be defended[138].

Explaining the slow-down in growth and the lack of innovation is a thorny subject with many problems still to be disentangled. It is obvious that a phenomenon of such complexity cannot have a single cause. However in conclusion we must emphasize some factors. We cannot ignore objective economic forces such as the slow growth of domestic and foreign markets for British industry at the end of the nineteenth century, and the fall in prices which cut profits and reduced the possibility of self-financed investment. Nor must we forget that the attitudes of entrepreneurs can be conditioned by the environments in which they operate. Certainly, a slow-down in growth, such as occurred after 1873, can become cumulative and perpetuate itself in a kind of vicious circle, by reducing all stimulus to invest, innovate and increase capacity[139].

However, one is tempted in the end to insist on less tangible and 'residual' explanations, to which many other theses point in the last resort, i.e. human factors. This means the shortcomings of British entrepreneurs on the one hand, and the handicap of Britain's early industrialization on the other. Indeed these two factors are linked, especially if one considers the second not only in the rather narrow field of technology, but also as it affected society as a whole, its structures and its outlook. Perkin has written that in the eighteenth century England was the only country to possess 'the right kind of society to generate a spontaneous industrial revolution'[140]. It is probable that the evolution of this society in the nineteenth century, and particularly the tendency for upper-middle-class businessmen to assimilate with the traditional ruling class of landowners – the 'gentrification' of industrialists – created conditions which were not as favourable as before to innovation and growth[141].

---

[138] In any case, as it has already been observed, we cannot blame pre-1914 businessmen for not having foreseen the dislocation in the international economy that the war produced. But, conversely, it is going too far to assert, as some historians have done, that, if there had been no war, the choices and decisions of these entrepreneurs would have appeared as perfectly 'rational' and correct; McCloskey, *Essays*, pp.309, 391–2.

[139] Saul, *The Myth*, pp.43, 53.

[140] Perkin, p.16.

[141] Ashworth, *An Economic History*, pp.42–5, on the other hand, sees an overall change in British society's structures and aspirations at the end of the nineteenth century, and this change, of which the fall in the birth-rate was one sign, lessened the economy's ability to adapt.

Select bibliography

It seems unnecessary to provide a substantial bibliography of British economic history in the Victorian era, so we shall confine ourselves to mentioning a few general works which are original and personal views rather than textbooks. They are studies which the author has used constantly and to which he is much indebted; he apologizes for not having made enough references to them, for reasons of space. These works carry bibliographies that were complete at the time of publication and the reader is invited to refer to them. The author has tried to supplement them on individual points in his notes by quoting the books and articles that have appeared in the last few years. In addition there is a bibliography which is thorough and complete:

W.H.Chaloner and R.C.Richardson, *British Economic and Social History: A Bibliographic Guide* (Manchester, 1976).

Here, in our view, are the basic works, in alphabetical order:

W.Ashworth, *An Economic History of England, 1870-1939* (London, 1960. In the series 'An Economic History of England', originally edited by T.S.Ashton).

G.Best, *Mid-Victorian Britain, 1851-75* (London, 1971. In the series 'The History of British Society', edited by E.J.Hobsbawm).

S.G.Checkland, *The Rise of Industrial Society in England, 1815-85* (London, 1964. In the series 'Social and Economic History of England', edited by Asa Briggs).

J.H.Clapham, *An Economic History of Modern Britain* (3 vols, Cambridge, 1926-38). A monumental work, out of date in certain respects, but which remains an indispensable mine of accurate information and intelligent ideas.

W.H.B.Court, *A Concise Economic History of Britain, From 1750 to Recent Times* (Cambridge, 1954).

P.Deane and W.A.Cole, *British Economic Growth, 1688-1956* (Cambridge, 2nd edn, 1967).

R. Floud and D. McCloskey, *The Economic History of Britain Since 1700* (2 vols, Cambridge, 1981).

J.F.C.Harrison, *The Early Victorians, 1832-51* (London, 1971. In the series 'The History of British Society', edited by E.J.Hobsbawm).

E.J.Hobsbawm, *Industry and Empire, from 1750 to the Present Day* (London, 1968. In the series 'The Pelican Economic History of Britain').

D.S.Landes, *The Unbound Prometheus: Technological Change and Industrial Development in Western Europe, 1750 to the Present* (Cambridge, 1969).

P.Mathias, *The First Industrial Nation: An Economic History of Britain, 1700-1914* (London, 1969 2nd edn, 1983).

A.E.Musson, *The Growth of British Industry* (London, 1977).

P.K.O'Brien and C.K.Kyder, *Economic Growth in Britain and France, 1780-1914: Two Paths to the Twentieth Century* (London, 1978).

S.Pollard and D.W.Crossley, *The Wealth of Britain, 1085-1966* (London, 1968).

Finally it is essential to know and use the following excellent collection of statistics, which are accompanied by notes and critical commentaries:

B.R.Mitchell, with the collaboration of P.Deane, *Abstract of British Historical Statistics* (Cambridge, 1962).

Index